I Do / I Don't:
Queers on Marriage

edited by
Greg Wharton and Ian Philips

suspect thoughts press
www.suspectthoughtspress.com

Cover image and design by Shane Luitjens/Torquere Creative
Book design by Greg Wharton/Suspect Thoughts Press
Print Management by Jackie Cuneo/Little Jackie Paper

First Edition: September 2004
10 9 8 7 6 5 4 3 2 1

To choices, and the freedom to make them!

Library of Congress Cataloging-in-Publication Data

I do/I don't : queers on marriage / edited by Greg Wharton and Ian Philips.
    p. cm.
  ISBN 0-9746388-7-0 (pbk.)
 1. Same-sex marriage--United States. 2. United States--Social life and customs.
 3. Gays' writings, American. I. Wharton, Greg, 1962- II. Philips, Ian.

HQ1034.U5I16 2004
306.84'8'0973--dc22

                                2004016826

Suspect Thoughts Press
2215-R Market Street, PMB #544
San Francisco, CA 94114-1612
www.suspectthoughtspress.com

Suspect Thoughts Press is a terrible infant hell-bent to publish challenging, provocative, stimulating, and dangerous books by contemporary authors and poets exploring social, political, queer, spiritual, and sexual themes.

I Do / I Don't: Queers on Marriage

I Do / I Don't:
Queers on Marriage
Table of Contents

Here Comes the Book...
A Foreword/Forewarning with Some Acknowledgments Thrown In
Mrs. Gregory Mead Wharton

Another book on marriage and queers... Why? And why now?

As to why now: It's not going away. Just last week, the California Supreme Court annulled Greg's and my marriage, along with 4,000 others that occurred here in San Francisco earlier this year; but the broader case of the constitutionality of California's voter-approved Prop 22 (which defines marriage—perhaps, you've heard this one before—as between a man and a woman) has only just begun to slouch its way toward the United States Supreme Court. (Don't hold your breath though; that final ruling could be over a decade away.) The Federal Marriage Amendment is either stillborn or cryogenically frozen (depending on whichever conspiracy theory shapes your worldview); but, as in every harrowing horror movie, the creature always returns. And the queering of marriage may not be the wicked wedge issue of this election, especially now that Kerry and Bush are focused on the war...in Vietnam; but states will continue to amend their constitutions, politicians will continue to make hay, and televangelists will continue to make bucks—millions of them—fending off the raiding bridal parties of Adam and Steve, Lilith and Eve.

So, why another book on marriage and queers? It's certainly not because there aren't enough of them on the shelves in 2004, and some excellent ones, too. In fact, three of the authors included in *I Do/I Don't* have books you may have read or may like to read (that's politespeak for *should* read): Davina Kotulski's *Why You Should Give a Damn about Gay Marriage*; Jonathan Rauch's *Gay Marriage: Why It Is Good for Gays, Good for Straights, and Good for America*; and Evan Wolfson's *Why Marriage Matters: America, Equality, and Gay People's Right to Marry*. (For rock-'em-sock-'em "I Don't" books, these two are must-reads: *That's Revolting! Queer Strategies for Resisting Assimilation* edited by Mattilda a.k.a. Matt Bernstein Sycamore; and *Unmarried to Each Other: The Essential Guide to Living as an Unmarried Couple* by Marshall Miller and Dorian Solot.) And it's not, as much as I'd like to say otherwise, that our collection of pro and con opinions on the issue of same-sex marriage is unique. Andrew Sullivan long ago beat us to that punch with his *Same-Sex Marriage: Pro and Con*, recently revised and reissued. Though there are big differences between the two. For example, you won't find Leviticus or Charles Krauthammer here.

Then why this particular book? That's easy. Talking points.

Not long after Greg and I left City Hall's rotunda as spouses for life, we started to get all manner of mail, e- and otherwise. (Not surprisingly in our everything's-for-sale world, the city had sold the mailing lists of the queerlyweds.) One of those emails asked us to come to the San Francisco Lesbian, Gay, Bisexual, and Transgender Center to learn from one of the national organizations about how to address the media. We would be "given" talking points to help us answer questions from friends and foe (and/or family) alike. And with those words, *talking points*, the imp of the perverse that sublets a part of my soul began to stir.

Now, I understand why some people, some groups would want to use talking points. They can be very effective in providing the appearance of a united, unstoppable front. Especially in the hands of the spinmeisters of the damned. Why if you watch enough TV, you'd never think the grandees of the Grand Old Party or the religious right ever disagree about anything. Onward Christian soliders, indeed. Further, since 9/11, the ministers of misinformation have been very successful at equating unity with strength and diversity (of opinion and pigment and sex chromosomes, etc.) with a ragtag rabble on the run.

And so I get how talking points are tempting, especially for the ever-ostracized. Goddess knows ideologues of all sides and stripes have bandied and bashed them about the heads of others for centuries. But if someone shoves something phallic and electrified in my face and shouts a question at me, I'm going to answer it, for better or worse, from the heart, even a rapidly beating one. So, I deleted the email.

But the imp within didn't forget, and finally, he got his message across. Four months ago, he wrote out the title of this book on a napkin and pushed it across the table to Greg during our Saturday-morning out-on-the-town publishers' pancake breakfast.

My imp of the perverse had heard his fill of the opinions of the talking heterosexual heads on TV. It was time to hear from those who they and their talking points were talking, and more likely, shouting, over: Queers.

And my oh my, do we have a lot to say on queers marrying queers.

Then again, I'm not surprised. Though we know a thing or two about silence, especially being silenced, if you fill a room with any number of lesbians, gay, bisexuals, transgenders, transsexuals, genderqueers, intersexed, you'll see we're far from a quiet folk. (Thank the Goddess!) Especially on an issue that is the equivalent of a flaming toaster hurled into the bathtub of the collective consciousness: queer marriage.

And oh how the tub boils and bubbles through the three hundred and eighty-some pages to follow. In fact, you, patient reader, must be tired of this foreword now and ready for some forewarning as you prepare to dip your toe in.

So, now seems as good a time as any to explain how this collection of "I Do"s, "I Don't"s, and "I Differ"s is organized. It's rather simple. It's alphabetical. Because just like queers, not every piece fits neatly in its category. And not all of these are essays even. The poems are easy to spot. But there's fiction, too. And vows and rants. Even some deconstruction and some mighty fine journalism.

And I definitely tried, like a rather nelly Noah, to make sure we had one of...every possible opinion and life experience. We asked over 400 people and received 175 pieces that became the 132 collected here. Some turned us down because they were too busy (we so understand), felt they didn't have anything to say that hadn't been said (fair enough), balked at the use of the word *queer* (we're San Franciscans and there is no other word that comes close to even attempting to include all the tribes here), and some were insulted by the fee we offered (it's wee as fees go, but most of the fees along with a percentage of the sales are being donated to five amazing groups: the ACLU, the Alternatives to Marriage Project, Freedom to Marry, the International Gay and Lesbian Human Rights Commission, and the National Center for Lesbian Rights). Fortunately, Greg was the ballast and kept Nelly Noah in check by reminding him that this book of a boat could only reach 384 pages without sinking.

But that's the last thing this book does: sink.

Thanks, Greg!

Speaking of Mr. Wharton, where is your husband in all this? you might ask. Doesn't he get to speak for himself? Trust me, if we'd had more room on this ark we would have kept our separate pieces along with an afterword by Mr. Wharton. Instead, like all good marriages, we compromised: I got to write the foreword and he got to have the photospread in *Unzipped* magazine.

Wait a minute, Mary! I know some of you want to shout. You led us through the whole foreword—from its Mary Daly-wannabe use of "foreword/forewarning" to its Judy Garland in *A Star Is Born* turn with the "I am Mrs. Gregory Mead Wharton" byline—with no plans of giving your personal opinion?!

Marriage. Is it for every queer? No. I'm pretty puritanical myself on the sacredness of a freely willed choice. Is it the mother of LGBTIQ struggles? No. Not if it leaves out those who don't marry. I especially disagree with the dictum that same-sex marriage is the end of gay liberation and the beginning of gay responsibility. I fear some within our community want to turn marriage into the latest great divide. The way to separate the normals from the freaks. The conservatives from the radicals. The God-fearing from the Goddess-worshiping. The plain joes and janes from the fairies and leatherettes. The merry monogamouses from the sacred sluts. The gay and lesbians from the bisexuals, transgendered, intersexed. The same mindset that is keeping everyone but those in Massachusetts from having the choice to marry.

Trust me, I may no longer be married in the Golden State of California, but I will always be a freak—a loud and proud one—wherever I go in this country. And if any of us queers aren't fighting to liberate all of us so we can each live a life of quiet or flamboyant dignity, how can we dare to call ourselves responsible. To put some oomph in some rather empty government rhetoric of late: No queer must be left behind. And I can think of no better way than by putting into nationwide practice many of the ideas mentioned in the pieces to follow about how we can make marriage one of many legal choices for affirming and enjoying our inalienable rights as well as honoring how and with whom we create our relationships. Queer and nonqueer alike.

August 2004
San Francisco, CA

And Now, Some Cake and Acknowledgments

First, Greg and I cannot thank each of the contributors enough for their great pieces and their great goodwill. Never have so many brilliant divas in such cramped quarters and under such tight time constraints caused so little fuss and created so much charity and clarity!

A special thank you goes to the never-praised-enough secret weapon of Suspect Thoughts Press: Shane Luitjens of Torquere Creative. He's designed every cover but one—and this one takes the cake!

Many thanks to the following fiercesome angels of literary heaven for helping us seek out many of the contributors: Toni Amato, Patrick Califia, Greg Constante, Heather Findlay, Abe Garland, Gina Gatta, Greg Herren, Krandall Kraus, Richard Labonté, Jeff Mann, Mattilda, Marshall Miller and Dorian Solot, Jonathan Rauch and the Independent Gay Forum, Tristan Taormino, Michelle Tea, Don Weise, and last, but never least, Paul Willis.

And Triple-Goddess-triple-crowns to Dodie Bellamy, Michele Karlsberg, Cheryl Rosenthal, and Jim Van Buskirk for using their supernetworker powers and bringing us a writers' colony apiece of amazing writers and poets.

And finally, my most heartfelt thanks and abiding love to Greg Wharton, who makes this press a dream come true for me and many other misfit authors.

I do, until the last book, the last scrap of paper and ink, burns away.

Notes to a Young Feminist
Dorothy Allison

A few years ago, there was a conference in Minneapolis on "Feminism and Rhetoric." I went as a doctrinaire, whiny feminist. The focus of my rant was directed at younger feminist theorists who were using an arcane language that I found an obstruction to my understanding. I thought not only was it arcane, it was an act of cowardice because they were talking in such high falutin' language no one knew what the fuck they were saying!

So I did my rant about how, if you people don't clean it up, we're lost—you can't keep talking in this language that none of us understands. I just laid into them. Then, feminist theorist Judith Butler gave her talk, and she changed how she spoke—it was as if she were doing a consecutive translation. For every one of those marvelous words she used, she provided an alternative that I actually understood! I did have to, like, listen really close, but I got it, and I followed along! Afterward, half-a-dozen young philosophy students went up to her and, being incredibly nasty and critical, tore her apart for the way she had delivered the talk.

Since then, I have made a study of language. I can actually understand what they're talking about when they say "normative." It's true that sometimes I have to make notes and go look up shit. It's also true that I have to drink a lot of coffee and Diet Coke. And I have to, like, focus. If you let your attention wander for an instant, you're into an entirely different philosophical category!

The specificity of the language is sometimes necessary because quite often the subjects being discussed are notoriously complicated, frighteningly dangerous and self-revelatory. Let me assure you that when our feminist scholars, philosophers, speculators, and thinkers use this language they're not always talking about a distanced subject but about their specific lives. The sex act they may in fact have committed, enjoyed, desired, or refused. They are standing naked, and the only thing holding them up, in some cases, is that complicated language.

What I don't hear at conferences is what did in fact bring me to feminism. So let's go back, let's begin: *Rubyfruit Jungle, Riverfinger Women, Meridian, Wise Blood, The Heart Is a Lonely Hunter, True Story of a Drunken Mother, Snapshots of a Daughter-In-Law, The Girl, The Salt Eaters, A Woman Is Talking to Death, Edward the Dyke, I Know Why the Caged Bird Sings, Memoirs of an Ex-Prom Queen, The Bell Jar, Big Blonde*, and authors like Judy Grahn, Elana Dykewomon, Alice Walker, Adrienne Rich, Carson McCullers, Audre Lorde, Lillian Hellman, and Joanna Russ.

What was the first feminist book you read? Not *Our Bodies, Ourselves* or *The Feminist Mystique*. No, take me back. All the way back. Take me back to the trashy books you read. Take me back to the stuff that you read and that you wanted to be. I'm 54 years old. To quote *Sex and the City*, I'm abso-fuckin'-lutely tired. I read theory. I read to train my language and to sharpen my mind. But I write fiction. I write fiction for a specific, deliberate, reasonable, old lesbian purpose. The world I love is not on the page. The world I understand is not reflected on the page. What made me a feminist were occasional glimpses of my real life on the page.

We can talk a lot about mother-daughter transgression and generational resentment for a good couple a million decades, but I came to feminism as a lover. Feminism for me was a love affair. I came to feminism as an escaped Baptist. Feminism for me was a religious conversion experience. I came to feminism as a hurt, desperate, denied child, and I would've killed for the feminist mama who would take me in her arms and make it all make sense. And I've been running after her ass ever since.

I do not necessarily believe that someone can make it all make sense. I am, in fact, in love with the feminist ideal of "get used to being uncomfortable, you'll learn something." That is what I need, want, ache for, and I believe absolutely in the future of feminism.

I do not construct feminism as an ethical or moralistic system. When I talk about justice, I am talking about institutions that have ground me and my kind, right down to rock, so far back that they owe me. They owe me as a working-class girl. They owe me as a queer girl. They owe me as a raped child. They owe me as a writer who had to raise money and who couldn't write for years because she had to raise money. Yet, I also know that that voice saying "They owe me" is the most dangerous bone in my body. It is a part of me that I have to resist. It is a bone I cannot stand on, feel, or shape. Instead, I owe you, my feminist sisters.

"Do you have a utopian vision of the future?" you ask me. I got a fucking utopian vision of the present! I live in Sonoma County. It's true; I live in the low-rent district of Sonoma County and, it's true, west of Napa. You know what they do with the poor people in San Francisco? They give them a bus ticket to my town. We have more social services than anything else. I live in Guerneville, a small town in northern California where people say a third of the population is queer. And more than a third of the population is dying. Not of AIDS, no, AIDS has actually gotten a little smaller in our town. What's killing us is cancer and drug addiction. And methamphetamine labs blowing up, because contrary to rumor, the return of cash to the capitalist system of America ain't happening in Sonoma County. Now methamphetamines—that's immediate cash. And people are dying because they're brewing it in the back of their trailer parks. My town, between tie-dyed T-shirts and methamphetamines, it'll keep going. And I confess, I buy as many tie-dyed T-shirts as I can stand. And I hold writing workshops for working-class kids. I like it that way. They've got to write short essays about why they identify themselves as working class. I still haven't gotten over the child who described herself as working class because she doesn't have access to her inheritance until she's 30—but I took her in!

All my friends down in San Francisco keep calling me and saying, "Get your ass down here and get married!" I put a message on my phone machine: "I've pierced her tit; I have tattooed her left thigh. I'll be goddamned if I'm gonna marry her ass!" I became a feminist because I wanted answers that were not easy moralisms. I became a feminist because I had been a Baptist. And let me tell you, when you leave Baptists, you are leaving some serious shit.

But when I got up in the morning and watched old George Bush on television talking about how he wants a constitutional amendment, I'm like, "Oh Shit. We gotta go get married." And I noticed something, in a phrase he used four times in his talk from the Roosevelt Room: "activist judges." How many of you know an activist judge? No, no, I'm serious—I know three. They're all dykes. One's from Colorado and two are from California. But I don't think that what I think of as an activist judge and what George Bush thinks of as an activist judge have any relationship to the same category.

Why do you become a feminist? Why do you grab hold of every book that speaks to your heart? Why do you want desperately to believe that there is a future? I have evidence in my own life that activism is an effective engine for change. I've got a banner: "Everything has been remade. Nothing has been remade. Everything is different. A little bit is different." It's complicated.

In 1981, I was almost fired from my job in New York City because someone from the Columbia University campus called my boss and said: "Do you know what she does at night? I can send you pictures!" My boss, an old red-diaper baby, said: "Send them; I'd love to see some of that! And I'm not firing her ass!" He kept that attitude when the same people called the people who had hired him. It was all part of the tumult associated with the 1981 "Sex the Scholar" conference but we didn't know that we were participating in a historical event. We only knew things were complicated for a while.

Things change, things stay the same, things are always in turmoil for people like us. Think back to the first book that gave you the notion that you could change your world. Whether you define your world as George Bush's world or your neighborhood or your family or your ex-girlfriends and the new ones you're looking at, I guarantee the book that you picked up that "empowered" you and gave you a sense of authority in the world was almost surely a feminist text. A narrative of revolution. A piece of someone's soul in which they spread their legs, took a strong stand, and stubbornly shared with you how they had changed their own life or endured their own life or made new the life they had been handed.

Last week, because the river rose and we got cut off, we all watched TV. And it made me think, what the fuck is it gonna look like when they make the movie of our life? Let me be clear about what I envision as the future of feminism. When they come around to make the movie of your life, when someone comes around to write the biography of you, as that feminist icon or that revolutionary, world-changing activist you are about to become, for God's sake, make it more than anything small or pretty or overromanticized. Make it as revolutionary as this tradition in which we speak has been. Make it so dangerous that people will be scared and unnerved when they read it. Take risks. Make illegitimate children. Get lots of lovers. Try some stuff! Make some difference. Without that courage, without that outside agitation, there will be no future of feminism. There will be no change in this country.

Oh, and along the way, read some novels.

Dorothy Allison is the author of Bastard Out of Carolina, Cavedweller, Two or Three Things I Know for Sure, *and* Skin: Talking About Sex, Class and Literature. *An old dyke, she was born in Greenville, South Carolina and makes her home in North California, with her partner Alix Layman, and her 12-year-old son, Wolf Michael.*

Originally presented as a talk at The University of Chicago's conference on the History of Feminism. First published in *In These Times*, April 27, 2004. Reprinted by permission of the author.

Lavender Wedding
Shane Allison

I'm convinced that I'll get married
in the gym of my old high school.
The ceremony will take place
on a beautiful spring afternoon
on Saturday 'cause Saturdays are
for weddings.
My suit will be "virgin" white
with a shirt of lavender and ruffles
at the collar.
The shoes will be platformed.
I'll reek of Brut and Afro Sheen.
My husband-to-be will look stunning
in his lavender Christian Dior wedding dress
imported from Paris.
I'll mow the hair from my legs like newly cut grass with a Lady Bic.
Pluck my chest hairs like feathers from a chicken.
Paint these lips with apple red lipstick.
I want all my closest friends
to come ornamented in those dresses
like they wore in *Footloose*.
The lesbians will come
as Wall Street tycoons
to remind me how
expensive all this shit is
no matter how many times I tell them
that money is no object.
I ask my daddy to give me away
if he promises to keep his hands off Aunt Tillie.
My mama will be the barer of rice and punch spiked with whiskey.
The priest will be a Michael Jackson impersonator.
The reception will be held at the house of Chicken and Waffles.
where Debbie, employee of the month,
will catch the bouquet.
Wally, the four-hundred-pound, stubble-faced cook,
who smokes stink cigars, where the ashes
occasionally fall in the blueberry pancake mix,
will have the pleasure of pulling
the garter belt from my husband's thigh with his teeth.
There will be no limousines 'cause if a Pinto was good enough for
my sister and her husband, it's good enough for me
and mine.

Shane "Dirty Bitch" Allison has been called a fag, a nigger, and a genius who has had poems and stories published in countless magazines, e-'zines, and anthologies. He is the author of Black Fag (Future Tense Books), *and* Cock and Balls (Feel Free Press). *He has a story forthcoming winter 2004 in* Best Black Gay Erotica (Cleis Press). *Marriage proposals should be sent to* starsissy31@yahoo.com.

First published in *Lynx Eye*. Reprinted by permission of the author.

Dear LGBT Activist
Charlie Anders

Letter dated August ~~1993~~ 2003:

Dear LGBT Activist:

As you may be aware, ~~gays in the military~~ gay marriage is the number one priority for LGBT organizations at the moment. This is a hugely important issue because it signifies mainstream acceptance of LGBT people. We can't be truly equal if we can't ~~slaughter foreigners~~ get married.

The forces of intolerance are massing to oppose us. They see ~~the armed forces~~ matrimony as a sacred institution with a glorious tradition. If we allow gays and lesbians to join, they claim, it'll drive red-blooded heterosexuals out of the ~~barracks~~ sacrament.

But we only aim to strengthen ~~the military~~ marriage by joining it. We want to make the same solemn commitment that so many Americans have made throughout history. Full inclusion will only help this institution to cope with the many challenges it faces in our complex new world.

Meanwhile, some extreme radicals who claim to speak for LGBT people may also try to hold us back. They may say, what's so great about ~~the miltary~~ marriage? It's a patriarchal institution designed to protect property rights, they'll argue. It has subordinated women and enforced social hierarchies. They'd have us critique it from the outside.

Those people are missing the point. LGBT people should be represented in every part of society. We deserve the right to make the same mistakes as everybody else. And including us will be one step along the path to making things fairer for everyone.

A scarce few decades ago, African Americans weren't allowed to ~~fight alongside~~ marry white people. We follow in the footsteps of generations of civil rights leaders when we demand full equality for everyone.

Whatever anyone says, we will not stop until we win this fight. We will throw open the doors and walk inside! History will look back and see that we never compromised! We demand our right to enter into this wonderful institution that will invite us to join together and kill ~~strangers~~ each other.

Yours in Pride,
—Name Redacted—
Executive Director,
Rights Are Fundamental

Charlie Anders (www.charlie-girl.com) is actually made of sushi, except for her brain, which is pure wasabi. She's the publisher of other *magazine (www.othermag.org) and the organizer of spoken-word series Writers With Drinks. Her first novel will be published in 2005 by Soft Skull Press.*

Come Brothers
Antler

Why should two pals cut their fingers
    and press the bleeding cuts together
        to pledge their bond,
When they can suck each other's cocks
    at the same time
        and swallow each other's come?
Instead of blood brothers, come brothers!
Isn't sublime 69 a better way
    to prove love?
But either way
Why can't our best boyhood friend
    be our best manhood friend
And a vow of lifelong friendship taken in boyhood
    between two 14-year-old boys
        last forever?

Antler, author of Selected Poems *(Soft Skull Press, 2000) and winner of the Witter Bynner Prize from the American Academy & Institute of Arts & Letters and the Walt Whitman Prize, was chosen to be poet laureate of Milwaukee during 2002-2003.*

A Modest Marriage Proposal
M.J. Arcangelini

for the bride, Laura Seelandt (06/28/48–05/04/04)

I have long held the belief that one of the ways gay people naturally fit into their societies, one of the important functions we can fill, is as priests, shamans, etc. On July 4, 1999, I finally got my chance to act on that belief. I was asked to perform a wedding for two heterosexual friends who had first met in my home eight years before. In order to legally to do this I went online and within minutes became an ordained minister of the Universal Life Church. I was now able to sign all the appropriate paperwork required by the government.

I was working with a priestess, who had much more experience at such things than I, and the two of us met with the prospective bride and groom several times to put together exactly the kind of wedding they wanted. We wrote our own text pulling in bits and pieces of things that were important to each of us. It would be spiritual without being religious. We even managed to work in sections from "Behold the Bridegrooms," the marriage ceremony James Broughton wrote for he and Joel Singer — my friends liked the idea of using words originally written to unite two gay men in their own wedding.

For the ceremony I would wear a colorful jacket which had been handsewn with raw silk and other fabrics by Gryphon Blackswan, an African American drag queen and friend who had died from AIDS several years earlier. Gryphon had really been into ritual and I could feel him smiling as I prepared to marry two people in one of his jackets. There would be a strain of queerness running through this straight wedding.

The ceremony was held outdoors in a redwood grove next to the Van Duzen River in Northern California. There were over 100 people in attendance, friends and family from both sides. I wasn't entirely sure how some of them would react to what we were about to do and was trying to prepare for potential Christian indignation. To be on the safe side, I did an invocation to Ganesh privately with the bride and groom before the ceremony itself.

Everything went according to plan. The four of us performed his/her role and things moved along at a good clip so the attendees wouldn't have a chance to get restless. Quickly we came to that part of the ceremony where I said, "And now, by the power invested in us...," and suddenly I felt something I'd never felt before and have not felt since. I almost stopped in mid-sentence as I was literally and abruptly vested with some kind of power. It was a physical sensation — strong, intimidating, and frightening in its unexpectedness; joyous in the way it seized me so completely, like a psychic full-body orgasm.

As soon as possible after the ritual I hightailed it down to the river. I found a comfortable rock and took off my sandals. Stuck my feet in the cool water to ground myself and sat there trying to figure out what had just happened. I could still feel a remnant of the power resonating through me, though it had diminished greatly. Ultimately I could find no rational explanation. It seemed too intense to have simply been an anxiety attack. I found myself unable to reach any clear conclusion beyond calling it "magick" and letting go of it.

Later that afternoon I got the bride and groom alone for a moment. I told them what had happened and made it very clear to them that I hoped they had really wanted to be married because after what I'd experienced during that ceremony I was convinced that they really, really were. This had been way more than mere theater. They assured me that they had really, really want to be married, and that they had each felt the power too.

I went to sleep that night knowing I wanted that feeling inside me again. I decided that I would go out and perform more weddings right away (I have yet to do another one...but I'm available). Beyond that, another thought formed: What had it felt like to be on the receiving end of that power rather than merely being its conduit? I suddenly couldn't wait to meet Mr. Right so I could get married and find out. I wanted to feel that same power coursing through me and my beloved uniting us in ways we'd never be able to understand.

Meanwhile, over in Hawaii, it looked like that might become a possibility. A lower court had interpreted the Hawaiian Constitution to outlaw discrimination of any kind—including allowing people of the same sex to marry. This gave hope to many of us, while sending others into a tailspin of panic.

Less than a year after performing that wedding, Pete Knight and the Christian right (sounding like a bad rock band) managed to get Prop 22 passed by a two-thirds majority of my fellow Californians. This new law very simply says: "Only marriage between a man and a woman is valid or recognized in California." I decided that, on a basic level, Prop 22 was a message from my neighbors and fellow citizens reminding me that I am not truly welcome here, but merely tolerated. It was a reinforcement of a sense of second-class status and additional license to the marginally sane to continue and perhaps escalate their queer-bashing and killing.

Gay marriage, which I'd never given much thought to, was suddenly a direct and emotional issue for me, especially since I was, by that time, in the kind of relationship that had me thinking wistfully along the lines of whatever might pass for my marriage options.

When discussion of Prop 22 came up before the election, some of my heterosexual friends and acquaintances told me things like: "What's the big deal? It has no real legal import." Huh? Or, "Just ignore them and they'll go away. You people make way too much out of these things and it only feeds the nutcases." Excuse me, but I'm the one the "nutcases" want to feed on, so forgive me if I'm a bit concerned.

My favorite comment was: "Don't you understand that what you're talking about here is a complete redefinition of marriage?" This from a friend, himself married several times, who was truly expecting me to agree with him. As near as I can see, marriage has been in a continuous process of redefinition for years, maybe centuries, mostly through the liberalization of divorce laws: same-sex marriage is just a natural progression of the ongoing process of redefinition.

Marriage appears to be a major dividing line among those who otherwise consider themselves tolerant and accepting. Many folks seem to support gay rights right up to that point, but then drop out saying something like: "But you have to admit, marriage is supposed to be between a man and a woman for the purpose of having children." And why do I have to admit that? Am I to ignore all that wonderful research John Boswell did and presented in his book *Same-Sex Unions in Premodern Europe*?

One thought I've had since is to take the idea further: marriage is solely for the purpose of procreating, play it out, and see where it leads us. If the intent here is, as alleged, to promote and preserve "the family" then why not go all the way?

I hereby propose that marriage only be allowed between a man and a woman who actually procreate. They will be given a certain amount of time in which to produce offspring, and if they have not done so within that time period, the marriage will be annulled and they will lose all the benefits automatically associated therewith.

Marriage licenses would have expiration dates, just like a driver's license or credit card. Proof of procreation (live birth) would have to be provided to the county clerk prior to the expiration date in order to make the marriage permanent. A certified birth certificate might do, accompanied by blood tests or DNA results attesting to the fact that these two particular people really did produce this specific child. I suppose some kind of life span requirement would be needed as well. The child would have to survive for at least a year, or some other reasonable period of time, in order to preserve the marriage.

What if the woman is pregnant but not yet delivered when the marriage expiration date arrives? A certified form filled out and signed by the ob-gyn attesting to the pregnancy under penalty of perjury would get an extension sufficient for the child to be born. After that, see above.

Adoption? Perhaps. Say your marriage is about to expire and you haven't conceived yet; your only option to annulment could be adoption. But this does present a small problem: single people and same-gendered couples can and have adopted children. Thus, it is questionable whether marriage is necessary to the adoption process.

What if a couple are trying really hard but it just won't happen? Sworn affidavits from fertility clinics attesting to the fact that the couple are actively attempting to procreate could be used to delay an annulment. But such delays would have to be limited lest they be used by the hopelessly infertile to merely prolong the fruitless union in a mere charade of true marriage.

You say you want to live with your beloved but don't want to have kids right away? No problem, just don't get married until you're ready to have a family—since "family," as traditionally defined, is all marriage is about. You can live together, open joint bank accounts, draft mutually beneficial wills, execute powers of attorney for health care, hold property as joint tenants, and in all ways present yourselves as a couple—you just can't get married. It's almost the same thing.

So that's my proposal. No half-baked lip service to tradition, no hedging, no discrimination: no marriages without provable, bona fide procreation.

Unfortunately this would mean that my friends' marriage, the wedding I helped solemnize, would be annulled, since they are blissfully beyond their breeding years. I wonder if that would make them feel less married? Somehow I doubt it.

So, here we are, post–Prop 22, post-DOMA with same-sex marriages having been performed in three states in clear defiance of the law, Massachusetts opening the floodgates, and constitutional amendment proposals popping up like mushrooms on cow pies, and here's what I'm thinking:

I do not need a government to tell me I'm in love or to validate any relationship I have. My beloved and I and our community, our chosen and found family, can and will provide all the validation we need.

I believe that should the time come when I decide I want to marry I will feel that same power I felt on July 4, 1999, and no slug-of-rancid-pond-scum who thinks he's got a direct line to Jesus, Allah, Jehovah or the president himself is going to be able to stop it. Such people will be defeated and shown as the ignorant and fearful relics they are.

I believe that we will ultimately prevail. I don't have to become a priest in order to fit into my society. We and our relationships will be recognized by our society for who and what we are. When I look at the history of this country I see a long and noble movement toward the recognition of freedom for ALL people. In the end justice and equality will prevail. I have to believe that. For me, there is no other acceptable option.

May 20, 2004

M.J. Arcangelini (www.sonic.net/~joearky), author of With Fingers at the Tips of my Words, *lives in Northern California and has been writing since age 11.*

Wedding Vows
Josh Aterovis and Jon Andrews

Josh's Vows:

Jon, when you first emailed me over three years ago to ask if the setting from *Bleeding Hearts* was Ocean City, I never dreamed that we'd one day be standing here. I remember the first time we met in person, how I felt as if I'd known you all my life. There was an instant connection, but it was still only friendship. I'd been hurt very badly before we met and I didn't know if I'd ever fall in love again, or how anyone could ever love me. But as I came to know you, I found myself falling more and more in love with you. As usual, it took you a bit longer to catch up. Remember how you told me you could never love me as more than a friend? I'm sure glad you were wrong.

When we were trying to decide on our wedding songs, Laura suggested a song we'd never heard before, "Stranger" by Melissa Ferrick. We agreed to it without really ever hearing it. When I did eventually listen to it, I sat there and cried because it so perfectly described the beginning of our relationship.

There's a line from *Les Misérables* by Victor Hugo that says, "The greatest happiness of life is the conviction that we are loved—loved for ourselves, or rather, loved in spite of ourselves." That sums up how I feel. You make me feel loved in spite of myself. I hope that I can always make you feel as loved.

So today as we stand here making public the commitment that we've shared for two and a half years, our choice is made. Our minds are clear and our hearts strong. This love means more to us than anything else in life. There is no person, precondition, or approval I value more than your love. There is no obstacle I would not overcome to reach you. When you need strength, I will offer mine. When you need words of encouragement, I will listen and provide support. When you need solace and comfort, I will understand. I place you in my heart today, before all others, and I give myself mind, body, and soul to our union. I welcome you as my partner in life. May our love forever keep us strong.

Jon's Vows:

Our relationship began when I redeemed a coupon you had given me for Christmas for "Your Heart." I am thankful everyday that I used that coupon. The last two and a half years have been the greatest, most amazing years of my life, and even though there have been some bumps along the way, and some obstacles to overcome, we have overcome them all together, and our love has grown stronger because of them.

Even though I was a little slow at the beginning, I soon came to realize how right we were for each other. When I first held you in my arms, it felt like you were completing a part of me that I didn't even know was missing. It was after holding you, that I knew you were the one for me. You complete me in a way that nobody else ever has or ever could. You are my soul mate.

As we stand here today, sharing our commitment to each other with those that we care most about, I want to start off our marriage the same way that we began dating: with a coupon. But this isn't the kind of coupon you redeem...hopefully. For as long as you keep this coupon, my heart, my mind, my body, and my soul will be yours. This coupon represents all that we are, and all that we will become.

It's a promise that we will work together to overcome any obstacles that life throws our way. It's a promise that I will support your dreams and goals, and strive to keep our lives filled with laughter and joy. And it's a promise that wherever life takes us, it will take us there together. Most of all it's a promise of our love and commitment to each other.

Josh Aterovis and Jon Andrews met when Jon read Josh's first book and recognized the setting. He contacted Josh and the two became friends, which developed into more. They held a commitment ceremony on August 9, 2004. Josh is the author of the Killian Kendall mystery series (www.steliko.com/bleedinghearts).

Marriage Agnostic
Cheryl B.

The summer of my 21st year I graduated from college, moved with my first love Pam and our gay male best friend Donnie to an adorable rent-stabilized apartment on East 6th Street by Avenue B. This was in the mid-nineties when you could still get two bedrooms in the East Village for a decent price. We all settled into our gay little abode as queer as can be. The only items in the apartment's communal closet were our clothes. Pam placed her baby butch uniforms of the day—long shorts and Jams sneakers-next to my color-coordinated baby-doll-dress-with-combat-boots getups. And Donnie's drag persona no matter how subdued, could never stay put, leaving a trail of feathers, sequins, and long brown strands of wig hair throughout the apartment.

To complete the lesbian tableau, Pam and I visited our local animal shelter and adopted two chubby cats: Sweetie, whom we named after the feminist Jane Campion film, and Sabrina, a homage to Sabrina Duncan, Charlie's dark-haired angel.

Pam and I relished making out on the streets of the East Village, in the dark corners of bars, and in front of churches just as they were about to release their Sunday parishioners. We were young, in love, and in your face.

I'd been working full time at NYU since my junior year to help pay the astronomical tuition and I remained on after graduation. The university offered domestic partnership benefits. Pam had no health insurance and no regular job—she just did freelance production assistant work as it came along—so I looked into getting her onto my health plan. Since we were already living together, we were great candidates for partner benefits. All we had to do was fill out a series of paperwork and register as domestic partners in downtown Manhattan. No appointment was necessary.

Although everyone I knew was supportive of gay rights, I was uncomfortable letting people know what I was doing. I'd been antimarriage my whole life after watching the misery in the relationships of most of the adults around me, particularly my parents union held together only by fear, lack of money, and Catholicism. "Screw that," I used to say when my friends in high school poured over bridal magazines, "that's nothing but institutionalized misogyny."

But there was my girlfriend waiting for me outside City Hall looking awfully cute in a suit jacket over ripped jeans, her shaved head gleaming in the afternoon sun. My stomach hurt and I felt a little shaky. Pam was my first relationship. I'd had a lot of sex before, a string of college fuck buddies, mostly stoner guys, but she was my first real lover. And as horrendous as our relationship was about to become, I had thought she was the "real thing."

Pam and I had bought each other rings a few weeks earlier, for our first anniversary. Nothing formal, we just came across a few we liked at the flea market. My ring was silver with a round, unusual yellow stone that had flicks of green and red. Pam's was onyx and long like a little shield on her finger. I nervously turned my ring over and over as we made our way inside. I have to admit here that I have a hard time with commitment in general (I've been known to agonize for weeks choosing a cellphone plan) and my palms were sweaty with anticipation.

I noticed Pam had a carnation tucked into the lapel of her jacket. Nice touch. I was wearing a semiclean short black dress covered in yellow flowers that probably needed to be ironed. I had asked if I could take a longer lunch break from my job that day for a "dentist appointment"—somehow I equated getting "married" with oral surgery.

Pam was much more into this than I was. Despite her butch exterior, deep down

I knew she harbored the desire to be a housewife, like her older sisters back in Ohio. She revered her parents' 30-year marriage and really wanted to stay home, bake, and raise children. Somehow, I had taken on the breadwinner role, and even as we entered the building to fill out the paperwork that would make us as married as two women could be in the State of New York in 1994, I felt incredibly uneasy about this.

We were directed down a long corridor filled with straight couples, some dressed up, some in jeans. One overly excited redhead in a humongous wedding gown, which seemed completely out of place in the fluorescent lighting, nervously paced the length of the hallway. The edges of her dress swooshed up against the walls. The redhead came complete with three bridesmaids in pink slip dresses. Bridesmaids were really unnecessary here. Only a single witness was required to get married and even that was not needed to get a domestic partnership. As we made our way down the heterosexual hallway, I could feel our distinct presence as "that lesbian couple."

At the very end of the hallway was the Domestic Partnership window. There was no line, no vows to exchange, just a few papers to sign that were stamped and signed by the city clerk. We paid our $25 fee and that was that. Pam and I were domestic partners and were given a semiofficial looking certificate that I could have made at home on my laser printer. Although neither of us said it, we were both a little blown away by the chilly ease of the process. We went outside, bought Good Humor ice cream bars from a vendor, and sat on a bench until it was time for me to get on the subway and head back to work.

Later that evening, my mother called to ask what I'd done that day. "Oh nothing," I answered. The coldness and lack of ceremony surrounding our union made it feel just that.

Like so much that happens in your early twenties, our lesbian bliss blew up as passionately as it had materialized. Donnie moved out, disturbed by our incessant fighting. And Pam became abusive, often berating me in public, physically restraining me and pushing me down stairs. She refused to get a job and spent most of the day watching television while I was at work. Fearing more physical violence, I decided to move out. This lead to a bitter custody battle over "the good cat" Sabrina, which I won. We said our tearful goodbyes about a year after we became domestic partners, the certificate still hanging on the wall in the living room next to a poster of k.d. lang.

After many fights over the next several months and Pam refusing to come with me or do anything to end our partnership, I returned by myself to fill out an Affidavit of Domestic Partnership Termination, a copy of which would be sent to her. As cold as our union had been, I was grateful for the swift way in which I could end it, this time with a $15 fee. Eighteen months after we sat on the bench eating ice cream, I walked through the same tiny park, a free woman.

To be honest, I hadn't thought about my domestic partnership experience until recently with all the talk of gay marriage in the media. And I began to wonder if we had been able to become legally wed back then would we have felt the need to do it? When the relationship ended, would I have been sued for alimony? Would the process of divorce been long, bitter, and expensive as most of the divorces I've witnessed? Of course, we were probably too young to make any sort of major commitment. [I've joked that there should be an age minimum of 28 on all marriages, 30 for having children—but that is the stuff of another essay.] And nobody should have to marry just to get health benefits.

The balance of my twenties, post–domestic partnership, was spent in a variety of relationships. I came out again as bisexual and realized that traditional monogamy was probably not right for me and grew as a sexual and spiritual being. I also attended countless weddings. Straight friends who in college had claimed they'd never walk down the aisle went all out—spending a small fortune, what could have been a down payment on a house, for dresses that made them look like self-contained parade floats. Women who hadn't set foot in a church in years were eager to receive Christ for the photo opportunities his proximity afforded them.

I would show up, completely welcome to bring a date of either sex as it was always pointed out, with my usual present, a $100 gift card for Crate & Barrel. After perusing the dizzying array of items on their wish lists — shiny, ergo-dynamic juice extractors, specially designed bagel toasters, '50s-style blenders, a yuppie picnic basket — I could never pick just one, so a gift card was the easiest option. I was also a little jealous — I wanted these things myself; didn't I deserve a set of crystal tumblers? I secretly concocted a similar list for my 30th birthday. My mother shot down this idea as tacky when I shared it with her. "Besides, what will they give you when you get married?" she asked hopefully. "I'm a mother. I can dream, can't I?"

As the gay marriage debate has unfolded, I have been of two minds. Of course I support gay marriage as a matter of equal rights and privileges. And I've rejoiced watching couples like Del Martin and Phyllis Lyon finally able to marry after 50 years together. It only seems right that everyone should have this option if they so choose to take advantage of it. On the other hand, I worry that this will become expected of us. Will we become just another marketing demographic for the wedding industry? Will there be no more edge to being queer? Will I be spending even more money at Crate & Barrel?

But the rampant homophobia that the debate has stirred up in the land of the free proves that we are far from being accepted as "that nice gay couple down the street" in most of America. I'm sick of hearing about the "sanctity of marriage" and the "foundation of American life." No matter how many "queer eyes" peer out at us from the TV screen, we homos are still not accepted. The fact that a constitutional amendment has been drafted to keep us from legally marrying is not only ignorant, it's just plain mean.

We all deserve the basic rights that marriage affords — who couldn't use a tax cut? But we also reserve the right not to participate in dominant cultural institutions, to live a counterlife with as much dignity as everyone else. Is marriage for me? Although I don't see it happening in the near future, never say never I guess. I realize I've probably posed more questions here than I've answered, but the one thing I can tell you for sure: Married or not, we all need love in our lives, the unending pursuit of happiness, and maybe a new juice extractor.

Cheryl B. is a writer who has performed her work throughout the U.S. and internationally. A native New Yorker, she lives in Brooklyn and online at www.cherylb.com.

Partnerskap
Bruce Bawer

"Are you married?" people often ask us here in Norway, where we now live. "Yes," I reply. They hear the answer knowing it comes with an asterisk: yes, in Norway—his country, their country—we're married; back in my own homeland, the United States of America, we're not.

Strictly speaking, Norwegian law describes what we have not as *ekteskap*, "marriage," but as *partnerskap*, "partnership." Only in the Netherlands, as of April 1, does actual same-sex marriage exist (though even there gay couples aren't fully equal: they're denied overseas adoption rights). Yet Norway comes close. Same-sex couples here aren't entitled to wed in Norway's state church (which seems headed for disestablishment anyway); we cannot adopt together (a matter now before Parliament); and our legal ties mean nothing abroad (which is something the Dutch can't do anything about either). Otherwise, *partnerskap* is equivalent to *ekteskap*. Over time, indeed, the use of separate words has faded, the word *ekteskap* increasingly being used—by ordinary Norwegians, and even on some official documents—to describe both homo and hetero wedlock.

Norway's *partnerskap* statute was our salvation. It gave us—a mixed-nationality couple—a place where we could live together within the law. In Norway, I have all the rights of any spouse of a Norwegian citizen, including health-care coverage and residency rights. Here we're family, each of us indisputably acknowledged as the other's next of kin—although every time we fly to the States we instantly become single again, and he's just another foreigner on a three-month visitor's visa.

Some would explain our two countries' striking policy divergence by pointing to Scandinavia's vaunted liberalism; yet in many ways Norway is quite conservative. The difference, I think, is this. Many Americans argue that recognition of same-sex marriage would outrage their "values." The U.S. was founded on abstract ideals, and for many Americans "values" inhabit an exalted, often religiously conceived empyrean far removed from their own real lives. Little wonder that, when same-sex unions are discussed, "marriage" in America can easily float free of reality and become the locus of images, at once absurdly idealized and highly conventional, that bear little resemblance to anybody's married life—and that leave no room whatsoever for the reality of homosexuals. It is, ultimately, for the sake of those bogus images that gay Americans continue to be legally marginalized, denied access to the most fundamental social right (and rite) of all.

Norwegians are more earthbound. Some may be uneasy around homosexuals, but are disinclined to exalt their discomfort to the level of lofty principle or to believe that such private attitudes should shape public policy. Realism is paramount. They accept the objective fact that homosexuals exist, and in a polity founded on equal rights and responsibilities, same-sex marriage seems to most of them only fair, reasonable, practical. The official *partnerskap/ekteskap* ceremony is striking in the unsentimental realism of its language, its emphasis on the couple's membership in and obligations to the commonweal. Hearing those words, on the May morning when we took our commitment vows, I felt myself to be a part of something mature, decent, and at once liberal and conservative—in the best senses of both words.

And I felt—and still feel—awed. Awed that we were able to enter Oslo's courthouse that day, say a few words, sign a paper, and walk out into the bright Nordic sun joined in the eyes of the law. It's something that many heterosexuals take for granted—and that involves rights they may never reflect on. For a gay American, it can seem nothing less than a miracle.

Bruce Bawer is the author of A Place at the Table: The Gay Individual in American Society *and* Stealing Jesus: How Fundamentalism Betrays Christianity. *His website is* www.brucebawer.com.

First published in *The Threepenny Review*, Issue 87, Fall 2001. Reprinted by permission of the author.

Marriage at Tiffany's
Kevin Bentley

"How about rings?" We were talking about Christmas gifts when I asked this, one eye on Paul's initial ring, a remnant of his last relationship. December had always reprised my grief over Jack's decline and hospitalizations in '87 and Richard's abrupt death three days before Christmas in '92, but by December '98 I'd had two very happy years with Paul—who fell in love with me without cold calculation of my HIV status—and I could help decorate a noble fir without remembering that ironic Charlie Brown tree twinkling by the nurses' station in intensive care.

"You mean *wedding bands?*" Paul said, taken by surprise.

The next day found us standing before the imposing stone facade of Tiffany's opposite Union Square in downtown San Francisco. Above the door, a verdigris Atlas hoisted an antique clock face. Time: that's what this was all about, wasn't it? As a long-term nonprogressor, I always wondered if mine was running out.

In the museum-like hush of the dark-wood-paneled store, we stood under glittering chandeliers and examined rings placed before us by a clerk whose smile seemed to indicate she found our mission as tender as any other couple's, and easily agreed on a pair of wide gold bands.

We picked the rings up on Christmas Eve. At the quiet landing halfway down the marble stairs from Will Call we paused spontaneously, fished the boxes out of their turquoise bags, took out the bands, and met each other's gaze, flushed and teary as any bride and groom at the altar or under the chuppah. "I love you," we both said, slipping the rings onto each other's fingers, then kissing. I had decided to believe in my future—and pledge it, one more time, to another.

Kevin Bentley is the author of Wild Animals I Have Known: Polk Street Diaries and After, *and the editor of* Boyfriends from Hell: True Tales of Tainted Lovers, Disastrous Dates, and Love Gone Wrong, *both Lambda Literary Award finalists.* Let's Shut Out the World, *a collection of memoirs, will be published in Spring '05.*

First published in *Poz* magazine, May 2004. Reprinted by permission of the author.

Forget Marriage, Have a Wedding
S. Bear Bergman

On the subject of gay marriage—which I cannot get through a workday without addressing, given my work as an educator and performer about queer and trans issues—I am deeply ambivalent. On the one hand, I'm beyond ashamed at the amount of money and time organizations like the HRC have spent on this issue, and at what could have been done with it instead (housing, health care, and education for runaway or throwaway queer and trans youth pops to mind, for example). I'm also not wild about the idea that economic and legal equity should be linked to marital status, especially when it comes to things like health care and parenting rights. On the other hand, George W. is dead against it, so that's a strong mark in favor, much like when Jesse Helms thinks your art is obscene—a good sign as far as I'm concerned. Plus the unfortunate fact that within our current legal system, marriage is the golden ticket to a lot of protections which many people I know deserve and would love to enjoy, however disgruntled I am that marriage is what gets you there. On the *other* hand (for marriage, she is a many-handed thing, with comparisons to the destructive god Shiva being not at all incidental to the argument) I wonder whether, as queers, we are taking a short-sighted swing at the wrong ball, much like the feminist movement of the '70s did in insisting on a marriage-neutral honorific rather than seeing the big picture, and insisting on a gender-neutral one. With all that money and time and work and passion, could we have managed to get universal health care, instead? And on yet another hand, what good does marriage do for people who don't have health insurance to share, or property to inherit, or any of the other trappings of the middle-class to protect within its, er, sanctity. Perhaps ambivalent isn't even the right word, suggesting as it does a binary (that very thing which I have devoted much of my activist life to kicking until it falls down), which my feelings about marriage are already not, even in one paragraph.

However. What I am not a bit ambivalent about are weddings.

My beloved wife Nicole and I had a wedding, a religious ceremony, on September 5, 1999. We had all the trappings, including my childhood rabbi, who Bat Mitzvahed me, officiating; a cadre of weepy relatives in attendance (from both sets of my grandparents on down to a brace of cousins of varying degrees of consanguinity); and a marriage contract, signed by both of us, the rabbi, and two witnesses—which is currently framed and hanging on our wall, and to which we both like to refer in times of marital tension: "You have to take out the trash/have lunch with my relatives/be nice to me!" one of us will cry; "It's in the contract!" There were unexpected guests and expected guests who never turned up (with ensuing place-card drama). There were toasts, there was dancing, a young boy got drunk and made an ass of himself. Even by the standards of my two Jewish grandmothers, who between them comprise a Standards and Practices committee the envy of any network, we were good and wed.

It was a wonderful thing. We got up in front of G-d and our 70-odd invitees and declared ourselves a unit to be going forward with, and they watched and were happy. Well, a whole lot more people than that watched, really, grouped up along the lovely old wrought iron fence and clapping and cheering for us, because we got married at the intersection of the two major streets in the middle of downtown Northampton, Massachusetts and made a big, queer spectacle of ourselves in front of a very lovely fountain on a warm, early autumn day. The first couple of any variety to have a wedding there ever, as it happened—Nicole had her heart set on that location, but it's public land. Two hundred and fifty dollars, three heartfelt letters, and a somewhat harrowing interview with the Counties' Commission later, we became the first people in the history of the incorporated city to get permission to use a public park for a private function. This is what I did instead of climbing a mountain or fording a river.

Weddings serve many functions for sure, and one of them—it must be said—is a winnowing process. Few things prepare you for a lifetime of living together like planning a major event, especially one as emotionally charged as a wedding is. There's all of that compromise and negotiation, all those interminable lunches with one's future in-laws, so many competing and often unharmonious visions of How Things Will Go. There is almost certainly going to be bald, naked Talking About Money, and at least a few exciting rounds of We've Always Done It This Way. There are so many things to decide, and everyone around you behaves as though these are certainly the most important decisions you will ever, ever make, a premise you must band together to resist or it will surely prevail. There are all of those *relatives*. Any two people, regardless of gender or sexuality, who still genuinely like one another after completing the Wedding Decathalon have gained skills which will serve them very well in the balance of their married life. I would really like for someone to do a study on divorce rates for couples who have had some sort of low-key City Hall ceremony or elopement versus the divorce rates of couples who have planned, and survived, a wedding. I would bet money that the wedding people stay together longer, simply because of the trial-by-fire required.

Not that we didn't contemplate eloping. Oh, we did. That's a different essay, but I'm glad we didn't, because having a wedding was an extraordinary, milestone, life-changing thing.

I didn't think it would be. Even though I committed myself fully to the wedding-planning process and developed opinions about napkin colors and was really looking forward to the whole party and most the people I liked all in the same place at the same time, I thought in my secret heart that being married would be like living together, except with nicer dishes. That seemed fine to me, as living together was really wonderful and I liked the dishes we'd registered for very much.

But something about the process of getting up in front of our families (those parts of them that chose to attend), and our friends and saying out loud and for sure and with tears streaming down our faces and in front of everyone that we were committed to each other, come what may, made something bloom in my soul. It made me look at Nicole with new eyes, marveling every time that this brilliant, beautiful woman had chosen to throw in her lot with me, and had been sure enough to say so in public, where people could see. And the raw, perfect energy of 75 people joyously affirming our choice to commit ourselves to one another nearly broke me open with how huge and vibrantly powerful it was; continues to surprise me with the ways in which it resonates between us, dimmer but undissipated. I felt…joined. And it was wonderful.

These days, because we live in Massachusetts, it seems to be a popular pastime even among people who attended our wedding to ask us whether we'll be getting married. When I say, as neutrally as possible, that we're already married, some people can't seem to resist saying, "No, I mean, for real."

I understand what they mean by For Real. They mean hospital visitation and her being my next-of-kin and all the rest of the much-discussed 1,000-plus rights marriage brings for a $35 license fee, except not at the federal level yet or maybe ever; they mean not having to carry my laminated copy of my power of attorney everywhere I go assuming I never leave the state, and maybe by the time we're eligible getting Social Security benefits, assuming that Social Security still exists in 35 years. I'm just not sure yet whether it's worth signing on for something I'm so conflicted about on the off chance that one of us ends up in jail anytime soon. Not to mention my instinctive, possibly genetic antipathy, as a Jew, to registering my modes of difference at the courthouse.

Instead, I think about the wedding canopy on the wall lovingly handmade in squares by our wedding guests, the wedding pictures which show several of my beloved cadre of Great-Aunts who are no longer with us, the ring on my finger and the look on my father's face and the nice dishes in the cupboard and my wife, a title she uses without a hint of irony, and I say, very gently:

"Trust me. It's for real already."

S. Bear Bergman is a theater artist, writer, book reviewer and gender-jammer; touring hir award-winning show Ex Post Papa *around the country. Ze has been heard and published in a variety of places, lives on the web at* www.sbearbergman.com, *and makes a home in Northampton, Massachusetts where ze is the very lucky husbear of a magnificent femme.*

Attack of the Gay Wedding Cake Toppers
Steve Berman

The metal door to the bakery's massive refrigerator, which resembled a vault more than anything else, opened slowly allowing the cool air to escape into the darkness. A flashlight beam sputtered followed by a woman's voice cursing in a thick Southern accent. She banged the flashlight against the wall and succeeded in bringing it to life once more.

Her thick arms slid milk cartons filled with 2% over to keep the door from swinging shut behind her. Then she went hunting, shivering not only from the temperature but with fundamentalist rage at what would dare happen at 3 p.m. the next day. Her flashlight finally found the cart carrying a three-tier cake.

Just looking at all the pink icing, the array of rainbow-colored piped rosettes along the edges, turned her stomach. Her malfunctioning pancreas rolled underneath the layers of snow-white fat along her midsection, as if aware that the amount of glucose in a single slice of that cake would be poisonous. Millicent Bouregard had to spit on the floor even though she knew it wasn't proper for a lady like herself.

The worst insult though to her, to the entire Bouregard family, and to the Lord Himself, was what passed for an ornament at the top. Two smirking grooms in white dinner jackets holding hands. Her hand shook and in the wavering light it seemed as if their expressions mocked her.

She turned the flashlight onto her heavy purse from J.C. Penneys ($9.99 on sale after she switched tags) and pulled out a handful of slender syringes. That young doctor in Birmingham, cheeky but at least God-fearing, always gave extras for her insulin. But each of the needles now was filled with ipecac. She began injecting it into the sides of the cake, cautious not to mar the fondant too much. Every so often, she would stop and glance up at the awful wedding topper. The dark eyes of the pair seemed to follow her every move.

Milli fanned herself with a slick magazine as she lay atop the duvet in the hotel bed. She reached for the mug of complimentary coffee and took a sip. Vera at the hairdresser always preached that a hot cup actually made the body cooler, but Milli had begun to think her as nutty as peanut brittle. Better to have a cool glass of buttermilk. Or be staying in a place with decent air-conditioning. Damn Earl's cheapness.

Any thought of food made her stomach growl. But she'd be damned if she'd take any part in a "rehearsal" dinner for those two sodomites even if one was sadly kin. Her poor sister…to deal with the shame every day of having such a godless child. She'd have to remember to double her prayers for family. Earl had gone down to the hotel bar and was probably cooling his heels over a bourbon and ice. Her hand shook the remote with anger.

In the darkness of the freezer things moved. Atop the tainted cake, first one then the other tiny grooms yawned and stretched their arms. They embraced and kissed, the one on the left bringing his plastic hands down to cup his partner's molded ass.

One reached down and dipped a hand into the icing and brought it to his partner's mouth, smearing the lips pink. The partner shook his head, as if disgusted by the taste. They both leaned down and put their ears to the icing a moment. Wiping his face clean on his sleeve, the right groom jumped off the top layer onto the next. His mate followed him down to the concrete floor.

Milli woke suddenly. She lifted her sweaty head and neck from the pillow. With the shades drawn, the room was utterly dark. The red glowing numbers on the clock radio by the bed showed 9:41. She looked to her right but could not tell if Earl slept in the double bed there. She listened and did not hear his trademark snore. Was he still down in the bar? She called out to him.

No answer. She sat up, chiding herself for nodding off. Her head felt achy from the humidity, the room still warmer than comfortable. She reached for the light and her hand brushed against something. Something that moved.

Milli yelped and quickly withdrew her hand. A rat! It could only have been a rat. She knew from her first impression of the motel that it was a horrid place. She felt around on the bed for the magazine, found it, and rolled the June issue of *Southern Living* up tight. She squinted, her eyes trying to adjust to the darkness.

The rat on the nightstand moved. It looked gaunt, standing up on its hind feet. She reached out with her makeshift club and swatted but the vermin moved faster than her, daring to jump onto the bed. She screeched once then again as she felt something dash across her bare legs. There were more of them!

She felt their little claws tug at her clothes. She began yelling, swatting the bed around her. One of them dug its teeth into her wrist and she lost hold of the magazine. Another began climbing up her blouse. The air suddenly seemed to be filled with two smells, a cloying sweetness and the tang of ipecac. She fumbled for the switch on the bedside lamp.

Light flared out from underneath the lampshade. What Milli saw on the bed brought a prayer to her lips but it quickly died when she saw what the little plastic figures carried. The silver blade of the cake server gleamed wickedly.

Earl opened the door to the hotel room. Too late he held up a hand and checked his breath. The bourbon left a strong stink on his tongue. Hopefully, Milli would be fast asleep. The room was dark and quiet. He shuffled slowly over to where he thought his bed might be, the one nearest the window.

He felt the mattress bump his bad knee and stifled the curse after the first syllable. He stayed still, hoping he had not woken his wife. Not a sound. He sighed in relief and sat down on the bed. He slid one arm back as he kicked off his shoes. His fingers brushed a leg.

Shit, he thought. "Milli?" he whispered. No answer. She had never been this sound of a sleeper. *Ahh, well, maybe all her fussing over this wedding tuckered her out*. First it had been writing congressmen about the wickedness of comic books and now this. He sighed while rising up and found the other bed, stripping down to his undershirt and boxers as quietly as he could.

Come morning, the phone's shrill ring woke him. Bleary-eyed, he reached for the handset, accidentally letting it slip from his fingers when he saw his wife in the next bed. Somewhere distant came the recording from the front desk announcing his wake-up call.

Milli sat up in bed still dressed. The skin of her round face was mottled, her eyes bulging almost as wide as her cheeks. Stuffed into her mouth was a large slice of wedding cake still dripping pink frosting.

The delivery girl entered the freezer and clicked the light switch. She gasped at the toppled cake on the floor. The layers looked trampled, the icing streaked. She did not want to be the one to clean up the mess, let alone tell whatever couple that their wedding would be minus a little something. What a way to start a new job.

All that would have to wait. She had to get the Bouregard cake loaded up in the van. She wasn't sure which one it was, but it had to be easy to spot. How many cakes would have two little grooms atop them?

Near the back she found them, standing proud on the peak of a round frosted bomb. She giggled slightly and smiled at the pair. As she carefully moved the cake to the empty cart, she felt her foot fall on something hard that crunched beneath her sneaker. She winced and looked down to find a traditional bride and groom topping, the plastic cracked in places, on the concrete floor. She glanced around to make sure nobody was watching, before kicking the fallen ornament out of the way and wheeling the cake out of the vault.

Steve Berman (www.steveberman.com) would certainly move to Massachusetts if he could marry that special guy. Currently he's single. Any rumor that he is channeling sexual frustration into writing fiction is a Republican plot to re-elect Adlai Stevenson. Steve's work has seen print of late in Best Gay Erotica 2005, The Faery Reel, *and the pages of* Xodus Magazine, *among others.*

Family Values, Anna Nicole, and Me
Chane Binderup

At my 5th birthday party, my dad filmed all of us kids with his Super 8 camera, interviewing each of us on what we wanted to be when we grew up. I sat on his lap in my little party dress holding my favorite doll "Pinky" and said that I wanted to grow up and be a mommy and live right next door to him and mom.

My first wife had the prettiest blond pigtails and the best porcelain animal collection. We were both six years old. "Two girls can't BE married," Sara's older sister admonished us as we prepared for the ceremony in their backyard hot tub. "Yah huh! Now read the vows to us!" we told her.

I encountered this same attitude two decades later when my girlfriend (a beautiful brunette who apparently collects only live animals) and I had our commitment ceremony. Some people came out of solidarity, because they loved us, though they did not believe that "two girls" should get married. Others did not come because they declared that although they loved us, they would not be witness to the "sins" that we were committing. Ouch! A handful of people came who actually supported us wholeheartedly. If it were not for these blessed few, angels really, the whole day would have been nearly impossible for me, with or without the cosmos my best friend was mixing me.

It was a stressful time when it seemed I could please nobody. It was hard enough to handle planning a wedding and making a major life commitment without also fretting about everyone else's homo "issues." While we heard nothing at all from close family members we had invited with much hope of their attendance (not so much as a card), others, with whom we didn't have much of a relationship, came out of the woodwork, upset that they hadn't been invited. "We have a lesbian plumber, how could you think that we would not want to come?"

Our ceremony was four years ago, four years before San Francisco began issuing same-sex marriage licenses, and before Massachusetts' Supreme Judicial Court ruled that a ban on gay marriages was unconstitutional. Before gay marriage seemed to be the only subject that radio talk show hosts cared about. Some of our close friends weren't even aware that gay couples couldn't legally marry. I remember a straight male friend of mine saying to me when he learned that our ceremony was not really legal, "You mean I can go get drunk and marry some one-night stand in Reno, and you two, who have this great, loving, relationship can't?" Yes hon, you, Anna Nicole, and J-Lo, but not us.

My partner and I have truly traveled light years from those bittersweet months leading up to our ceremony. We have made it through those difficult first two years (i.e., the turf wars); we have learned how to fight fair (most of the time); and we have weathered a couple of huge storms, making us stronger as a couple and individually. In fact, one of the most positive elements about having had a ceremony is that a gay partnership ages fabulously. Meaning that, to the outside world, it looks better and better the longer it lasts. It is absolutely amazing what even a few short years can do in changing people's minds and hearts about gays when they see a loving couple committed to each other going about their daily lives.

We have come to find complete acceptance from most of the members of our collective family, and until recently I thought that that was enough. The issue of legal marriage for gays and lesbians had slipped off my radar screen. Although I have always been 100 percent in support of the legalization of gay marriage, I guess that it ceased to be a big issue for me. My partner and I have a strong relationship, we have a domestic partner certificate, we have had legal documents drawn up, and we were living a happy, comfortable life close to my family, just like I had always wanted. What the hell did I care that some president I never voted for wouldn't allow me to legally marry my girl?

Then came the mommy part. My partner and I are in the final stages of picking out a sperm donor. We have the lucky boys narrowed down to 16. Sixteen profiles stacked on our kitchen table, which will be narrowed down to the top three and then just one. This has been a process several years in the making, starting when we first talked about having children a year or so before we had our ceremony. When it came down to a stack of donor profiles on the table, however, I suddenly got cold feet and freaked out about the whole thing. All those fun, internalized-homophobia monsters that I thought I had rid myself of crept in again, growling at me that it was selfish of me to give life to a child that would perhaps have a tough time because he or she had lesbian parents. Even my internal rebuttals to those monsters were monsters in and of themselves. *Hey, even drug addicts can have kids that turn out well*, I thought. What the hell was happening? I'm not suggesting that drug addicts are lesser people; my point is that my internal arguments focused on my being capable of being a good parent despite being a lesbian. This was my wake-up call that legal marriage for same-sex couples is an absolutely necessity.

For the most part I feel like the lovable, well-adjusted, contributing member of society that I am. I am good enough, smart enough, and gosh darn it...blah blah blah. Without getting too therapy-speak, I have to say that I know that not having my relationship legally recognized affects my self-esteem, even if my "monsters" only come to a head from time to time in the safety of my own room. Legally, my partner and I have all our ducks and docs in a row. A legal marriage might save us the cost and hassle of such things as adopting one another's birth children, but I don't even care so much about that. What I care about is equal recognition of our relationship and our family under the law. I want my children to grow up in a family where not only do they know that their moms love each other and them very much, but that their family is just as good as any other kind of family—damn it!

I know that a legally recognized marriage is not going to rid me of every last scrap of my internalized homophobia. Even if Mr. Bush suddenly had a change of heart and decided to officiate over one big, fat, nationwide gay wedding ceremony, not everyone is going to accept our unions as legit. (Take a minute and try to picture that though, just for grins!) Gay kids will still be made fun of, there will still be groups out there that try to cure us, and there will still be churches that condemn us to hell. But by having our rights equal under the law, I think we take huge steps toward protecting gays and lesbians and our families. Perhaps it's not very revolutionary, but I'm still that little girl who wants to be a mommy and live next door to mom and dad. And I think it's only fair that my family should be seen as equal to any other.

Chane Binderup lives in Shasta County with her partner in a pet-majority household, and is currently working on her first novel. She has written about gay and lesbian issues for The Arcata Eye *and* Curve Magazine, *and was an editor for the LGBT travel guide company* Damron. *She and her partner are busy planning a family, and with any luck the humans may once again gain control of the house in 2005. You can contact Chane at:* binderup@sbcglobal.net.

The Grooms Wore Matching Sound Bites:
How Our New Paltz Marriage Made Us Media Poster Boys
Jay Blotcher

Millions of people were at my wedding. You were probably one of them.

My husband Brook Garrett and I were one of 25 same-sex couples married by New Paltz Mayor Jason West on February 27, 2004. The broom-jumping was beamed across the planet, reaffirming the maxim that the personal is political—especially when you're a homosexual and a second-class citizen in George W. Bush's America.

As a veteran activist for gay rights, I know the value of a well-placed quotation. It can change minds, lives, policies. When I heard that a platoon of TV trucks had rolled into New Paltz the evening before the wedding day, I felt the familiar surge of energy I once knew as a street activist. I knew we'd have the attention of the world—however briefly. I felt obliged to craft the most effective sound bite possible for the assembled media—and make it sound utterly spontaneous.

The stakes were high. President Bush had just proposed his Hate Amendment to the Constitution the previous Tuesday, proving you can never go wrong with facile pandering to bigots. I wanted to deliver the proper rebuke. So, up until the moment we ascended the stage to join Mayor West that afternoon, I mulled over variations on the perfect declaration.

But nothing came. This usually loud-and-proud homo, never at a loss for a sharp word, was overcome. By the supportive crowds. By the unexpected warmth of the February day. By the simple joy of our "I do"s. When we were pronounced "husband and husband," I was completely overwhelmed. I stood quietly by my groom, clutching my bouquet. This was no mean feat; ask anybody who has witnessed my motormouth at a demonstration.

But my beloved Brook had the perfect response: he began blowing kisses to a cheering crowd. It was the perfectly understated gesture for this reserved man. The media loved it. Cameras popped. Video rolled.

We received the lion's share of the wedding media coverage that day. (In hindsight, I should have leaned into the bank of microphones before us and sneered: "Well, President Bush, here we are—the happy, loving couples you are trying to protect marriage from!" It might have worked, misplaced preposition and all.)

The Associated Press photo of Brook and I ran in more than a hundred newspapers. I was able to squeeze off a comment for reporters afterward and was quoted in the AP story accompanying the photograph. My winning comment? "This country was founded on a revolution," he said. "And this is a revolution, but it's a revolution of love."

CNN captured our glowing faces and replayed the segment for months afterward. (But they only ran our wedding kiss a few times; subsequently, it was cut.) All the major stations ran similar clips of us, hoisting our bouquets in triumph. (Our favorite was seeing our smooch on *The Daily Show* as the lead-in to a riotous story on gay penguins. Only then, we knew we had arrived.)

A decade ago, such a public declaration of homosexuality would have earned us embarrassed averted glances. Two decades ago, it would have lost us our home or jobs. Now, it sparks an endless chorus of "mazel tov!" from Ulster County neighbors, family, friends and even strangers. Change is good.

In the days that followed, reporters called our house, asking for interviews. Brook had had his fill, he informed me; he was officially off-limits to media. So, I responded to the many requests, explaining where gay marriage fit in the context of equal rights.

I argued as to why civil unions are not an acceptable compromise. I insisted on the importance of turning a private moment into a public spectacle.

After the tenth interview, I was emotionally exhausted. After all, this was not mere small talk; I was justifying my life and my actions, all the while making a case for gay marriage in America. Not for a moment do I think an ill-chosen word from me would derail the movement. But one wants to make a good impression. Why should The Fab Five get all the attention?

The resulting media coverage was almost entirely favorable. Yet another significant change that stands in sharp contrast to the past, when gay people could expect being trashed by "objective reporters."

Honestly, the only discouraging words came from gay friends. Some felt gay marriage marked the final collapse of our already-hobbled queer imaginations. Others groused because they had never found the perfect mate—and certainly didn't need another reminder of it.

When I was the media chairman for the New York City–based founding chapters of ACT UP and Queer Nation, I learned what civil rights leaders had known for years: the success of a movement often centers on how effectively you convey your cause to the media. In a world now saturated by infotainment, the equation is even more important.

I'm reminded of the 1991 documentary *Truth or Dare*, in which Madonna makes a great show of being spontaneous while cameras swarm around her, capturing every angle of her carefully orchestrated public persona. Her lover at the time, Warren Beatty, had outgrown the need for such media adulation and sat beyond camera range. At one point, he taunted her, saying, "Why say anything if it's not on camera?"

When it comes to gay rights, being on camera remains the most powerful statement one can make. One day we'll attain our equal rights—not queasy-making compromises crafted by Rove or Romney. When that day arrives, I will happily retreat with Brook into our private lives and private joys. But until that happens—and the Federal Marriage Amendment hearings suggest that halcyon day is still in the distant future—I'll keep parading before the cameras as queer as can be. I'm a media whore for all of the right reasons.

Jay Blotcher has been a professional homosexual since 1982. His rites of passage have been colorful ones: he has worked at The St. Marks Baths and The Saint, written for regional and national gay newspapers and magazines, served as a publicist for numerous New York City gay and AIDS organizations, produced three documentaries, and belonged to the activist groups ACT UP and Queer Nation. In late 2001, he launched Jayboy Greetings, a line of art cards sold in 14 stores nationally. Blotcher is a manic collage artist and spends his free time poaching images from old books and magazines. He and his husband Brook Garrett relocated from New York City to the mid–Hudson River Valley in July, 2001. Visit his website, which contains his greeting cards and selected articles, at www.jayblotcher.com.

First published in *InsideOUT* magazine, May/June 2004. Reprinted by permission of the author.

Gay Rights, Civil Rights
Keith Boykin

The only thing more disappointing than hearing black leaders speak out against same-sex marriage recently is hearing black gays and lesbians make the same arguments. The arguments are as simple as they are misleading.

You can't compare gay rights with civil rights, they say. Dozens of no-name black ministers across the country have stepped in front of cameras in recent months to win their 15 minutes of fame by repeating this transparently ridiculous bumper sticker slogan.

Of course you can compare gay rights with civil rights. According to Webster's, to compare simply means "to examine the character or qualities" of something "in order to discover resemblances or differences."

There are similarities between the civil rights movement and the gay rights movement, just as there are differences. But to compare civil rights with gay rights doesn't mean the two are identical. Unfortunately, when black ministers hear "compare," they think they hear "equate," which means "to make equal."

I've searched the Internet far and wide, and I've yet to find a single national LGBT leader who equates the civil rights movement with the gay rights movement. That's because nobody makes that claim. Not HRC, not NGLTF, not Lambda Legal, and not anyone in the national leadership.

There are plenty of racial problems in the gay and lesbian community, but this isn't one of them. The whole comparison complaint is a straw man created by the white religious right primarily for the purpose of inciting black opposition to gay rights.

Then there's the issue of religion. Since the days of slavery, the black church has played an enormously influential role in shaping black values. The church, like many in the black community, tends to be politically progressive but socially conservative.

That explains why black ministers have been front and center in the recent marriage debate. But there's one major problem with the religious objection: Gays and lesbians aren't asking for religious marriage; they're asking for civil marriage. Civil marriage does not involve religion at all. But once again, the religious right wants to get African Americans upset by misleading blacks about the "gay agenda."

It's bad enough to hear a black minister parrot the arguments of the religious right. It's even more frustrating to hear the same complaint from black gay men and lesbians.

Worn down by white racism and black homophobia, many black gays and lesbians aren't eager to take on the marriage fight. That's not our issue, they say. But when your own minister holds a press conference to condemn you, it is your issue.

Two months ago, a black minister in Chicago told *The New York Times*, "If the KKK opposes gay marriage, I would ride with them." Dozens of other black ministers have gone on national television and radio programs to condemn homosexuality in the past three months. If that's not enough to spark black LGBT activism, I'm not sure what is.

Some black gays and lesbians understandably fear that the focus on the marriage issue will divert our attention from other important challenges facing our community. But what are we really doing about those other issues? Many of us don't vote. We rarely contribute to our own civil rights organizations. Our community AIDS organizations are struggling. And we aren't holding protests on anybody's picket lines. If somebody could tell me what the black LGBT agenda should be, I would gladly support it. But, unfortunately, we're not actively pursuing any agenda.

Meanwhile, black gays and lesbians are under attack. Like it or not, there's a battle going on across the country. It doesn't have to be the first or the only battle we fight, but we do need to fight somewhere. Why not start by defending ourselves when we're attacked?

Keith Boykin is president of the National Black Justice Coalition (www.nbjcoalition.org), which works to build alliances between blacks and gays on the issue of marriage equality.

This column originally appeared on *PlanetOut.com*. Reprinted by permission of the author.

Delicate Monsters:
Talking with Myself About Gay Marriage
Christopher Bram

My boyfriend and I have been together for 25 years. Neither of us is terribly excited by the idea of gay marriage. We have friends who love it and others who are appalled. Draper and I feel more casual about it. We don't want to get married ourselves (we met with a lawyer fifteen years ago and he set up the necessary wills and legal protections), but we're not going to stop you.

All right, "we" is a highly unstable word, and Draper and I are not one homogenized mind. We agree more than we disagree, but I should focus on my own thoughts here. As our country goes marriage mad, I wonder why I am so nonchalant, curious yet detached. I'm going to explore a few ideas in an attempt to discover what I really think.

Marriage: a kind of friendship of interest to the police.
—Robert Louis Stevenson

Until recently, late in the 20th century, marriage was virtually mandatory for everyone. The West was as adamant about it as the Third World. A man without a wife was not a real man. A woman without a husband was a nonperson. That's no longer true in secular countries. More and more people live alone or in nonromantic households. More and more straight couples live together without the blessing of church or state.

Not only is marriage no longer required, there are fewer benefits to being married. Not enough companies offer decent health care to their employees anymore, much less to their employees' spouses. Most couples, straight as well as gay, include *two* workers, so individuals have their own Social Security accounts. And so on. (One exceptional benefit, however, is when your lover is a foreign national. Straight people can turn lovers into citizens simply by marrying them. We can't.)

Now that marriage is no longer a necessity, it's become more important as a symbol. And symbols are very interesting, not least because we are free to choose or reject them.

Love is not so much an emotion as a situation.
—Laurence Sterne

The world is an unreal place. We want companions to provide a few landmarks to let us know where we are. Friends help but a long-term mate is even better. Yet a mate can be just as unreal, so we often require some kind of act or rite or magic words to make the bond less ephemeral, less existential.

Progressive types who oppose any kind of marriage argue that it brings the church and state into our bedrooms. Which it does, but that's not how it feels. The experience of getting married is more like a social ritual that pins down a slippery emotion. Such as a funeral. I'm not being satirical. Love is as powerful as grief; a wedding can shape and name love just a funeral can shape and name loss. A wedding is a beautiful thing, and much less conclusive than a funeral.

Two heads, four arms, four legs—
Such a delicate monster.
—The Tempest

When Caliban, a very rough monster, speaks these words in Shakespeare's grand play about love and forgiveness, he's referring to two men lying in a heap on the ground. But one can't help thinking of a married couple.

Shakespeare is full of great marriage matter. There's "Let me not to the marriage of true minds/Admit impediments" from Sonnet 116, for example. His comedies often end in multiple weddings. The entire state of Massachusetts on May 17, 2004, when gay people were suddenly free to marry, resembled nothing so much as the finale of a Shakespeare comedy. My cousin Maureen got married to Meg, her lover of many years, that morning in a city hall on Cape Cod. Their stories about the festive day were absolutely exhilarating.

But the wonderful metaphor of marriage is also a legal fact, and legal facts involve lawyers.

I like lawyers. Some of my best friends practice law. My sister-in-law, who I adore, is a lawyer. However, I get very nervous whenever an enterprise requires an attorney. A few years ago a friend was involved in a small business contract that bound him to a financial partner he came to despise. It took them forever to dissolve the contract. And what is marriage but a very small, very personal business? More than one gay or lesbian attorney has quipped in recent years, "When gay marriage is legal, I'm getting out of legal aid and into divorce law. That's where the money will be."

This spoils the metaphor for me.

It is not good for man to be alone.
—Genesis 2:18

One thing I love about gay marriage, without reservation, is how the very idea of it infuriates Christian conservatives. Liberal Christians respond more loosely and sanely, but conservatives—evangelicals, fundamentalists, Mormons, and so on—go bananas. That's because the concept strikes not just at their idea of gay people, but at their idea of themselves. The human race is full of sin, but conservatives have somehow decided that the gravest sin is homosexuality. Since they're not homosexual themselves, they can feel assured they are among the righteous, even if they sometimes think impure thoughts, cheat in business, cheat on their spouses, neglect their children, or skip church on Sunday. Suddenly, gay people can marry too, and the good Christian must ask him or herself, "Is my life so different from theirs? Am I really so much better? Can I still count on heaven?" It has to hurt, to have your chief guarantee of eternal life snatched away, leaving you with the fear that you still might burn in hell after all.

Marriage is a fine institution — but who wants to live in an institution?
—Groucho Marx

I must confess that, as a novelist, I *love* gay marriage. Novelists tend to be descriptive rather than prescriptive in our morals. All we want is a good story. Where would the Victorian novel be without marriage? Where would postwar American fiction be without divorce? I can't wait to see what new plots and story lines gay marriage will provide.

However, I don't expect it to produce a radical change in perception or behavior. That's probably the chief reason for my laid-back attitude. The change in perception has already occurred. Twenty years ago, gay marriage would've overturned American assumptions about gay people: Oh wow, they love and live in couples too. Now, however, many straight people, especially those who can look honestly at their own marriages, know gay couples are often like straight couples, no better and no worse.

People will behave much as they did before, only under different names. Some gay people will marry, others won't. Some marriages will work, some will go down in flames. Love is difficult with or without lawyers. A few years ago Andrew Sullivan argued that gay men needed marriage so we would learn to keep our dicks in our pants. Since then we have discovered that Andrew—with his love of chat rooms, sex lines, and testosterone injections—is the one with the wandering penis problem. However, I can't imagine a wedding ring will make him or anyone else more restrained than they already are. (A straight woman friend recently confessed that she found married men's wedding rings very hot—when they weren't married to her anyway. Some gay people are sure to find the band of gold even sexier than tattoos or pierced nipples.)

Marriage has loosened up in this country without entirely disappearing. Now it's loose enough to include us. It's neither the end of civilization, as many Republicans claim, nor the guarantee of equal rights and domestic happiness that its giddier celebrants hope for. But gay marriage is going to happen, no matter what you or I or Jerry Falwell say. There are no good legal or logical reasons against it—and we have reached a point in social history where people can actually listen to logic.

Let me close by wishing the new couples all the happiness in the world, warn them they will have bad days as well as good days, and hope they understand that it never hurts to know a good attorney.

Christopher Bram is the author of eight novels, including Father of Frankenstein *which became the Academy Award–winning movie,* Gods and Monsters. *His most recent novel is* Lives of the Circus Animals. *He grew up in Virginia and attended the College of William and Mary. He was a 2000 Guggenheim Fellow and winner of the 2003 Bill Whitehead Award. He lives in New York City with his partner, filmmaker Draper Shreeve.*

Fuck Gay Marriage...
NO, on Second Thought... Fuck Gay Marriage...
Tala Brandeis

Gay Marriage is like:

Jews praying for Zyklon B, "please god please let me shower soon..."

Palestinians worshiping the butcher of Syria, Israeli Prime Minister Ariel Sharon...

Iraqis petitioning to be inmates at Abu Ghraib...

Trotsky begging Stalin for a Kremlin Summit...

The Sioux, Apache, and Comanche thanking "The Great White Father" for the genocide, murder, torture, and scalping of Indians by the U.S. Army...

Black folks fighting each other for first place in line to be locked in chains, thrown in the hold of a ship for weeks, and be sold into slavery...

Liberals begging the Bush regime to suspend the Constitution... (See, they've done that one.)

I go too far you say. You just want your lover to have medical care on your policy, to obtain the tax benefits of joint filing, to help your kids fit in better at school. To let the world know you're just like them, normal.

The benefits of marriage. Medical care is a right. You're reading that correctly, I didn't stutter, I didn't hedge that statement with shoulda, woulda, coulda... Medical care is a right. So what is the proper response to a lack of health care? Marriage? You say, "I just want to alleviate the problems we have now." Fine, what is the rest of the world supposed to do for health care, including all those folks who think marriage is a contract with the state and not your lover? Or, is the health of the world not your problem?

The income tax was originally and rightly intended as a tax solely on the rich as method of redistribution of wealth obtained through monopoly business practices. A TAX ON THE RICH. Actually the rich must bear the primary burden of taxation if they expect to continue to make a profit. (Oh, we tried that... Let's see, where we are now?)

The benefits of marriage. You're just like the others, normal. Great...you're normal. Yeah, that's what we should all work at being, normal, marginal, zero intelligence, hiding in front of the television, afraid to go out to the juke joint cause there are too many niggers waiting to kick our asses, steal our cars, money, stereo, computer, clothes, bullshit, horseshit, and chickenshit. Stop waiting for someone to steal it and throw it away. Give it to your local neighborhood street person. It'll make you feel different, but then you won't BE normal if you have feelings of having connected with a, "gasp," street person. So what if you feel "good" about giving something away? So what if you feel "guilty" about giving something away?

Seriously, what's the benefit of being normal? Aside from perfecting your "ostrich in the sand" look, nothing. Anyone normal is already dead. The culture may only stagnate through the auspices and indifference of the normal. The culture may only change and mature through the harmony of the pervert, the abnormal, the genius, the eccentric, the radical, the witch, the shaman, the queer, the fag, the dyke, the one looking for something new, better, more interesting, more implicit, more explicit. Get your ass out there and become involved in Art and Science at the personal-interpersonal level. Who does that better than minorities, the ones on the edge, the ones who FAIL TO FIT IN to the majority paradigm? Why would or could anyone who thinks, who uses their brains ever identify with whiteness? Bland, beige, movie popcorn…versus hard, funky, stanky, slippery jive-ass butt-thumping ugly-bumping grind. The one you choose says how "normal" you are. Seriously, humans are more like the Bonobo than the Chimpanzee, but the Bonobo em-bare-ass the stuffy and Chimpanzees are less likely to fuck up the program. So to speak.

Stop watching movies and make some. Stop listening to music and make some. Stop looking at art and create some art. Goddamn fucking do something. Stop bitching and get active. Connect with more people than your simpleminded jealous, bitchy, adoring partner. Oh fuck you don't have time. Make time. Sorry honey, I've got to get laid tonight…I'll bet he'll be more interested in being more interesting the next time you want to do something. See, competition is a good thing, it makes us THINK…and then act on those thoughts. You'll get to find out just how great your girlfriend is in terms of her response to your getting laid. If he's jealous, mean and vicious, toss the fucker. If she finds ways to intrigue you with her wit and fantasy, so much the better, just be prepared to do the same for her after she tricks next time.

What would you rather have; equal pay for equal work or a thousand dollar refund from the IRS? How about your lover on your medical policy or an end to racism? What other rights do you have? The right to an education of your choosing, lifetime education. The right to food. The right to leisure. The right to shelter. What prevents you from exercising those rights? Which are more important, these rights, or the sacrament of marriage? Fuck the church.

Commitment is a wonderful thing. To what purpose really would anyone who has a functioning brain bring the state into their bedroom and more importantly, their joint finances? That's it, THE STATE. Capital letters.

What does marriage provide? The state is now in your bedroom in very old and conservative ways. Most importantly the state now has an interest in how the two of you regulate your finances. Your ability to make contracts with and between each other are more limited and must include the institution of marriage from a legal perspective. If you and your husband/wife have disagreements, one of you may force the other to court in ways you may not have dreamed of prior to marriage. I guarantee you if you have any problems with communication and you must go to court over the issues, you will both wind up as losers. Who in their right mind would invite the state into their finances, into their relationship? Well, that begs the question, does it not?

Let's look at THE STATE. Other than corporations, what does the state represent? THE STATE IS: Anti-Communist. Anti-Socialist. Anti-Labor. Anti-Abortion. Anti-Liberal. Anti-Conservative. Anti-Tradition. Anti-Republic. Anti-Democracy. Anti–Bill of Rights. Anti-Constitution. Anti–Declaration of Independence. Anti-Freedom. Anti-People. Pro-Corporation. Pro-Conformist. Pro-Life. Pro-Greed. Pro–State Terrorism. Equipped with a manifesto to maximize profit at the expense of the people and the environment… That's who you're letting into your bedroom and your bank with marriage. Why the fuck would anyone want the state in their finances? Even if you're straight. What's the purpose in anyone getting married? Who would voluntarily place themselves in a position of chattel slavery? Slavery is the essence of marriage. A man's possession, HIS wife and children. Ownership. You say that's not what marriage is NOW. I say you're a fucking idiot. You're especially an idiot if you think an institution developed around the concept of slavery changes in the minds of people in a few short decades. Ownership. Marriage. Synonyms. So, which are you, the possessor or the possessed? Likely the both of you are possessed.

What an absolutely fabulous English colony we live in. How marvelous that we can embrace outmoded Victorian traditions as queer people. You say we live in a free country… You're an imbecile. Free people can choose their form of government, have the right to revolution, the right to life, liberty and the pursuit of happiness. If you believe slavery is freedom, you've been brainwashed and you want to belong, to normalize, more than you want to enjoy life. If you believe a country that can't enact a constitutional amendment guaranteeing equality for over half its citizenry is free, you're a perfect dupe. (The U.S. failed to pass the Equal Rights for Women Amendment to the Constitution.)

How many people died for the eight-hour workday? Five? Ten? One hundred? No, more than twenty thousand people died in the United States for your eight-hour workday. Is marriage more important than time to enjoy your partner? Will marriage bring your community better working conditions, better health care, cheaper housing, a larger paycheck, a more equal share of the profits? It is our right to have enough time to rest, relax, and take it easy. Is one week a year enough for you? Two or three months a year would be more appropriate. Include a one year sabbatical every ten years and work begins to look like fun. It is your RIGHT to relax. It is your RIGHT to fucking get high once in a while. It is your RIGHT to enjoy life, to sit and have some time to just let thinking disappear and connect with what is in front of your eyes. Does marriage provide that for you? If it does, you've got your eyes on a pile of shit and you're missing the world.

A union between two people. Oh and that just twists your nuts, doesn't it? What about other forms of union? You know, a triad, or a collective? Can they get "married"? To what purpose would a collective clusterfuck want to get married?

Fuck the emotional state of "bonding" through a ceremony that in any way shape or form includes the state. What is wrong with people? Have your brains turned to mush? Are you such neo-liberal-conservative-yuppie-scum you must follow the dictates of the church-state hydra?

Oh we're married, we can do that now, isn't that wonderful… Excuse me while I wipe up the vomit and then your arrested-development ass. Yes, yes, get married, join the military (loser), become a cop (pig), a therapist (the rapist), a lawyer (seriously afraid of authority), you know, be part of the problem, not part of the solution. Get a life. Really. Seriously. Quit fawning over *American Idol* and make your own music; sing for fuck's sake. Quit watching the fucking Giants and go play some sandlot baseball. Stop sucking the corporate tit and get a fucking tattoo already. Make yourself incapable of conforming to social mores and learn how to be yourself. Remember the horny, dripping wet cunt you used to be/have before you got "married"?

What makes anyone want to "settle down"? When did you lose your spark for life? When did you stop looking for the next fuck? All right, why should you be looking for the next fuck? Well, it makes us different from those who feel the need to breed. How much more honest is it to acknowledge the reality of being human and wanting hot sexual adventure? What form of fucked-up patriarchy is it that says only married men can fuck around and get away with it? Why should anyone have to "get away" with fucking around? Where is your pride in being queer, a dyke, a fag, a sexual being? Just throw away your pride and get MARRIED???

What keeps you from having a life partner and still tricking?

What really pisses me off is sodomy is still illegal in many places in this country, that queers and fornicators may be legally stoned to death in some countries. What could you be doing to end homophobia, gay suicide, queer-bashing and queer murder instead of focusing on the fucking church sacrament of reactionary marriage. I mean if you had to do something to advance the health and well-being of the greater number of people, you would have to prioritize your activism and place things like worker's rights, racism, slavery, sexism, and homophobia ahead of marriage.

Get a fucking divorce and let me know how wonderful the "marriage" ride was...
Okay, flamethrower off... I'll step down from my soapbox now... Happy Trails.

Tala Brandeis (www.talabrandeis.com) is a revolutionary leather dyke in an open 11-year relationship with her lover Anne Williams. I've organized unions, and done anti-Nazi work. I've been a sex worker and...I am a sex-educator, a biker, a writer, a photographer, and a tattoo artist (www.talatattoo.com). I'm studying bass guitar. Perverts are the bearers of genius. Let's have more perverts acting as perverts...

Over the Rainbow:
Gay-Movement Organizers Obsessed with Fighting for Same-Sex Marriage Seem to Have Forgotten Their Roots in a Quest for a More Liberated World, One They Shared with Feminists Who Viewed Marriage as Hopelessly Patriarchal
Michael Bronski

Marriage rights mania is in the air. First, there was the decision by the Ontario Court of Appeal to grant same-sex couples the right to marry, and to urge the Canadian government to change its definition of marriage so that gay and lesbian couples from every province can wed. Then the U.S. Supreme Court ruled that gay couples have the right to have sex, prompting Justice Antonin Scalia to fulminate about "the so-called homosexual agenda" and warn: "This reasoning leaves on pretty shaky grounds state laws limiting marriage to opposite-sex couples." And if the Massachusetts Supreme Judicial Court grants gay and lesbian couples the right to marry when it rules in *Goodridge et al. v. Department of Public Health*—a decision is expected any day now — the marriage debate will be all we hear about for the next 20 years. Hell, maybe the Bravo network will even commission a sequel to last summer's hit reality miniseries *Gay Weddings*. (The network could combine it with *Queer Eye for the Straight Guy* and call it *Queer Cupid's Bridal Makeover*.) But even if the Massachusetts court doesn't decide in favor of the plaintiffs in *Goodridge*, full marital equality for gay and lesbian couples is in America's future. The Pew Research Center reported last week that 38 percent of those polled said they backed the idea of gay marriages, up 11 percent from seven years ago. Meanwhile, an NBC/*Wall Street Journal* poll from November 1999 found that 66 percent of the public believes it's only a matter of time before queers win the right to marry.

All this can be only good news for a queer activist like myself, who's spent 35 years advocating for gay rights, right? Well, no. Let me explain: I've made a career out of political organizing and advocacy of gay and lesbian issues. I joined New York's Gay Liberation Front less than a month after the Stonewall Riots, and I've been working on queer issues ever since. While I can appreciate why winning the right to marry will be seen as a bringing down the walls of a heterosexual Jericho, I also view it as a limited, very small victory.

My problem is not with queer people getting legally hitched, per se. Any change in our culture that brings fuller equality under the law—as mandated by the Constitution—is a good thing. Queer couples who want to marry should get the same benefits now offered only to heterosexual couples. My problem is that gay political organizing seems to have become *obsessed* with winning the right to marry. I fear that queer political organizers have been caught up in the exhilaration of the moment and that they're not looking into the future—or the past—as much as they should. I fear that for many people, winning the right to marry has become the raison d'être of the movement, not only its alpha but especially its omega. Indeed, cultural and political commentator Andrew Sullivan, author of 1995's *Virtually Normal: An Argument About Homosexuality* and the editor, with Joseph Landau, of 1997's *Same-Sex Marriage: Pro and Con*, has proclaimed, "When we get the right for same-sex marriage, we have done all we need to do, we can just pack the movement up and close it down."

I don't want to sound like some cranky old radical—a parody of the aging socialist in some Lower East Side café who complains that nothing good has happened since Lenin published *What Is to Be Done?* in 1902. Yeah, I know. Too late. But bear with me.

Institutional memory in a social movement is both good and necessary.

When the gay-liberation movement formed in 1969, we had a broad, expansive vision of social justice. We wanted to change the world and make it better—not just for gay men and lesbians (this was before bisexuals and transgender people were fighting along with us), but for everyone. We wanted to find alternatives to the traditional structures under which we were raised, structures that many of us found insufficient to meet our needs and desires. We aligned ourselves with other movements and learned from them. We got "Gay Is Good" from the Black Power movement's self-affirming "Black Is Beautiful." From the new feminist movement, we learned that patriarchy—especially when it mandated compulsory heterosexuality—was as bad for queers as it was for women. And we also believed, like many feminists, that marriage was, at its best, an imperfect institution, and, at its worst, a dangerous one.

With such history feeding my politics, I am amazed that the feminist critique has been completely lost in the current debate over marriage. Especially since many of the lesbians now working to secure the right to marry came out and came of age in the early 1970s. Today, there is a complete misconception about what feminists saw as the problem with marriage. It wasn't just that prevailing state laws meant that men had the legal right to rape their wives; or that domestic violence wasn't taken seriously; or that most jurisdictions forbade women from signing legal contracts without the consent of their husbands. It was that marriage privatized intimate relationships, hindered community interaction, and regulated sexuality. The feminist critique of marriage sought to promote personal freedom and sexual liberation. It chafed against the notion that the only valid relationships were those that had been endorsed—and financially supported—by the state. The feminist critique of marriage, signed onto fully by the Gay Liberation Front, made clear that the state had no business telling us what we could do with our bodies (especially with regard to reproduction), what we could do in bed, or with whom we could do it. We understood that what the state allowed, or sanctioned, was in the state's interests, and not ours.

These were not crackpot ideas coming from the lunatic hippie fringe. They were at the center of a very lively public debate about the best ways for women and men to lead their personal and sexual lives. In 1970, Kate Millett's *Sexual Politics*—in which she seriously questioned the idea that marriage was necessary for personal happiness or the successful raising of children—was a *New York Times* bestseller; Millett herself was featured on the cover of *Time* magazine. Other books—Shulamith Firestone's 1970 *The Dialectic of Sex: The Case for Feminist Revolution* and Dorothy Dinnerstein's 1976 *The Mermaid and the Minotaur: Human Malaise and Sexual Arrangements*—were widely discussed in the popular press. In 1971, Nena and George O'Neill published *Open Marriage*—a how-to guide for people who wanted to expand their ideas about intimate relationships. It sold over one million copies in less than a year, making its authors instant media stars. The culture was desperately hungry for alternatives to traditional sexual relationships. Ideas about communal living, extended nonbiological families, and collective child-raising were also in the air: nobody was saying, let's get rid of marriage, but they were extraordinarily interested in exploring alternatives to it.

For me, the gay movement was a factory in which alternative visions of everyday life were dreamed up and then shipped out to the rest of the world: rearranging the ways we think about love, making oral sex a permissible topic for heterosexual discussion (though Bill Clinton took care of *that* for us), teaching heterosexual men and women that they could dress in a less restricting, more comfortable manner. Gay liberation, along with the feminist movement, was also a primary catalyst for radical social change. We told mainstream society that there were plenty of other options and that they should loosen up.

All this, obviously, has changed. The gay movement today has gone out of the radical-social-change business and taken up a franchise in the "let's just fight for equality" business. Not that there is anything wrong with equality—hey, it's a basis for democracy, even if democracy has a hard time attaining and maintaining it—it's just that it doesn't move the world forward at a very fast rate.

My primary problem with the current obsession among gay-rights groups like the Human Rights Campaign and the National Gay and Lesbian Task Force is that marriage still poses the same problems it did in the late 1960s: is this the best way for most people to organize their most intimate relationships, and does marriage ultimately make people as happy and productive as they might otherwise be? Well, given the 50 percent divorce rate, the ongoing epidemic of domestic violence among straight *and* gay couples, and the number of people who seek marital counsel from the likes of Dr. Phil, Dr. Laura, and Dr. Ruth, not to mention the vital role fantasies of conjugal cheating play on television and in Hollywood, I would have to conclude that marriage falls far, far short of its exalted reputation.

So why would gay people even want to get married? Part of the answer is that in a world wracked by homophobia, getting an official okay on your relationship feels great. It is validating, and it mutes some of the hurt and pain inflicted on so many queers by their families, neighbors, co-workers, and society at large. Most of us will seek almost any remedy for pain, anything that might make it go away, or at least make us feel better. This is evident in the numbers of same-sex couples who have gone to Vermont for civil unions or crossed the northern border to Ontario or British Columbia to be legally wed in Canada. Neither Vermont civil unions nor Canadian marriages have any legal standing in the rest of the United States (though a Nassau County judge in New York ruled earlier this month that a gay man had legal standing—based on his civil union—to file a wrongful-death suit after his partner died while receiving treatment for a broken leg). But the symbolic meaning of such legalities is very compelling for the couples who seek them out. And it is no surprise that this should be. In our culture, marriage is a powerful expectation. Marriage is so much the expectation and norm that even heterosexual couples have to explain why they *don't* want to get married. It is what we are all brought up to want and never given much permission to question. It is a cultural myth many of us still embrace, despite all the evidence suggesting that "happily ever after" is more aptly applied to fairy tales than marriages. For some couples—straight and gay—getting married is simply easier than not getting married. It is a learned cultural response that is easier to give in to than to fight.

There is nothing intrinsically wrong with queers buying in to the marriage myth—although it does strike me as odd, given that we have managed to do so well without it for so long. What I do find irritating is that the fight for marriage rights has become such an idée fixe for both the gay movement and gay culture. It is now the elusive Holy Grail of gay freedom: when we are granted same-sex marriage, we will have finally achieved transcendent acceptance. In the early 1970s, we had continuous, vibrant community discussions about how best to enact the new freedoms we were discovering. In those years, we rejected myth after myth embraced by earlier queer generations: that we had to be private to be safe, that our sexual desire was a form of mental illness, that we were doomed to hell, that we had to replicate the most staid heterosexual relationship patterns to have any chance at personal happiness. Rather, we thought we could create a better world, one more in tune with our needs and desires.

I hear very little discussion now—in the gay press or in our national organizations—about the intricacies of how queer people feel about marriage.

Everyone agrees that gay people must have equality under the law, but do we ever hear from people who don't want to get married? From people who think their relationships are fine the way they are now? From people who have found that monogamy doesn't work for them? From people who feel their lives have been seriously encumbered by having kids and being in a traditional relationship? From people who chafe at the idea that under the traditional definition of marriage, monogamy is not only expected but mandated? In my 54 years, I have had several long-term, very successful relationships. None of them was monogamous, because neither I nor my lovers wanted to be—but they were faithful. Most gay men I know (and not a few lesbians) share similar sentiments. Are we just not the marrying sort? Maybe we should be campaigning for open marriage, or marriage with a tricking-on-the-side option, or the we-just-want-the-economic-benefits-but-have-no-intention-of-actually-being-traditionally-married marriage.

But this isn't how it works. You don't win the right to marry by telling the world that queer people's lives are as confusing, messy, tattered, and complicated as heterosexual lives. You win the right to marry by presenting to the world, and to the courts, the most acceptable, most homogeneous, most lovable, most traditional couples (with kids if possible) you can find. And given that marriage is, for everyone, a form of sexual regulation, it is also important to present to the world the most conventional images of gay sexual behavior. Nowhere is this better exemplified than in the writings of William N. Eskridge Jr., the noted gay legal scholar who has been a major theoretician and proponent of full marital equality for same-sex couples. In 1996's *The Case for Same-Sex Marriage: From Sexual Liberty to Civilized Commitment*, Eskridge argues that, along with providing equality under the law, marriage would be of enormous social and psychological benefit to both queer and heterosexual communities, since it would regulate gay-male promiscuity. "Gay marriage will have a civilizing effect on gay men," he argues. Aside from the idiocy of this argument—as if heterosexuals have ever allowed marriage vows to curb their sexual wanderings— it is also deeply, profoundly homophobic.

Eskridge pleads for equality under the law by reeling out the same stereotypes that have made gay people second-class citizens. His theory embodies everything we thought was wrong with marriage in the 1970s: it is not about love and commitment— it is simply about regulating sex. Indeed, in Eskridge's world there would be two kinds of gay men—good ones who had sex in marriage and bad ones who had sex outside of marriage; not all that different from the '50s-era stereotypes of "good" and "bad" girls that feminists condemned as repressive and destructive. Most interestingly, Eskridge's views are not on the fringe. He is one of the most frequent commentators on winning the freedom to marry in the gay and mainstream press, and his archconservative, destructive views on sexual morality are almost never challenged. Eskridge's sales pitch for queer marital equality is based on a lie. And while I understand that the marriage battle requires "perfect" queer couples to act as poster children, I also think we have abdicated our responsibility *to ourselves* to debate the pros and cons of the matter. Not only aren't we talking about new visions of how we might want to live our lives, we aren't even talking about how we actually live them now.

In this age of marriage mania, I miss not just the vigorous public and community discussions but the visionary impulses that fueled the early movement. Why aren't we having demanding and intelligent debates over whether we want to fight for marriage or something similar to, say, the French *pacte civil de solidarité*—which essentially gives marriage rights to any two people (gay, straight, the sexually involved, or those who are just roommates) who want to declare themselves a legal couple? That legal arrangement would also grant us all equality under the law, as well as enlarge our idea of what family might be. Some activists have argued that such a radical proposal would stand no chance of becoming law in the United States. But the reality is that you get only what you organize for—five years ago same-sex marriage was unthinkable, 35 years ago antidiscrimination bills were unthinkable. The queer movement did not get to where it is now by thinking small. Activist and writer Patrick Califia has written, "Years ago, when we spoke of gay family we meant our community, now we mean parents raising children in the suburbs." And I have to wonder, with the fight for marriage in full swing, are we thinking large or small? What do we gain? What do we lose?

Marriage has become such a fixation in gay politics that I fear we may lose touch with other equally, if not more, important issues. Yes, queer legal groups like Gay and Lesbian Advocates and Defenders, who are litigating the *Goodridge* case and who litigated the Vermont case that resulted in civil unions, are doing incredibly important work. But that nearly every other queer legal and advocacy group has made marriage its priority strikes me as intellectually lazy. It's the I'll-have-what-they're-having fight rather than the this-is-how-to-make-the-world-better-for-everyone fight. Fighting for marriage is like fighting over yesterday's leftovers rather than coming up with something new and better. Even as we fight for the right to marry, there is still so much to do. We can't even pass a federal nondiscrimination bill, much less make the streets safe for transgender kids who are being murdered in their own neighborhoods. So much energy is being expended on marriage that we might not have the resources to fight for other issues in the future, both near and far.

It is tempting for social movements to become consumed by their own obsessions. The early women's movement focused entirely, fetishistically, on suffrage for nearly 70 years. When that battle was finally won, the movement nearly died and—despite so much more to be accomplished—did almost nothing until the late 1960s. Could this happen to the gay-rights movement? Only time will tell, but I do know that a movement only moves forward when it is filled with healthy debate and dissent, when it has visions of the future, and when it acknowledges its past.

As an old-time gay liberationist, I find the frenzy around marriage organizing exciting but depressing. I would never have imagined that a movement that started out in the bars, the streets, and in public cruising places could have come this far. The gay-liberation movement had a vision of radical change and making the world a better place. Securing the right to marry will make the world a better place, but it will not change the world. Heck, it doesn't even change marriage. In the end, it is such a small gain for such a big fight.

In 1969, we didn't just want—as we said then—a piece of the pie we had been denied for so long. We wanted to take over the bakery and produce a huge array of tasty, extravagant, nutritious, luscious, and inviting foodstuffs for queers and everyone else. I don't think we ever imagined that our movement would one day be happy to settle for such small crumbs, no matter how sweet.

Michael Bronski is the author of several books including The Pleasure Principle: Sex, Backlash and the Struggle for Gay Freedom *(1998) and* Pulp Friction: Uncovering the Golden Age of Gay Male Pulps *(2004). He is an independent scholar and journalist and has been involved in the gay movement for 35 years. He is a frequent Visiting Scholar at Dartmouth College.*

First published in *The Boston Phoenix*, August 1, 2003. Reprinted by permission of the author.

Something Borrowed, Something Blue:
Is Marriage Right for Queers?
Victoria A. Brownworth

Who gets to decide whether same-sex couples should be granted the legal right to marry? Is this a civil rights, morality, or cultural issue (or all three)?

Let us presume same-sex marriage to be, first and foremost, a civil rights issue, as morality and cultural mores are far more flexible and delineated by normative standards of a majority, not the minority. From a civil rights perspective, is it truly democratic to allow a majority to determine the civil rights of a minority? Between the early 1600s and 1865 when the Emancipation Proclamation was signed, black Americans were disenfranchised by slavery (only a member of the white majority could enfranchise or make "free" a black man or woman). That disenfranchisement continued relatively unabated in most sectors of the United States until 1954 when the U.S. Supreme Court struck down segregation in the landmark ruling of *Brown v. Topeka Board of Education*. In 1964, institutionalized racism was finally made illegal in all public arenas when the Civil Rights Act was signed.

Women were relegated to second-class citizenship and disenfranchised through a range of legal stratagems from the early 1600s in the U.S. until 1920, when the Nineteenth Amendment gave women the right to vote. But women did not receive fuller legal status until the 1962 U.S. Supreme Court ruling in *Griswold v. Connecticut*, which made birth control available to women, and the controversial 1973 ruling in *Roe v. Wade*, which made abortion in the first trimester of pregnancy accessible to all women and termination in the second and third trimesters available under some conditions. Further legislation allowing women to divorce, prosecution of domestic violence, and affirmative action all furthered women's enfranchisement into the male-dominant society. However the 1976 vote on the Equal Rights Amendment, which would have given women full citizenship under the Constitution, was narrowly defeated. As a consequence women remain less than fully enfranchised in the U.S. in 2004 and sexism still pervades, particularly in the workplace where women continue to make only two-thirds what men do for similar work.

In July, 2003, the U.S. Supreme Court again made civil rights history by voting in *Lawrence v. Texas* to abolish the arbitrary imposition of sodomy laws against same-sex couples. Writing for the majority, conservative justice and George Bush Sr. appointee, Anthony Kennedy wrote that sodomy laws unfairly penalize same-sex couples. Kennedy wrote that the very arbitrariness of their imposition created an atmosphere of discrimination that led inevitably to societal antagonism and even violence against lesbian and gay Americans. The Justice argued that the U.S. Supreme Court had been wrong in 1986 when it ruled to uphold sodomy laws against same-sex couples in the case of *Bowers v. Hardwick*.

Kennedy's assertion that the Court had erred and had thus contributed to discrimination against a considerable demographic of American society was a huge civil rights step for queer Americans. (Sodomy laws have been used not only to arrest men and women for consensual sexual acts, but also as a predicate for denying other civil rights to lesbians and gay men. Sodomy laws have been used repeatedly as a basis for denying women legal custody of their children.) What's more, Kennedy wrote in his opinion that same-sex couples deserve equal rights under the Constitution to the "pursuit of happiness" — a pursuit which would be impeded by random enforcement of sodomy laws.

One of the three justices who dissented in Kennedy's opinion, Antonin Scalia, countered that in making this ruling the High Court was inevitably opening the door to equal rights for lesbians and gay men (which he opposes) and that the Court's ruling would give legal credence to the case for gay [sic] marriage. As it happens, Scalia was correct. Several months later a lower court in Massachusetts ruled that prohibiting the marriage of same-sex couples violated that state's constitution and thus same-sex marriage would be legal as of May 2004.

The U.S. Supreme Court ruling led to a groundswell of activism on same-sex marriage, much of it from heterosexual politicians. The then-newly elected mayor of San Francisco, Democrat Gavin Newsom, began issuing marriage licences to same-sex couples mere weeks after he took office. Newsom noted that he could not in good conscience bar same-sex couples from experiencing the pleasures of marriage that he and his wife enjoyed. A range of communities throughout the U.S. followed Newsom's lead—in New Mexico, New York, Wisconsin, Utah, and New Jersey, among others. In the months leading up to the legal marriages of same-sex couples in Massachusetts, these unions (which some called sanctioned because they were approved by the mayors of their towns and which others termed acts of civil disobedience and which a series of judges eventually halted) flourished across the country with far less opprobrium than conservatives would have wished.

Then on July 10, 2004, President George W. Bush threw down the culture wars gauntlet in his Saturday morning radio address by calling for an immediate constitutional amendment defining marriage as heterosexual: "between a man and a woman, a husband and a wife." According to Bush if "activist judges" (like his father's appointee and the Massachusetts and New Jersey courts) are allowed to make marriage "a mere legal contract," they will divorce it from what Bush termed its "cultural, religious and natural roots," and "the meaning of marriage will be lost and the institution weakened."

Bush's statement was more than a little suspect, following as it did a series of political setbacks for his administration that demanded he reach out to his conservative base as the 2004 presidential campaign moved into high gear. The president's comments also seemed to fly in the face of the groundswell that had not abated: same-sex couples were marrying, legally in Massachusetts and extralegally elsewhere. Equally important, however, was the fact that there was less backlash over the Massachusetts law than had been expected. Unless Bush's proposed amendment passes prior to 2006, there are no grounds for stopping the legal marriages of same-sex couples in Massachusetts until a referendum can be voted on in that state—which will not occur prior to 2006. By that time, argues Rep. Barney Frank (D-MA), citizens of Massachusetts who were against same-sex marriage will have had ample time to witness those couplings and see that none of the irreparable damage alleged by conservatives to be incipient against the institution of marriage or society as a whole will have occurred.

Bush may have also broadcast his attack on same-sex marriage because the same day as his radio address, gay and lesbian couples in New Jersey were lining up for domestic partnerships, which had just been made legal in the state, making it the fifth state to afford same-sex couples either domestic partnership, civil unions as in Vermont or, as in Massachusetts, legal marriage.

In 1994, I wrote an essay entitled "Tying the Knot or the Hangman's Noose: The Case Against Queer Marriage" in which I queried why lesbians and gay men were pursuing marriage (and at that time, the military—it only took a few wars and a lot of killing from the Bush Administration to get queers firmly off that soapbox, I've noted). In 1994 I was unequivocal in my denunciation, asserting that marriage and the military were two of the most oppressive and repressive institutions in human history and wedding ourselves to them politically and socially would not alter that fact. Both were bad—not just for us, but for everyone.

More than a decade and much social and political change later, my feelings about the military remain unchanged. On marriage as an institution my perspective hasn't changed, but my view of same-sex marriage as a civil right have.

Marriage is inarguably, after war and torture, the world's most repressive social institution. Throughout most of the world, in particular Africa, Asia, the Middle East, and Central and South America, women and girls are victimized by marriage in a myriad of horrific ways. In Africa prepubescent girls are married off to men older than their grandfathers. On that continent, too, the practice of female genital mutilation (FGM—the usually violent and unanesthetized removal of the clitoris) and infibulation (the cutting off of the labia and sewing shut of the vagina) are endemic and as essential to marital tradition for women and girls there as wearing something borrowed and something blue to the wedding is for brides in America. India has some equally sickening marriage traditions: girls are routinely married off to men of their parents choosing (sold off is more accurate; dowries remain an elemental aspect of marriage in the world's most populous nation). Sometimes girls balk at such arrangements and reject them. This often results in those girls being splattered with acid by the prospective bridegroom to make them unmarriageable. Frequently, soon after the marriage, the husband's family becomes discontented with the woman's dowry. An epidemic of bride burnings have resulted. In-laws try to disguise such attacks as kitchen accidents; the practice is so widespread, however, that laws have been instituted in the last decade specifically against bride-burning. Also banned after centuries, yet still in practice in most rural areas of India, along with bride burnings, is *suttee*, the throwing of a widow (still alive) onto her husband's funeral pyre.

In most Muslim countries FGM is a component of marriage, as are so-called honor killings in which a bride's own family will murder her if she is even thought to be adulterous, lesbian, or has been raped. The reason for honor killings: in Muslim society such acts reflect on the manhood of the fathers, brothers, sons, uncles, and cousins in a woman's family. These murders of women and girls are rarely prosecuted (nor are the men implicated in either adultery or rape usually prosecuted). In Nigeria in 2003, a woman was sentenced to death by stoning because she had been raped and had borne a child by a man other than her husband. The strict Islamic law of Sharia, which obtains in many countries like Saudi Arabia, requires a woman be stoned or signifies other forms of execution for any presumed crime—adultery, lesbianism, rape–that occurs while she is married. (The woman is tried by a religious court, not a secular one, if she is tried at all.) Throughout the majority of the world today married women have no recourse against violent husbands; neither domestic abuse nor rape in marriage are considered crimes anywhere but in the U.S. and Europe. In several states in the U.S. as well as in parts of Europe, Asia, and the U.K., married women must get their husband's permission before they can have an abortion, even if their health is at stake. In India, Pakistan, and China, women are regularly forced by their husbands to *have* sex-selection abortions so that they do not have female children.

The reasons why marriage can only be viewed as a repressive and oppressive institution through which women are routinely and often brutally victimized thus is manifold. Which does indeed beg the question of why queers would want to be associated with it.

When President Bush made his statements on July 10, 2004, he asserted that allowing gay [sic] marriage would "redefine the most fundamental institution of civilization." Maybe yes, maybe no, but given the short compendium of what marriage is in much of the world today, can anyone reasonably argue that marriage as it stands in 2004 desperately *needs* to be changed?

When I was 17, I married a man. The reasons why I did so were complex. Thirty years ago I could not envision a future life as a lesbian. I had already experienced a tremendous degree of discrimination as an out lesbian in my all-girls high school, where I was expelled for my involvement with another student. My parents were upset by my lesbianism, although they were unequivocal in their declarations that my sexual orientation was merely a phase because, in the words of my father, "You're pretty and boys like you."

I *was* pretty and boys *did* like me, but the issue of my sexual choices at the cusp of what was then called gay liberation (I came out in ninth grade a few months after the Stonewall Rebellion) was confusing. We had no models then for queer lives that were led in ways that were not disturbingly marginal because the people leading those kinds of lives were shut tightly in the closet while those who were flamboyantly out were, when I was a teenager going to queer bars, men and women on the fringes of society.

As I stood before the priest with my husband-to-be, a nice Catholic boy from a solid working-class immigrant family, I hoped that some member of our wedding party (half of whom were gay—I'd met my husband through his gay cousin when we were in Gay Activists Alliance together), some member of our families (his parents were opposed to our marriage), or one of our friends, gay or straight, would stand up and protest our union. But we were pronounced husband and wife and as I walked back down the aisle, now with a new name and a new place in the world, I knew with grim certainty that I had made a terrible error.

The marriage was short-lived. The experience of being married was for me, as a woman, disturbing from the moment I turned to walk back down the aisle. The first time I received a piece of mail on which my name appeared as Mrs. John Smith, not Ms. Victoria Brownworth, I broke out in hives. *Who was Mrs. John Smith?* Where was *I* in that name? (My husband had not expected me to change my name, although 30 years ago few women kept their "maiden" names. He just didn't want to change his own.) I never experienced that thrill of being a new bride that I had been led to believe growing up as a girl was something all women felt when they married. I did not yearn to be half of a whole—I ached to be the whole I thought I was prior to becoming someone's wife, which was, I now saw, a position as adjunct to the *real* person, the husband. Even though that was not really my husband's perspective, it was certainly the view of everyone around us—society as a whole, our families, our friends, our church.

No doubt my experience is somewhat anomalous because I really was a lesbian and had no business marrying a man. No doubt my husband was equally unhappy because I was not the wife he should have (rightly) expected. But my experience of how the world changes in mere moments when one marries was, I believe, an experience shared even as you read this by women around the globe. In marriage as it has been instituted, which was indeed as a legal contract, despite President Bush's lack of knowledge of the history of the institution, women are ceded to men, either as outright property or as sexual and child-bearing chattel. It has actually only been since after World War II in the U.S. and other Western nations that marriage has been more than a legal contract. Although small enclaves of the highly enlightened discussed the idea throughout the nineteenth century, the concept of marriage for love, marriage for companionable connection, marriage for the pleasure—not profit—of being part of a couple, is relatively new, a twentieth-century ideation. So new is it, in fact, that laws are still catching up to that evolving reality. Even divorce (which many of those conservatives who denounce same-sex marriage as perilous to the institution have gone through, some more than once) has only been a legal option for women since the twentieth century, although it was available to men centuries earlier.

What would be different if we queers married? How would same-sex couples avoid all the vicissitudes of marriage that have been part of that institution for centuries?

In the years that I was a voice arguing against gay marriage on platforms with noted proponents of it, my dissent focused on the wrongs inherent in marriage as it had been defined. Marriage was (and still is in most of the world) a social contract devised solely to control women. Men were not bound by its confines; women were shackled by it. Why would queers embrace an institution which was, as its history proclaimed, as bloody and dehumanizing as slavery?

We cannot negate the long, insidious, oppressive and repressive history of marriage when we talk about wanting it for ourselves as lesbians and gay men. And just as heterosexuals need a better argument for denying it to us than that tradition dictates it is for men and women, lesbians and gay men need a more complete argument for embracing it than merely that if straight people can do it, we should be able to as well. That *ipso facto* argument worked about the enfranchisement of women and blacks because they were denied so much within white, male society—every aspect of their lives was limited by their social status.

That lack of equal social status is also true for lesbians and gay men; the very tone of Justice Anthony Kennedy's ruling in *Lawrence v. Texas* resonates with how much lesbians and gays men have been denied in straight society. But does marriage fix that, does it promote equality in areas other than queer relationships versus straight relationships?

It does not. We still bear the mark of discrimination in every other aspect of our lives, from where we live (or are allowed to live) to where we work (or are allowed to work). The violence against us merely for who we are is pandemic and the more obviously queer we are—butch lesbians, nelly gays, the transgendered—the more likely we are to be victimized. *Lawrence v. Texas* may have been the queer version of *Brown v. Topeka Board of Education*, but we have yet to see our version of the 1964 Civil Rights Act.

All of which makes the debate over same-sex marriage complex. Undeniably marriage grants lesbians and gay men legal rights (and responsibilities, an aspect of the marriage contract we rarely hear discussed in the dialogue over marriage rights) they have not previously had access to in our society. To that extent legal marriage seems, unequivocally, to be a step in the direction toward full enfranchisement. As conservative gay writer Jonathan Rauch argues so persuasively, marriage creates kinship irrespective of birth or lineage—nothing else on earth can do this. That, of course, is both the joy and the responsibility, the "for richer and for poorer, in sickness and in health," element of the marriage contract. Marriage is the quintessential legal and social partnership. That, finally, is the only true argument for marriage that can be made, irrespective of its dreadful historic past and embracing its complex but often joyful present: It denotes our kinship and legalizes our connection.

In reconsidering my position on marriage I come away from the polemic still confused. I acknowledge the contradictions of my evolving position: I remain vehemently opposed to the oppressive nature of marriage as it is imposed upon and subjugates women around the globe; but I embrace the idea of an evolving concept of marriage in which two people—in this case lesbian and gay male couples—engage in the kinship denied them in our heterosexist culture and society. As an anti-assimilationist, I do not want to see our queer culture subsumed by a mimicking of straight culture and what I consider to be largely abhorrent straight values. We have our own rich culture born, like that of black Americans, from our legacy of oppression and we should be proud of it, we should celebrate it. Part of our culture, just as with black Americans who were denied the right to marry for centuries, is our strong bonds of queer "family," including our lovers, our spouses. (Black Americans marry less than any other group—fewer than 20 percent of black couples marry as opposed to 80 percent of white couples.) We already have *kinship* in the deepest sense, but legalizing those bonds provides us with some of the civil rights we have been denied—some quite basic, like the right to our own children or the right to be with our sick or dying spouses. Same-sex marriage also grants us something we have been denied for centuries and which many of us ache to have, no matter how politicized and radical our views might be: social approbation. As Rauch asserts, marriage brings with it community. I experienced this during my brief marriage to my husband which lasted for only 2 years, yet I never experienced it with my lesbian spouse with whom I lived for over 12 years. As Mrs. John Smith, a whole world of social approval was opened to me; his family didn't like me but embraced me as his wife. Yet as the longtime lover of another woman I was always an outsider in her family, and she in mine. I could readily declare my marriage to John Smith to anyone if I so chose and risk nothing more than social accolades. But if I declared the spousal nature of my relationship to Jane Smith, I put myself *and* her at risk of social opprobrium, discrimination, and even violence.

I do not presume that an expansion of same-sex marriage laws in states beyond Massachusetts will vitiate the ingrained prejudices of a majority of Americans toward queers. Racism still obtains in the U.S. despite the many laws passed to rectify the legacy of slavery and oppression of blacks in America. Sexism still pervades our society no matter the many gains feminism has wrought over three decades. I do believe, however, that marriage allows for a formalizing of our relationship to each other as queer couples and thus makes us public in a way we have not previously been. We are united as a queer community by witnessing queer marriages (even if we don't know the people involved) just as heterosexuals are. When we see ourselves on the evening news in joyous embrace of our love for each other—both couples newly minted and couples of decades' long standing—we experience a jolt of recognition: These are *our* lives being celebrated, *our* kinship being validated, *our* long struggle for equality being recognized. We needn't be proponents of marriage, queer or otherwise, to revel in the symbolism of our public status after so many generations having been relegated to the closet. The witnessing of these couplings is much like the witnessing of pride marches: Our numbers are vast and seeing our community in all its diversity (the marriages in San Francisco, for example, ran the gamut from activists who had been coupled for over fifty years to young tattooed and pierced couples in butch-femme regalia, a panoply of races, ethnicities, ages, and abilities that spoke to the multiplicity of queer community and relationships) is emboldening and invigorating—it breaks the silence about our lives in very public ways. It also shows that lesbian girl or gay boy in Middle of Nowhere, U.S.A. what I could not envision for myself as a queer teen in the era of the closet: a shared life with a queer partner, a life in queer culture and queer society that was as full and fulfilling as those of my straight counterparts, a life that could celebrate queer kinship, embrace queer family.

George Bush promulgates the theory that marriage as an institution will be weakened if same-sex couples are allowed to participate in it. Decades earlier we were told by other American leaders that allowing blacks into white schools or to drink from white water fountains or sit at white lunch counters would somehow lead to the destabilization of American society. We were told that if women—with their flightiness and lack of intellectualism and education—were allowed to vote they would choose badly and we would all be lost as a nation.

These legacies of racism and sexism are what have damaged society. Heterosexism and homophobia continue to harm our society as do lingering tinges of racism and sexism. Equality never hurts a nation; oppression always does.

Bush is correct, however, when he states that allowing same-sex couples to marry will weaken the institution of marriage. It most certainly will do so, and that will make marriage a far better concept than it previously has been. Same-sex marriage will further limit the sexist construct of that institution because now male couples will be wedded (men tend to demand the entitlements they have always been accorded in patriarchal culture) and lesbian couples will more than likely refuse the social inequities built into marriage as a contract. The possibilities exist for same-sex marriage to recalibrate the institution, balancing the gender inequities and making it a true coupling of equal partners.

When the majority seeks to undermine the rights of any minority one has to question why. Fear of losing one's own status, fear of being less powerful is usually the answer to the question of oppression. As queer Americans are more open about their lives and their culture, as more of majority America sees not just how vast our numbers are but how diverse, it is my firm belief that we, as have blacks and women before us, will prevail in our quest for civil rights. Segregation has always worked to maintain oppressive social constructs. If one doesn't see the oppressed minority one doesn't have to address one's fears about difference. For generations black Americans *had* to deal with white America, but white Americans could avoid blacks if they chose. Likewise queer closeted America has always had to operate within the purview of straight America, while straight Americans remained ignorant of who we were and how many of us there were. But democracy is an evolving political theory and within a democracy there is no room for institutionalized oppression, nor institutionalized segregation.

Ironically, it is the desire among so many formerly closeted queers for the symbols of normalcy, the cant of social approbation, that have led them into the spotlight, to be seen by straight America. In the small working-class town of Asbury Park, New Jersey, clerks began handing out marriage licenses to same-sex couples who applied for them in March 2004 while hundreds were being married daily in San Francisco. This was a major story on the local TV news in Philadelphia, where I live, because the stations cover the South Jersey area. What struck me at the time was first how the couples themselves were definingly ordinary working-class women and men and then how the straight folks in their town seemed to care very little that this civil disobedience was going on. The clerks shrugged as they handed out the licenses and asserted that if it didn't say they couldn't issue them in the state statutes, then obviously they could.

Asbury Park is Middle America by any calculation. Small town, hard-working folks with—presumably—small town values. Yet inarguably the majority of the town could not have cared less that queers were marrying. A live-and-let-live philosophy obtained in that town clearly delineated by what the townsfolk perceived as insider status: the queers in their town were hard-working Janes and Joes like themselves. If they wanted to marry, let 'em. In Asbury Park, working-class community defied segregation.

All this suggests that in embracing the concept of same-sex marriage, queers cannot ignore its limitations. Not everyone wants to or is even able to marry. And any social or legal alteration in this one arena does not necessarily presume that other civil rights will evolve. Those rights must be worked for, and hard, for all queers. We cannot take the assimilationist perspective that if we can get married, then that is all that matters—let someone else work for the other elements of our civil rights. In embracing the responsibility of marriage we must also take on the responsibility of queer civil rights, a far headier agenda than two people's coupling.

The question of whether marriage is right or wrong for queers is, to a degree, an insoluble query. Marriage has always been oppressive; whether we perpetuate that legacy or utterly alter it remains to be seen. But for now we deserve the opportunity to try. And we certainly deserve the opportunity to validate our kinships and mitigate our own oppression with access to the rights every heterosexual takes for granted.

Victoria A. Brownworth is a Pulitzer Prize–nominated journalist and Lambda Book Award winner whose syndicated columns appear in a multiplicity of newspapers and magazines in the U.S. and abroad. She covered the U.S. Supreme Court for several years as a reporter and received numerous journalism awards for that coverage. She is the author of 11 books, including the award-winning Too Queer: Essays from a Radical Life *and editor of 12, including the award-winning* Coming Out of Cancer: Writings from the Lesbian Cancer Epidemic. *She lives and works in Philadelphia, where the Constitution was conceived and written.*

Homeland Security
Cynthia Burack and Laree Martin

Today is the day: it is Monday, May 17, 2004, and the first same-sex marriages "fully sanctioned by law" in the United States are being performed—and protested—in Massachusetts. I would like to say I've been waiting for this outcome since I came out nearly 30 years ago, but that would be a lie. Honest now: I've never wanted to get married, even when I was a little girl. At eight I solemnly informed my mother that I would never marry or bear children, and I've kept that latter promise all the way through the gayby boom.

Like many of my compatriots in the LGBT movement, I am willing to defend marriage for those who desire it. And it makes sense that many of us do. The abysmal system of social provisioning in the U.S. can make marriage nearly as imperative for any particular individual as it historically has been for women as a group. And, as we all know, the legal benefits of marriage are nothing to dismiss lightly. In these respects, our political culture and institutions often lag well behind others in the "developed" world. Beyond these prosaic issues, we want to marry to share our love with a lifelong partner, to publicize our joy to our families and communities, to have children or give our children another adult who will love them, to solemnize our commitment, and to solicit the blessings of a favored deity. Put defiance into this mix, and we want to marry for all the right and rational reasons. But we are at a disadvantage when we list the reasons we want to marry. Having been denied that right, we may be more likely to come right out and say that legal benefits like health insurance and joint filing enter into the cost-benefit analysis. This is, of course, a faux pas in discussions about marriage. It isn't that straight people don't also consider the substantial legal and financial benefits of getting hitched. It just isn't polite to talk about such things in the context of the sacred nuptial, and doing so can make us look cunning and instrumental. We're not. Or at least not any more than straight people who collect the benefits (and liabilities) of marriage while they're deflecting our attention to other matters—family values, for example.

Of course, in the end it all comes down to our personal convictions, situations, and feelings. During the recent season of sporadic same-sex weddings, Betty, my "mother-in-law," called to ask me and her daughter Laree if we intended to fly to San Francisco and queue up for a lawless wedding. At the time we were enjoying an unusual interlude together in the Midwest, and we had to admit it hadn't occurred to us. Would we get married? Well, on the one hand we've been together for nearly a decade now, and we've never lived together full-time. Shouldn't we do that first? On the other hand—well, there are several issues on the other hand, including our commitment to one another and our goal to some day reside in the same city (perhaps even in the same household). But then—and I need yet another hand for this—there are all the things that have always bothered me about marriage: the divisions of labor, the inequities (particularly those that the marriage bond itself might solidify and render invisible), the forms of bad behavior its presumed indissolubility might breed. All these points make it difficult for me to decide what same-sex marriage *is*—is it the most radical or the most conservative of all social institutions?—to say nothing of what I might do or not do with it.

Even so, if my partner asked me to marry her I suspect I would. And I might even cry like a girl.

Cindy's the theoretical one of us, not that I'm incapable of creating hypotheticals, considering the philosophical, or letting a passionate vision of the future be my direction in life. When it comes right down to it, though, I know what marriage is and why couples who partner with the same sex need it. The five darkest years of my life were spent married to a partner whose sex was opposite mine. We had the blessings and well wishes of our community, our churches, and the government. There were no requirements of us to bear and raise children to obtain the legal status and benefits of marriage. Had we chosen to formalize our union under the common law instead of under the civil code, we only would have had to reside together for some statutory period, hold ourselves out to the public as being married, and consummate the relationship sexually. So I've always been curious about why anyone really cares whether two men, two women, or one man and one woman join to marry. Mostly I think it's just what we're used to—it's traditional. We like tradition. And if just anyone could go off and marry whomever she pleased, well! What would that do one of our most Honored Traditions?

Last week I steamed a little while a colleague of mine related a story about one of the women in her office who was relocating under the same policies I contend with in my federal employment. The Defense of Marriage Act clearly defines a "spouse" for the purposes of any law in the U.S. Code to mean one man and one woman married under state law. Since the tax codes drive relocation benefits, the woman was surprised to find that the moving company refused to move the belongings of her live-in lover with whom she'd been living-in-sin for years. She figured that those years entitled her to have him treated as a spouse. "His" things and "her" things were, in many cases, easily distinguishable to even the least observant moving professional, though, and she was listed as unmarried on their paperwork. His name was on the house deed, so she was only going to get the benefit of reimbursement for half the closing costs as well. Her solution? She took Mr. Right by the hand, went to the nearest justice of the peace, and got hitched. Problem solved. No longer sinners, they were entitled to the full benefits of relocation under the tax code and her federal employer's policy. How romantic! How fortunate for them that they had a penis and vagina between them to qualify for these benefits!

My partner and I are short one penis, and in the eyes of the law, we've got a vagina to spare, although it doesn't feel that way to us. Thus, we do what we can to even up the odds. So that we can both benefit from the tax savings that property investments bring, we purchased our main residence jointly. If we decide to sell it the next time my employer relocates me, Cindy will have to file a quitclaim deed, which will mean we incur substantial fees to refile the deed in my name only. And the moving company will gladly move all our household goods, because it really is hard to tell "her" things from my things unless you bother to check shoe sizes. It would be nice just to go get married.

We sort of already did what we could do as residents of Washington, DC. On March 21, 2003, we filed in the District of Columbia as domestic partners with my mother, Betty, present to share our joyful ceremony. The process pretty much reflects DC government, which is better than it was several years ago, but still... Turns out there's an office you go to where a clerk signs you up and gives you a certificate after you wait for them to figure out how it's supposed to work. Maybe it's the same for marriage licenses, but it's not the same room, that much I know. We were couple number 25 to sign up. The benefits of being domestic partners in DC are few and mostly flow to employees of the District whose partners are eligible to participate in its health care plan. I think the only benefit Cindy and I actually gained was that we knew we'd done everything within the means allowed to us by our government to demonstrate that we are committed to being together and taking care of one another through illness and poverty and whatever other adversity may strike. We exchanged rings, had a hug there in the little room that we agreed not to call a closet (although it easily could be mistaken for what it once must have been been), and took my mom out for lunch.

It was important to us to take a legal step of some sort to tie us together more formally and to make someone other than our friends and family acknowledge that we are a couple. If we ever decide that we can no longer fulfill our commitment to one another, we have to go back to the clos...I mean, the office in DC and file dissolution papers to let everyone know we're no longer domestic partners. I think that's a good thing. After all, in the weeks prior to becoming domestic partners, Cindy and I found it necessary to vow that we would, under no circumstances, change our sex, become members of the clergy, or announce either in therapy or on national television that we were straight. All of these things had happened to lesbians we knew personally or to lesbian icons with whom we identified.

In my view, relationships are hard to keep together because it's easier to walk out and start new than it is to bear the pain of forgiving and being forgiven. Marriage itself, the social expectations for the solemnity of the vows of marriage, and the state support provided to marriage through cooling-off periods in most divorce laws all help to force couples away from flight when fighting for their relationship might seem unbearable. Except in cases of physical and emotional abuse, I agree with these laws and expectations. Marriage stabilizes relationships in society, and the benefits that flow from that stability are equally beneficial to lesbian and gay couples and the communities in which they live. I generally resist legal and moral constraint; nevertheless, marriage would be good for me. Marriage provides a sort of due process. Under the rules of marriage and divorce, my partner can't take away some of the things I value most in life—her companionship, caring, support, and love— without giving me notice and an opportunity to be heard. U-Hauls can be packed up and driven away just as easily as they can be loaded up to move in, you know. Did I mention I have abandonment issues?

Cynthia Burack teaches at Ohio State, one of the last Big Ten universities to resist extending full domestic partnership benefits to its employees. When she isn't teaching she travels around the country to be with her partner and two cats.

Laree Martin is an executive in the United States Postal Service. She is temporarily away from her office in Washington, DC, where she and her partner make their home.

Marriage: Thanks, but No Thanks
Rachel Kramer Bussel

I have never dreamed about getting married, never had those visions of myself walking down any aisle in the long, blindingly white dress, veil covering my eyes, promises of forever floating in the air. Even when I was a little girl, my fantasies running rampant about actors like Ricky Schroeder, my boy-crazy, lust-filled mind didn't want the ring or the ceremony. I occasionally dreamed of babies, or even setting up house, but never being a bride. And not much has changed in the ensuing 20 years. If anything, having lived through many wondrous as well as difficult relationships, I'm even more certain that there is no wedding march in my future, be it to a man or woman. As I watch all those around me, straight and queer, rushing to the altar, that decision still hasn't changed.

Partly, my negative association with marriage is the result of growing up with not only divorced parents, but divorced grandparents, and slowly seeing other family members split over the years. My aunt and uncle, who I proudly wobbled down the aisle and doled out rose petals for as their flower girl? Split. My great-aunt and her husband — split up long before I knew them as a couple. I've seen more than enough long-standing relationships and marriages end, some amicably and some not, that the promise of "till death do us part" seems all too much like wishful thinking and not a true commitment. Who can be so omniscient as to predict the future?

To me, the cultural imperative to be married, paired off, settled down, not only has never appealed to me, but the way it's pushed upon people, especially women, has made me want to run screaming in the other direction. I feel fortunate in that being a queer, mostly polyamorous person has given me an easy out from that. I don't tend to date people who'll be pulling out a small velvet box while we're out to dinner. And for that I'm grateful; I can get to know and enjoy my lovers without trying to figure out exactly where it's all leading. When I start dating someone new, whether a man or a woman, I don't have to immediately revert to *Rules*-girl mode and figure out how to get a ring on my finger. Part of what is so insidious about marriage is precisely all the rules surrounding it, the cost and the formality, the showy nature of wedding hype that obscures the simple but all-important love it's meant to celebrate.

And yet for all that cynicism, I am not immune to true love, which at its best marriage does celebrate. I find myself wiping back tears at weddings, and especially seeing all the happy brides and brides, grooms and grooms, beaming out at me from San Francisco or even in my own state of New York. The looks on their faces after getting the chance to live out the moment they've been waiting for seemingly forever are enough to make anyone reconsider marriage as only a problem rather than a solution.

Ultimately, I don't truly believe in marriage for myself, and I'm quite distrustful of what that precious piece of paper can do for anyone else. I'm skeptical about the promises it holds out before us, glittering gems that may be cracked and faulty once you get too close. How can marriage possibly live up to our impossible dreams and plans for it? And yet I can't say that queer folks shouldn't be allowed to marry. Equal-opportunity failure or success should be ours, and it seems to me that by stating so plainly their opposition to same-sex marriage, the Republicans and conservatives (not to mention the so-called liberals and others pushing for "commitments" and "domestic partnerships" versus "marriages") are making themselves look foolish and pushing those in the middle further to our side. It's one thing to question the institution of marriage and especially the ways that institution is put on such a fucking pedestal, but it's another to have the right to that pedestal, whether it eventually topples or not, denied to people simply because of the sex of their partner. All of the antigay marriage arguments instantly fall apart and are so laughably untrue—that marriage is for procreation is one that is particularly ludicrous—that they could make almost anyone an activist.

To me, marriage is already so fraught, first with its cultural imperative, then with its impossible notions of forever, along with my family's history, that is has always felt like pretty much a nonissue for me, and I often find myself shaking my head in confusion at the clamoring for marriage as such. In fact, I'd be more likely to commit to some sort of ceremony called anything else but marriage, since the word to me signifies so much of what is wrong with our cultural notions of love—that it be public and sanctioned and done in a very specific, highly contrived way. Like so many things that are thrust upon us, I have more trouble with marriage as a concept and institution than I do with it in reality. When I see alternative weddings of all sorts, queer and Goth and any marriage where the people throw those cultural imperatives in the air and create their own traditions and meanings, I'm encouraged because I think those marriages have a stronger chance of surviving and thriving. I gave a speech at my mom's wedding last year and meant every word of it. I cried and was touched and moved not because I suddenly believed in marriage as savior, but because I believed in the people standing in front of me. Marriage should never be about an ending (though it's certainly treated that way by many), but a beginning. Women are still taught that marriage is about finding some man, any man, to do the deed, the prize for a lifetime of dating, rather than having that search be an enjoyable experience in and of itself. When marriage is treated as the final puzzle piece to one's life, it seems like an inevitable anticlimax.

Clearly, I am no big marriage fan. When I was on the board of my local NOW (National Organization for Women) chapter, in charge of the Lesbian and Bisexual Rights Committee, a woman came to us wanting to organize a protest in favor of gay marriage. I had very mixed feelings about devoting my time and energy to a cause that is simply not at the top of my list of things queer people need. I did it anyway, and while we got nowhere near the turnout that the recent protests in favor of same-sex marriage have received, it was still a thrill to see how many people supported the issue. And yet, why shouldn't they? That one seems like such a no-brainer to me that anyone not supporting the rights of same-sex people to marry is simply a throwback to an antiquated (and highly utopian) vision of what marriage is.

Sometimes I forget just how deeply ingrained the notion of the necessity marriage is, and think that we've finally reached that time where people can be free to marry or not, live with others, be gay, queer, what have you. And then I'll hear someone say something like "now I'm not single anymore," referring to their marriage, and realize all over again that marriage is the true marker in our society for whether one is partnered or not. For those with that kind of narrow-minded vision, we are single, or married, end of story. No matter whether we are in love, or live with someone, or are in multiple relationships, if there's no ring, it doesn't count, and this kind of insulting thinking cuts across issues of sexual orientation. Opening up marriage to gay and lesbian couples in many ways will only reinforce these provincial notions; those egalitarian enough to "accept" same-sex weddings will then place that same pressure on queer people that straight people are already subject to.

I would like to have hope that marriage can one day be more about love and personal commitment than taxes and dresses, pressure and approval. That instead of a costly, stress-inducing affair, a wedding can simply be a celebration amongst friends and family and community. I write this as a person who deep down, below all the cynicism and doubt I have about marriage as an institution, has a deep romantic streak, who does cry at weddings when I can see the looks of true love and devotion passing between the faces of the attendees and participants, when I witness the radiant smiles beaming out from across the country of the dual brides and dual grooms having their commitments sanctified by their local governments. But the word *marriage* to me is one of those big, ugly words like *monogamy*, fronting a belief system that, no matter how alternative we make it, ultimately privileges some over others. Until being married or not is treated equally, from the workplace to the family, I won't be making it a priority that same-sex couples be able to take that step. It should be the right of all of us, but it should also be an equal choice among many. And don't expect to see me walking down an aisle near you anytime soon. Then again, life has a funny way of working out sometimes. Give me a few years, and I just may change my tune.

Rachel Kramer Bussel (www.rachelkramerbussel.com, lustylady.blogspot.com) *is senior editor at* Penthouse Variations, *reviser of* The Lesbian Sex Book, *and editor of* Up All Night: Adventures in Lesbian Sex. *Her writing appears in over 40 anthologies including* The Best American Erotica 2004, *as well as* AVN, Bust, Curve, Diva, Penthouse, Playgirl, On Our Backs, *and* The Village Voice.

I Know I Shouldn't, but I Probably Will
Patrick Califia

Please forgive me if my opinion about gay marriage is based on my unhappy experience with a heterosexual version of that hoary institution. I am speaking, of course, about my parents. My devout Mormon mother's sole act of rebellion was to marry an unsuitable boy who had enlisted in the Navy instead of going on a mission. What could you expect? His family had been in "The Church" only three generations, compared to her pedigree which included founder Joseph Smith, the second president, Brigham Young, and a handful of apostles and other high-ranking Latter Day Saints. She wanted to go to art school, and her farming family laughed at the idea of wasting good money on sending a girl to college. The day after she collected her high school diploma, she flew to Hawaii to marry her one and only boyfriend.

She spent the next 21 years of her life regretting that decision. My dad worked hard in coal mines and construction sites, and he did not want to spend one of his precious days off sitting on hard wooden benches waiting for the miserly Mormon sacrament of torn-up white bread and tap water. He swore. He chewed tobacco and spit on the sidewalk. He got speeding tickets. He drank coffee and Coca-Cola. He liked sex. (I was later to discover he liked it so much that he had a second, secret family.)

Mormon marriages are for time and all eternity. Not only are bride and groom sealed together in this manner, so are their children. If everybody doesn't get to the Celestial Kingdom, the status of other family members is jeopardized. My mother stayed with my father through daily outbursts of verbal abuse and physical outrage, through occasional drinking binges, six pregnancies, and moving house every other year as he followed jobs around the country.

She decided to leave him one night when she found my little brother crying because he believed that his father didn't love him. I'm not sure why this was the straw that broke the housewife's back, because all of my dad's children had spent many nights in the same miserable condition. Money was certainly a factor. Half of her children had left home, which meant that she could barely eke out a living working at a sewing factory and cleaning motel rooms.

My mother went to night school, learned how to type, and landed a secretarial job at Brigham Young University. She was eventually promoted to a management position there. When my father sent divorce papers, she signed them. But she never went on another date. My dad remained the only man in her life. And she once observed to me, only half-jokingly, "He thinks he's gotten away from me now, but he's mine. For time and all eternity."

It is to shudder.

Five years seems to be the upward limit of my tolerance for keeping the same lover. Two years seems to be about as long as I can maintain sexual interest in the same person. I don't have my mother's religious faith to inspire (or coerce) me into forming a lifelong attachment, much less one that stretches out into infinity. A couple of attempts at monogamy failed miserably, mostly because I didn't see why I should tolerate jealous rages about the time I spent with people I wasn't fucking. If I am going to be punished, let me be punished with a happy memory of sweaty butt-sex and flogging in my mind.

When I begin a relationship, I am always pretty clear about what I don't like about my lover, and I know why I will leave them long before that begins to seem like a necessity. This one has too many cats. That one could never balance her checkbook. Another was an alcoholic. (And another, and another.) There has been one exception to that rule. One man I thought I would be with forever, which is why I agreed to parent a child with him. We still see each other quite frequently, but we broke up several years ago. My only lifelong relationship is probably going to be the one I have with my son, and with a few friends who tolerate my lack of thrift, sexual restraint, regular sleeping habits, temperance, or modesty.

My rational self tells me that there are many excellent reasons why half of all heterosexual marriages fail—and more than half of all same-sex couples seem determined to win equal rights to matrimony (and divorce and child support and alimony and custody battles). While I wholeheartedly support same-sex marriage, I wish the queer community would spend a little more time wondering why it doesn't seem to work very well for straight people. I also wonder why there can't be some form of legal recognition for people in polyamorous relationships. What business does the state have in mandating monogamy or offering only one type of legal agreement between adults who are sexually involved with one another?

Until quite recently in the West, marriages between people who owned property used to be arranged by families that wished to make more profitable arrangements for their titles, lands, and businesses. With the rise of industrialism, growth of the middle class, and the flourishing of the novel came a competing notion that each individual should select his or her own mate, and do it because they had fallen in love. This beloved was idealized as a soul mate. Only one per customer, and a perfect fit. Romeo and Juliet are often touted as the archetype of such romantic love, but I wonder if Shakespeare wasn't actually pointing out how stupid it was to believe that a marriage could succeed if the bride and groom's families were violently opposed to it. The love in *Romeo and Juliet* is as stupid as it is intense, and consequently doomed. Shakespeare understood that passion is ephemeral and lacks all common sense.

Nevertheless, romantic love has become the new secular religion. People want the same thing from a spouse that they used to want from God. We want someone who will provide us with a life purpose and replace our hollowness with meaning and vitality. This compatible roommate and movie date is also supposed to be the source of great sex, material comfort, assistance with child-rearing, and caretaking in illness or age. This person has supposedly looked deep inside us and understands our hidden pain and yearning. Once they possess this intimate level of knowledge, they are supposed to be drawn to us even more deeply, rather than flee in horror. And until this person arrives, we are supposed to feel lonely, incomplete, frustrated, and unfulfilled.

I don't think so.

What I know in my bones is that staying with the same person will make you unhappy. I saw my mother do it for two decades. I'm sure she told herself that she kept her marriage together for the sake of her children, but she never polled her offspring for their opinion. I have no doubt that my mother and father were deeply and madly in love with each other when they got married. Was it marriage that destroyed their affinity? No, although the demands of poverty, work, children, and housekeeping were harsh and didn't help. By the time my mother was 26 years old, she had six kids. The only thing I could keep track of at that age was my pot stash and the cupboard where I kept my cat's food.

Their religious and temperamental differences were what did them in. My dad wanted a woman who would get turned on sitting in the car while he drove fast, a woman who would drink and party with him and laugh at his jokes, someone who would enjoy trips to Las Vegas and camping out. My mother wanted a stable husband and provider who would escort her to church, greet the visiting teachers once a week, attend priesthood meetings, lead the family in prayer, and dote on her for keeping us all in clean clothes and meals. My mother often infuriated me when I was a teenager (who caused a scandal at Sunday School by telling everyone I was never going to get married) by telling me that she should pick my mate, because people used to be happier in the days when marriages were arranged. In her case, I think that is probably true. But as a willful 18-year-old, she never would have accepted a man that would have made her happy once she became a mother. She wanted to have her bad boy and then tame him. Her lack of success in that experiment has not discouraged me from repeating it.

I'm a jaded, disabled, and cranky 50 years old. I can barely stand having somebody else in my apartment long enough to clean it. I will not share the remote control to the television, and I do not care if those pants make your ass look fat. I have filled my living space with bookshelves and computer equipment. There's barely enough room for *me* to sit down, so don't imagine you can leave so much as a toothbrush here. The only "commitment" I've made is to get my voice mail and return calls once a day, and I usually fail to keep it. My cat likes company more than I do, since she views visitors as potential acolytes in her temple, whom she interviews and then dismisses as unworthy. I think she may have the right idea.

If my life and the lives of most of my friends are any clue, the queer community needs more help with breaking up than it does with forming attachments. Even those of us who have found a partner we want to elevate to the status of spouse have probably chalked up a lot more separations than matrimonial debuts. We have found no gracious way to acknowledge that our needs have changed. The brutality we exhibit toward a departing lover affects everyone around us. How many times have we all seen entire networks of friends torn apart by a hurtful parting of the ways? Would these unhappy occasions escalate so quickly or contain so much malice if we did not expect impossible things of love in the first place? No one can tolerate losing all of the things that love promises us, but love also cannot really sustain these outrageous expectations. The fault is in the paradigm, not the person.

Part of my reluctance to fall in love again comes from unpleasant memories about what happens when I hate myself for being attracted to somebody who treats me badly, or I hate myself because I no longer want to have sex with a person who has remained loyal and devoted to me (albeit in a parasitical and irritating fashion). I once did a seminar on sexuality for a group of Metropolitan Community Church pastors-in-training, and when I suggested that we create a ritual to acknowledge a breakup, one of the consecrated dykes said huffily, "The church is about bringing people together, not pushing them apart." I could only shake my head. Is it good for the faithful to believe that God will abandon us if we tell the truth about a relationship that has gone stale or become destructive? Shouldn't queer spirituality affirm the courage that it takes to acknowledge a shift in feelings? As a therapist, I see as much personal growth occur after uncoupling as I observe when two lives are joined together.

Our reluctance to deal with the unwelcome fact that people tend to grow apart makes me view gay marriage as an incipient public relations train wreck. You can bet that newspapers and television stations are going to love nasty same-sex divorces every bit as much as they loved the happy couples in camp wedding attire at San Francisco's City Hall. If you felt damaged when your last boyfriend ran off with the contents of your joint checking account, the stereo, and your favorite Plexiglas cock cage, wait till you see what that mean little fucker can do to your peace of mind with the help of a sharp divorce attorney.

I say this without making any claim to being able to uphold my own ethics when a love affair turns into a shoot-out with Teflon bullets. I too want the pretty vision of perfect happiness that our delusions about romantic love have promised. I don't want to be lonely or horny. I want someone to see my higher self and help me to become a better (and richer) person. I wish someone besides me would dust all these books and figure out what to make for dinner. I'd love to have my life filled with witty conversation and excellent oral sex. I want someone I can depend on forever and ever, no matter how bad it gets. When my unrealistic expectations are crushed, I become nasty and punitive. I don't want to see that person or talk to them ever again. The man or woman I wanted to possess utterly and receive all good things from becomes the most loathed and despised individual on the face of the earth.

What I've got now is a life where I receive some of the things I want, some of the time, mostly from friends who have proven to be more reliable than the objects of my crushes. "Like" has proven to be much more soothing, dependable, and accurate than "love." Sex remains an iffy proposition. I am searching for sexual pleasure without the intoxication of romance. But I'm not optimistic about this because in the past it's been love that sweeps away my sexual inhibitions and transmutes awkward and comical physical conjoining into molten angelic bliss. I don't think my heart can stand any more bliss at the moment, however. I'll settle for a really good orgasm and somebody who gives me a sincere hug before he goes home.

Oh, but I know the warning signs. A person can only live according to rational principles for so many days, weeks, and months. Then the heart, no matter how much scar tissue it bears, takes over.

Sadomasochism is in part the culprit here. It's very difficult to open someone else's skin without feeling your own heart gape wide to receive their offering of pain and blood. The same flesh that yearns and deserves to be bruised also pleads for tenderness from the keeper of the whips and fetters. The illusion of master and slave blends seamlessly into the illusion of lover and beloved. Once you have a perfect offering on your black leather altar, it's hard to let it go. Why not repeat the ritual, and seek epiphany together once more? To arrange any session, no matter how casual, is a form of courtship. Binding and punishing, chiding and exploiting the orifices of the subject, very quickly acquaints you with all that is squalid and yet staunch in the victim's character. And who can resist someone who has seen you do your worst, who still longs to follow and serve you? I can—but not often, and not very cheerfully.

Somebody will appear who has an extra sparkle. One of the masochists I bring home will display an uncharacteristic desire to fuck me senseless, and I'll be lost. They'll probably even have a motorcycle. I will take wry note of every cliché, and yet I'll be caught up in the undertow of optimism and rejoicing. "I've never felt this way before," I will tell someone, and mean it. Because telling the truth is not the same as The Truth. Their favorite idioms and intonations will creep into my speech. I'll feel wonderful. I'll write them poetry. I won't be able to leave their zits alone. I'll be crushed if they are angry with me, and crazed with hunger when we are separated. They will be allowed to borrow my books. I'll believe that they have brought a true and lasting happiness to my arid life. When requiring their attention, I will say, "Bear, come look at this." A collar will be chosen and locked around a willing neck. I will propose.

I dread it. It's right up there with Death and Taxes. Unavoidable, unfortunate, and horrid. The foolishness of it, the excess, the insanity. Love will make my cozy bomb shelter of a life look like a prison. No wonder hatred is intermingled with any serious attraction.

Patrick Califia (www.patrickcalifia.com) is a therapist and dad as well as being a prolific author. You can see more of his essays in Public Sex *and* Speaking Sex to Power. *He lives in San Francisco, where he has a monogamous relationship with a tortoiseshell cat.*

A Queer Wedding Indeed
Anne Campbell

You have to dig a little deeper to see us as a queer couple. We live in a small, rural town in western Massachusetts. Drew's clearly a man, beard and all; I'm clearly a woman; and people stop us in public to tell us how much our toddler daughter looks like her dad. We just smile and say, "Do you think so?"

But just a few months before we met, Drew had his first testosterone shot and began his transition from female to male. I had gone through a series of boyfriends as a teenager, then a series of girlfriends as a young adult, and on to a few FTMs and other significant others of unusual gender. We met on the Internet, embarrassingly enough, on a mailing list for gender oddballs like ourselves.

After a false start to our dating relationship (we met in person, and were both so shy that we each thought the other didn't like us), a friend knocked our heads together, and within six weeks we were engaged.

Our closest friends congratulated us with cautious optimism. I'm sure they thought we were out of our minds, getting engaged so soon, but we had decided on a long engagement of two years, just in case. We did all the usual things: poring over bride magazines, deciding on a location, registering for gifts, getting Drew fitted for a kilt by a charming old Scottish gentleman who kept calling him "Richard."

The first sign of trouble came from an old friend of Drew's, who was in a long-standing lesbian relationship with a woman who also had another male partner. The couple declared that they were boycotting our wedding, because if they couldn't get legally married, why should we? We were obviously exploiting heterosexual privilege.

Drew pointed out that we were not heterosexual; that we were only able to get legally married because of a loophole in California law; and that we were unable to get partner benefits from my work because we weren't married yet, while they enjoyed that privilege as a lesbian couple. No dice; we were still the enemy, and we haven't heard from that couple since.

The second bump in the road came from my parents. I had been enjoying a rare period of good relations with them, and we went to visit them for Christmas. Everything went splendidly, and we announced our engagement on Christmas Eve. My mother took me aside and gave me a speech. "I was always sure that there would never be a husband good enough for my daughter. But I just love Drew! I'm so happy for you. But tell me, what happened to the lesbian thing?"

I explained that Drew was an FTM. She chewed on that for a while, and all went well until a few months later, when she flew out to visit us in California...for two and a half weeks. Suffice it to say that everything unraveled, and by the time she went back home, she was convinced that Drew had me brainwashed into a life of unspeakable depravity, and that he was a charlatan masquerading as some parody of a man. She has insisted on calling him "she" ever since, beard and all. Scratch a few more family members off the wedding guest list.

Drew's mother, on the other hand, was delighted for us and gave me her own wedding and engagement rings, which had been made too small for her by her diabetes. Over the course of the engagement, she signed her letters "Mrs. Campbell," then "Mrs. C.," then "Mom."

Our friends grew more and more supportive as the wedding drew closer. Even the ones who were skeptical about the institution of marriage because of their own parents' divorces all buried their doubts in our case.

Acquaintances were a mixed bag. The straight ones treated our wedding just like any other, asking about the flowers and the catering. Some of the queer ones did the same. (Our downstairs neighbors, a drag queen and a leather daddy, asked "What are the wedding colors?" We answered, "Hunter green, of course." "Of course!" they cheered.) But many others seemed to treat the wedding far more casually, and even with a little disdain, as if we were undertaking something strangely old-fashioned and unnecessary.

In the summer, we lined up at City Hall with some trepidation, hoping that there would be no drama about the marriage license. As it turned out, because Drew's driver's license showed his gender as M, we were duly rubber-stamped and the worry was over.

When the wedding weekend rolled around, our guests from out of town arrived. My grandmother came from Boston with her best friend, and Drew's mother and godmother came from Missouri and New York, respectively. My own best friend came from Maine, and two friends from Seattle. Everyone met up for dinner on Friday night, and the four older ladies were old friends right away.

The wedding morning on Saturday was a dream. We had just a dozen close family and friends gather by the rosebushes in our back garden, and the ceremony was over in a flash. After a celebratory brunch, Drew and I checked into a weird and charming little hotel.

Then it was Sunday, the day appointed for the larger wedding reception. The caterers arrived with no tables to put the food on; they had thought we had tables, and we had thought they would bring them. We dragged every flat surface available, from kitchen table to ironing board, into the garden and put tablecloths on them. The florist, who was Jewish, shook hands with the Palestinian Christian caterer, whose forearm was tattooed with a map of Israel labeled "Palestine" in Arabic. The pastry chef remembered the florist from when they worked at the same strip club together. Somehow everything got arranged, and the guests started to arrive.

I am quite certain that we had the most motley crew of wedding guests ever assembled. Aside from our out-of-town guests, we welcomed: co-workers and their spouses from my big Silicon Valley employer; Drew's co-workers from Damron, the queer travel guide company; parishioners and clergy from my predominantly gay and lesbian Episcopal parish; and assorted other gay, straight, leather-inclined, and Goth friends and hangers-on.

In a few hours, the guests had eaten as many falafels as they could hold, the wedding cake had been cut, the toasts made, and the garden was empty again.

Marriage changed everything, and still everything was exactly the same as before. When friends would ask, "How's married life?" we joked that it was "just like being engaged, except we don't have to plan a *wedding* any more!" But somehow that piece of paper, and much more significantly, the public vows, have cemented our whole lives. I can't imagine that there were ever days when I wasn't married to my great love and best friend. We've attended a number of weddings before and since, gay and straight, legal and not, and I'm always struck by how monumental that change is. It's the same for every couple (or it should be): permanent love, unerring commitment, the genesis of a new family.

Our almost-three-year-old daughter asked at the dinner table the other night, "Marriage means...?" Drew said, "It's when two people promise to live together forever." I added, "And love each other!" That was answer enough for her, so why is it so hard for us adults to grasp?

One photo in our wedding album sums up the culture clash that was our reception. In the background, Drew's elderly godmother is chatting with the rector and priest associate from my church, next to a group of Damron friends, who are dressed in everything from khakis and vests to a stained T-shirt, jeans, and a penis pendant. Our friend Patrick, wearing a leather vest to show off his tattoos of butterflies, flowers, and a topless Cretan snake goddess, is sitting back-to-back with my grandmother, who looks a little queasy.

It was a queer wedding indeed.

Anne Campbell is a spouse, mother, student midwife, birth doula, Web designer, and toymaker in idyllic western Massachusetts.

Bad Arguments for Gay Marriage
Dale Carpenter

With the country still simmering after the Massachusetts court decision that could extend marriage to gay couples, it's time to separate the chaff from the wheat in the arguments for gay marriage.

There are several good arguments *for* gay marriage. Among these are the stability and commitment it would encourage in gay relationships and in gay life generally. That would benefit everybody, gay and straight.

There are also some bad arguments *against* gay marriage. An example is the selective logic of the procreation argument, which holds that nobody is required to procreate in order to marry, except gay couples, who can't procreate, and so must unfortunately be excluded.

We should acknowledge, however, that we ourselves have been guilty of making some bad arguments *for* gay marriage. Here are three:

Bad Argument #1: It's All About the Benefits.

The most common argument for gay marriage emphasizes the harm that's done to gay couples by excluding them from the protections and benefits of marriage. Among these are tax benefits, settled property division and presumed child visitation and/or custody upon death or divorce, testimonial privileges in court, hospital visitation, and health benefits extended by private employers or governments to the spouses of workers. Someone has tallied over 1,000 marital benefits and privileges. Give us all these goodies, too, the argument goes.

Benefits are indeed part of the story about why it's wrong to exclude gay couples from marriage, but they are not the most important part of it. Some of the benefits of marriage can be replicated—at some cost and inconvenience to the couple—through wills, trusts, and contracts.

Emphasizing the riches of marriage misses the richness of marriage. Very few people marry in order to experience the magic of filing a joint income tax return. They marry because, in our tradition and history, marriage is the way couples in a community signal the depth of their commitment to one another. Their family and peers reciprocate by supporting and celebrating that commitment, which in turn reinforces it. Everyone understands the stakes.

If the benefits were all that mattered, civil unions would be an adequate substitute. Yet, "We're unionized," simply does not have the powerful social significance of "We're married." So let's argue for the benefits, but let's not stop there.

Bad Argument #2: We Have a "Right" to Marry.

Another common argument for gay marriage is more legalistic, and less functional, than the first. It tends to emphasize the discrimination in the marriage exclusion, holding that gays have just as much "right" to marry as heterosexuals.

The problem is that, while a reasonable legal argument can indeed be made for gay marriage, it is unlikely to persuade anyone who isn't already convinced that gay marriage is a good idea or at least not a bad idea. Legal conclusions follow, they do not create, arguments on the merits of an issue.

Another problem with the rights argument is that it tends to channel our efforts toward courts, where the issue will not ultimately be won, and away from legislatures and from the hearts of our fellow citizens, where it must be won. The comparatively easy work of writing briefs for judges and their clerks will not substitute for the hard work of persuading the people we're right.

Bad Argument #3: Gay Marriage Will Revolutionize Society, and That's Good.

This perspective was recently expressed by sociologist Kersti Yllo, a professor at Wheaton College in Massachusetts. "We need to acknowledge [conservatives'] argument that gay and lesbian marriages have the potential to change civilization as we know it," says Yllo. "And that will be a good thing."

There are at least three versions of this argument. One holds that heterosexuals have screwed up marriage and gays will do a better job. But gay couples, I predict, will suffer divorce rates just as high as their straight counterparts. There will be instances of gay spousal abuse and infidelity, just as there are for straight couples. Gay marriage is not the cause of the problems with marriage, but neither is it a solution.

A second version of the revolution argument maintains that gay marriages will be less "stifling" and perhaps more "open-textured," offering a healthy alternative marital model to straight couples. What is primarily meant by these euphemisms, I think, is that gay male couples will play around more.

I doubt the rate of publicly "open" gay marriages will be very high, for reasons I've offered elsewhere. Further, whatever that rate, I doubt it will have any effect on straight couples because gay couples will comprise a tiny percentage of all marriages and because women will continue to demand monogamy in opposite-sex marriages.

Moreover, if gay marriage did have this "liberating" effect on straight marriage, that would be a good argument *against* gay marriage. Sexually open relationships are on average less stable and lasting than monogamous ones. Introducing even more instability into opposite-sex marriages would be terrible for the relationships themselves and for the children they often produce.

The third version of the revolution argument holds that gay marriage will undermine traditional gender roles under which wives do housework and husbands make money. Like the better-living-through-adultery fallacy just discussed, this argument assumes a huge effect from a small cause. Besides, gay couples are often not radically different from straight couples in their division of labor. Finally, traditional marital roles have already declined to a great extent.

While Arguments Nos. 1 and 2 are just bad when offered by themselves, Argument No. 3 in all its versions is just plain bad.

Dale Carpenter is a professor at the University of Minnesota Law School. He also writes a bi-weekly column, OutRight, for gay newspapers.

First published in the *Bay Area Reporter*, December 11, 2003. Reprinted by permission of the author.

Step Up
Margaret Cho

Step up your game. No matter who you are or what you feel about homosexuality. If you are gay, lesbian, transgendered, bisexual, bi-curious, metrosexual, heterosexual, celibate, hermaphrodite, a satyr, a succubus, a fucking human being—and especially if you are a fucking human being, and really want to live in a country where all people are equal—not separate, not "civil-unionized," not lied to about your rights—realize that same-sex marriage will not harm you. It will not make gay people more "gay." It will not make you gay unless you already are. It will not make your children gay, unless they are anyway. It will not change your life in the least, unless you are gay and want to marry your partner. Then it will transform your life, because it will change your status from second-class citizen to first, where we should be.

If we are not absolutely strident, insistent, unflinching about lifting the ban on same-sex marriage, if we settle on our presidential hopefuls fence-sitting position of "civil union," then we might as well forfeit the Constitution, cross out all the amendments, knock down the Statue of Liberty (it was a gift from France anyway—those peace lovers—who needs 'em?), reverse *Roe v. Wade*, pretend Stonewall never happened, reinstate Prohibition, not let women vote, derail the Underground Railroad, bring back slavery, take out all the tea bags from Boston Harbor, give Patrick Henry death instead of liberty, because he's fucking dead now anyway, knock Paul Revere off the horse, realize that George Washington lied, albeit posthumously, besides, all those dudes had slaves anyway, get back on the Mayflower and go back to England.

The only problem would be trying to bring the Native Americans back to life and restore their nations that we so cavalierly destroyed in our own pursuit of religious "freedom."

Without the reality of same-sex marriage, there is no freedom. This is not an argument about homosexuality, God, what is in the Bible, what is in your moral value system, or what you feel is ethical. It is a no-argument zone. No spins here, not in the least. It is about upholding the idea that we are the representation of freedom in the world. That to be an American is to be free. Unless we have same-sex marriage legalized and recognized by every state, then we are not free. We are hypocrites, for we are allowing a certain group of our population freedoms while denying others those same rights. It is discrimination and that is that. If the theocrats successfully ban same-sex marriage, then what is next? What rights go up in front of the unjust jury then?

Shout out to the NASCAR dads: If maintaining the "sanctity of marriage" is what is going to keep you in support of George W. Bush, remember that your little boys and girls sitting next to you now at the races will be old enough in the next four years and going off to fight another needless war to lose their lives for a country that you falsely believe is free.

A vote for Bush is a bullet in your kid's head. I know it is harsh, but it is true. I am trying to help you out. Think before you vote. Now more than ever. It is life or death. Literally.

To all the Democratic candidates: Take a look at Gavin Newsom and what is happening in San Francisco. Have the brass balls to truly be an American. Marriage is a right not a privilege. It is time to see who really qualifies to run "The Home of the Brave."

Comedian Margaret Cho has launched three sold-out national tours in the past five years, turning each into a concert film. Her newest tour, State of Emergency, will address the political state of our nation this fall. Always incorporating activism in her comedy, Cho has been honored by NOW, GLAAD, AALDEF, and the ACLU for her efforts to promote equal rights for all and her courage to speak out about the dangerous policies of the Bush administration. Cho has also started her own marriage equality resource site at www.loveisloveislove.com.

This column originally appeared on *MargaretCho.com/blog*. Reprinted by permission of the author.

My Old Man
David Christensen

Saturday, February 14, 2004

My favorite kind of weather: gray, rainy. It's very quiet out. Today is our ninth anniversary, the ninth anniversary of our first fuck. And it's Valentine's Day, too— hokey, but true. Is it terrible that we haven't planned anything romantic? We don't exchange gifts anymore, either.

We lounge around the living room with the cats, drinking coffee. Scott reads the paper. I read *Disco Bloodbath*. I see the lesbians across the street, already up and playing with their kids. Scott says City Hall is issuing marriage licenses to same-sex couples. Gavin Newsom authorized it. They're going to stay open through the three-day weekend to accommodate as many people as possible. Huh? We're stunned. We sort of laugh. What's the point if it doesn't provide any actual rights? I've always agreed with Joni Mitchell: *We don't need no piece of paper from the City Hall, keeping us tied and true…*

We don't do much until dinner. We both really need to crash this weekend. Things have been so stressful.

Dinner at Fino is fun, but the only topic of conversation is gay marriage. All the other diners are straight couples on Valentine's Day dates. Carol brings her friend Joan the Jewelry Designer. They want to know what we think of gay marriage, and if we'll get married. "Get married" sounds so stupid I can't even say it. We try to explain our doubts and lack of interest without sounding too negative, but it's hard. I don't even really know what I think. I don't want to seem like a downer; the excitement around this thing is palpable. I say I haven't seen many examples of good marriages, so why would I want to get married? Plus, we don't want to feel like we have to emulate straight people in order to gain respect. Carol says she wants to throw us a ten-year anniversary party next year.

After dinner, we go to Julie's 30th birthday party at Jade bar. We're among the first to arrive, as usual, because we want to leave by 10. Early to bed, even on weekends. I talk to Renata for quite a while. She wants to know what we think about the marriages. I say I've heard it could be dangerous for same-sex couples to get married, because they might lose the rights they already have through California's domestic partnership registration. Wrong answer. I see her face drop. Kate, a girl I haven't met before, bubbles over telling me how many of her friends just got married. I smile and fake enthusiasm. When Paul arrives later, he tells me his partner is now a father—he donated his sperm to a lesbian, and the baby was born just a few days ago. I think Scott and I are the only gay people in this city who aren't married with children.

Monday, February 16, 2004

Since City Hall began issuing licenses, about 2,000 same-sex couples have been married. It's huge. People are coming from all over to do it, and there's the predictable media frenzy. On the front page today are two white, 30ish Ken dolls, with perfect skin, perfect hair, and perfect teeth, getting married at City Hall, each with a baby strapped to his chest. They're the poster couple. I'm getting calls and emails from friends, either announcing their marriages or asking about ours. Strangely, no one in our families mentions it. Scott's dad calls with an update on his mother's health. He seems like he has a question to ask, but doesn't ask it.

I'm afraid that all the gay people we know will get married. Where will that leave us—"living together"? "Single"? I was just getting used to "partnered." Will there be tiers of gayness, more than there already are? Will Scott and I be considered less gay than those who are married, or less respectable? Will we have to attend hundreds of wedding receptions and bring presents? I've always hated weddings and spending money on wedding presents. It's so unfair. Why should I have to buy gifts just because some teenagers fucked without a condom? And then they get instant respect and benefits just because they're married. And then they get divorced a year later and keep the presents...

We hang around most of the day, reading, playing with the cats. Larry invites me to perform the Brahms Clarinet Trio later this year. I haven't played it before, so I get the score and start working on it. It's beautiful.

We have dinner at Bill and Daria's. Janet, another guest, tells us that she'll address the issue of gay marriage at the Christian school where she teaches, risking complaints from students and parents. She's already had complaints for expressing liberal views. All she wants to say is that not everyone has the same beliefs concerning how people may live their lives. She's not advocating either side.

Later at home we notice that poor Bev's flea allergy is worse, and she's licking at the fur on her legs. We need to take her to the vet soon.

Tuesday, February 17, 2004
Back to work after the three-day weekend. Everyone talks about gay marriage. People ask me excitedly if I got married. I want to laugh, or shout, NO ONE GOT MARRIED! IT ISN'T LEGAL! Of course, the Michaels and the Peters were among the first couples to get married. I tell Jack I don't want to get married, I think the whole thing's stupid. He says he and his partner will. He says it's not so much about marriage per se; it's civil disobedience. I have to admit he has a good point. It's exciting to think of thousands of people engaged in this, and now other cities in other states are considering the same thing. Is this the beginning of a huge movement?

Maybe Scott and I should get married. But Scott has to go out of town later this month, and he'll be gone for a week. I think we're too busy until he leaves, and then my sister's coming to stay. Would we have to dress up? And then we'd have to tell our friends, and then people would want us to have a celebration, and they'd be disappointed if we didn't. We'd have to invite everyone to make sure we didn't offend anyone. I don't know—I don't really feel like planning a big social event right now.

Thursday, February 26, 2004
Jack and his partner were supposed to get married over the weekend, but now you have to have an appointment—you can't just show up. He says it takes a whole day to make the appointment, and the appointments are several weeks out. I'm pretty sure we won't be able to do it now. I have the number, but I won't have time to call.

People from all over the world are sending flowers to the couples standing in line. Rosie and Kelli fly in and get married. City Hall bumps the little people off line to let the beautiful people in. Local celebs too, like Sharon Smith and her latest. Gavin Newsom is in the news everywhere. People are surprised that he took this action, especially so early in his tenure. In spite of my mixed feelings about gay marriage, I'm glad I voted for him.

During my sister's visit, she never asks if Scott and I got married. No one in our families mentions it. What if we had been married? I don't think our families want to know, and they certainly wouldn't want to celebrate or recognize our marriage. If we got married, I don't think I'd tell them. It would just be uncomfortable for everyone. They might feel obligated to do something nice, but I'd know they were really feeling put out, and then I'd feel guilty. And it would be embarrassing for them, because other people might ask about us and they'd have to tell, or lie.

On my walk home from work I overhear a woman on the street say, "We're considered a blended family." What the fuck? I feel like watching one of those weird Elizabeth Taylor movies, like *Secret Ceremony*, but I can't find one on. I eat a handful of white chocolate chips from Trader Joe's—they taste like wax. I eat another handful: still waxy. I eat some organic dark chocolate—only a little sharper. I always get bored like this when Scott's gone. I can't imagine what I'd do if we weren't together. I love him so much.

Monday, March 1, 2004
Scott gets back from his trip this afternoon. We have martinis at Trax, then beer and pizza at Magnolia. Back at home we watch *Queer Eye* and drink 12-year-old Balvenie, the double-cask kind. Scott's talking about redecorating our flat. I get hungry again and make a chocolate Atkins shake with Carnation malt powder in it. I want more Balvenie 12, but it would probably taste bad after the shake.

Monday, March 8, 2004
I don't feel well today so I stay home from work. I watch *All About Eve* on TiVo and finish the white chocolate chips. They don't taste so waxy today, and lying there eating and watching the movie feels so luxurious, it's better than sex! I wonder about that weird voice Marilyn used—the words aren't clearly formed.

At one point I go out for groceries. I notice that everyone on the street has one or two of those tiny dogs, those trendy tiny, super tiny-tiny fucking dogs. How can a trend hit the realm of pet-owning so hard? Suddenly everyone in the city has this dog. I saw a man in Metro bar with the tiniest dog in his shirt. It sure got him a lot of attention.

Thursday, March 11, 2004
City Hall's been ordered to stop issuing marriage licenses to same-sex couples, so I guess it's over, at least for now, but there's speculation that the marriages will be upheld.

After work we make manhattans and watch an American Masters special on Balanchine. It's good. There's supposed to be another one soon on Joni Mitchell.

Did we just sit around on our asses and miss out on the most important historical and political event in our lives? Yes. No. Have we become too jaded and cynical? Are we too self-involved? No. Maybe. Are we afraid of commitment? Are we unsure of our relationship's future? Maybe. No! Are we so furious at straight people and white people and middle-class people and Republicans and married people and parents and politicians and home owners that we can't even think straight? Yes. No. Probably.

I've finished learning the Brahms and start working on several Hindemith sonatas for another program. Bev keeps licking at her fur, and her legs are quite bare. She looks pretty funny (or sad). We use a bug bomb and extra doses of Advantage, which seems to help, but we'll probably need to get a professional exterminator at some point. I'm not sure when we can, though.

David Christensen is a musician and an instructional designer. He lives in San Francisco's Haight Ashbury district with Scott, Bev, Deb, and Lee-Wu.

The Prong of Permanency: A Rant
Cheryl Clarke

This piece is written from my perspective as a dyke (a perspective I've been writing from for 25 years). I do not name each of the communities who have broadened and contributed to the gay and lesbian movement for liberation, i.e., bisexual, trans, questioning, ambiguously/ambivalently sexed and gendered people; for gays and lesbians are in the vanguard of this movement for marriage equality. Regardless of how our partnerships have enriched, restored, and rehabilitated communities all across this country, gays and lesbians are the focus of this critique. And so, I won't hold back.

Their Eyes Were Watching God, a foundational black women's literary text written by Zora Neale Hurston in 1937, comes to my mind these days, especially the character Nannie. "Love is the very prong colored women gets hung on," Nannie tells her 16-year-old granddaughter, Janie, the novel's protagonist, whom she quickly marries off to a bachelor three times her age. Like "love" for black women, permanency for gays, lesbians, and other same-sex variants is the very prong we "gets hung on" when the arguments for marriage equality come up. We want that *forever* thing or the *thing* forever. We use the law, land, and furniture to make it so, don't we? Long demonized by/in the West, lesbians and gays long for longevity. "Longevity has its place," said Martin Luther King prophetically and critically, shortly before his untimely murder at the age of 39. Admittedly, permanency has its place—replacing "promiscuity," the other, sexier *p*-word still applied to our communities. But let's not turn our whole movement over to the locking-in of the same-sex dyad. Need we dedicate our pride marches to marriage, as was the case in this year's New York Pride March? "We decided we had to attend the parade this year. We had to let people know we're here," said one 20-30-something New Paltz–married lesbian and her partner. First of all, young sister-dyke, it's a "march" not a "parade." Secondly, we've had a movement for 35 years, letting people know we're here. Can't help it if your pride was just born yesterday. This dangerous and ahistorical speaking and thinking burns me in our march toward marriage—or bust. This desire for permanency is driving us into state-sanctioned marriages. Same-sex folk want to be able to deploy marriage in as equivalent a way as opposite-sex folk do to bind each other to their relationships. Our pride marches could have been dedicated to ending the war in Iraq or the homophobic torture of Iraqi prisoners of war at Abu Ghraib, or to getting homeless youth off the streets 50 percent of whom are queer, or lobbying against the cutting of funds to fight HIV/AIDS.

I am calling upon bulldaggers, dykes, faggots, feminist femmes, fierce sissies, and other outrageous progressive queers to have a major multicultural sexual liberation confabulation to take our movement back from liberals. Because marriage equality with its rhetoric of sameness is not why we came out of the closet in 1969 or before. We came out to dismantle marriage as an institution. (Yeah, like gays in the military; we shouldn't be prevented from joining because we're gay—but our whole movement shouldn't be contravened nor the lives of those queer service people endangered because liberal queers want to make political hay.)

Yes, I want permanency as much as the next queer. Who wants to risk being left when we're old and ugly. But must we sabotage our liberation just so that six-figure-salaried gay or lesbian elopes across the border to Massachusetts to lasso his/her six-figure-salaried lover into nuptial oblivion and tax shelters. And, yes, as I said above, lesbian and gay partnerships have changed the cultural, political, and material landscape of this country. But must we be married? And even if we are together 12,

17, 28, 32, 40 years as the lesbian and gay couples suing for marriage equality in New Jersey are—and I am full of admiration for them—we still want to lasso our partners into that vain institution, where the church and state converge and congeal.

Marriage trivializes our partnerships.

Even though more than half of straight marriages in this country end in divorce, we still want leaving and taking up with the next same-sex lover with a SUV (or U-Haul) and a good dental plan to be just that much more difficult for our lovers. But according to the May-June issue of *The Advocate*, divorce attorneys are gearing up to handle gay and lesbian divorcés. I am almost ready to agree with Double-Ya: get a constitutional amendment to preserve marriage for heterosexuals. Let heterosexuals have it. Marriage is a bankrupt remnant of the bondage of women and children. Remember also, marriage was denied enslaved black people, and was even denied interracial couples in many Southern states until the 1970s.

Even heterosexuals, except those in Hollywood, think we're bonkers to invest in it.

Let us, the queers—and anyone else who wants to constitute a domestic partner relationship or civil union with whomever you choose, if it be your next-door neighbor—have those benefits that automatically accrue to married heterosexuals (and now married homosexuals in Massachusetts for the time being where institutions and corporations have rolled back domestic partner benefits for same-sex couples because we can get married now). And better yet, if we had universal health care, perhaps fewer of us would be so caught up in the marriage syndrome.

I tried out my premise of permanency on a dyke couple, I'll call Y. and B., who have been together for 19 years, are raising an 11-year-old daughter, own property together, and are both professionals with good insurance plans and politically against marriage. They laughed in all the right places when I read this piece to them, but Y. disagreed with my premise:

"I'll tell you why we want marriage," Y. proffered.

"Yeah, why?" I asked.

"Self-hatred."

July 1, 2004

Cheryl Clarke is an unregenerate lesbian-feminist, poet, and author of four books of poetry, Narratives: Poems in the Tradition of Black Women *(Kitchen Table: Women of Color Press, 1983),* Living as a Lesbian *(Firebrand Books, 1986),* Humid Pitch *(Firebrand Books, 1989), and* Experimental Love *(Firebrand Books, 1993). She was an editor of* Conditions, *a feminist literary journal for women with an emphasis on writing by lesbians, from 1981-1990. Her book,* After Mecca: Women Poets and the Black Arts Movement *will be published by Rutgers University Press in January 2005. Her new manuscript of poems,* Corridors of Nostalgia, *is slated to be published by the award-winning independent press InnerLight Publishing of Atlanta.*

Taking It to the Courts: A Game Plan for Marriage Equality
Matthew A. Coles

Marriage equality isn't a new issue, but until recently, it didn't look like a very promising one in the near term either. The ACLU's Minnesota affiliate brought the first case demanding marriage for same-sex couples in 1972. We lost, as did other cases brought in the '70s and early '80s. In the early '90s, there were what first looked like promising new cases in Hawaii and Alaska. But both of those provoked drastic reactions: voters approved amendments to state constitutions effectively denying marriage to same-sex couples.

But at least four things have changed. First, some courts finally broke through the ice. It began with the Vermont Supreme Court decision that brought about civil unions, then the Canadian appeals courts' decisions that opened up marriage in British Columbia and Ontario. Those were followed by the Massachusetts Supreme Court decision in the *Goodridge* case, which finally brought marriage for same-sex couples to the U.S.

Second, public understanding of gay relationships keeps getting better. When the first case was brought in 1972, most people didn't even know gay people had relationships. The AIDS epidemic probably did more than any other single thing to change that. And every year, more and more Americans realize that gay people do have relationships, relationships that are as complicated and deeply significant as their own.

Third, the Supreme Court's decision last year in *Lawrence v. Texas* made marriage the primary lesbian, gay, bisexual, and transgender issue. Sex and relationships have always been at the core of the movement for LGBT equality. It is sex and relationships that make us different, and so sex and relationships have always been at the heart of discrimination against us. Before *Lawrence*, Americans could always say that our sex and relationships could be—and in some places were—a crime. *Lawrence* didn't just take that argument away. With a vehemence unusual in Supreme Court decisions, the Court said gay people have the very same right to sex and relationships that heterosexuals have. And that begged the marriage question; if gay people have the same right to relationships that straight people have, can society deny them marriage?

Gavin Newsom, and then Jason West in New Paltz and the county commissioners in Portland, finished the job by transforming the issue from an abstract question about social policy into a very tangible question about real people's lives. The stories and images that came out of those cities captured the attention of the country. Perhaps more importantly, they formed eloquent answers to our opponents. It is hard to argue that lesbian and gay relationships are transitory in the face of couples that have been together 20, 30, even 50 years. There is no better answer to the claim that a critical purpose of marriage is creating a place to raise children than same-sex couples taking their vows along with the children they are raising. And perhaps most eloquent of all, the lines of people waiting in the rain to get a chance to marry in San Francisco proved that it's a lie when our opponents charge that gay people aren't really interested in committing to one another.

But if marriage is the right issue, and this increasingly looks like the right time, it is not a sure thing, at least not in the immediate future. The politics of marriage make it clear that even if we succeed in heading off widespread public opposition to marriage for same-sex couples, we are still going to have to rely on courts, at least at the start, to make any progress. The constitutional law of marriage makes it clear that we have to be careful about how we use the courts.

In-depth research shows the public is divided roughly into thirds: 30 percent generally support us, 36 percent are strongly opposed, and about a third are unsure. That middle third is movable. But more important here, that middle third doesn't care very much about the issue at all. No matter how the folks in it feel, the issue is not going to influence how they vote. And among those who are committed, our opponents have many more people who feel much more strongly, who will vote and donate to politicians on the issue. That means that political institutions, at least for the time being, are much more likely to get in the way of marriage for same-sex couples than they are to help it along.

American constitutional law is dominated by the idea that courts, because they are not democratically chosen, should be hesitant to use their power to overrule legislatures, presidents, and governors. Typically, they abandon that general attitude of restraint only when a law appears to discriminate against a traditionally disadvantaged minority or the government appears to be violating one of the explicit rights set out in a constitution.

The difficulty with marriage is that American courts haven't decided whether they believe gay people are a traditionally disadvantaged minority. There is enough room in the doctrine about what a disadvantaged minority is to fight about it. And marriage isn't mentioned in the federal or most state constitutions in so many words. If it is nonetheless part of a constitutional right, it has to be because it is implicitly protected by due process. But getting courts to be tough about implicit rights isn't so easy. The rules are notoriously slippery, and slippery rules are exactly what you don't need when you ask courts to wade into politically controversial issues.

The Supreme Court's decision in *Lawrence v. Texas* should have gone a long way toward resolving questions about both discrimination against gay people and the protection of intimate relationships. But like most Supreme Court decisions, *Lawrence* didn't go far beyond the question in front of it—which was the constitutionality of laws that made same-sex intimacy a crime. And the Court made a point of saying it was not deciding the marriage question.

Since so much is still unresolved about what the Constitution really says about marriage, courts that are hostile to gay people are unlikely to be helpful, and courts that are uncertain about marriage are likely to be unpredictable. This means we have to be choosy about where we bring cases. There are serious downsides to bringing cases and losing, especially at this early stage. Courts don't readily reverse themselves. It will take longer to get marriage for same-sex couples in states that have a court decision on the books saying the constitution doesn't require it. Decisions like that also make it harder for us to use state constitutions to protect gay students and gay parents. And to keep the marriage fight moving ahead, we want to win as many early cases as we can. If there is a clear trend, that will be helpful with uncertain courts. A string of losses will make the job much harder, and make it take longer.

We want to go to courts that already have a history of protecting lesbian, gay, bisexual, and transgender people. We want to go to courts where judges have relatively more experience working with constitutional questions. The more a court studies the issue in depth, the better our chances. But most state courts are populated with commercial lawyers who rarely see a constitutional law issue after they leave law school.

And we have to stay out of federal court, at least for the time being. Any case that raises a federal issue can potentially go to the U.S. Supreme Court. Four members of the current Court told us in the *Lawrence* opinion that they do not think the Constitution requires states to let same-sex couples marry. That means we would have to get the votes of all five of those who have yet to say what they think. And a bad decision... Well, it took 17 years to undo *Bowers v. Hardwick*, the 1986 decision that upheld laws making same-sex intimacy a crime. And that was record time for a turnaround at the U.S. Supreme Court. To make matters worse, most of the lower federal courts these days are far more conservative than the Supreme Court.

The course seems fairly clear. We should bring cases in 6 to 10 states, in state courts on state grounds, where the history and makeup of the high courts give us a decent chance of winning. That process is under way. As I said above, there are cases in progress in New Jersey, Oregon, California, New York, and Washington, with a few more being prepared. If we succeed in getting most of those states—particularly economically important states—to rule that same-sex couples cannot be excluded from marriage, we can begin using those decisions to begin asking other states, through courts and eventually legislatures, to do the same.

But the court strategy will fail if it is not accompanied by a political strategy. Hawaii and Alaska were not singular; one way or another, the constitution of any state can be amended to overrule a court or to take away its power to decide an issue. Good court decisions must be politically sustainable. In some states, that may mean defeating attempts to have the voters amend their state constitutions; in others it may mean preventing a judge from being recalled, or supporting officeholders who refuse to back constitutional amendments.

That brings us back to the great truism of American law: no court victory ever makes lasting change unless the public is convinced, at a minimum, that the principle on which it stands is right even if some of them don't much like the outcome. The good news here is that the public can be convinced.

Much of that middle third I wrote about earlier consists of Americans who are uncomfortable with same-sex couples, but whose bedrock belief in fairness will overcome that discomfort if they believe we make the same commitments they do, but are then treated unfairly.

That case—the case for fair treatment based on commitment and discrimination—is one that has to be made to the public as a whole by the same-sex couples of America. They have to show America that the commitment is there, and that the consequences of treating people like legal strangers are dreadful.

Some people won't be careful about choosing their battles. Cases will get filed in courts where there is really no reason to think we can win, and cases will raise federal issues long before the federal courts are ready to deal with them. If we are lucky, those cases won't do too much harm.

But nothing will help us if we fail to lay the groundwork we need to make decisions ending discrimination against same-sex couples politically sustainable. That means this civil rights battle, like every great civil rights battle, will not be won by visionaries and lawyers, important though they may be. It will be won by ordinary people convincing their neighbors to do the right thing.

Matthew Coles has been Director of the ACLU's national Lesbian & Gay Rights and AIDS/HIV Projects since 1995, and has been involved in the LGBT civil rights movement for nearly 30 years. He was one of the main architects of the challenge to Colorado's Amendment 2, which culminated in the landmark U.S. Supreme Court decision in Romer v. Evans.

First published in the *ACLU Lesbian and Gay Rights and AIDS Projects Annual Report*, 2004. Reprinted by permission of the author.

Two-Sixteen-Ought-Four
Sherilyn Connelly

00) This is not an apology.

01) It was a very, very long Monday, starting at 7 a.m. in the rain. It had been sunny and beautiful for the last few days, until it was *our* turn to stand in line outside City Hall.

02) By 2:30, the paperwork was turned in and the fee was paid.

03) Just what is Gavin Newsom, the controversial new mayor of San Francisco and ostensible architect of this mad rush of same-sex matrimony, *up* to? What's his angle? Is it just the notoriety? How is this going to help his career, exactly? He is most certainly *not* doing this out of the kindness of his heart or any particular love for queers. To put it mildly, I do not trust him. I voted for rival Tom Ammiano in the main election and Matt Gonzalez in the subsequent runoff, and performed at fundraisers for both. I would do it all again if I could, and I still wish Tom had won. Gavin is not our hero just because we're getting married. There's something vaguely Faustian about the whole affair.

04) The actual ceremonies took place in the City Hall rotunda. At the front of the line of people volunteering to witness was a fairly average-looking fellow—maybe straight, maybe queer, certainly innocuous. Immediately behind him was a large, bald, and seemingly gay man carrying a camera. Guess who I picked. (Many moons later, I discivered my gaydar had been malfunctioning and he is, in fact, hetero. Regardless of who he boinks, he takes great pictures.)

05) Food was provided by do-gooders and well-wishers. Problem was, most of it was sugary junk food—not exactly the best thing when you're standing on concrete for hours on end. The thought very much counted, however.

06) We realized that if we got in and got married—and we weren't going to believe it until it happened—this would be the third anniversary we observe. The first is in honor of the day we officially became a couple: July 10, 1999. The second is the day we became domestic partners, June 29, 2002. It was Pink Saturday, the day before Pride Sunday; so that one's a floating holiday for us, the last Saturday in June regardless of the actual date. February 16, 2004 would be the third. The couple immediately ahead us nodded, saying that this would become their third observed anniversary as well. I'm sure there were many, many others.

07) The City is making serious bank off of us—the staff is largely volunteer, and each of the thousands of couples is paying around a hundred dollars. I'm no good at math, but it's a lot of money in a short period of time. That can't be the only reason they're doing this, though.

08) Two days before, we had a threesome in a hot tub at a party. Getting married now did not feel contradictory.

09) How many of us are risking our domestic partnership benefits?

10) Sometimes, when I'm talking to a straight person I've just met, I refer to Katrina as my girlfriend rather than my wife. It's just easier that way. Not because they might say, "How can you have a wife? You're a woman!" Rather, they might think to themselves, "Aha! You have a wife! You *are* really a man!"

11) The Very Ill Little Dyke. I saw her on one of my occasional walks around the building. None of us looked *well*, really, since it was sickness season and we'd all been standing the rain for hours, but she was bad. A cold for sure, and possibly the flu. She should have been home in bed, heavily medicated, not sitting out in the rain. Dedication, in the classic sense.

12) A lot of people brought their own witnesses. We, however, did not plan that far ahead. Just as well; nobody should have to wait through all of this with us. I briefly considered asking San Francisco fixture Frank Chu, this planet's ambassador to the 12 Galaxies — anywhere there's a crowd in San Francisco, you'll find Frank in his dark glasses, holding high his sign with its incoherent message of intergalactic justice — but decided against it. The day was surreal enough already.

13) I greatly resent the notion that we got married in order to show the world that queer couples are just like straight couples. Y'know what? The only thing that makes us like a straight couple is the fact that one of us has a dick. Otherwise, we create a different beast entirely, and I've never suggested otherwise.

14) Will divorce figures be changed? Will straight versus queer stats be reported? If so, you can bet they'll be twisted and repurposed as proof positive that queer marriage is evil.

15) I made sure to bring my checkbook along because of what happened at our domestic partnership ceremony: Checks only. I'm glad cash *is* an option today, because I don't like the idea of our marriage being ruled invalid before the check even clears.

16) A girl with a camcorder asked if she could tape the ceremony. We said yes. Aside from her and our photographer/witness, I detected at least three other people taking pictures as Katrina and I vowed to each other. For people not in wedding clothes, we were no doubt very striking. Of course, we were both gothed out, not to mention I'm six feet tall and was wearing vinyl pants.

17) If I'm bashed, or either of us is hospitalized for any reason, the other will have visitation rights and the ability to make medical decisions. I don't see why I need to explain *anything* beyond that.

18) Our friend David West happened to walk by, and he stood in line with us for about an hour. He was a capital-C communist back in the day, and even though he and the Party are no longer an item, he still keeps the social agitation faith — he considers being arrested in antiwar demonstrations to be no big deal, just fighting the good fight. I respect the hell out of him, and the fact that he supported what we were doing meant a lot to me. (I asked David if he knew which window Dan White used when he snuck into City Hall to assassinate Supervisor Harvey Milk and Mayor George Moscone. He did, and pointed it out. A lot of history has happened in this building.)

19) *scene missing*

20) Our friend James proposed to his girlfriend Jyllian at their New Year's Eve party on December 31, 1999. This is an excerpt from what I wrote in my diary in the wee hours of January 1, 2000:

This sort of thing has a tendency to result in the unmarried couples asking themselves why THEY haven't gotten hitched yet. Of course, it isn't an option for us; if someone told me that to save my life I had to get married as a boy, I'd ask for a Dylan quote to be put on my tombstone, and then haul off and shoot myself so fast they wouldn't even get a chance to ask which song. Anyway, it was nice to see that Katrina has very much the same attitude about it as I do: it's swell for other people, and their wedding is already being greatly anticipated, but it's not something either of us want or need to do. She's already been down that road once, and I've never wanted to. Indeed, that was a point of contention between Kim and I from the early days; she wanted to get married, and I didn't. I was rather content just to be together, not seeing what difference the piece of paper and ring on the finger meant. Granted, for most people it's not even those symbols so much as it's the ceremony and pageantry and pomp and fucking circumstance. Spare me.

Most likely my distaste for the concept of the wedding ceremony stemmed from my association of marriage with divorce. My parents got divorced, their friends got divorced, my friends' parents got divorced, and, perhaps most significantly, I attended my brother Joe's wedding only to watch his marriage deteriorate from day one. As it was happening, I couldn't help thinking that on top of everything else, it must have been humiliating to have the memory of their wedding fresh in so many minds. Maybe it's related to why I don't handle praise very well: it makes your inevitable failure that much harder.

The wedding says *Yes, this is it, this is the person, this is the one that I'm going to spend the rest of my life with, so I'm going to make this big huge elaborate spectacle proclaiming it to god and fuckin' everyone, and the divorce says whoops! never mind.* At least praise comes from an outside source. The wedding was *your* idea.

I know that not all marriages end in divorce. I believe Jyllian and James are going to stay together forever. They've both been through enough in their lives and have come together at the right time, when they need each other the most. They love each other, there's no question of that. Kim and I loved each other, too, but we came together when we very young, and at least one if not both of us still had a lot to learn about ourselves. Even if I hadn't transitioned, I believe we still would have broken up for simply having grown apart. We were perfect for each other at the time, but not by eight and a half years later. We couldn't have been. Joe and the mother of his children, I've always suspected, got married at least partially because the fundamentalist Christianity they embraced at the time required it in order to do normal human things like sex. (Is there a worse reason to get married than just to have sex and/or make babies? No, there isn't. Next question.) Maybe they even loved each other at first, but it must be hard to tell whether you can really be intimate with someone if you can't get close to them until after you've gotten married. Whatever the reason, their marriage dissolved four years later, and his two daughters call someone else "Daddy."

So, from my observation, nothing about getting married seemed to make a bit of difference as to whether or not the couple stayed together or how they felt about one another, so how could not getting married make a difference? Do two people who don't get married, by definition, love each other less than two people who do get married? I just don't see it. Never have.

21) The mailing list. *That's* how The City is paying for all this, judging from the recent influx of wedding-themed junk mail: "I just wanted to send my warmest congratulations for your blessed union..." Ugh. Isn't there an opt-out list or something? No, probably not.

22) They won't all last. That's a given. Being a snarky bitch every once in a great while, I could just tell by looking which ones were doomed. I decided that the older they were, the better chance they had. Of course, being in our early thirties, we're on the riskier side of the curve.

23) When we arrived at a friend's annual Valentine's Day-slash-Anniversary soiree on Saturday, we discovered it had mutated into their wedding reception. I'm sure there were many such re-jiggered parties all throughout the City.

24) I'm a performer. I love a crowd, and there was one ready and willing on the steps of City Hall, greeting every couple. When the doors opened and we stepped outside to the cheering throng, I raised our freshly printed marriage certificate up high. I worked the moment for all it was worth, for all we were worth.

25) As we made our way down the steps, someone offered us a piece of cake. I declined. A couple more steps down and a bag of Hershey's Kisses–type candy was offered to us. I was feeling guilty for having turned down the cake, so I reached in and took a piece. Unfortunately, I spazzed when I took my hand out of the bag, and the piece of candy went flying like an individually wrapped bullet into the forehead of a nearby well-wisher. Painfully, from the looks of it.

26) I grew weary of long lines many years ago. It always amazes me to drive past a nightclub and see people standing in line out front, devoting their precious time to possibly getting in. It makes no sense to me. I would do this for very few things.

June 12, 2004

Sherilyn Connelly (www.sherilynconnelly.org) is a San Francisco–based writer. She has been featured at events such as K'vetch, The Unhappy Hour, and LadyFest Bay Area, and hosts the shows Wicked Messenger and Lit at the Canvas. Her theatrical forays include acting in productions of Night of the Living Dead, The Hitchhiker's Guide to the Galaxy, *and* Zippy the Pinhead, *as well as adapting and directing a live-action* Twilight Zone *episode. She also co-produces the cult public access show* kittypr0n, *which you should watch.*

Speak Now or Forever Hold Your Pee
Dana Cory

Saturday February 14, 2004 — Outside San Francisco City Hall (corner of Polk & McAllister)

"I really have to pee."

"You should have gone before we left."

"I did, honey, but that was three hours ago."

"You don't think we should get married?"

(*sigh*) "That's not what I said — I'm just expressing my desire to empty my bladder before it pops."

"There's the pay toilet across the square."

"No thanks, junkies live in it. And you know I can't stand filthy public rest rooms."

"Sweetie, you don't *know* that junkies live in it because you haven't gone over to check. The toilet is self-cleaning — they use them in Europe. I think you're pee-shy."

"Oh, yes — Europeans are soooo well known for their hygiene. And I am *not* pee-shy."

"Hover."

"What?"

"Hover. If it's as filthy as you think it is, just do the hover-pee."

"I hate the hover-pee!"

"Because you're pee-shy."

"I am not!"

"Are so."

"Am not!"

"Are so!"

"*Excuse me ladies, but are you sure you should be getting married?*"

"Fuck off, faggot!"

"Oh, here we go. Sweetie, please don't swear at the other people in line just because you're pee-shy. I'm very sorry, sir, and I'd appreciate it if you'd please mind your own business."

"*What-ever!*"

"Honey, why do you always do that? Don't apologize for me! He's being an ass."

"No, sweetie — *you* are being an ass. He's being observant, and once again I'm being the CoDA peacekeeper because I'm the Taurus and you're the Aries...ass."

"Maybe he's right, maybe we *shouldn't* get married."

"I knew it! You're not fully committed to this relationship!"

"At the moment I'm only committed to tapping a kidney before my teeth float away!"

"*You* proposed to *me*, remember? (*sob*) Don't you love me?"

"I know, I just, oh god, don't cry....I'm sorry, honey. I do love you, but I *really* have to pee."

"You love me?"

"Yes, honey, I love you and I want to marry you."

"Oh, sweetie! I love you, too."

"We're good? Okay...Now if this line would just move a bit faster."

"Uh, sweetie, why is that woman waving at you?"

"Which woman?"

"The counterprotester with the Honk for Hunky Gay Jesus sign."

"Where?"

"There, across from the three Christian-protester guys."

"Oh, shit!"

"Why is she coming over here? Do you know her?"

"Fuck, fuck, fuck!"

"Sweetie, what the hell is going on here?"

"I can explain—"

"Hey, sexy! You are the last *woman I expected to see here! I can't believe you're getting married!"*

"Excuse me—who the hell are you?"

"Ah, honey, this is Toni. She and I, um, when you and I were separated last fall—"

"YOU FUCKED HER?!"

"Goddess, did she ever! Say, would you two like to get together for a playdate someti—?"

"Bitch, I will knock you down!"

"Whoa there, honey! Punching people—not your style. Toni, get out of here—please!"

"Whatever. This is so The L Word. *(mouthed) Call me."*

"How could you fuck her?!?"

"Honey, we were broken up!"

"For two weeks!"

"Oh, like you didn't date while we were separated."

"No, as a matter of fact I didn't. I still loved you, so I didn't go fucking every skanky ho I met!"

"Okay, one: Toni is neither skanky nor a ho. Two: I don't love her and our one date meant nothing to me. Three: I'm sorry—I do love you and you mean everything to me. Four: I really have to pee."

"Then do it."

"Do what?"

"It."

"Um, like 'sex' it? Here? In line?"

"No—go pee."

"What?!"

"You need to do something to prove to me how sorry you are for fucking around."

"So you want me to piss myself?!"

"Yes. If you love me, you'll do anything I ask to regain my trust."

"Except that! You're fucking insane!"

"Do you want to get married?"

"Yes, but not soaked in my own urine!"

"Is she serious? Ohmigod, you two should not get married!"

"Fuck. Off."

"This is a private matter."

"Not if you're gonna act out your water play next to me, beeyatch."

"Step off, man, or I'll piss on you instead!"

"I'd like to see you try! Girls aren't exactly known for their aim!"

"Oh, I have just about fucking had it today! Honey, you want me to piss? Well, here goes. I'm gonna drop trou right here right now and spray this whole goddamn lawn!"

"Sweetie, stop! I didn't mean it! Pull your pants up!"

"Oh, no! Nothing's gonna stop me now! Just lemme get the ole boxers down and—"

"Next!"

"What?"

"Oh, Sweetie—it's our turn!"

"Next couple please! Come on, people are waiting!"

"Oh, shit! Lemme pull up my pants!"

"No time, let's go!"

"Okay, okay...Shuffling to my wedding with my pants around my ankles. Great."

"I love you, sweetie!"

"I love you, too, honey. Pants or no pants."

"Honeymoon—where?"

"Ladies room—there!"

Dana Cory (www.danacory.com) was born into a show business family on an Easter Sunday and (due to the overmedication of her mother) was very nearly named "Bunny Basket." Since that preverbal close-call, Dana has grown up to perform and write comedy, professionally making fun of herself and everyone else. She resides in San Francisco, but will travel anywhere to say funny things in exchange for money.

Sometimes a Queer Notion
Wayne Courtois

In the beginning, there was To Look.
Wherever it appeared, it made green fields barren,
And caused cattle to die in their tracks.
So the starving men swore to avert their eyes from each other's nakedness.

If I ever forget that there are millions of people who care about what I do with my penis, I need only consult my local newspaper, the *Kansas City Star,* for a reminder. Over the past several weeks—I'm writing this in June 2004—there's been a flurry of activity at the highest levels in the State of Missouri. In mid-May, the Republican-led legislature passed a proposed amendment to the state constitution, banning gay marriage. Missouri already has a law against gay marriage, but supporters believe that the one-sentence amendment—"That to be valid and recognized in this state, a marriage shall exist only between a man and a woman"—would better withstand a legal challenge.

Democratic Governor Bob Holden couldn't wait to place the amendment before the public; he wanted the vote to be part of the August ballot. So did all the other Democrats. As a rule, no one bothers to vote in August, when party members don't run against each other. But if the proposed amendment were to appear on the November ballot, it would draw Republicans to the polls in droves. And they would not forget, while squashing gay marriage like a bug, to vote for all of their favorite fascists as well.

After a period of uneasy peace, along came To Touch.
As bad as To Look had been, To Touch was a thousand times worse.
It made great fissures open in the earth, swallowing nations whole.
Oh, yes—To Touch was as bad as bad could get...

In October of 1986 I moved from New York to Kansas City—cries of "Are you crazy?" notwithstanding—to live with my first husband, whom I'll call Burke. On the night I arrived at the airport, he stood waiting at the gate, and we looked at each other as though we were meeting for the first time. He wore charcoal gray slacks and a light gray sweater; he'd abandoned his Jheri curls in favor of a natural look, and his beard was more full than when I'd seen it last. He was altogether handsome, and seemed to be shyly looking up at me even though I was shorter. I was exhausted, but an excited child jumped up and down in me, and I waited no decent interval to get close enough to touch him. A pat on the shoulder was what I had in mind, but he pulled me close and crushed me against him. My knees went weak and I thought I'd crash to the floor if he let me go.

The house that we rented belonged to a young straight couple who were trying to make a career out of buying curiously neglected, ruined little houses, restoring them, and selling them for a profit. But profits were scarce, and the couple had resorted to renting out this house—a salmon-colored crackerbox with a barn roof—because they were running out of money and had just about worked themselves to death.

When Burke and I moved into the place, it had no kitchen—only the space where a kitchen had been, with no floor and no windows. The back porch had been torn away, leaving no access to the small, steep backyard, and there was no furnace. Only three rooms were finished: the living room, with a hardwood floor and elegant powder blue wallpaper; the upstairs bedroom, which was as large as my apartment in New York had been; and the upstairs bathroom. We kept a secondhand refrigerator in the makeshift dining room, along with a microwave oven Burke had bought instead of paying his share of the first month's rent.

At bedtime we listened to *Hearts of Space* while we rocked gently in the king-size waterbed Burke was renting by the week. I felt an indescribable sense of peace as I looked at him, his outline barely perceptible in the streetlight seeping through the white curtains. I couldn't get enough of his skin; I'd press my whole length against him as we slept like hibernating bears in the swiftly cooling nights. He had a clean, intoxicating smell that took me a while to identify. Finally I had it: he smelled like a *bookstore*—like freshly cut paper and scrubbed wooden shelves.

This, surely, was all I would ever need to know of love.

When Democratic Governor Bob Holden sent a proclamation to Republican Secretary of State Matt Blunt, calling for an August 3rd vote on the gay marriage ban amendment, Blunt refused to start the process of setting the election, claiming state law required that he first receive the signed amendment passed by the legislature. (As bureaucracy would have it, there wasn't time to get the signed amendment to Blunt before the deadline for setting the August election.)

At that point, Democratic Attorney General Jay Nixon stepped in, bringing a lawsuit against Blunt to force the issue. When a circuit judge refused to order Blunt to place the amendment on the August ballot, whether he had received the signed amendment or not, Nixon appealed the decision to the Missouri Supreme Court—which declined to take the case until after the Missouri Court of Appeals ruled on the matter.

As bad as To Touch had been,
There was yet one thing worse, that could never be forgiven: To Love.
It brought down fire from the sky.
And men who dared To Love learned the lessons of the damned.

My relationship with Burke began to deteriorate quickly. I tell myself to this day that it was no one's fault. He just happened to be a compulsive liar, the kind who couldn't tell the truth about anything—his origins, his work history, or even the time of day. Unable to hold down a job, he was also on the brink of being arrested for several years' worth of parking violations.

Then came the night when I stood in our makeshift dining room, facing Kev, Burke's former roommate—Kev of the ultrapale skin and bushy blond hair—and a friend of Kev's, just as skinny but darker, with a mustache sprouting in all directions.

"What do you dickheads want?" Burke was saying, for they had just burst into the house, after pounding on the door hard enough to rattle the upstairs windows.

"You know what I want, fucker," Kev said.

It could have been Kev's finger poking his jacket pocket toward Burke's face, but I believed instantly that it was a gun. I stopped breathing, could only force my next breath when it was long overdue. "What do you *want*?" I squeaked.

Kev took the gun from his pocket. He kept it aimed at Burke, but the sight of it, so flat and unglamorous in his hand, had a galvanic effect on me. I wanted to be everywhere in the room, to find all points of safety at once. But all I could do was make a beeline toward Burke. "Burke," I squeaked again, "what do they *want*?"

Burke only growled.

I backed up against the wall next to the refrigerator. I was hardly removed from the scene, but for a half-second I felt a detachment that allowed a different picture to suggest itself, one of hairy warriors in animal skins circling a fire while grunts and screams echoed in the background. Once I had lusted for this, the Great Male Dream with its *fuck*-language, the *ur*-language of men with more passion than brains. And like so many things I'd wanted, it only struck me dumb when I finally got it. The dream held nothing but the sour taste of hormones, and a sense of my genitals as achingly vulnerable.

"...*fuck* out of here," Burke was yelling at our guests, "before I call the fuckin' cops!"

Kev barked, "That's a fuckin' laugh." He reached past the microwave oven and yanked its plug from the wall.

"Is that what this is about?" I asked. "You want to steal our microwave?"

"Your big dumbass friend is who stole it," Kev snapped.

I looked at Mustache, who was still glaring at me. "Who are you, anyway?" I asked.

"That microwave's half mine," he growled, as if that was all I needed to know.

Kev waved his gun again. So *this* was how people got killed: it wasn't about a million-dollar drug deal, or passionate, mind-bending love; it was about a barbecue grill, or a big-screen TV...or a microwave oven, like the one my husband had stolen from his ex-roommate, telling me later he'd spent the rent money on it. And as I watched the wavering muzzle of Kev's gun—charcoal gray, with no sparkle or finish—I knew it was all over between Burke and me. The lie about the microwave was the last lie of its kind that I ever wanted to hear, and I never wanted to be threatened by a gun again.

So great, so instantly gained was my resolve that I immediately began to calm down. Kev wasn't going to kill us; he only wanted to get his property and leave. When neither Burke nor I moved, he put the gun back in his pocket and cradled the microwave oven in his arms. He couldn't resist a final threat as he backed toward the door that his husband was already opening: "Fuck with me again and you're history."

A very few minutes later I was saying to Burke, "I'm leaving you."

He looked at me, his eyes hooded, the shape of his mouth revealing nothing. But he knew it was true. I was leaving him and his crazy ways and this crazy unfinished house, and there was nothing he could do about it.

On May 24th, the Court of Appeals sided with the Secretary of State, ruling that the gay marriage amendment did not have to appear on the August election ballot just because the governor wanted it to. Attorney General Nixon immediately filed an appeal with the Missouri Supreme Court.

On June 3rd, the Missouri Supreme Court surprised everyone by siding with the governor and attorney general. The *Kansas City Star* announced: "In a victory for the Democrats, Missourians will vote in August—not in November—on a proposed constitutional amendment to ban gay marriage."

Even Pollyanna couldn't fail to see the cynicism here. The court struggle wasn't about gay marriage at all—it was about whether Democrats or Republicans would have the upper hand in the fall election. Never has a civil rights issue been more blatantly used as a political football.

To Look, To Touch, and *To Love had hauled mankind to the brink of Hell.*
Then To Marry *appeared.*
And men, struck dumb, could only look at each other.
To Marry. That two men *should* marry...
It was the end of everything, the extinction of the planet, the unwinding of the universe back, back to its beginning, a sparkle in God's eye.

Better to have never existed, than to let this shame come to pass.

It's easy to say, now that I'm with my second husband and we've been happily settled down for 15 years, but...

When I think back on my first gay marriage, that's exactly how I see it—as a marriage, nothing less. As much of a marriage as the one I have now, even though that first one failed. To me, that's the point of wanting marriages that are full-fledged and legally sanctioned: we should be able to marry for good reasons *or* bad.

Repealing the sodomy laws may give me the right to fuck, but I want more. I want the right to *fuck up.*

Now, that's a queer notion if there ever was one.

No wonder the fascists are afraid.

On August 3, 2004, an overwhelming 70 perent of Missouri voters approved an amendment to the state constitution banning same-sex marriage. As many as 11 other states will vote on similar provisions in November.

Wayne Courtois (www.waynecourtois.com) is author of the novel My Name Is Rand, *published by Suspect Thoughts Press. He lives in Kansas City, Missouri, with his second husband and two cats, both adopted. Email him at waynerman@aol.com.*

mrs.
Dani Couture

according to her mother, it all went downhill
after the bride chose carrot cake. icing
sopping down the walls, bits of brown cake
rolling slowly across the floral print wallpaper.
her mother's hand clenched, still stuffed
with the guts of the wedding cake, waiting
for a target. outside, the bride's disco stilettos
aerate the lawn, give a full view of the gifts
beneath her cocktail dress. partial mohawk
gone limp gives her head cherubic appeal—
picture perfect profile. pink lips, slightly parted.
the photographer has already run out
of film, and the garter is still on.

On September 27, 2003, Dani Couture was legally married to her gorgeous wife, Sarah. Dani
is a Toronto-based writer whose poetry, reviews, and interviews have appeared in a number of
Canadian journals and magazines. This is her first venture south of the border. Dani's online
residence is www.danicouture.com.

Do I Know You?
Jameson Currier

Dear Richard and John,

Thank you so much for sending me the invitation to your Impending Grand Nuptials. I'm very honored and touched to be included as part of your Great Day. And I'm certainly impressed by all the grandeur and the expense of the Big Occasion you are mounting. (The invitation alone could become a museum piece — Heavy-weight paper! Embossed borders! Gilded edges! Translucent Insert!) You must be planning an Elaborate Affair for Hundreds — a four o'clock wedding ceremony on the beach followed by dinner and dancing in town. I'm already dazzled and excited! And I just love that "Festive Attire Requested" bit. No black tie necessary! No suits and neckties that no longer fit me because time and gravity have taken their toll!

But I must confess right up front that I can't exactly place the moment — or place — where we met and bonded enough that you would be so generous to include me in your Special Celebration of Commitment to One Another. Are you the Rich who works out at my gym or Rick-the-personal trainer who gave me his cellphone number a few weeks ago? There is a Rick-with-a-goatee who lives in the apartment two floors above mine. Is that you? Or are you the Richard who works on the floor beneath me? You're not the Dick with the huge cock and the sling on East 53rd Street, are you? Or Richard the therapist that I met at the Townhouse about two years ago (and who had that fabulous loft)? I'm certain you're not the Ricky I hired as a hustler last fall — he would need a lot of work before he could land into such nuptial bliss as what you are up to — I mean, even those *Queer Eye* boys would be hard-pressed to convince him to dry out and sober up enough to say, "I Do," but, then again, he *was* a beautiful piece of work, with a dick that could get as hard as a good dick can get... And a rich man could certainly entice him into sticking around for the Next Big Thing he could try... Is that you? Are you that Dick? That Ricky? That Richard?

I know there was a friend, Rick, from my ACT UP days, but he is long gone from this planet and that can't be you. And then there was another Richard who was on my phone tree list — that's not you, is it, after all these years? Or are you that older Richard, the Richard I met at the Man's Country baths back in the late 1970s? My God, that would make us both, what? — well, almost ancient and shriveled-up and certainly almost-off the marriage-market list!

So it must be John whom I know — Is this John from the Black Party in 1995? (The guy in chaps I gave such a long, delicious blow job to in the balcony?) Or the Jon who was the volunteer at the March on Washington in 1993? (We shared a bagel together while waiting to head down to the Mall). You're not the JJ from the Gay Pride Parade in Manhattan back in, well, 1986, are you? (Jonathan James Something-Or-Another, as I recall...the guy who was an ex-boyfriend of my ex-boyfriend — the one who was in the hospital at the time and didn't live much longer that summer?) You're not Johnny, the chorus boy, whom I dated briefly when I was just out of college, are you? Or are you the Jonathan I had the three-way with back in the early 1990s? You're not the John who was married to Sharon-Lee, are you? — the guy who swore he was going to get a divorce from his wife and wanted me to fuck him a second (and third) time the night we hooked up. You can't be John from Hewlett-Packard — that really well-built dude who showed up at my apartment to fix more than just my printer — he told me he was really straight, but didn't mind having sex with a guy and so he did — have sex with a guy — me — and more than once, too, as I recall. This isn't you, is it?

So maybe it is Richard I know after all. Are you the Richard on Perry Street with the beautiful nine-inch cock whom I greedily devoured one night in 2002? The one with the massage table? Or are you the Dick I had a blind date with (about 4,000 blind dates ago)—the guy I met at Starbucks on Eighth Avenue on April 16, 1999 (and who, by the way, looked nothing like the photo he emailed me in advance). Are you the Richie from the summerhouse in 1985 I fooled around with when our boyfriends weren't around? Or the one on 14th Street in 1991 with a gold Labrador and who liked to do watersports in his bathtub? You can't be Richard-the-Republican I slept with at the Warwick—I mean, he would have had to have gone through a lot of therapy to come out of the closet, you know—but, then again, that was something like 15 years ago, so, well, it could be you? Are you that fucked-up Dick?

Come to think of it, there was the John I shared a heart-pounding hand job with during a van ride from the Miami airport to Key West in 1983 (when that near-monsoon canceled our flight and we were driven south in the blinding rainstorm courtesy of the airline). Or did I meet you on the rooftop of Kevin's apartment building on the West Side during his Fourth of July party back in—what—1979? The John with the big blue eyes who was a really great kisser? I hope you're not the John I threw up on during the boat ride around Manhattan when my boss was retiring in 1987. (Who knew gin and tonics could be so deadly on an empty stomach and a swaying vessel? But then you were so sweet—we went back to your place and showered and fooled around for like, well, hours and hours and hours and hours.) Is this you again, after all these years?

Whomever you are, how ever I know you, I am so glad you have each found your Significant Other, and I am thankful that whatever past I shared with either (or both) of you did not make a strong enough impact for you to abandon your quest to find your True Soul Mate For All Eternity and thus, you found Each Other. I am so looking forward to being present at your Special Recognition of Commitment Between Two Gay Men and listening to you exchange your Vows of Companionship—especially, after all the time and memories that have passed between us (unless you're the Richard from the chat room I met last week—then we simply have to smile and nod and keep our little secret, huh?—consider it one of those things that bachelors do before they get hitched).

So, *Yes*, absolutely, I've enclosed my RSVP card (prestamped by you, no less, how *truly* generous). And of course, I'll be sending a thoughtful gift along before the Big Date happens—a quick Google search already shows that you are registered at Bloomies, Tiffany's, and Crate & Barrel! But my big, burning Question of the Day—the one I am saving up to ask when we meet again—is not really How did *We* meet? but How did *You* find each other? How did *The Two of You* meet? How did it happen? Where did it happen? Details, details, details, dearies—I want to know all the facts. (Because, God knows, I've been trying to meet someone just like you for decades! I have been a Husband Hunter from my Gay Day One!)

I'll also be bringing lots of Kleenex with me to the Big Event, expecting to sob my eyes and heart out because of your fortunate happiness and new marital ecstasy. I'll share my tissues with any one who needs one, you know, and I'll have a few unused condoms in my wallet, too, just in case there is someone who might be interested in seeing what happens. You never know who you might meet next—he could be Mr. Right, after all. Then again, even if he's not—even if he is just Mr. Right Now, I'm not too old yet to overlook a new adventure—and you never know what else you might find along the way... As I always say (and probably said to you), it's good to keep an open mind and be ready for the possibility to change.

All my best and see you soon,

xoxoxo
Jim
(aka James, Jameson, Jimmy, Jamey, JC, or just plain J)

Jameson Currier is the author of a novel, Where the Rainbow Ends, *and two books of short stories,* Dancing on the Moon *and most recently,* Desire, Lust, Passion, Sex. *He is still single and lives in Manhattan.*

A Message from Piki & Poko:
Queer Marriages in StarLand
David Cutler and Mark Ewert

Hello, Earthpeople!

Lately, we've been watching your TV-news on our magic star-bracelets! Every time we watch, we see people talking about "Gay Marriage"! Some are saying, "DO!" but others say "DON'T!"

This made us wonder about "gay marriage" in StarLand. Did it exist? Was it legal? Would we be invited to one? What dresses would we wear?

We journeyed to StarLand's Bubble-Library to find out more. Imagine our surprise when Ms. Neenu, the liquid librarian, informed us that not only was gay marriage legal in StarLand, but there were over 750 ways to do it!

Here are some of StarLand's fave gay ways to "tie the knot." Which one do you like the best? Wouldn't it be fun to get married in the Corn-people way?

"Arranged Arboreal Enemy Marriage":

Many parts of StarLand are covered with forests of sassy, effeminate trees. In anthropological terms, these trees form "elective kinship systems," a.k.a. families-of-choice; thus, effeminate trees band together in groups called "groves." Groves nurture and support their own members, but engage in fierce rivalry with other groves in such arenas as fancy-dancing, foliage costumery, and party-hosting. To ensure excellence in its members, a grove matriarch may opt to join one of her saplings with a sapling from a rival grove in an "Arranged Arboreal Enemy Marriage." The two young trees are transplanted close together, so that from the earliest age they are schooled in all the moves and countermoves of their enemy-spouse. Root-systems vie with each other for soil and nutrients, while leafy branches strive as the trees see who can throw the most "shade." At the age of 15 rings, the two trees will have their first public melee in a grand "Budding Out" Ball hosted by their respective groves. Trees from far and near will show up to watch the wedded enemies perform their most funky, trunky maneuvers. The passion expended in such tournaments can become truly legendary.

As Madame Sarsaparilla, matriarch of the Hazyseed Grove says: "The more they strive, the more they're alive."

"Commerce-based Demographic-Polyamory":

All over StarLand, one can hear the plaintive mating cries of mobile, sentient vending machines. The most popular machines are the "Gender Venders," sophisticated units that sell all the trendy new genders the customers of StarLand demand. Older Gender Venders offer gender classics such as "Azure Male Diminutive," while more cutting-edge machines experiment with such gender-models as "XXL Re-Female Clementine," and "Pale Hyssop: Excited/Undecided."[1]

Anyone who buys a gender from a given machine is considered married to it; thus, a very hip unit can be united in marital bliss with vast swatches of the population, i.e., marketing-segments.

---

[1] Please note that all StarLandic gender-terms can be, at best, only *loosely* translated into any given Earth-language.
[2] See translation note, above.

The lyrics of one very popular advertising jingle/nuptial hymn goes something like this: "Buy buy buy, bi bi bi, with and by...ME!"[2]

"Recombinant Maizal Meme-Sharing":

The Cornunons are a highly advanced, space-faring race of giant corn kernels, who live in familial groups known as "cobs."

In Cornunon biology, DNA is done away with entirely. Cornunons find the very idea of genetic inheritance repugnant; for the Cornunons, what matters most is not an individual's genes, but his or her *memes*. In essence, a meme is any sort of really compelling idea. Some of the memes most prized by the Cornunons include syndicalism, atonal music, and the ur-recipe for vegan cookies.

Once in every Cornunon's life, he or she hopes to voyage unthinkable interstellar distances in order to exchange memes with the great Cornunon Poetess Cornnudra 4à3b. Such a colloquy is said to be orgasmic in the extreme. The memes a Cornunon receives from the Poetess are then taken back and shared with his or her cob-mates. As a species, the Cornunons are endlessly revitalized by this constant flow of thoughts and ideas.

(One Cornunon informant said that the closest thing humans have to Recombinant Maizal Meme-Sharing are anthologies such as this book.)

David Cutler and Mark Ewert are the co-creators of the Internet's favorite animated series, Piki & Poko, Adventures in StarLand *(www.pikiandpoko.com).*

You Can Keep Your Rights, I Already Gots Mine!
Sven Davisson

For Larry & Trevor married February 15, 2004

The licensing of marriage is the last uncomfortable intersection of law and religion left in our increasingly secular society. Marriage is, on the one hand, a religious ceremony—one of the three great rights common to all denominations of the priestly classes—and, on the other, a contractual union with appendant civil oversight and regulation.

Within the milieu of religion, marriage bestows a cultural recognition and support of the solemn promise of two people to live together in mutual love and respect. As an ideal, it is the moment when one's small community of faith, friends, and family join together in celebration of a life shared.

As a civil contract, marriage is codified in over 1,000 federal "automatic" benefits and countless more in the state and private sectors. With licensing certificate in hand, the couple becomes a unit, which is everywhere predefined in the laws that govern everything from inheritance to privacy protection and access.

This uncomfortable intersection leads to an uncomfortable, and highly inappropriate, collusion between lawmakers and religious leaders. The religious estate of our republic sees marriage as a purely religious issue—the civil license merely being a recognition of nonsecular solemnization—ignoring the numbers of people who obtain a civil marriage, only, without interface with clergy. For their part, the secular leaders view marriage as much more than the act of licensing clerks, recognizing that it creates a legal class with more privileges and responsibilities than any other in our society.

When debating civil unions, the Vermont legislature admitted to being confused as on one day a religious leader would advise them against the proposed bill, while on the next another religious leader would speak in favor of the bill. It was obvious from the legislators' comments that their collective confusion arose out of their inability to glean a consensus of religious understanding from the various positions articulated before them by the line of religious authorities. In a recent *Newsweek* editorial, Anna Quindlen posed the question, "In a secular nation, why should church leaders be required to acknowledge civil marriage—or, for that matter, be attended to when they pass judgment on what they will not acknowledge?"

The real crux of the "gay marriage" question is not a religious debate. It is, rather, a wrestling for the retention of one of the last areas of religious control of secular life. Ultimately the question of marriage legislation is a secular one, positioned squarely in the domain of law and codified social custom. The spiritual solemnizing of unions is a religious question, while the licensing of a special coupled class of society is not.

Recently a colleague asked why gay men and lesbians would want to fight for marriage anyway. On the surface, it does seem a lot of energy to lay claim to the summit of an anachronism. It is, however, one of the last great vestiges of exclusion directed at a colonized people. One cannot help but feel something akin to the Berlin Wall being torn down, as each new town is added to the list of gay marriage havens… On the other side, the last stalwarts desperately trying to hold on to a history and golden age that never really existed.

The opponents of gay marriage argue that the concept erodes the foundations of the very concept of marriage itself. They paint an image of marriage that claims to look backward into time immemorial at a continuity of glorious union—pristine, perfect, and biblically sanctioned.

The truth, of course, is that modern marriage has no historic antecedents. The history upon which they choose to premise their arguments never existed. In the 21st century, marriage is about love and commitment—a construction that would have been unthinkably scandalous in proper society just 100 years ago. For the centuries prior, marriage has been a contract of property and inheritance with little or no relation to the practice today.

Just a little over 30 years ago, interracial marriage was illegal in much of the United States. When it was legalized nationally, the country was less divided over the issue than it is today over the question of gay marriage. Unlike current polling, at that time an *overwhelming majority* of the country opposed interracial marriage. A Gallup Poll conducted in 1968 showed that fully 72 percent of the country opposed interracial marriage with 48 percent openly expressing the opinion that it should be criminalized. It is no coincidence that Massachusetts governor Mitt Romney is using a 1913 anti-interracial marriage law to prevent nonresidents from marrying in his state.

As an observer of this debate, the critical point in the current events and court rulings is a subtle, but vitally important, shift in the rubric of power in the debate of gay rights (so called). I have long been ambivalent about the notion of demanding rights, as I see a large, unintended, side effect being the ironic, and often self-defeating, empowering of others to bestow rights. This has allowed the far-right to control the debate for the last 20 years, by casting the demand for equality under the law as a fight for "special rights" and asking the loaded (rhetorical) question of how far should the "expansion" of "rights" go. In this environment, courts are deemed symptomatic of an "activist judiciary" when they have the hubris to interpret the self-evident truths of our founding fathers as applying to *all* peoples.

Regardless of whether the members of the Enlightenment could foresee what they were setting in motion, courts are now beginning to correctly interpret the reach of those rights. The authors of the Declaration of Independence acknowledged that no mortal could ultimately bestow rights on another, leaving that to the avowed purview of a mightier universal power. It may seem like a subtle shift, but asking someone to give you what you already have, only gives them the power to withhold it.

When the Supreme Court overturned their own *Bowers v. Hardwick* (1984) ruling in *Lawrence v. Texas* (2003), the debate transformed overnight to a question of existing rights. This decision stands in sharp contrast to earlier legislative efforts easily cast as attempts at articulating new rights or extending novel protections. Justice Scalia, in his dissenting opinion, correctly observed that the Court's overturning of *Bowers* called into question the "validation of laws based on moral choices" including, in his list of examples, same-sex marriage. For once, I actually agree with a Scalia opinion, though he and I are at complete odds as to whether this change bodes well or ill for society. Without question or exception, in a modern, secular country laws should *never* be based on "moral choices."

The Massachusetts Supreme Judicial Court was the first to correctly extend *Lawrence v. Texas*, ruling that exclusively intersexual marriage laws are unconstitutional (*Goodridge v. Department of Public Health*, 2003). In their decision, the court acknowledged that "many people hold deep-seated religious, moral, and ethical convictions that marriage should be limited to the union of one man and one woman, and that homosexual conduct is immoral. Many hold equally strong religious, moral, and ethical convictions that same-sex couples are entitled to be married, and that homosexual persons should be treated no differently than their heterosexual neighbors." The court ruled that "the State may not interfere with these convictions, or with the decision of any religion to refuse to perform religious marriages of same-sex couples." They held "these matters of belief and conviction" to be "properly outside the reach of judicial review or government interference."

The court's response to the Massachusetts Senate went further, giving reality to Scalia's deepest fears, stating "neither may the government, under the guise of protecting 'traditional' values, even if they be the traditional values of the majority, enshrine in law an invidious discrimination that our Constitution [...] forbids." The court saw clearly that the existing state marriage law created a class relegated "to a different status." In rejecting the Senate's proposed compromise legislation outlawing same-sex marriage while, with the same stroke of the pen, creating "civil unions" — same as marriage in everything but name — the Massachusetts SJC could deduce no rationality in creating a segregated group. In their response, they observed, "The history of our nation has demonstrated that separate is seldom, if ever, equal."

Apocalyptic queer American novelist William S. Burroughs observed prophetically in *The Western Lands*, "The more familiar something becomes, the less it will incite fear and hostility... But, and it's a big But, a certain percentage of individuals, varying with environment and context, act in the opposite direction: the more gays come out into the open, the more hysterical and frenzied and often violent they become." We are now living in both interesting and dangerous times — a time when a respected civil rights leader like Coretta Scott King can declare: "A constitutional amendment banning same-sex marriages is a form of gay bashing." The attacks from the Right certainly will become more violent as their position becomes more desperate and untenable. At the same time, a more insidious, and potentially more damaging, threat lurks beneath the surface of the cultural debate. In the long term, what price will we pay as a "people" for assimilation and acceptance?

Gay culture is both myth and reality — but the same can be said of all cultures throughout time and place. A culture is little more (or less) than artifice developed from within (and all too often marketed from without) that assists in binding a group together rather than by ethnicity, religious belief, or clan heritage. This process is vital for the self-preservation of a colonized people, which, as Joan Nestle observed, gay people are. The inevitable homogenizing process of assimilating to a dominant culture may prove an even greater threat to Queer cultures — new and modern as they are, lacking the pull of centuries of contiguous heritage and the support of familial tradition. Couple this with the fact that we lost a generation before they had a chance to become our cultural elders and the situation becomes more precarious. It is my hope that we, as gay men and lesbians, will do as we have done before and take the mythic "I Do" and make it our own in all of *our* irreverent, Queer culturally affirming, camp glory.

Sven Davisson is editor of Ashé! Journal of Experimental Spirituality, *an online quarterly which he and his partner founded (www.ashejournal.com). He has a degree in Queer Theory. He, his partner Chris, and their menagerie of dogs and parrots currently live on an island off the Maine coast. Website: www.svendavisson.com.*

Change
Robbie Daw

1
"There are some bad people on the Rise,"
Morrissey used to sing to us
On those long summer days in 1989
When we were 15.

We'd sit cross-legged in the woods
Behind the community college
With the Ouija board between us,
Trying to summon ghosts.

The summer inevitably faded
Into school, and we were
Torn apart from each other by
The social rules of Senior High.

I still listened to all our tapes
And I wondered if you did, too,
With your new friends.
But I knew in my heart you probably didn't.

2
In college we all drank coffee
And talked and talked and
Talked and one night at Kevin's
I saw you and we made faces at each other.

We did homework in the lounge
And I imagined us getting married
And having a house and fireplace but
It was 1995, and we couldn't get married.

It was a naïve ideal I guess
And I should have paid more attention
When I could see that you were
Getting bored.

When the semester ended
And you waved goodbye as I drove
Off into the summer, I still smiled
Though I knew it was over.

3
When I finally met You
It was only a few months
Before the world shook
And I'm still haunted by that day.
We sit around for hours

And don't have to talk and talk
And talk and talk to communicate
And You even had some of those old songs.

I'm sorry for the time we went
Downtown and You wanted me to
Get fitted for a ring and I balked
And got embarrassed.

Because after all the years
And mistakes with others who
Can't even touch You,
It's us in the house with the fireplace.

4
I got your wedding invitation
In the mail and sent you an email
Saying I couldn't come
But that it was nice to hear from you.

You wrote back and we remembered
The woods and the tapes,
Some of which we later replaced
With CDs.

I wrote and told you about him
But it somehow seemed less
Because you were getting married
And he and I couldn't do that.

After a few weeks we lost touch again
But I realized that I still had You,
And it wasn't inconceivable that
Times were changing.

Robbie Daw is a writer and photography editor for Instinct. *He fled the greenery of western Pennsylvania for the mirage of Los Angeles in the late '90s, but often returns home to Pittsburgh to keep his sanity in check. His boyfriend and two cats usually keep him busy when he's not writing.*

For Whom the Wedding Bells Toll
Christian de la Huerta

My earliest romantic fantasies were about women: movie stars, famous singers, or magazine cover models. I even had a crush on one of my mother's friends. In contrast, my earliest sexual memories were about men, even before I had a real clue about the nature of sex. Yet throughout my youth, and as I developed a sense of identity as a gay man, not once did it occur to me that I could get married. Even as a boy, some deep part of my self unconsciously knew that marriage was not an option for people like me.

At least not then.

Marriage and My Family

I was brought up in a Catholic family, one of nine children — further evidence that the "Vatican Roulette" is not very effective. My teenage years were one long depression. Deeply conflicted about my budding sexuality and the religion that utterly denied it, I eventually had to make a gut-wrenching, existential choice between who I was and the spiritual tradition in which I was raised. At 19, I fell in love for the first time and discovered the difference between having sex and making love. The choice became clear, and the rest is history.

Right around this same time my older sister got married. In fact, we both left home within a few days of each other. In retrospect, the contrast of our respective departures from the family nest is startling. Pat enjoyed a beautiful church wedding and a festive reception; she and her husband Juan received the love, support, and acknowledgment of family and friends, not to mention lots of presents.

A few days later, my first lover Harry and I slunk out of our respective homes in virtual secrecy, dragging a small U-Haul behind my old Nova, filled with our few earthly possessions. Instead of starting out our relationship with multiple toasters, blenders, and other brand-new kitchen accoutrements, we had a few mismatched plates and utensils our mothers had pieced together as we left to be "college roommates." At the time, the inherent unfairness never crossed my mind.

Besides its religious and legal aspects, marriage also has a social element. There is great affirmative and bonding power when two people ritually express their love and commitment to one another in front of their tribe of friends and family. And yes, gifts do help a young couple get started on their life together — that's the whole idea.

Is it possible that the "bonds" of marriage — including their five kids — have supported my sister and her husband to stay together? Harry and I, in a relationship bound by secrecy and eventual conflict with his family, and struggling to support ourselves financially while going to school, "divorced" after three years.

Agents of Change

Queer people often serve society by fulfilling certain spiritual roles and functions (which I outline in my book, *Coming Out Spiritually*). Among other things, we are outsiders, healers, keepers of beauty, priests/shamans, agents of change. As outsiders, we hold up a mirror in which society can see itself and test its limits. In many ways, we propel society's forward movement and help it decide what its limits are. We are scouts of consciousness: those who go first. We take ten steps in a given direction, and then the rest of society will look at us and say, "Well, we don't know about ten steps, but we might take three or four." The issue of marriage today is a perfect example of this. Just by virtue of being who we are, and wanting to be included in this institution, we are forcing society-at-large to reevaluate the meaning of marriage.

In the last year, there has been endless discussion in the media and around the watercooler about marriage; a barrage of articles and several books have been published analyzing its history. Suddenly everyone knows that, for example, marriage was not made a church sacrament until the 1200s. At the same time that politicians rant about the "sanctity of marriage," by now many of us are aware that originally marriage was about property and paternity, economics and politics. Romantic marriage is, in fact, a very recent development in human history. We also know there is a difference between civil and religious marriage.

In forcing society to ask the question, "what is marriage for and what does it mean to be married?" queer people serve the greater good for everyone. For, even if painful and difficult, arriving at the truth is always good.

A Change of Heart

My own perception of marriage has evolved. I idealized and romanticized it in my youth, while seeing it as untenable because of my sexual orientation. Many years and several relationships later, when the issue of civil marriage rights for gays and lesbians began to rise in the public consciousness, I decided that marriage was not for me. I considered marriage a heterosexist construct, a patriarchal invention to establish paternity, determine inheritance and property rights, establish the dominance of man over woman. I had no use for any of that.

Then, a few years ago I attended the commitment ceremony of my friends David and Alfredo. Witnessed by friends and family in a beautiful San Francisco garden on a gorgeous afternoon, they professed their love for each other in a heartwarming ceremony officiated by an openly gay retired Episcopal bishop and an openly gay Episcopal deacon.

That afternoon, for the first time in my life, I decided that perhaps someday I might like to get married. For some straight people this might be hard to comprehend. Things like the right to get married or the right to hold your beloved's hand in public without fear of threat or personal endangerment are taken for granted by most heterosexuals. That is what constitutes a heterosexist society. Most people do not realize that gays and lesbians have spent a lifetime translating song lyrics, poetry, movies, and novels to fit our experience.

Things changed last year. A few months after the Supreme Court outlawed sodomy laws, the Massachusetts Supreme Judicial Court made marriage available to all people in that state. Suddenly, surprisingly, and unexpectedly for most of us, same-sex marriage leapt to the forefront and heart of the culture wars, polarizing religions and threatening to become a wedge issue in our national elections. In San Francisco alone, more than 4,000 same-sex couples were married in 2004, though the legality of these unions is still being disputed in court. As of June 2004, more than 10,000 same-sex couples have taken their vows in San Francisco, Portland, Massachusetts, and Canada.

When San Francisco Mayor Gavin Newsom courageously opened the door to same-sex marriage early in the year, my partner Markus and I, who had fallen in love three years ago, seriously considered joining them. Yet the more we thought about it, our sense was that we were not ready. "If it wasn't for this window of opportunity, which will close at some point," we agreed, "we would choose to wait." We decided to do just that.

A couple of weeks later, Bush came out publicly in support of amending the

Constitution to define marriage as between a man a woman. For the first time in U.S. history, rights would be diminished, rather than expanded; and my rights were being singled out. I was angered. I thought: "I work hard and pay taxes; I am an American citizen and love this country. What right does he have to keep this from me?" Though I hadn't thought about it this way before, no longer was I willing to accept second-class citizenship.

I was on a business trip and called Markus from the road. In what was probably one of the least romantic proposals in recent history, I said: "Look. I know we talked about this, but I've been thinking... Wanna get married? It won't be the 'real' one, of course, more of a political statement. We can think of it as our 'engagement' and then have the real, spiritually based ceremony a year from now."

What ensued over the next few days was interesting and surprising. All sorts of "stuff" came up. As engaged heterosexual couples have discovered for centuries, it is one thing to look at marriage theoretically and another to stare directly at the possibility. Practical questions came up that we had never considered or thought about. We both knew, for example, that once hitched we would legally share all property accumulated from the time of the marriage. But what about debt previously accrued by the other partner? And then, of course, the underlying question surfaced: Is he really "the one" for me?

A part of the heterosexual condition that had previously eluded me suddenly dawned. When marriage became a possibility, I realized that, at least in part, I was terrified at the prospect of getting married. The depth of the commitment, the legal entanglements, the vows of responsibility in the face of friends and loved ones...suddenly it all took on a different dimension.

I mean, sure, there are over 1,400 benefits that committed partners in same-sex relationships are denied that most opposite-sex counterparts take for granted. And, needless to say, I believe that to deny someone the right to visit their life partner in the hospital or to inherit the home they both have shared and payed down for years is unfair, discriminatory, and unconstitutional.

But I just wasn't prepared for the jarring sense of "Oh my God!... What am I getting into here?"—that gripping fear of terminal conclusiveness that so many have felt as they approached the altar. I understood for the first time what countless heterosexual males have felt when marriage looms, and why not a few hetero females have become "runaway brides" when the critical moment arrived. I identified with the heterosexual experience in a way I never had before.

While wrestling with all those questions, the California Supreme Court halted the process. The window was shut. I felt sadness, disappointment, and, well, to be totally honest, relief.

For now, Markus and I keep working on our relationship, and watch with interest what is unfolding—legally, socially, and spiritually—around our country and world regarding the institution of marriage. I keep seeing images in the media of ecstatic couples from San Francisco, Portland, and now Massachusetts. More than anything, I think those pictures of real people, of average Americans waiting patiently in line for hours—sometimes overnight—braving the weather and finally reveling in their joy will help turn the tide. And I think back to that afternoon when David and Alfredo's commitment to one another was witnessed by all, an afternoon where it appeared that the birds and even the clouds overhead had joined in a celebration of their real, human love.

In an example that queers are not in any way exclusive to the spiritual archetypes of which I write, one hetero couple I know is pushing boundaries and taking things a step further in redefining marriage for themselves. They took their rings (symbolizing their "possession" of each other), tied them to a helium balloon, and released them back to the Unknown. Yet, the truth is they remained married legally, and continue to enjoy the many benefits of that legal institution.

Which is the point.

Christian de la Huerta's Coming Out Spiritually *was chosen by* Publishers Weekly *as one of the ten best religion books of 1999. His writing has appeared in* OUT, The Advocate, Genre, *and other publications. Christian is founder of Q-Spirit (www.qspirit.org), and a professional speaker, seminar leader, and retreat facilitator.*

My Big Fat Gay Wedding
Maggie Dolan

I'm not sure how I feel about gay marriage. It's not that I don't believe in it because "I Do." I just wonder how the advent of gay marriage will change the idea of a wedding ceremony, as we know it. If my gay wedding is anything like my love life, then we're in for a bumpy ride.

Truth be told, I never really saw myself as a commitment ceremony type of gal. Now this just gives my stepmother something else to nag me about. "When are you going to settle down and get married like all those nice girls down in Provincetown?"

My father on the other hand will not be as supportive. The one thing he accepted and even enjoyed about my alternative lifestyle was the $20,000 he saved not having to marry me off. I can see it now, I give him the good news that I'm getting hitched and the wheels will start turning. He'll tell me that I'm much more butch than my fiancée and based on that fact her parents should pick up the wedding tab. Could this be a new tradition and if so will we see more femme lesbians just trying to save their folks a little money?

Don't think that I am completely without tradition. I've had a "hope chest" ever since I was nine. I'm not talking about a cedar box filled with china patterns and taffeta that reeks of mothballs. My hope chest goes something like this, "I hope my chest doesn't get any bigger. I hope my chest doesn't get any bigger." That dream was crushed by my 36D underwire, but I digress.

If I do elect to take the plunge, I imagine that the rest of my family will help out in any way they can. I envision my sister's choice of a photographer. She'll mistakenly assume that S&M Photography Inc. refers to Showers and Marriages. All the photos of grandmother will include a ball gag and harness. It brings a whole new meaning to the term "capturing the memories." This will also take care of the "something blue" business; does something black and blue count?

Gay marriage could prove to be the catalyst for many new wedding traditions. For instance, ushers will no longer ask wedding guests if they are from the bride or groom's side. The most appropriate question would be "Are you a relative of the top or bottom?"

We may see a new generation of wedding favor gifts. While my friends and I would find engraved Swiss Army knives both fun and practical, others might think it in poor taste. Perhaps a more thoughtful and sentimental gift would be "Maggie and Mary—September 5, 2005" rainbow-colored temporary tattoos.

Will the gay community have their own set of wedding songs? I'm particularly fond of "The Bride Wore Birkenstocks" and who doesn't get misty when they hear the lyrics "Going to the courthouse and we're gonna become spouses for life"? We must also address the needs of our vegan couples and throw out the Chicken Dance. Perhaps Usher or Janet Jackson can choreograph a more apropos dance. The Tofu Twist has a nice ring to it. DJs across the country will be heard saying things like, "Boys, please put your shirts back on. This is a wedding reception not a T-dance."

I would be remiss if I did not address a few issues that men might face in the age of gay marriage. Can any self-respecting gay man truly wear white? I foresee the *GQ* Bridal Issue, and yes it is a double issue. *Men's Health* and *Men's Fitness* will carry articles such as "Limber Up for a Wedding Night He'll Never Forget."

Gay marriage may put a whole new twist (no pun intended) on the ring exchange. We may have to remove the exchange of rings from the ceremony altogether. Some boys will get the wrong idea, and it won't be long before Tiffany & Co. starts selling matching cockrings complete with engraving. My sympathies go out to the ring bearer.

I speak for all lesbians when I say that there is nothing more excruciatingly painful than a bridal shower. Well, nothing yet. Can you imagine the Gay Man's Bridal Shower? Thirty queens eating finger sandwiches, making ribbon bouquets, and drowning in a sea of gifts from Neiman Marcus, Pottery Barn, and Williams-Sonoma. Need I say more?

Yes, it's all too much for this lesbian to take. For now my status will remain "Maggie Dolan, Party of One." And down the road, if that should change, I'm registered at Good Vibrations.

Maggie Dolan (dolanmaggie@hotmail.com) is a writer and comedian. She lives in San Francisco, California.

Bound, Not Gagged
Neal Drinnan

Dearly beloved, we are gathered here today to join these...people in...I dunno...senseless tradition...easily containable and politically manageable population units...a temporary alchemical phenomenon in which ardor may be keen but will surely fade and may move quickly to hostility and acrimony?

Who doesn't remember those immortal Tammy tracks, "I Don't Wanna Play House" and "D.I.V.O.R.C.E.," and is there any man or woman here today who has any just reason why they've never dreamed of that once-in-a-lifetime soul mate ideal? I certainly have, but I have also dreamt of having sex with Johnny Depp or running into George Michael in a public toilet or winning the lottery or the Pulitzer Prize. They are fantasies, and it is important to remember the difference between fantasy and reality. Isn't it? It might just be that no one person will ever be everything marriage infers they should be, and what the fuck is marriage anyway? Huh?

Being queer has offered me a rare objectivity and a somewhat clearheaded approach toward the limits of limmerance, and I would like to share these today however hostile it may make the gay marriage advocates. Let me first say that I believe absolutely in equal rights for homosexuals. I believe wills made in sound mind should be rock solid and should not be challenged. That people should be allowed to make whatever declarations they want to each other and be legally recognised as significant others (if they choose), but marriage? Are we MAD? I've always thought that one of the best things about being a fag was that I'd never have to do it. I've always secretly sniggered at those poor straights who seemed doomed to it. I thought we were lucky *not* to have it. Oscar Wilde never had a good word to say about it, though I'm sure that was more to do with the unfortunateness of his being a homosexual married to a woman. Of course it was also he who said God created homosexuals so the truly gifted wouldn't have to be burdened with children. I wonder what he'd say if he knew of the zeal with which those rug rats are now being pursued?

I'd like to run through a few basic ideas here—so the hopeless romantics, gold diggers, stalkers, and bunny-boilers amongst you might choose to go no further with my particular line of poo-pooing the current gay agenda. The ideal of marriage even amongst straights is so flawed, fallible, and fraught with angst, I can't believe we would be foolish enough to mimic it. Roughly 50 percent of straight marriages end in divorce and probably the other half of those that don't, would, if money, position, and children weren't involved. Dare I say it, *marriage is an institution...and who wants to live in an institution...ba boom.*

Marriage has always worked as a way of sharing fortunes and power, containing wealth and continuing family lines, but its central tenets of monogamy and vows of lifelong devotion cause even more misery than the churches that impose them. *Love* is one of the most overused and poorly defined words we have in our language. If Eskimos can have 50 words for snow, it's anathema to me why we don't have at least 12 for love. It can describe everything from how we feel about our parents, our friends, our pets, our children, our addictions, or our partners. There's filial, platonic, chemical, maternal, and paternal. It means so many things that in an increasingly litigious world we should perhaps be issuing a legal disclaimer, tailoring our every declaration of the word to its relevant components.

This is a moderately infatuated kind of love and the bearer of this contract is entitled to visit twice weekly, share meals, the bed and bathroom for no more than 48 hours, and if the aforementioned infatuation lasts until summer, a shared vacation may be considered. NOTE: this voucher is not redeemable for cash.

Now if you think this is turning into a cynical diatribe from a bitter queen who's had one too may gold-digging boyfriends, you'd be very wrong. I think love is the most important thing in the world, possibly the only thing worth anything at all. I think forgiveness sets everybody free, and I think if you love someone you should set them free too. Love must always be about freedom. It will not flourish in and cannot endure any other conditions. This is a fact. We are naïve to think we can make it do so.

The declarations people are expected to make on their wedding day are both impossible and damaging. They consign us forever to feelings of guilt and inadequacy. Life and the universe are in constant flux and to vow to love someone in the same way forever is not something anyone is capable of sustaining. Today's truth can become tomorrow's lie, and lies take even more energy to sustain than the truths that went before them.

I'd like to list some anecdotal tidbits of information I've found to be true of urban gay relationships in Australia. These findings are primarily extracted from men, but "lesbian bed death" is a common enough discussion point amongst my lesbian friends.

1) The highly sexed honeymoon period of a relationship lasts between 6 and 18 months.
2) The average sexual relationship lasts between 3 and 5 years.
3) Long-term couples, however affectionate they may be toward each other, seldom have much (or any) sex with each other past the first 5 years.
4) Long-term couples, either by agreement or through deceit, are seldom monogamous.

What is doubly intriguing about that list is that most married, straight people will look at it and feel a certain affinity with us homos. Problem is, they've declared to each other, in front of God and all of society that they will forsake all others 'til death do them part. They have been sold an illusion by the church, by the government, and most importantly by an industry that makes billions of dollars making "that special day" just perfect. They've also been sold it by the lawyers who are waiting at the other much more unhappy end of that marriage to help strip and redistribute all the assets.

From what I've seen of straight marriages and gay partnerships, there's a much greater likelihood of gay couples holding on to a few shreds of the love after the affair is over. Why? Because they never expected as much to begin with. They hadn't been duped by Hollywood, romance novels, and advertisements into thinking forever was the rule and not the exception.

When married straight couples have awoken from their period of enchantment, their limmerance and infatuation, they realize they've been duped. They no longer desire each other yet cannot discuss it because they vowed they always would. They can't have sex with anyone else either so they experience more and more guilt; they feel like sleazebags because they have perfectly natural sexual desires outside of the marriage. It is then that the shrinks, sex shops, and self-help people get their cut of the deal. Hundreds and thousands of dollars are spent by these couples finding out what's wrong with themselves and seeing if there's not some way to bring back that loving feeling. The porn, the lingerie, the books on loving too much, the Mars and Venus, the vibrating rubber penis, the dog-eared guides to hot monogamy and the empty Viagra bottles. Or maybe there's just an uncomfortable silence and ongoing credit card charges from some filthy internet site they can't work out how to unsubscribe from. The churches and counselors will tell couples they have to work at the relationship, and we all know how much fun *that* is. And the doctors will prescribe antidepressants that take away anxiety and with it, desire and the ability to ejaculate. The TV will placate disgruntled spouses with real-life shows about younger, more attractive people falling in limmerance and shagging while the supermarkets and fast food shops will sell them all the food and ice cream they will need to get them fat and render them sexually invisible.

Because Love is Strong as Death
And Jealousy as Cruel as the Grave…
Song of Solomon 8:6

Aside from family and property, marriage is also designed to contain jealousy. *To forsake all others.* This rather begs the question, Should we really be basing our most intimate personal contracts around our most unattractive erroneous zone? Jealousy. Marriages fall apart because of an "infidelity," when it seems to me they should be strengthened by them. Certainly the idea of sharing partners is completely out of the question to most people, and I find this in itself bizarre. If an itch is allowed to be scratched once in a while, doesn't the marriage stand a better chance of surviving? Perversely, jealousy does not ensure fidelity even from the jealous partner. And most couples seem to silently or tacitly agree to keep their infidelities from each other, the rationales and justifications behind this no doubt playing havoc with their head whenever possible or sublimating itself into some crevice of the psyche as they go about paying lip service to a system through which they've already become a casualty.

Forever happens one day at a time and marriage makes us lazy; it allows us to become complacent about who we are with and who we are when we are with them. It denies us the verve of possibility. Attraction, chemistry, and friendship are constant possibilities; marriage tends to make any relationship other than the marital one suspect. Love changes constantly; sometimes it vanishes beneath the waves and doesn't surface for hours or even days. On the oceans of limmerance, weather conditions are notoriously capricious and so many have been lost at sea.

It never ceases to amaze me how enduring and strengthening my partner's love has been for me these past eight years. I think I would have left me by now if I could. We've been through up times and down times, like everyone, and I don't think I'll ever leave him. But if we do get old together, we will do it having confronted all our demons while gathering to us a great many angels. If we'd not let each other take lovers or experience the sudden bursts of infatuation which bloom like wildflowers or magic mushrooms along the roadside of life, we'd be much smaller for it. We have no role models for our sort of love, no guidelines. There are no TV shows or commercials that celebrate the emotional anarchy we choose to live with, and sometimes it would be comforting if there were. I suppose most people like to have everything set out for them. Why else would people kowtow to the tyrannies and absurdities of orthodox religions? I suppose homosexuals are no different, and I don't expect my radical bohemian notions of love and freedom to be adopted by your average Joe or Joanne.

In arguments for the institution of marriage, homosexuals tend to revise the whole concept anyway, picking and choosing this bit or that bit and tempering anything they don't like, indicating that its conventions aren't necessarily agreeable to begin with. Heterosexual marriages manage to embrace all sorts of double standards and corruptions in order to continue receiving the tax cuts, rebates, probates, and respectability that accompanies them, but homosexuals are naïve to think that "marriage" will make them any more respectable in the eyes of their enemies or any less marginal in the eyes of politicians. So why not have the courage to create a model of union that defies the strictures of wedlock? Are homosexuals not in a position to make love the real reason for their union and can they not teach heterosexuals a lesson or two? After all, if the *Queer Eye* guys can put the sparkle back into dull hetero romances, surely we should be leading the way in love contracts.

Don't get me wrong, I'm not averse to donning the glad rags and cheering the happy heteros as they take to the aisle — and there's a lot to be said for the white goods and crockery you get as presents on the magic day. But for me, I'd rather choose my own dinner set so I can ensure there are always plenty of settings on the table. As Auntie Mame said, "Life is a banquet and most poor sons of bitches are starving to death."

To have and to hold is one thing, but if we have to have "marriage," can't we call it something else: spliced, tied, clasped, lovelocked, rooted, bound? Not gagged.

Neal Drinnan (www.nealdrinnan.com) was born in Melbourne, Australia, sometime in the 1960s. At 17 he abandoned his education for the lure of life's more ephemeral things. (They lasted longer than he thought they would.) He has worked in publishing and journalism for many years. He is the author of three novels — Glove Puppet, Pussy's Bow, and Quill — as well as The Rough Guide to Gay and Lesbian Australia. Readers who find themselves shocked by the morality of his tales should perhaps spare a thought for the author and his diligent research. While people bicker and argue queer politics on the Net, he's at the coalface of modern gay social intercourse. Drinnan is generally polite, well-spoken, and well-read (although not necessarily well-behaved). And, like vodka in tonic, he mixes freely and sometimes even glows in the dark.

Holy Matrimony!
Lisa Duggan

The political storm over marriage is now intensifying as gay couples wed in San Francisco and President Bush vows to stop them with a constitutional amendment. Gay marriage threatens to wreak havoc as a "wedge issue" in the November elections, but it isn't entirely clear which party's prospects will be promoted, and which damaged, through marriage politics this year. Progressives certainly haven't figured out how best to enter the contentious and confusing public debate. Widespread anxiety over changing demographics and contested social norms is producing the background noise for a relatively volatile political calculus on all sides.

If Britney Spears' high-speed annulment and the competitive gold-digging with a sucker punch on TV's *Joe Millionaire* are any indication, concern over the state of the marital union is justified. Statistics confirm what entertainment culture spectacularizes—marriage is less stable and central to the organization of American life than ever. There are now more unmarried households than married ones, and a variety of formal and informal, permanent and transient, solemn and casual partnership and kinship arrangements have displaced any singular, static model of domestic life. Political responses to these changes have long been polarized between those who want to bring back Ozzie and Harriet and those who are fighting for the democratization of state recognition of households, along with equitable distribution of services and benefits to Americans, based on how we actually live rather than on some imagined, lost ideal. But today, in part because of the public's own ambivalence, the major political parties have been reluctant to come down firmly on either side of this divide.

What is most vexing the political parties right now is same-sex marriage. The Republican electoral alliance is split on this issue. On the one hand, hard-line religious and moral conservatives have been working to rigidify the boundaries of "traditional" marriage and to shore up its privileged status. These groups are now pushing to pass a constitutional amendment defining marriage as between "a man and a woman." On the other hand, libertarians, states' rights advocates, and social moderates prefer to retain conventional gendered marriage but support allowing some diversification of forms of partnership and household recognition at the state level. They oppose a constitutional amendment as a federal imposition on the states, or as just too mean to help Republicans during an election year. The religious and moral right appears to be winning out in the wake of the Massachusetts Supreme Judicial Court's decision that the state must extend civil marriage to same-sex couples. Bush, however grudgingly, fulfilled his promise to the Christian right when he announced on February 24 that he will support a federal marriage amendment.

With their convention in Boston, and Massachusetts Senator John Kerry the likely presidential nominee, Democrats will be fighting any "too liberal" charge associated with gay weddings by noting their opposition to same-sex marriage (the only remaining candidates who support it are Al Sharpton and Dennis Kucinich), while opposing a federal marriage amendment and emphasizing support for civil unions and domestic partnerships. Their carefully calibrated rhetoric will urge tolerance without questioning the supremacy of married, two-parent families. Indeed, the Bush administration's recent proposal to spend $1.5 billion promoting marriage, "especially" among low-income populations, has not encountered energetic opposition from many Democrats, who have supported like-minded efforts in the past. Progressives, meanwhile, are struggling to articulate a small-*d* democratic politics of marriage that demands full equality for lesbians and gays without accepting the logic of the "family values" crowd.

It may be tempting to see this squabble as an example of symbolic politics, with the debate over the future of marriage potentially displacing bigger and more significant battles over war and peace, taxes and fairness, corporate greed and good government. But state regulation of households and partnerships does in fact affect the basic safety, prosperity, equality, and welfare of all Americans—it determines who will make medical decisions for us in emergencies, who may share our pensions or Social Security benefits, who may legally co-parent our children, and much more. It's just hard to sort out the real issues from the smoke screens as the rhetoric heats up this election year.

Moral conservatives have so far taken the lead in the struggle to frame the meaning of the "marriage crisis." In their apocalyptic imagination, the stability of heterosexual unions and the social order they insure are threatened on all sides—by the specter of gay marriage, by women's independent choices within and outside marriage, and by government neutrality, toleration, or support of single-parent and unmarried households, especially among the poor. But wait! It gets worse: As Stanley Kurtz argued in *The Weekly Standard* last August, "Among the likeliest effects of gay marriage is to take us down a slippery slope to legalized polygamy and 'polyamory' (group marriage). Marriage will be transformed into a variety of relationship contracts, linking two, three, or more individuals (however weakly and temporarily) in every conceivable combination of male and female."

I'm not sure, given the rise of transgender activism, just how many combinations there are of male and female. But the dystopic vision is clear. Moral conservatives want to prevent courts and legislatures from opening a Pandora's box of legal options—a flexible menu of choices for forms of household and partnership recognition open to all citizens, depending on specific and varying needs. Such a menu would threaten the normative status of the nuclear family, undermining state endorsement of heterosexual privilege, the male "headed" household, and "family values" moralism as social welfare policy.

The problem is not that any such flexible menu is currently available anywhere at present. What has emerged over decades of political wrangling at the municipal and state level is a hodgepodge of legal categories—civil marriage, civil union (with the same state-level benefits as civil marriage but without the portability from state to state, or federal recognition), domestic partnership (with fewer benefits than civil marriage), and reciprocal beneficiaries (which carries the fewest benefits). The categories are neither equivalent nor open to all. Civil marriage, thus far (and until May in Massachusetts) open only to one man and one woman who are not close blood relatives, carries the most specific benefits and mutual responsibilities (more than 1,049 automatic federal and additional state protections, benefits, and responsibilities, according to the federal government's General Accounting Office). It endows couples and their children with both real and symbolic citizenship rights at the highest level. Civil union (in Vermont) or domestic partnership (in 5 states and over 60 municipalities) has been made available to gay and lesbian couples and sometimes to heterosexual couples who choose not to marry (or not to have to divorce) as well. Only the reciprocal beneficiaries status has been available (in different versions in Hawaii and Vermont) to close relatives, or those with no proclaimed conjugal bond. It has so far provided the most limited benefits, but it is in some senses the most radical innovation. It potentially separates state recognition of households or partnerships from the business of sexual regulation altogether.

The right wing's fear of a "slippery slope" suggests some ways that this eclectic array of statuses might move us in a progressive direction. Kurtz himself, citing Brigham Young University professor Alan Hawkins, sketches out what is to him a distasteful scenario:

> Consider the plight of an underemployed and uninsured single mother in her early 30s who sees little real prospect of marriage (to a man) in her future. Suppose she has a good friend, also female and heterosexual, who is single and childless but employed with good spousal benefits. Sooner or later, friends like this are going to start contracting same-sex marriages of convenience. The single mom will get medical and governmental benefits, will share her friend's paycheck, and will gain an additional caretaker for the kids besides. Her friend will gain companionship and a family life. The marriage would obviously be sexually open. And if lightning struck and the right man came along for one of the women, they could always divorce and marry heterosexually.
>
> In a narrow sense, the women and children in this arrangement would be better off. Yet the larger effects of such unions on the institution of marriage would be devastating. At a stroke, marriage would be severed not only from the complementarity of the sexes but also from its connection to romance and sexual exclusivity — and even from the hope of permanence.

Gee. Sounds good. Then consider how such arrangements might benefit women, children, and others even more substantially. What if there were a way to separate the tax advantages of joint household recognition, or the responsibilities of joint parenting, from the next-of-kin recognition so that such rights might go to a non-co-resident relative, a friend, or a lover? And what if many benefits, such as health insurance, could be available to all without regard for household or partnership status? The moral conservative's nightmare vision of a flexible menu of options might become a route to progressive equality! That could happen — *if* all statuses could be opened to all without exclusions, allowing different kinds of households to fit state benefits to their changing needs; *if* no status conferred any invidious privilege or advantage over any other, or over none at all; and *if* material benefits such as health insurance were detached from partnership or household form altogether (federally guaranteed universal healthcare, for instance, would be far more democratic and egalitarian than health insurance as a partnership benefit). Meanwhile, the "sanctity" of traditional marriages could be retained and honored by religious groups and families, according to their own values and definitions.

Efforts to stop any such democratization of households have escalated steadily ever since a Hawaii state court decision conjured up visions of legitimate gay weddings in 1993. Thirty-eight states have passed legislation or constitutional amendments restricting marriage to heterosexual couples. In 1996 Bill Clinton signed the federal Defense of Marriage Act, designed to prevent any future state-level same-sex marriages from carrying the federal recognition and portability that civil marriage has so far guaranteed (though many believe DOMA is vulnerable to constitutional challenge). The proposed federal marriage amendment, with more than a hundred sponsors in the House and a handful of supporters in the Senate so far, would go much further than DOMA to write marriage restriction into the Constitution. Depending on the final wording, and the results of inevitable litigation over its interpretation, the amendment might also put a stop not solely to gay marriage but to all diversification of partnership and household recognition. In one stroke all the hard-won civil union, domestic partnership, and reciprocal beneficiary statuses could be wiped off the books, leaving civil marriage, restricted to heterosexual couples, as the sole form of recognition available at the federal, state, or municipal level (and possibly at private businesses and organizations as well) throughout the country.

Fortunately for advocates of partnership and household diversity, a marriage amendment faces a long, steep uphill battle as supporters struggle to pass it, first in Congress and then in three-fourths of the state legislatures, before it can become law. Many conservatives are clearly leery of the expensive, acrimonious battle ahead. George W. Bush withheld his own endorsement of the amendment until after his State of the Union address, in which he chose to emphasize his plan to promote conventional marriage instead.

To many, this looked like election-year strategy—an effort to pander to moral conservatives without giving them the explicit approval they craved. And surely such tactical concerns are shaping every word uttered by Bush on this issue. But it would be a mistake to attribute this administration's interest in marriage promotion solely to such motives. There is a deeper commitment to preserving gendered marriage, on economic as well as moral grounds.

Bush's marriage-promotion initiative isn't new; it first appeared in the welfare reauthorization legislation passed by the House two years ago, which is now before the Senate and may come up for a vote as soon as this spring. Bush's $1.5 billion package, to be used to hire counselors and offer classes in marital harmony, extends the commitment contained in the 1996 welfare "reform" bill, passed under Clinton, to "end the dependence of needy parents on government benefits by promoting...marriage." Women and children, in other words, should depend on men for basic economic support, while women care for dependents—children, elderly parents, disabled family members, etc. Under such a model, married-couple households might "relieve" the state of the expense of helping to support single-parent households, and of the cost of a wide range of social services, from childcare and disability services to home nursing. Marriage thus becomes a privatization scheme: Individual married-couple-led households give women and children access to higher men's wages, and also "privately" provide many services once offered through social welfare agencies. More specifically, the unpaid labor of married women fills the gap created by government service cuts.

Besides being sexist and outdated, this model of marriage is not exactly realistic. Relatively few men today earn a "family wage," and employed married women are not able to care fully for dependents by themselves. Marriage promotion, moreover, has not proven an effective means of alleviating poverty and reducing the need for government benefits. But even without any measurable economic impact, the effort to promote marriage among low-income populations works at the rhetorical level to shift blame for economic hardship onto the marital practices of the poor rather than on the loss of jobs, employment benefits, or government services.

Republicans and Democrats are by and large in agreement that as social programs are whittled away, gender-differentiated marriage (heterosexual, with different expectations for women and men) should take up the slack. Clinton's marriage-promoting welfare law embodied this principle, which also helps to explain the ambivalence of conservative and centrist Democrats toward genuine gender equality in marriage (illustrated in the retro discussion of the proper role of political wives in the current presidential campaign) and their opposition to gay marriage. So there is an economic agenda, as well as surface moralism, attached to calls for the preservation of traditional marriage. The campaign to save gendered marriage has some rational basis, for neoliberals in both parties, as a politics of privatization.

Unwilling to support gay marriage, defend Judith Steinberg's remote relation to her husband's now-defunct presidential campaign (though Laura Bush did so), or openly attack marriage promotion as public policy, the Democrats are left with lame advocacy of second-class status for gays, mandatory secondary supportive roles for political wives, and public silence about welfare policy. No viable Democratic candidate has yet been able to shift the frame of reference to escape a weakly defensive posture on these issues. So it's left to progressives, both within the Democratic Party and outside it, to formulate a clear, positive vision of how best to address the needs of real households for state recognition and social support.

But progressives are divided, too, in their approach to marriage politics. The hateful campaign to exclude same-sex couples from full marriage rights creates tremendous pressure on gay-rights advocates and supporters to emphasize access to civil marriage as a core right of citizenship. A few marriage-equality advocates have continued to call for the multiplication of democratically accessible forms of state recognition for households and partnerships, and for the dethronement of sanctified marriage as privileged civic status, but many have couched their advocacy in language that glorifies marital bliss, sometimes echoing the "family values" rhetoric of their opponents. The "Roadmap to Equality: A Freedom to Marry Educational Guide," published by Lambda Legal Defense and Education Fund and Marriage Equality California, begins with the kind of banal American Dream rhetoric that appeals to some gay people, but misdescribes, annoys, and even stigmatizes many others:

> Gay people are very much like everyone else. They grow up, fall in love, form families and have children. They mow their lawns, shop for groceries and worry about making ends meet. They want good schools for their children, and security for their families as a whole.

The guide goes on to recycle some of the more noxious views routinely spouted by conservative moralists:

> Denying marriage rights to lesbian and gay couples keeps them in a state of permanent adolescence... Both legally and socially, married couples are held in greater esteem than unmarried couples because of the commitment they have made in a serious, public, legally enforceable manner. For lesbian and gay couples who wish to make that very same commitment, the very same option must be available. There is no other way for gay people to be fully equal to non-gay people.

No other way? How about abolishing state endorsement of the sanctified religious wedding or ending the use of the term "marriage" altogether (as lesbian and gay progressives and queer leftists have advocated for decades)? In a bid for equality, some gay groups are producing rhetoric that insults and marginalizes unmarried people, while promoting marriage in much the same terms as the welfare reformers use to stigmatize single-parent households, divorce, and "out of wedlock" births. If pursued in this way, the drive for gay-marriage equality can undermine rather than support the broader movement for social justice and democratic diversity.

Meanwhile, critics of marriage promotion, located primarily in feminist policy and research organizations, are working to counter rosy views of the institution of marriage. The National Organization for Women's Legal Defense and Education Fund has documented the planned flow of money and services away from poor women and children and toward conservative organizations, contained in the proposed welfare reauthorization bill (see *www.nowldef.org*). A group of academic researchers and professors organized by Anna Marie Smith of Cornell University, Martha Albertson Fineman of Emory University, and Gwendolyn Mink of Smith College have created a website to circulate critiques of marriage promotion as a substitute for effective social welfare programs (*falcon.arts.cornell.edu/ams3/*

npmbasis.html). As they point out, "While marriage has provided some women the cushion of emotional and economic security, it also has locked many women in unsatisfying, exploitative, abusive and even violent relationships." Their research findings and legislative analysis demonstrate that "federal and state governments are transforming the burden of caring for our needy sisters and brothers into a private obligation."

The agendas of lesbian and gay marriage-equality advocates and progressive feminist critics of marriage promotion don't necessarily or inevitably conflict, though their efforts are currently running on separate political and rhetorical tracks. Given the rising political stakes, and the narrow horizons of political possibility, it seems imperative now that progressives find ways to make room for a more integrated, broadly democratic marriage politics. To respond to widespread changes in household organization and incipient dissatisfaction with the marital status quo, progressives could begin to disentangle the religious, symbolic, kinship, and economic functions of marriage, making a case for both civil equality and the separation of church and state. They could argue that civil marriage (perhaps renamed or reconfigured), like any other household status, should be open to all who are willing to make the trek to City Hall, whether or not they also choose to seek a church's blessing. Beginning with the imperfect menu of household and partnership statuses now unevenly available from state to state, it might not be such an impossibly utopian leap to suggest that we should expand and democratize what we've already got, rather than contract our options.

Such a vision, long advocated by feminist and queer progressives, may now be finding some broader support. Kay Whitlock, the national representative for LGBT issues for the American Friends Service Committee, circulated a statement at the National Religious Leadership Roundtable last fall that argued, "We cannot speak about equal civil marriage rights and the discrimination that currently exists without also speaking of the twin evil of coercive marriage policies promoted with federal dollars... For us, it is critical that the LGBT movement work for equal civil marriage rights in ways that do not further reinforce the idea that if a couple is married, they are more worthy of rights and recognition than people involved in intimate relationships who are not married." The statement continued, "We do not want to convey the message that marriage is what all queer people should aspire to. We also do not want the discussion of marriage to overwhelm and suppress discussion about a broader definition of human rights and basic benefits that ought to accompany those rights."

This seems like a good place to start. The question is, How can arguments like this be heard in the midst of the clamor against gay marriage on the right, when Democrats are reduced to a timid whisper and gay groups are too often sounding like the American Family Association? Might it be possible to tap into an undercurrent of dissatisfaction with the current state of the marital union—and appeal to the public's understanding of the enormous distance between rhetoric and reality on this subject? Politicians pay lip service to conservative family values, but voters do not always bolt when their actual lives fail to conform to the prescriptions—as Bill Clinton's enduring popularity despite repeated sex scandals demonstrated. Polls show widely contradictory public views on the subjects of marriage and divorce, adultery and gay rights. Questions with only slight wording changes can yield widely differing results. Why not muster the courage to lead the public a little on this issue? Civil unions, considered beyond the pale only a few years ago, are now supported by many conservatives. The political center can and does shift—and right now, it is particularly fluid and volatile in this area.

In the current climate, progressives might profit by pointing out the multiple ways that conservative marriage politics aim to limit freedom in the most intimate aspects of our lives—through banning gay marriage as well as promoting traditional marriage. Given current demographic trends, it couldn't hurt to ask: Why do Republicans want to turn back the clock, rather than accept reality? And why can't Democrats find some way to support law and policy that advances the goals of intimate freedom and political equality, even during an election year?

Lisa Duggan is a historian, journalist, and activist. She teaches in the American Studies Program and the Center for the Study of Gender and Sexuality at New York University, and is author of Sapphic Slashers: Sex, Violence and American Modernity, *co-author with Nan Hunter of* Sex Wars: Sexual Dissent and Political Culture, *co-editor with Lauren Berlant of* Our Monica, Ourselves: The Clinton Affair and National Interest, *and most recently author of* The Twilight of Equality: Neoliberalism, Cultural Politics and the Attack on Democracy.

First published in *The Nation*, March 15, 2004. Reprinted by permission of the author.

An Application for Divorce
Dean Durber

In his 1969 "A Gay Manifesto," Carl Wittman warned against the dangers of assimilation and the mimicking of straights. He wrote:

> To accept that happiness comes through finding a groovy spouse and settling down, showing the world that "we're just the same as you" is avoiding the real issues, and is an expression of self-hatred. (71)

A decade later, John Shiers added: "Once we can explode the myth of the perfectly adjusted person who only needs to find the 'right' relationship for everything to be hunky-dory, we will have come a long way!" (153). By the 1990s, we saw the emergence of the "str-8 acting" gay man, an identity critiqued for its blatantly intense loathing of sexed and gendered positions at odds with the ideals of heteronormativity (Harris 59). But homosexuals have always mimicked straights. If not ever quite as "normal," they have always been as *normative* as their heterosexual counterparts. The bid to marry is just one more attempt to reaffirm the truthful existence of the normative homosexual type alongside the truth of a similarly normative heterosexual being.

Back in 1971, Dennis Altman insisted that "[l]iberation would involve a resurrection of our original impulse to take enjoyment from the total body, and indeed to accept the seeking of sensual enjoyment as an end in itself, free from procreation or status-enhancement" (99). In this same book, *Homosexual Oppression and Liberation*, he went on to argue that "[g]ay liberation will have achieved its full potential when it is no longer needed, when we see each other neither as man and woman, gay and straight, but purely as people with varied possibilities" (154). In the wake of the post-1960s gay liberation movement and its progression into a discourse of rights, there has been no eradication of the concept of a homosexual category as distinct from a heterosexual opposite. There has been no metamorphosing of man or of woman. Within the movement today, there is no distinctively audible attack aimed against the normative interpretation of our sexual desires within a sexed-body model. Even as it seeks to increase tolerance of homosexuality in the culture, the gay liberationist discourse offers no substantive and operative attack against the restraints placed on understandings of corporeal pleasures by the naturalisation of the homosexual-heterosexual binary itself. On the contrary, its tactics insist that only a public pronouncement of one's true homosexuality can work to override the discrimination effected within this binary. It therefore continues to demand that all bodies that engage in same-sex sex come out, now as "gay."

The visibility of gay culture over the past three and a half decades has brought us no closer to a utopian future of sexual liberation. The decriminalization of certain corporeal acts naïvely aligned with homosexuality—sodomy, for example—and the protection of homosexual rights now enshrined in legislation do not free us from a former space of oppression. The oppression felt by us—bodies that have sex with same-sexed bodies—is not the result of being undermined or attacked by a pervasive heterosexuality. The closet we often exist inside is not created by a homophobic world. Rather, this oppression and this closet are merely the aftereffects of an acceptance that bodies can be divided into sexual types according to the things they do, and that these divisions speak the truth of who we are.

The issue of the morality and legitimacy of homosexuality may still be widely disputed in our culture, but the notion of the existence of the homosexual type is not.

Regardless of the diversity of judgements attached to same-sex sexualized contact — irrespective of whether one, on the one hand, abhors it or, on the other hand, constructs a lifestyle in which it plays a central and positive role — there is a general agreement in Western culture that a body's anatomically determined sex is the primary focus in our pursuit of sexual pleasures; and that a person can therefore easily and correctly be defined as a "homosexual" (or as a "heterosexual") according to the sex of the person with whom s/he enjoys sexualized contact. This suggests somewhat of an ironic agreement between gay rights campaigners and those who advocate a cure for homosexuals through medical or spiritual intervention. The gay movement needs the homosexual category. It needs the definition of all same-sex sexualized contact as "homosexual" in order for it to have an object on behalf of which it can speak. It needs bodies that are willing to conform to this model of sexualization. It needs an oppressed homosexuality and oppressed homosexual bodies in order to have something and somebody to liberate.

I have no doubt that gay marriages will, at some point in the near future, become socially accepted and legally approved. It may take different countries and different states a while to come to the table. Some may insist on sitting alone much longer than others. But, such acts of blatant discrimination cannot survive in democratic systems which espouse equality and which, with much unnecessary struggle along the way, must always therefore eventually face up to the ideological promise therein. The acceptance of — or tolerance of — gay marriages — is far less of a threat to the normal social structure of Western culture than the alternatives to this kind of union.

To ask that the culture now accept the right of the homosexual to marry another of its own kind is to ask that it continue to read our bodies in the very categories of sexuality that have already been constructed around them. Such a request does nothing to critique the understandings of sexual pleasures that have become accepted as absolute truth in our culture. For Western culture to permit two members of the same-sex to form a union that is similar to that already promoted as ideal for two members of the opposite sex is less of a radical shift than considering what other forms of unions, sexual or otherwise, we might wish to validate. In the application for the marriage of two homosexuals, we see not a transgression of sexual norms, but rather a reaffirmation of the way in which all bodies must be sexualized.

In his discussion of "The Gay Awakening," Paul Berman has suggested that the reason for the emerging popularity of the notion of identity politics was the ability it had to offer a safe space for those who were terrified by what their radical demands had created and by the positions in which this radicalism had placed them (156-59). Similarly, Michael Bronski asserts:

> This process of social containment, presenting less-threatening forms of social change through commodification, developed for two reasons. As much as people wanted and enjoyed these new freedoms, they also viewed them as a potential threat to the existing social order. Caught between the desire for pleasure and the security of a tightly ordered society, they were comfortable with a compromise that allowed limited freedom without fear of disorder. (69-70)

The safety on offer here is more than what Julia Creet has explored in her anxiety over a lesbian identity: that a homosexual identity can function politically "as a defense against re-incorporation into heterosexuality or into the categorization of what more accurately might be bisexuality" (186). Rather, the safety of being gay offers comfort from the fragmentation that comes with challenging assumed norms about the ways in which one is able to understand self. To know "I am gay" helps to reaffirm the capacity of an autonomous "I" to know of self. It helps us to continue to believe in our natural sexualization. Even those of us who have questioned compulsory heterosexuality are now scared by what the alternatives might offer. It would seem that we would rather marry into an eternity of compulsory homosexuality than struggle to keep on finding new ways of doing intimate and sexual relationships with others.

With the signing of any marriage act that permits for homosexuals to legally wed, these terms that claim to speak the truth of our sexual desires will be more efficient in the controlling and disciplining of our pleasures. At the moment when we stand up in front of a crowd of family and friends and declare "I do," we will be attesting to the truth of the historical and cultural confinement of our pleasures within the homosexual category. We will be consenting to being forever homosexuals without questioning the limitations now imposed upon us and upon our pleasures as a result of this tolerated confession. And wherever homosexuals are known to be, so too can there always be laws telling these types what it is they should or should not do. Those of us who make public declarations of our homosexuality will always be knowable to the world as "homosexual." Being knowable means being controllable. Just as laws change in favor of bodies, so too they can just as easily turn against them.

It is not my desire to have my sexualized pleasures handed over to such arbitrary and flimsy methods of control. I care not for the granting of licenses that permit me to be what I am already expected to know myself to be. I would rather seek to file for a divorce from this homosexual being, and thereby exist in a space where I might be permitted to define my sexual pleasures outside of the demands that these pleasures must signify the entirety of my being 'til death do us part.

Dean Durber is a PhD candidate at Curtin University in Perth, Western Australia. His short stories have appeared in anthologies such as Best Gay Erotica 2003, Straight? Volume 2, *and* Boy Meets Boy.

Works Referenced:
Altman, Dennis. *Homosexual Oppression and Liberation*. Ringwood, Vic.: Penguin Books, 1973. Berman, Paul. *A Tale of Two Utopias: The Political Journey of the Generation of 1968*. New York: W. W. Norton & Company, 1996. Bronski, Michael. *The Pleasure Principle: Sex, Backlash, and the Struggle for Gay Freedom*. New York: St. Martin's Press, 1998. Creet, Julia. "Anxieties of Identity: Coming Out and Coming Undone." *Negotiating Lesbian and Gay Subjects*. Eds. Monica Dorenkamp and Richard Henke. New York: Routledge, 1995. 179-99. Harris, Daniel. *The Rise and Fall of Gay Culture*. New York: Hyperion, 1997. Shiers, John. "Two Steps Forward, One Step Back." *Homosexuality: Power and Politics*. Ed. Gay Left Collective. London: Allison and Busby Ltd., 1980. 140-56. Wittman, Carl. "A Gay Manifesto." *Come Out Fighting: A Century of Essential Writing on Gay and Lesbian Liberation*. Ed. Chris Bull. Vol. 67-79. New York: Nation Books, 1969.

Happily Ever After
Amie M. Evans

I grew up in a small town in eastern Pennsylvania where the passage of time was marked by weddings and deaths, not months and years. "Marriage" was a game kids played on rainy days in playrooms with dress up box items—plastic flowers, discarded First Communion veils, and costume jewelry. Getting married was a public and community event that announced a girl was a Woman; it marked her entrance into adulthood. There are many things about marriage and my childhood that I don't understand fully even as an adult, but, even then, I did understand that marriage was a passage, a doorway, to something bigger than itself. In addition, people would refer to *my* wedding as a milestone, thus ingraining the date of the spectacular celebration into local lore. Nothing was more important to me when I was a child than community acknowledgment and grand spectacles involving me as the centerpiece. A wedding promised me both of these things rolled into one.

I started planning the specifics of my wedding when I was in fifth grade. I labored over all the details: which white, oversized dress; what color, puffy-sleeved, tacky bridesmaids' gowns; what kind of exotic flowers; where to have the ceremony—outside vs. church; what type of transportation for the wedding party—horse-drawn carriages or white limousines. I ripped countless photos from *Bride Magazine, The Bride,* and *Your Wedding* and created a "Wedding Planner" scrapbook into which I pasted all the pictures of potential dresses, flowers, and tuxedo options and other important notes on topics such as appetizers, cake toppers, invitations, table-seating arrangements, and reception etiquette to be considered in more detail for the actual planning of *My* Big Day. My girlfriends, most of whom now know that I am a lesbian and no longer speak to me, were angry at me for not choosing them as maid of honor for the future wedding. This was serious business; we were all 12-year-olds and being picked as maid of honor for some distant wedding for which the groom was yet unknown was much more important on the social scale than *not* being picked last in gym class for kickball. My future wedding was already providing me with social power. And that after all is what weddings were about—social power. Those aren't the words I used at the time to describe the transformation, but having a wedding was the cultural marker of becoming an adult, social agent. Granted, the agency was received by becoming Mrs. So&So, and not by virtue of any talent, skill, or accomplishment of one's own, but, hey, I was 12.

I wasn't the only one planning my wedding; most of my female friends were planning their wedding days too. For me, the Wedding Day was a gala celebration, a star-studded event with fancy clothing, rented tuxedos and cars, a live band, an extravagant nine-course dinner, and extreme excess. But most importantly, everyone would be paying attention to me—snapping photos, fussing, newspaper announcements—and I'd get to go on an expensive vacation to a tropical location when it was over.

It wasn't until I was in 8th grade that I noticed most of the women I knew who were actually married worked at dead-end jobs, carted two or more kids around, and had husbands who worked in factories, and had time to hunt and party, but were seldom actually around to do husband-chores or watch the kids. These women, after the flash photography, white dress, and three-tier cake were gone, had very little freedom or opportunity in their lives. I started to become aware of inequality within the structure of the marriages that made up the small world I lived in, and more importantly I started to notice that husbands were by definition *men* and after the wedding-day party, you were sort of stuck with them. It was around this time, coincidentally, I'd also discovered that the girl-next-door, who was butchier than any of the boys on the block, was also the best kisser in the neighborhood and she only kissed me. It was clear to me at the time that what I really wanted was to marry *her*. This wasn't a problem for me, because in my fantasies at least, I could slip her into the groom's role for the wedding. And, from years of playing house with her, it was also clear she'd make a much better husband than any of the boys I currently knew. It did, however, create a problem in my real plan of a Big White Wedding and a "Happily Ever After" life. While I didn't have a vocabulary that included "lesbian" or a working understanding of the socially constructed sanctions against homosexuality, I knew on a gut level that society didn't approve of my desire for girls, and I was sure my family wouldn't pay for a wedding involving me and another girl as the main players.

By the time I hit high school, black-and-white gowns for bridesmaids were in vogue. I was dating boys, and silently lamenting secret crushes on my girlfriends. I took a stance, at least publicly, considered far left by my friends, that marriage—and weddings by association—were a plot to undermine women's agency and hold us captive and I was not get married. I was going to be a movie star like my idol Annette Funicello.

Inside, in the deepest, darkest secret parts of myself, I knew both of these statements weren't true. I longed for a white wedding dress, a rented set of tails, a vintage limousine, and more flowers than the local neighborhood church had ever seen. I also knew that I'd never be a movie star and I'd never spend the rest of my life with a boy. Annette of *Beach Blanket Bingo* fame was selling Skippy peanut butter on TV, and while I had always wanted to be her, I'd never been able to solve the Frankie Avalon problem. I couldn't find a female understudy to be *my* Frankie; and without Frankie what was Annette? An overgrown Mouseketeer hocking peanut butter sandwiches on white bread to mothers who wanted the best for their kids.

Flash forward to the late 1980s and I'm in college. I've acquired an academic understanding of cultural theory, a feminist vocabulary, and I'm an out lesbian destined to be a newspaper reporter. These forces align, leading me to rip to shreds the institution of marriage. Marriage was an archaic, patriarchal form of enslavement for women all done up in white bows and flowers. It allowed society as a whole, and men specifically, to exploit women's work and devalue women's labor. Gone were any wide-eyed illusions of love, lifelong companionship, and community acceptance. Marriage was institutional robbery reducing women to second-class citizens. All well and good, but as a lesbian, marriage had been ripped violently from the list of options open to me. It was easy to hate marriage; it didn't matter what I thought about it or what I wanted—like so much else, it seemed society wouldn't allow me to have it.

Marriage moved out of my life circle as I graduated college. All my old high school friends were married or not speaking to me; the friends I made after college were mostly queer or already-married heterosexuals. Marriage seemed like a Third World country—something you heard about on the news, but were never forced to actually deal with directly; so you could easily forget it existed. It slipped out of my life, my memory and thoughts purged it completely. It wasn't something I had to deal with or consider even critically.

Marriage came back into my life in the form of Commitment Ceremonies in the 1990s. These queer versions of marriage—unacknowledged by state or church—were said to be cutting-edge and radical, but still I felt they were a paler shade, a shadow of the "real" thing that I was banned from having because of the object of my love. I told myself and others that they were an imitation of heterosexual marriage, no different then playing at marriage as a child. Yet, they pulled at my old desires and dreams. I felt joy for my friends, but no envy as I had when I lost the right to marriage by coming out.

The Spring of 2004 hit like a ton of bricks as Massachusetts was forced by the Supreme Judicial Court to allow gays and lesbians to marry. I, like the rest of the nation, was tossed, wearing a small, questionable life preserver, into the turbulent sea of conflicting emotions and high-rising tides of anger and joy. My Wedding Planner had long since been tossed into the trash, but the hope those pasted photos and yellowed pages had held, I was shocked to discover, still exists within me. I was and continue to be confused by my deep desire to marry my partner. I admit part of what I feel is the old dream of a large party with me and her as the centerpieces. But, when I force myself to examine that stirring desire, to scratch at the vanity and superficialness of Marriage, The Party itself, I discover what I knew so long ago in my childhood. Marriage is a formal, institutional stamp of approval on love. Not crush love or lust, but a contract issued before friends and family, before government and god (if you believe), that two individuals are united as one. It is a formal announcement that they plan to share their lives—good and bad times—together, and care for each other body, soul, and mind until death do they part. Behind the formality and mundaneness of those words is the *truth* about marriage. By marrying, we publicly declare intent to our motivations and actions. The intent is a truly adult one and universally understood. "This is for real, folks," we say together at the tops of our voices. "I love this woman more than anything else in the whole world and plan to spend the rest of my life with her. I want the whole world—my friends, my family, the government, the gods—to know, celebrate, and acknowledge that we two are bonded together as one."

Being married is a rite of passage. You come out the other side changed mentally and emotionally. And while many of the legal implications of marriage for gay and lesbian folks can be reconstructed with a number of well-written and court-filed documents, the power of the affirmation that the ceremony bestows on the two individuals and their immediate family (whether blood or constructed) cannot be reconstructed without the public ceremony and the social acknowledgment a legal marriage bestows on the couple's position and psyche. Despite all that I know about institutional and social power, despite all that I know about the love my partner and I hold for each other, I want a wedding and a slip of paper from the government stating that we are a couple joined forever through a bond of marriage.

I have two female friends who have lived together since they were in college—to be exact for 25 years. One of their parents, when told of the upcoming wedding referred to their relationship as "special" but added "marriage is for a man and woman." There is nothing "special" about queer love relationships. They are exactly like heterosexuals' relationships. My partner and I have been together a mere six and a half years. We own a home and two cars together. We care for a dog, two cats, and three birds together in lieu of children we could have but don't want. We plan out life choices, career moves, and vacation trips together. We fret about retirement, money, and extra weight gained together. She takes out the trash and does the dishes, and I cook and do the shopping. We share a queen-size bed in one bedroom, and we have sex—lots of sex—that I later turn into dime stories and hope her parents don't ever read any of them. We laugh and cry. We hold each other when we watch movies together. She is my god, my love, my life, and I wouldn't give her up for anything or anyone.

The only thing that is "special" about our relationships and thousands of others like them is that individuals, like my friends' parents, religious leaders, government officials, and high school bullies, don't want to acknowledge that our love is identical to their heterosexual love. Maybe I am wrong about this. Maybe there *is* something special about our queer love. Maybe what everyone is afraid of is that our (queer) love is stronger than their (heterosexual) love. *Our* love has managed against all odds to come into being, to exist, to grow, and to bear fruit when the whole mass media machine, our own families and friends that we hold closest to us, god in all his many multitude of forms and institutions, and the laws of the land have worked both consciously and unconsciously to continually attempt to stop, to sabotage, and to kill our love. Maybe that is the most "special" thing in the world — a love that won't stop, won't die, and won't give up in the face of what would seem to be insurmountable odds.

My partner and I haven't directly discussed marriage. We have toyed with each other in public about making an "honest woman" out of me, and have agreed in private to discuss it "soon." I am not sure how or why she feels whatever it is that she feels about marriage. I am not sure how I will explain to her the desire to publicly declare my love for her in a white dress in a public venue. I am not sure what we will do about the "Marriage Question." But I know this, whatever we decide as a couple to do, I will always love her the same, and I will forever be grateful to have had the chance as an adult to truly consider the "Marriage Question" as a valid viable option for my lesbian life.

Amie M. Evans (pussywhippedproductions@hotmail.com) is a white girl, confirmed femme-bottom who lives life like a spontaneously choreographed performance. She is the founder of The Princesses of Porn with the Dukes of Dykedom, PussyWhipped Productions, and Philogyny: Girls Who Kiss and Tell. *She is a published literary erotica writer, experienced workshop provider, and a burlesque and high-femme drag performer. She graduated Magna Cum Laude from the University of Pittsburgh with a BA in Literature. She is currently working on her MLA at Harvard. She firmly believes that queer liberation cannot happen through mainstreaming which demands the fringe elements of our community be isolated and marginalized and that sacrificing our queer sexuality in order to achieve a false sense of equality is not a valid option.*

The Marriage on My Toast
Douglas Ferguson

So far, I've been with my partner, Paul, for 12 years. Sometimes, when I think of the concept, "Until death do us part," I think: *That's simply not good enough.* I need to be with Paul a helluva lot longer than that. I need to be with Paul long after death, long after the Galaxy has gone supernova, and existence no longer exists. The idea of being apart from Paul fills me with a melancholy. And I know he feels the same way I do. If any two people deserve to get married, it is definitely the two of us. But whenever someone asks us if we will get married, Paul and I both reply with an emphatic "No."

Our reasons for not wanting to get married aren't politically motivated. We're not radical queers spewing manifestos about why gays aren't meant to marry because we're designed for sin. In fact, we support gay marriages. But because we live in Canada—arguably one of the most progressive countries in the world—Paul and I have never met any real opposition when it comes to our union. My parents love Paul like a son, and Paul's parents, in return, love me. Our work and health benefits support the both of us as legitimate partners. If we felt that our union wasn't going to be recognized any other way, then perhaps we would get married simply as a means of survival.

Our reasons for not wanting to marry have to do more with our observations of straight marriages. When I think of marriage, I think about my older brother John and his wife of eight years. More specifically, I think about their wedding.

Because my family has no real religious convictions, my brother had agreed to appease Lana, his bride-to-be, by having a Roman Catholic wedding. When John and Lana met with the priest to arrange the wedding, the priest discussed his stance on marriage in general. Although John is not Roman Catholic, the priest gave the wedding his blessing. It was after he approved of John that he explained his stance on both gay and interracial unions, which, of course, he was fervently against. Having one brother who is gay, and another brother—my identical twin—dating a black girl at the time, John was not impressed by the priest and began to have second thoughts about having his marriage recognized in a Roman Catholic church. After the meeting, my brother paid a visit to my parents. When my dad asked how the meeting went, John said, "We're going to be married by Father Hate."

There was even concern expressed by Lana's parents about Paul's and my attendance at the wedding. I suppose they were concerned that I would wear a full-length ball gown, or that Paul would bugger me in front of everyone at the reception. Whatever the case, there was so much bullshit surrounding the wedding that nobody in my family was looking forward to it—not even the groom.

The day of the wedding ceremony, Paul, my twin brother Don, his girlfriend Jennifer, and I had arrived late. Not wanting to interrupt the ceremony, we discreetly seated ourselves on an empty bench against the wall at the very back of the room, and quietly watched the ceremony. Part of the wedding involved a ritual that made use of a gold-and-red-velvet crown. The priest made the sign of the cross three times, placed the crown on the groom's head, took it off, and then put it on the bride's head. The crowning symbolizes several things, and the obvious symbol is one of victory.

The crowning ritual, however, did not make me think of the holiness of marriage, nor of victory. Instead, my first thought was of those Imperial Margarine commercials, where one of the actors would bite into a slice of toast and—*ta-da!*—a crown would appear on his head. Because my twin bother and I share that psychic link that twins have, he was thinking the same thing. We turned to each other, and at the exact same time that I said "margarine," he said "butter." The two of us got an immediate case of the giggles. Paul and Jennifer shook their heads at us. This only made our giddy state worse. The harder we tried to contain ourselves, the harder we laughed. The other guests turned their heads and leered at us disapprovingly. When the pain of trying to suppress our laughter became too much to bear, I left for the bathroom, where I tried to contain myself. I simply could not be in the same room as my twin and remain calm. By the time I wiped away my tears of laughter, took several deep breaths, and composed myself in front of the mirror, I had missed most of the ceremony.

It was only during the dance that I had a chance to personally congratulate my older brother. He looked exhausted and was quite drunk by this time. When I asked how he was doing, he put his arm around my shoulder and said wearily, "I'm tired. Very very tired." He has remained tired ever since.

Whenever people ask me if Paul and I will ever get married, I think about my brother's wedding. I think about the commercials with the Imperial Margarine crown. And I think that marriage, like margarine, is just a marketing gimmick for the ever-hungry consumer. Despite the commercial's message, margarine doesn't give you the status of royalty, and neither does marriage. Marriage is as meaningless to me as the brand of spread on my dinner rolls. They're both low in nutrition and high in preservatives.

My relationship with Paul won't take on a higher level of significance if we get married. We are no less committed to each other just because we don't have rings on our fingers.

Our refusal to get married is usually met with looks of confusion and disappointment. Now that gays and lesbians are getting married, Paul and I are expected to march up the aisle. Ironically, some people—both straight and gay—had more respect for our relationship when the government didn't recognize gay marriages. Because we have no plans to marry, our relationship is suddenly questionable. It means nothing that we've been together longer than most couples of our generation. In the past, we have never needed to explain our same-sex relationship to anybody. But now that the laws are changing to permit gay marriages, we are obligated to explain our non-wed relationship all the time.

I have seen happy marriages. My parents have been wonderful role models for how great a marriage can be. I aspired to (and achieved) the same quality relationship with Paul that my parents have with each other. But after seeing the false, pretend relationships that many other couples have, I know that good marriages are exceptional. It's ridiculous to believe married couples are more committed to each other than unwed couples. At least unwed couples *choose* to be together; they are not bound by the contract of marriage to commit to one another.

I worry that if gay marriage becomes common, there will be future generations of queers getting married only because they are conditioned to believe that their relationships mean nothing otherwise. And because of the social expectations of marriage, there will be just as many queer couples as there are straight couples forced to wear a crown that doesn't fit them. What a noble victory that will be.

Douglas Ferguson is a Saskatchewanite, currently residing in Calgary, Alberta. His short stories have appeared in all three Quickies *anthologies (Arsenal Pulp Press). His novel* The Forgotten Ones *will be released by Suspect Thoughts Press in the near future. And despite Doug's scrawny frame, his partner, Chef Paul Orr, assures that he's well fed at all times.*

An Attempt to Rewrite a Rant Against Marriage...
Originally Written After the U.S. Supreme Court Ruling Invalidating Remaining Sodomy Laws
Steven Finch

for FA: "When people ask what I think about gay marriage, I say I believe in gay divorce."
And for BV, who writes the best rants

1. In spite of — or perhaps because of — the facts that I was raised a Protestant; that, as a Boy Scout, I went along with the others in our troop to any given church on any given Sunday when we went camping; that I did all my university studies in Catholic institutions; that I've worked for and with Asian Indians; that I've known people from all parts of this world; and that I've studied philosophy: I am a nonbeliever, 100 percent.

2. All notion of religious or civil marriage as it exists today should be abolished or, at least, rethought. Neither a church nor a state has any business at all in a private relationship between two (or more) persons of whatever sex who love each other. Whatever legal transactions need to be made between such unions can be done before a lawyer. Cermonies to celebrate such unions are fine, as long as no "authority" prevails.

3. Two books — John Boswell's *The Marriage of Likeness* (that also covers non–same-sex unions) and George Ryley Scott's *Curious Customs of Sex & Marriage* — should be required reading for everyone.

4. As long as a "union" — same-sex, heterosexual, or a mixture of both — is made on the basis of love and devotion, there should be no logical reason for that union not to be able to adopt and/or give natural or scientifically assisted birth to children. As far as the "family" name of a child of such a union is concerned, nothing could be more simple or obvious: each child (and eventually each adult) will have a composite "family" name, as is the case in Spain. For example, the child of a parent, mother or father, adopted or "natural", whose family name is Steele-Parks and another whose family name is Rosenfeld-Moore will have the family name Steele-Rosenfeld or even Rosenfeld-Steele.

5. I've shared my life and love with a person of the same-sex for almost 30 years now. I will never have children, even adopted, and will never marry that person, even if given the possibility. While researching my original rant, I came across the following etymological coincidence that I hope will make the mere idea of same-sex marriage even more ridiculous: so as not to mix up same-sex unions between two women or two men, a legal union between two women should be officially called a "matrimony" [via Norman French from Latin *matrimonium* wedlock, from *mater* mother] and a legal union between two men should be officially called a "marriage" [from Old French *marier*, from Latin *maritare*, from *maritus* married (man), perhaps from *mas* male] — my apologies for not putting in the proper accents!

6. Unless I'm mistaken, the preponderant reason for demanding the legalization of marriage between two persons of the same-sex found its raison d'être when partners of persons with AIDS were not allowed to stay together owing to the parent(s) of that

person with AIDS. All that I will say here is that, if the two persons, the two "partners," are adults—i.e., of age—the parent(s) of the person with AIDS, or whatever illness/disease, should have absolutely no decisional weight over the patient's wish, written or orally transmitted.

7. I'll end this rewrite here, on what will most likely be the most controversial of all seven points. It comes in two parts—one concerning religion, in particular Christianity, and the other concerning the "State." According to Christianity, all sex is "unclean" (for those who doubt this, Dr. Daniel A. Helminiak's book—the "Millennium Edition"—entitled *What the Bible Really Says About Homosexuality* is also required reading), so why should a union of whatever sexual makeup ask for the Church's "blessing"? As far as "citizenship" and "equal rights" are concerned (and my question/reasoning may appear oversimplified to many), why should any individual, let alone partnership, seek the permission of a government when, especially today, anyone in his/her right mind knows perfectly well (or should) that his/her state and national governments have very little respect, if any at all, for their citizens and citizens' "rights"?

Poet and translator Steven Finch is American by birth and Swiss by adoption. As a poet, he has been published in, for example, Boyhood: Growing Up Male *(University of Wisconsin Press); as a translator, he was, for example, the first person to have translated into English all six of the poems of Jean Genet* (Treasures of the Night; *Gay Sunshine Press). When 17 years of age, he came close to being married twice; since 1976, he has been "wedded" to a Spaniard named Miguel, with whom he now shares a house over 300 years old and a minpin named Niña.*

Against Gay Marriage
Gay Shame San Francisco

Queers should be offended every time Gavin Newsom is praised for marrying the gays. Hardly the selfless act of "civil disobedience" it is portrayed to be, this risk-free political stunt was merely a step toward building Newsom's political empire in San Francisco and paying back the conservative gay politicians and voters who were so essential to his election into the mayor's office. Newsom carefully calculated his move to jump in at the climax of the process, thereby avoiding taking part in any of the work involved.

One must remember how little concern Newsom has demonstrated toward queers. On February 6, 2003, he threw a lavish fundraiser at the LGBT Center, charging $125 a head, in order to court the powerful gay vote. Peaceful Gay Shame protesters were brutally bashed by the SFPD just after police escorted Newsom through the doors. The police riot, which left one person missing a tooth and with blood streaming down her face, was merely a spectacle for Gavin Newsom and his band of ruling-class socialites to watch as they sat safely inside the Center. Neither Newsom nor any of his supporters made an attempt to stop the violence. Since Newsom has refused to make any statement condemning these acts of the SFPD, we can only assume his complicity in the violence.

So why are gays so set on honoring and flattering this straight, white, privileged man for patronizingly granting them the "right" to marry? Surely some of the same people who raced to City Hall to tie the knot this February are those same queers who only ten years ago would have proclaimed that marriage is violent, racist, and homophobic—serving as one of the central institutions necessary for organizing a misogynist, sexist, and oppression-ridden world—a world that has no intention of building anything resembling supportive communities.

Throughout history, queers have made some of the most important challenges to the institution of marriage. Marriage is not a civil right. It is an oppressive institution that is forced upon people's lives. Marriage is an institution created by religious men to sustain their domination over the entire world. Obtaining the "right" to marry is not going to give gays equality, decrease homophobia, or challenge any structure of power, as marriage activists would like for us to believe. Rather than liberating us, it will be one step further toward absorbing us into the violently heteronormative culture that wants us either assimilated or dead.

The rhetoric behind the gay-marriage movement reveals its true intent. Gay-marriage proponents have explicitly defined their agenda as a way to transform gay identity into something more palatable to the heterosexual world, and to gain access to the privileges that come along with that approval. It is a desperate attempt to obtain validation from a violent, abusive culture with the sole aim of reaping the benefits from the very abuse and violence that oppress queers in the first place. In doing so, the gay-marriage movement is participating in the erasure of the radical queer struggle that has been the real force toward queer empowerment and a politic that challenges mainstream culture's hegemonic ideas of normalcy.

Clearly, the institution of marriage does not represent ideas of human relationships that queers need. Surely queers can find more genuine, meaningful, and safe ways to express our feelings to one another. Whatever happened to the time when being queer was a challenge to misogyny, gender hegemony, and the imperialist, bloodthirsty status quo?

The benefits promised by marriage rights belong to everyone, not just those people who conform to a specific form of state-sanctioned coupling. Every slut, whore, single person, polyamorist, and pervert deserves the rights that are reserved for married couples, as does every marginalized person in the world, not just those who have submitted to the tyranny of the mainstream.

It's disappointing and frightening that gay marriage has taken attention away from so many more pressing issues — war, education, and homelessness, just to name a few. It's sad that all of the time, money, and resources spent on gay marriage couldn't have been put to use providing support for those queers marginalized from the gay "community." The gay-marriage media circus successfully enabled most people to forget that Newsom's agenda centers around consolidating power and control in the hands of a ruling-class elite and punishing San Francisco's homeless for allegedly interfering with tourist dollars. While gays were getting married: the department of Alcoholic Beverage Control shut down a renowned gay cruise bar for allowing sex to take place on the premises; Newsom allied himself with monster-landlord Angelo Sangiacomo to try and evict hundreds of people from Trinity Plaza, one of San Francisco's largest affordable-housing units; a state budget passed that will decimate welfare, education, health care, and other social services; the U.S. Government engineered a military coup to overthrow the only democratically elected government in the history of Haiti.

Queers should realize the inherent contradiction in supporting Gavin Newsom's elitist political agenda by fighting for such a meaningless symbol of normalcy. It only leaves all other marginalized folks in the dust while the real issues are being silenced and ignored.

Gay Shame San Francisco is a Virus in the System. We are committed to a queer extravaganza that brings direct action to astounding levels of theatricality. We will not be satisfied with a commercialized gay identity that denies the intrinsic links between queer struggle and challenging power. We seek nothing less than a new queer activism that foregrounds race, class, gender, and sexuality, to counter the self-serving "values" of gay consumerism and the increasingly hypocritical left. We are dedicated to fighting the rabid assimilationist monster with a devastating mobilization of queer brilliance. Gay Shame San Francisco is a celebration of resistance: all are welcome. Visit www.gayshamesf.org.

Elephants Who Need Elephants
Jim Gladstone

My parents went to Puerto Rico for their honeymoon. Until I was ten years old, I was certain that they'd traveled there in a yellow hot-air balloon. I would have sworn to you that my father had projected images of the liftoff during our Sunday-night family-room slide shows. I forget the context of the conversation in which my mother disabused me of my odd imagining, but I remember suddenly realizing how I'd come up with the image in my mind: It was the wedding of Babar and Celeste, Jean de Brunhoff's picture-book pachyderms, King and Queen of the country of the elephants. They were my proto-parents, a long-trunked twosome, whose quarrel-free coupledom I'd generously transferred onto my own less-gentle-souled mom and dad. My primal image of marriage was Babar and Celeste's nearly identical heads, topped with yellow crowns, taking to the air in the wake of their wedding.

You can have your Streisand, boys. I've got a Babs of my own. Growing up with Babar and Celeste as my icons of romance was a lucky stroke of fate. Their bodies, like their heads, were strikingly similar. Yes, there were the scenes in which The Old Lady, Babar's urbane benefactress hooks up the big guy with a green three-piece suit and a bowler. And there are pages on which Celeste wears a lovely flowered frock. But before these clothiered images arrive, before Babar brings the garb of "civilization" back from Paris, the elephants are all naked…and in every respect but overall size — which distinguishes adults from children — they all look exactly the same (For those unacquainted with the de Brunhoff oeuvre, Babar and his cohort hail from a jungle which is conveniently adjacent to the City of Light and all of its fine shopping opportunities).

Recently, reading back through Babar, I noticed that everyone of those naked elephants, adult and child, has large ears and tusks. They're males, all of them, never mind Celeste's fancy French wedding dress. But even setting this ironic wrinkle aside, I never thought of Babar and Celeste as a man and a woman. I thought of them as elephant and elephant, two of a kind, in love and uplifted.

For as long as I can remember, I've wanted to honeymoon in a hot-air balloon. I imagine a partner and I floating not so high above the ground, able to see our friends and families raising their eyes skyward, smiling and waving to us. I want to know that we are tethered to their gravity, not leaving the orbit of the commonplace, but celebrated for our desire to briefly rise above it, for letting the idea of a storybook romance — the ideal of a perfect union — lift us for a little while. I want to see how it lifts everyone around us.

Idealism lets us rise, even as we know we're bound to the mundane, even as we know we're going to struggle all our petty earthbound struggles. Idealism is the thing that makes us cry at weddings; idealism juxtaposed with the hard-earned knowledge that we can never achieve ideals…and juxtaposed yet again with the fact that we're going to take another run at them nonetheless.

Every wedding is an exquisitely awkward marriage of idealism and acceptance. Which in and of itself is a case for same-sex couples, isn't it?

Cockeyed optimism is not to be underestimated. It may be the secret of human nature, something pure buried under all the bitterness to fuel our forward motion. In good time, when I meet my guy, I'd love you to have your rice at the ready. And throw in a peanut or two for luck.

Jim Gladstone thrives on variety. His latest book, Gladstone's Games to Go, *is a collection of over 60 no-equipment games that's been called "a dense, effective weapon against boredom"* (The Trentonian) *and named one of the hot books of Summer 2004 by* The Advocate *(which suggests that losers of the games be forced to strip). His prior book was the award-winning novel,* The Big Book of Misunderstanding, *and his next — as editor — is the gay short story anthology* Men & Ink: Hot Tattoo Tales *(Summer 2005). A new novel is perpetually in the works, but distractions, excuses, and fiscally sounder opportunities are vexingly ever-present. Tons of Jim's past writing — including dozens of book reviews — can be found by poking around on his website* www.GoGladstone.com.

On the Difficulty of Confiding, with Complete Love and Trust, in Some Heterosexual "Friends"
Thomas Glave

But then by now you have learned that when referring to them — indeed, even when thinking about them, as you often do — you must suspend the word "friends" between quotes. You have learned by this time (or ought to have learned by now, given all that they have already shown you, that you have plainly seen) that, when using the word to refer to them — to those particular heterosexual people who claim to be your "friends" — you must distrust the word; regard it and them askance and with all suspicion. For when, given what they have revealed to you over the years of your "friend"-ship, were you ever completely certain that they truly were friends? That they really considered you and others like you an actual person, not an aberration? Not something experimental and "interesting," nor one of "those people" who can be so funny, so acerbic and outrageous and — when?

And so it has been true that from time to time — often — you have wanted to confide in them. Very much. Of course. You have wanted to tell them how things were and might have been for you that week, that month; on those two clear days between ponderous rain during which you waited for and spent time with *him* — the man you loved at that time, hoped to love; were working so hard at loving. That man whom you desired, about whom you thought and dreamt and — yes, whose most intimate smells you summoned beneath you and beside you as, alone, on so many nights and tepid afternoons, you rubbed yourself back and forth on those spreading sheets and imagined being with him, within him, beside him, for what would have been still more secret and unknowable time. Between rain showers and clear days, nightfalls and loping dawns, you wanted so much to tell them how those hours passed for you in so many ways and how they passed — the minutes, interludes, silent stretches — for him. But those confidences would not have been all. Surely you would have wanted them to know how the hours had passed for another friend severely in love (but will he never stop yearning? some of his friends had wondered); for a friend caring for a sick lover (but when will he himself take time out to rest?). You would have wanted to tell them about that ex-lover recovering from a gay-bashing, about that other friend distraught over his mother's illness, and — of course! — about the new acquaintance hell-bent on enjoying the hell out of this club, or no, *this* club, he had laughed, let's hit *all* of these clubs, let's dance until —! (And how that laughing man had held on to you and pulled you in his direction with the zest of someone utterly free, you remember...how you and all the others in that evening's company had laughed in return, not entirely easily, and accompanied him, twirling, for a night of sheer abandon and joy.) You have wanted to tell all of these things and more to the married couple whose photograph you once lovingly nestled on your dresser in between cherished leavings of the dead and souvenirs of the sea; as you have wanted to do with the engaged couple who departed last week for Martinique, or with your dear woman friend and her man "partner" — all of whom have claimed to be "friends" and all of whom have been kind to you on several occasions, it is true, and clearly care about you in some way.

And so why wouldn't you tell them? Why would you choose not to confide in them about the first time you noticed the soft creases in a youngish man's face, that testified to how he would appear to the world when he reached 60 years old, if he lived that long? The creases that appeared somehow only when he spoke, wistfully, about adopting children with a man for whom he cared but whose continued presence, for so many reasons, could no longer be guaranteed? That wistful yearner shared with you exactly the sorts of things you have so longed to tell them: how, for instance, you have loved one man in particular so much, for the longest time, even as—not surprisingly—you have dreaded loving him so much. You have loved him, you have wanted to tell them, as assiduously and imperfectly as they have cared for each other—the wife her husband, the husband his wife, the woman and man each other. Their flaws in loving are yours, too, and his, and everyone's. Regarding them, you wonder: did they, so community-supported ("But they really do have a perfect marriage, such lovely children," etc.), ever fear making a life together in the way that you, today, fear making a life with him? (Yes, for you cannot forget how, only two weeks ago, he gazed so serenely at you and asked if you would be with him—"Will you be with me?" he asked.) Did they ever cower before the expectation of two lives lived lovingly, intimately, steadfastly together? What would their fear have felt like— smelled like? How would it have (or would it have) trembled and itched at the tips of their fingers? Would they, feeling the dampness of a humid rain-soaked afternoon or the aggregate salt of years, eventually have regarded each other in the way you trust you never will regard him, and wondered if, after all these years, they had done "the right thing"? Wondered if they had each finally received what they had always hoped for and wanted, in the ways they had hoped for and wanted it? Would they have said, as you might hope to say, *But all right, then. Because this is—yes, no mistake—what we always wanted. What we have. Each other, and more.* And how, how you would like to ask them all these things, and share that untold number of your own, but you cannot. Not with this woman or this man, because—

Well, but there they are again, as they have always been, responding to your imminent disclosures with the same reactions. The same slightly clenched fists (*why* must he speak about these things and those people? the fists say. Isn't it enough that we care about him? Why does he have to bring all of *them* into it? their furrowed brows tell you once more). The same glazed-over eyes—no, we don't want to have to imagine, when he speaks about *desire*, how *those people* have sex with each other— please, no! Then that familiar hooding of their eyes; their voices sand-thickened; that awful twitching somewhere south of the nose, and the chin, at the sullen edge of its own precipice, half-mastedly holding its own against outrightly communicated disgust. Now your hands and throat itch toward providing some sign that you wish to speak about him; about what it has been like and will be to be with him. As you privately exult in the sway-swing of his hips when he walks toward you or away from you, you note how they, halfway attendant, clear, once more, their throats; you see how their eyes roll (to where, or whom?) and how, just so skittishly, they hem and haw about how the dishes simply must be cleared from the table right now (the end of a dinner party to which they invited you, at which few other nonheterosexual people were present). They mutter, not entirely disingenuously, about how the children must now be put to bed, because well, yes, they would sleep down here in the living room if we let them, can you imagine?—and then we'd never be able to talk amongst ourselves, would we? And, of course, what they imagine you have to say in all its filth and perversity (words they would never use in front of you) isn't fit for children's ears—it never is, they have made tacitly clear time and time again. And so as you stutter toward some form of speaking, you learn that they must make some urgent phone call—yes, to Kuala Lumpur, Port Said, Dar es Salaam, Dallas! Or no, they must tune in to some critical TV show—an epic series on the melting polar ice caps or the latest word on the continuing chemical ruination of inland seas. They must wash their hands, vacuum crumbs off the tablecloth—crucial tasks, hell to pay if they aren't done—or they must run out quickly, very quickly, for something earlier forgotten. It will be a loaf of bread this time, although you are certain that you saw— didn't you?—two full, fresh loaves in the kitchen, atop the gleaming white refrigerator, as usual right next to the tongue-clucking Swiss-fashioned clock...

Is it painful? Their avoidance, awkwardness, and downright rejection of you and those for whom you care? Well yes, of course. Of course it hurts, deeply. Severely. As always, you would rather not witness their mouths drawn down along the edges, their eyebrows raised not in anticipation but in the dread of *Please don't talk about this now*, their faces say, *we just can't handle it*. You would rather deny that their faces are plainly stating that they positively *do not want* to know that part of you that has everything to do with deep feelings for other men; with the essential human need to love, to desire, to be loved. But we don't want to (and so will not) imagine it, their eyebrows say. We're better off not knowing, and we wish that you would have enough decorum not to *force it down our throats*. And what an image, you think. As if you, nonsoldier and complete pacifist, never a torturer for even one day in your life, could ever, outside of intimate and consensual engagement, successfully force anything down anyone's throat.

And here you recognize imposed upon you, by way of their stiffened backs and taut brows, a form of exile; ostracism; a delivery of *almost* diplomatically wrought shaming and exclusion that, through a nearly invincible intransigence, banishes you to that most pernicious place: to an outer region of silence where shame, caressed and fortified by prejudice, may triumph. Suddenly, aware once again that you are not welcome to speak intimately with these people about your most pressing vulnerabilities, you feel keenly outside that warm locale where human beings frequently exist most vibrantly, in the realm of animated and intimate, vulnerable conversation; the place where imagination is engendered, amplified, and reconfigured; the place where we all imagine and re-imagine loves, losses, hopes and hopefuls, the chances we took and didn't take, and every regret and joy clutched fast between them. It is there, outside the warm place of deep imagination even as you feel yourself still strangely in their presence (for you are still present; you did not stalk away, nor—for whatever reason—viciously curse them), that you now watch them. Watch them as they kiss and cuddle—the woman her man, the husband his wife, the fiancée her affianced. You watch them as they kiss publicly: in a mall, in a movie theater, out in the open on people-thick streets. You marvel at their complete lack of self-consciousness as they neck in all those places, completely oblivious to the possibility of the danger that rarely (unless, in the United States, they are a black-white interracial couple) threatens them. They appear so free, so unencumbered by doubt, concern; unfazed by the who-might-be-wielding-a-baseball-bat-just-around-the-corner type of worry that, not without great reason, has stalked so many times before you and other women and men queers you know. You marvel at how they, as the world's personified definition of what love *should* be, take the display of their affection and its pride of place so much for granted. You know, as they cannot, that (unless they are an interracial couple) they will never know the quick release of a publicly held hand as a group of hostile-looking young men approach. They will never know the fury of angry voices shouting at them that their love is not "real," or that it is "filth," "an abomination," "a sickness." To them, all those billboards and TV commercials and films and popular songs extolling "love," illustrating the "correct" kind of intimacy—same-race, same-class, opposite-gender couples, and invariably (although not always) young faces—will be above question; for that, you know, is what the world, the world that they know and you know, the same one that formed us all and which continues to preside absolutely over too many of our imaginations, *wishes to see*. And then you marvel once more at the fact that, for every particle of ire you have choked within yourself over their smooth disregard for the unparalleled human rights they enjoy—human rights they rarely, if ever, view in such a context— you have never, up until now, confronted them with your feelings. You have never told them how it makes you feel when, thinking nothing of it, she refers to him as "Honey," he to her as "Sweetie," but both of them swiftly close their faces and cringe when you do the same, in their presence, with him. You have not yet told them how stallions' hooves have viciously kicked at your temples every time you heard the spittle in a passing woman's comment: "Oh, is he into men? What a waste"; every time you heard another woman's angry lament that "all of 'our' black men are either in jail, dead, on drugs, or gay" (and hopefully this last time you heard the word "gay," not "faggots"). You have never discussed the disgust and contempt you felt when—in a locker room, in some other unrelievedly macho space—you were privy, *again*, to a round of boors braying about how hot she was last night, fucking Christ, did you see her tits in that blouse, Jesus, and what a pair of legs on her, and that ass, man, did you see? Even as you were repulsed by their heavy-testosterone straightstudman talk (which bore an alarming resemblance to some forms of gaystudman talk), you couldn't help but grimace at what you knew would be their absolute repugnance were you even to mention in their presence how lovely his bikini-shorted buttocks had appeared to you the week before, how his hands had moved over you through the dappling of that afternoon and *well now but then how utterly wild you became, a fully-grown man, when the bending evidence of his desire all at once about-faced and saluted his bellybutton that way merely because you had, once again you had*...of course. You see once more their eyes closing down as, your face already returned to the thick-misted forests of that private time, you ascend off the ground in a memory of what exactly he whispered into your neck last night as you held him and he told you (of course). You envision their arms tightly folded across their chests, fit to demolish their hearts, as you speak of feeling married to this particular man. You remember the feeling, and yearn so much to share more with them, but will they welcome it? Will they beckon you with a "Please do" and a "Come, tell us how you live"?

Some will, of course, and some won't. Most so far haven't. Most—even those who have fancied themselves "liberal," "modern," and "broad-minded"—have, until now, tossed you and other queers off with a simple "Umff" of disinterest, or the lackluster "Oh, really? Huh" wholly devoid of ingenuous, generous engagement. They might have been sophisticated enough not to pitch the old "But why must you talk about it—" (And what exactly is the "it"?) "—and be so blatant?"—but, well, small cheers for that underwhelming achievement. How could you explain to them, in a way they would finally understand, that—as only one example of a prevailing "master" hetero societal script—a woman's pregnancy is and always will be, irrespective of her actual sexual and romantic interests, a public and widely accepted confirmation that sex, actual *sex*, occurred between a man and a woman? How could you make clear to them that even if a woman prefers the companionship of other women, her visible pregnancy will automatically "heterosexualize" her to those who know nothing, or wish to dissemble that they know nothing, of her personal life? How could you make definitively evident to them that, along the way, such a woman will without doubt encounter all too many people only too willing to "forget," in the face of the pregnancy that has "heterosexualized" her, that she is in fact a woman who prefers her own form of same-gender intimacy? How could you make them understand all these points and more, even as you labored to make them apprehend that the sort of sex they take so much for granted—"normative," opposite-gender sex—is precisely the sort of which society in large part (at least in the public legislating sphere) approves, albeit much more so within the confines of heterosexual, preferably monogamous, marriage? As citizens of the world of generally sanctioned, even championed, sex, they would care to hear little or nothing of your transgressive wish—a wish you have heard other men express when speaking about the men they cared for—that he could get you pregnant, or you him. For what would it be like, you have often wondered, to carry his child? To have received him in that way; to have felt, after the shudder and the gasp and the melding of his various parts with yours, his body-hot fluids racing through your insides and on to the places where a child-creature would be formed, held, fed, and protected; the places your man's body did not possess, would never possess. What would it be like to feel his child-thing growing within you, as you watched yours grow in him? To see and touch and kiss his belly ballooning over the months? To gaze, close up, at his nipples swelling, increasingly sensitive, as nausea and the violent need to retch roused him from bed early each morning? To feel the intensifying kicks of that sightless foal that, at the nine-month road's end and another road's beginning, would charge whinnying into the world, causing you, as the first sign of that small head emerged from you, to throw back your head and part your legs, as women have done for millennia, with a scream… But no, you certainly cannot confide such a pondering to them — not to those heterosexual friends, no matter how friendly, to your face, they appear. They would laugh you out of court, and maybe even (but you should be so lucky!) revile you as a pornographer. But then you know also that few homo men would care to hear such a wondering either, ashamed as so many have been and continue to be of their own private parts, and most especially of their private parts that, so effectively, receive, and grip, and hold.

It is still possible that it all will end differently. Possible that trust and love between you, in spite of everything, will somehow emerge. How, you are not entirely sure; nor are you completely certain, in this moment, that you care. For the while, you are content to revel in a morning of sun and dust motes. In a bedroom, on the uppermost floor of a house somewhere, far from any town or city; many living things outside and all around flexing and shouting out their names in deep green, as the air fairly groans beneath its weight of summer, redolent heat, and the lively snaps and whistles of the re-awakened natural world. You remark how the motes flout their freedom in the rays that slant without fail each early morning through the nearer bedroom window, as you push yourself more immediately into him — whichever him he will by this time have become — and smell, squeeze, nuzzle. Your belly presses into his back; he sleep-smiles upon feeling your knuckles' hitchhike across his broad plains. You both are happy enough holding and being held in this way for all these minutes that will stretch into an hour, or two, or four. You are pleased when you remember the orange juice that awaits you in the refrigerator downstairs, and the coffee, and the delicate, smoothly folded rolls. When a photograph comes into your mind — one once kept on your dresser, lovingly nestled in between cherished leavings of the dead and souvenirs of the sea — it is enough for you to murmur, No. Not now. Perhaps not ever. Enough for you to disremember the young, happy, smiling couple in the picture, and their laughter as, beneath tossed flowers, you also laughed and begged them to hold still, please! while you focused the lens and they kissed, through which act (although they might not have known so at the time) they became more of themselves, and more still. For now, holding him and drinking in the sun's outrageous flirting with the day, it is gratifying indeed to dismiss them and a few others like them from memory: she grown more dusty now, ample about the hips, and he slumped everyplace except in his body. Over the years, they have become more part of that other world — that world of which, at least as part of their company, you have become less and less a part, as you have insisted on talking more about him and yourself; on showing and sharing him and yourself; on taking pleasure in the company of others who have had similar tales to relate about past disharmonies, and who too have moved on. Whatever else might happen, you know that for just these hours that will shortly transpose themselves to something else yet again, this quiet joy that you feel — over the day, the tawny flirtatious sun, the feeling of your knuckles across his plains, and his breath, now and then, just beneath your neck—can be enough. Enough to vanquish memories of censorious eyelids, apoplectic ahems, twitching *Please don't bring it up* brows and fearful hands safeguarding children. Enough to carry you back to the hours of yesterday and last week that will shortly become the minutes of this unfolding time, when you will once more look at him as you did before...as you always have before. When he will return your gaze. When neither of you will need to ask the question to which you both know and have long known the answer, the answer you have already told each other so many times without needing to say it, that, once more, moves right there, without words. And moves again. And settles. And yes.

Thomas Glave is the author of Whose Song? and Other Stories *(City Lights) and the forthcoming* Toward Nobilities of the Imagination: Essays *(Minnesota).*

Excerpted from an essay that originally appeared in *The Massachusetts Review*, Vol. 44, No. 4 (2003). Reprinted by permission of the author.

Divorce
Robert Glück

While everyone in the city is getting married I am getting divorced. Always ahead of my time, I am engaged in bitter disputes over property while others merge their bank accounts. Always in the avant-garde, I avert my eyes from Chris while they gaze at each other with unguarded expressions. Our relationship will be truly over when I can look at him again. The life we had planned together fell apart—a feeling of desolation as strangers seem to buy our union, our derelict property. I find random sex while they discover monogamy. I resent the time that promiscuity takes, it's a grievance against Chris, though now I'm locating people who want to make pleasure happen in a body like mine. Search for: older, bear, daddy, and avoid those who take these designations seriously. The Australian who wouldn't shut up—aye mate; the vice president in charge of ATMs erotic massage in Pleasant Hill—first he said destiny brought us together, then he declined to see me again; the Irish dance teacher who didn't call back; the architect who wanted to harm my nipples; the numerous heavy guys with average penises who think they have well-endowed swimmer's bodies. I am mildly obsessed with internet dating while other people return each other's phone calls and emails as though that were normal. While everyone else in the city is making a legal vow I wonder how to go about canceling ours. I search through drawers for the official paper and try to determine which government office to call while they are drawn to the marriage bureau in City Hall. While the horns are honking. While friends throw rice. While reporters take notes. While the parties get underway, I weep in my garden, watching it bloom for the last time. I'm afraid to leave this garden because I put too much of myself in it. I am hanging onto this environment like the alien at the end of *Alien*, clinging by its toenails to the ship hurtling through space. Why are there no parties with gifts for divorce? Where is my party, now that my household is ripped in two and I actually need the new blender, TV, vacuum. While they give each other courage I have stage fright, that is, who am I now? Where are my lines? Who can I talk to, emphatically awake in the hours of the night while they sleep annealed skin to skin. Awake and without resistance because there is no one to recognize me. While they are buying sheets together I sleep on my side, a haystack of papers and dirty dishes in his place on his side of the bed. While they are setting up house in each other's consciousness, I learn to banish Chris, don't think about him one way or another. While they are planning to have a child my son is caught in the middle. Fine, I'll go say hello to Chris' relatives when they come to town. Do you think you can do it? Get divorced? The new couples are walking in the front door of Noah's ark while I sneak out the back like a thief. They are becoming more than the sum of their parts while I am becoming less than one. Their friends are getting to know each other while my friends choose sides.

Robert Glück is the author of nine books of poetry and fiction, including the two novels, Margery Kempe *and* Jack the Modernist. *His new book,* Denny Smith, *was published by* Clear Cut *in February 2004. He's an editor of* Narrativity, *a website on narrative theory:* www.sfsu.edu/~poetry/narrativity/issueone.html.

Undone
Daphne Gottlieb

When San Francisco Mayor Gavin Newsom (who we tried to keep out of office with all our hearts) spurned national law and declared that San Francisco would issue marriage licenses, I was living with my —.[1]

It was a few days shy of our nine-year anniversary.[2] We'd been together for all but five years of what I consider my "adult" life, if you start counting at 21.[3]

We were deadlocked, trying to decide whether to go get married or not. It was like trying to decide whether to go get expensive sushi or not. Or buy a new sex toy we might not like. Actually, it was not like that at all.

We were going through a rocky period; a relationship mood swing. It was the kind not unfamiliar to anyone who has been in a relationship that has lasted more than two years recognizes as transient. Even so, each time you think, "Uh oh. It's over."

We went back and forth on the marriage thing: Oh yes, Oh no, Uh oh. We fretted privately and together. Marriage was important. Marriage was assimilationist. This was an important historical moment. This was tokenism.

The fact is, we'd had this conversation many times over nine years. And we'd decided that commitment ceremonies—though they can be really swell—weren't for us. They lacked any real legal reason to spend that kind of money—limos but no power of attorney, flowers but no bulletproof custody, champagne but no tax break, no deal. Not our kind of spending. Despite excited exhortation by some friends and enthusiastic hints from parents and siblings, we had demurred for almost nine years. We slyly told them we'd prefer to live in sin. After all, that's exactly what my mother proposed to my father, albeit under different circumstances.[4]

So. My — and I were choosing to live in sin, sort of. And, I figured, so did I. I chose to not suburb this, not soft-pedal this, not palliate this, not "my roommate" this. Because she was my wife, I called her, for a while, my "wife." Which was a grand political statement and a love letter all in one. Until we could actually get married.

And then there it was: Our anniversary, Valentine's Day, and now we could be, like, legit. Obviously, I needed strong ammunition. I took aim at her hatred of tradition. "Oh, no," I said. "I'm not going to marry you until you unless you get down on one knee and propose." We both laughed and I thought it was over. I breathed a deep sigh from laughing and relief. And then she, who I had seen over nine years in sickness and health, who I had seen richer and poorer, shocked the shit out of me.

She got down on one knee and took my hands in hers.

"Do you remember," she said, "the early days of Queer Nation?" Yes, I said, I did.

"Do you remember," she asked, "going into malls for kiss-ins and asking straight girls if they wanted to make a statement?" Yes, I said, of course I did.

---

[1] I write — because, after being with her for nine years, living together for six, she was hardly my girlfriend, and much more than my lover, not my significant other and not my partner, thank you. She was my (love). And if legally she was my "domestic partner," so be it. But she really was my — (love).

[2] According to Chicago's Public Library, that's the, um, modern Leather anniversary.

[3] Which I think is generous. There was someone I met before I turned 21 who I pledged to spend the rest of my life with. It would have worked out, had I died at 22. I think it's a common phenomenon. At least five in ten. Do you really want what you want at 21 to be what you want at 41? Not me. Even if it's the same person, maybe you want different things.

[4] They'd been married more than 20 years. He was dying. Living in sin seemed good enough for me if it was good enough for them. Of course, the last time they tried to have sex, the Jehovah's Witnesses interrupted them, but I can hope for better. Or maybe laughing is just fine.

"And," she asked, "if they said 'yes'," she said, "you'd kiss them?" Yes, I said. I remembered. "If," she said, "you want to make a statement with me, I would love to make a statement with you."

The world stopped for a minute for me.

"So," she said. "Do you want to make a statement?"

"I don't know," I said, wailing into tears. I'm not sure how long I was crying for. Only that I wasn't crying alone.

Later that night I called my brother, an attorney in Los Angeles. "You know what's happening in San Francisco," I said. "This round probably won't hold up," he said. "I know," I said. "But I might get married anyway," I said. I explained the best reason for getting married I'd heard—the one that had convinced me: The courts would soon put a stop to these marriages, but there were couples all over the country who wished to get married and could not be in San Francisco for reasons of privilege of one sort or another—money, safety, and otherwise. We should, the argument went, get married on their behalf. Represent them in the statistics taken. We should do it for those who couldn't. My brother listened, then laughed. "You do realize," he said, "that these are just about the only circumstances under which I can see you getting married."

At some point, though, here's what happened. I wanted marriage to mean something beyond resistance. I wanted my wedding—our marriage—if we chose it—to be the celebration and the pledge of fusing two lives together. I didn't want my wedding to be a test case. I want promises made in love to mean more than litigation.

There are photos of me at the age of five or so, wearing a veil and a wedding dress, playing dress-up. Not so many years ago, this was good training for the best a girl could expect from her life. For some, maybe that's still true. And though my mother wished desperately for me to choose the doctor costume first, the bridal getup had the better hat.

For me, the expectation of marriage was something so deeply ingrained early on that no matter my fear, dislike, and critique of it as an adult, the promises of a happily ever afterness still sing in my cells once in a while. And I'm ashamed to admit this. Because it feels shallow to me, like getting hot to mainstream porn, like wanting something from Old Navy even though you know it was made in a sweatshop, like somehow being the same as everything you thought you'd spent your whole life fighting against.

The truth is, I was never married. But I have been divorced. Even though all that I can correctly say is, "We split up." If I said "divorced," maybe co-workers would have looked at me differently when I crept in late to work, red-eyed, and suddenly stumbling heaving-chested to the bathroom. Or when I didn't come in at all. I don't know that their opinions were any different than if I'd been married to a man. I really have no way of knowing.

She took the apartment. We split up the cats. She took a sublet. I found a roommate, found an apartment. We tore our lives, our hearts apart and then I called her sobbing: I'd had to sign a form at work to end her health care on my form. The form said "Termination of Domestic Partnership." I called her through choked throat, tried to explain. She tried to make it better. We hung up.

And then the certified letter arrived at her door, notarized. Not even needing her signature. In (I believe) Saudi Arabia, you used to be able to get a divorce by saying "I divorce you" three times. All it takes in America now, if you're queer and a registered domestic partner, is a notarized signature. If you're not registered, it takes even less.

I have never written marriage vows. Here are, belatedly, my divorce vows. My dear — who shared my heart for nine years, who will be in a part of my heart always:

maybe, regardless what happens, there was a special love, a special fight in having to have had to get the power of attorney, to have had to garner the domestic partner status through two different agencies, to have had to correct the "roommate" slips, to have written the next-of-kin name in on forms with no legal protection. I jumped through these hoops with you, and I regret that our forever came sooner than the oldest ages we could reach. If there ever was a marriage vow I could give you, could have given you, it is this: I wish for your happiness every night as fervently as I wish for my own.

And, should your new someday love lead you that way, I hope you'll invite me to your wedding.

San Francisco–based performance poet Daphne Gottlieb stitches together the ivory tower and the gutter just using her tongue. She is the author of Final Girl *(Soft Skull Press, 2003),* Why Things Burn *(Soft Skull Press, 2001), and* Pelt *(Odd Girls Press, 1999).*

Same-Sex Civil Marriage
Rabbi Steven Greenberg

This affidavit was submitted by Rabbi Steven Greenberg for use in Canadian lawsuits seeking recognition of civil marriage for same-sex couples. It is a response to a previous affidavit by Rabbi David Novak.

In five Canadian cities, Toronto, Montreal, Ottawa, Calgary and Winnipeg, legislation is being introduced to extend civil marriage rites to same-sex couples. I was asked to offer a short response, stating my opinion on the issue as an Orthodox rabbi. The opportunity to write about this matter triggered my own thinking about the areas where religion and public culture rub up against each other.

My Response

1. I am an ordained Rabbi of America's largest Orthodox Rabbinical Seminary, Yeshiva University's Rabbi Isaac Elchanan Theological Seminary. I held an Orthodox pulpit early in my career and have been a Senior Teaching Fellow at CLAL-The National Jewish Center for Learning and Leadership since 1985.

2. I have been asked to address the religious basis for the extension of civil marriage to homosexual couples. The usual split on this issue has been between the religious right and the secular left. The religious right desires to see certain religious values (in this case, exclusive heterosexual marriage) reflected in the society at large, while the secular left wishes to keep the public square free from specific religious values which undermine legitimate individual freedoms.

3. Marriage as an institution has deep roots in every religious tradition. However, the very idea of "civil marriage" was both a blow to the authority of the church (which until then was the only venue for enacting a marriage) and a direct import from religion into secular/civic affairs.

Orthodox Jewish Law—Halacha

4. The Hebrew *halacha* is translated as Jewish law. It is derived from the verb "to walk." Halacha is a society-building enterprise that maintains internal balance by reorganizing itself in response to changing social realities. When social conditions shift, the halachic reapplication is not experienced as "departure from the law," but as the proper commitment to the Torah's original purposes. While that shift in social consciousness in regard to same-sex relations has not occurred in Orthodox communities, it surely has in the larger society. Orthodox rabbis are beginning to understand that their gay and lesbian congregants are not freely choosing to be gay, but are simply discovering themselves to be essentially different.

5. Under Orthodox Jewish law as it currently stands, same-sex marriage is not permitted. The religious rites of kiddushin can only be enacted between two Jews, one male and the other female. While the rejection of homosexual relations is still normative in most Orthodox communities, halachists are beginning to include in their deliberations the testimony of gay people who wish to remain faithful to the tradition. New halachic strategies, I believe, will, in time, appear under these changing social conditions.

6. Orthodox Judaism places many restrictions on marriage that differ from those placed on civil marriage. Interfaith couples cannot be married. Indeed, a number of couples that might desire the state of matrimony, under Orthodox Jewish law, could

not be married. The traditional Jewish community does not marry a male member of the priestly lineage with a divorcée or a convert, nor can a child of an adulterous union marry any Jew at all.

7. Despite the fact that civil marriage is offered to each of these couples, one hears no protest from the Orthodox community over the violation of its sensibilities. Orthodox communities have grown accustomed to the challenges of living in secular societies. Orthodox synagogues in Canada, were they to hire an "improperly married" or intermarried individual, would recognize the civil marriage and provide the appropriate marriage benefits for such persons. Rabbi Novak's speculation that Orthodox Jews would reject civil marriage were same-sex marriages included runs counter to the Orthodox community's historical acceptance of civil marriage as an institution governed by secular society.

Marriage Is Not a Natural Institution

8. Marriage is an institution structured by societies. All marriages are "according to the laws" of some communal body that honors them. They are a feature of civilization, not nature. Marking homosexual marriage as contrary to some natural laws is reminiscent of the justifications put forward in the U.S. for laws prohibiting interracial marriage.

9. Moreover, all sorts of ideas about marriage have changed. Abraham ended up with a wife and a concubine, Jacob with two wives and two concubines. In the Talmud, the famed scholar Rav would travel and call out, "Who will marry me for the day?" This custom of "day marriages" was common in Babylonia among those men who could afford them. While surely not ideal, the rabbis of the age did not protest this use of marriage by one of their most revered teachers. Families are always a subset of the society of which they are a part. Marriage, likewise, is conditioned by the values and sensibilities of the social context. As society has come to understand the essential unchosen nature of same-sex desire, the offering of new forms of matrimony that support such couples would seem consonant with a contemporary sense of justice and social responsibility.

10. Same-sex marriage, like marriage generally, is a conservative institution expressing lifelong commitment, caring, love, and support. It is fundamentally not about rights, but about duties. Central to Orthodox Jewish teaching is the importance of family. The rejection of gay coupling is hardly an expression of family values. Indeed, it is just the opposite. It is surely in the interest of families to support such unions that glue us all together by the force of our loving commitments to each other.

11. While it is true that procreation is one of the intents of marriage in our society, same-sex marriages would not prevent such endeavors any more than heterosexual marriages require them. Surely we would not claim that sterile couples or couples who choose not to produce children are not "really" married. Under Jewish law such couples might not be fulfilling the duty to reproduce, but that would have no bearing upon the legitimacy of their marriage. Moreover, adoption and surrogacy offer to gay couples the same potential as they do to heterosexual couples unable to reproduce.

12. Gay people cannot be asked to be straight, but they can be asked to "hold fast to the covenant." Holding fast to the covenant demands that gay people fulfill the mitzvot that are in their power to fulfill. Same-sex couples cannot procreate without outside assistance, but there are other ways to build a family and a marriage.

13. The wisdom of a religious practice lies not in the number of people that support it. Rabbi Novak raises the issue of the size of a religious community to impugn the views of Reform Judaism. It seems unimaginable to me that a Jew, a member of a religion that has endured such relentless persecution coincident with its

minority status, should invoke this notion. As a minority religion in North America, the religious marriages of Jews are given civil recognition despite the fact that they are not in keeping with the beliefs of the majority. The comfort Rabbi Novak draws from allegedly being in the majority regarding religious views on same-sex marriage is frightening.

Civic Institutions Are Crucial for Religious Freedom

14. While religious organizations might have a hard time admitting it, the institution of civil marriage is one of the public frameworks that allow religious communities to thrive. It allows synagogues and churches to do what they do, to restrict or extend membership and offer or deny access to their services and rites according to their principles. Civil alternatives for contracting a legally recognized marriage insure the freedom of religious communities to shape their own rules. Without civil and diverse religious alternatives for contracting a legally recognized marriage, those who do not conform to religious rules would put great pressure on religious organizations to change.

15. Civil marriage provides an umbrella under which we all can live, despite our very passionate differences. The state ensures that marriage is not denied to anyone based on a couple's particular religious beliefs or their lack of any religious beliefs. Civil recognition is extended to secular marriages and to marriages according to diverse religious traditions, practices, and beliefs, including to persons who do not meet the criteria of one or more religions. Conversely, the state does not require any religion to marry anyone who does not meet its criteria (for example, an Orthodox rabbi cannot be compelled to marry a Jew to a Gentile). This situation is not a cause for concern, but rather for celebration. That the civil concept of marriage and diverse religious conceptions of marriage can coexist not only demonstrates the ability of civilly recognized marriage to be flexible and to be separate from religious practice, but it also ensures the ability of religious marriage to choose its own course. That is certainly a victory for freedom of religion.

Rabbi Steven Greenberg received his BA in philosophy from Yeshiva University and his rabbinical ordination from Rabbi Isaac Elchanan Theological Seminary. He is a Senior Teaching Fellow at *CLAL (the National Jewish Center for Learning and Leadership) and has conducted hundreds of leadership-training programs for communal lay and professional leaders in over 50 cities in North America. Steve is a founder of the Jerusalem Open House, the Holy City's GLBT community center, and he continues to serve as its Educational Advisor. Steve appeared in Trembling Before G-d, *a documentary about gay and lesbian Orthodox Jews, and has joined the filmmaker, Sandi Simcha DuBowski, in carrying the film across the globe as a tool for dialogue and community organization. He has finished a book entitled,* Wrestling with God and Men: Homosexuality in the Jewish Tradition *(University of Wisconsin Press, February 2004), which explores biblical, rabbinic, medieval, and modern Jewish responses to same-sex relationships.*

* CLAL is an independent North American–based organization dedicated to preparing Jewish leaders to respond to the challenges of a new era in Jewish history.

This originally appeared on *www.CLAL.org*. Reprinted by permission of the author.

What's Love Got to Do with It?
Aaron Hamburger

What's all the fuss about?

I still don't understand why gay marriage of all things has become the central concern of the gay-rights movement, any more than I understood in the early '90s why gays in the military was such a burning issue. Back then, I wondered why activists dedicated to the freedom to love would work so hard to enable people to join an organization whose object is to kill. Now I wonder why a community that currently makes its own unique familial configurations free of governmental or societal encumbrances would want to enslave itself so it can be like everyone else.

More importantly, I don't understand why these two hot-button issues have become more important than passing straightforward legislation guaranteeing nondiscrimination in housing and employment, basic issues of survival. Not only are these kinds of laws desperately needed, but they also affect a greater range of people, since not all queer people want to get married. (And many of those who do may not have found a potential candidate.) Nondiscrimination laws would also be more practical, more palatable to mainstream America, and therefore more possible.

So why has the gay-rights establishment gone for hot-button issues like gays in the military and now gay marriage in such a big way? Certainly equal rights in housing and the workplace is far less glamorous than gays in the military or gay marriage. Also, I suspect that issues of discrimination affect poorer and rural gays more than their wealthy urban counterparts who are concentrated in cities where gays are protected by local civil rights laws. Wealthy urban gays, who are more likely to drive political agendas than rural gays, have a more vested interest in reaping the financial rewards of marriage than federalizing protections they already enjoy at a local level.

The push for gay marriage, however, isn't just financial. I came to understand the emotional impact of the issue while on a blind date several years ago. We'd barely opened our menus when my date, who'd recently been dumped by his boyfriend of four years, asked for my views on gay marriage. He believed that had gay marriage existed, he and his ex-boyfriend would not have broken up because they'd have had to go through the lengthy process of disentangling themselves from each other, legally and financially. In other words, they might have stayed together to avoid deciding who gets the sofa. When I pointed out that perhaps a relationship grounded in sofas might not be the most stable to begin with, it became clear there wasn't going to be any second date.

It's an argument I've heard several times since: if gay marriage existed, my boyfriend and I would be staying together, but since it's not, we're not.

To which my response is, in that case, thank God gay marriage doesn't exist. If the institution of marriage is on the rocks (which is debatable), it isn't because of our corroding moral culture, as many conservatives allege. Rather, the reason more marriages fail now as compared to years ago is that with the advances of feminism marriage is no longer a binding financial contract. Both men and women feel less need to tough it out in a long-term relationship that's clearly a failure. True, there's more pull to stay in a marriage that isn't working than in a "domestic partnership," but that's largely a matter of tradition, which is mostly what marriage is about anyway.

As for the legal rights associated with marriage, they are ridiculous and ought to be abolished for straights and gays alike. Society has no business trying to manipulate people's private relationships with free handouts. If matrimony is really as great as it's cracked up to be, then it ought to be its own reward. Why prop it up with artificial legal supports? And as for marriage's vaunted reputation as a society stabilizer, how do we square that reputation with the epidemic of domestic violence in this country, particularly among immigrant communities in which the traditional family model is prevelant and divorce is discouraged?

Love is a funny thing, famously compared to "a piece of ice held fast in the fist." It isn't suited to being hemmed in by the stringent shapes of laws. Getting married for love sometimes works out, but it's never a guarantee. After all, what happens when love cools? For a couple to stay together, they have to have mutual needs that are met by their relationship. When two reasonable adults can no longer find a way to make their relationship serve those needs, the best thing for all parties concerned is for the relationship to be dissolved with as few obstacles as possible. That dissolution may cause some short-term pain, but it can also result in long-term personal growth as well as true happiness that has nothing to do with financial dependency or sofas.

It seems to me that we gays have it about right when it comes to long-term relationships. If two gay people want to get married today, they can, by arranging a private commitment ceremony that isn't recognized by the government. The rest of the world ought to be imitating us, not the other way around.

Aaron Hamburger is the author of The View from Stalin's Head, *a short story collection about post–Cold War Prague. His writing has appeared in* The Village Voice, Time Out New York, Poets and Writers, Nerve, *and* Out *magazines, and has won several awards, including a fellowship from the Edward F. Albee Foundation. His next book, a novel set in Jerusalem titled* Faith from Beginners, *will be published by Random House in May 2005.*

Take These Men
Brent Hartinger

A couple of years ago, when my partner Michael and I decided to hold a ceremony to celebrate our commitment to each other, most of our friends told us they didn't know what to expect. We told them it would basically be a wedding between two men, but the truth was, we didn't know what to expect either. Straight people talk about "the gay agenda" like there's some kind of newsletter. It might be easier if there were.

We did know we wanted to "publicly affirm our relationship," even if we weren't exactly sure what that meant. In some vague kind of way, it just seemed hypocritical of us to insist that our friends and family treat our relationship with the importance we feel it deserves when we'd never told them—formally and in so many words—just how important it is.

But almost immediately, we found ourselves floundering. Once a heterosexual couple decides to get married, they're suddenly whisked off into a whole Pirates of the Caribbean full of traditions, with underwater tracks guiding them from one event to the next. Look over there—it's Wedding-Shower Cave! Now here we go, down Invitation-Selection-Process Waterfall! And now we come to Burning-Village Rehearsal Dinner!

Our boat, on the other hand, had no track whatsoever. For a long time, we drifted aimlessly. We weren't even sure what to call the damn thing. A wedding? A commitment ceremony? We briefly considered just calling the whole thing off.

Then the unexpected happened. Our friends, some gay and some straight, started taking our wedding...seriously. In fact, they took it far more seriously than we were taking it ourselves. It was the first thing they'd ask about when we went over for dinner. Had we set a date yet? Had we picked out a place? Two heterosexual couples threw us a shower-of-sorts—lots of wine and Thai food, great gifts like panniers for our bikes, and not a blender in sight. And a couple of my straight male friends began planning an "alternative" bachelor party—a whole weekend of intellectual debauchery that would include plenty of chemically assisted musings around a raging bonfire on the beach at midnight.

In other words, now that we'd foolishly said the words "commitment ceremony" out loud to our friends, we were suddenly obligated to go through with it.

When we finally sent out invitations, people warned us to expect some shrinkage in our guest list. Sure enough, two or three people had unalterable conflicts on the date we were proposing: a Nobel Peace Prize being bestowed, an audience with the Pope, or something along those lines. But everyone else we invited desperately wanted to come.

By now, of course, we had found a place, and were starting to plan the ceremony itself. Traditions? There was nothing stopping us from using them if we wanted (well, except for our lack of garters). At the same time, we didn't feel confined by them either—the way every single heterosexual couple we've ever met seems to have felt before their weddings. We now saw that we had the best of both worlds; we were the bisexual hermaphrodites of the wedding set.

Where we had felt aimless before, we now had a direction; best of all, it was a self-chosen one. With each new idea, our ceremony felt less generic, less interchangeable with other weddings, and more like a ceremonial representation of *us*. Why *couldn't* we have our pagan friend lead us and our friends around a garden giving us the Blessing of the Four Winds?

We held the actual event on the deck of a huge house on an island in Puget

Sound. In a nod to potentially confounded parents, we chose a (wildly liberal) minister as our officiate. We started by singing some songs, including a couple embarrassing ones that I wrote for the occasion. Then a few close friends spoke movingly, the minister said some words of his own, and we all walked down to the beach where everyone made a wish for us, then threw a single flower out into the ocean. We both admit to tearing up a little as we watched the floating blossoms streaming out into the setting sun.

Then the ceremony was over, but the best was yet to come. During dinner and around the bonfire afterward, we had friend after friend come up and tell us how honored they were to have been invited. Several people told us how glad they were they had been able to bring their kids—that they had desperately wanted their children to see that there are different kinds of relationships in the world. And couple after couple, gay and straight, also told us they considered our relationship to be a role model for their own.

A role model? That's when it finally occurred to us. We hadn't needed to tell our friends and family how important we are to each other. They already knew.

That's also when we learned a profound truth about weddings. They aren't about the couple saying anything to friends and family. They're about friends and family saying something to the couple: that they are valued and appreciated, an important part of the community. We had it exactly backward. Stupid us.

Of course, despite our ceremony, we're *not* married—not in any legal sense. All over the rest of the world, countries like Norway, France, Spain, and Canada have listened to the obvious concerns of their lesbian and gay citizens and granted them marriage or marriage-like rights. But in the United States, only a handful of states offer lesbians and gays any form of marriage, which the federal government and most other states have refused to recognize. On the contrary, conservatives—those great champions of "states' rights"—are now, of course, trying to amend the U.S. Constitution to specifically forbid any state from *ever* offering any same-sex marriage rights, even the limited ones that some states now offer. Many Republicans—and they *are* all Republicans—even have the audacity to accuse us of wanting "special rights."

Why do marriage rights matter? Anyone in a long-term gay relationship knows the answer. It's the petty little concerns, like the possibility of being denied access to a hospital room when your partner is about to die. Or the chance that, should one of you die, antigay family members will suddenly demand to inherit half the property of the surviving partner. (Don't scoff—this happened to one of our friends. It was one of the most evil things I have ever witnessed.) And don't get me started on tax advantages or Social Security benefits.

But for the time being, we live in an age of "don't ask, don't tell," where many heterosexuals insist, as if magnanimously, that they're willing to tolerate us, just as long as they're never confronted with any evidence that we exist. Big of them, huh? Still, I suppose I should be thankful, because plenty of other Americans aren't even willing to do this. Most of the Republicans pushing for a constitutional amendment are also on record as supporting same-sex antisodomy laws: laws that make consensual sex between people of the same gender—what Michael and I call "making love"—a crime.

Why would the famously compassionate, "new" Republican party take such bigoted, uncompassionate stands? And why would their broom-butted representatives bring out their big guns against even the slightest trifle of a domestic partnership law? Well, they usually argue that the mere acknowledgment of our relationship is somehow a threat to their families and their community. It makes me wonder what they're families are made of anyway. Styrofoam? Tissue paper? Snow?

The Republicans can think whatever they want. Funny thing though.

When my partner and I got married, it made our family, and our community, that much stronger.

Brent Hartinger is the author of Geography Club, *a two-time Book Sense Pick and IRA Notable Book; he has also adapted the book for the stage, and a feature film is in the works. Brent's other books include* The Last Chance Texaco, *about foster kids in a group home, and* The Order of the Poison Oak, *a sequel to* Geography Club *due in February 2005. Brent lives near Seattle with novelist Michael Jensen, but he'd much rather you visit him online at Brent's Brain, his website:* www.brenthartinger.com.

First published in *The Tacoma Morning News Tribune,* June 2001. Reprinted by permission of the author.

The Whole Fairy-Tale Princess-Bride Thing
Kristie Helms

Do you see me? Sitting here with my hands over my ears?

LA LA LA LA LA LA LA LA LA

I can't hear you. Ask me again. Ask me one more time, "So when are you guys getting married?"

LA LA LA LA LA LA LA LA LA

I can't hear you. I can't hear you. I can't hear you.

Since it became legal in Massachusetts on May 17 for same-sex couples to get married, getting married is all anyone can talk about. I've sat in on conversations about which caterers to hire, whether or not honeymooning in Provincetown is cliché, if it's gauche for a couple who has been together for 27 years to register for china, and what exactly it is you wear to a lesbian wedding, that you didn't wear to the 12 others you've already attended.

Now that it's legal for us to officially get hitched, it's hard to ignore that ever-present question, "So when are you guys going to get married?"

It's also hard to answer that question. Because while it's wonderful that my partner and I now have the choice to marry in our own state and I can legally entertain the romantic visions of lacy wedding dresses and picture-perfect receptions that dance in my head, the truth is that I've yet to come up with one good reason to sign a piece of paper declaring us wife and wife. Or partner and partner. Or spousal unit and spousal unit. Or "Party A and Party B" as the newly minted Massachusetts Marriage Licenses declare it.

We're lucky enough that my partner is still able to get medical insurance through my company's domestic partner policies and our wills cover those pesky property-transfer rights. I have no more interest in legally taking on her debt that she has in mine, and we've already decided that my inability to ever say that I'd pull the plug on her if she were in a vegetative coma means that her best friend is her health care proxy. On the other hand, my by-the-numbers engineering major sister is going to make sure that no one ever overrules my wishes to lay dramatically in any coma in which I might find myself with fabulous hair and a lacy nightgown just like Hope on *Days of Our Lives*—for at least as long as my lipstick stays fresh.

And the thing that's most likely keeping me from rushing to the altar? Is the fact that I've already been married.

My best friend has a theory that all young girls should produce, direct, and star in their own theatrical production whenever they turn 18. That way they can get the whole fairy-tale princess-bride thing out of the way early on and without the legal hassles or pressure to choose a buffet or served-plate-style reception dinner.

No one ever presented this as an option to me, and seeing as how there was a severe shortage of theater space in my small hometown in Western Kentucky, I did what any good Catholic girl who just wanted to see what was at the end of the gravel road leading out of town would do—I got married. My particular princess-bride moment came the week after I graduated college. I was 21 with hot-rolled, Aqua Net–ed hair and a handful of *Country Bride* magazines to match. I had a maid of honor and four bridesmaids, each outfitted in floral cotton dresses with matching bouquets. I wore a white dress with a long, white train and a pillbox hat with a flowing veil. We hired a high school kid to work as the DJ and kept a keg in the back room of the reception hall. For those of you keeping a record at home—we chose a buffet-style dinner.

It took five years, $600 for the movers, and $1,500 in legal fees for me to get out of that marriage. During those five years, my marriage had gotten me exactly where I wanted to be. Out of Kentucky and into New York City. Toward the end of that particular five-year period, I was on my way to church. (Pardon me here. I have to point out that being the good, if not slightly clueless, Southern, Catholic girl, I had chosen a church located in Chelsea because I liked the dramatic way they celebrated the Epiphany. Lots of red banners and incense. It was incredibly genius. Yeah, clueless.) So on my way to church that Sunday in 1998, I ran into two gay men. They were dressed in identical angel outfits with halos and white wings and they looked stunning. They asked me where Sixth Avenue was and I told them. They ran off and yelled back to me, "Happy Pride, honey!"

I followed them instead of going to church and I never looked back.

Less than a year later, I had hired my attorney, pawned my wedding ring, and dated as many of Manhattan's most eligible lesbians as I possibly could. I had gone to the DMV and various federal agencies on my lunch hours in an attempt to reclaim my maiden name, had gotten my own checking account, and rented my own apartment that came complete with my own utility bills.

I wasn't clueless anymore, and I was definitely never going to lose myself in a relationship again.

The fact that the federal government, my church, and until recently my state government wouldn't allow me to walk down an aisle made it easy for me to keep my own identity in all the legal ways that I found difficult to reclaim after my first marriage. When I finally found the woman I'm going to spend the rest of my life with, my checking account stayed my own, I kept as many of the utility bills as I wanted, and while I did eventually move out of my apartment and into our house, there was not even a question of whether or not I'd keep my own last name.

I was able to enter into the relationship as myself.

While I've figured out how to stay myself within a partnership, I'm not so sure how to do it in a marriage. I'm not sure it's possible. The day-to-day stuff is easy. She cooks dinner and I clean afterward. I pack our lunches to take to work and she makes sure I down a multivitamin every day. I'm in charge of filling out all forms, handling all bureaucracies, and dealing with whatever take-out place we order in from on Friday nights. In return, she mows the yard. It's hugely equal in my eyes, but it's something we've negotiated every step of the way. It literally took us months to decide whether or not the last person to use up the roll of toilet paper had to replace it, or if we could just move the toilet-paper storage area from the hall closet to under the bathroom sink, rendering the whole replacement issue slightly irrelevant. (We chose the latter.)

These are the things that make a relationship. The things that make a commitment. These are the things that allow you to negotiate your couple-hood on a daily basis, while still retaining your complete individuality. We queers have no ready-made, media-controlled role models, no Ricky and Lucys, no Ward and Junes, no Mr. and Mrs. Howells to look to as the Way Things Are Supposed to Be Done. So we get to make them up ourselves. Our expectations become our own—not society's, or our parents' or our religions'—because we negotiated them on our own over the dinner table.

When you sign a piece of paper, however, the state officially steps in and gets to set the expectations. You become a single unit, joined as Party A and Party B into state-sanctified couple-hood. She becomes part-owner of my car and I become part-owner of her house. The Powers That Be at Visa, Discover, and American Express through the power vested to them by the Commonwealth of Massachusetts, consider your credit lines forever joined. And I have no idea if my handshake of a deal with my sister to keep me looking fabulous during any unanticipated comas would hold up under the weight of a signed, sealed, and certified Marriage License.

I want to be with my partner because I choose to be—not because it would be too much a hassle to hire a lawyer to get out of it. I want to wake up every morning (knowing there is a full roll of toilet paper waiting downstairs for me) and know that she chooses to spend another day with me because she loves me, because I make her smile, and because we share a history of care and intimacy that no one will ever come between. I want to be with my partner because I know that she'll make sure I take a multivitamin every morning and I'll always make sure there's fresh coffee ready on the table when she stumbles out of bed.

Maybe someday I'll come up with a good reason to involve the Commonwealth of Massachusetts in our relationship. Maybe someday my company will stop offering domestic partner benefits or my sister will decide it really is a good idea to pull the plug on someone in a coma. Maybe I'll decide it's time to have another big theatrical production, or at least need a damn good excuse to showcase my hot-roller-and–Aqua Net skills. But until then, I'll just keep popping my multivitamin every morning, cleaning up after dinner, and loving my wife each and every day of our lives— without a piece of paper telling me I have to.

Kristie Helms is a Southerner who keeps moving farther north. Her first novel, Dish It Up, Baby, *was recently published by Firebrand Press. Her work has also appeared in* Utne, The New York Press, *and the Lambda Literary Award–nominated* Pinned Down By Pronouns. *Her online diary, now at* www.DishItUpBaby.com *earned a 2001 Best Writing Award from* Diarist.net.

I Do
Kris Hill and Karen Stogdill

Kris Hill and Karen Stogdill were scheduled to be legally married in San Francisco City Hall on the 25th day of March 2004. Instead, they simply got a refund of their filing fee after the courts halted the marriages. However, nearly seven years prior, on June 25, 1997, they did have a marriage ceremony to proclaim their commitment to each other and to seek recognition and support from their families and friends.

The wedding, which took place at Tilden Park in Berkeley, California, was relatively traditional in format — Karen wore a tux, Kris wore a wedding gown — and the vows they exchanged echoed those chosen by many couples before them (sans the religious references.) Given that the marriage had no legal status they also executed wills and financial and health care powers of attorney. Later they registered as domestic partners under California law and drew up an explicit partnership agreement detailing their understandings of their obligations to each other. The partnership agreement specifically states: "As a lesbian couple living in the USA we do not share the same legal rights as heterosexual married couples. However, we do see our union as a marriage. It is our intention to treat any disposition of our assets — should it occur upon death, or upon dissolution of our marriage for any other reason — as it would be treated if it were a disposition of assets of a heterosexual marriage as determined under the laws of the United States of America. This includes embracing the concepts of jointly held property, of equal rights to all earned income, and of the right to alimony if determined to be appropriate by mutual agreement or through arbitration as outlined herein."

Since Karen and Kris are both professionally involved in the field of taxation, and Karen's background is in pension law, they know that it is not actually possible to achieve true equality with heterosexual couples even if it is stated as a goal. It is these rights that are sought by Kris and Karen and many others in the current political movement to legalize gay and lesbian marriages. And it is often these rights that Karen and Kris first espouse when asked by family members or others as to why it is important to be able to marry. But it is really not only about the financial aspects of marriage; it is also very much about love and emotional commitment. It is about the ability to create something more as a couple than can be created alone.

Karen — I Do

The torrid affair replete with steamy sex letters and even steamier phone sex was not the only lure reeling me in to San Francisco back in 1989. It was also my search for the elusive lesbian marriage.

Having come out of the closet (at least my internal closet) amid the feminist movement of the 1970s college campus, "lesbian marriage" or marriage in general, was anathema to the collective goal. The vital feminist analysis of the patriarchy illuminated so well the historical ills of heterosexual marriage — women as chattel — barely a step above slavery. And although Linda Shear performed on stage at the Michigan Womyn's Music Festival in a white wedding gown, it was Holly Near's ode to nonmonogamy that set the behavioral expectation of my lesbian community. It was in this climate that even as we celebrated our tenth anniversary my lover refused to make a spoken monogamous long-term commitment. We didn't plan to ever break up. At that point we were living our lives as though we would never break up (joint checking accounts, joint cars, etc.), but there was no overt commitment. And though I was typically the one to have a romp on the side, I knew even then that I wanted so much more. And so it was after 11 years together that I ran away from home (San Antonio, Texas, at the time) and away from a woman that I loved, and rushed headlong into the fog of San Francisco.

But the throes of passion apparently clouded my vision. For instead of finding my sought-for lesbian marriage I found myself in an extremely destructive love triangle. My new lover was physically committed to me and emotionally committed to her ex. And so my first five years in San Francisco were a nightmare of tears, drama, fear, and heartache. Thank god (goddess) there's a therapist on every corner in the Land of Oz. By the time I extricated myself from the nasty affair I was even further away from believing in my elusive lesbian marriage.

After months of self-imposed reflective isolation I again began dating, but this time I was the one holding back, keeping things casual. By dating more than one person at a time, by dating people in open relationships who already had a primary lover, and by dating transcontinentally I managed to not confront the marriage/commitment question for a while. But as many gay men's ideas of relationship were transformed by the AIDS epidemic, so too did tragedy and death awaken my complacency.

Gayle and Mary Kay lived in the upstairs railroad flat of our Castro Street apartment building. The welcoming home they created was a refuge for me during my darker days and their commitment to each other was a shining example. Their partnership exuded vibrancy, love, warmth, domesticity, and commitment. Their loving example was proof to me that what I sought was indeed attainable. But it was Gayle's sudden death that finally jolted me into action.

In February 1995, Gayle was diagnosed with advanced ovarian cancer. And even the extensive medical knowledge of her lover's nursing career, and the help of friends who were doctors, couldn't stop the cancer. In April, two months after her diagnosis, and a few days before her 35th birthday, Gayle died. I will always be grateful that I was able to be there at her death, and that I was part of the group of friends who provided round-the-clock care for Gayle (and Mary Kay.) But even more, I will always be grateful that while her life and her relationship with Mary Kay gave me hope that a loving lesbian marriage was possible, Gayle's death galvanized my resolve to find it for myself without further ado.

It was that August 1995 that I placed my "marriage wanted" ad in the *San Francisco Bay Times*. This time I was determined not to fall in love with a girl who didn't believe in marriage. And although we might not know immediately if we would wed, we would at least share the goal of finding a spouse.

They say the perfect "soul mate" ad gets one response: While I'm not sure I believe this to be true, my ad only got two responses, and as it turned out I only met one respondent, my future wife, Kris. I required a written response; literacy and intelligence are important qualities to me, not just a sexy voice and hot first date. I was lucky—I got both sex and brains!

Our first date was at La Mediterranée restaurant on Noe Street. Kris beamed those beautiful blue eyes at me and told me exactly what she was looking for (in explicit detail.) She also said that she believed in marriage and very much wanted to get married (so much so that she had been engaged to be legally married to a man and had called the wedding off only a month before the ceremony when she realized that she would be marrying the wrong person). However, from there she landed into her own destructive fling which had recently ended. Now, although she still wanted to be married eventually, she desperately wanted first to just have fun. Her ground rules for the first six months—no doing laundry together, no talking about the dry rot in the bathroom, and no serious conversations—just fun! You can imagine my surprise then when less than two months later she casually asked, "So, what in life is important to you?" It's a miracle we did eventually marry when, caught off guard, and in keeping with our original agreement, my flippant answer was "sex, motorcycles, and football!"

Kris — I Do

From the moment I was assigned this essay, I could see the stakes were high. Failure to produce a sincere, articulate exposition of my deepest personal beliefs about the subject — worse, failure to produce anything at all — would mean not only disappointing my partner's tax clients (the editors of this anthology), thus impairing professional relationships, but would also land me in serious romantic trouble with the woman I love most. And it was our anniversary, too.

Oops, already messed up — I wasn't *assigned* this essay, I *volunteered* for it, some time in the Massachusetts-San Francisco frenzy. Well, and why not? Why not contribute my two-cent squeak to the chorus of voices clamoring for legal status — especially since some of our friends still can't understand what all the fuss is about, even *after* we lecture them on the tax advantages. (Wow, what more do you want — tax benefits! Come on, people!)

But then Karen showed me her essay, and it was so articulate, and so full of feeling, and so moving that I just...choked. Because I don't want to *compete* with Karen (and here's my hot tip for wannabe marrieds: don't compete with the person you love — let them be better than you are at the things they are good at. For example, Karen is much, much better than I am at driving, making small talk, and staying on a schedule, and I just appreciate Karen's excellence in these things and try to stay out of her way when she's doing one of them), but it did seem that my efforts needed to be *worthy* of Karen, who was proceeding to demonstrate just how much better she is at being romantic than I am.

So there I was, with my *voluntary* assignment to write "What Marriage Means to Me" and suddenly the feeling in the pit of my stomach resembled most the one when you have to write "Why I Should Be Promoted This Year" after you have just really screwed something up at work.

It occurred to me that I might need to forget about Actual Reader Karen for a moment and find a different Ideal Reader...someone who actually needed to hear why I want to be legally married. Mom...too easy at this point; Jerry Falwell, too hard. Then I had it! My legions of wonderful tax clients — young, recently married straight people who without exception *could not believe* what I was telling them about California's community property law and its effect on their taxes. I think it's reasonable to infer that they had no conscious intention of making the legal and economic commitment that they actually did make — they didn't even know about it. No intention without knowledge — good enough for Aristotle, good enough for me.

Not just the community property law, either. I'm no attorney, but I think "to have and to hold" translates pretty evenly to "my bad credit is your bad credit" across state lines. Certainly the IRS understands that "my back taxes come out of your seized bank account" pretty well.

So what is it that my clients — they really are wonderful, by the way; they just failed to check out this one little thing — would have been committing to, had they actually understood what they were doing when they did it? I think they would have understood that the legal commitment was the outside, real-world expression of the emotional promises they made when they stood up and said they would keep loving each other.

Perhaps people don't mean wedding vows as a promise. Perhaps they just say *I'll love you forever* and mean: I can't foresee a time when I won't think that you are wonderful. Maybe because few people now use the traditional marriage service, the words don't remind them that marriage is a commitment to the other person.

For better, for worse: I commit to making our marriage work even if it's hard.

For richer, for poorer: I commit to an economic partnership with you.
To love and to cherish: I commit to nurturing you with care and affection.
Till death do us part: This commitment is for my lifetime.

The commitment of marriage is to put the marriage first. A very wise man I worked with once told me that you should never take a job without getting your spouse's commitment to whatever efforts or compromises that job will take, and that if you can't get her commitment *you don't take the job*. Because the job, or the career, only exists to benefit the two of you. The two of you as a unit—you and me against the world, as the song says. Don't take the job anyway and tell her that she'll see the light someday—that's putting you first. But don't take a job you hate because she wants you to—that's putting her first. Put the *marriage* first. Ask: what will it take for us to stay together?

Yes, put in all the qualifiers you are itching to attach—"in a healthy way, no abuse, no stifling the other person, etc., etc." I'm not going to argue with all that—I'm not saying you have to stay even if your spouse is beating the crap out of you. But if you are reasonably sane, and so is your spouse, and you are anything like me, then this advice is for you: Put the marriage first. You, and your spouse, will flourish more inside the marriage than you will outside it. The commitment of marriage will give you room to grow and plan and will enable you to get more done with your life than you would ever think possible.

Economic partnership means both of you get rich or poor together, and each of you does his or her best to make the partnership productive. Nurturing the other person allows them to flourish and nurture you in return. Making a commitment till death parts you forces you to stop thinking of your own good as separate from that of your spouse—you need to make the marriage work, because you are going to be here.

This is an emotional commitment. But it may be risky to make this kind of emotional commitment without legal protection. If the two of you decide that the best thing for both of you is for only one of you to have a demanding (if hopefully lucrative) career, or to have the babies, or any other unequal division of labor, then unless you are married, the law will not treat you as a "unit" if something happens. Something may happen, after all—perhaps your beloved will start beating the crap out of you, and you'll have my permission to leave. But what will you be able to take if you leave? If you don't have legal protection, you may as well keep dividing the bills up 50/50 on the refrigerator door, the way you would if you had no emotional commitment at all, and could split up the pots and pans at any moment.

And that's why I want to be *legally* married. We stood up in front of everyone and promised "for richer, for poorer." But people who get *legally* married really do make a commitment that they (generally) can't get out of: to share the property they acquire during marriage, to be responsible for each other's debts, to share the retirement plan. When Karen and I tried to cover all of it in our domestic partnership agreement, we were appalled at how many details there were. And (being tax people) we were even more appalled at the bad tax treatment when unmarried people have to divide property. (Here's a tip for unmarried people who have to write these agreements: when you are drafting the property-settlement guidelines, think of it as what you will have to do if your beloved joins the Moonies. You'll be more inclined to be fair in that case than if you treat the property settlement as the necessary outcome to a cheatin' heart.)

Frankly, we just want there to be an easy, civilized alternative to writing up all these legal documents. *In sickness and health*: a.k.a., for us, the Durable Power of Attorney for Health Care. *For richer, for poorer:* a.k.a. ditto for Financial Matters. *From this day forward: paperwork, till death do us part.*

Karen & Kris—We Do, We Did, We Want to, Please Let Us!

Did our relationship change after we made the marriage commitment to each other? It most certainly did. In fact we were both a bit astonished at how immediately we felt the change. And since then the love and commitment have grown deeper every year. We are clearer about putting the marriage first and also more practiced at it. We just celebrated our seventh wedding anniversary and so far neither of us has had to invoke the mandatory counseling should things go awry. But rest assured we will if or when the time comes that we need assistance to get back to a healthy place in our marriage. Because after all, you can't always do it all alone. We need counselors to help us out in times of emotional trouble. We need politicians to forge new legal ground to resolve the current inequities. Both can be messy, but both are critical. (Don't forget to vote this November!)

Kris Hill's prior published work includes a fascinating article about the alternative minimum tax capital gains rate in Tax Notes Today, *and an equally compelling article in* Passthrough Entities *on donations of S corporation stock. She is gainfully employed as a tax accountant at Deloitte & Touche, LLP. Kris sits on the back of Karen Stogdill's motorcycle.*

Karen Stogdill is temporarily living in Washington, DC, having arrived there via Indiana, Texas, and California. She makes her permanent home in Berkeley, California. She's been in the tax profession for more than 20 years, first focusing on retirement plans and then progressing to individual income tax. She has her own tax practice serving individuals and small businesses. Prior publishing experience includes a weekly column in her college newspaper and more recently a tax geek article in a trade newsletter. In the off-season you might catch her donning her leathers and riding off on her motorcycle. She is a long-term member and past president of the Sirens' Motorcycle Club of San Francisco. In 1997 she married (sans legal status) Kris Hill.

What If It's Not Gay, Not Same-Sex, and Not Really about Marriage?
Thea Hillman

This is a talk I gave at the 2004 Whole Earth Festival in Davis, California. Gavin Newsom and I had both been invited to speak about gay marriage. I had been told that he didn't feel qualified to be the only voice on the subject at the festival, so the event organizers invited me to speak as well. I was hardly qualified but knew at the very least I could offer a unique perspective. In the end, the mayor didn't attend the festival — to the dismay of many in the audience who had come to thank him. The talk was well-received, nonetheless.

I think all of us here know the importance of what Gavin Newsom has done in San Francisco. I think we understand his courage. I know I appreciate him comparing his relationship with his wife Kimberly to the relationships of gays and lesbians. So, first, I want to say thank you. Thank you to Gavin Newsom. Thank you to Kimberly Guilfoyle Newsom. Thank you to every gay and lesbian couple that got married at City Hall while they could.

But second, I have to tell you: Marriage has never felt so sad to me as it does right now. I feel disappointed that we're fighting for something called gay marriage or same-sex marriage.

Gay marriage, same-sex marriage. The fact that these terms are used interchangeably, and that they are used at all, says so much about how little many people understand about my life.

Both terms — gay marriage and same-sex marriage — erase my experience and my body. And they exclude me from the rights associated with marriage.

Let's talk about gay marriage first:

Two years ago, my brother and his wife were to be married in Oakland, at the courthouse. My lover at the time and I arrived early and approached the desk to find out if the rest of the family had arrived yet. Before we could even speak, the woman behind the desk asked us, "Are you two here to get married?"

You know why that happened? Because my lover is very masculine. To many, she looks like a man. She gets mistaken for a man all time. In fact, despite her sex anatomy, she may be closer to man than woman. She identifies as both, and calls herself transgender. That day at the courthouse, she and I looked like a heterosexual, male-female couple to the woman behind the desk. We didn't look gay and we didn't consider ourselves gay. And so I wonder: How is the term "gay," as in gay marriage, defined? How is it defined by the gay-marriage proponents, and the opponents? Is it two people getting married who are the same gender? Well, I'm certainly not the same gender as my lover. She is transgender and I am not. Is the marriage gay if the two people are the same-sex?

Let's talk about same-sex marriage.

How far could my transgender lover and I have gone toward getting married? What if they had failed to check her ID for the letter *F*?

As for me, I am intersex, which means I was born with sex anatomy that someone decided isn't standard for male or female. People with intersex are often confusing to the world around them when it comes to defining sex. Is sex decided by chromosomes? It's now known that at least 12 chromosomal combinations exist in newborns, including X, XX, XY, XXX, XXY, XXXX, and XXXYY, and five other combinations that would make your head spin and make it very hard to determine sex simply by chromosomes.

Even when the person has the good old XX or XY, sometimes there are hormone variations, like a body that doesn't respond to testosterone—and that intersex person has a very different body than their XX or XY chromosomes might suggest. Is sex determined by presence of reproductive anatomy like testes or ovaries? What about when these are missing or when they are found in nonstandard combinations, like ovaries and a penis? Is sex determined then by external anatomy, whether someone has a clearly distinguishable penis or vagina?

Today, all over the country, doctors are determining the sex of intersex babies by how effectively the genitals will work for heterosexual sex. If the penis is too small for penetration, it gets removed and the boy is turned into a girl. If the clitoris is so large it encroaches on penis territory, it gets reduced. If there is no vagina or a small vagina, it gets enlarged to the extent that it can accommodate a penis. This is done to children, and babies, mind you, who have no say in what's being done to them, nor have many of them had the chance to express to the world what sex they feel they are. These decisions, made early and without the consent of the child, have a huge bearing on who the intersex person will be able to marry later on in their life, regardless of who that person feels they are or whom they want to marry.

All of this leads me to wonder how same-sex or gay marriage has anything to do with my lovers who are transgender and my community, which is made up of many people whose bodies and lives belie the supposed binary that society is so hell-bent on maintaining. I'm not even addressing here the experiences of transsexuals, people who have legally changed their sex, and whose sex and therefore marital rights are called into question when it's convenient, and whose custody, inheritance, and other marital privileges are regularly threatened or denied.

When we grant a person rights, whether it's marriage or anything else, based on who they sleep with, by whether or not we understand their sex anatomy or whether or not we think it's standard, and by whether or not we feel a person's gender fits into what we consider standard, we are discriminating against them based on the limits of our understanding. Said another way, we are discriminating based on our own ignorance.

There's a reason that the religious right was so scared when the Supreme Court struck down the ban on gay sex last June. The case represented a major reexamination of both the rights and acceptance of gay people in the United States. The court went much further than it had to in overturning that Texas law that said states could punish homosexuals for having so-called deviant sex. In overturning it, the court could have argued that gay people should have equal protection under the law, the same protection that heterosexual people have. But it went even further. It went as far as to say that the government doesn't belong in the bedroom of consenting adults. It didn't say married adults, as the state of Texas had wanted it to; it said consenting adults. The Texas law that banned gay sex was ruled an unconstitutional violation of privacy. And this, I believe, is the key to obtaining our rights.

Here's why this ruling is so important to me: When it comes to society's understanding of my body and my life, I believe that our concepts simply aren't large enough. Our concepts aren't large enough to include the idea that people deserve rights even if we can't define or understand those people. The majority of white, straight, wealthy lawmakers and Supreme Court justices will never understand me, my partner, or what I do with my partner in the privacy of our bedroom. And you know, I'll probably never understand what they do in their bedrooms, either. I'll probably never understand their idea of marriage, but the thing is, they don't have to suffer because of my lack of imagination, or my ignorance. And with this Supreme Court ruling, neither should I.

But here's what I'm scared of: In *Lawrence v. Texas*, the landmark case where the

Supreme Court overturned the ban on gay sex, a long list of legal and medical groups joined gay rights and human rights supporters with friend-of-the-court briefs that argued that times have changed since the court said states could punish homosexuals for having what it called deviant sex. These friend-of-the-court briefs said times have changed since the 1986 decision and the court should catch up.

This kind of thinking, that rights are dependent on society's progress, on social acceptance of difference, scares me. Not very long ago, it was illegal to marry someone of a different race. Interracial marriage was considered deviant, abnormal, bad for children, and bad for America. Today, my queer relationship is considered abnormal, deviant, and is not recognized by the government, the courts, or by much of society. Do I have to wait for society to catch up before I'm allowed to marry? Do I have to wait for some senator in Iowa to understand my sexuality, my body, my trans lover's gender before I can have access to the rights of marriage? I can't wait. I just can't.

My solution to the same-sex, gay-marriage question? As long as marriage offers civil rights, and legal, social, and financial benefits, take sexual orientation, take gender, and take sex anatomy out of the equation. Keep the government and the courts out of the bedroom, and out of the underwear of consenting adults. What happened in Texas was true justice and we need more of it. The Supreme Court could have stopped at equal protection, saying gay couples should be allowed the same rights as straight couples, but instead they went further. It said the right to privacy means the government can't regulate relationships between consenting adults. I believe we need language to take this concept further, into our fight for basic human rights.

We need language that includes and protects the basic human right to loving relationships for people with intersex variations, transgender people, poor people, people of different nationalities, people in configurations other than a couple, and people who don't want to get married. Obviously, I believe this language won't include the words "same-sex" or "gay," and it probably won't even include the word "marriage." This fight against discrimination of queers and others who don't fit the current state-sanctioned marriage mold is larger than gay or same-sex marriage. And that's why the religious right is fighting it so hard. There's liberation for a lot of people at stake here. We need language that includes the diversity of people being denied their rights. Until each of us incorporates new inclusive language into our arguments and uses it, we will be excluding many people we need to win this fight.

Thea Hillman is an activist and writer who raises awareness about sexual variations, society's fear of difference, and alternatives to the current medical model of treatment for intersex. Her book of poetry and fiction Depending on the Light *was published in 2001. She lives in Oakland. For more information, visit* www.theahillman.com.

...The Second Time Around
Walter Holland

I grew up in the fifties and sixties in Lynchburg, Virginia. Marriage for me was an institution better suited to quiet colonial houses with boxwood hedges. I met my partner, Howard, in New York City in 1987 at the beginning of the AIDS pandemic. This came after the seventies and years of the Women's Movement, disco, club life, and liberating social rebellion. Marriage was "out" and "living together" was "in" with "bi" the new chic password.

In the late eighties, however, having a partner seemed a necessity. Like the survivors of Hitchcock's *Lifeboat*, the gay community was stuck in the same small dinghy—evil queens and all—leathermen and clones—and the only thing to do was to focus on the bare necessities and row. Everything was chaotic. Tempers were flaring. There was the sense of sink or swim. We were under threat, vilified by the "general population" and the conservative government. Straight marriage seemed like a gated community, a bastion of smugness with drawbridges up and moats flooded. Gays were left outside the walls to die.

Howard and I protested together, marched together, and slept on the same hardwood floors. Meanwhile, married moms and dads came and tossed their sons' lovers out of the hospital and whisked their dying offspring off to the pastoral reaches of America. Married folk locked up shared apartments and auctioned off lifetimes of memories. Straight married lawmakers removed children and deprived natural parents of custody. We heard the rhetoric: "chosen lifestyles," "moral abominations," and "the sanctity of the family and the church." Howard and I wedded twice en masse (a display even the Moonies couldn't have better orchestrated) in front of the Treasury Building in Washington, DC.

Both of us were survivors of "near-marriage encounters of the complicated kind." In the seventies Howard had put down his Uzzi one morning, stopped milking the cows on his kibbutz and said goodbye to his Jewish-American intended (who used to dress up as a Howard Johnson's hostess to serve breakfast in northern Israel). He came back to New York and hired a psychotherapist. At the same time, I said a sobering "no" to my girlfriend whose mother was breathing down her neck for a decision, ready to whisk her back overseas for further husband-shopping should I decline.

My parents gradually accepted Howard. As the *Love! Valour! Compassion!* generation, we dealt with midlife crises, sexual jealousy, adultery, like any other normal American couple. What had started as a political statement, a radical experiment, and a life raft on a stormy symbolic sea, settled into "we're just like everyone else—now shut up and watch *Ellen*."

We shopped at Pottery Barn. We bought from Gracious Home. We puttered upstate in rented cars, browsed for antiques, visited friends who hosted country cookouts. We talked of illusions lost and desires suppressed and found our lives as soapy as any drama on daytime TV. We ran into old tricks or steam-room studs in the checkout at Safeway, watched our fellow gay fraternity buy Snackwell's cream sandwiches and wasabi peas. Life seemed idyllic and traditional. Subaru SUVs, new decks for the weekend house, high quality Dolby sound systems, DVD players, and the ubiquitous gay rainbow flag were everywhere.

In the mid-to-late nineties "commitment ceremonies" appeared. Howard and I were invited to our first in Columbia County, NY. Our friends, Hal and John, were united under a giant oak which they had adorned with ribbons and affirmations. A rabbi and an Episcopal minister recited a scripted ceremony that the grooms had written. Hal and John dressed in linen white. It was a beautiful day and under the tent we each sat at prearranged tables and participated in the "country hoe-down" wearing our complimentary cowboy hats stenciled with their names. Children ran through the house. Babies cried. Family relatives got drunk. Single gay men cruised the band and the caterers. Hal's sister cried. John's brother got drunk, and Howard and I ate cake and dished with a few other guests about the shindig's ultimate cost and the grooms' collective incomes.

From Fire Island to the City, gay couples abounded. The Gay Boomers had settled into households with dogs in tow and the occasional baby nestled in the tattooed arms of the Dads. Rings eagerly were displayed on hands at the gym. Domestic partnership became a reality in New York City, conferred by City Hall. Howard and I went and spent a few hours being processed. Party after party introduced us to the "new gay parents," lesbian couples and successful male professionals talking about PTAs, private schools, and more. Would-be parents analyzed the rigors of the "blender method" (mixing sperm and throwing to chance in vitro fertilization), "surrogate shopping," and "the troubled-teen-adoption-options."

Even my mother, sensing her own mortality, called me in early 2000 to ask if Howard and I considered having children. It seemed her final pronouncement of validation on our relationship (she realized our family line would die out on my watch otherwise). In saying "no" to her, I seemed to set a million family skeletons rattling in the closet. I, for one, couldn't see myself as a parent; couldn't relinquish the childlike insecurities and stomach the weary demons that had long plagued my mind and imagination, nor had I become gay to subscribe to things conventional. Howard, on the other hand, would have been a practical and devoted father.

The Clinton years were indeed the "Gay Decade." The media pumped gay chic over the airwaves and marketed it to the masses. Handsome men in twosomes occasionally began to turn up in the background of 30-second spots for cars or vacation cruises. Our very-pregnant neighbors down the hall (the West Side being the "home of the triple-stroller" — the "Hummer of prams" — and spawning-ground for the metrosexuals) accepted us as the complementary gay couple. Junk mail from charities and misguided lawfirms addressed us as "Mr. and Mrs." Phone solicitors continued to call asking for the "Mrs." of the house.

In academia, Queer Theory had "constructed" both Howard and me into a virtual simulacrum of married heteros, the de rigueur binary inverse. We were analyzed for our essentialist features and saddled with a century's-worth of sexual history and cultural imprinting. The authentic was gone, the signs and referents were scrambled, and even if we had wanted to get married, there was no certainty that the process had meaning anymore or a "context." There was no "there" there. "Outside" was "inside" and "in" was "out."

With my mother now dead, the family house disposed of, my father on his ninth life (traveling the world — he can't sit still), one sister divorced, the other a widow, and one with two daughters on their way to living together with boyfriends then getting married, Howard and I were established parts of the clan.

I took my medical benefits from his plan (although he was federally taxed on the price the company paid out in group insurance premiums — it was considered extra income) and for years we shared the same joint accounts, credit cards, mortgages, and maintenances. We'd been reviewed by two co-op boards in New York City, a process which seemed akin to any pre-Cana the Catholic Church could devise. If we'd weathered and passed all these hurdles, it seemed pretty self-evident that by any stretch we were already "hitched."

But as the new century dawned and 9/11 cast its terrible shadow of anxiety over the land, social unrest has risen and conspiracy theories within and without abound.

Evil seems to be stalking the country, concealed by the most unassuming among us. Difference is suspect and the old rhetoric of antiliberalism—the "defense of the family," the "rooting out of the moral rot within"—seems to have returned. Scapegoats and scape clauses are being searched for. The latest constitutional amendment on the sanctity of marriage seems on the fast track. Those wedding cakes hither and yon with two wax grooms holding hands or two radiant brides seem destined to end up as kitsch on the dustheap of American cultural history.

Howard and I did not line up at four in the morning in Boston, nor fly across the country to the harbor front of San Francisco. We did not endure the jeers of born-agains nor receive floral bouquets from a waiting crowd. Rosie O'Donnell has not knocked on our door yet to give her congratulations.

The truth is this is a newer sort of activism for us, one that apes the very evil that back in the seventies we were persuaded to revile. Truly the issue has energized some of our younger out-generation, who look at the laws against same-sex unions as Germans at the Berlin Wall. They see it as the last glaring artifact of exclusion (along with the "don't ask, don't tell—except during a war" military policy) to be torn down and cast aside. However, just as the East Germans soon found out, having the whole enchilada is not always what it's cut out to be. Getting a McDonald's in your neighborhood or being able to listen to William Hung at all hours of the night is not as desirable as keeping the imaginative edginess of underground dissent and radical otherness.

Driven from the Catholic Church after college when I was counseled by a local priest that if I didn't "act" on my sexual preferences, I could live happily ever after in the eyes of the church (i.e., hypocrisy as a model for faith), I never found "marriage" appealing.

The Church has never welcomed my type back to the altar. Dogma seems its bedrock (apparently the sun still revolves around the earth and the earth's a square cube in the center of the universe).

As a pure civil ceremony, marriage presents a legal institution and an economic contract, which comes with a lot of social baggage and inane, hysteric, fuss. In recent months I have seen the dissolution of three "straight" marriages. I have heard from the ex-spouses as they debate and disagree and seen them break up before my very eyes.

Howard and I have been through two wives with one straight friend and a host of stops along the way from dating, lusting, to re-marriage-re-marriage. Who are the bureaucrats and functionaries that are extolling the virtues of marriage? It's rough and tough out there! The fur is flying in the Fatherland and the soccer moms have more than dinner on their stove (the hubbies all take Viagra). The Beav' has moved on to crystal meth, Ward's gone postal, and June's a multitasking CEO of Hewlett-Packard. All this is to say that the American social landscape has long since changed. The country has progressed and the laws must change with them.

I don't need a paper from the government validating my commitment to Howard. I may need a paper, however, to visit him in the hospital, hold on to his apartment, care for his kids. The point is America is a practical country, a pragmatic land, where freedom was a right and democracy an experiment. It was always meant to push toward new frontiers and new borders, not to retreat into fear and dig trenches. Church and State were separated. If this is being changed (and an amendment to the Constitution certainly reeks of it!), then those of us in the new theocracy would like to know so that we can get our rafts and fishing boats readied.

It's not about marriage at all. It's about the civil experiment; it's about freedom being explored and acknowledged intelligently. It's also about the pragmatic. If Howard and I as a couple can't do what the couple down our hall, who are married, can do, then the laws must be changed. After 16 years of living with him, I would say we are an institution (if not in the Gay National Historic Registry, then besting the average record for straight-marriage longevity).

Walter Holland, PhD, is the author of two books of poetry, A Journal of the Plague Years: Poems 1979-1992 *(Magic City Press, 1992) and* Transatlantic *(Painted Leaf Press, 2001) as well as a novel,* The March *(Masquerade Books, 1997). His poetry, essays, short fiction, and reviews have appeared in various anthologies, journals, and magazines, including* Rebel Yell; The Columbia Anthology of Gay Literature; Bend, Don't Shatter: Poets on the Beginning of Desire; Christopher Street; The James White Review; The Harvard Gay & Lesbian Review; *and* Art and Understanding. *He currently teaches American Literature at The New School in New York City and works as a physical therapist.*

I Do, I Do My Baby and My Baby, My Baby Do Me
Michael Huxley

Like the song goes, "I believe in love." My parents, after all, were a devoted couple for 60 years. Thank god my father was well into the midstages of Alzheimer's when my mother died, for I don't know how he would have endured his loss otherwise.

I began training for marriage in childhood. From my earliest recollection I've had one best friend at a time—always male. And those friendships, without exception, included some form of sex play until puberty put an abrupt end to that aspect of the pattern—for a time. Until my "wild days" in the early-to-mid '70s, my "mad existence" as a single man more than enabled me to make up for lost time.

A sucker for sex appeal, at 22, I fell in love with a gorgeous, semihomeless alcoholic 12 years my senior. You can imagine how much fun my believing that love alone would change him turned out to be. I baled after a year of abuse and abusing, a full-blown souse myself. Moved 1,000 miles away. Either that or one of us would have wound up dead.

Never the same after *that* one!

A sucker for brilliance and talent, I forged ahead. My next lover was a rather well-known concert pianist, 11 years my senior—the affair orchestrated during my first stab at sobriety (1975-1980). Playing my beauty and smarts *almost* as well as he did Beethoven's *Appassionata* sonata, I became altogether smitten with my Parisian-educated Brazilian inamorato who adored me *almost* as much as he did his career. I mean, how *could* he treat me like a mere acquaintance backstage, surrounded by his wealthy, classical groupies after his performances, having insisted that I attend his every concert? Me, who had won accolades of my own for connecting all the dots in my 12-step periodical!

I began tricking out, seeing that, in our 18-month liaison, he never did entrust me with his house key, let alone the one to his back door...

I never confessed my infidelity, even when he did me the favor of suggesting we "go our separate ways." I was shattered, had never been dumped before. My mother, noting my dismay, handed me a Valium, and *my* but didn't I get over "Giancarlo" in a hurry! I still can't help but wonder if he ever made the leap out of the closet, as his numerous hits on the Web don't provide that sort of information.

A sucker for beauty, brilliance, *and* talent, I met Paul Marquis (one year my senior) in a Detroit barroom in 1977. His Eagle Scout mastery of tying the knots that bind not the least of his many talents, Paul is French, and as such, loves to fight, *especially* for justice, yeah...

One evening, a couple of years into our life together, we were having dinner with my parents, the topic du jour being gay rights. Our touching upon the political imperative that same-sex marriage be legalized in the actualization of that goal, my mother, though quick to agree, added: "But you have a hard nut to crack, there."

I have never been able to fathom how couples of divergent political philosophies survive—Mary Matalin and James Carville, the traitorous Maria Shriver and her automaton of a husband notwithstanding. Perhaps it is because Paul and I are such committed partners in outrage: socialists, pinkos, disestablishmentarians, misanthropic humanists, self-described dichotomists who survived the remainder of the '70s and the '80s, and all that time frame's attendant clichés.

We survived my meretricious fall from grace off the wagon that lasted from 1980 to 1985. We survived our fashionable addiction to cocaine. We survived our two-year dabble with an "open relationship."

We survived the plague.

We've survived in sickness and in health, for richer and poorer. We raised Paul's two children from their early teen years on, built a successful business, counted our unhatched chickens, retired to Florida, and have begun new careers.

How "married" can two people be? Our stock response to the astonishment new acquaintances never fail to express at hearing we've been together for 27 years is: "We're registered at Delta Airlines if you'd care to remember our anniversary. And by the way, we *both* 'do the cooking,' just in case you're wondering."

When asked if we plan to "make it legal," we present a unified front in answering, "No, our relationship isn't IL-legal, last we heard…"

Sometimes love *is* enough in abiding uncomfortable laughter and conciliatory pats on the back.

But before I continue, allow me to state that we are hyperaware that homosexuals will never be recognized as equal citizens without securing the right to marry—fuck that "civil union" bullshit—and we will be the first in line to vote for proposed legislation that would ensure that right, and/or the first to show up at demonstrations to protest opposition to it.

But exercising the shorter list of constitutional rights homosexuals are privy to does not negate the facts that Paul and I are children of an idealistic zeitgeist, one in which time has long since weeded out the peace-and-love poseurs from the true advocates of change who took to heart such words as "We don't need no piece of paper from the city hall…keeping us tied and true," and that we have become an anomaly in clinging to, in *growing in* that belief. Hell, the esteemed Ms. Mitchell herself succumbed to marriage (and subsequent divorce) since composing those lyrics; but hey, in my book, enduring art always supersedes the artist who created it.

Since the most excellent editors of this collection *asked*, here we go—and yes, I am also speaking for my beloved spouse, with his preapproval.

We do not believe in the "sanctity" of marriage because, for starters, we are wholly agnostic. If the concept of sanctity is in any way associated with the concept of "truth," then the current divorce statistics are far more "sanctified."

As feminists, we believe that the institution of marriage still connotes ownership, and in so doing perpetuates inequality between partners. We feel that homosexuals, in buying into this, relinquish their opportunity to change what's gone wrong with humanity and reinforce heterosexist prototypes—most blatantly observed in the slave/master dynamic so glorified in homoerotic literature.

Please note that, in these "liberated" times, the great majority of women still choose to take their husband's family name, or hyphenate—relegating their surname to middle name status, which is a practice that women have done for many generations, minus the hyphen. What percentage of men adopts their wives' hyphenated names? Even those women who retain their own name, will, with very few exceptions, bestow their husband's name upon any children the union may produce (before the statistical likelihood of the happy couple divorcing) without as much as a second thought. I *still* hear "I now pronounce you *man and wife*" on TV weddings (that noisome and obligatory "happy ending" tacked onto every final episode)—even on enlightened programming such as HBO's *Six Feet Under.*

Of course when it comes down to who gets what in the divorce courts, the "sanctity" of marriage suddenly doesn't mean shit. Yet without "god's blessing," *nothing* is perceived as valid by a society whose approval every dreamy-eyed, star-crossed pair of lovers (Or is it cross-eyed lovers?) seeks when they bleat and baa down the rigid center aisle of unblinking conformity.

Oh, but the *flowers* are so pretty!

I reiterate: My spouse and I believe that homosexuals will never achieve equality in the eyes of society until our right to marry is secured, and we will vote and protest accordingly. We will, nonetheless, never marry, for why on earth would we seek the approval of a society that, for many many reasons, we do not approve of?

Do we seek the *option* to marry? Of course! Why, I'm still naïve enough to find the very *controversy* offensive! But let's face it, guys, marriage implies monogamy. Just watch Jerry Springer or Maury Povich if you don't think so. And let us assure those of you who haven't tried it that long-haul monogamy is a bear. Why do you think the stereotypic "groom" on TV sitcoms is so oftentimes portrayed as a bumbling moron of last-minute reticence?

Just be forewarned: Beginning on Day One of our hard-won victory to be as miserable as everyone else on this increasingly resource-depleted planet, the society whose approval we sought will be sweating with the effort to keep the record straight, tracking stats on the homo divorce rate. And "god" forbid it should reflect a higher number than the hetero percentage because, if we're not exemplary little boys 'n' boys and girls 'n' girls, they're liable to take our *candy* away...

So be pretty damned sure that's what you *really* want, and not some *Will & Grace* fantasy trip foisted by a power structure that conspires to create hit shows about gay-flavored heterosexuals on commercial television networks.

Mom was right; we do have a hard nut to crack. (Paul Marquis and I have been cracking each other's for 27 years now, and oh how we love to compare notes about the gorgeous hunks we see every day that we'd so love to fuck if human beings weren't the only flawed species on this planet and the universe were a different sort of reality altogether. Why just the other night Paul had sex with Chris Keller from *Oz* in a dream, the lucky bastard.) Hmm...27 years: still less than half the amount of time my parents shared.

When I came out in 1973, it was with the noble conviction that sexual orientation, like race and gender, is a nonissue. Because society's contrarious dictum concerning such matters has ensured that pissed-off idealists *remain* PO'd, I would like to offer the following blessings:

George Carlin bless Oprah and Stedman.

Sinéad O'Connor bless Tim Robbins and Susan Sarandon.

Vanessa Redgrave bless Goldie Hawn and Kurt Russell.

Too bad about Woody and Mia, but y'know what? Gore Vidal bless my parents, and (what I know of) Paul Newman and Joanne Woodward, and Ian Philips and Greg Wharton—this last couple for having taken a courageous political stance early in 2004.

And Paul and Michael bless Michael and Paul, just *because*.

And Bill Maher bless everyone else whose love for another human being dwarfs such ballyhooed common denominators of traditional thought like, "Don't tread on me," which translated means: "Cross this line and I'll fucking kill you."

Yep, marriage ain't for everyone, but...Paul and I certainly don't have any strong feelings about it.

Having accepted the position of Editorial Director at STARbooks Press in April 2002, editor/author Michael Huxley has compiled four anthologies of literotica thus far: Fantasies Made Flesh; Saints and Sinners; Men, Amplified; *and* Wet Nightmares, Wet Dreams. *He resides in Sarasota, Florida with his longtime spouse, Paul Marquis. Feel free to contact Michael at* mhux@flf.org.

Of Course I Do
Debra Hyde

One of the first lessons I learned in life was that family is where you find it. In my parents' case, that was in England during the mid-1950s. My father was stationed there as part of the NATO postwar forces and, during that time, he and my mom were lovingly adopted by my uncle Norman and my aunts, Rosemary and May. It would prove to be a familial tie that would last decades.

As a child, I learned that, no, they weren't my blood relatives, but my parents had accorded them familial standing without reservation and with much affection. Later, I would learn that my uncle and aunts had found each other while serving in the British ambulance corp. There, in the midst of the Second World War, during a time of bombs and rubble and death, they found each other.

As my siblings grew up, we grew curious about our English relatives. At first, we voiced a simple "Why hadn't any of them married?" Later, when we learned that Uncle Norman had purchased a laundromat for our aunts, our interest grew more cagey. Why hadn't Uncle Norman married either of *them*? My parents stood silently by, never answering us fully out of respect for our British relatives' privacy, leaving us to create our own mythology. We decided for ourselves that Uncle Norman had loved them both so much that he could never bring himself to choose between them.

It was, of course, a wildly romantic notion. And years later, after discovering queerness, I garnered the real answer: My uncle and aunts had, in reality, formed an alternative family. And my biological family was fortunate to benefit from their familial love and care for decades.

Indeed, I owe my very identity to my aunts. Before I was born, my mother's desire to high-femme her daughter-to-be was so great that she had planned to saddle me with a name so antiquarian that it carried images of frills, curls, and lady-like curtsies: Priscilla.

But my aunts saved me by pointing out that my nickname would be "Prissy," a name ripe for sneering. Even worse, kids who didn't like me were bound to hurl "Pissy" at me. Horrified, my mother swiftly changed my name to Debra. For which I, in both my childhood tomboy persona and my adult neither-butch-nor-femme queer-loving bisexual self, am forever thankful. (My inner child, the trannyfag, also sends his gratefulness.)

With such lessons starting with my very birth, it's no wonder that on a cold winter's day, a middle-aged me would stand on the steps of Connecticut's state capitol building holding a sign that proclaimed "Straight Mom for Marriage Equality."

Surrounded by 2,000 others people who agreed with me, I used my heterosexual privilege to make a point. I had to. I had to stand as a countervoice to the well over 4,000 presumably straight people who had gathered a week earlier, demanding a Defense of Marriage amendment. I could not let that demonstration—and that desire to further institutionalize prejudice—go unchallenged.

There I stood in allegiance to my queer loved ones and in opposition to straight prejudice. As I did, college students aimed their cellphones at me, took my photo, then waved to me, smiling. A butch dyke spotted my sign and cheered me on. Later, she would get me in a fierce, solidarity-giving hug. An air of accomplishment surrounded us as we made ourselves known. Afterward, when I ordered up a cup of tea before heading home, the guy at the coffeehouse saw the event sticker on my coat and asked me how the rally went. "I wanted to go but I had to work," he said, adding as he handed me my cup of tea, "but my friends were there."

And, in old racist terms, I would've never guessed him as queer folk; he passed so perfectly in straight world. I hope I passed equally well in his. And that someday passing itself will pass into oblivion.

Here, in Connecticut, there's a tension in the air. As a border state to Massachusetts, we're well aware that local forces against queer marriage—largely Christian denominations of both the conservative mainstream and evangelical, charismatic persuasions—have begun pressuring the state to act. But for far longer, a group of activists for marriage equality have quietly worked for social justice with state law-making committees. The judicial department has already been asked—and has answered—just what rights queer folks have been denied by virtue of their orientation. It started with hospital issues, grew to include an examination of probate inequalities, then finally in terms of second-parent adoption and marriage inequality. The codified law has been explored thoroughly and, I suspect, in a depth most U.S. states have yet to contemplate.

In the process, the state government discovered how prejudice proliferated in the deficiency of some 2,000 laws. Already, some next-of-kin issues, such as wills and hospitalizations, have been ameliorated and equalized.

But despite this new awareness, the tension remains, and I expect I'll have to carry my "Straight Mom" sign again in the near future. When I do, I will hold it to honor the many queer individuals who have graced my life.

Specifically, I will carry the sign for my dear friend Lynn. In high school, we were fellow musicians and close friends, me with my gender-neutral (even then) oboe, her with her soft-butch trumpet. After reading a collection of the letters between Tchaikovsky and his patroness in which he had poured forth the torment of being homosexual, I told her how terrible I thought it was that anyone should ever have to live in a closet. Weeks later, Lynn tried to come out to me. Unfortunately, I wouldn't recognize Janis Ian as a lesbian icon until years later. I missed Lynn's cue.

Today, Lynn is a Methodist minister. She advocates from within for both marriage and ministerial equality. For her, I will hold the sign.

I will carry the sign for my son's friend, Danny. At 21, Danny has just graduated from the special-ed school he and my son attend. As someone with Asperger's syndrome, an offshoot of autism, Danny is incapable of looking you in the eye when he talks, but he carries a Nsync concert DVD and a large plastic sandwich bag filled with boy-band pictures with him everywhere he goes. And he knows Asian muscleboys like you wouldn't believe.

I'll carry the sign for Danny because I adore him and resent the fact that the law gives him more legitimacy to marry as an autistic individual than as a gay man.

I will hold my sign up to remember Anna. During a bitter divorce, her spouse went to Child Services and sacrificed their children to the foster system because he loathed her interests in leather sex. Today, Anna lives with and loves an MTF transsexual. She openly advocates for transsexual rights in a world that's even more hostile to transfolk than it is to other sexual minorities, all while carrying a painful, personal burden foisted upon her by an insensitive and narrow-minded system. I will carry it in the hope that Child Services has overcome its own ignorance and reunited her with her own children. (And Child Services should know better, what with the number of throwaway kids who are tossed because they're queer.)

I'll hold my sign up for my cousin, Mary Ellen, and her partner, Susan. Mary Ellen is actually an uncle-by-marriage's niece, but when she came out to her own family, it caused such discord that she moved to Florida. When my dad and his siblings began to retire to Florida, they discovered her there and adopted her and Susan into our family. Two years ago on the sad occasion of my mother's death, I welcomed Mary Ellen with a huge hug and much thanks. Weeks earlier, she had knocked on my mom's door, flowers in hand, on what would turn out to be my mom's last Mother's Day. It was a gesture I will never forget, one that I'll honor by carrying the sign—especially since the state of Florida isn't likely to give her and Sue equal rights anytime soon.

Once again, family is where you find it, what you make of it, and how you appreciate it. Its examples never end.

My "Straight Mom" sign actually honors countless other queer folk beyond those I've singled out here. It starts with my beloved queer writer-friends in Northampton, Massachusetts and includes all the queer folks I worked with in corporate America, lived with in college dorms, and known about town. And it recognizes those young queers I remember, from Sherry, that baby butch who bravely started wearing camouflage to high school in 1973, to Tommy S., who in sixth grade was a flaming queen-in-waiting, biding his time till puberty made him outrageous. Innumerable; these experiences are innumerable.

Of course I want my queer loved ones and friends to have the right to say "I Do" and to be awarded all the benefits that come with the exchange of vows. I want them to have the same rights I do, regardless of whether they'll choose to exercise them. When I first became aware of gay rights as a teen, I saw people joining up and becoming suddenly visible. I saw them fight against social oppression. And immediately I saw it in the same light I saw the civil rights struggle. It made sense then and it makes sense now. The fight for marriage equality is simply the penultimate step in a long upward struggle for legitimacy and inclusiveness.

Feel free to stand against marriage if you wish. Go ahead and question it as an institution. As a minor-league sex radical, I'm more than willing to acknowledge its many faults and shortcomings. But before I can even consider the question of whether marriage should be institutionally dismantled, I must—I absolutely must—fight for all Americans to be accorded access to it, and as long as my queer loved ones are excluded, their fight for greater rights takes precedence and priority over whether marriage is viable as an institution.

As I write this essay, I've just lost a dear friend to a years-long battle with cancer. Tonight, my family will attend her wake; tomorrow, the funeral service. And I'll remember how, in healthier times, we sat together folding her laundry and talk turned to the topic of loving your kids, no matter what. It would be the one time Nick and I would talk about queer rights (and one of the few times a straight mom would openly broach the subject with me). Nick told how she had walked into adulthood with much of the prejudice of her Catholic upbringing, only to find herself re-evaluating it when a gay friend had come out to her in the workplace. During the months she comforted him after his lover of many years left him, her perceptions would shatter entirely and a new mosaic took shape.

"His feelings were just like mine," she told me as she explained what exactly changed her mind about queer folk.

His feelings were just like mine. That was the humanizing moment for Nick, seeing a gay man's heartbreak and feeling it as if it were her own.

I write about Nick not just because she is one of the few straight mothers with whom I've had this pivotal discussion, but because Nick was the first "where you find it" family member of my adulthood. She was the "serious girlfriend," the ex who came before me, yet she and my husband remained friends. Because they actually forged a friendship out of their previous relationship and because that friendship was so genuine, I did not want to disturb it. So I followed the example set long ago by my gay uncle and lesbian aunts: I welcomed Nick as family. She became one of my bridesmaids; my husband was an usher in her wedding; we would become godparents to her son, and she and her husband would return the honor for our kids.

Life's early lesson came full circle.

Every experience I've had in forming and keeping alternative familial bonds, in witnessing queer love and family, and in seeing straight people embrace their own realizations about sexual equality makes my belief in marriage equality resonate more deeply. Every instance confirms it and strengthens it. And it reminds me that it remains my good fortune that I can claim that my family is, thankfully, everywhere.

Pride colors, included.

Equal access to equal rights. It's as simple as that for Debra Hyde. You can find her erotic fiction in any number of major anthologies and witness her convictions in action at her sexblog, www.pursedlips.com. She's most proud, however, that her kids can recognize a marriage-equality sticker when they see it.

Johnny Does Not Want to Marry Me
Francisco Ibáñez-Carrasco

De-Icing the Cake

Don't I deserve to be celebrated by my girlfriends as a bride festooned in tickle-me pink taffeta and showered with emollient lotions and fragrant orchids and frilly presents? Don't I deserve to be told by a mother-in-law to "always keep $500 in the bank— just in case—'cause men are dogs"? I have been a queen all my life; don't I deserve the pageantry and the royal icing hard-on of my bridegroom searching under my fluffy gown? Or conversely, don't I deserve to be taken out by my gym and workplace buddies on a stag night to get hammered? They would tramp me around town, getting crazier and crazier, tie me up hugging a tree, bare-naked under a minty-fresh polyester negligee, and I would be scorned with a friendly sneer by a pudgy police officer who caught our sophomoric party. He would pat us on the back, like a father to a child, and tell us to finish off our stag party at home. Don't I deserve to be hauled upstairs by my best bud, my Mercutio, the one not yet married because he is too busy getting an MBA and lots of pussy, the strapping 6'2" Polish hockey player who drove me home in the bluish dawn light, got me to my bachelor pad, undressed me, plunked me onto my crumpled sheets and collapsed by my side, laughing, shirtless, resting on one broad shoulder, laughing a bit more, but our eyes glazing, our tongues humid, and our breath reeking of scotch as he closes in on me. In two days I will be married. We were hammered. Isn't it all about getting hammered? Something between my tongue and my upper fillings hardens like royal icing.

Spectacle and Market-Choice?

Johnny does not want to marry me. I want to marry him. Seldom do people who agree in principle disagree so forcefully in practice. This has generated some friction in our two-year-old household and in our seven-year-old relationship. Although no extended family member has gone all Capulet and Montague on us, they have volunteered strong comments, some benign and some offensive ("So you wanna a big party, eh?"), some thoughtful and some too serious. I want to get married and Johnny does not, but we all seem to be feeling a great deal of ambivalence. Let's look at the reasons…

Marriage is available. Why not use it? I wanted to get married because a new law exists; it is like a brand-new tool. Ursula Franklin, a Canadian thinker, said that when we have a hammer everything begins to look like a nail. Sometime after my initial (and Catholic) glee at the possibility of marriage, I still hear the bells in articles and stories ringing with the archaic trappings of heterosexual marriage. Once the nail is in, it is hard to get rid of it, and it mostly comes down to an ugly divorce between nail and wood, between the egos fastened together on the shingles of a constructed house—the clauses of life insurance, the purchased appliances and pets (and sometimes children). This is not to say that there do not exist those who marry because they want to be with each other and find it a respectful way of showing their covenant to others and to themselves. Just as there are those who marry because they have money and can afford the heterosexual multimillion-dollar industry's wedding pageantry with its guests and food and bridesmaids and royal icing. I would want to get married because the law exists, but I do not want to get divorced because the law exists. I want to have my cake and eat it too.

I am one of many, probably, who thinks about divorce or separation as a failure.

Johnny, who possesses a heightened sense of justice, does not want to get married. He has seen the ethical implications of this long before I started writing my first line. In 2004, queers do not need to get married simply because marriage has become one more choice in a Wal-Mart of tool options for good living. We start to need neither Botox nor Cialis simply because they are available. We live, however, in "spectacular" times; everything is on display as if we're living constantly in the glass house of a reality show. We want to be the spectacle, the exploitative truth, the exposed gaze; we need to be part of this spectacle simply to show that we can.

Care?

I give myself to one man each time I fuck with one man, and I give myself to many if I fuck with many. Queers (and this includes males and females) share ourselves with many, even though we still do it with tremendous moral fear, social guilt, and at considerable biological risk. If not a virtue, the practice of promiscuity amongst queers should be upheld as a no-nonsense rule because it entails care for oneself and the others—each time, in each new body, in a river of salt and tears and fluids. Promiscuity entails consensuality and maturity. Coercion, fear, and self-repression make condoms fissure and hearts break. Queer promiscuity can be caring and careful, interesting, and worthwhile, and at times it can be messy and melodramatic. I have heard that monogamous marriage is exciting too, and I believe it. Promiscuity and marriage are not at odds; they sleep in adjacent rooms. I have heterosexual friends with lovely wives whose platonic relationship with their best hockey buddy would never be questioned. They do not put each other's dicks in each other's mouths. But is carnal sex the only measure of promiscuity? Or, asked in a different way, Is the enjoyment of one single body for all eternity the true measure of monogamy?

When Johnny and I accepted to live together, pool resources, fight, clean our toilet, and sleep in one bed, we were both accepting to lie with the ghosts of many—dead or alive—whose DNA signatures are inscribed under my nails, in my warts, in my herpes outbreaks, in the HIV in my bloodstream. The 1980s' safe sex fear-mongering message, "when you fuck one, you fuck many" (worded nicely back then), wasn't completely off the mark. I am his "Six of Twenty" (and he is my "One of One Hundred"—and I am being modest here), as in the character from *Star Trek: Voyager*, Seven of Nine. If one in the community feels the joy, the envy, or the pain, we all do. If I get married and I am happy, we will all be happy. But will we all be happy? Do queers care for each other this much? Or are we too complacently content with the sexy moniker "queer," the TV shows, the common-law rights, and other democratic hand-me-downs? Are we allowed to care for each other this much? I think Johnny is right. We should postpone the wedding until queers show that we care for each other and not for the ritual or the covenant that supposedly envelops us in a rising bubble. Marriage throws us in bed with the community at large; thus, marriage should legitimate our carnal community, communication, and communion instead of being a bill of moral clearance. Marriage should prove that we can be deeply individualistic, pursue our pleasure and desire, and that we are, at the same time, in profound solidarity with each other. Choose to marry the mob once the mob chooses to accept that they will be living with you. We come full circle, our living our promiscuity, as our unwedded couple does not seem too different from the way that normal heterosexuals live their marriages.

Serotriage?

If love is a battlefield, queer marriage may be a form of serotriage. Johnny and I are serodiscordant. Two people marry even though one of the partners is crazy, in a wheelchair, or worse, poor. People love and marry each other, and these are said to be great equalizers. Probably love is the great equalizer, but romantic love is fleeting and unions tend to abate if not cemented in affection and respect. I have lots to gain by marrying Johnny. I have a disability; I might die young (I have been waiting for 20 years now); and having been near the gates of hell and back, I want to have somebody to hold my hand, clean my shit, and probate my will (and the debt attached to it) without killing my dignity with smothering pity. However, Johnny is a smoker and works painting walls perched up on high ladders. If something happens to him, this "security insurance" would be shot. I would personally go and kick him on his deathbed for ruining my plans about my now-uncertain future. I've already buried one lover in 1993; I don't need more widowhood. Ah! I get it. This is why we probably marry: to acquire an existential sense of security that all our critical scenarios will be covered. Still, we are mostly alone, trapped in our victim-like and/or celebrity-like personalities, and the slow burning of our flesh. No one can save us from our destiny and ourselves. Damn it. Well, I wanted to marry to announce to all those AIDS bitches and victims out there that I had been able to lasso an HIV-negative man, but marrying to seek revenge on the world and my misfortunes or to have a trophy–construction worker–Anglo-blond-stud husband are not good reasons—they are boomerangs! Marrying to protect an illusion is not a good idea—an illusion that I do not need anyone else, that I am out/above/beyond the sexual market, that it does not matter that the anti–HIV drugs are taking a toll on my mirror image with fat redistribution and weird side effects, that I have left all banality, vanity, and the sexual treadmill behind. No husband by my side will save me from disease, depression, or that testosterone-based sense of competition, with others, with destiny, with myself. Johnny is wise and noble, and he saves himself for bigger battles than marriage.

Family?

Queers have raised their own children or other people's children for generations. Haven't homosexuals lived in couples of good uncles, or "good friends," for years? Serving in silence their godchildren and servicing their fathers. With the advent of AIDS, we told ourselves a sinister but truthful maxim: "Silence equals death." Does this maxim apply to those who would rather not announce and implement their relationship of convenience, love, sadomasochism (or some/all of the above combined) as a legal marriage? The privileges of marriage—understood as the heterosexual contract—have always existed to be reaped by those who already bring into the covenant shitloads of social privilege. If we had not been this damned poor, if I had not been this old already, if I had not been HIV-positive and Johnny a smoker, I would have married to have children. (I think of my mother as queer in this respect.) My mother was a single mother in the 1960s in Chile where it was still a stigma. Isabel bedded a young married man (who dated her on the side) and gave birth to me. Isabel never saw Victor again. She wanted a child so she could become what was seen as a whole woman in that society at that time, a society in which a female was either a virgin mother or a virgin whore. She also expected not to be left alone—we all want someone to vouch for us in the world in our time of need—and the stereotypical but supple umbilical cord between a (Latino queer) son and his mother is a monogamous relationship I trust as invincible. If I had married Johnny and we had adopted a child, I could have been a whole man, maybe. Maybe I could have later forgotten about Johnny or he could have taken off with some sweet seven-year-itch or become an alcoholic or, worse, could have left me for a young woman. I honor my mother's decision to give birth to a child for practical and loving reasons with the help of an accidental sperm donor. She never expected anything from this married man; she never saw him again in her life; and she never spoke evil about him or any other boyfriends. Maybe this is why I became a slut. I wanted to become pregnant and worked so hard at it; the intention was good: to form a family, my family, though the necessary hardware was not in place. By the time the legal right of homosexuals to adopt children and marry came, I was too late in the race; I had collected a bit more sperm than necessary. But I did have a family of sorts, a motley crew of friends and enemies I have nurtured over a lifetime.

Convenience?

I want to get married without complications, and certainly I'm too fucking poor to be thinking about taxes and the possibility that Johnny might hate me one day and sue me over the custody of our neurotic cat, Lucy. I live from pay cheque to pay cheque. Under Canadian laws, we are bound by common law already; he can sue me for whatever little I have today if he wanted. It sounds like we have to marry simply on good faith and a wing-and-a-prayer that things will be fine between the two of us. Looking at the heterosexual track record this may be possible; straight couples marry and keep at it for over 50 years, but what I see in that is a compassionate companionship, an oasis against the eroding sands of the day-to-day. My dream of marrying a hard-footed male who comes home to find me at the kitchen, barefoot, pot holder in hand, gripping a steaming casserole of tuna and crumbled potato chips, aroused by a quick kiss, douched and ready to be mounted vigorously in the course of a romantic evening becomes liquid that quickly slips through my fingers. Queer marriage looks to me now more like the type of dyke relationships we used to love to mock: *What do dykes bring to their first date? A U-Haul.* I want to get married to share the mortgage, the family members we detest but endure over the holidays, to debrief at the end of the day after work, and to attend the memorial services for the sudden cancer deaths of longtime heterosexual friends who seemed to have had it all— gorgeous, endowed, rich, and talented. Johnny says that if these are the reasons we want to be married, we're married all right—why would we need a ceremony? I hadn't realized that I got married the day I moved into this house in plain view of the neighbors, our friends, my mother, my co-workers, and the government. I wish I had worn something prettier that hot summer day. We were sweaty, pumped, driven, and so horny at the end of the day. What were we thinking? We should have taken the whole moving ceremony more seriously.

I Dream of Johnny

Doesn't practice make perfect? I have rubbed men so many times to see what genie budges from them. When we find a new tool, we think it can be used for anything and everything. We need to recognize that marriage is actually less like a sacrosanct ritual and more like a new set of social tools recently made available to queers. Historically, it has been used to preserve bloodlines and wealth. Artificial insemination and test-tube babies and sperm banks have done away with some of its utility. Those, however, who have applied for bank credit as singles and at other times as one of two employed partners can attest to the notion that marriage is used as a "measure of (hu)man(hood)." Aside from this, marriage is a debunked ritual and covenant, made a mockery and a mess of in the Western societies. Yet, if we are prepared to accept that marriage has not outlived all of its social usefulness, then this social tool of marriage— akin to the suffrage to elect our civic representatives—might still be useful. If practice makes perfect or at least improves our public good as civic individuals, we should still get into queer unions because there is a good chance we might improve our collective social lives. No, we should not get married just because we can—this is one of the accusations I hear from across the table when the subject is brought up and I state I want to marry Johnny—but we should get married because it is only by making good use of this social instrument that we can build our version of gay marriage as a viable social institution.

The maxim "The master's tools will never dismantle the master's house" could be true here, and I reckon that my view of queer marriage is utilitarian. But cut me some slack; I'm seeking a place to begin. I wouldn't like to live in a country where I am not allowed to become a permanent resident and later a citizen with the right to vote. I am prepared to meet the criteria selected to become a citizen and a voter. In fact I met it when I became Canadian in 1991, and as such I have made my share of mistakes and my share of good choices. Similarly, if I were married, I wouldn't expect it to be any different. I believe that if one has the right to vote and does not use it—as many neglect to do—one is contributing to a fraying of the civic network by not participating in it. By the same token, I believe that only by marrying another man and by making use of this social tool to build a covenant that is neither reactionary nor smarmy—that could uphold some of the significant sexual mores of our queer culture such as promiscuity and perversity—and only by participating directly and taking the risk of it being recognized by all communities, can we take our chance on this beat-up social institution of marriage. Johnny says that he supports any queer couple who wants to get married, but he will not marry me. I feel that he supports others but not me. This ambivalence leaves us both straddling the white picket fence of society.

Love?

I want to get married because it means that I would give myself to one man forever in body and soul. I write this and I squirm. And not fuck anyone else anymore? The sweet bi Italian young man at the gym who leans over in the shower stall to expose his rosebud every Tuesday? The tall thick-mustached, strapping garbage collector who looks at me with disdain as I expose myself at the rear bathroom window on the second floor and spits with fury in the early morning light and hurls the refuse and spits again, steaming thick spit, and climbs up the robust truck? Half a block away, at the corner of 2ⁿᵈ Avenue, he looks back and up to my window again. And spits. So many men, so many infections, so little time. Let's try another formulation of the same idea: I want to get married so I will have someone to call "my own." I write this and I squirm. Great expectations. I expect this one man—or a platoon of gentlemen in serial monogamy—to fulfill, if not every wish of mine, many of them: sexual, emotional (financial?), etc. This man is to abate my solitude, my cravings, and to support my petty ambitions and my crazy dreams. I chastise myself for accepting anything less, for capitulating and conceding. I say to myself, *I think less of my partner because he is my second choice, a compromise, the lesser evil.* My first choice for a suitor (Justin Trudeau on cold days, and when feeling randy, Ashley MacIsaac) might never come, and I am too scared to wait alone, feigning sturdiness and dignity in a virtual bathhouse cubicle online, in every blind date with a toad that never metamorphoses, at every rave or art opening, head up high, nose in the air, dignified, crawling on all fours, seriously believing that the leather master who is dogging my ass *really is* a young dominant bisexual man who sits open-legged in chaps and smokes cigars throughout the day. Or I say to myself, *I would have too little self-esteem to rise to the occasion when a real man comes.* My contrived dreams and the stereotypes we gay men twirl in the heads of our dicks make me chuckle. I look down onto our garden. I see Johnny tending his flowers in his worn-out Dickies, the sun shining on his fair face, aging beautifully; I see Lucy the cat circling him mischievously; and I see that my second choice is not even close to a fairly-tale prince but is so fucking real that I could burst into laughter and tears and melt at his feet every single time.

Francisco Ibáñez-Carrasco was born in Santiago de Chile and has lived in Canada since 1985. His novel Flesh Wounds and Purple Flowers: The Cha-Cha Years *was published by Arsenal Pulp Press in 2001. His short stories included in North American erotica anthologies are gathered in a volume titled* Killing Me Softly: Morir Amando *and was published by Suspect Thoughts Press in 2004.*

Reporter Covering Right's Reaction
to Gay Marriage Loses It
Rik Isensee

CAMBRIDGE, MA—Dozens of same-sex couples marched into history today as they obtained marriage licenses and married legally for the first time in the good ol' U. S. of A. The states of New York and New Jersey immediately promised to recognize their marriages as the floodgates of a new era of gay civil rights burst open to resounding cheers.

But of course somebody had to piss on their parade: "We will never recognize gay marriage!" swore Davy Doolittle, member of California's state legislature. "It's immoral, it's sacrilegious, it undermines the family!" and all the other whiny gripes we've heard over and over again in this never-ending dispute. I just hope the Supreme Court cans every one of the states' antigay marriage laws, just like they did with the antimiscegenation laws back in the sixties.

Oops, that's not very objective reporting, is it? But sometimes a reporter's gotta do a little editorializing, or he goes bonkers. The same old ridiculous claims and homophobic diatribes—Good God, what's going to happen next, are we gonna let Joe Schmo marry his dog?

And what kind of example are we setting for our children? My Lord, what would happen if they saw people who actually loved each other form a committed relationship? The family faces imminent destruction! We're going the way of Rome, or Sodom and Gomorrah! Every great civilization that's fallen because of its inner corruption, all caused by men giving each other a wank—Oh, please. You'd think the sky would fall in, the way they carry on about it. If I recall, Rome didn't fall until after it converted to Christianity. Light that cigar and puff on it.

The truth is, these homophobes are afraid their own kids will start getting bright ideas. Once they know gays can get married, why, they'll all want to become gay, too! They already copy every gay fashion that comes down the pike, so what's next? If you give any legitimacy at all to these perverts, the next thing you know they'll want to marry your son. Everyone knows they're out to recruit every kid this side of Hoboken into their sordid lifestyle—and maybe your own son will turn gay just to spite you!

Well, we've all heard this claptrap before, and frankly, I'm weary and bored with it. Maybe I'm burnt out covering the Bible beat, and I need to take a breather by reporting on mineral extraction, or Serbian iconography. My editor says I gotta get a grip; if I can't maintain a more objective tone about these episodes, he's gonna transfer me to the Guinea pig–caught-in-the-plumbing beat.

But these self-righteous, Bible-beating, blathering idiots really goad my gizzard. Why the next thing you know, they'll be claiming that all gays want to do is piss in their coffee and give them AIDS. As if they didn't have better things to do, like get on with their lives.

These nutcases should get a job, get a life, get a wife! Every repressed desire in their own misguided disgruntled minds gets projected onto gays. It's all so transparent, it's ludicrous. Like the old canards that the Negroes are gonna rape our women, and the Jews are gonna eat our children.

Yeah, right. Everyone knows what gays really want more than anything else is to suck on some straight guy's dick, who in any case usually just lies back and enjoys it, like who really gives a fuck what gender your mouth is? A blow job is a blow job.

Rik Isensee is the author of The God Squad, *a spoof on the "ex-gay" movement, and* Spank the Monkey, *where this essay originally appeared. In real life, he practices psychotherapy in San Francisco, and has written three self-help books for gay men. Check out his website:* www.rikisensee.com.

First published in *Spank the Monkey — Reports from the Front Lines of Our Quirky Culture,* Unlimited Publishing, 2003. Reprinted by permission of Unlimited Publishing.

The One Ring
Aaron Jason

"...and in the darkness bind them"
—J.R.R. Tolkien

"What if the One Ring is really a wedding ring?"

"I can see where this is going."

"No, seriously, think about it."

"You're going to tell me that the whole *Lord of the Rings* hubbub is about a wedding ring? If this is another of your queer-theory tirades—"

"You don't know what I'm going to say."

"Let me guess, something about the One Ring being a symbol for Frodo and Sam engaged in some sorta gay marriage, right?"

"See? You made the connection!"

"A little head-cradling and maybe a parting glance or two hardly means anything."

"That's because you've only seen the movies. Much more happens in the book, which you'd know if you read it."

"I couldn't get past page 110. I didn't think *anybody* could."

"Regardless, the Ring is the perfect symbol for gay marriage."

"We're talking Hobbits here, right?"

"Think of traditional wedding bands. If the man's is thicker than the woman's, then what about us? Which are we supposed to wear?"

"Take your pick, really. How about identical ones?"

"No, don't you see. That's why the One Ring is so perfect for us. One that's shared. It's a union, a same-sex thing."

"Like Frodo and Sam, right?"

"Again, from your lips."

"But didn't that Lucas Haas wear it all the time? He hardly shared it with What's-His-Bucket from *Rudy*."

"What's-His-Bucket was Sam. And it was Elijah Wood, not Lucas Haas."

"Well maybe it should have been. He seems more Hobbity."

"Sam helps out, but Frodo's really the more dominant of the two."

"More so than a butch gardener?"

"Sam may seem butch, but he's quite domestic; always cooking, cleaning, and pruning."

"So the top gets the ring most of the time? Which means what, that I'll have it on odd days and you even? Besides, Sam is such a masculine name. Frodo sounds so, well, girly."

"Both their names are perfectly ambiguous. How many Frodos do you know, male or female? And as for Sam, well, think Samantha from *Bewitched*. Or anything with Samantha Morton. Or Mathis for that matter."

"Or Martha Plimpton?"

"My point exactly! The name is sexually fluid."

"Sexual fluids and Martha Plimpton?"

"It doesn't matter which one of us, or whatever couple in general wears the ring. As long as it's worn. Besides, it's really only in the twentieth century that grooms began wearing rings. For thousands of years it was only the woman. The Greeks thought that if a ring was placed on the third left finger, that it connected to the heart via some vein. And Tolkien knew his Greek."

"But I thought that Gyllenhaal guy always wears it on his index finger?"

"It's not Jake Gyll—forget it. This is beyond Frodo and Sam. Think about Gollum."

"What the hell *was* he anyway?"

"He was once like a Hobbit but was perverted by the Ring."

"Perverted, eh? So he's a symbol of gay divorce?"

"No, no. He's an even *better* symbol for gay marriage. Remember, he's got two sides: He used to be good Smeagol, then turns into evil Gollum. But his dual nature never really leaves, that's why it resurfaces in the end. He's good and bad, master and slave, masculine and feminine, yin and yang all rolled up in one. And all thanks to the One Ring, a ring that marries his natures together. Remember when he argues with himself?"

"You mean in the second movie? Or the third? I'm a little fuzzy on that one."

"No wonder. You slept through *Return of the King*."

"The book or the movie?"

"Both it seems."

"It was long. I tried."

"You slept through it twice."

"Well things go down hill after the first. That Viggo just gets grimier. And frankly I like Gandalf as a crusty ol' hippie smoking out with Hobbits, not when he's all white and holy like Christopher Lee—who looks much too much like Cher with that white wig. Hey, maybe that's the gay connection you're looking for. Cheruman."

"Cher?"

"Certainly gayer than Gollum."

"Don't you remember first seeing him in *The Hobbit*?"

"The book or the cartoon?"

"Both. He was sitting by a pool and talking to himself so lovingly just like Narcissus. And who could be gayer than Narcissus?"

"Cher? Okay, okay, I know. And Tolkien knew his Greek, right?"

"How about that deep, dark cave Gollum lived in. It's like he was in the closet and came out. Came out to reclaim his Ring, reclaim his right to marry."

"Himself, that is. Nice. Look, you have the right to reclaim your senses while I donate your Sedgwick books to the local thrift. He doesn't even *wear* this wedding ring of yours through most of it. So even if he *is* gay, how could he symbolize marriage?"

"It just goes to show that in marriage, we lose our identity. And only when its symbol, the ring, is cast off, our individual selves return. So if you and I are going to merge completely, we need only one ring."

"Oh yeah, this circular logic certainly rings true. So tell me, why doesn't Frodo just marry himself?"

"He has Sam."

"We're back to that again, eh? Full circle?"

"You might say that."

Aaron Jason's work has appeared in Men on Men 7, Blithe House, HGMFQ, Washington Square, *and the prize issue of* The Mississippi Review. *He is fiction editor at* Lodestar Quarterly *(www.lodestarquarterly.com) and teaches at Cal State Hayward in the Bay Area.*

A Tale of Two Marriages
Matt Kailey

I've been married twice in my life—just like almost everyone else who is legally allowed this type of union. One marriage rarely seems to be enough, does it? But people who can legally marry get to make up for those who can't—almost as if they're thinking, "I'll take mine and, well, since you're not using yours…"

The first time I married, the wedding took place in a church, at my fiancé's insistence, and was presided over by a conservative minister who refused to allow my two song choices—"Somewhere" from *West Side Story* and "Time in a Bottle" by Jim Croce—because they were too secular. He finally relented, grudgingly, on a song called "One Hand, One Heart," which I don't even remember but that I threw out there as sort of a grab-bag pick. The vows were directly from the Bible, including some verses from the Song of Solomon about love being patient and kind. My fiancé, along with the minister, orchestrated the wedding—what would be said, what music would be played, what vows would be taken—because he wanted me to become a good Christian woman, and he wanted our home to be a good Christian home.

A portrait of a flaxen-haired, blue-eyed Jesus hung on our living room wall. Jesus was watching over us—he was watching the anger, the threats, the emotional and physical abuse that constituted this good Christian marriage. It didn't work out.

My second marriage took place in a friend's backyard, overseen by a judge who married us with a beer in his hand. I wore a pair of white jeans decorated with rhinestone studs and a matching vest. My husband wore khakis and a plaid shirt. It was a wonderful, secular marriage that lasted as long as it possibly could, given the emergence of my gender issues, which eventually led to my gender transition and the inevitable divorce. But I will never forget this incredible man—a man without a bigoted bone in his body, a man who believed that everyone was equal, that everyone was good, that everyone was valuable and deserved equality under the law.

Two marriages. One was holy, sanctified by the church and by God. But curiously, that extra "benefit" did little to make it a marriage of love and happiness. Now there's nothing wrong with a holy union of any kind. But the idea that God is going to make a marriage solid, workable, or wonderful just by having it meet certain standards of approval is as off base as the religious arguments that are used to deny same-sex couples the right to make the same mistakes that straight couples do—arguments such as:

The Bible does not condone same-sex marriage. Maybe it does, maybe it doesn't. There are so many interpretations of the Bible that we can find just about anything in its pages to use in whatever way we please. The Bible also says that those working on the Sabbath should be put to death. But yet George Bush encouraged us to shop to fight terrorism, and all the malls are open on Sunday. So if we live by the literal Bible, we will have to kill everyone working in the mall on Sunday. While the Evangelical Christians are busy doing that, I think I'll go to one of my friends' commitment ceremonies.

Men and women were meant to marry because opposite sexes complement each other. Hmm. My friend has been married for years, and the last time her husband complimented her was when he told her that her butt was finally getting a little smaller. No, wait, I don't think that's what it means. Men and women *complement* each other—they balance each other out (not counting my friend's big butt, which tends to tip the scales in her direction). But they seem to have trouble doing this on their own.

An entire genre of literature has been built around the fact that men and women are from different planets, that they can't even understand each other, let alone balance each other out. I'm not sure exactly how this one works, but I do know that it's a lot easier to drive my friend to the bookstore to buy these books now that her butt has shrunken.

Marriage is for procreation. If this is true, marriage is in serious trouble indeed. If we stick to this argument, almost no woman over the age of 50 should be allowed to marry. If two people in their 70s fall in love, they're just shit outta luck. Taken to its extreme, we would not only deny marriage to older Americans, but we would have to test every single person who applied for a marriage license for fertility. Hysterectomy? Sorry. Next, please. Low sperm count? Come back when those little guys start to be fruitful and multiply. And even if two people got a clean bill of reproductive health, we would have no idea whether or not they would be able to produce a child together. In that case, there would be two options: we could either insist that they have sex prior to the wedding until the woman gets pregnant, thus proving that, as a couple, they can conceive, or we could issue a temporary marriage license — one that expires in, say, two years. If the couple has not been able to conceive a child within the two-year grace period, the marriage license would be revoked and the union would be put asunder. So what if they're in love — they couldn't produce the goods. Under this argument, love doesn't seem to have a whole lot to do with marriage.

God made Adam and Eve, not Adam and Steve. Yes, but Eve ate the apple and brought sin into the world. Steve wouldn't have touched it. It would have destroyed his abs. On the whole, we would have been better off.

All of these arguments have a basis in religion. There hasn't been one legitimate argument set forth against same-sex marriage based on anything but the Bible and what God supposedly wants. Now I can certainly provide a book full of details about the holiness and unholiness of my own first marriage, but I will only sum it up to say that if that's what God wanted, then all marriages should be outlawed for good before someone gets killed (in fact, many already have). But I don't believe for a minute that a truly benevolent God, which seems to be the god of choice for most religions, would begrudge anyone a happy marriage. He or She might, however, disapprove of hatred, prejudice, discrimination, and violence being spread in His or Her name.

Matt Kailey is a Denver journalist, author, and public speaker. His first book, tentatively titled Just Add Hormones: An Insider's Guide to the Transsexual Experience, *will be published by Beacon Press in the spring of 2005. He can be reached through his website at* www.mattkailey.com.

Lincoln's Birthday
Davina Kotulski

It was Lincoln's birthday
He would have been 190-something years old
The writer of the Emancipation Proclamation
The leader who unshackled this country from the misery and suffering
    of human slavery
A white man who saw the humanity in those of African descent,
While the white majority only saw inferiority.
Did he not say "A house divided cannot stand"?
I wonder what he would say about today's country divided on marriage
    for same-sex couples.

A large wall has stood for hundreds of years
Built with bricks of hate, but mostly ignorance
Dividing those who love openly
And those whose love dare not speak its name

It was a fresh-faced mayor
Who did more than mouth his pledge to defend the Constitution
Against all enemies
He actually read the document he had sworn to uphold

Then, seeing the injustice of the wall and noting its cracks
Wielded a mighty hammer
In the name of justice for all,
And I was there that day.

It was the fifth year that I had come to San Francisco City Hall
To ask for a marriage license with my unlawfully wedded wife, Molly.
We had had a wonderful ceremony with 150 family members and friends in 1998,
But we wanted the legal protections.
The 1,049 federal and several hundreds of state rights that come with marriage.

For five years in a row I stood at the marriage license counter
Waiting to be served,
Stuffing my humiliation as I turned to comfort my weeping Molly,
A put-together attorney in many areas,
But unable to hold back the tears when the clerk handed her the paper
"One unmarried man and one unmarried woman"
Year after year.

I knew that one of us could walk out on the street
Grab a stranger of the opposite sex and be married in moments.
I have seen nongay friends and co-workers marry and divorce and re-marry
In the almost eight years we have been together.
I have watched celebrities marry for a joke,
People marry for millions on TV,
Seen inmates at the prison I work at marry,
And know that child molesters, death row inmates, and serial killers can marry,

While she and I have been denied.

I had my couples therapy class define marriage.
They spoke about love, commitment, respect, and companionship.
These things were nowhere on the marriage form.
The form said "man and woman only."

For five years we were denied,
Turning around to see others laughing and rejoicing
As they filled out their marriage license applications,
And said "I do"s,

But then,
On Lincoln's Birthday
It all changed.

Instead of disapproving faces,
There were smiles,
We were welcomed in
Given a number and a form to fill out.

We raised our right hands and surrendered $82 to the clerk who kindly
Verified all the information.

I looked into my bride's eyes and felt my heart and spirit lift as I
Heard "By the power vested in me, by the State of California, I now
Pronounce you spouses for life."

It all happened so fast.
I wonder if they could have predicted how many of us wanted
        that wall to come down,
To join our straight brothers and sisters on the side of martial bliss.
Did they know how many of us took it seriously?
Ready to get legally married with only 30-minutes notice.
Could they have predicted the crowds of people willing to stand out all night
        in the beating rain
That would come from all over the nation and from foreign countries
        in the days to follow?

Our friends started pouring in from 90 miles away,
Racing as fast as they could, as soon they heard about it,
To make their marriages legal,
Before someone changed their mind.

I watched as the wall so massive,
Separating me from my straight brothers and sisters,
Separating me from my humanity,
Began to teeter.

I listened as Mayor Newsom stepped out of his office to speak with news reporters
And declared that the wall was an unnecessary figment of our imagination,
That gays and straights were equal,

More similar than different,

And I cried when he said
That if we would all read the Constitution
We would know in our hearts
That the Constitution did not allow for this kind of discrimination.

February 20, 2004

Davina Kotulski, PhD, psychologist, and author of Why You Should Give a Damn about Gay Marriage, *has deep roots in the freedom-to-marry movement, from fighting the Knight Initiative to her work with Californians for Same Sex Marriage, Marriage Equality California, and the Freedom to Marry Coalition. In October 2004, she will travel with the "Marriage Equality Express" from San Francisco through America's Heartland to Washington, DC, for a National Marriage Equality Rally. She is a key organizer for the Marriage Equality Express and Marriage Equality Rally. Kotulski has appeared with her wife on CNN and in Newsweek, Time, and USA Today, and is featured in the movie* Freedom to Marry. *She is currently working on her next book* Love Warriors: The Freedom Fighters of the Marriage Equality Movement. *For more information go to the website* www.marriageequalityca.org.

Love: An AIDS Odyssey
Gil Kudrin

The moment that I met Michael is etched in my memory, as are all the moments that have changed our lives. For a year, I arrived at The Living Room, a drop-in center for people with HIV/AIDS, every Thursday night around 6:00 p.m., to work the AIDS information hotline. My buddy Gordy worked the first two hours of a four-hour shift then left for Thursday night support group. I attended the sister group on Tuesdays.

In order to get to the bathroom, I needed to walk through the room that was actually our living room. Whether any one of the eight or nine other people in the meeting noticed me, I will never know. But I am certain that the very second Michael's eyes met mine, I knew — we knew — that our long search was over.

I rushed back to the desk to catch Gordy before he left. He knew Michael! Now I had a name. Was Michael HIV-positive? Yes! Since being diagnosed myself, I had dated too many men who were not and who in the end were never able to negotiate a life at the edge. What was he doing here? Volunteering to organize an Ohio AIDS Coalition Healing weekend I was scheduled to attend in two weeks! No more questions or answers, Gordy was off to his group.

I spent the next agonizing hour waiting for the meeting to break up. I had been working various hotlines since 1978, and this was 1990. Trying to do a good job was more than a little distracting. And to those who called that night, I apologize...but this was beyond my control. The meeting broke up and the committee filed out one by one, many anxious to get their cigarettes lit. Michael made it halfway across the threshold. As my heart sank he stopped, turned around, came over to the desk.

"My name is Michael," his hand reaching for mine.

"I'm Gil Kudrin."

"I know."

Those were two of the most beautiful words that I had ever heard. Understand that this was years before my ACT UP days. Few people in, or out of, the HIV community knew who I was, but someone in that meeting did and Michael had asked if anyone knew me. Several minutes of nervous conversation established that we would both be at the Healing Weekend in two weeks. Great, no one had to ask for the first date!

This was too good to be true. Which we all know means exactly that — it *was* too good to be true. Eighty-five people with HIV/AIDS and twenty facilitators in the safety of a retreat center in the woods of rural Ohio for three days. Michael and I flirted briefly on our way to and from workshops on Friday and Saturday. Saturday night was reserved for those with great talent and those with too little to be compelled to sit quietly at the back of the room (Mercifully, I fall somewhere between the two). A look across the room was all that was needed for Mike and I to head for the door in unison.

After three hours of walking in the cool, fall evening along wooded trails, of easy conversation, and of even easier making-out, we made our way back to the main lodge where the evening was ending. Much to my surprise (who am I kidding...I was a 31-year-old gay man) there was a very angry man waiting for his boyfriend. Someone I had never seen before. As I said, it was too good to be true. Obviously, Michael was the only one who thought he wasn't seeing anyone seriously. Gordy was witness to the entire scene and kept me in stitches for the next two hours recounting the entire situation, noticing that this was the first time he could remember me wearing red and that the color was quite becoming on me. I couldn't be too upset. I was too focused on my health and already had someone to snuggle with.

I had been assigned a young, first-time participant named Matt to look after. Matt showed up with 12 T-cells and a heart of gold. A normal immune system would have found Matt with nearly one hundred times that number. Friday night we slept in the barracks-like cabin to which we were assigned. Late Saturday night found us curled up together under a blanket in a corner of the main lodge.

On Sunday, before we left, Michael apologized for the night before and noticed a diamond ring with four stones on my ring finger. I assured him that not only was I not involved with anyone, but I had bought myself the ring, having grown tired of waiting for the right man to provide me with one. I might have even mentioned that it was designed in such a fashion that if someone (finally) noticed the empty spaces between the stones, they could certainly feel free to add another carat or two without offending me in the least. Okay, as pathetic as it sounds today I did mention it. He left with my phone number and my heart.

He called. I don't remember where we ate that night, nor if we even saw a movie. What I always will remember is waking up in the middle of the night finding his side of the bed empty and soaking wet. I made my way to the kitchen table where he was sitting with his cigarette. I then lit one myself. Like it or not, I was involved with someone who was at the precipice of AIDS progression. In 1990 we called it ARC (AIDS-related complex). My original "230-T-cells-years" had blossomed into 870, and were staying there. Mike's hovered around 200 and the night sweats that came every night were heralding things to come.

It seems that one night together was all that he could manage. I was hurt, but even today I can't tell you why. Only that a week later, after being coaxed to a night of Halloween parties, I went home alone to cry myself to sleep. Even though I had a very lifelike monster mask, everyone knew who I was. I had been a bodybuilder for many years, and ten years of HIV had taken most of my friends, but not the body that seemed at times to be more of a curse than a blessing when it came to being taken seriously. In my heart, even wounded, I knew that, well or not, Michael and I were meant to be together.

Over the next five months, depending on my self-esteem, I would attend local AIDS events where I knew that I probably would see Mike. I had moved from the front desk at The Living Room to facilitating a new Wednesday-night support group. Turns out my education didn't go to waste after all. I averaged around 20 men and women in an open-ended group. This meant that there was a variety of people each week. Some new, to replace the dead. Some just well enough to come back. Some taking the frightening first steps to meet other people with HIV.

One Wednesday night I walked into the room to find Michael filling one of the chairs. (In a small town word travels fast, especially in a population reaching out to one another.) Again, I am sorry to anyone who might not have received the attention or care they needed that night, but I tried to keep him out of the mix. Professional boundaries are difficult to keep in times of plague.

After group ended, the two of us stood in front of The Living Room having a cigarette. I just couldn't do this any longer. I looked over at him and asked if we were through with this "thing" that we had been doing and if it was all right to get on with what it was we were going to do! The corners of his lips curled up slightly and his boyish grin lit up an otherwise darkened street...and we moved in together that night. Oh, no, we didn't call it that at first. Our friends would have thought that we had lost our minds. The official date came several months later. And in the time that is AIDS... that is an eternity.

One day I noticed that Mike resembled one of the comic strip characters I loved as a child. Not only did I enjoy the story, but I had a bit of a crush on the main character — Dondi. Although we were raised only 35 miles from each other, and had a difference in age of only five years, Michael seemed to have few memories of his early childhood he could share with me. Being the first of ten kids in an Irish Catholic family, who could blame him? We set off to the public library to dig up some microfilms of the character I had fallen in love with as a child. Even the research librarian recognized the resemblance (*www.toonopedia.com/dondi.htm*).

Our days together became increasingly filled with joy and sorrow. So many of our friends were dying during the early 1990s. At times we would lose four people in six weeks. We never answered the phone after 10:00 p.m. It could only be bad news. Amazingly, we managed to not only live through this, but to thrive. We shared so many things. However, we seemed to do this apart from the rest of the world. (*Pain* seems too shallow a word for the losses we shared. Even our doctor died.) But throughout this period, our careers melded together.

I had been working for nearly 20 years at a local hospital in the maintenance department. I had finished my degree by taking night classes and was poised to move on with my life right before I was diagnosed with HIV. Having only 200 T-cells, I had no choice but to begin on AZT, the only drug we had then, and give up my career aspirations. Then, Michael opened a door!

Paul Monette, Victor Brown, Michael, and a dear friend began a small company, Nightsweats & T-cells. This was an extension of Michael's fledgling screen-printing business and meant to make shirts that reflected the horrors toward which most of America turned a blind eye. We all became moving billboards. As our name grew, we slipped further into the poverty that accompanies HIV/AIDS and trying to run a small business...no profit...no paychecks. Our HIV-positive employees always got paid; we seldom did. We survived on my paychecks from the hospital, Michael's credit cards, whatever charity we qualified for, and a wave of goodwill from all across the United States. (This all happened before the advent of protease inhibitors. No FUCKING cocktails thank you, boys and girls! This is CHEMOTHERAPY! I have since taken in excess of 100,000 pills to Michael's nearly 150,000.)

Then something happened. We witnessed the millennium together and joy began to outweigh sorrow. Small pieces at a time, but we reveled in it.

Paul is now dead, so is Victor. Their dear friend and founder of the business was a casualty of AIDS who didn't die. She just went away to lick wounds that won't heal in a thousand years. Matt's dead, so is Christopher, Mike, Andy, Les, Kevin, Joseph, John, Mark, Harry, Kenny, and hundreds more that made up our lives. Michael and I have persisted, and now when we view the AIDS Memorial Quilt we see dozens of our shirts sown into the panels of people who were too close to forget and too numerous to name.

We now live a comfortable life; however, it is little comfort in the wake of such tragedy. Nightsweats & T-cells has taken on a life of its own. It can be said that we feel that we serve the company more as its guardians, not as its owners. Our love has taken on a life of its own as well. Michael likes to say, "We have even outlived our sympathy!" Our bodies have been ravaged by the treatments meant to save us, but sometimes if the light is just right...just right...I see the boy I fell in love with a hundred years ago on an October evening in Ohio.

On February 27, 2004, Michael and Gil took the only legal option in Ohio for gay couples and registered as "Domestic Partners" in Cleveland Heights. They live in an apartment above the Nightsweats & T-cells shop (www.nightsweats.com) with their 13-year-old dog Mountain.

Excerpt from *Dirt Roads and Loon Calls*
Greg M. Lanza

Ever since Matt first began dreaming of it, he knew exactly the wedding he wanted: outdoors, dusk, the vows offered under a big tree. There would be white everywhere, and he'd be surrounded by the people who meant the most to him.

And now, the beauty and accuracy of it all overwhelmed him. A long, white train separated six rows of white chairs on each side of the aisle. White candles ran along the entire length of the train; the only source of light breaking through the dusk, leading the way. White ribbons adorned the surrounding trees and at the end of the train, a Priestess dressed in white stood behind a pillar-style altar. Three white candles burning on the altar symbolized the Triple Goddess. And there, dressed in a white unbuttoned shirt and linen pants, barefoot, stood Sean, looking more gorgeous than any man ever had a right to look. Matt was not the only one crying.

Matt turned to Kris. She too was all in white—a flowing sleeveless blouse with a long skirt. She too was barefoot.

"Ready?" Matt nodded and they began to slowly walk the aisle.

Everyone in attendance had been given a white rose to hold. Matt took a deep breath, allowing the scent to overtake him. As he walked, he noticed all the people who had come to be a part of this day. His sister Emma stood at the end of a row, her arm outstretched. Matt paused, took both her hands, and they hugged and kissed and cried together.

"Oh, Em, thanks for coming all this way."

Emma wiped a tear from Matt's cheek and said, "Go get married."

His best friends, Mary Beth and Donald, stood together in the second row. Their hands flittered as they both wept, and Mary Beth said, "You sleazy skank! You made my makeup run!" Matt blew them both a kiss before stepping forward into the arms of his mother, who stood at the end of the aisle.

"Mumms." He and his mother hugged for what seemed like forever.

"My baby is getting married." She stroked the back of her son's head while covering him with kisses as she had since he was a child.

"You've grown into such a wonderful man", she said, "but I always knew you would because you were always my wonderful, loving son. I am so proud of you."

Tears streamed freely down Matt's cheeks as he gave his mom a last squeeze and whispered, "Thank you for teaching me how to love."

"All right, well let's get going!"

Matt's grandmother stood next to his mom. She was laughing and wrapped Matt up into a big, bear hug. She wasn't crying; never had. Matt wasn't sure what he'd do if she did.

Matt took Kris' hands and kissed her on both cheeks. "Thanks for bringing me this far."

"I'll always be right here," Kris kissed Matt back and stepped off to the side, leaving Matt with his mother and grandmother.

Matt's grandmother was the only one who insisted on wearing a colored skirt, and Matt knew he couldn't overrule her, even at his own wedding. She carried a white lily and wore a blue skirt with a white blouse.

He and his mom and grandmother all clasped hands. For Matt, this was the second-most-important part of the ceremony, for they symbolized the three faces of the Goddess: Maiden, Mother, and Crone. Matt didn't share this with them, however. He knew they might not have agreed to participate had they understood their respective roles. Matt didn't want to beat them over the head with his pagan ideals.

Yet it was his wedding, and there were only so many compromises he was prepared to make.

But here, now, Matt had his moment. He said a silent prayer of thanks to the Goddess while the Priestess gave him a knowing wink. After a moment, the two women walked him over to Sean who joined his hands and completed the circle.

The candles burned a little brighter as Matt felt the power held within that circle. Then, his mom and grandmother let go and took a step backward, leaving Matt and Sean clutching hands. "I love you," Sean said and as he and Matt locked eyes, Matt saw the future there, the past, and the present. In them all was love; love like he had never dared hope for, love he never knew himself capable of feeling.

They faced the Priestess, her fiery red hair pulled back in a simple braid. "Your journeys have brought you to each other, here, today, in love. But the journey does not end here. You've walked a long way, alone and now together. Take comfort in knowing that from this day on you shall never walk alone. Be mindful of each other, appreciate each other, and always remember love is not the destination. It is the journey. I wish you good journey."

Matt and Sean turned to one another, hands lying in hands, both smiling. Matt took several deep breaths and fought against the urge to remove one of his hands and cover his mouth; a nervous childhood habit that stayed with him through adulthood. This was not the time for nerves. Sean, as well as the loved ones present, deserved to hear the words as loudly and as clearly as possible.

"Want me to go first?" Sean whispered, leaning in and winking.

Matt gave his hands a squeeze.

"And rob me of my grand opening? Never."

Sean kissed him on the cheek and as he pulled back, couldn't resist saying, "Well get on with it, will ya?"

Matt smiled as he tightened his grip on Sean's left hand.

Matt had written and rewritten his vows hundreds of times over the past four years, before they were engaged, before they even talked about marriage. In the past few weeks he wrote and tore up revision after revision, wanting to say everything Sean and their love meant to him and what their future would bring, while being entertaining, funny, and moving, and all in the space of two minutes. He wrote, read to Kris, wrote again, practiced in front of the mirror, and agonized over these next few sentences until he finally had written exactly what he wanted to say.

He then proceeded to rip it up and forget it all.

"Sean, as I stand here today, with you in this place, surrounded by the people we love and this beautiful land, I can't help but know that we've done this before. Countless times over countless lives and in various ways, we have stood before those we love and trust and declared our love to each other. I know this because it would take more than one lifetime for me to show you just how much I love and need you in my life; with me, by my side, inside me always. And surely it would take even longer for us to discover all there is to know about each other."

Matt's eyes never left Sean's, and the love and strength he found there allowed him to speak without breaking down.

"There is no one I would rather walk through time with, grow old and start anew with, face life's joys and despairs with than you; you who I have loved since before I knew you; you who have been with me long since before you had a name; you who have touched my life and my heart in more ways than I could possibly know; you who I share myself with, give my all to; you who I shall love until the universe no longer exists; you who are me and not; you who are my husband, my best friend, my soul mate. You have all that I was, all that I am, and all that I will be in this life; and I promise to spend the rest of this one, and countless others, showing you everyday how much my life, my heart, my love is yours."

Another deep breath, a broader smile, and a single tear trickled down his cheek, but Matt had said everything he needed to and could see that Sean had heard it all.

"I'm supposed to follow that?" Sean said loud enough for all to hear. "But you're the writer in the family, Matt, not me. I've never been that creative, at least not with talking. But there are a few things I know with complete certainty. The first time we met, you blasted me through a wall, and you've done it every day since. Each time you smile at me or even look at me I feel your love, and my heart answers in a way that tells me it was made to love you.

"Now you're the one who deals with past lives and magics and Priestesses and all that, and I love you for sharing it with me. But all I need to know about you, us, our love I learn everyday, here, now, in our present. I told you once that I knew I was in love when I never got bored with someone. Matt I have never been bored with you, not for one second. Every day, every minute you're surprising me, showing me something new, and I never get tired of learning. You're still the first person I want to see in the morning, and the last person I want to see at night, and between the two, when we're apart, it doesn't feel good, and I don't feel right until we're back together. We can talk all day and when I go to sleep my last thought is usually, 'I forgot to tell Matt something,' but I smile because I can reach over and hold you and watch you sleep till morning when I can tell you what I forgot." By now Matt's tears were falling freely, though his smile never wavered.

"So you tell me we've done this before, and I believe you, but I'm more concerned with this life, this time, and making it the best life possible for you, for us. And I promise to spend the rest of my days loving you, supporting you, walking with you, and will truly feel blessed for having shared my life with you. I love you, Matt, in every way I know, and in some I don't, and I'm a better man because of it."

Sean wiped a tear from Matt's cheek and whispered, "How was that?"

Matt took his face in his hands, kissed him on both eyes, and said, "It'll do."

They kissed tenderly and Sean's body next to his felt like an inferno, as if a wall of flame had surrounded them, isolating them from their loved ones and the Priestess. Matt was in no hurry to return.

Eventually he heard his grandmother's voice bellow, "Will you save some of that for the honeymoon? It's a wedding, not a dental exam!"

He and Sean, as well as the guests and the Priestess laughed. Matt reluctantly pulled away and the two stared at each other for another few seconds before turning their attention back to the Priestess, who was waiting sheepishly to pronounce them married, as if she or any other force in the universe ever really had a say in the matter.

Greg M. Lanza has been working to makes schools safe for GLBT students for most of his 29 years. When not actively trying to change the world, he listens to Stevie Nicks, re-reads The Mists of Avalon, *and works on his own novel-in-progress,* Dirt Roads and Loon Calls.

An Agitation on Gay Marriage Expressed in Motes
Daniel W.K. Lee

Gay Nuptials
Fuck "marriage"!
It's all about the wedding!

Gay Nuptials with a Chinese Groom
(CORRECTION)
It's all about the wedding banquet!

Gay Wedding
Where else
do we register?

Gay Chinese Wedding Banquet
You should fast.

Gay Newlyweds
Shouldn't we be
having more sex?

Gay Honeymoon
It's your turn
to play the virgin.

Sex After Gay Marriage I
We still have threesomes.

Sex After Gay Marriage II
Barebacking is ggggreat!

Sex After Gay Marriage III
Though we are monogamous,
I somehow seroconverted.

Gay Anniversary
Lose track of the years.

Gay Divorce
I do.

Daniel W.K. Lee is a poet-artist based in New York City. He is chronically single, but has an uncanny ability to attract men who want to cheat on their relationships with him. Fans, stalkers, and exceptional conversationalists can reach him at strongplum@yahoo.com.

My Kansas Family
Sharon "Vinnie" Levin

On a sunny afternoon in 1997, I stood up in front of G-d and everybody I knew and told Kristi Parker that I would love her forever, no matter what, until I died.

I meant it.

Even though we were poor by any standard, I wanted a wedding. A real wedding—and through barter and luck I got it. One hundred and fifty guests in a friend's backyard, a custom-made, long, flowing, white gown (in which I looked stunning, by the way), a tiered cake (mine had Winnie the Pooh marrying Mickey Mouse on top), a band, and a ten-minute ceremony. Oh, and a beautiful bride. I had a very beautiful bride.

My mother-in-law fought with us about a wedding, mostly because we were poor. The victim of a failed straight marriage, she couldn't see why we wanted the spectacle of it all. If I were a man marrying her daughter she'd have argued the same way, I know. But the truth is, a lot of lesbians and gay men have asked the same question: Why do you have to *do* that?

I can answer that question. I have to do that because I *really* want to and I can do whatever I want. Don't you read Richard Bach? I wanted the white gown—it looked so good—and I wanted the flowers and I wanted the people and the cake and the singers and the ceremony and the band. But most of all, I wanted the woman I love more than anything else in the entire world to know it, more than she could know from day to day. More than she could know from cards and flowers.

The act of marriage, to me, is serious business. I felt ugly in junior high and high school. I felt out of place so much of my life. When I figured out that I was gay everything fell into place. But I'm the kind of person who can love like crazy, and it's too much for most people. It's gotten me into my own kind of trouble before. But Kristi got it. She understood me and she complemented me in a way no one had. And even though she was from Kansas and I from Philadelphia, and she was scared to death of me in the beginning because I'm a little louder and more forthright than a lot of people here in Kansas, she knew just a few weeks after we met that she wanted to be with me forever, no matter what, until she died.

Don't you see how huge that is? How wonderful? It's one thing to say this to someone when you're in your bed or the living room, but standing up in front of G-d and everyone and saying it out loud leaves me speechless. Unless you've felt that kind of wonderfulness, you probably *don't* understand why I wanted to do it. When Kristi and I got married, we had been together for three years.

Seven years later, Kristi and I have a beautiful son who's about to turn three. He is the light of our lives. More than ever, Jack is the reason we want our marriage to be recognized by our country and our state. This is unlikely in Kansas until our legislature is forced by the U.S. Supreme Court, which we assume will happen one day. But my marriage is more stable than that of many straight couples I know. I think that we have a better idea about what's at stake than most. And we're happy. And that's what matters.

Sharon "Vinnie" Levin lives in Wichita, Kansas, with her wife of ten years and her two-year-old son. They own and operate Liberty Press *(www.libertypress.net), Kansas' statewide lesbian and gay newsmagazine.*

A Very Deerdog Wedding
Ali Liebegott and Anna Joy Springer

Ali: My favorite part about the hysterical antigay protestors is when they say, "Next they'll want to make marrying animals legal!" I love animals and often think of marrying them. Having tiny tea-and-crumpet parties with my animal husband or wife.

Anna Joy: "I'm an animal! Have a tiny tea-and-crumpet party with me! How come we never have a tiny tea party anymore, just you and me? Animals don't even drink tea. And crumpets? When have you ever seen a Bonobo eating a crumpet?" In the few months since the marriage, it's been nag, nag, nag. Not her, me. "Don't use the paper-towel, use the cloth towel." "Save that plastic County Fair cup; it'll be good for iced tea." "Why not try that libido hand cream." I have a horrible problem with nagging, like I've got a problem with snacking and impulse buying. Right now I'm eating salty mixed nuts. By way of transition, let me advance the argument that us queers are like a bag of mixed nuts. Don't get your feelings hurt. I mean like, viva la difference. However you spell it. Let a thousand flowers bloom or schools compete or what have you. And if both polygamy and interspecies marriage are legalized, we can merge identities with the whole damn farm.

Today, July 4, 2004, Ali and I sat at the kids' table to eat our fake burgers on the patio of my uncle's vacation condo. When my aunt came out to oil and comb my cousins' sea-gnarled hair, everyone clammed up. I'd just been telling one of my cousins, "Look, when you need to get away from all this algebra homework, you'll always have a place to…" My aunt, an adult, had invaded. She tugged at my cousin's hair, admonishing, "Remember what we talked about with Aunty B—. We don't talk about our parents with others." My cousin said, "Yes, mama," in a nearly impercievably sarcastic tone. Ali and I sniffed back giggles, conspiratorially. Not to, by insinuating that we aren't total grownups because we're not straight, set the whole idea of dyke or womanly adulthood back 200 years.

Ali: But even further than 200 years ago was the Miocene Period when Reeve's Muntjac, a tiny fanged barking deer supposedly evolved from a deerlike mouse. When Anna and I first started going out, I lived in Brooklyn in this wonderfully solitary apartment that still had Miocene period linoleum. Anna would visit from San Francisco and want to go to museums in New York. No one I knew in New York went to museums. We were too busy drinking alcoholically. So, after a few dates of sitting in bars, Anna dragged me to the Natural History Museum. That's when we met "deerdog," a.k.a. Reeve's Muntjac for the first time.

Anna Joy: Like some Tennessee Williams character in the less-serrated early hours of a gin binge, I'll say now, a little pleased with myself, that my unmarried nagging ("You have to take a femme on dates. That's what lovers do when femmes fly all the way across the country to visit. We have to go to museums and things…") led us right down the garden path and straight into the spiky visage of deerdog, and thus, commingling of debt, revisitation of unresolved childhood traumas, morning naked dances for dogs, and olfactory-intimacy. It led to our queer illegal fetishy marriage. Nature, soothing or horrifying, is a powerful aphrodisiac (i.e., leather and rubber and horses). At the Natural History Museum, Ali wanted to see all the deerlike creatures, the ones I always ignored at zoos, thinking they were boring and herdlike. In that section, we met deerdog. He was taxidermed in a regal-yet-militaristic stance in his shiny silk-leaf diorama. Little fangs poking over the sides of his lower jaw and round rocks shoved under his thumb-size hooves. I watched Ali fall in love.

Ali: Was it that I loved deerdog or that I knew that five years from that day I would have my own fanged, barking wife at home, behind a red velvet rope?

Anna Joy: It was more like four and a half years, Ali. And speaking of conceptual and/or velvet ropes, the point is, I'm inhumanely possessive and everyone knows it. Which doesn't mean I can't share you with deerdog, but just that I need to own a big chunk of you. I'm a double Taurus and an only child who grew up nagging her straight butch-looking single mother. I'm "the" femme in the relationship, in any relationship. In deer terms that means my fangs are shorter and I need more space. In people terms that means I wanted to have a wedding ever since I learned to make perfect rows in the preschool rug with the mini-mommy rolling sweeper. Ever since I built my first Lincoln Log cabin and tried to stuff my Barbies in the window. Their pointy toes poking out. I was engaged at 16. I tried to marry just about everyone I loved, and I tried to love more people, so there'd be more to try and marry. I only exchanged vows with two of my loves. One was Juli, my best friend, who's also a femme, and the other was Ali, who's not a femme and never thought about getting married before I came along. (Hunting like shopping, loving like winning.) Juli got her "girl" friend Paula to go up to SF for the big illegal marriage-a-thon, too. We had a festive four-woman double wedding, just like in Barbie days. Not really *just* like Barbies, who never sleep, but only use beds to clash plastic mounds and make birdy sounds. Unlike Barbies, we were butch and fat and Jewish and broke and mainly, we needed lots of sleep. Instead of sleeping, on February 18, we drove all night long from San Diego to get to San Francisco in time to doll up and get in line outside City Hall.

Ali: Rarely will you see the Reeve's Muntjac "Get in line" or be monogamous. The males need more than one doe and often have several does around in various stages of pregnancy. Both male and female muntjacs are great lickers and have extra-long tongues. When Anna and I left the museum and got back to my apartment in Brooklyn, we looked online obsessively for this thing the sign at the Natural History Museum had called "Deerdog—Deer or Dog?" Butch or Femme? Museum or dive bar? We'd have to go to the hills of Thailand to look for deerdog in its natural habitat. But Anna and I were just starting out—butterfly larvae—who knew if little deerdog would gobble us up and reduce our population 30,000-fold? In the meantime, we fell in love. What trite words. We drank gin in the morning until my ass got hauled off to AA and I learned how to buy groceries before she came to visit and take her on dates to the Yonkers County Fair.

Anna Joy: It's a queer little animal, the Muntjac. Part dinosaur, part mouse, part deer, part dog, sneaking through the Asian underbrush. It could be a symbol for something even more expansive than Ali's and my love.

I hate it when ethics philosophers talk shit about animals, as if they know animal phenomenology or about all creatures' workaday lives. I can't believe the nerve these assholes have, bragging that we humans "choose" while nonhuman animals "react." What*ever*. I don't know about you, but I react all the time. For instance, when Ali just let slip her desire to fuck twin strippers next week (that's what the whole very subtly coded message about male deerdogs needing more than one doe and often having hundreds of pregnant stripper does just waiting around in their panties and lip gloss…etc.) I did not choose, via my ever-expanding freeness of will (freedom to shop), to think, *Shit Ali, the strippers all share one buck because they aren't so excited by* male company. *You understand that. They need him to keep out of their hair.* Rational, instinctual reaction. I spit on the intellectuals who pretend an intimate understanding of animal minds and desires. And Darwin, and his whole theory based on competition and scarcity rather than interdependency and symbiosis, I spit on that too. I am femme, hear me bark like a deer.

Ali: Once I used to like to spit on the walls of my high school. There was one particular high-gloss wall that people liked to spit on. It's easy to spit after drinking orange juice. I hate and spit on all those little cocaine-addict/child-molester/philosopher/ academic/corporate flunkies who talk shit about animals. Like people who say it's the koala's fault for getting run over and killed by a pickup truck. Kudos, Anna Joy, for your spitting! (Does anyone truly know what *kudos* means? Did Darwin?) PS, I don't really know what I'd do with twin strippers. I bet you that probably what I'd do is try to charm them with pictures of Reeve's Muntjac. "But it's a tiny fanged barking deer," I'd whimper. How come these philosophers never talk about the people who try to sell mops at county fairs? I love "miracle" demonstrations and the obvious waste of salt/pepper and soda. How fun to consciously pour a bunch of soda/salt/pepper onto the floor, then drop in a handful of dog hair and mop it up with your miracle mop! These mop and sponge people are amazing with their headset microphones and one-liners. I looked over at Anna's face at the fair yesterday and I watched it light up with joy at each clean stroke of linoleum. Like shedding Dalmatians, deerdogs can live in apartments, too, but they're very stinky.

Anna Joy: Very stinky. Kudos to you, too, Ali, for rhetorically aligning child-molesters and animal-hating philosophers. I'm certain our reading audience will understand the passion behind that parallel and forgive its reach. What about the animal-molesting, child-hating philosophers? I'm talking nonconsensual animal-molestation. What about them, Ali? How would you like to hear story after story of terrible rape-filled fawnhoods from your deerdog girlfriends like you're accustomed to hearing from your human ones? But let's not split semantic hairs, especially when we agree, my love. We agree about the miracle mop sellers, the sublimity of a county fair, the healing properties of goat-hugging, and that it's better to be kind to people and do good work than it is to be a pontificating OverMan. We agree about so many things, let's finish this bit of propaganda so that we can go gloat about our generosity and righteousness while we couple like the stinking mating pair we've become.

Ali: Since Anna Joy refuses to tell you the story of how the hand of GOD reached down into our little world of love and blessed us, at all places, at the Yonkers County Fair, I'll tell you.

I've just found out *tonight*, only hours ago, that Anna Joy enjoys and partakes in FRENCH DISCO!!! Also, this is the first time we've ever written anything together. I think because I always return to putting animals in little outfits and Anna always turns my animals in little outfits into objects of social analysis. My wife. I cried when I married you. Do you remember, how I cried uncontrollably in City Hall? The wedding photograph lies. It gives me the same face I had when I was two-seconds shy of barfing on the neighbor's floor when I was eight. Big chubby face, giant pre-barf eyes. But really I was falling from one illuminated place to another. Or, really, I couldn't believe that there were still even more illuminated places to fall with you.

Anna Joy: Well, you see, that's how Ali wins. She always wins, a noble foe. Children, for a partner, find yourself a noble foe. Or a noble doe, but why pick? I'm not going to address the tears or God or any of that here, for an audience of strangers. I'll leave that to you, my poet. Let me just back up to the diorama at the Natural History Museum. I love to watch you, love. But, who knew I'd love to watch the watchers of the things you watch.

It's why, after we got off tour and you were in New York and I was in San Francisco, I'd watch the playoffs (or whatever) at the bars, knowing you were watching the Mets too. I hated sports, but I loved you. I watched the sports fans watch your team. I watched them cheer and cover their eyes—and strangers talked to strangers and touched them—several thousand invisible cubicles dissolved in the sports bar while I watched your team almost win. The game was our moon.

But back to the Yonkers Fair. I was surprised to learn that on the East Coast, "Freak Shows" are still legal.

Ali: Why must we continue writing this drivel when what I want is to take your words, my opiates, and retreat to my little underbrush, secreting urine and dung and climbing up young saplings to snap off and give to you. "Next thing you know they'll want to marry an animal." What if they want to *be the animal,* Dr. Laura? (Who wants to be a doctor by the way?) I've had a terrible pain between my ass cheeks for the last three days, and I'm secretly hoping I'm growing a tail. That God is giving me a tail—but can I pick what kind, please? You'd be surprised by the size of the Muntjac tail. Tiny, tiny. You'd be even more surprised by its thin legs—unbelievable anyone could walk on those. It was hot at the Yonkers Fair as we wound our way through the booths, seeing signs for a real freak show with "Bearded Lady" and a "Fat Lady." Then we came to an animal freak show. "Cow with six legs," "Two-headed Goat," "World's Smallest Deer." It was one dollar. I looked at Anna Joy, my young little pup of a girlfriend, and said, "Whaddaya think?"

Inside we walked from one too-small pen to the next. "Cow with Six Legs" was black and white. She had four regular legs and two other tumor legs growing out of her back. They were flaccid, looked boneless, as she lay on the ground in that 100-degree New York heat under a sign with COW WITH SIX LEGS! scrawled out in thick black pen. There were lots of things in jars. Preserved lizards and snakes, stacked on a shelf. And the taxidermed plaque with two goat heads affixed. "Does it have two brains?" said all the voices. "Does it eat out of both mouths?" We were depressed and sat down next to WORLD'S SMALLEST DEER. It was hard to find WORLD'S SMALLEST DEER at first, but he eventually crawled out from behind his green plastic kennel, past his plastic bowl filled with Kibbles 'n Bits. We'd already seen many unhappy animals, like the baby panther panting on its back in a small aquarium, with a fan blowing on the glass. I was one too, in the haunted house where our little car went through a metal trailer full of black-light skulls, and then, in pitch black a filthy damp mop dragged across my forehead. It was truly a scary moment. "Why is it eating Kibbles 'n Bits? Why would they give a deer Kibbles 'n Bits?" cried Anna Joy. "I don't know. I don't know." My response to the cruelty of men. He came up to us. Walking gingerly on his tiny pencil legs. He came up and pushed his nose against the chain-link fencing. We petted him and petted him and talked to him. Twenty minutes passed like this and then his long pink tongue came out. He pushed his nose through the bars and began licking.

Anna Joy: His pretty little tongue, lapping Ali's palm like it were a mango or an ocean, then turning to me and licking my cheek. I opened my mouth and he licked me there, his tongue tasting salty and metallic like Ali's sweaty hand. He turned back to Ali, who'd pressed her cheek up against the fence, for some face-licking. It was the first time I'd seen his profile, close up. I gasped. "Ali, look!"

Ali: And that's when we saw his fangs. "Deerdog!" we cried simultaneously. "Deerdog!" We looked at each other and then at the ceiling of yellow tarp that housed the animal freak show at the Yonkers County Fair. Deerdog in Yonkers, eating Kibbles 'n Bits, blessing us.

Anna Joy: Whether this is late-capitalism or not, whether or not there's a God, and whether and how we clumsily mimic heteronormative aggression/consumption patterns, we feel blessed, which is not a bad way to feel. We've intentionally involved ourselves in our culture's weird mating rituals, just two more bozos on the bus, because the alternative—feeling doomed and superior—is best left to the young and the drunk. Aging sensitive lesbian schoolteachers, we laugh, we lick wounds, we pet things, and we take turns barking and bleating, hooting and growling.

Ali Liebegott's book-length poem The Beautifully Worthless *is forthcoming from Suspect Thoughts Press in February 2005, and her work has appeared in numerous anthologies and journals. In 1997-1999, she toured the country with the amazing and historic Sister Spit's Ramblin' Road Show. In 1999, she was a recipient of a New York Foundation for the Arts Fellowship in Poetry. She's finishing two books right now: an illustrated novel about duck feeders called* The Crumb People *and a novel called* The IHOP Papers. *She currently lives in San Diego with her beautiful and brilliant ball and chain, Anna Joy Springer.*

Anna Joy Springer, a beautiful and brilliant ball and chain, has little fangs and barks like a deer when excited. Teenage fans call her "The Bird Lady," because she writes, almost exclusively, about birds. Before moving to Sandy Dayglo to teach at Eileen Myles' School for Wayward Writers, she did lots of femme jobs, made neon sculptures, sang in "legendary" punk bands Blatz, The Gr'ups, and Cypher in the Snow, and read her purple prose with Sister Spit. She currently tongue-lashes misogynists, writes weird and lengthy cross-genre messes, and ponders the many species of love, radical performative pedagogy, and the gyre of ethics in konsumer kapitalism. She loves Ali.

The Kiss Seen Around the World
Michael T. Luongo

I am probably one of the most antimarriage gay men you can find in the world. And I literally am all over the world. I am a travel writer, and I take the view that being gay is a gift from God—allowing me to be free, live and do as I like, which is to travel all over the world, finding boyfriends and lovers in as many ports of call as possible. Why some gay people want to mess things up by getting settled and being domestic, getting married and arguing in shopping malls about matching shower curtains is beyond me. Isn't that the punishment God gave straight people? And I know that once they are married, that is what straight people do. I was once, a very long time ago, a manager at a suburban New Jersey J.C. Penney in charge of those shower curtains that straight people would argue about.

So, whenever I hear about gay marriage, I generally roll my eyes and think, well that's nice for some people if they never go anywhere. But not for me. Still, the topic is inescapable, and it amazes me the new twists on it that some gay magazines take to keep the topic fresh, and how it comes up in some of the most casual conversations with people gay, straight, or simply unknown. But one place where I least expected to get into intelligent conversations about gay marriage made me think that maybe all the fuss over this issue is worth it. That was Kandahar in Afghanistan, a city perhaps better known for the Taliban toppling walls over gay people than enlightened conversations about gay marriage.

I was in the city to look at those toppled walls and some other aspects of Afghanistan's secret gay history for *The Out Traveler* and several other publications. My first night in town, I wound up at a wedding. No, not a gay wedding, a straight one, but local custom dictates men don't mix with women, so it might as well have been.

As part of Afghanistan's rapid rebuilding since 9/11, a new marble-encrusted wedding hall has opened up in Kandahar. My friend in that city, a local journalist named Suleman, was curious to see the inside of the structure. Being a foreigner gave me license to do whatever I wanted in town, so we sauntered in, inviting ourselves to the party. We found ourselves in a giant hall with about 500 men. Many of them, like my friend's friend whom we wound up sitting next to, were very handsome. That and this rigid same-sex separation were fine by me. I think such customs made being a gay foreigner here more fun.

The place was noisy and chaotic. Most of the men were in the traditional camise, a two-piece ensemble made of an oversized broadcloth shirt and what I likened to genie pants. I was in one too, trying to blend in, though most people knew I was a foreigner. There was no sign of the groom, which is normal here. He's the only man allowed in the women's hall. Since this will be the only time in their entire lives they'll ever be surrounded by so many women, most Afghan grooms blow off their friends and male relatives at their wedding.

I don't remember exactly how it started, but as soon as we were talking with Suleman's friend Rameen, the conversation turned almost immediately to the topic of gay marriage in America. Rameen first began by asking me about marriage customs in the USA, and about how they might differ from what I was seeing here. Without hesitation, and perfectly naturally, he then asked me if I had ever been to a gay wedding. I was surprised by the ease with which he could discuss the subject, but I knew immediately why he knew about it at all. That nonstop coverage of gay marriage you find in your homes on CNN, BBC, MSNBC, and everywhere else is beamed by satellite into living rooms here in Afghanistan, and of course, the rest of the world as well.

This was the same wherever I went. It seemed any Afghan with a television was aware of same-sex marriage in America. It was an odd curiosity to Afghans, yet it wasn't a concept completely unfamiliar to people from Kandahar. Army commanders had often been rumored to "marry" the young soldiers they kept around as playthings. Such "immorality" was part of what gave rise to the Taliban. Thus, it wasn't hard then for them to understand the idea, but what amazed them was the openness of the images, the loving tenderness between the men and the women onscreen. And even, seemingly, the government approval of the whole thing.

This went far beyond Kandahar though. In the capital of Kabul, where the international rebuilding process means there are a large number of expats, you'll find a sizeable foreign gay population, along with signs of a local gay scene. Some of these expats had told me that they had gotten into great conversations with men about same-sex marriage. Glenn and Jeff, Americans affectionately known as the "Gay Couple of Kabul," told me of their Afghan gardener who hoped one day to find a man to settle down with. "I want to be a modern man, like you and Glenn," Jeff told me the man had said to him. With images beamed by satellite into his living room, the young man was developing an understanding of how to look for gay couples all around him, even in Kabul. He wanted to model himself after Jeff and Glenn's lifestyle. While in my experience most Afghans can pick up on homosexuality, were it not for the omnipresent gay-marriage coverage, the young gardener might not have had the words to discuss the topic with Jeff and Glenn.

I also found it easier to come out to other Afghans I had known for a long time. I had met two men who once worked as translators for friends at CNN on my first trip to Afghanistan in 2003. Over dinner this year, same-sex marriage came up, and I decided this was a perfect segue into coming out to them. They were, of course, intrigued, and we began a rapid-fire conversation on the topic. Some of the questions were naïve, like who gets to be the woman, but it wasn't out of evil. In the end, I was happy that our conversation, and our friendship, had gone to this level.

It seemed no matter where I went in the country, Afghans who had seen gay marriage covered on television were curious about the topic. Still Suleman in Kandahar put it best when he explained to me how much he liked the happy images of men and women kissing on the steps of San Francisco's City Hall. "Homosexuality is about power here," he explained, referring to the army commanders who use these relationships as control over their young soldiers. "But in the West," he continued, "it's about love and romance, and that is the best thing of all."

If media coverage of gay marriage can bring about comments like that in Afghanistan of all places, imagine what it does for Peoria, Des Moines, and Bensonhurst here at home? I'll still take the single life all around the world, but keep up the gay-marriage coverage. It's been leading to some interesting conversations for me.

Michael Luongo is a New York–based travel writer, editor, and photographer who loves visiting unusual gay destinations in Latin America and the Middle East. He is an editor of numerous books and a senior editor at Haworth Press in charge of the Out in the World series on GLBT travel literature.

I Would Rather Be Dead
Than Living in Baltimore
Jason Mahanes

I would rather be dead than living in Baltimore.

The phrase looped through his mind like a red shirt in the dryer. The other things in there clanked and rattled and called out for Advil or something stronger. He couldn't recall the feeling of not having a headache.

Of all the definitions of marriage, this one is surely the best: To place two ropes along side of each other so that they may be grasped and hauled on at the same time. To join two ropes end to end so that both will pass through a block.

He rehearsed the line: a haiku riddle aphorism joke puzzle. It was a pastime. Or else it was past the time of action. He felt certain he'd lost the initiative, was now object to the world subject.

To think of the future was to think of the past's conception of the future. The present had ceased to touch its forward edge. Time washed forward in exactly the manner of driving late at night when you realize your last blink has failed to end and the alarm in your mind has failed to rouse your lids and your conception of what is before you becomes increasingly provisional with each passing foot, and your fingers twitch, and your thighs clench, and your breath has gone, but your lids and the eyes have disappeared into the dark place, and you know the abrupt tin-slashing is imminent, and impossibly distant, and this time you might miss it altogether like last time.

Does marriage preclude hurting you? Because that would be a deal-breaker. How about myself? If married, can I any longer be obliterated? There are some assurances you'll need to be able to make. I have expectations. Above and beyond what happens now and what is happening. There is by nature a change that must occur, and how can you put quantitative measures on qualitative judgments? Amount or intensity?

And all this time as inattentive as your eyes have been, your foot has never faulted, even to drive you incrementally faster, and somewhere near here the freeway curves through the words that conceal the houses your friend's parents bought and left to their no-account sons and daughters, and somewhere around you. There are cautious midnight drivers caffeine-keen saying to their wives or cellphones: that guy's drunk or high, watch him drift, a danger.

My local courthouse is not really a courthouse at all. Like most things, the institution has outgrown itself. My local courthouse, or what I'm calling my local courthouse, is beside, or next to, the giant new building that replaced the old, classic or true courthouse. The old courthouse was razed, and, presumably, the new modern facility was erected in its place, then fortified recently, now, I assume, the building that actually houses the courtrooms, so properly the courthouse. Somewhere in all this, the office where one goes to license a marriage, or certify a birth or death got moved into a low one-story brown brick bureaucratic modernist building, my local courthouse.

And when you continue on without the lines that hem you in, they'll be the ones to scream tires and pull to curbs, to come running down embankments, to shuffle through beaded safety glass, to explain it all to the paramedics and then again in dramatic fashion to the drowsy cop. They roam the highways at every hour in search of the touching. Empathic after the fact, brutalists lusting in their muted, taped-before-a-live-studio-audience way.

The first time I woke secure in the fact that it is impossible to die simply. IT requires drama of the three-act variety. It is impossible to die by withdrawal. I woke covered in, surrounded by surprisingly unsharp glass. April promised extravagantly.

When married, once married, while married, during marriage, wed.

The feeling reserved for babies, amnesiacs, coma survivors and failed suicides. The multiplication of gravity. The afterglow of the futility of self-destruction. The affirmation of the negation of agency. The cosmic joke. The residue that sticks to you like smoke. The best worst fuck of your life, except you're a preteen with a crush and your mind skips from foreplay to cuddle.

It is amazing how the thing worked itself out in his mind, falling asleep the instrument and the goal, a seamless, or nearly so, transition from one to the same. Elegant even. And subtle, even to him, that the spiral of thoughts—the ideation: *too many of the wrong books*—had occurred or been occurring, a sure sign. The simple fact of the matter was, or is, that he, as always, hadn't realized until after the fact.

It is fitting that a seaman would have a healthier conception of marriage than a poet.

Jason Mahanes is an experimental artist originally from Baltimore. He currently lives and works in L.A. His work in a variety of media is archived at www.letterj.com.

Virginia Fantasia
Jeff Mann

Spring morning in Blacksburg, Virginia:
hedge of blooming lilacs, golden drift
of white-oak pollen,

                               and this listserv note
announcing that the General Assembly
of this great state, state of Washington and Jefferson,
state where I was born,

                         has just passed
the Marriage Affirmation Act, which prohibits
civil unions and outlaws "any partnership, contract
or other arrangements that purport to provide
the benefits of marriage."

                      I smash a coffee cup, I call my sister
for legal advice, ask about the complications of changing
state citizenship, but West Virginia, it turns out,
is much the same on this score.

                    11 am—
Creative Writing/Poetry: I read my students Mark Doty's poem
"Charlie Howard's Descent," in which hoodlums throw
a young gay man off a bridge to his death.

                          In between
the first class and the second,
in the men's bathroom, second floor of McBryde Hall,
I'm washing my hands when I see, in the mirror over the sink,
FUCK YOU FAGGOTS, large black letters
inked into the wall of a toilet stall.

                      Afternoon's end,
a guest lecture in The Appalachian Family and Its Environment,
I'm talking about mountain cooking—ramps, creecy greens,
brown beans and cornbread—the foods I grew up on,
the foods that make me feel safe and at home
in these hills, I'm wondering what the members
of the General Assembly of the Commonwealth of Virginia
will be enjoying for dinner tonight.

                      Walking back
to my office, I pass young men playing basketball: pale,
shirtless, sweating, remote. I press my face,
my yearning, into the pink blossoms of an apple tree
and think of King Arthur, wounded, floating off to paradise,
the Isle of Apples, where strife's a stranger
and every appetite's answered.

                    Dinner with friends,
a visiting writer's reading, then home, tired, to sip single malt,
grade a few student journals. In bed by 10. Tomorrow,
the drive up to Charleston, another weekend with John, but
tonight alone, loving the solitude and silence,
far from those I love and those I hate.

Night breeze wafts
the curtains in. I strip, light a candle, take from its wall-mount
Aragorn's elven hunting knife, curved scimitar engraved with elvish
"Foe of Morgoth's Realm." For a minute I stand
                                                    before the mirror
naked, studying the salt-and-pepper goatee, hard-won muscles,
tribal tattoos. What I loathe most is any constriction that limits
what this body might choose. What I love is
                                                    the world
reimagined, revised. I stretch out on the bed, cold blade sleeping
in the silver hair between my pecs. I run my fingers over
the etched elvish, the sharp edge, rub the band of gold
about my left ring finger, and close my eyes. I fondle
these irreconcilables side by side:
                                    Wedding
amidst blooming rhododendrons, atop the overlook at Turkey Spur,
John in his conductor's tuxedo, I in my Maclaine of Lochbuie kilt,
dirk at my side,
                and
Aragorn atop me now, smiling in the candlelight, lean and hairy,
his long hair falling over my face, his beard brushing my lips,
                                                                and
every man I have ever wanted, in the classroom, on the street, in
the bars or in the gyms, an eternity of touch, endlessly various,
perpetuities of sweat and candlelight,
                                    and
Clover Holler, perhaps, in the lap of the mountains, a farmhouse
with a porch, John's flowerbeds, maples burnt-orange with autumn,
biscuits and gravy on Sunday mornings, slate trivets and canning jars,
                                                                and
this knife brought down again and again,
the last No silenced, a heap of heads, the ravens' eyeball-feast.
I want a warrior's well-deserved rest, drowsing
by the hall's hearth-fire, bare shoulder to shoulder,
beard married to beard, darkness welded to light,
golden quaichs of Drambuie or mead, toasting the end of our enemies.

Jeff Mann (www.english.vt.edu/~jmann) *grew up in Covington, Virginia, and Hinton, West Virginia, receiving degrees in English and forestry from West Virginia University. His fiction, poetry, and essays have appeared in many publications, including* The Spoon River Poetry Review, Prairie Schooner, The Big Book of Erotic Ghost Stories, Rebel Yell, Rebel Yell 2, The Hampden-Sydney Poetry Review, Crab Orchard Review, Best Gay Erotica 2003 *and* 2004, *and* Appalachian Heritage. *He has published three award-winning poetry chapbooks —* Bliss (*Brickhouse Books, 1998*), Mountain Fireflies (*Poetic Matrix Press, 2000*), *and* Flint Shards from Sussex (*Gival Press, 2000*) — *as well as a full-length collection of poetry,* Bones Washed with Wine (*Gival Press, 2003*). *His collection of essays,* Edge, *from Haworth Press, and his novella* Devoured, *in the anthology* Masters of Midnight: Erotic Tales of the Vampire, *from Kensington Books, both appeared in 2003. Another poetry collection,* On the Tongue, *will be published by Gival Press in 2006. At present he lives in Charleston, West Virginia, and Blacksburg, Virginia, where he teaches creative writing at Virginia Tech.*

We're Here, We're Queer, We're Married. Yawn.
Meredith Maran

While my friends lined up in the rain to get married in San Francisco, I wondered: If this is what we've been fighting for, why do I feel so ambivalent?

In early February I left home in Oakland, California, for a one-month writing fellowship in upstate New York. A few days later I got a frantic call from Katrine, my girlfriend of seven years. "Honey! Come home quick!" she said. "They're doing gay weddings in San Francisco! Let's get married!"

"Again?" I asked. Katrine and I were already the most-married couple we knew. We'd exchanged vows and rings for the first time two years ago in February, alone in bed à la John and Yoko (but without the press coverage); again the next year at a celebration our friends and family threw for us, officiated by my Baptist-minister son; and once more when we registered as California domestic partners a few months later. We registered for our fourth—and, we thought, final—marriage when we visited Katrine's family in France last summer, where we applied without fanfare for *le Pacte Civil de Solidarité*, which offers more legal rights than *concubinage* (domestic partnership) but fewer than *mariage*.

"For real this time!" Katrine said. "This might be our only chance!"

There was no TV where I was, and the nearest newspaper was a ten-minute walk away, but I hardly needed the news feed to be aware of this turn of events. Every time I plugged the phone cord into my laptop I found new wedding announcements bouncing around my in-box. I hadn't seen that much excitement—or that many exclamation points—on my computer screen since Ellen came out on national TV.

"It's official!!" wrote the gay dads across the street, whose unofficial commitment ceremony I'd attended many years ago.

"We did it!!" wrote a friend in her 20s, enclosing a photo of herself and her blushing, butch bride toasting each other with donated champagne on the bouquet-strewn steps of San Francisco City Hall.

"All day long I hand people their rings and cry, cry and hand people their rings. So much joy...it's restoring my faith in the human race," wrote a straight, normally self-contained friend who'd served as a volunteer witness at 24 ceremonies and counting.

"Great news! Louise and I got married!" bubbled my agent, who'd waited in the rain for six hours to marry her girlfriend of 17 years, with whom she was now co-editing a photo book chronicling the wedding blitz. Amy had delivered plenty of "great news" to me over the years, but no book deal had ever made her sound this happy. "It felt so right—so much bigger than the two of us. You should come home, Mer, even if it's just for one day," she urged me. "This could be the best thing you ever get a chance to do."

I cited the price of last-minute plane tickets. I maintained that the fellowship was the chance of a lifetime, too. I reminded Katrine and everyone else that she and I were already as married as two people could be. When the mayor of New Paltz, New York, started performing same-sex weddings I extended a perfunctory tit-for-tat invitation of my own ("Honey! Come here quick! They're marrying gay people in New York!") and was uncharacteristically acquiescent when Katrine proved no more willing than I to cross the continent for a quickie queer wedding. Marriage is all about compromise, I proclaimed loftily, when San Francisco started offering same-sex marriage appointments and Katrine got us one for the next available date, seven weeks later.

"It's not like you to be so unromantic," wrote a friend who knows that "uncompromising" is my not-so-secret middle name. "Or so un-activist," she added. "What's up?"

My friend had a point. Why wasn't I hopping aboard the lesbo love train?

As the happy virus spread from state to state, I went on reading the daily front-page gay-wedding stories, gazing at the daily front-page gay-wedding photos, waiting for a stab of sorrow, a ripple of regret, a frisson of romantic or activist fervor to kick in. It never happened. Instead, I felt a growing and disturbing sense of, well, disorientation.

I'd had that feeling before: seeing the once-militant gay-pride march morph into the faggots-are-fun gay parade, watching *ER*'s Dr. Weaver having a baby with her girlfriend on one major network and Ellen DeGeneres hosting her own talk show on another, hearing the pundits remark that supporting same-sex civil unions had become a mainstream position. Being warmly greeted on Sunday mornings by my son's Christian church-mates, who know that I'm his lesbian mother.

I felt I should be relishing these fruits, so to speak, of the gay movement's labors. Instead, as one city after another started issuing same-sex marriage licenses, as the progress of the gay-rights movement became nightly dinnertime conversation, as the straight people around me started casually conversing about their same-sex flings and fantasies—as the gender-inclusive dream I'd spent much of my life fighting for seemed to be coming true—I had a strange, nostalgic longing for what I'd known to be the natural order of things: hets on the inside with the door locked behind them, homos on the outside, banging to get in. Even if we weren't *really* sure we wanted all those trappings of boring-ass straight life; even if we secretly *liked* the compulsory creativity of our "commitment ceremonies" and fabulous family configurations; even if we wouldn't have dreamed of asking the state to sanctify our love (unless, of course, it refused to), this was the world as we knew it—the us-vs.-them rules of the one game we'd been invited to play.

The goal of every social-change movement—or (gag me with a chakra) personal-growth process—is its own obsolescence. So why wasn't I celebrating all the gains, both personal and political? Maybe because I felt I had too much to lose. For better and for worse, living as an "out" mom, an "out" neighbor, an "out" writer had given me an identity and an address to go with it; a sometimes scary but stable spot on the outskirts of town, on the margins of the mainstream. There's a steep price to be paid for being gay in America, and the compensation package—at least for those coastal big-city dwellers who can take advantage of it—is what those hard-earned dues buy us. Being gay got me the secret password to the in (out) places only queer people go, the in (out) jokes only queer people know. Why would I want to share those membership benefits with hets who haven't paid to join the club?

And as I settle into middle age, being gay has become more than a built-in, nearly effortless expression of my activism—it's become one of the few cool things about me. But how cool can it be to be gay when macho straight guys swoon and preen, allowing themselves to be fluffed and petted by screaming *Queer Eye* queens on national TV, and giggling gay-day marchers chant, "We're here! We're queer! We've got our own TV shows, Mary!"? How cool can it be to be gay when the love that dared not speak its name makes lead news headlines and campaign hay? If the world is as ready as it seems to open up and let us in, will we—will I—lose the edge we got from being out?

My greatest hopes and worst fears were realized when I came home to a changed world—well, a changed Bay Area, anyway. Suddenly it was retro to be hetero. Straight friends I ran into asked if I'd gotten married, eager to horn in on the joy; gay friends displayed marriage certificates and wedding photos where "Hate Is Not a Family Value" posters and rainbow flags had once hung on their walls.

A week after I came home from the retreat I went to open a joint savings account at our local Bank of America. "My wife and I are saving for a vacation," I told the young, meticulously manicured, straight-appearing teller. I sneaked a peek to gauge her response, and witnessed...absolutely none. "Oh, did you get married in San Francisco?" she asked nonchalantly, bringing to a screeching halt a lifetime of uncomfortable silences, defensive conversational maneuvers, and elaborate explanations. "Even though Katrine's not here to sign, I'll put both of your names on the account," she offered before I answered. "After all, you guys are *married*."

Since our first wannabe wedding I'd made a point of publicly referring to Katrine as my wife, gulping down my fears to face the dry cleaner's confusion, the haircutter's horror, the mortgage broker's veiled hostility in the interest of a bit of political provocation. Now the four-letter word I'd winced to use when I was legally married to a man but tossed around like confetti when I was illegally married to a woman— the word that only a few weeks ago had sparked nervous laughter at best, animosity at worst—triggered friendly smiles, congratulations, or no reaction at all. Now I had something even stickier to swallow than my fear: my ambivalence about the kinder, gentler, less homophobic world I'd been so sure I wanted. Who will I be, I found myself wondering, if it's normal to be who I am?

I didn't have long to wonder before reality kicked in. My first clue was the sound of my sweetheart calling me to her desk, her voice choked with tears. Together we read the email that had just appeared on her screen. The sender was the San Francisco city clerk. The subject line was "Supreme Court Decision." The date was March 12, four weeks before our wedding date. The message was brusque.

"By order of the California Supreme Court, the San Francisco County Clerk has been ordered to discontinue issuance of same-sex marriage licenses. Therefore all previously scheduled same-sex appointments are now cancelled."

"I knew it wouldn't last," said Katrine. "I wanted to *really* marry you," she cried.

"I wanted to really marry you too," I answered, surprised by the clutch in my throat that told me it was true. It struck me then that my ambivalence might have been more self-protective than I knew. Maybe I didn't want to join the party in case the neighbors complained and the cops shut it down. Maybe I found it easier to live with the world as it was—homophobia and all—than to risk living with the perilous hope that it might actually get better.

As the love fests were aborted in one city after another and the front-page profiles of ecstatic newlyweds were replaced by stories of honeymoons harpooned by homophobia, Katrine and I decided to console ourselves with a weekend honeymoon. Checking in at a bed-and-breakfast in a tourist town three hours from home, we instinctively assumed the position: standing an ambiguous distance apart, looking at each other with ambiguous eyes, speaking to each other in ambiguous tones. For the next two days—hesitant to hold hands as we strolled through the picturesque streets, scoping out the vibe in each restaurant before we fed each other bits of food, kissing only in the privacy of our overpriced, Laura-Ashley-on-steroids room—we were painfully reminded of how many risks we still take, how many prejudices we still challenge, just by being ourselves outside the Bay Area post-wedding-boom bubble.

Even inside it, where life is about as same-sex-safe as it gets; even now, when the Bay Area's still in the blush of mass-wedding afterglow, I don't kiss Katrine goodbye on the front porch if the neighbor's watching. I write an acknowledgment to her in every book I publish, but the bio on the more visible jacket flap always says, "Meredith Maran lives in Oakland," as if I live there alone. When I quote or mention Katrine in the talks I give, I sometimes tell the classic "queer lie for the straight guys," referring to her as my wife only when I'm confident that being gay won't keep my message from being heard, or me from being invited back.

Same-sex sitcoms, homo home decorating shows, gala gay days, and other sure signs of progress notwithstanding, being gay is still far too exciting for most people— including me—in most places most of the time. Until that changes, we'll have being bored to look forward to.

Meredith Maran (www.meredithmaran.com) is the author of the bestselling books DIRTY *(HarperSanFrancisco, 2003),* Class Dismissed *(St. Martins Press, 2000), and* What It's Like to Live Now *(Bantam, 1995). She also wrote a children's book,* How Would You Feel If Your Dad Was Gay? *She will be happily married to her fiancée of eight years as soon as that becomes possible.*

Originally appeared on *Salon.com*, April 19, 2004. Reprinted by permission of the author.

Marching Nuptials
(or Don't Be a Bride, Eat One)
Janet Mason

Thinking of gay marriage in the midst of NY Pride,
How could I knot? Marriage is everywhere
from the HRC petitions to the hand-holding lesbian
sporting "I'm taken" on her red tee. So am I in a
manner of speaking, but she's not here
and there are so many others, that I would not advertise
as I march with the drummers, my 6' 2" stature
raised three inches by my tiara, "genuine rhinestones"
bragged my girlfriend when she gave it to me.
I am the same height as the bride-to-be in his white veil
and chiffon tutu teetering on his three-inch platforms,
white satin, of course, a gaggle of likewise attired girls
with bulging crotches, and that is what I like about
Pride in NY, the blur of it all, gender surprises,
parade marchers gawking at sidewalk onlookers
where, in midtown, an old woman wrapped in sari
watches, her face set but eyes gleaming as they
beam into mine, and I think about marriage again,
hers, most likely arranged, and even though things
(in some places) have changed, the sanctity of the state
still does not appeal to me, but here I am marching
down Fifth Avenue in 2004, "Lick Bush" slogans
everywhere, and John Kerry blue-and-white stickers
on denim-clad asses. In the Village, streets narrow, people,
rainbow flags drape fire escapes, confetti showers,
and a woman on the sidewalk waves a "Marry Me" sign
madly in my direction, while pointing with her other hand,
and jumping up and down, and I, suddenly regal, smile,
curtsy and accept, before marching on, thankful for the
barricade between us. And when all the fun is over,
dinner with friends, the Rubyfruit after-party spilling
onto sidewalk, then home to my lover, 21 years now,
we're planning a trip to see her parents next weekend:
I'm still thinking about gay marriage.

Janet Mason is an award-winning writer. Her literary commentary is featured regularly on
This Way Out, *an international Queer radio syndicate aired on more than 400 radio stations
in the U.S. and also in Australia, New Zealand, and throughout Europe. She is the author of
three chapbooks of poetry, two from Insight To Riot Press. She has finished a memoir and is
working on her first novel. She lives in Philadelphia and can be reached at
janetmason3@msn.com.*

David McConnell

They got married. How strange! Almost like joining a cult—with the rings and the self-deprecation meant to convey, "Don't worry. We're still the same people." But they had a rosy contentment, which looked, in a certain light, smug. At times, they were giddy and tried to make a joke of the whole thing. Pecks on the cheek were giggly reminders that they were authorized by church and state to have sex now. Which is why the wedding—a big, public coming-out ceremony in front of all their friends and family—was so intensely embarrassing for them. Their hearts raced; a fit of laughter made them stumble over the vows they'd written. They were private people. They'd really rather have been camping alone together in Manitoba. The public aspect, the coming out, struck them as a necessity, nothing more. But much later, when they'd started using those ancient honorifics, husband, wife—purely as a joke, of course—they decided that the coming-out part had been good. When the embarrassment burned off, a residue of pride was left. That was my sister and her husband.

When gay people marry, the scenario differs a little. First, sex doesn't hover cutely over the ceremony, because everyone assumes gay-marrying types are the least-sexual gay people. Whether that's true or not (probably not), gay marriage is definitely not about sanctioning sex. Second, marrying isn't a reflex for gay people. There's no unexamined submission to an embarrassing public ceremony just because it's what's done. Gay people who want to marry really want to marry. To them the public aspect of marriage isn't a painful necessity but the whole point. It's a bigger, better coming-out opportunity. An article of faith among gay people holds that anyone who doesn't publicly avow their sexuality is in the state of sin called the closet. Which makes it awkward for people like me, who find marriage weird, to wonder, even to themselves, why would anyone care? I don't want to sound like a sinner.

All marriages strike me as weird, unreal—suits of invisible clothes that couples, straight and gay, ask you to admire. I realize I'd better honor their delusions, because believers are as powerful, as prone to rage, as they are insane; so I do. I offer congratulations, always hoping to see a glint in the eye that tells me—Ah!—it's all a joke. But even when they're joking, as my sister and her husband did with their bouquets of smirks, it isn't all a joke. They think marriage is real. Millennia of tradition and plenty of documentary evidence, including last year's joint income tax returns, back them up. Somehow it isn't enough to convince me. All that tradition and paper only make marriage seem too insisted-upon, too from-above, too abstract—in short, even less real. Other abstract states of coupleness don't prompt the same disbelief. Boyfriend, girlfriend, longtime companion, weekend lay, even the icky "partner," all of these make sense precisely because they're just words used by people in quick-and-dirty (or fumbling-and-thoughtful) descriptions of themselves. Marriage doesn't describe you; you describe yourself into it. When someone introduces "my husband" or "my wife," I feel I'm cast in the role of patient neighbor introduced to little Megan's imaginary friend. Pleased to meet you! Analyze it, if you wish; shake your head at my cussedness, my state of sin, my lack of seriousness; but any time we try to fit ourselves to words rather than fitting words to us, I see willed ignorance.

Gay people have played with vows and rings and honey-I'm-home domesticity for years. I used to sigh, thinking it funny if a touch cruel, like children mimicking the village idiot. I didn't grasp how much longing the jokers put into their game, much more like children mimicking their parents. I thought, maybe this gay-marriage movement is meant to wake us rudely from our delusions. Maybe gay couples are getting married in the spirit of a satirical performance piece. They hope to prove the extreme-right right for a change by undermining the institution of marriage through their marriages. They're like me, I thought. They don't see an institution but a transparent cloud-palace purling in the rising heat. So when my gay friends got married, I wanted to laugh. How strange! They didn't crack a smile. Their eyes were proudly dull.

The delusional cult they've joined is, of course, our society. Mass delusion of this sort is—I guess—the property of the masses, and they're entitled to fight for it when it's withheld. But I find the spectacle weird. Gay people must be weary. They must want to stop thinking for while. The tired doctrine of marriage looks like a safe place to rest, and in the palace bedrooms are soft beds for enchanted sleep.

July 4, 2004

David McConnell is the author of The Firebrat. *He lives in New York City and is at work on a new novel.*

Pray for Me, Muffy
Mike McGinty

"We are gathered here today…"

These are words you usually hear in a church, but which are starting to echo resoundingly in the courts and in the halls of Congress, thanks to the contentious debate over gay marriage.

It amazes me that so many people would choose to vote for candidates based solely on their stance on this one issue. Kristian (Wow. Can that be her real name?) Mineau, president of the conservative Massachusetts Family Institute, recently said of her group, "Our theme is 'Remember in November.'" Apparently, what government leaders are doing about poverty, drugs, crime, and education doesn't figure as prominently in those folks' minds as what I'm doing with my genitals. Would that I could garner as much interest in them from fellow patrons at my favorite gay bar on Saturday nights.

My mother, a big Bush supporter, has begged me not to be a "one-issue voter." However, when that one issue is equality under the law, I can't be anything but. Any candidate or incumbent who stands for less than "equality for all" doesn't deserve to be an American citizen, let alone hold public office. Let alone serve as President of the United States. I don't care how many of his constituents support him; it's just wrong and goes against every principle this country was founded on. Every principle I swore to uphold during my six years in the Navy. Every principle we are supposedly fighting for in Iraq.

One of those founding principles is separation of church and state. But tell that to the Catholic Church, who has made a statement encouraging its faithful flock to cast their votes based on candidates' stance on homosexuals at the altar. But it's a free country, sort of, and pedophiles and child abusers and those who protect them so that they are free to repeat their heinous crimes are entitled to express their opinions.

Just as Raymond Flynn, former mayor of Boston, is entitled to express his: "Homosexual couples are not the enemy. (Yeah, right. Then why don't you go home and watch reruns of *Cheers*?) The enemy is the legislators who ignored and betrayed the people of Massachusetts by not giving them an opportunity to express their point of view." You mean the legislators who stood up for equality in the face of bigotry, fear, and hatred? The legislators who upheld the law of their state Supreme Judicial Court? Do you really think the people of Massachusetts—or any state—deserve anything less, Mr. Mayor?

In May, a vocal group of citizens held a rally against gay marriage at the Capitol in Phoenix. People dressed all in white carried signs, bowed their heads in prayer, and held their hands aloft to the blue sky. Their signs read: "Preserve Marriage." But where were these people when Britney Spears got hitched, and divorced 22 hours later? Where were they when the first drive-thru wedding chapel opened its cargo-bay doors? When Elizabeth Taylor took her seventh husband? When Anna Nicole Smith married that rich geezer on his deathbed? Don't try to tell me all of these stunts were okay because the people involved happened to be heterosexuals. Because there was nothing okay with any of them. Nothing at all.

And don't tell me that if I get the freedom to marry another man today that I'm going to want to marry my dog tomorrow, and my ironing board next week. We're talking about two people in love, sharing their lives together, so let's stay relevant—

shall we?—and try not to trivialize the issue at hand. This line of reasoning is completely devoid of logic and only serves to further show just how desperately opponents of equal rights will cling to any thread they can find in an attempt to unravel what they don't understand.

The same goes for, "Well then, why don't we just legalize acts like murder and rape?! Where does it stop?!" No thinking, sane person can draw a substantive parallel between gay marriage and taking lives or violating people.

And by the way, I'm not even asking these people to understand me. Hell, my own family doesn't understand me. They don't know why I'm gay, why I have the feelings I do for people of my own sex. Neither do I understand my parents and siblings in their attraction for the opposite one. We don't have to understand each other in order to respect each other's right to live the lives we want. We don't even have to understand each other to love each other. Even Hollywood, so often accused of being vapid and shallow, shows us that. Need proof? Rent any Tom Hanks—Meg Ryan movie and watch the sparks fly.

As for what might happen to the very fabric of society if gay marriage were legalized in this country, remember the Great Copenhagen Marriage Crisis of 1989? That's because there wasn't one. How about the Norwegian Hetero Horror of '93? Never happened. Probably because the forward-thinking citizens of those countries have something called a life.

And don't get me started on Utah. That "Do as I say not as I do" state is leading the way in attempts to pass antigay marriage legislation. Utah! Founded by polygamist Mormons whose leader, Brigham Young, had 20 wives; some put the number as high as 50. I guess they lost count after a while. How convenient that they lost their memories, too.

You've heard all of these arguments before. The sad fact is, they either fall on deaf ears, or amount to nothing more than preaching to the choir. In other words, people make their decision on this issue very early on, and generally cannot be swayed one way or the other. I am never going to get Muffy Van Horn of Cleanlife, Texas to see things my way. She is never going to stop incensing me with her insistence that, as a gay man who wants to enjoy the same rights as every other American, I am somehow "less than," and as such I am undeserving of those rights. Muffy and I, we will never see eye to eye. She will always "pray for my soul" while I will always marvel at her odd aversion to tolerance and her uncanny ability to call herself an American while fighting so vehemently to deny freedom. That's what stops me cold and leaves me sick to my stomach.

To me, the bright spot in all these "pray-ins" and hate rallies, the right-wing rhetoric, the venom-spewing pundits, the So-Called Christians, and the plain, old redneck fear, is history. I look back on the fights to end slavery, win women's suffrage and civil rights, repeal laws against interracial marriage, and other hard-won causes and I can't help but feel hopeful that one day, despite all the ugly opposition from all the ugly people in this country, we will finally just grow up enough to leave each other alone.

When that day comes, and, God willing, I fall in love with a man and we decide to get married, I will walk down the aisle with tears of joy and pride streaming down my face. I hope my Republican, Catholic parents will be there to witness it. And my Evangelical sister. And my Southern Baptist brothers with their Southern Baptist wives and their Southern Baptist children. I would want them to see, firsthand, that when you come right down to it, gay marriage isn't about politics or equal rights or even religion. It's about looking at another human's face and seeing a full, unchecked, surprising joy there and, in so doing, feeling a little bit of that joy yourself.

That, ladies and gentlemen, is really why we are gathered here today. Today, and every day.

Mike McGinty is a Clio Award–winning ad copywriter in San Francisco. His essays have been published on Gay.com, Outsports.com, SiliconMom.com, and in the Noe Valley Voice. *He has also contributed to* American *magazine,* Bookmarks, *and, ironically,* San Francisco Bride. *He recently finished a memoir, and is currently at work on his first novel.*

Marriage: The Carny Come-on
Skian McGuire

Step right up! Get your gen-u-wine 100 percent legally valid imitation traditional heterosexual marriage!

Yes, you too, lesbigay gentlefolk, you too can be the proud possessors of that proverbial ball and chain! It's been okayed in Canada, it's virtual in Vermont, and coming soon to a commonwealth near you — the time-honored institution of marriage! Tell, me folks, why buy a civil union, accepted only in one tiny New England state, when, for the price of a marriage license, some hothouse flowers, and a handful of rice, you too can shackle yourself to a contract recognized by every government on earth?

Yes, folks, you too will soon have every societal privilege previously accorded to only the heterosexual majority, you too can savor the same socially approved marital bliss that your parents enjoyed — or if not your parents, perhaps your mom and your stepfather, or maybe your dad and your stepmother, or at the very least, your father and his third wife, the former Miss Pottowatomie County with silicone implants and color by L'Oréal, generally regarded by his business associates as a trophy.

You heard me — marriage. In the true-blue American tradition of seeking out new markets when the old ones dry up — in the spirit of that greatest of American industries, Big Tobacco, now peddling its wares in the Third World where no one lives long enough to get cancer anyway — now that nobody cares anymore except Christian fundamentalists and the bridal industry, wedding bells will soon be ringing for lesbians and gays from sea to shining sea, from Las Vegas to Niagara Falls, Visa and Mastercard accepted. Yes, folks, God bless America, where every child can grow up to be monogamous, and every consenting adult will be able to wed the man or woman of his or her choice; America, the land of the drive-thru chapel and the quickie divorce, where soon every citizen will have the right to tie the knot but only holy rollers and queers will want to.

Yes, folks, marriage. Faster than a 30-year mortgage, more powerful than a speeding U-Haul, able to leap age, class, and cultural incompatibilities in a single bound — soon, brothers and sisters, lesbians and gays will share the thrill of putting on the yoke, and gettin' hitched! After decades of fighting to be assimilated, now, at last, we're finally going to get exactly what we deserve!

Step right up and get your gen-u-wine 100 percent legally valid imitation traditional heterosexual marriage!

(This message has been brought to you by the Association of American Divorce Lawyers.)

Skian McGuire is a working-class Quaker leatherdyke who lives in the wilds of western Massachusetts with her dog pack and her partner of 22 years. Her work has appeared in Best Lesbian Erotica *and other places, including* The Big Book of Erotic Ghost Stories. *She's a past winner of the Amazon Slam in Boston and recipient of several Cambridge Poetry awards for performance and written poetry.*

Our Gay Wedding
Mara McWilliams

Renee and I were married February in San Francisco City Hall, along with thousands of other happy couples. The event itself was simply beautiful from beginning to end, despite the pouring rain and freezing cold. Hundreds of us camped out around City Hall in the cold and rain for the opportunity to be issued a marriage license and get legally married, even if the marriage might only be legal for a few days.

My partner and I and our daughter Serena arrived at City Hall at 10:15 p.m. Sunday night to stake out our spot on the cold sidewalk surrounding the building. Within five minutes of arrival, the rain started to trickle down and resigned moans filled the air.

We had brought sleeping bags, padding, a camping chair, a propane heater, thermos of coffee, an ice chest, and some snacks. We didn't expect the rain and were grateful for the single mini-umbrella that was stashed in the trunk.

The couple next to us, William and Eddie, were less prepared than we, as were many couples who flew in from around the world. They huddled together under a single large umbrella with a single sleeping bag covering their legs. Eddie had flown in from Utah to get married to his love, William. We talked about the adventure we were all embarking on in the name of love, and although drenched, everyone was excited.

Our car was parked right next to us and our eight-year-old daughter was snugly situated in a sleeping bag in the back seat watching a DVD, calling us on her walkie-talkie, taunting us about how dry she was! Couples around us laughed and we bonded like family. Serena soon fell asleep in the back seat, and we settled in for a long, wet night.

Thirty minutes after our arrival, people began walking around handing out bottled water, cookies, and chips. The individuals handing out these simple luxuries were not part of the line, but supportive citizens of the city of San Francisco who believed in our commitment not only to each other, but our commitment to equality for all.

By midnight the City had porta-potties delivered to the corner and not a moment too soon. I should note that the City didn't know there would be an influx of 4,000 people to a single city block for the chance to wed. Yet, we were there, and the City responded with compassion, doing their utmost to meet the needs of those waiting to be married. A San Francisco Police Department van slowly circled the building all night to keep us safe.

Throughout the night, people, just regular people who wanted to help, continued to come around passing out free hot coffee, hot chocolate, oatmeal, umbrellas, trash bags so we could try to stay dry, HOT PIZZA, bottled water, juice, donuts, muffins, and cookies!

We were so deeply moved that these individuals and couples (straight and gay alike) were willing to brave the elements with us in order to give us support. I thanked a man, and he said, "I'm not ready to get married yet, but I wanted to thank you all for what you're doing for us." I said, "Thank you again," and he said, "No, thank YOU." Literally, I felt that Love was a living and breathing entity surrounding all of us.

I honestly do not know what time City Hall opened on Monday morning; I was exhausted and excited and hoping that we would be able to get married. We had been turned away the previous morning at 9:00 a.m. because City Hall was processing licenses as fast as possible, but could not keep up with the overwhelming demand.

This morning we were anxious, yet time was of no matter.

The halls within City Hall were filled with anxious brides and grooms and cheers of congratulations. Ladies rushed to the bathroom to dry off and fix their makeup; many held flowers that they had brought with them the night before. The building was alive with love and excitement. The volunteers greeted us with broad smiles and encouragement; many of them walked up and down the line with orange juice and water, as the wait once inside City Hall was still to be 90 minutes. Six different volunteers came by and checked our completed application while we waited in line, to make sure it would be correct when we reached the clerk's office.

The atmosphere in the clerk's office was downright festive. Volunteers called out "Next patient!" or "Next victim!" to keep the applicants and paperwork flowing quickly.

When we received our marriage license there were tears of joy in my eyes. As we walked down the hall, license in hand, passing the line of people still waiting, people yelled and cheered their congratulations and we proudly held it up for all to see. We were quickly escorted to the rotunda and had our ceremony with our daughter Serena as our maid of honor. Despite the scores of people in the building, it was as if the only people there were my new bride Renee and Serena. After proceeding to the Clerk Recorder's office, we received our completed license and proudly walked out the front doors and down the steps of City Hall. People cheered and shouted their congratulations while passing cars honked their support. Walking down the steps with my new wife and my daughter, marriage license in hand, I felt elated and liberated!

This experience did several things for me. It gave me a feeling of liberation, validation, and equality to which I believe all gay people are entitled. It also restored my faith in humanity. I saw that there are still people who care enough about others to commit truly selfless acts. This was about our right to marry, but it was also about the legal recognition of love and the overwhelming support the people and the city of San Francisco have yet again shown the worldwide gay community. Thank you to all the kind and generous people who handed out the simple comforts of warm coffee and trash bags and the like! We really were so grateful for your kindness!

I would also like to thank the City of San Francisco, Mayor Gavin Newsom, Mabel Teng, and all the of the generous volunteers who made ours and thousands of other marriages possible: you are to be commended for your support, kindness, and compassion. You are heroes!

Mara McWilliams (www.maramcwilliams.com) is a Bronx-born, California-raised outsider artist and the author of Outta My Head and In Your Face. *Mara is bipolar and for most of her life she has fought the demons associated with mental illness, self-injury, addiction, and eating disorders. Mara now resides peacefully in California with her wife Renee and "their" daughter Serena. Through treatment, medication, art therapy, reading, self-cognitive behavioral therapy, and peer-counseling, Mara found peace. Her life for now is beautiful and more balanced than she ever thought would be possible. It is her desire that by sharing her experiences with this illness and expressing her feelings through painting and poetry, she can help de-stigmatize mental illness.*

First published in the *San Jose Mercury News*, March 2004. Reprinted by permission of the author.

The Lavender Picket Fence
Tommi Avicolli Mecca

"The expression (familia) was invented by the Romans in order to designate a new social organism, the head of which had a wife, children and a number of slaves under his paternal authority and, according to Roman law, the right of life and death over all of them."
—Philip Janison, "Sybil Leek and the Nuclear Family," *Radicalqueen* #5, 1974

How well I remember those good old days of queer political manifestos written in a favorite hangout or on the living room floor of a compañero's dusty Bohemian apartment. They served as our primary means of communication with each other and to a lesser extent with the outside world.

In the early '70s, I was involved with several queer groups, among them Radicalqueens, a Philadelphia transgender collective that viewed "gender as a primary source of oppression." The group had a rocky relationship with the post-Stonewall, mainstream gay-rights movement (as opposed to gay liberation) that in many ways was looking to assimilate into the dominant culture.

Radicalqueens was in the forefront of questioning not only why boys and girls are assigned different and unequal tasks in our society, but also the very existence of such cherished institutions as marriage and the nuclear family. In our often-controversial magazine, *Radicalqueen*, we as a collective espoused the not-so-new idea (Marx and Engels beat us to it) that marriage and family were the means society used to control behavior, sexual and otherwise.

To wit: "We can trace all power systems, all invidious economic relations and even the fact of oppression itself to the prototype in the subjection of women in the family." (Janison, *Radicalqueen* #5)

So I find it perplexing that 30 years later we have a gay-rights movement wanting nothing more than to perpetuate its own version of the nuclear family via gay marriage. This push for the lavender picket fence has spread like wildfire across the country ever since San Francisco mayor Gavin Newsom, not to mention the Massachusetts Supreme Judicial Court, gave the nod to issue marriage licenses to queer couples.

The San Francisco City Hall marriage scene was a glorious event, no doubt about it. In just a few weeks, over 4,000 queer couples (including comedian Rosie O'Donnell and her girlfriend Kelli Carpenter) tied the knot before a court injunction filed by right-wing religious groups put a halt to the largest act of civil disobedience the city has seen in a long time, perhaps in its entire history.

As much as I celebrated these weddings, I often found myself wondering what in the world we as a community were doing. I have nothing against anyone getting married. If this institution is going to exist, it should be open to everyone. The same goes for gays in the military. I am opposed to the very concept of an armed forces. Since the Vietnam War days I have worked to change the world so that armies will one day be obsolete. But I will defend someone's right to participate in either institution.

A lot of benefits come with both military service and legal marriage. Working-class kids get a chance at an education and job skills in the military, as unfortunate as it is that they have to learn to kill in order to do so. Married couples receive over a thousand rights that single folks don't have. Yet, why should married people gain privileges that I as a single person do not have? What makes the act of saying "I do" so monumental that it should instantly bestow all of these benefits? A reward for those who fall in love and are ready to commit themselves to each other?

Marriage was never about love. Back in the days before Hallmark and soap operas, it was about property rights. That is, the right of a man to possess and control certain things: land, wife, children, and slaves, among them. The Romans' word for family (*familia*) originally referred to a man's collection of slaves. Later it was adapted to mean all of the man's possessions, including property, wife, children, slaves, etc.

Unlike the song lyric, love and marriage don't always go together. In America today, nearly 50 percent of all marriages end in divorce, a figure that's even higher in California. The majority of missing children are abducted by partners in a messy breakup. A large percentage of child abuse (sexual and otherwise) occurs within the family. Then there's domestic violence (two to four million women a year), the physical and emotional abuse of queer children, etc. Clearly marriage has not been an altogether civilizing force, as the right wing has been asserting since the gay marriage debate began.

What the institution of marriage and family has done effectively, as Engels and Marx observed over a century ago, is to enforce society's conditioning onto children and produce generation after generation of loyal workers, churchgoers, and fodder for the military excursions of a current government hell-bent on controlling oil and other natural resources throughout the world.

It's not a pretty picture.

With gay marriage it may not get any prettier. Will parents push their gay children to settle down and marry? Will the pressure to take the walk down the aisle force young queers to settle for Mr. or Ms. Second or Third Best? Will queers who don't marry be considered failures, just as my unmarried godmother was? "Poor thing, she never found the right man." Objects to be pitied and whispered about. Will gay life transfer to the suburbs where the white house with the lavender picket fence is the acceptable style of life and cruising in parks and bars in the inner city the choice of "those other kinds of queers"?

Will divorce end half our relationships each year? Will we face alimony fights? Custody battles? Will our celeb split-ups make the front pages of the tabloids? Will our relationships be major storylines in the soaps: Juan and Joey, their tragic love story continues on *All My Children*; Sally and Moesha get married while Sally's ex plans revenge, today on *The Bold and Beautiful*.

More importantly, will the establishment of gay marriage open up the institution itself so that people who are involved in threesomes and communal living arrangements can also be recognized legally as families? What about those living together who don't want the marriage license?

I would feel more enthusiasm for the gay-marriage movement if it stood with the struggle for national health care for all, as well as the fight for affordable housing through such means as community land trusts and limited-equity co-ops, two ways to guarantee that the land cannot be speculated on, the major reason for the high cost of housing in this country. I would be less uncomfortable with the assimilationist aspects of gay marriage if the movement expressed support for workers (including queer ones) who are struggling for higher wages to support themselves or their families.

Unfortunately I suspect that when gay marriage is finally given the highest court's stamp of approval, a majority of gay marriage advocates will slip off to their houses with the lavender picket fences to raise 2.3 turkey-baster or adopted kids. For them, gay marriage is the end of the struggle and that's fine. It's still an important right to be won. For me, though, it's a part of a larger movement that is about ensuring that all people in this country have guaranteed health care, housing, food, clothing, and other necessities of life. It's part of a human rights movement that will not end until the means of production belong to the workers and war is something children only know about from history books.

As gay liberationists in the '70s, we advocated complete freedom to make love to the partner of one's choice. We believed that relationships need not be restricted to just two people. We celebrated communal living, extended families, and other loving human arrangements. We felt strongly that government had no right recognizing or denying anyone's relationship, that it should stay out of the business of marrying altogether. If only we had stayed that course.

With gays in the military, we can have out queers torturing prisoners at Abu Ghraib. With gay marriage, we can have our own Al and Peg Bundy or Archie and Edith Bunker. We can be just like our parents.

It's not my idea of progress.

Tommi Avicolli Mecca is a longtime southern Italian/American queer troublemaker and socialist whose writings have appeared in magazines, newspapers, and anthologies since the early '70s. He is author of Between Little Rock and a Hard Place *and co-editor of* Hey Paesan: Writings by Italian American Gay Men and Lesbians.

Two Men in Search of a Label
Sean Meriwether

The conservative dam that has prevented same-sex marriage is beginning to crumble—Hawaii, Vermont, Massachusetts. We are finally getting people to understand that we are after equal—not special—rights, and that barring same-sex unions is in itself unconstitutional since the objections against it are founded on religious pretexts. Now we're ready to rush down the aisle to proclaim our love and commitment to the person of our choosing, to be bound spiritually *and* legally, and be pronounced…*what*?

It might seem a niggling point to be made, especially while we're fighting off American conservatives who want to "protect the sanctity of marriage" by denying it to the same people they accuse of being hopelessly promiscuous; but the sad truth is there is no precise terminology to describe a same-sex marriage or the individuals in one.

Since we are refining the definition of marriage from "one man, one woman" to "a loving commitment between two consenting adults," we should also distinguish the difference between a heterosexual marriage and a marriage between two people of the same-sex. Though we have adopted some of the traditions of a heterosexual marriage—ceremonies, vows, and of course, gifts—we are in fact reinventing the institution in our own image. To give a more accurate understanding of what we mean to each other, as well as to define our relationship within society as opposed to husband-wife couplings, we should have simple and encompassing words for the individuals in a same-sex marriage that everyone will be able to understand.

How often have you been asked to define your relationship in heterosexual terms, being asked by some idiot "Which one's the wife?" meaning "Which of you is the submissive one?" The terms "husband" and "wife" are not just tied to heterosexual marriage, they are gender- and role-based words. Husband is not just the male in the relationship—the word also implies a masculine role of the one in charge, the designated decision-maker and provider; while its counterpart wife implies the one who takes a more submissive role, the caretaker and nurturer. Husband is distinctly male, wife distinctly female; you could easily substitute male and female for those two words without losing much more than the relationship between them. Though we've come a long way as a society to break these gender stereotypes, the truth is they still exist.

The majority of same-sex relationships are not constructed on gender-based roles, but more frequently on equal footing. It is normal for two men or two women sharing a household to divide the chores and responsibilities of daily life and childcare between them based on their schedules, ability, and desire. In our household, Jack does most of the cooking, I do most of the cleaning, and we equally share the responsibility of bringing home the bacon. It is not one person's job to act as the "wife," doing the stereotypically feminine household chores, nor is it to act as the "husband" in the masculine-defined role of provider. We define our own relationship rather than allow gender-based expectations implanted in us by society to define it for us.

To that end, the terminology designated to same-sex relationships has been "partner" based. We have a series of gender-neutral words stemming from legal documents, for this has been a legal and political battle, but these compound words do not accurately capture the true spirit of marriage. Domestic partner, life partner, and significant other are fine terms for designating a legal arrangement between two individuals, same-sexed or not, but they are too emotionally distant in meaning for me to describe the person I share my life with. Though husband and wife might be gender-loaded words, they automatically convey the significance of the relationship with a sense of family, as well as create a new entity out of the pairing; husband and wife form a *married couple*, the sum is greater than the parts.

It is up to us as a community to agree on words that we use to define the individuals in a same-sexed marriage. Whether there should be separate words for men in a gay marriage, or each woman in a lesbian marriage remains in question, but the topic should be opened for discussion. It is important in the infancy of sanctioned same-sex marriage to set down the words now so that we can more quickly establish the validity of our relationships, and perhaps assist in gaining victory over our opponents by distinguishing the difference between "traditional" marriage and our own.

In the meantime, Jack, never at a loss for words, dubbed us "blovers," short for "brother lovers," after being told by a number of people how much we looked alike. It's a term we use jokingly between us, especially when we are similarly dressed. Perhaps as an alternative solution we will continue to define our own words for each other, as we define our own relationships, and one may even argue that this is a better solution than fixed terms like husband and wife, our heterosexual predecessors. However, I believe it is in our best interest as a community to set down the terms we use to define our own relationships, in order to build a foundation of understanding not only for ourselves, but for our new roles within society.

Sean Meriwether's fiction has been defined as dark realism, his subjects rooted in the peculiar nature of everyday life. His work has or will be published in Lodestar Quarterly, Love Under Foot, *and* Quickies 3. *He is currently working on a collection of short stories and a novel. In addition to writing, he has the pleasure of editing two online magazines,* Outsider Ink *(www.outsiderink.com) and* Velvet Mafia *(www.velvetmafia.com). Sean lives in New York with his blover, photographer Jack Slomovits, and their two dogs. If you are interested in reading more of his work, visit him online at* www.seanmeriwether.com.

Two Steps Forward, One Step Back:
Don't Let Marriage Rights End Support for All Families
Marshall Miller and Dorian Solot

Part I: Joy

Few moments in the recent history of social change can match the exhilaration inside Boston's Old South Meeting House on November 18, 2003. The Supreme Judicial Court had just handed down its decision stating loudly and clearly that yes, Hillary Goodridge and her partner, Julie, had the right to civil marriage. The mood inside the church was electric: After years and years of activist sweat and tears by those present and countless more around the country, our side had won a victory. A big one.

The victory was a political one for the gay, lesbian, bisexual, transgender (GLBT) community, but it was also a deeply personal one for same-sex couples who had all but given up their dreams of being able to marry their life partner. Our own mental photo album is now filled with snapshots of cheering and screaming on that autumn day, followed by touching memories of our friends Gail and Betsy's wedding, and the online video *The Washington Post* produced about the marriage of our friends Robyn and Peg. Even us two Alternatives to Marriage Project activists who have chosen unmarriage for 11 years and counting, got all teary and sentimental watching these weddings.

The great thing is, we're not the only ones who have seen happy gay couples marrying. Thanks to television and radio, the entire country has now watched and listened to same-sex couples marrying at Cambridge City Hall, on P-Town's sandy beaches, and on Northampton's rolling hills. Americans know that same-sex couples can marry in Massachusetts, and that many of them are thrilled to do so.

Yet, like any major event in the news, most Americans probably aren't aware of the extent to which the victory in Massachusetts was the cumulative effect of many small victories. Some, like Ellen's coming out or civil unions in Vermont, made national headlines. Others were barely noticed by the mainstream press, but significantly improved the quality of life for GLBT people. One of the most important of these has been the decidedly unsexy, yet profoundly important, implementation of domestic partner benefits.

In 1982, *The Village Voice* newspaper became the first employer in the country to officially offer domestic partner benefits to its employees. The company already had an unofficial policy of covering employees' unmarried different-sex partners, and a GLBT employee group successfully argued that their partners should receive equal benefits.

Since then, interest in domestic partner (DP) benefits has exploded, with over 7,300 companies offering domestic partner benefits, and new ones adding them each day. These benefits provide the same benefits (health, dental, and often family leave, bereavement, and other "soft" benefits) to employees' domestic partners and their children as were already available to employees' spouses and children. Over the 20 years since DP benefits first arrived on the scene, employers have begun to realize it's in their best interest to offer them. The benefits have been found to help companies attract and retain the best employees. One survey of 279 human resources professionals representing 19 industries found that domestic partnership benefits were among the top three most effective incentives for recruiting new hires. Also, if an employee's family has health coverage, it's more likely that employee will be at work rather than home dealing with a partner's health crisis.

Part II: Concern

Given the popularity of domestic partner benefits, you can imagine our concern when Beth Israel Deaconess Medical Center, Babson College, and the city of Springfield, Massachusetts announced they were yanking their DP benefits policies in light of same-sex marriage in Massachusetts. Now that same-sex couples had the option of marrying, these employers said, we will no longer recognize their domestic partners as members of their families for purposes of health benefits. If you want to maintain access to the same medical care you already have, you'll have to tie the knot.

Beth Israel and Babson had same-sex-only DP policies, making only same-sex couples eligible, rather than couples of any sexual orientation. This is not standard business practice: 92 percent of employers offering DP benefits use an inclusive definition of "domestic partner" that makes benefits available to both same-sex and different-sex couples.

The city of Springfield had this kind of inclusive policy. Before same-sex marriages were recognized by the state, this city told heterosexual unmarried couples who fit the definition of domestic partners they would not be forced to marry for health benefits. Once Massachusetts started recognizing the marriages of same-sex couples, though, the city announced that employees with domestic partners covered by its policy—both straight and gay—had 90 days to get married or lose their health insurance.

In response to these employers, 11 major national GLBT organizations signed a joint statement calling on Massachusetts employers to maintain their domestic partner benefits. They provided thoughtful, detailed reasons to preserve DP benefits, pointing out that the benefits were not originally intended as a stopgap measure until same-sex marriages were recognized by states, but as a way to "provide fair and equal treatment to the growing diversity of employees' families, both married and unmarried."

While the announcement of the end of these employers' DP policies was of great concern, even more worrisome was they way in which the decision was touted. Jerry Berger, a spokesman for Beth Israel, said the decision was "a way of celebrating the equality of gay couples and heterosexual couples." The New England GLBT newspaper *In Newsweekly* ran an editorial entitled, "After Marriage, Show Domestic Partnerships the Door," arguing that "domestic partnership benefit programs are not only unnecessary, but they undermine the continued fight for full marriage equality." The people making these arguments may consider themselves supporters of GLBT relationships and families. But they seem to have forgotten about GLBT employees who work in Massachusetts but live in another state; those advised by a lawyer or accountant to postpone marrying because of the legal and financial conflicts it would create on the federal level; those for whom marrying would mean losing a pension or survivor's benefit from a deceased spouse; those who choose not to marry (like growing millions of heterosexual couples) for political, religious, or personal reasons; and countless other situations that remind us that marriage is not a one-size-fits-all solution. Full equality means offering DP benefits as well as marriage licenses.

Part III: Strategy

Those charged with managing the public perception of the fight for the right to marry have a difficult task on their hands. On the one hand, in survey after survey, a majority of the general public consistently says it doesn't approve of same-sex marriage. There are signs of hope: younger people are more likely to be in favor of equal marriage rights, as are those who know a gay or lesbian person. But 38 states have adopted Defense of Marriage Act legislation, refusing to recognize same-sex marriages granted in other states.

On the other hand, aside from the marriage issue, Americans have become markedly more accepting of GLBT people. Public acceptance of gays in the military grew from 51 percent in a 1977 Gallup Poll to 80 percent in 2003. Approval of gays as elementary school teachers grew from 27 percent in 1977 to 61 percent over the same period. A 1999 Gallup survey showed that 59 percent would vote for a well-qualified presidential candidate who was homosexual, up from 26 percent in 1978. Just a few years ago no one had ever heard of a "civil union." GLBT activists should consider it a major victory that in the four years between the Bush-Gore election and the Bush-Kerry election, the platform of most mainstream Democratic party candidates includes support for civil unions as a way to provide legal protections to same-sex couples—short of marriage, of course.

This disconnect between a public that clearly says it doesn't want GLBT people, or at least G and L people, to be discriminated against, but also doesn't want them to marry, speaks to the symbolic power of marriage. Same-sex couples in Vermont argued vehemently that they needed access to civil marriage because of the legal rights and protections it provided. When the state created civil unions to provide the same state-level legal rights as marriage, suddenly couples were arguing they wanted the *m*-word itself, not just its legal cloak. For that same reason—the distinction between legal equality and symbolic equality—many nongay Americans stop short when it comes to supporting marriage rights for same-sex couples, even if they are generally tolerant of GLBT people.

The practical problems with shifting public opinion given these conditions are plainly evident in an online advertisement as part of the Human Rights Campaign's "Millions for Marriage" campaign. Available for viewing at *www.hrc.org/millionformarriage/hospital_commercial*, the ad invites the viewer to imagine a gay world in which a straight man is informed that his wife is in a coma, but he can't see her because the state doesn't recognize their marriage. As the man sits, stunned, the words, "Hospital visitation: Just 1 of over 1,000 rights granted to a legally married couple" appear on the screen. The add closes with the HRC equal sign logo and the phrase "support equality for all Americans."

In the press release touting this ad, HRC President Cheryl Jacques said, "No American should ever have to experience being blocked from visiting their partner at the hospital room door... But without the right to marry, all too many couples have been denied this right." Yes, it's true that no American should ever have the experience of being blocked from visiting their partner at the hospital room door. Any archaic hospital policy that still limits "family" to blood and marriage is sorely in need of updating.

This no-brainer—that people should be able to choose who is by their side in medical emergencies—is even recognized by the primary health care accreditation organization in the U.S., the Joint Commission on Accreditation of Healthcare Organizations (JCAHO). In its standards for hospitals and health care facilities, JCAHO defines "family" as "the person(s) who plays a significant role in the individual's [patient's] life. This may include a person(s) not legally related to the individual." The GLBT legal advocacy group Lambda Legal provides information about how to file a complaint with the JCAHO regulating body if one of them refuses visitation to a domestic partner or other family member.

So if one's goal is to obtain hospital visitation privileges for same-sex couples, there are at least three ways to bring it about:

(1) secure marriage rights in all 50 states

(2) pass hospital visitation bills in state legislatures (in Rhode Island, for example, you can name up to five people who should be treated as "immediate family" for the purposes of visitation in a medical facility)

(3) hold hospitals to the standards set by their own accrediting organization.

Not only are #2 and #3 easier to obtain at this point, they actually take the further step of recognizing that hospital visitation shouldn't be based on blood or marriage. As a result, they include unmarried different-sex couples, unmarried same-sex couples, and other "alternative" family forms like stepfamilies, polyamorous families, or other types of GLBT family forms, such as two moms and two dads parenting together. Legal marriage isn't the easiest or even the best path to hospital visitation rights.

That's not to say that the HRC is making a mistake by using the emotionally powerful hospital visitation issue as a means to sway public opinion on marriage. But just as with domestic partner benefits, we must be prepared for the inevitable result: a general public that's told that once gays and lesbians have the right to marry, they'll finally have all the rights and protections they need. Therefore, the logic goes, there's no further need for any policy that recognizes unmarried families or provides rights to single people—gay, bi, or straight. Including same-sex couples in the definition of marriage doesn't change the underlying problem that hospital visitation shouldn't be based on marital status in the first place.

While it may be difficult, surely it's not impossible to fight the war for equality on two fronts. The first is to continue and win the highly visible campaign for same-sex couples to be allowed to legally marry. The second is to change policies and laws so they don't discriminate on the basis of marital status. There's simply no reason why married people—in same-sex or different-sex marriages—should pay fewer taxes, receive more workplace benefits, and get thousands of other perks and bonuses simply because they have rings on their fingers. Legalizing same-sex marriage doesn't rectify much broader inequalities.

The GLBT community has long argued that domestic partnership is not an acceptable substitute for marriage. Likewise, marriage is not an acceptable substitute for domestic partnership. We need same-sex marriage, yes—it's a basic matter of civil rights that everyone should be able to make the same choice whether to marry or not. But we also need other ways to recognize GLBT families, unmarried families, nontraditional families. Despite the current excitement about marriage in the GLBT community, the overall trend in the United States is *away* from marriage. The average American spends the majority of his or her adulthood unmarried. The number of unmarried partners living together is skyrocketing.

So, we'll be there with bells on to share in the excitement as states come to their senses about same-sex marriage. But before and after that happens, we'll be advocating for fair and equal treatment for all kinds of relationships and families— married or not.

Marshall Miller and Dorian Solot are the founders of the Alternatives to Marriage Project (www.unmarried.org), a national organization for people who choose not to marry, cannot marry, or live together before marriage. They're the authors of Unmarried to Each Other: The Essential Guide to Living Together as an Unmarried Couple, *a book for people of all sexual orientations.*

Rainbow Bridge
Tim Miller

I am standing in the middle of the Rainbow Bridge that crosses over Niagara Falls. There is an American flag to my right—naturally—and a Canadian flag to my left. The bridge makes a graceful, leap—rainbowlike, I suppose—over the rushing torrents of the Niagara River. There are lots of tourists who want to be photographed with one leg in Canada and one in the U.S. They want their legs spread wide; they want to be ripped opened by that hot throbbing U.S.-Canadian border. Well, I should just speak for myself, I think.

I'm here to plan my wedding, my big fat GAY wedding, with my partner Alistair, here in the middle of the Rainbow Bridge. We'll be married just two inches over onto the Canadian side where gay people have rights. What place could be better to get married, right? The scene of the crime, Niagara Falls—all those millions of weddings and honeymoons over the decades! It's the prime locus for unjust heterosexual marriage privilege! Niagara Falls on the Rainbow Bridge! Who knew they had made a homosexual bridge between Canada and the U.S. For moi, it seems. It's so culturally sensitive!

When you're at the Falls, you can't help but imagine all the bad things that could happen. The Maid of the Mist might hit a rock, sink, sending the yellow-slickered tourists plunging to their deaths. The plump white Observation Balloon from the American side over Goat Island pops a panel and spills everyone into the Niagara River and over the American Falls, onto the rocks below. We can witness the meltdown of the heterosexual family unit; husbands push their wives over the falls, wives shove their husbands. Fed up parents throw their children over the wall into the torrents below. There go Bobby and Suzie! Anything can happen at Niagara Falls!

Everywhere I look here, I see recently married straight couples walking in rented tuxes and wedding gowns. The straight couples promenade down the path, gracefully receiving smiles from all who pass. They look like shabby Balkan royalty. Alistair and I have already bought matching Prada tuxes for our wedding—we maxed out all our credit cards on them—and we put the tuxes on and take them out for a test drive, walking hand in hand along the Falls promenade. It's weird how when we walk past the American tourists no one says anything nice to us. In fact, a weird woman from South Dakota smoking two cigarettes at once actually spits at us! Where are all the other gay couples?

I'm here on the Rainbow Bridge for a very good reason. I'm getting ready to take the plunge. No, I'm not going to fling myself off the bridge; I'm not that much of a drama queen. But there is a plunge coming. Alistair and I are planning our future marriage here in Niagara Falls, Canada. Even though we are planning this wedding day, there is a huge clock hanging over our heads, ticking down to when we have to leave America. Since in America gay couples have not one single federal right respecting the humanity of our relationships, and since Alistair is from Australia and we can't get married so we can get Alistair a green card and stay together in the U.S., we have to leave the fucking country. For a gay couple like us, the Rainbow Bridge is the perfect spot to really see how we are treated in the U.S. We can do the math here. Over to my right in America, lesbian and gay couples don't have a single federal right respecting their relationship. Over to my left in Canada, they have rewritten hundreds of laws to include gay couples in the definition of spouse, and gay couples have complete equality of civil marriage rights. See, for a gay person, when you leave the U.S. and step into Canada, that's when you enter the free world!

I am balanced between the Maple Leaf Candy and the Kentucky Fried Chicken, feeling all existential and ripped in two. And as so often happens in moments like this, I start to hear bagpipes. Oh, God, it's Alistair's Scottish father come to stop our wedding. One of Alistair's sisters must have tipped him off. He's going to come up with all his drinking buddies from Glasgow to stop me from marrying his youngest son. He's going to rush out onto the Rainbow Bridge, waving his highlander broadsword and shouting, "Ach, you dirty devil, you'll not have me wee bairn Alistair Duncan McCartney."

But wait, it's not Alistair's dad. It's a Canadian bagpipe orchestra! About 30 people in kilts with bagpipes. It's the Niagara Falls, Canada Police Department Bagpipe Orchestra! They are being led by some guy in an eighteenth-century town crier costume. He steps onto the middle of the Rainbow Bridge, pulls out an elegant scroll, and rings his bell. "Oyez! Oyez! Oyez!" he cries as the bell clangs. "On this Victoria Day, in honor of HRH Elizabeth II of the United Kingdom and the Dominions of Canada and Australia, I welcome you to the 42nd Annual tug-of-war between the police of Niagara Falls, Canada and the police of Niagara Falls, America." Three dozen buff and hunky Canadian cops march out onto the bridge dressed all in black, with neat berets. They look like sleek, sexy otters—I mean, OT-TERS! They are carrying a huge rope over their shoulders, thick as an anaconda. The U.S. police department team arrives a moment later. They're working a whole other look, sort of a sky-blue-polyester-jumpsuit, too-many-doughnuts, changing-planes-at-Memphis-International-Airport kind of look.

At this point, 138 Boy Scouts from Troup 883 of Wexford, Pennsylvania, suddenly surround me and the crazy synchronicity of what is happening becomes a bit too much. Let me do a checklist: I am standing here at Niagara Falls, historical heterosexual marriage destination, as I ponder gay marriage, about to be tipped off the edge of the United States, forced to leave with Alistair, and feeling tugged in two, watching the U.S. and Canada have a tug-of-war on the exact borderline between the nations on the Rainbow Bridge, surrounded by the Wexford, PA Boy Scouts—yet another organization that only in America discriminates against gay people. What comes next—Jesse Helms on a broomstick spelling out in smoke, "SURRENDER, TIMOTHY!"?

BANG! The game is on. The U.S. makes an immediate move and almost drags the Canadians over the line; but the Ontario cops dig their feet in, every Canadian sinew tensing, and slowly pull the U.S. team closer, closer, and finally over the line. Canada has won the first round. It's going to be the best two out of three. It takes them a while to get set up for the second match. The rope is straining so tight it looks like it's going to snap and decapitate the sunburned head of the Scout Master of Troop 883, Wexford, PA. And I realize that I am the rope being pulled to the breaking point.

Oh, God. I realize something scary about myself. I realize I want Canada to win this tug-of-war. Oh, aren't I naughty? Aren't I being such a bad American? But I don't just want America to lose this little game of tug-of-war. I want all our huge outstanding bills to be paid. Just a few little debts we owe. Like for 250 years of human slavery that created the nation's wealth. Our huge overdue debt to the native people we took North America from. The fact that we are 4 percent of the world's population and use 35 percent of the world's natural resources. For the 85 countries we have invaded in the last century or so. I don't know about you, but I'm sick of our country's racist, sexist, gun-loving, faggot-hating, red-baiting, health-care-denying, sodomy-criminalizing, gas-guzzling, war-mongering, carbon-dioxide-spewing, wealth-grasping shit! I realize I have become a daytime TV cliché—I'm stuck in an abusive relationship with the U.S. America slaps me and I say, "Thank you, Land of the Free." The U.S. slugs me and I say, "I'll have two lumps, please." She kicks me and my partner Alistair out of the country and I say, "You're too kind."

The U.S. is slowly pulled over the line and loses. The Canadians on the bridge roar as they win the best two out of three. The Americans do what Americans do when we lose: have an out-of-body experience, pretend it never happened, slink off and look for someone much weaker than us to beat up on. The bagpipes cry out as everyone marches back to their side of the border.

I look at the departing, defeated U.S. police team. They march back to the U.S., which will not be my home much longer. I look to Canada, the civilized world beyond, England, our future home past the horizon. There on the Canadian side, I see a Planet Hollywood and a Hershey's Kiss the size of the Goodyear Blimp draped over the facade of a fine old Canadian hotel. Alistair takes my hand; soon it will be our wedding. Surrounded by bagpipes, I turn and walk with him back over the Rainbow Bridge. With Alistair's hand in mine, the drums and bagpipes swirling around us, and rain definitely falling on my parade, we walk slowly back to Canada.

Tim Miller is a solo performer and the author of the books Shirts & Skin, *and* Body Blows. *He can be reached at his website:* http://hometown.aol.com/millertale/timmiller.html.

Originally appeared on *Nerve.com*, June 2, 2004. Reprinted by permission of the author.

Commitment
John Mitzel

As I write this text, the legislators at my state house (Massachusetts) are sitting as a constitutional convention, which they do every year, I think, and they have a number of items on their plate. One item is the issue of "gay marriage." A recent decision by the majority of the judges on the state's highest court maintained that the state could not refuse issuance of marriage licenses to same-sex couples. This decision set off an uproar and as a result attempts to amend the state's constitution are in play at the convention, mostly to define marriage as the legal union of one man and one woman, at a time that is. The constitution of Massachusetts is 224 years old, and it was written in a way that makes it difficult to amend. Other states have different procedures, and a good number of them have already changed their constitutions to recognize "marriage" as exclusively a mixed-sex union, including, most recently, my native state of Ohio—and didn't Gov. Taft, yes, I know, another Taft, seem overly eager to enshrine discrimination in his state's premiere document? And the current president of these United States has brought his heft and gravitas to the conversation, in favor of an amendment to the U.S. Constitution to do what Ohio solons have done to theirs. I wish the current occupant of the Oval Office would find it in his heart to take up my position on this public issue, which is something along the line of the late Emma Goldman's.

The state house has been a circus as this "debate" goes on. Advocates for "traditional marriage" are present as are substantial numbers of same-sexer supporters. It is a development long past mere political tinkering; the discourse is now emotion-laden. All of this has come as a surprise to me. Actually, one of many surprises. The first surprise was that the marriage issue would so suddenly become the top item on the famous Gay Agenda. It has been kicking around for over 30 years. I recall a picture from the early 1970s, printed in one of the then few gay publications, of two guys being turned away by some town's official, after they had applied for a marriage license. That scene has been repeated many times, with other couples. But the tides of change can erode even the most obstinate obstacle. But I thought other issues would be first up. There are issues of employment discrimination, health-care funding, an epidemic to confront, and the ridiculous Don't Ask Don't Tell policy of the military. But the marriage issue is now rattling around the country, and little Massachusetts is getting beat up on for being Leader of the Pack.

Marriage is a peculiar institution, as are most institutions. Many participate nonetheless—think Rev. Moon with his wholesale marriages. Marriage has its perks and its downsides as well. And there are all kinds of marriages. Between my two brothers and my parents, I think there are a dozen marriages, or close to it, in my immediate family; so I've had the opportunity to see the variety of opposite-sex marital options. (My sister-in-law has had six husbands! Margaret Mead once opined about the option of polygamy and polyandry. She noted that in our culture, such phenomena exist; it's just that we do them serially rather than all at once.) So, marriage, to quote the late Zelda Fitzgerald, seems to be a movable feast. It occurs to me that the role of the state in these affairs is to process an equitable outcome. If two individuals wish to settle down with each other and become a couple, the various benefits and perks accorded to one should be offered to all. I believe that this is how other societies have addressed this issue. Other societies—in my effort to be polite, they will be nameless—seek civil remedies to matters of inequity. In our culture, unlike the others, we are still encumbered by the large presence of religious influences and the dash to majoritarianism. Some of the folks at my state house, in support of "traditional" marriage, had signs that read: "Let The People Vote!" Under my state's constitution, once the pols do their thing, amending the document, then the good *volk* get to weigh in at the ballot box—yes or no, vote now! But should the good *volk* vote—in a climate of emotion and religious hysteria—on matters of social justice? Isn't our political system designed, in many ways, to prevent this from happening?

What I still don't get, and probably never will, is why many people are so emotionally invested in their own take on marriage. In marriages, there are sex acts involved; there are often children involved; there are finances involved. Everyone, well almost everyone, gets tired to some degree of his or her nearest and dearest over time. But so many lack compassion. So many seem to have no clue. So many seem to have punishment—a favorite theme among many religious—on their minds. And, of course, a lot of them just hate queers to begin with and would be content to have the lot of us gone for good. Something to remember, even on your wedding day.

My position? I think people should pursue happiness. I am not part of a couple and probably never will be, though you never know. But for all those persons who are content to be couples and do what couples do—settle down, be domestic, raise children, be involved in community activities, etc.—I would expect nothing less than my state legislators, sitting as solons or as constitution amenders, to stand up—think a production number from *A Chorus Line*—and bow and say, "Thank You." And then do the right thing, which can be, for the lot of them, an iffy thing.

John Mitzel was a founding member of the Fag Rag collective, and has been a columnist for The Guide *magazine since 1986. He is also the proprietor of Calamus Bookstore* (www.calamusbooks.com) *near Boston's South Station.*

First published in *The Guide* magazine, March 2004. Reprinted by permission of the author.

Reality Orientation/Idiot Country:
In Which Marshall Sharpens His Tongue on the Opponents of Same-Sex Marriage
Marshall Moore

Wedding bells are ringing in Massachusetts. Brain cells are dying in the provinces. Gay marriage became legal in the Netherlands a few years ago. Queen Beatrix threatened to abdicate for a day; if she carried out her threat, the rest of the world didn't notice. And Holland didn't sink into the sea. Belgium legalized it next. The cupid fountain didn't stop pissing and the Atomium didn't collapse. Canada, in its fractious way, has kept its position near the forefront of human rights issues one province at a time. In British Columbia, Ontario, and Quebec, gay couples can wed; in the remaining provinces and territories, where no one lives, they can't. Sweden and Spain are in queue. Even Taiwan has made overtures toward legalizing gay matrimony. Here in America, where nothing can be accomplished without a lawsuit, we're going to see a summer of love and litigation; perhaps a few more states will become places where queers can officially be human. Look outside. See those big blue shards of sky falling? No? Funny about that. That must mean the world hasn't come to an end.

The religious loonies I understand. You can't grow up in small-town North Carolina without tripping over an old rugged cross every 20 feet or so, and without scorching your eyebrows on all the hellfire and brimstone. Some people need to believe Jesus is pulling their puppet strings. It's easier than thinking. What I don't understand is the gay antiassimilationist canard that Marriage Is Bad for the Movement. The sixties ended. The Republicans took over, with aid and comfort from the Religious Right. No matter what kind of political skulduggery may have been behind Gavin Newsom's decision to let gay couples say "I do" several months before the term "Boston marriage" took on an updated meaning, the antimarriage queers' fuzzy rhetoric about transforming a corrupt heterosexual institution is going to prove as effective as trying to change the course of a hurricane by farting at it.

Homosexuality is no more a new script for society than left-handedness is. It's not a radically different state of existence unless that's what you make of it. Anyone who maintains that queers are inherently unlike straight folks is missing two important points: *heterosexuals are not all alike either, and they are not the enemy.* If deep down inside you want to be coupled up with and married to someone of whatever sex — if that arrangement will satisfy your needs, if it's what you've always dreamt of — then why shouldn't that option be available? Straight or gay? Why should committed couples deprive themselves of necessary legal rights and protections for the sake of radical but vague ideals put forth by people who have probably never owned property and never will? And, perhaps more fundamentally, why should any so-called advocate presume to tell gay people how they ought to live?

I didn't become gay to change the world, as I once heard a lesbian activist say, because I didn't become gay. I just am, and that fact is the foundation upon which this entire debate rests. I didn't have any choice in the matter. Having a homosexual orientation isn't a *choice*. The only element of choice comes into play when you recognize you're gay and choose to live consistently with the way you're made. It's challenging at times, but it beats the hell out of the lies and misery of the closet. It's also not a fetish, as the right-wingers appear to believe. It's not an arrangement us homos make to get a steady diet of blow jobs and butt-fucking. That said, I'm not willing to accept an inferior status (or turn my nose up at marriage just because it's what breeders do and we should be above that), and I don't have much patience with the fuzzballs who seem to believe I should be something I'm not, just because I'm gay. That's no different from what the religious fundamentalists are up to.

In my ideal world, marriage and civil unions would exist side by side. In my ideal world, church and state would be divorced but still on cordial terms. For those who want a religious ceremony, in a church whose leadership and congregants embrace same-sex couples, marriage should be available. Those who want the legal recognition without bringing religion into it could opt for civil unions. The same rights, responsibilities, privileges, protections, and prestige would appertain to both. However, America in the early-to-mid Zero Decade is not even close to my ideal world. The United States is the new Imperium, with the government whored out to corporate interests. Our militaristic opportunism in the Middle East may win us fresh petroleum fields to exploit, but we're paying for these resources in blood. The only difference between the year 2004 and Orwell's *1984* is better shopping. Since we're not going to get a new gay-inclusive Constitution like South Africa did (hell, it would be nice to have our original one reinstated), we're going to have to live with assembling our civil rights one fight at a time.

The idealism of the activists who want to *build community* and *transform marriage* is naïve in the context of our new world disorder. It overlooks the reality that our government is a juggernaut incapable of being influenced by anyone with less money than, say, Warren Buffett or Bill Gates. Wanna cause social change? Don't bother writing your congressperson because your letter won't get past a 22-year-old page who's working on Capitol Hill for the summer and can't read. And for your own sake, don't bother protesting too vehemently. The Patriot Act has more or less superceded the Bill of Rights, and your freedoms of speech and assembly have been reduced to nostalgic abstractions. Wanna live in the America you used to know? Move to Australia. Wanna make sure you can make medical decisions for your partner and not be turned out of your own house by his or her blood relatives in a worst-case scenario? Preemptively sue someone. Or get married. Marriage isn't a panacea for all the obstacles facing gay people, but it's a step in the right direction. What about gay couples marrying won't be transformative, anyway? Marriage will be transformed whether the God 'n' Country Club like it or not, because *it's no longer working for straight people*. If you doubt me, look at divorce statistics. Transformation may not happen the way the antiestablishment fringe dwellers want, or on their timetable, but it will happen. It has to.

As far as building community is concerned, the ideal of gay cohesion overlooks the fact that any community comprises people who have differing levels of investment and participation. Some people simply want to come home at the end of the day, shut the door, check their investment portfolios, and be done with the outside world. Those who want to join organizations, boycott corporations, eschew meat, and protest in the streets should absolutely do that. Gay or straight, not all of us are joiners. Where on this continuum any gay man or lesbian lands is up to him or her to decide. And *community* is being used as a red-herring issue in the marriage debate. Why does it have to be an either/or situation? How could communities not be enriched by the stability—and quiet advocacy—of legally married couples?

When I came out 15 or 20 years ago (it was a process with murky beginning and end points), the word used to refer to one's significant other was "lover," which sounded spurious and illicit, and generally made my skin crawl. As we all do, I ached to find somebody. Grow up lonely, always hearing you're defective because of a difference you didn't ask for, keep getting beaten up because of it both at home and at school, and a void opens. Just as the galaxy is supposed to contain an immense black hole at its center, my psyche has organized itself around a complex dark structure from which little light escapes on certain days. (But then, I live in Seattle; at times, it's easy to forget that sunshine exists here.) Some people, similarly constructed, anesthetize themselves with drugs and drink. Others ricochet from relationship to relationship, always bouncing but never coming to rest. Somehow I managed not to turn into a lush, but where men are concerned I'm a train wreck. I lived with R—, an alcoholic mama's boy who couldn't hold down a job to save his life, for about a year in my early 20s. Less than a year after we broke up, I met F—, a foreign student on an expiring visa. Ended up moving in with, and supporting, that one. It was hell. While living with him, I met D—, my ostensible Mr Right. D— and I spent six years in a strange push-me-pull-you orbit, connected but not quite connecting. He said he wanted to get old with me and I believed him. Then he told me he was in love with somebody else, and it destroyed a part of me. I met A— while the wreckage from D— was still black and smoking, and invited him to move in with me four months later. Yes, it was a rebound. Shortly before we broke up, what was left of me met and fell for J—, a Canadian who seemed to be into me but then one day suddenly wasn't. Yes, that was another rebound, and I'm still raw from it. You could cut your hand on my jagged edges. I'd have married all five of them. Only with J— was it actually a possibility. We even discussed it. I'd rather live in Canada than the United States, and gay marriage is legal in British Columbia. But that relationship ended on Valentine's Day 2004, and I made things worse by picking a fight with him afterward. In the first four cases, it's ironic that I was saved from myself by institutional discrimination. Thank God or Somebody (Hephaestus will do, or Sedna) I didn't marry any of them. In addition to commitment, marriage sometimes means divorce, and divorce means alimony; I'd rather wash shards of broken glass down with Iraqi crude than write any of them a monthly check. In the case of J—, we could have gotten married and I'd have happily moved to Vancouver, but it wasn't to be. I'm not in a rush to get married because I've finally figured out I'm not husband material at the moment, but when and if the right man comes along (especially if he's not an American citizen, and immigration is an issue), I'd like the chance.

I have not yet heard a convincing reason why it should be any other way.

Marshall Moore is the author of the collection Black Shapes in a Darkened Room *(Suspect Thoughts Press, 2004) and the novel* The Concrete Sky *(Haworth Press, 2003). For more information about him, please visit his website at* www.marshallmoore.com.

My Sister's Wedding
Eileen Myles

Last May, the following message appeared in my AOL mailbox:

Hey Eileen:
Judy and I are getting married Saturday morning. Isn't it wild? I never thought this would
happen in our lifetime. Finally an advantage to living in Massachusetts!
Love & Kisses,
Ann Marie, Future Married Woman!

Now I won't say that my sister and I are not *close*, but looking back in my files, I find her wedding announcement among other messages from her with subject headings like "Best Chicken Joke Ever," and maybe a bunch of political emails, nothing that would indicate that despite the fact that we shared a room for 18 years we are now intimate friends. Though Nancy and I are some kind of friends, maybe friends that have been trying and failing for years to stay consistently close, but truly what I most often say about my relationship with my sister to other people is that we are gay. A few years ago I had a girlfriend who owned a house in Massachusetts, and we invited my sister and her girlfriend for Thanksgiving and when they came I realized that I was the only person in my crowd who had a gay sibling. It was so great. Part of the practice of our sisterhood at that time was her coming to P-town with her girlfriend and spending Thanksgiving or weekends with us — though actually my girlfriend didn't get along very well with my sister and her girlfriend. It turned out my sister and I were in lesbian relationships that didn't necessarily fit with the other's, so that's where our relationship got stuck for a while. Though I remember when I was on the Sister Spit tour in New Orleans that same summer and I took a ferry across the Mississippi River and I called Nancy from there and that felt close. I remember standing on the payphone at Algiers Point and telling her I wanted Jell-O and I knew she would know what I meant. It got better when my girlfriend and I broke up, but nothing's really pushed my sister and I to another level till this announcement. Cause what would I do? I mean of course I would go. My friends in California just got married and they had a big party and their families came but in some ways it was difficult. I mean for them with their families. But it was still a big dyke party, an opportunity to stand outside at night and eat and talk about our new haircuts and again, I was glad I had gone. I had had something else going on that night, a reading, but naturally I cancelled. I wasn't going to miss my friends' wedding party, though in the event of their wedding, the wedding itself wasn't the issue at all. It was the fact of it that was important. I actually needed to *go* to my sister's wedding. *It* was different. When I emailed her back that of course I would come she was a little shocked, but "thrilled." There had never been something I could give my sister. I mean in college there was a Peter, Paul and Mary concert I should have gone to with her, but I cancelled to do something with my friends. But we were adults now. What could I do for her? Change my will? I think about that. I have some kind of insurance and sometimes I think I would give some to my girlfriend, and some to my sister — and what about my brother — and his sons? Yes, what about his sons — both of them. Are wills when you express relationship — or what? I have gone to weddings when people invited me for the hell of it. And I went because I just wanted to say I like you, or else just what fun to fly to Denver. And another time, no twice, flying to the South both times to go to the weddings of my girlfriend's college friends, but all of these people were straight. I was there as a date, a lesbian date, sort of a freak at a heterosexual wedding, my girfriend looking like a normal woman and I her man in a suit, a woman, getting looks as I walked into the ladies' room, always returning to a cluster of men flirting with her, then eyeing me weirdly. Weddings are a trial, always reminding you of what you're not, being occasions for the married folk to say how healthy they are, by including you. Though they can't. They never truly can. You're like the thumb. At my sister's wedding I was like a pun. I flew to New York, finding the cheapest fare I could, and then I drove. Getting out of New York took hours, and then I had to pull over I think, just being so exhausted, and yet too exhausted to sleep, waking back up, finding a Dunkin' Donuts, buying a couple of those mugs because it's hard to find good ones. My sister and Judy Nietzche were getting married at the Northampton Center for the Arts. They got married with nine other couples. It was funny because they are really not dykes with a community, instead they point at houses in their various neighborhoods where odd couples of women lived and died, and identify with those women who lived together and alone for years. None of their friends who came to the wedding were lesbians, mostly women that worked with Judy and none with Ann, or Nancy, as I call my sister, so I was the sole representative of our side, and I got there before anyone and saw all these other lesbians couples with a little bit of family, maybe a fag or two. Actually the event wasn't intended to be all dykes, just a group wedding, but no men applied. It was a plain enough room on the third floor that I walked up and down. I had two disposable cameras, and the room was full of chairs so I started draping my possessions, figuring I could save space for us, that's what I could do. The front row was for "the brides" and there were pieces of paper on each seat, and one said Judy and one said Ann and that's when I began to cry. I really shook, I felt very alone, and happy for my sister. *She's really doing this*, I thought. *It's real.* I couldn't get over it. For a moment I was mad at my girlfriend, not because she didn't want to do this. But because she wasn't here. It was a very moving moment. My heart was jumping out of my chest. *What if I die?* I kept looking out the window and finally they came. There had been a lot of talk about outfits. Nancy and Judy might have gone shopping and they looked funny in everything they put on. I strongly advised my sister to go as herself. She has some class things with Northampton lesbians. I insisted T-shirts were right and Nancy's I think had Wonder Woman on it and it was bright and Judy's was bright too. They were like adamantly silly. They go camping. They like birds, and nature, and kind of keep to themselves. Why would such women wear suits? For who? They liked the minister, a woman who had agreed to marry all of them. I met a bunch of their friends. I felt famous and charming, glad to be me. It seemed like such a good time to be butch. In my way I was the butchest thing in the room. It wasn't like I was so tough. It was just that I so belonged to my lesbian sister, her proud lesbian brother, and I now could have all this love toward my lesbian sister-in-law, Judy. I could ask her to take care of my sister, which she already does, but there was never a moment where my older sisterness was allowed to ask for that and receive a grin and know that the conversation fulfilled a need for me and this other woman to agree that my sister was worth taking care of and it was happening. It was like an occasion had been constructed to give me a place to acknowledge my sister and my relationship in relationship to theirs. If there had ever been competition between me and Judy, there had never been a place to put it aside. I was glad my girlfriend wasn't here now. When the ceremony started all the women said in unison that they would do what the minister was asking. *Will you hold her all the days of your lives?* "Yes," said 18 tearful women. My sister was crying, Judy was crying, I was crying, Rachel, Judy's daughter, was crying. She had lived with them when she was in high school and it was not easy. But this was easy. Because Rachel was there too. It was more like a confirmation than a wedding. It was also funny. Because the minister had asked the women to say something and they all said it and cried. And now the minister asked "the other woman" to say something. And everyone laughed. Because there was no other women. Everyone had already said yes. It was a group agreement. It just didn't have to go back and forth. That would have made no sense. But my sister and Judy had lived together for 14 years, which is a very long time. I thought about how sad it would be when one of them died. Too sad, really too sad to think about but it's in the ceremony. It asks you to think about that and you're there all alone with it, one by one, very serious. And then you go to the party, very serious eating of food. I was exhausted. And none of Judy's sisters came to the wedding, but they all came to the party. That was all very nice. Her mother didn't come either and asked that my sister and Judy not put their names in the paper and not have their picture taken so they told the newspaper photographer that, which was a little sad. They weren't in the group portrait. It was Judy giving her mother something. Can you imagine that thought being at the other kind of wedding, that the mother would ask the daughter to assist her in her shame? Though I'm sure they do do that some other way. Just the fact that she's marrying a man. It's almost like those weddings happen for an entirely different reason. It's like history, an opportunity for heterosexuals to create, but for my sister and Judy history had already happened. The wedding was a moment to celebrate their past. It wasn't the bond.

I got a letter later on from my sister saying she was never sure I cared about her and now she was.

Eileen Myles is currently working on a novel, The Inferno, *and she has written the libretto for an opera,* Hell, *which will be soon in a theater near you (fall 2004). Otherwise, she's been doing a lot for a long time.*

The Butch That I Marry
Lesléa Newman

"Hey Flash," I whisper to the prone body lying beside me in the dark. "Flash. Flashy. Flash-Flash. Flasheroo. Flashkins. Flashmeister." But it's no use. It's 12:01 a.m. and my beloved is fast asleep. I haven't the heart to wake her, even to wish her Happy Anniversary. Yes, it's been six blissful years since Flash and I became wife and wife, but I remember our wedding as though it were yesterday.

Before the wedding came the proposal, of course. We'd only been going out for two months when Flash got down on one knee and asked, "Will you marry me?" I got up on two elbows, peered over the side of the bed, and asked, "Where's the ring?" Flash, having none, quickly looked around her bedroom and offered instead a good-luck onyx stone that she'd had for years. Not the kind of rock I'd hoped for, but I accepted nevertheless and immediately started making lists: people to invite, people not to invite, the menu, the music... Flash wanted to celebrate our engagement in a different, more traditional manner, but I pushed her aside. "There's no time for that now," I said, reaching over her back for a pen and pad from the nightstand. "We've got a wedding to plan."

In the weeks to come, I kept waiting for Flash to surprise me with an engagement ring. When none appeared, I started dropping hints. I sang "Diamonds Are a Girl's Best Friend" when we showered together. I said, "Give me a ring sometime," instead of "Call me later," when Flash left my house for work. When Flash asked if I had plans for Saturday night, I said, "As a matter of fact, I have a previous engagement." All to no avail.

Finally Flash and I took a trip to our local lesbian jeweler to choose our wedding rings. In all the excitement of choosing matching bands, the matter of an engagement ring was simply forgotten. Flash wanted us to start wearing our rings right away, but I was stern. "Nothing doing. We can't wear them until we're actually married."

"Can we at least try them on?" Flash asked. We did and they looked gorgeous. "Let's just wear them out to the car," Flash said, and I relented. "Let's just wear them out to brunch," she said. "Let's just wear them until I take you home." "Let's just wear them while we're doing the nasty." Needless to say, from that day forth we never took off our rings. Not even when I brought Flash home to meet the folks. You would think that my mother, who notices everything, including the one gray hair in my left eyebrow ("You really should touch that up") would notice a gold band on the fourth finger of her only daughter's left hand and say something about it. Especially since said daughter's new "friend" was wearing an identical ring on the fourth finger of her left hand as well. But you see, my family actually invented the "Don't ask, don't tell" policy, and has been practicing it for years. Flash was amazed. "You mean you're not even going to tell them about the wedding?"

"Of course not," I said. "Then I'd have to invite them."

"You're not inviting your parents?" Flash was aghast.

"You're not inviting yours," I reminded her.

"My parents are dead," Flash pointed out, as if that was any kind of excuse. Then her face took on a look of concern. "Who's going to give you away?" she asked.

I didn't hesitate. "My therapist."

"But," Flash was visibly pale, "I thought it was traditional for the femme's family to pay for the wedding."

I kissed her cheek. "You're my family now," I said, throwing my arms around her. Flash was so moved, she didn't know whether to laugh or cry.

In the months to come, Flash and I met with a printer, a florist, a photographer, a caterer, a bartender, a DJ, a band, a rabbi, a hairdresser, a dressmaker, a shoemaker, and a tailor. We compiled a huge guest list, since after all, our wedding was going to be *the* social event of the season. But when our caterer informed us that her sliding scale started at $23 a plate, we quickly realized who our 75 closest friends really were. Not that any of them bothered to return the little reply card enclosed in their invitation complete with envelope and LOVE stamp. A week before the wedding, our caterer was tearing out her hair. "You've got to tell me how many guests are coming," she cried. I tried to explain that lesbians think RSVP stands for "Respond Slowly, vs. Promptly," but she was not amused.

On the morning of the wedding, I went off to have my hair done and my nails polished. At ten o'clock I returned home and began to dress. I had just fastened one stocking to my garter belt when the phone rang. Mitzi, who had come over to help, answered. "It's your mother," she whispered, covering the mouthpiece with one hand. I grabbed the receiver, frantically. My mother never calls me on Sunday mornings. "Who died?" I asked.

"No one," she answered. "I just woke up thinking about you, so I decided to call. So, what's new?"

"Nothing."

"So, what are you doing today?"

My mind raced. What could I tell her? I remembered that old fiction-writing adage: I lie in order to tell the truth. I decided to try the opposite and tell the truth in order to lie: "Getting married."

"Very funny."

Phew. I knew she wouldn't believe me. "Listen, Ma, I got some people here. I gotta go," I said, hanging up the phone. I fastened my other stocking and continued getting dressed. Soon I was covered from head to toe in silk and rhinestones complete with something old (my grandmother's brooch); something new (my dress); something borrowed (a tampon from Mitzi); and something blue (the string on the tampon). Flash, who looked stunning in her cream-colored satin shirt and black tuxedo pants, also had her period. We'd never bled together before, and promptly decided that the simultaneous shedding of our uterine walls was a sign from the goddess that our union was meant to be.

Then before we knew it, *the* moment had arrived. Flash and I stood under the chuppah, her Best Butch to our right, my Dyke of Honor to our left. We were surrounded by our loved ones who all wore their finest: everything from combat boots, cutoff shorts, and nose rings, to high heels, velvet gowns, and diamonds. And those were just the boys. The girls wore their best Birkenstocks, drawstring pants, and T-shirts with slogans on them like, "But Ma, she *is* Mr. Right," or "Monogamy = Monotony" depending on their point of view. Flash and I faced the rabbi, who started the ceremony by saying that the two of us looked beautiful and very much in love. Of course I started to cry. Then the rabbi started to cry. Then Flash, who is too butch to cry in front of me, never mind before 75 of our nearest and dearest, proceeded to have an allergy attack.

When things calmed down, the rabbi continued. Flash and I said our vows, exchanged rings, sipped wine, and kissed. Then the rabbi emptied the wine glass, and with great ceremony, wrapped it in a napkin, and placed it on the floor for Flash to crush. I caught Mitzi laughing out of the corner of my eye. Later I asked her just what was so funny. "You left the price tag on the bottom of the wine glass," she said, still giggling. "Even from across the room I could see that it was 50 percent off."

"So what?" I asked, indignant. "You think I would let Flash break crystal I paid retail for?"

After we were pronounced Butch and Bride, the party really went wild. Flash and

I were hoisted up on chairs and paraded around for all to see. Our friends toasted us and danced circles around us. The food was so fabulous, even the vegetarians couldn't resist diving into the swan-shaped chopped liver centerpiece. Both wedding cakes (one traditional, the other sugar-, wheat-, and dairy-free) were divine. I tossed my bouquet and Flash threw my garter. We smiled so much our faces hurt. At the end of the day, we drove off to a nearby hotel. I didn't want to take off my wedding dress yet, so Flash worked around it. We fell asleep in each other's arms, and we've slept that way ever since.

I sigh with contentment and look at the clock on the night table. It is now 12:27 a.m. and Flash is still deep in dreamland. I decide to let her sleep. There'll be plenty of time to celebrate later today. Maybe I'll even surprise my beloved with breakfast in bed. But the surprise is on me. When I open my eyes I see a vision of loveliness: Flash, handsome in her silk bathrobe, stands before me holding a breakfast tray. "Happy anniversary," she says, setting the tray down on the bed. I ooh and aah over the fresh coffee, the bagel and lox, the red rose. "What's this?" I ask, holding up a small gift box.

"Remember the night I proposed to you?" Flash asks. I nod my head, dreamily. "I never forgot what you said."

"I said yes."

"No you didn't." Flash says. "You said, 'Where's the...'"

"Ring! Oh my God!" I tear open the box and gasp at the sweetest, most stunning, most beautiful diamond ring I have ever seen. At last, the rock I have always wanted. "Is it too late to get engaged?" Flash asks. I grab her by the neck and kiss her in reply. My butch. I think I'll keep her.

Lesléa Newman (www.lesleanewman.com) is the author of 50 books for adults and children. Her titles include: Out of the Closet and Nothing to Wear; A Letter to Harvey Milk; Still Life with Buddy; Write from the Heart; Jailbait; She Loves Me, She Loves Me Not; *and* Heather Has Two Mommies. *She is married to Mary Grace Newman Vazquez.*

Do You, GLBTI, Take Str8 Acting...?
Geoff Parkes

"Gay people have a right to be miserable too."
—Chris Rock, on gay marriage.

Being somewhat gay and somewhat not (when you're post-queer, it's difficult to be somewhat anything), I'm only somewhat sure of how I feel about gay marriage. After all, marriage is not meant to be a happy affair—that's what affairs are for. Nor does gay abandon lend itself easily to the notion of 'til death do us part. If we were honest, to ourselves and to the divine drag deities who rule our lives, 'til Babs tours again would be much more appropriate a vow. And think of the material benefits—every time La Streisand drags her ass on the road, you get to renew or renege your vows, and either way, it's occasion for a party with gifts. Bridal showers, golden showers—it's all good.

I live in the antipodes—and no, that's not the next island over from Fire. In Australia, we too have a rabid homophobe with all the charisma of a vomiting cane toad running our country. No I don't mean the Queen—she stays out of our politics and we rarely question Prince Charlie's desire to be reincarnated as a tampon. Fair trade. No, John Howard, conservative Christian with a party full of prima donna bigots and *Brigadoon* fans, has been a pus-drenched blight on our nation for far too long, and throughout his unspectacular career as chief truckler he's never been shy to exploit the most base prejudices of the Australian public (and we have many). He won his first election because we were sick of the other guy, the second by frightening city folk that the indigenous population (all 2 percent) were going to take their houses away, and the third by locking up refugees fleeing from Saddam Hussein and the Taliban whilst maintaining that 3,000 boat people a year meant Australia was being flooded by foreigners. "We'll decide who comes to Australia" was the electoral slogan, and boy they flew it high.

But, like our cousins in the Coalition of the Killing, we have another election coming up, and things aren't looking great. There are no weapons of mass destruction, very few photo opportunities (that's what happens when most of the Aussies are secret service), people are a little bit angry that the price of medication is going up and the public health-care system is dive-bombing quicker than a smart bomb on a crowded Baghdad market. So what's old Johnny pull out of his pocket? A motion to reassert, via federal law, that marriage is between a man and a woman.

Never mind that no one in Australia has argued, with any great success, that it isn't. Nor should thinking folk object when we realize that, unlike in Europe and the U.S., no one's really been pushing for a change to the law. Capital city fags are far too concerned with property-value rights and superannuation, whilst rural folk like me bow on our knees when a Pedro Almodóvar flick comes to town for one night. More relevant in the past has been Howard's attempts to change the laws to prevent lesbians having access to in-vitro fertilization programs, and to prevent all folk who aren't hetero from adopting kids from overseas. Lord knows what would happen if two loving parents helped a defenseless kid, a victim of circumstance and poverty, to grow up to be tolerant and accepting of diversity. It's simply un-Australian.

And to reassure you that we are a democracy, the opposition Labor party agrees with the government and looks set to pass the bill in the Senate. The National Party politicians (who represent most of rural and outback Australia and who share power with Howard's Liberals) have already said they'll campaign hard on the issue—apart from there being no issue because only seven federal politicians are arguing otherwise—at least it will keep the heat off the local cow-fucking brigade.

But because the personal is political, the pubic is public, and some of my friends are exchanging dildos for doorknobs and white powder for white lace, my own view of marriage is that if people want to pledge their love in front of people they care for, and want to provide free food and drink and opportunities to check out how hot other guests look in or on evening wear, who am I to say marriage is a ridiculous leftover from dark-ages ownership and represents a gross selling out to breeding rituals whilst "real" queers are still getting bashed by schoolmates or raped because all they really need is a man to set them straight? And what my personal choice is, and what your personal choice is, and what the choice is of anyone over the age of consent who loves and believes in the salvation of love when our world seems so utterly devoid of love, well, that choice ain't the government's choice to make, nor the choice of the slobbering syphilitic religious right. They're wrong. Choice, freedom, difference—that is what our contemporary democracies are founded on, although idea has always differed from practice. But the government has no right to tell me whose ring I put on my finger, no more than I have the right to tell Liza Minnelli to stop. Just stop.

Back in Oz, John Howard's argument is that same-sex marriage demeans the idea and the institution. He thinks that because Jane and Jennifer say I do, Bill and Mary's marriage will somehow be rendered unstable, less meaningful. If John is so worried about Bill and Mary, why doesn't he take steps to reduce the current divorce rate? And I don't mean by making divorce illegal.

Final words go to my 84-year-old grandma. We were waiting for *Passions* to come on one afternoon, and I asked what she thought of the government's idea. "Their idea is gay marriage is demeaning? I bet if you poked a stick around their private lives," she said, "you'd find plenty that was demeaning. Does that mean that my past or my marriage is demeaning? No... I think if people want to get married, they should. Politicians be damned." And their poking sticks too.

Geoff Parkes wrote Fuct & Fiction *and runs* Loggedoff.net; *he would like to walk up the aisle to the sounds of "Bat Out of Hell."*

First Love, Commitment, and Partnering:
The Handfasting
Christopher Penczak

Our first love and, in particular, our first gay love is definitely a rite of passage. All relationships bring us something from which to experience, share, and grow, regardless of the outcome. Our first experience is one of the most important, be it first kiss, first sexual experience, or first actual relationship. Each is a milestone that transforms us significantly. Recognizing the personal and spiritual significance of each event is important.

If we desire a life partner, and find one, that relationship can be the most transforming of them all. A long-term commitment places us in situations that force us to grow, expand our awareness, and move beyond our sole needs, to create a home for the relationship. Although not always easy, the rewards can justify the difficulty. In most societies, the act of partnering is celebrated by the community through what is now called a marriage. Unlike simple lovers, a marriage asks the community to recognize and support the public relationship. Many in the gay community refer to their partners as "lover." Although very true, I always found that funny. Having an astrology background prior to a deeper experience in the gay community, I noticed how astrology always divided the two, having a separate space, or "house," in the chart for partners and another for lovers.

Astrologically, and personally, the two have very different energies. When two people make their commitment public, it transforms the experience, although for those who have been together for a while the transformation is subtle. My partner, Steve, and I lived together for a few years, and had been together for many years before we had a public ceremony. Nothing seemed to change, but looking back on it many months later, I realized the dynamic of the relationship changed slightly, presenting new challenges, as well as new growth.

In witchcraft, the marriage rite is traditionally called a "handfasting," referring to the binding of hands together that is an important aspect of the ritual. Although some extreme Wiccan ministers view it as a binding of souls together for this life and all others, most moderates, myself included, feel the loose binding of the hands symbolizes the conscious choice of two to walk together on the road of life. Most witches believe in reincarnation of some sort, and feel we are not wise enough now to know what we will need in all lifetimes. Decisions made in this lifetime should only be for this lifetime. If you are "meant" to partner with a soul throughout eternity, you can renew your vows in each lifetime.

Part of the tradition from the Celtic background is a year-and-a-day trial period for the partnership. In this time, a couple really discovers life as married partners. The trial period is much like the time of study for an aspiring witch, before truly committing to the path. The process starts with an initial handfasting ceremony, usually done in private. After the year-and-a-day period, the couple renews the handfasting as a more permanent commitment, typically through a more public ceremony and celebration. If the couple chooses not to continue after the year and a day, there is no guilt in the dissolution. It is considered wise to own up to your feelings and make life more pleasant for all concerned rather than stick to a decision because everybody expects it.

Another beautiful part of the ceremony is the jumping of the broom. Jumping the broom can be found in many traditions. The broom symbolizes the threshold. Witches often put their ritual brooms, used for cleansing a space, on the edge of the circle.

When a couple jumps the broom, they are "jumping" into their new life together as a couple. Many brooms are made with an ash or oak handle, with the plant broom, itself, as the bristles, which are tied together with willow. They can be decorated with magical keepsakes and are put over the couple's hearth. Other popular plants used in the ceremony are rosemary, for remembering your love in times of difficulty, and rose, for love. Some make the handfasting cord from a garland of rosehips, for passion and desire in a marriage.

The most wonderful thing about handfastings is that most Wiccan ministers will perform handfastings for gay couples. Some are ordained ministers, for couples who can legally marry. I hope that someday all gay couples will have the legal right to marry, but at the moment, we do not. Many Wiccan priestesses and priests will also perform ceremonies for those who are not on the pagan paths. I feel the rites of handfasting and commitment are very important to the gay community, but many couples feel they cannot have it, and others say they don't want it, and don't need what the straight world needs. Perhaps they really don't, but some say it out of spite. But rituals and ceremonies are part of our rich history as queer people and it's time to reclaim them, on our own terms, with our own definitions. If you don't want to define your partnership in traditional marriage roles, then don't. Your partnership is between you and your partner and can be whatever you make it. Ceremonies are ways to acknowledge the importance of the commitment between you, celebrate it, and ask for the support of the family you have gathered around you. They can be simple and short ceremonies, or elaborate with formal receptions. Through commitment, we work on our relationship development, and thereby develop and mature our soul.

The Handfasting Ritual

Use this ritual, very close to my own handfasting, to inspire your own handfasting rituals. In my own ritual, we involved many people, including parents, covenmates, and good friends, to act as our "bridal party," call the quarters, bring up ritual tools, and recite blessings.

- Couple enters the circle from the east, for new beginnings.
- The HP/HPS (high priest/high priestess) casts the circle.
- The HP/HPS calls the quarters. You can call particular deities or animals to bring their blessing to the handfasted couple. You could use a call such as:

> To the north, I invite the element of earth and the great Bear to join me. Please bring strength and stability to this couple. Hail and welcome.
>
> To the east, I invite the element of fire and the great Lion to join me. Please bring courage and light to this couple. Hail and welcome.
>
> To the south, I invite the element of air and the great Crow to join me. Please bring wisdom and clarity to this couple. Hail and welcome.
>
> To the west, I invite the element of water and the great Dolphin to join me. Please bring love and healing to this couple. Hail and welcome.

- If outside, scatter a clockwise ring of flower petals around the circle, for the blessings of life and the element of spirit.
- The HP/HPS calls the divine:

> I invite the Goddess, God, and Great Spirit to this sacred rite. May you guide and witness this ceremony, and this couple through their life journey together. We invite all spirits of Perfect Love and Perfect Trust into this space.

- Burn a love incense of some kind, such as rose. (Optional)

- The HP/HPS says:

  [Names of couple], you are about to step into the destiny you chose before entering this life; to make a promise of commitment, the fruits of which you will carry throughout this lifetime and others to come. Knowing this, are you prepared to continue?

  Couple responds with:

  I am.

- Lighting the Family candles: If each partner has a family member present, such as a parent, or a loved one who is like blood family, the family representative comes up to the altar, and lights a candle for that family. Colors of the candle should match the clothing/theme of each partner. The HP/HPS says:

  May we have the families come together, to light the sacred candles to represent these two sacred families.

- Exchange of vows: To each partner, the HP/HPS says:

  Do you [partner's name], take this man/woman to be your husband/wife, your partner for life? Will you remain at his/her side when life is good, when it is filled with challenge and fear? Will you laugh and dance with him/her in joy? Will you share his/her burdens, dry his/her tears, and hold him/her to your heart when he/she doubts himself/herself? Will you share his/her dreams, support his/her ideals while holding fast to your own? If you can promise these things, without reservation or hesitation, please answer by saying, "I do."

- Personal words of commitment: The couple says their own words or vows to each other if desired. The HP/HPS says:

  At this time I ask you to offer your own words of love and commitment.

- Great Rite: The couple can perform the Great Rite together if they wish. They can drink from the chalice together, and share it with the group if they choose. I prefer to keep the chalice between the couple only.

- Exchange of rings: You can have family members or "best men/bridesmaids" bring up the rings. To each partner in turn, the HP/HPS says:

  [Name], place the ring on [Name]'s left hand and repeat after me: "I, [name], pledge to you my troth, with total and unconditional love. I will love and honor you from the depth of my heart, in this life and all others. Please accept this ring as a sign of my love."

- Binding of cords: The HP/HPS wraps cords around the couple's held hands and says:

  The binding of hands is a powerful ceremony uniting two hearts together as one, yet retaining their individuality. The cords are wrapped loosely around the hands demonstrating the free choice of each to walk hand in hand, in sacred union to the journey's end.

- Lighting the Unity Candle: The couple lights the main unity candle from the flames of the two family candles. The unity candle can be any color the couple wishes. HP/HPS:

  The couple will now light the candle symbolizing the unity of their two families.

- Jumping the Broom: The couple, still handfasted, jumps the broom together, jumping into the west, the land of love. HP/HPS:

  It is now my honor to invite you into the most magical transition, as you jump the broom from solitary life into the union of partnership.

- Rosemary Blessing: The HP/HPS gives each partner a sprig of rosemary. HP/HPS:

  I offer each the gift of Rosemary, the herb of remembrance. Keep these sprigs in a place where you will be reminded of your love. Call on Rosemary if ever you feel doubt, and be reminded of your love.

- Pronouncement: The HP/HPS says:

  With the sacred power invested in me, I pronounce you life partners. You may seal your vows with a kiss.

- Complete the circle, thanking all present, release the quarters, and release the circle.
- Couple exits the circle from the west, for happy endings.

Christopher Penczak is an eclectic witch, author, and teacher residing in New Hampshire with his husband, role-playing-game designer, Stephen Kenson. Christopher is the author of several books including Gay Witchcraft, City Magick, *and* The Inner Temple of Witchcraft. *He initiated a project to use magick for equal civil rights for same-sex couples in the Magic for Marriage ritual. For more information visit* www.christopherpenczak.com *or* www.magicalactivism.org.

Excerpt from *Gay Witchcraft* by Christopher Penczak. Reprinted by permission of Red Wheel/Weiser, Boston, MA and York Beach, ME. To order, call 1-800-423-7087.

Wabi-Sabi
Elissa G. Perry

1.

My cousin and I are making sandals out of wallpaper samples and ribbon. These are our toys. Her father is an architect. Her parents are arguing downstairs. We go on with our creations. The ribbons adorning our toes and ankles match those in our braids. We are not old enough yet to have had relaxers put in our thick manes. Pippi Longstocking is still the style for us.

If we were at my house, we'd be doing experiments with worms and my microscope. If my father, a pharmacist, were home, my parents might be arguing too. We would go on with our play/work, already aware that pretending all was fine was what was expected.

"I'm never getting married." My cousin had snuck into the bathroom and retrieved a color of nail polish to compliment our Ferragamo-*cum*-gladiator slippers. We knew Ferragamo was the best. They were the shoes our mothers fawned over when we went window-shopping after ballet class on Saturdays. "Married people are always unhappy. They don't have fun." Sometimes we wouldn't pretend with each other.

I thought about this and watched her draw the brush over her toenails, careful not to get the bronze lacquer on the newly sanded hardwood floor. I could picture my mother laughing, my father too, but not with each other—only with us kids or with their friends.

"Me either." I decided then and there. "I'm going to have lots of friends and two kids, maybe three, but I'm never going to get married." This felt good and I kept going with it. "We will live near each other and eat over at each other's houses."

My cousin smiled and blew on her toes while she handed me the polish.

I didn't tell anyone else of my revelation. I knew the nuns at my Catholic school wouldn't like this, but it wasn't their business. What did they know about marriage? No more than anyone else who maybe grew up surrounded by one but never had one themselves.

Someone from our church got married later that summer. I don't remember who, a Murphy, a Simpson. A daughter of one of the really nice neighborhood families that frequented my father's drugstore. She wore a big white dress and a veil. She let me touch it and hold her flowers.

She had to promise to obey 'til death parted them. I didn't like it. They were one in the eyes of God, Father Henning said. I had decided two months earlier that I didn't care about the eyes of God since I asked if our friend Fadia was going to hell because she was from Lebanon and not a Catholic. Sister Thomas said yes. Not even my grandmother was a Catholic, and what about my father's friend who was Jewish? She looked down and shook her head. If I had known the expression intimately, I would have exclaimed that it was all bullshit. Instead, I decided that I didn't like her or God or anyone that tried to tell me what to do or that my friends were going to hell.

I told my mother the next day, that I was never getting married. "Don't you want to have a family?" she asked me. "I don't have to get married to have a family."

This business of not liking God and reducing Him to him made room for a lot of alternatives in my logical mind. I knew how babies were made. God said that to do that one should be married, but who cares what god said? "Question authority," isn't that what my father said?

"Well why don't you want to get married?" she asked next. I was standing on a step stool in the kitchen juicing lemons for lemonade. "Married people fight all the time and the dress is itchy and you have to obey some man and obey God and obey all these other people and laws and stuff, don't you? It all sounds ridiculous to me." Ridiculous. This was my new favorite word.

"Well that's a big decision. You might change your mind someday. But maybe not." Her voice trailed off into the ribbons of barbeque sauce she poured over the ribs. She went outside to the grill. It was too hot to cook indoors in the summer. Too taxing on the window air-conditioning units, my father said. Too taxing on the electric bill.

I was dragging the step stool back to the counter where the pitcher stood, heavy folding metal in one hand, the sugar container in the other, when my father came into the kitchen. I managed the balance. I wouldn't ask for help. "Lissa do it self." I am still reminded today that this was my first sentence.

I climbed the stool and poured the sugar into the lemon water. "What are you doing, QT?" my dad asked around his pipe. In 1976, neighborhood drugstores were still closed on Sundays. "We had a bunch of lemons so I'm making lemonade!" I said it with an exaggerated cuteness. I knew I was Daddy's girl.

I also knew he wouldn't like my revelation. I'd have a good 15 years to hear about how much he didn't like it. I calculated such things in my mind, fascinated with the new understandings adding and subtracting brought to things. When he was uncomfortable with something, everyone around him was just as uncomfortable for twice as long. This was not as clear then. I had no language for it. But I knew what to do. I pretended everything was perfect.

"Sounds good." He replied and went back to whatever he was doing in some other part of the house.

2.

We hadn't talked about it in the interim but seven years later, my cousin updated her plans. We were watching Luke and Laura get married. "I'm going to get married but not in a church. Churches are weird." We had been going to church with our aunt. Dresses and stockings required. "I'm going to get married on Grandaddy's farm."

I liked the sound of that. "Me too," I told her. "But I'm not wearing a dress. I'm wearing overalls and no shoes." I saw the whole thing. I had on a ragged straw hat. A white shirt, overalls with the legs rolled up to midcalf, and no shoes. There was a girl there too in a simple white cotton dress, but I didn't tell her that part. No one else was there. Just me and the girl. We both wore two braids. The light was golden, just before dusk. That was perfection.

"I think maybe in some trees, not in a field," she went on. "And I'll wear a dress but not a fancy one. It will be simple but pretty. I'll make it myself." I imagined her in the woods and was happy for her.

"I'm hungry. Let's get Granny to take us to McDonald's." She hopped up off the couch as *Luke and Laura's Theme* played.

"Okay." I pretended everything was perfect.

3.

I was watching Madonna flirt with Isabella Rossellini on MTV when the phone rang. I fished for a cigarette and answered it. It was my cousin. She was coming to San Francisco for graduate school. Could she stay with me 'til she found an apartment.

I exhaled. I hadn't seen her since high school. I was 23. She knew I was gay. She knew I lived with my girlfriend. She was my cousin, pratically my sister.

"Okay."

I ran into a friend from an artists' collective when we were on the street. She was cold to my girlfriend and friendly to my cousin. "What was that about?" my cousin asked.

She doesn't believe in interracial relationships. I began to explain the whole East Bay/City black lesbian thing, but before I got to the next sentence I heard my cousin exclaim, "Wow! I mean I know among my friends and heterosexual people that's frowned upon, but I would have thought that with the whole other layer of oppression a sort of anything-goes attitude would be more prevalent." She paused. "That's cool."

I didn't know what to say. I did not pretend that everything was perfect. We rarely saw each other during the three years she lived here.

4.

My partner and I are planning a wedding reception for our closest friends, a heterosexual couple I've known since childhood. They eloped in January. We are elated and want to throw them the best party possible. It's at the home of queer friends of theirs.

It's February and now queers are getting married too.

We are wishy-washy. It's exciting. "Should we go down to City Hall?" we ask each other periodically.

For what? we wonder. The refrain goes like this:
We already made the pledge to one another.
It's not going to be recognized anywhere else.
Who cares? Do we care who cares?
There are bigger things to worry about. If this becomes a focal point of the election and Bush wins again because of this, then won't we be doing a disservice to the larger picture?
We don't want to be some test case and have to file suit to be recognized.
We don't care who else recognizes that we are married. We recognize it. We registered with the city, then we registered with the state, is another piece of paper going to make a difference? We are married in our hearts.

We do:
Promise to respect, cherish, love, and care for my sweetie until death do us part.
We don't:
Wish to camp out in the rain, in a long line of queers desperate to have this promise recognized by government, wringing my hands, clinging to a complicated hope that we will squeeze into the log before a judge orders a halt to our temporary rights.

On the subject of rights — there are other ones about which we worry with much more fervent urgency.

1. The right of black people in Florida (everywhere) to have access to their polling places. The right of black people to have their votes counted.

2. The right to choose, even though neither of us have had a sexual relationship with a man in at least 15 years.

3. The right to talk on the phone without the threat of unwelcome ears.

4. The right to communicate with anyone about anything without the possibility of being reported as some sort of suspicious character by an eavesdropping other who does not share the same opinion or doesn't know of or care about the context of our words.

5. The right to be represented in the world by a leader elected by the people.

6. The right to be governed by a group of responsible, thoughtful people

driven by a desire to serve all of the people, not by a religion skewed to serve the profit margin of a few.

And what's wrong with "Civil Union" as long as the rights are the same? A marriage license is a legal arrangement regulated by government. Therefore it is civil. It is also a union. Civil. Union. Civil Union. Maybe we don't want the historical baggage of marriage attached to our relationship. Why do people want to be married with the title "marriage" attached to their union so badly? To be "equal" to heterosexuals. What a ridiculous goal in life. Should we want to be equal to men? Should my partner want to be equal with Christians? Should I want to be equal with whites? That seems a pretty dire prospect for a vision of society. Shouldn't we want better than those limiting labels for everyone? Shouldn't we be models for redefining what it means to be committed to another human being? But I digress.

So…Marriage.

My sweetie and I were delighted to hear the news. I tapped the memory of what if felt like to know that I had found and made a promise to my life's partner to give a truly heartfelt "congratulations" to the queer newlyweds we knew, but another part of me wanted to ask "And? So what exactly does that mean?" As the laughs and giggles, hoots and hollers filled the damp days and nights, we both remarked how we could already hear the refrains. "You're married, you're not married, you're married, you're not married." "Liberals are ruining family values." "Preserve the sanctity of marriage by voting for me, George W…me, Orrin Hatch…me…" What's more threatening to marriage: *Who Wants to Marry a Millionaire?* and *Elimidate* or Joe and Steve who want the same rights as other committed couples?

On the subject of commitment—a group of six of friends, including my partner and myself, from five different cities, with different cultural and religious backgrounds, and three different sexual orientations (gay, bi, and straight) racked our collective brain to think of one heterosexual couple who had been married for more that 15 years and was still happy. In 20 minutes we came up with two married couples who had each been together over 30 years. Only one was still happy though. In the case of the other couple, those who knew them thought that both parties should be committed (to an institution other than marriage) and perhaps medicated.

On the subject of medication—my partner's aunt came to visit from her suburban New Jersey home with her new husband. She was recovering not only from a horrific car accident in which she was creamed on the freeway by someone trying to find a CD, but also from chemotherapy and a battle with cancer. It was the height of marriage hoopla and San Francisco's City Hall had been on the news in every nook and cranny of this nation and many others. Her only remark on the subject was, "If people are allowed to talk on the phone, headset or not, and drive, then the two of you should be able to get married. Stupid people driving is a much bigger danger to the American people if you ask me." We laughed. What a great comment. We felt recognized, loved, even appreciated in some odd way.

I don't know, maybe we'll find the perfect field some day. I don't think my partner will go to Grandaddy's field in East St. Louis to do the deed. We've talked about it. Maybe in a few years on our tenth anniversary… Or maybe we'll just keep talking (and laughing, and teasing one another) 'til death do us part. Isn't that the point of marriage anyway?

5.

My cousin lives in L.A. now. We've seen each other a few times in the last three years. Things get better each time. We had dinner together when I was in SoCal for one reason or another last fall. She had just come from her boyfriend's brother's wedding on Long Island and had lots of stories. We laughed and laughed and laughed at the ridiculousness of some people. She told me if she and her boyfriend ever got married she would want me to be her maid of honor. The title caused some place in the back of my mind to shudder briefly—maid of honor, matron of honor, person of honor, best person? My partner and I had been together for six years and officially partnered with vows for five.

But this bristle, lasting only a nanosecond, was quickly subsumed by overwhelming joy. I even got a tear in my eye. Who am I?!

I smiled the rest of the night. It no longer mattered that I was gay or that I was with a Jewish woman. Her latest boyfriend of three years is Jewish.

We had champagne. We reminisced. We resolved that we were not our mothers' saviors. We argued over the bill.

"You look great. I mean really, really good," she told me as we hugged goodbye.

The next day her boyfriend asked her to marry him. She said yes. The wedding will be in the woods. I will be the maid of honor. There will be ridiculousness. There will be no church. And all is just fine, perfectly imperfect, wabi-sabi.

Elissa G. Perry—writer, performer, educator, agitator, geek, and slut for big brains—is of African and Choctaw descent. She is committed to attempting work that causes people to ask questions and inspires people to seek answers to those questions. She lives in San Francisco with her life partner/best and only girl. She has published several short stories, interviews, and other writings in anthologies, journals, and magazines including Black Silk, Beyond Definition, Butch/Femme, Clamour, Girlfriend Number One, Sinister Wisdom, Patterns, *among others.*

Get Me to the Church...Never!
Felice Picano

Before I came out, I was having a nice affair with a woman at college. We enjoyed each other's company, we had enough sex to keep horny 19-year-old me happy, and we did wacky and wonderful things like dancing up Broadway at 4 a.m. and roasting a duck and eating it with our bare hands, with only a bottle of wine to accompany it.

Then she went and spoiled it all. She wanted to get married.

Comprehending I couldn't shake this idea out of her head, I quickly found her an older guy, a veteran, also in our classes, and fixed them up on a date. After a year or so they married, moved away, had three children, and in time, divorced and remarried correctly the second time.

In my experiecne it usually takes one bad marriage, sometimes two or three, before you do it correctly. My parents for example did it right after 35 years of marriage and a messy divorce.

At the age of 19, I would have eaten live babies before I married anyone. And this, mind you, before I came out.

In fact, the closest I ever felt to the actual state of being married to anyone was at the memorial service of my beloved friend of the previous 16 years where I was unquestionably treated by my friends and his friends and co-workers and even some of his relatives as though I were his widow. Or was that widower?

It wasn't a terrible feeling, but it also lasted about two hours. Then, I was single again.

The truth is, I'm not and I never was "the marrying kind."

He was, however, "the marrying kind."

He'd been with one lover since he'd come out in college. Brief period of a year and six months as he unhappily played the field. Then he was more or less with me for the rest of his life.

Looking at his astrological chart, it was clear he'd always be "married."

Sometimes we lived together, sometimes we didn't. But that depended upon who had how much money at the time. After the first few years, we pretty much always vacationed together. We spent summer weekends and vacation weeks together at my Fire Island rental. If I were on a national book tour, he'd arrange to meet me at the end of it, for a pleasant weekend. If he were off at some legal conference, I'd arrange to meet him at the end of it.

After a few years, I always knew it was him on the telephone without having to pick it up. Someone asked how. I would answer that the phone's ringing just sounded like him. Contrarily, if I wanted to speak with him but wasn't sure if he was at his office, on the road, or at court, I'd think hard and within fifteen minutes he'd phone me.

We spoke a minimum of three times a day on the phone. Sometimes as many as ten times. If we were a continent apart, we'd talk on the phone until he fell asleep. Today I don't have anyone I speak to even once a day. Sometimes I'll speak to one person once a week. Seldom more.

We had an open relationship. We'd decided to be friends first, throughout and last. Because friends always tell you what's wrong, or what they think you said or did wrong, or ask your advice, or come to you to share fun times and things and people and come to you when you or they are in trouble. Also because friends are always honest, no matter the consequences. We remained friends until his last conscious minutes in Cabrini Medical Center. I never lied to him and he never lied to me.

Once he became an attorney—he switched careers in his mid-thirties—he'd advise me as a lawyer. He was a very good lawyer. Also a completely ethical lawyer. Despite this, he was soon earning a great deal of money. When we'd first met, I'd been on a career high, and I was the one earning lots of money. I'd told him then, Don't worry if I spend more now; later you'll spend more. It will even out. You'll see.

It had begun to even out when he died.

Even when we weren't living together, I'd get antsy and suddenly feel trapped and need more independence. That's how we started having every second Tuesday of the month off from each other. At first we didn't tell each other where we were going or what we were doing. Then, because we were friends first and you always tell your friend anything weird or funny or unusual that happens, we began telling each other about those elements from our "nights off."

In the middle of all this, I developed a boyfriend, in much the same way and with many of the same results that most people develop a bad cold, although mine lasted a little longer. Unlike him, the boyfriend was about 99.44 percent of my ideal physical type. He agreed and he said he thought my boyfriend was "cute." I dumped the boyfriend when he became more interested in him than in me.

Some time after, he too developed a boyfreind, who—unlike me— was about 99.44 percent of *his* ideal physical type. As far as I was concerned, his boyfriend wasn't even "cute." He did, however, have a temper, and since he was Sicilian American, he and I began calling his boyfriend Etna, after the volacano outside Palermo. A few months later, and after more experience, we changed his boyfriend's name to The Child. Not Our Child. Just, The Child. The reason for that oughtn't be too difficult to work out.

Sometime later, when he was dying, he made me promise to watch over The Child. I said I would even though I knew I wouldn't. I didn't. In fact, after the memoiral service I only saw The Child once more.

I was alone 31 years before I met him. I was with him 16 years. And I've been alone again 13 years since he died.

I was never married and I never intend to be.

Why should I? I had a friend.

That's more than most people can say.

In 2004, Haworth Press put out the reprint of Felice Picano's sci-fi masterwork, Dryland's End, *and The University of Wisconsin Press published Picanos' novella,* Fred in Love.

Walt Whitman Married Us
Jeff Poniewaz

When I first fell in love, it was with my same-age best friend around puberty. To my great sadness, after an exciting year during which swapping hand jobs evolved into swapping blow jobs, he cooled toward my erotic ardor for him when he turned to girls. He stopped seeing me when we graduated from grade school and I went to Catholic all-boys high school and he went to the co-ed public high school. After high school he went to Vietnam, after which he got married and fathered three sons. After highschool I went to the Milwaukee branch of the University of Wisconsin, where I met Antler.

Whereas I first fell in love during my last two years of grade school, Antler first fell in love during his last two years of high school. The friend he loved during adolescence, like my best friend during puberty, was straight and Antler's love went unrequited. During Antler's and my lonely teen years, living unbeknownst to each other at opposite corners of the greater Milwaukee area, we were both consoled by Whitman's poetry. Especially by his promise in "So Long!": "I say you will yet find the friend you were looking for."

Before we met and became each other's best friends, Antler's best friend and my best friend too was Walt Whitman. Luckily, we both did find the friend we were looking for and in the last year of our teens. In 2006, we'll celebrate 40 years together.

When I first met Antler in a UW-Milwaukee poetry class in spring of '66, our love of Whitman was our common bond, and thereafter his "We Two Boys Together Clinging" was "our song."

> We two boys together clinging,
> One the other never leaving,
> Up and down the roads going,
> North and South excursions making...
> Eating, drinking, sleeping, loving...
> No law less than ourselves owning...
> Fulfilling our foray.

The spirit of that poem—the spirit of Whitman, not some Christian or other organized-religion ritual—is what made us inseparable lifelong friends. Whitman married us without need of official recognition of any kind—without invitations requesting RSVP and without need of "bat-eyed and materialistic priests" he denounced in "Song of the Open Road" (yet said he didn't despise in "Song of Myself"). To this day, Walt is for each of us our ongoing best friend aside from each other.

I risked hell to read *Howl* while in early-'60s Catholic high school. When we became friends, I got Antler into Ginsberg and he got me into Corso and Ferlinghetti. Ginsberg's Whitman elegy in *Howl* was our favorite poem by a living poet.

Hearing Ginsberg read at UW-Milwaukee in February '67, annunciating sanity and compassion amid the madness of the Vietnam War, confirmed us in our vocation to be poets, a vocation we first heard in Walt's "Song of the Open Road." We were impressed that both Allen and Walt dared to include same-sex love in the spectrum of subjects they addressed, yet were highly respected, even revered, as towering poet heroes despite their respective uptight times.

Now I teach at UW-Milwaukee a course I devised and named Whitman &

Ginsberg: Liberating American Bards. On occasion I bring my camerado to class as a special guest: this man named Antler who Ginsberg called "one of Whitman's 'poets and orators to come'" and who won the 1985 Whitman Prize of the Whitman Association in Camden, New Jersey, an award given "to the author whose contribution best reveals the continuing presence of Walt Whitman in American poetry" and which commended him for his Whitmanesque "affectionate comradeliness toward all beings."

Though the notion of getting married seems as unnecessary to us as it would to a pair of best-friend boys who stick together just because they're best friends and don't need any other reason, as we get older we do see the practical wisdom of having the same rights in regard to each other that a pair of married heterosexuals have. Especially the right to take care of each other without interference from each other's family, to visit each other in hospital, to fully inherit each other's literary and other possessions, and to enjoy whatever other legal benefits.

Whatever provides for that equality—whether marriage or just registered domestic partnership—it's about time it become available to same-sex mates. Whatever form it takes, it hopefully will take gays further from lonely promiscuity and closer to the day envisioned in Whitman's 1871 essay "Democratic Vistas," in which Whitman envisioned same-sex mateship (camerado-hood) as essential to achieving true democracy, which he glimpsed on the horizon like a Moses glimpsing some promised land. His term for same-sex love, "adhesive love," sounds quaint nowadays but he used that phrase long before Scotch Tape, in the sense of the closing line of his "Song of the Open Road": "Shall we stick by each other as long as we live?"

I end with the prophetic passage from "Democratic Vistas" that Allen Ginsberg quoted as epigraph to his 1975 National Book Award–winning *The Fall of America*:

Intense and loving comradeship, the personal and passionate attachment of man to man—which, hard to define, underlies the lessons and ideals of the profound saviors of every land and age, and which seems to promise when thoroughly develop'd, cultivated and recognised in manners and literature, the most substantial hope and safety of the future of these States—will then be fully express'd.

It is to the development, identification, and general prevalence of that fervid comradeship, (the adhesive love, at least rivaling the amative love hitherto possessing imaginative literature, if not going beyond it,) that I look for the counterbalance and offset of our materialistic and vulgar American democracy, and for the spiritualization thereof. Many will say it is a dream, and will not follow my inferences: but I confidently expect a time when there will be seen, running like a half-hid warp through all the myriad audible and visible worldly interests of America, threads of manly friendship, fond and loving, pure and sweet, strong and life-long, carried to degrees hitherto unknown—not only giving tone to individual character, and making it unprecedentedly emotional, muscular, heroic and refined, but having the deepest relations to general politics. I say democracy infers such loving comradeship, as its most inevitable twin or counterpart, without which it will be incomplete, in vain, and incapable of perpetuating itself.

Jeff Poniewaz teaches Literature of Ecological Vision and Whitman & Ginsberg: Liberating American Bards via UW-Milwaukee. His book Dolphin Leaping in the Milky Way, *which Allen Ginsberg praised for its "prescient Whitmanesque-Thoreauvian verve and wit," won him a PEN Discovery Award.*

Somewhere in the Middle
Jim Provenzano

I was channel-surfing on my parents' TV the night before the Senate vote for the Federal Marriage Amendment, put forth as an obvious red herring by the Bush administration to distract gullible Americans from the shitpile of lies, deceptions, and utter fraud in occupying Iraq, all to the tune of hundreds of thousands of legislative dollars wasted on what's already going on in state after state.

Divorced adulterous Republicans are once again tossing us around like a political football.

In between watching the news, I switch around to annoying infomercials, MTV's *Jackass*, and some Cinemax soft-core straight movie where the actors laughably simulate heterosexual humping.

It's strange to watch, and stranger still in the living room of my childhood home. What is all this crap on cable (something I don't bother with back home in San Francisco)?

Home. Where is home? What is a home? Is my apartment a home, or just a place where I live? Where would I be if I had a partner? And what would he be doing now? Instant-Messaging me? Visiting Ohio with me?

My parents serve as the best example of how to keep together in a marriage, through all sorts of problems, which is why I'm starting to spend more time visiting them, and helping them fix up their house.

The secret to their marriage's longevity? Televisions in separate rooms. I hop between my mother watching *Iris* upstairs and my dad watching a baseball all-stars game downstairs. In between visits, I drag a few cement blocks in from the garage to support the sink in the basement, where I had the privilege of cleaning out the floor, which had been coated in silt from a recent flood.

We spend dinners together, and a few prime-time hours and afternoons together, on the porch or in the living room. Every now and then, we see gay people on TV— *Will and Grace*, *Queer Eye for the Straight Guy*—but mostly it's straight people talking about gay people on the news.

By the time they go to bed, my parents and I have discussed the day's preposterous news: a straight teacher sent to jail for molesting girls; the local university has just torn down an entire block of homes that used to be my paper route, to make way for a student parking lot; oh, and some Baptist minister is "offended" that gay rights are being compared to the black civil rights movement.

Why isn't the minister upset with Republican Gov. Romney in Massachusetts dredging up an antiquated law to oppose gay marriages, a law that was used to prevent acknowledging interracial marriages? But more important, why aren't any gay people being interviewed on any news shows?

Even Hillary Rodham Clinton, on C-SPAN, tells her fellow senators that they should have been focusing on preventing divorce instead of banning "same-sex marriage." She doesn't even bother to use the word "gay."

Like the hideous 2000 election, and the strange millennial new year, and now this obscene vote to tag on discrimination to the Constitution, I seem to gravitate toward my parents' home at the same time as momentous and eventually disturbing events.

There's something about the dependability of my parents. They stuck together. I've always admired them, but never realized I could be like them.

In the past, the revolution called, just outside my door. In New York, I lived in the heart of the East Village. Wigstock, ACT UP and Queer Nation protests, and the Tompkins Square Park riots, were only steps away. We were fighting for basic survival. Marriage? Can we stop dying and getting assaulted first, then worry about becoming soccer dads and moms?

Perhaps I'm a bit tired of spontaneous yet meager protests planned for the usual route near my San Francisco home: from the Castro to City Hall. Here we go again.

In February, as Valentine's Day brought hope to thousands lining up at San Francisco's City Hall, I only had to walk downhill from my Bay Area home to witness another revolution.

But it was stopped abruptly by a state court, and tossed about callously by a Hollywood actor–governor who "doesn't care one way or another." The San Francisco marriages were halted, like a short list at Ellis Island.

I think, as brave as Gavin Newsom may be, that perhaps he tossed gay and lesbian couples a bone that he knew would be yanked away. Perhaps that piece of paper may not mean a thing, but it meant enough for a few thousand couples to wait in line for, in the rain.

Perhaps, since I couldn't stay all those days and watch the events unfold, my doling out a box of belated Valentine's Day cards (*Lord of the Rings* and WWF; hey, they were on sale at Walgreens) wasn't enough of a gesture of support. Perhaps I was supposed to do something more. Send another email petition, write my senator, protest even.

Perhaps most of the couples lining up to get their partnerships officiated never showed up for the protests I devoted my earlier life to, because they were too busy being domestic, and at the time didn't think "in your face" protesting was right. Perhaps some dusty piece of radical rhetoric about "mimicking the patriarchy" still clings to the back of my mind.

These days, I'm sorry, but somewhere between the 367th emailed gay-marriage news report from Rex Wockner, and the 40th email from my usual gang of "concerned friends" who send such emails, I just didn't have time to protest.

I thought I'd done my time in the trenches. Having spent the past 15 years focusing on becoming an accomplished writer of mostly gay news, arts features, and fiction, I thought I was contributing. But every time some thug like Bush gets elected, most of what we've fought for, what I thought I worked for, seems like a few droplets of water on a raging brushfire.

Between California and Massachusetts, I'm sitting here in Ohio, somewhere in the middle, in a state that jumped to ban marriage before gay activists had a moment to even propose it.

My mom and I stay up a bit later than usual, and after watching an episode of *Six Feet Under*, where Nate learns from a psychic that his wife may not be dead, we watch the *Queer as Folk* episode where Michael and Ben trek to an apparent Valhalla of gay marriage, Canada.

They do it while riding in an AIDS fundraiser. I update my mom on the plot, that a corrupt fundraiser walked out on the event, forcing the characters to create their own AIDS Ride. "That sounds like that series of articles you wrote," she says. I remember being criticized by some people for writing them, for anticipating what would eventually happen, then, eventually, feeling some small form of vindication when it did.

My mom says she's so happy Sharon Gless is doing another good show. She says I should be proud of my work. She hopes I find a man like the guy in *Queer as Folk*. I tell her, if he's anything like Robert Gant, I'd marry him, no problem.

I'd like that. I really would. I'd like to meet a man, or be a man worthy of waiting in line in the rain to officially marry, and I mean a marriage that's legal, permanently. But something tells me it's going to have to happen in a civilized nation, and this one isn't it just yet.

And besides, unlike all my articles and stories, I think I missed the deadline.

Perhaps if I'd spent a little less time trying to fight for the gay community, and a little more time working toward my own life, I could have dragged my hubby to this house, to meet my parents, work on the yard, show him where I grew up never even thinking I could get married.

I'd proudly show him off at the Wal-Mart, at the grocery store, at the July 4th celebrations, just to rub it in, show these small-town people just who they were so afraid of.

Before bed, I check my email.

On Yahoo News, Sen. Rick Santorum, one of the most monstrous of antigay Republicans, has dredged up has-been singer Pat Boone to rally support for this insidious proposed assault on that tattered document lying under glass in Washington, DC.

And I wonder, Is that what they want, people listening to Pat Boone as some sort of authority figure on what's best for American politics? The man who posed for a photo showing his cock sticking out of a hole in a box? Is that his idea of family values?

Is that the best they can do? Is the utterly corrupt Republican Party so pathetically desperate to shift our collective attention away from their own faults? Will there ever come a day when they stop using gay people in such an unscrupulous manner?

Not today, where all across the country, those smug right-wingers are sleeping soundly, eager to rise up and do their alleged duties.

I shut off the computer, sneak downstairs for a snack, and wish I could brush it all aside, think of my apartment a few thousand miles away as warmly as this house, where my family lived, and lives.

I think of all the chances I didn't even know I had to build such a home with another man; of waking up with him in my boyhood bedroom, mowing the lawn, watching the news as a herd of strangers in Washington decide our fate and toss another football, then switching the TV off, escaping to the porch, where we sit, waiting, holding on, watching fireflies as the night grows dark.

Jim Provenzano is the author of PINS *and* Monkey Suits, *and writes the nationally syndicated column "Sports Complex." Visit his website,* www.myrmidude.com.

Marry Me A Little
Andy Quan

I never fantasized about marriage.

I don't remember the first wedding I went to, but I did go to a lot of wedding banquets. They were opportunities which my whole family awaited, so tempting that we'd even sit with our dreaded relatives and risk being seated next to an old village lady who spoke no English and would fill our plates with not what we wanted—an extra bowl of shark's fin soup! Taro-stuffed duck! Thinly sliced abalone!—but with big slimy Chinese mushrooms and smelly cabbage.

If that seems like a digression, really, it's not. We were there for the food. Who cared about the bride and groom, the ceremony that had taken place that afternoon, the bride's three changes of clothes during the ceremony? We hardly knew these people. Were they 2nd or 3rd cousins? And Dad had explained clearly: the gift we give is money. The money is equivalent to the amount of money that they'll spend to feed us.

So, my early memories of weddings: economic exchange.

My brother's wedding reinforced this. I was amazed at how excited my father's generation was to hand down wealth to the next generation in the form of kitchen appliances, artwork, dinner sets. And because I knew I was gay, and was beginning to understand what that meant politically and socially, I was also pissed off. Marriage was a way to transfer wealth from the old to the young. If you played by the rules. If you fit in with what they wanted their young to be.

No matter that those weddings ended in divorce sometimes. Often. My brother's for example (although he has now remarried, and to a wonderful woman). When my first college friends to get married were asked their reasons, they explained that they'd done so much in their lives that hurt their parents, they thought they wanted to do something to make them happy. My gift to them was both heartfelt and unintentionally cynical: a song that I wrote and played for them at their reception. Its chorus? "All that one has to give in this life is one's self." My other college friends chipped in to get them a cappuccino maker. Their divorce, with a daughter now part of the equation, was bitter. More recently, I nagged at a friend: "You're not making us go to another wedding and reception, are you? A THIRD one?! Please tell me why you're getting married again." "This time's for love," he replied, a dreamy expression in his eyes. "This one's for love."

So, I have a few reservations about marriage in general, which carry over to queer marriages.

On the other hand, I've been watching the development of this issue for years, and perhaps closer than most. I was a gay activist from before I left my teens. I figured out early that declaring a struggle for antidiscrimination laws didn't sound very compelling, and equal superannuation benefits was neither understood by nor relevant yet for me and my peers. Therefore, one of the first political songs I wrote was "The Right to Love," followed a number of years later by "Fight for Love." In Ontario, Canada in 1994, we fought for (unsuccessfully) a complex set of changes to provincial law, but our rallying cry was for "Equal Families." If we were going to achieve social change, then we'd talk about what society understands, or purports to understand: Love. Relationships. Family.

A few months later, I flew off to start my first professional job as the only paid employee of the International Lesbian and Gay Association in Brussels. As editor of their quarterly newsletter, I chronicled for two years the advent of domestic partnerships in Denmark, Sweden, Norway, Finland, and the Netherlands as well as in various cities and municipalities. There was a great sense of celebration in these achievements rather than the feeling that these partnerships were second-class. I think the Scandinavians are a practical people, and felt less need for the symbolism of marriage as long as they got the benefits from it. Besides, journalists around the world didn't make any differentiation, and called them "gay marriages." While I never really believed that we'd achieve marriage, the battle for it was everywhere. In individual American states, in European parliaments, in the demands of grassroots organizations from Brazil to Latvia.

During this time, I heard counterarguments, mostly from gay men from an older political movement who asked why we should be aping a deficient straight institution, about the power of gays and lesbians to create new forms of relationships and communities of friends, about ensuring that gay sexuality remain free and untamed, about prioritizing other issues like age of consent and antigay violence.

And still, gay marriage marched on, steadily, one step backward and two forward. After Brussels, I lived in London for two years, and during this time, friends suggested that I should stay in Europe and that in order to do so, I should get married. "Lots of lesbians you could trade citizenships with, maybe place an ad…" However, I knew a number of binational gay and lesbian couples making pleas to the Department of Immigration so they could be together. It felt sad to me that I could try to pretend to be straight and get married to stay in the country when my gay friends were in danger of being separated from their partners.

I left London for Australia. Australia was one of the first countries anywhere to recognize de facto relationships, and it was felt by activist groups here that having lesbian and gay relationships recognized as de facto would be the best strategy. Incremental change, including work toward antidiscrimination laws and equal rights and benefits in the workplace or other spheres, would lead to fuller equality. However, the momentum of the legalization of queer marriages in Canada, and the huge booming discussions in the USA have reached our shores now; and there's debate between those who wonder why Australian gay and lesbian groups aren't fighting for gay marriage as a first priority and those who believe that other battles are more winnable and important, especially in a political climate where our prime minister seems to truly find us distasteful.

Meanwhile, some part of me does believe there's something sacred about partnerships and public oaths. So, if we're to embrace this idea of marriage whole-heartedly, are we thinking about the responsibilities that come with marriage as well as the privileges? I've also witnessed and read about so many unhappy marriages. So, are we looking at marriage critically? Whether public commitments and the worship of an idea of "marriage" mean that people commit to or stay in relationships that are without love or benefit. Most of all, I hate the way marriage privileges state-sanctioned partnerships over those who are, by choice or not, single. I've always felt it tragic that some of my straight women friends feel themselves less or unequal to those who have married.

I wonder if I feel I do not want to get married because I fear commitment. Or is it that I romanticize love so much that I don't want to risk its public failure? I also wonder in what circumstances marriage would make my life easier in terms of tax benefits, immigration, and other legal areas. As an ideal though, I'm not fussed about it. I know this is because I never absorbed mainstream expectations and desires, as I always felt apart from the mainstream. For this reason, I kind of admire those who demand marriage as an equal right and privilege. A sense of entitlement to justice for gays and lesbians is a good thing.

I also like the idea of gay marriage as inspiration. While an Indian activist commented recently, "when we're being beaten black and blue, the first thing is survival. And then we can think of legalizing marriages," this doesn't necessarily contradict a situation where knowing that gay marriage exists elsewhere gives hope to those living in countries where it's hard or impossible to have a gay or lesbian identity. At the same time, it's important to think about the different contexts around the world for lesbian and gay rights and how marriage and partnership fit into this. The particular polarized climate in the USA and the political and cultural and religious beliefs of its peoples bring a fire and passion to this issue of gay marriage which may be similar in other parts of the world, but is definitely not the same.

Still, lesbian and gay newlyweds are changing the definition of marriage at the same time that this battle is reminding us of how change is possible and probable. When I heard the news about Canada, I felt a secret teary pride thinking that the lobbying I did ten years ago in my fresh-faced early twenties may have contributed to today's victory. And rather than getting tied down to a sacred institution, couples seem to be swinging it around in the air and catching it in a way that's sweetly profane. Maybe we can make sure that the institution of marriage works for us in the midst of our complex created families, open relationships, and other nontraditional pathways. Maybe it's not a bad thing for marriage to be used in any way that suits us: to honour and celebrate our relationships, to challenge laws in other countries and states, to demand an equal piece of every pie, to flip the bird to American presidents and Australian prime ministers and have great big fabulous parties. I'd love one myself, wouldn't mind the gifts, and would love an excuse to invite friends from overseas. And while I've never wanted to wear a wedding dress, nor rent a tuxedo, a full nine-course Chinese wedding banquet for everyone I know would be divine. Just don't tell me that joke again about gay men being entitled to bridal registries.

Canadian-born Andy Quan was the coordinator of the International Lesbian and Gay Association from 1994-1996 and has since worked for HIV/AIDS organizations in London and Sydney. He is the author of Calendar Boy *and* Slant, *and his fiction, erotica, and poetry are published widely. Say hello at:* www.andyquan.com.

Always a Cultural Deconstructionist, Never a Bride
Carol Queen

I'd solidified my convictions about marriage and kids way before I came out as queer. My early philosophy was influenced by the countercultural mores of the 1960s as well as the abysmal example of Mom and Dad. I pretty much had these sentiments down by the age of 12, and mind you, I hadn't even heard of Emma Goldman yet: I was going to fuck anyone I pleased when I grew up; I wasn't going to marry anybody; and bringing children into a postnuclear world was a karmic error that would follow the perpetrators past the grave. Nothing that's happened during the ensuing 35 years has done much to change my mind.

None of this means that I decry the solace and pleasure of family (I even recognize that a scant few of us came from nurturant and delightful families of origin). I appreciate the drive that draws so many of us together as partners. I even understand why you people want to pull pictures of your kids out of your wallets. See, look at these photos of my cats! Aren't they precious? Look, this is Teacup, walking through a carpet tube! She's so smart! And Bracelet holding a stuffed bear with her paws—did you ever see anything so cute?

Hey, I'd even send 'em to college, if they wanted to go. Fortunately, I've chosen a species to love that doesn't need a degree to succeed in life. But I digress.

From the time I began to go to slumber parties, where I invariably was the only girl present who didn't want to wait to have sex until she was married, I've looked askance at engagement rings and bridal showers, crudely decorated honeymoon cars and the sticky-sweet taste of wedding cake. (I used to feel the same way about bachelor parties, too, until I worked a couple of them. I never jumped out of a cake, though. That's so retro.)

Even when I came out as queer (I knew about Emma Goldman by then), I was in no hurry to plan my wedding. Ironically, the reason I came out to my dad had to do with a lesbian wedding, a lovely little outdoor ceremony planned by my college Gay Studies teacher during summer break. I had to get my dad's permission to go (in those days he paid for everything, including bus tickets to weddings), which involved me telling him what prompted the trip in the first place: When I had finally let loose that Jill was my *Gay Studies* teacher, and she was marrying a *woman*, my dad violently crumpled the newspaper he'd been reading and yelled, "Jesus Christ! I suppose that means you're a homosexual!"

"Bisexual, actually, Dad—but if you can only imagine things one way or the other, thinking of me as homosexual will be fine."

Jill and her lover had a nice little ceremony with tasty cake, which I figured presaged a higher quality of marital commitment than the typical heterosexual. I'm sure it was good while it lasted, but within a few years they had broken up.

(Let's spend another minute considering the question of cake, since I am so obviously fixated on it. They make that vile icing perfectly white and "sculptable," and damn the flavor. Doesn't that in itself telegraph a *huge* warning about marriage?)

I wondered what it must feel like to call someone "my wife" (or, for that matter, "my husband"—I couldn't really picture either). My mother's career as a wife effectively ended her autonomous dreams, and she wound up an unhappy alcoholic stuck in a tiny, uninteresting world. "Husbanding" didn't seem so great either, when it meant you had an unhappy alcoholic and two unhappy kids to shepherd around.

In the queer world, we called each other "lovers," an appellation I couldn't imagine my parents ever using. Straight people de-emphasized the connection between partnering and the erotic (well, the older ones did, anyway—the ones who got married; in those days there were scads of heterosexual lovers too, also under the philosophical influence of Emma Goldman). Queers re-emphasized the sexual, especially the boys, who had their own special bathhouses wherein they could do precisely that. The word "lover" had another kind of larger political significance, too, as in: "An army of lovers cannot fail." I firmly believed (Jill and her wife to the contrary) that we were redefining what it meant to be together, rejecting hetero ways in favor of erotic personal affiliations based on the value systems of people who saw and treated each other as equals. Such coupling (or triplings, for that matter) would not fall prey to the sex-role stereotyped problems to which straight marriages were heir.

Later we had to alter the slogan a little, to "An army of *ex*-lovers cannot fail." But I quickly adjusted, because I had figured out that queer lovers could in fact fail, and spectacularly; but if you stayed on good terms with your exes, after the obligatory and hopefully brief period of hating them for ruining your life, you could get back on footing perhaps even firmer than when you'd been together.

Granted, as we congratulated ourselves on avoiding the pitfalls of hetero gender-role sterotypes, three things were happening: Many hetero people worked very hard to discard those stereotypes and to remake marriage as an institution; queer people rediscovered how hot gender roles could be; and some queer people put their noses to the grindstone so they could step up to the altar and call each other "husband" and "wife."

Having come of age, and come out, in the heady years just after Stonewall, when more queer men I knew joined Faggots Against Fascism than wanted to join the army, I always viewed the assimilationist queer folk around me with bemusement. I respect pretty much any queer organizing, even the Log Cabin Republicans (if only because of the childish fun it is to point and laugh when their favored candidates mistreat them time and time again). It is clear to me, with 30 years of hindsight, that every kind of queer organizing has moved us out of the shadows, although I have not always personally appreciated the type of limelight some have chosen. But I could never have predicted that joining the army, getting ordained, and getting hitched would be the big issues they are as the new century dawns.

Certainly oppression in any context is wrong. Naturally queer folk are irritated when straight people get benefits denied to same-sex partners. There's nothing to *like* about being discriminated against—except, perhaps, the way that discrimination forces anger, creativity, shows the way to the road less traveled. As we have seen time and time again, pissed off (or even simply irritable) queers making a point can cause the culture to shift—sometimes not a lot, often not enough, but these shifts are no less significant for that. Queers who flounce off to live our own lives often find straight people eventually come tugging at our coattails, wondering what we're doing, how we're doing it, if they should do it too. Who doesn't have a wistful "straight but not narrow" friend who's confided, "I wish *we* had a parade"?

And don't even snap back, "Butcha *do*, Blanche; you have the Macy's Thanksgiving Day Parade, the Rose Bowl, and every other fucking parade all fucking year." Because what Poor Wistful Straight Friend really means is: "I wish I could celebrate my sexuality like you do."

Yes, the correct Gay Studies answer is: We do this because we have to. We do it because the larger culture doesn't celebrate us at all (well, at least before *Queer Eye for the Straight Guy* it didn't). We do it to flaunt—for each other, mainly, but sure, you can watch from the sidewalk. We do it to create ourselves, celebrate ourselves, make ourselves visible as big and loud and proud and *here*. In the old days, pups, we did it for those reasons even when some of us wore paper bags over our heads. (Yes, I attended more than one demo in the '70s where paper-bagged queers shouted, "2-4-

6-8, gay is just as good as straight"—proud enough, but also worried about keeping their jobs if they were to be caught on film by a TV crew. I always said we ought to all wear Groucho Marx noses, but no one ever took me up on it.)

But then the next question is, If heteronormativity is still so ubiquitous that it needs no Straight Pride parades, whom will we become if enough of us squeeze our asses onto the park bench of Normalcy? Because you know that's what the military/marriage nexus is all about.

I took my friend Arugula DeVoon, a female drag queen, to the 1994 March on Washington for LGBT Etc. Etc. Rights. She had come out in San Francisco and was, like me, an alumna of the Lusty Lady Theatre, a peep show that allowed women of all sexual identities a place to grow larger-than-life femme personae, even if they strode in wearing Doc Martens. Arugula had never been to a predominantly political queer march before, and she was excited to be there. She wore a 1950s foundation garment with the cups cut out so that her own very splendid breasts could serve as the garment's focal point, and she had personally sewn a couple of zillion strings of pearl Mardi Gras beads onto it. She didn't ride the Metro in this getup; she changed in the rest room beneath the Lincoln Memorial. There we encountered a lesbian from the Midwest, or perhaps the DC suburbs. She was wearing a sweatshirt with fuzzy protruding pussy willows on it (I do not think any irony was intended), and a mullet. She did *not* appreciate the excellent beauty of Arugula DeVoon; in fact, by the time Ms. Mullet was finished ranting, Arugula was in tears. The gist (I bet you can already guess): "I'm here to march for my civil rights! When they see *you*, it'll ruin everything!"

Sobbing as we trekked up to tell Abraham Lincoln what had just happened, Arugula managed to say, "I thought this was about letting people be *themselves!*"

If some of our elder philosphers—Harry Hay, Judy Grahn—are correct, queers are here to culturally diversify every society into which we emerge. We are here to expand the very notion of what "being ourselves" can mean. Many of us are also here to devote more of our life's energy to cultural production (art, teaching, and so forth) than to producing the next generation. Instead of raising it, we help birth the alternative ways of seeing that the next generation (or the one after that) will embrace.

Fortunately for Arugula, the Sisters of Perpetual Indulgence were up on top of the Lincoln Memorial, and they welcomed her as a lost sister. As speaker after speaker trashed Bill Clinton for his absence from DC (the putatively progay president had flown the coop when the people who helped elect him started to arrive), queer after queer from all over the U.S. rushed up to Arugula and asked to have a photo taken with her. "I've got to send this to my mom!" gushed one guy. And of course when she, with her Mardi Gras bead accents, met up with the fags from New Orleans, it was homecoming all over again.

Note to Missy Mullet: Not only is Arugula better-dressed than you, she has more pride. Pride is supposedly what brings us to things like marches. And when this culture gets comfortable with Arugula (and all the men who are dressed like her), they won't even *notice* you—except perhaps to say, "Eccch! Pussy willows!" But I'll tell you what—when that happens, you'll have some civil rights you don't have now.

Civil rights, snivel rights. Again, I am not suggesting these goals are completely inappropriate. I don't want a world where fiercely independent people never fall in love, never create family (whatever that means to the people involved in creating it). I want every one of us to be able to care for our lovers, make the lives we want, in the way that works best for the kinds of people we are. I don't want us or our partnerships to be second-class.

However, any queer who has set her or his sights on traditional marriage hasn't been paying attention. Look, I know how much fun it is to go all Martha Stewart and impress your grandma—and I even know that some of your grandmas would dance at your weddings. But marriage is in crisis in this culture, just like Pat Robertson said—it's just that *we're* not the ones who put it there. A vote for gay marriage is a vote for gay divorce—don't ever forget it, nor how quickly legal supports can turn into legal bonds. Really, go talk to a bunch of divorced people before you decide hetero-style marriage is where it's at. Is there any chance you've been watching too many screwball comedies?

Even the touted "queer marriage" alternatives—domestic partnerships and civil unions—require us to assent to a less tightly corseted version of marriage. Now we may be getting somewhere. But, interestingly, in some places these alternatives are open *only* to same-sex couples. My partner Robert and I can register as domestic partners in San Francisco, for example—but we can't with the State of California, until we're senior citizens. (Huh?) To the extent that a domestic partner agenda is created as an alternative for those who *cannot* legally marry, it does nothing but shore up the notion of marriage. It isn't a real alternative at all.

"Why don't you get married, then?" Bi-identified queers with other-sex partners hear this all the time. Well, let me ask you this: If you had one lover who was white and one who was not, and the law only allowed you to wed the caucasian one, would you? (There *were* such laws in the U.S., and not so long ago.) Why would I want to sanctify one of my relationships (or potential relationships) when I can't get the same respect for the other one? For that matter, why would Robert and I want to take advantage of a cultural perk so many of our friends are disallowed? We don't. Not to mention the fact that we're more likely to want a third (maybe even a third and a fourth) person to join our life than to live monogamously. Not many people (including promarriage queers) are quick to say the state should allow us the same marital privilege if "us" equals more than two.

I recently read a long article from the conservative *Weekly Standard* arguing that the reason to oppose gay marriage had nothing really to do with gays, but rather because once gays could marry, how would we stop the polyamorists from wanting the same thing?

Emphasizing marriage rights in a queer community where many people have chosen alternative relationship configurations, including living single, cuts off or de-emphasizes all the other ways we can choose to relate to one another. Unless we mindfully make marriage one choice among many, many equal choices, we've elected to minimize diversity. We should have dozens of choices; for when the mainstream queer-rights movement clamors loudly for marriage, it masks all of us for whom that isn't a great goal; it does not honor our difference.

Oh, but you say you don't want to be different? Butcha *are*, Blanche, ya *are*. Not only that, lots of heterosexuals are as well. The queer movement was truly the key in the closet door, but what those of us worrying about being normal don't realize is that it wasn't just homos and genderqueers in the closet. Everybody was in there! Even *heterosexuals* did not want to live *Leave It to Beaver* lives. I find it deeply ironic that while the LGBT movement focuses its resources on the enormous battle that is gay marriage, straight people are busy signing up for polyamory workshops, renting *Bend Over Boyfriend*, and identifying as queer because *they think we hold the key to living free lives!*

We all need more choices rather than fewer. I won't be the least bit disturbed, really, when one of those choices is gay marriage—unless our other choices have shrunk and not grown. There are as many ways to be wedded as couples (and triples, and more-ples) who want to commit to each other, even more reasons than insurance, inheritance, and love, and the bottom line is, we live in a culture that puts barriers in the way of even heterosexuals who want to create authentic, lasting, and equal partnerships.

One of those barriers is marriage—it does not facilitate, though sometimes it cages. It does not create what was not already there. If you have chosen someone, and you don't wake up every morning knowing your commitment is strong and your love real, your love as permanent as it will be, how will marriage help you? If you *do* have such a relationship with someone (or more than one), how could marriage make you cherish it more?

Our cultural rituals create. But they also exclude. And I find no joy in the Ms. Mullets of the community, who cling to the values of a rejecting culture and proceed to reject others in turn. That culture is in crisis anyway, and desiring to join it more or less on its own terms seems to me like swimming toward the *Titanic*. Write yourself a ritual, throw yourself a party, put on a tux, stand barefoot in the Pacific, invite all your friends. Hell, insist that your mother buy you a toaster. But don't get all romantic about Church and State. They don't feel the same way about you.

Carol Queen practices the Zen of queer marriage: while she doesn't believe in it, she's got a Universal Life Church ministry card and isn't afraid to use it. But are you sure you don't want a nice commitment ceremony with your cat? Carol is the author or editor of many books, stories, and essays; visit www.carolqueen.com *for her bibliography and much more.*

First published in *That's Revolting! Queer Strategies for Resisting Assimilation* (Soft Skull, 2004). Reprinted by permission of the author.

Power of Two:
The President's Stealth Defense of Gay Marriage
Jonathan Rauch

In endorsing the passage of a constitutional amendment that would restrict marriage to the union of men and women, President Bush established himself as the country's most prominent advocate of same-sex marriage.

To be more precise, he established himself as the most prominent advocate of the best arguments for gay marriage, even as he roundly rejected gay marriage itself. Consider the words that he spoke in the Roosevelt Room of the White House on February 24, 2004.

"The union of a man and woman is the most enduring human institution...honored and encouraged in all cultures and by every religious faith." Correct. Marriage is indeed the bedrock of civilization. But why would the establishment of gay matrimony erode it? Would millions of straight spouses flock to divorce court if they knew that gay couples, too, could wed? Today, a third of all American children are born out of wedlock, with no help from homosexual weddings; would the example gays set by marrying make those children's parents less likely to tie the knot?

Children, parents, childless adults and marriage itself are all better off when society sends a clear and unequivocal message that sex, love, and marriage go together. Same-sex marriage affirms that message. It says that whether you're gay or straight—or rich or poor, or religious or secular, or what have you—marriage is the ultimate commitment for all: the destination to which loving relationships naturally aspire.

"Ages of experience have taught humanity that the commitment of a husband and wife to love and to serve one another promotes the welfare of children and the stability of society." Correct again. And the commitment of gay partners to love and serve each other promotes precisely those same goals.

A solitary individual lives on the frontier of vulnerability. Marriage creates kin, someone whose first "job" is to look after you. Gay people, like straight people, become ill or exhausted or despairing and need the comfort and support that marriage uniquely provides. Marriage can strengthen and stabilize their relationships and thereby strengthen the communities of which they are a part. Just as the president says, society benefits when people, including gay people, are durably committed to love and serve one another.

And children? According to the 2000 census, 27 percent of households headed by same-sex couples contain children. How could any pro-family conservative claim that those children are better off with unmarried parents?

"Marriage cannot be severed from its cultural, religious, and natural roots without weakening the good influence of society." By "roots," Bush had in mind marriage's traditional definition as male-female. But at least as deep as marriage's roots in gender are its roots in commitment. Marriage takes its ultimate meaning not from whom it excludes but from what it obliges: "To have and to hold from this day forward, for better, for worse, for richer, for poorer, in sickness and in health, till death do us part." For gay people to join other Americans in embracing that vow only strengthens "the good influence of society."

Yes, letting same-sex couples wed would in some sense redefine marriage. Until a decade ago, no Western society had ever embraced or, for the most part, even imagined same-sex marriage. But until recently, no Western society had ever understood, to the extent most Americans do today, that a small and more or less constant share of the population is homosexual by nature. Homosexuals aren't just misbehaving heterosexuals. Fooling straight people into marrying them is not an option. Barring them from the blessings of marriage is inhumane and unfair, even if that is a truth our grandparents did not understand.

So today's real choice is not whether to redefine marriage but how to do so: as a club only heterosexuals can join or as the noblest promise two people can make. To define marriage as discrimination would defend its boundaries by undermining its foundation.

"Government, by recognizing and protecting marriage, serves the interests of all." Correct yet again. A marriage license uniquely bestows many hundreds of entitlements and entanglements that publicly affirm the spouses' mutual responsibility and that provide them with the tools they need to care for each other. Far from being just a piece of paper, a marriage license both ratifies and fortifies a couple's bonds. And marriage, like voting and other core civic responsibilities, is strongest when universal. It best serves the interests of all when all are eligible and welcome to serve.

"Our government should respect every person and protect the institution of marriage. There is no contradiction between these responsibilities." Indeed, there is not. Allowing and expecting marriage for all Americans would show respect for the welfare and equality of all Americans, and it would protect the institution of marriage from the proliferation of alternatives (civil unions, domestic partner benefits, and socially approved cohabitation) that a continued ban on same-sex marriage will inevitably bring—is, in fact, bringing already.

The logic of Bush's speech points clearly toward marriage for all. It is this logic, the logic of marriage itself, that Bush and other proponents of a constitutional ban defy in their determination to exclude homosexuals.

"In all that lies ahead, let us match strong convictions with kindness and good will and decency." Amen. And let us have the courage to follow where our convictions and our compassion logically lead.

Jonathan Rauch, a senior writer for National Journal magazine and a writer in residence at the Brookings Institution in Washington, is the author of Gay Marriage: Why It Is Good for Gays, Good for Straights, and Good for America.

First published as "Bush's Case for Same-Sex Marriage" in The New York Times Magazine, March 7, 2004. Reprinted by permission of the author.

Gay Marriage Menu
Alan Reade

The discussion on gay marriage in 2004 is amazing to me. I thought maybe by 2034 we'd be seeing this discussion. But 2004? This seems strangely anachronistic, like looking out your window and seeing those flying cars from *The Jetsons* going down your street during rush hour. Hoodathunk?

The discussion around same-sex marriage rights brings up a very personal ambivalence that started a decade ago. At 25, I got "married" to another guy in a ceremony we designed. I was ready to "partner up," and I didn't give a rat's ass about whether it was socially sanctioned.

But in a way I did care—I cared about how my friends and family would view the legitimacy of our union and hoped that we'd be seen and accepted as any other couple. In Seattle, where I lived at the time, that was pretty much the case. But we never tested out people's tolerance levels for gay couplehood outside of our urban comfort zone…in Mississippi, for instance.

Anyway, three years later, we split up. I think it was partly due to the pressure we put on ourselves to act as a "married couple." As though there is any proper way! (J.Lo, Britney, Zsa Zsa—need I say more?) I think I was more interested then in the idea of marriage—the social status that went with the union—than in staying the course. Although I must admit, I really was surprised when our relationship came to an end. I'd thought at one time we'd end up in the old fag's home together.

So jump forward ten years: We are in the post-sodomy-criminalization (PSC) era, and partly because of that landmark Supreme Court decision (and to the constant chagrin of the Bible-fanatics and crazies that pass as "conservatives" in this country), gays are able to make strides toward gaining marriage rights. But only in Massachusetts, Portland, San Francisco, and a few other places so far, and who knows how those battles will turn out.

I do firmly believe that in time this particular culture war will be won, however. Just look at how long it took interracial marriages to be accepted (remembering that the late sixties was when the ban was abolished by the Supreme Court—not *that* long ago), and now we accept that as normal. Well, most of us do, anyway. It takes time, persistence, and a "normalizing" of public opinion, but we'll get there.

I am partnered with a guy from India, who is abundant in talent and love but lacking in a green card. If we were heterosexual, I could marry him and keep him in the country. Instead, we have to rely on work visas to keep him in the U.S. Given the facts, it seems like I would be a poster child for gay marriage!

And yet, I have ambivalence: First, I'm not so interested in mimicking 100 percent a heterosexual institution that grew not out of the idea of *companionship*, but out of the idea of *property*. For most of its history, the institution of marriage was a way for dynasties to hold on to land, for families to hold on to things, and for men to hold on to women, as things. The idea of romantic love in marriage, or even of church involvement in marriage, is a fairly new concept in human history. (Although you wouldn't know it from the "must find Mr./Ms. Right" directive that seems to permeate culture in the West today.) Also, heterosexual marriage is badly in need of an overhaul. Would you get on a carnival ride or jet plane that had a 50 percent failure rate? Well, folks take the "marriage ride" with those odds all the time.

Second, there's that lingering "first marriage" for me. If I married my partner, would I be doing it for the right reasons? And what are they? I know the wrong reasons would be to get approval from folks who would never approve of me anyway. Or to do it for a new china set. Bad, bad, bad! Truthfully, I would want to make sure to do it for the legal reasons and for reasons that make sense to both of us. And that takes some soul-searching, away from the incredible pressure I feel in the Bay Area at this time for gay men to call every trick who spends more than two nights with them their "husband."

Finally, I can't help thinking at times, *We're queer, dammit! Can't we come up with something better?!*

But marriage is what we've got to work with for now. And, since Western Civilization (at its best, anyway) has become more or less a menu of individual choices, here is what I would like on my "gay marriage menu," please. My "Yes!" category includes things I would like to see recognized as part of gay marriage across the board. For the stuff in the "No!" category, I think we need more flexibility and individual choice—the "No!" is a "No!" to *automatically* making those things a part of all gay marriages. I mean, what good is being queer if we aren't going to expand on the idea of what it means to be married?

YES!

• Immigration rights for spouses. Because personally, honey, we don't have time to move to Canada right now.
• Automatic "next of kin" medical visitation rights and automatically conferred power of attorney.
• Automatically granted family medical leave.
• Joint property rights that do not need a mountain of paperwork to confirm.
• Joint tax filing without having to do battle with the IRS.
• Commonplace registries for brides and grooms at Home Depot, Crate & Barrel, and various mainstays of quality life in the U.S. (But no Wal-Mart.)

NO!

• Approval of the big churches. Do you really expect them to be on the cutting edge of this particular issue? Ultimately, reality TV has more power over what people in this country believe in anyway.
• Having some kind of "social parity" with heterosexual married couples. Have any of your married or single hetero friends ever had a problem accepting you or anyone you've dated? No? Then what do you care about keeping up with the Married Joneses? If yes, drop your friends and get new ones.
• Automatic monogamy. Note that I said "automatic." I am including lesbians in this one, but this one is mostly for the menfolk. For some couples, monogamy works, but I am not convinced that all gay men are suited for a lifetime of sex with only each other. (I know most heterosexuals aren't, if the divorce rate is any indication.) Maybe biology isn't destiny, but it sure seems to drive the bus sometimes.
• Bad tuxedos and hideous bridesmaid uniforms. Come on, people! It's not even campy anymore!

Regardless of how the legislative battles go, I do expect the gay-honeymoon market to be a big-ticket item in the coming years. So if you plan to propose, you'd better think ahead about your flight, hotel, and rental-car arrangements, before he or she says yes. Also, then you have a plan of action if he or she declines.

Alan Reade (www.alanreade.com) is a writer and performer whose satiric work has been presented to worldwide obscurity in tiny performance spaces in the U.S. and abroad. His biggest hit so far was Bear-A-Go-Go! *a burlesque comedy about big furry guys and the men they entice. Alan is about to unleash his newest comedy about the B-side of the queer-marriage debate,* Bad Gays, *on the Bay Area and the world.*

LoveStud Converted
Shar Rednour

I didn't, I don't, I won't! I never thought I would get married. I preached against it. I wholeheartedly advocated for the single girl. My book *The Femme's Guide to the Universe* is basically the "Single Dyke's Guide to the Universe" — so I can say, ahem, I really did *write the book* on being single! I believe in being the best "you" you can be — and constantly compromising and giving yourself over to another person's whims does not make you the best "you" you can be. Sorry.

I could have sex, file my nails, discuss the weather, and go on my way without a second thought. Good sex. Checked in, feeling my body and emotions sex. Even cry sex. But think of this moment lasting forever and me making any big promises to you??? No, Darling. I don't think so.

I used to argue with those hopeless romantics. They inevitably thought that I'd had some bitter breakup and was sour on love. Oh no. I believed in love always. But I did not and do not think that love is worth enslaving your life over. And you see, that was the only example of love I had in my life. I have absolutely no stories of true love in my family. None. Only "It'll do love" at best and fucked-up abusive love at worst. I was the opposite of sour. My mama raised a leader and a problem-solver, so I figured I would solve the problem of all these women being enslaved to a love that transforms them into being men's nurses and maids and in our blue-collar class often the money-makers, the check-balancers, and the spiritual heads of the household. I would figure out solutions to mating and preach it to gals. I did and still do.

As far as society accepting the queers and giving us rights. Well, of course I wanted that. I used to think that marriage between a man and woman being sanctioned by the government was stupid altogether. I don't like the government being in people's private lives as a rule. But when I thought about it, I realized that yes, in general, mating and making families really does help our society. And in theory, we as taxpayers and members of a community have less burdens (crime, health costs, happier world, etc.) if family/mates are taking care of their loved ones. And studies show we live longer (that's simply because the women — referring to my family again — don't let the assholes, I mean men, die. They make 'em go to the doctor and get blood-pressure pills and all that). So if straight people get government benefits for marriage then I wanted my full and equal right for us queers too — even if I thought I would never use them.

Back to the single life. So I definitely had some love along the way but not anyone that I would change my life for or make any promises of forever to. How silly, I thought, if you make that promise you can only meet it or mess it up. There's no going beyond the minimum. There's no 200 percent — unless we discover how to contact the afterlife. And I'm a 200 percent-er kinda gal. I like to go to the extreme. You don't get to go for extra credit with marriage.

But then one night, I went to Club Cream, the sex club I was helping Carol Queen and a hottie named Rita, produce. I love parties and events, but I'd had a hard day and didn't even want to go. I cussed through doing my hair and pulling on my half-naked outfit. (A black satin faux corset, a little fluffy see-through skirt, black faux suede boots with shocking fuchsia insides and garters with stockings of course.)

To cut to the chase, so to speak, Jackie Strano kissed me and my knees went weak. I had to sit down — on her lap Queenveniently — and I saw stars. Like those ones in cartoons. My soul felt at rest and my body seized as it released a tension I'd never even known it held. Being consumed by our love, the passion, would have been enough to indeed make me a slave to her, and if she were a bad person, or a person who wasn't healed in this world enough, it coulda gone ugly. The Goddess knows what screwed-up messes I would have gone through with her just for our passion-love-lust-soul-heart-consumption. But as it turns out, we are compatible as well. As my mother noticed right away: We truly are soul mates. And we both have faced our demons enough so that they don't hurt the other person beyond repair (not to say they don't need more wrastlin' with in this lifetime). Contrary to my previous beliefs that I couldn't be the best me I could be with another person chained to my leg—I am better than ever with Jackie. It's a cliché but it's true. And it's not a chain; it's like a violet, silky love rope that can be short or long but securely there. We make each other better. So simple, so love-songish, so artist-passionate. Maybe some of those those songwriters and artists in history have known this kind of love. Maybe it's the artists and freaks who can't hide it. Who are overwhelmingly compelled to share it and shout it and display it.

I was just in Hellinois, by the way, and got into an argument with my father. He was saying that he didn't understand why the likes of Rosie O'Donell and Ellen would "flaunt their sex lives and ruin their careers." He, believe it or not, is one of the people who didn't know Rosie was gay until she flat out said so! I told him it's not about the bedroom, Dad; we don't want to be in a cage of lies. He said, "Why? I don't talk about me and your mother's sex life in public." I said, "Neither do they, but don't you mention Mom when you discuss where you went for the weekend or in your daily routine??" And I realized that no matter what, there are so many people who have some idea in their head of what a minority is and fit the sterotypes to that. Or repeat ridiculous sayings they heard on talk radio. We as queers need to remember that we must not assume that our logic or reason will just naturally occur to the uninformed homophobes. We must still explain, educate, and argue with them, even though it's not necessarily what I want to be doing in this lifetime.

As for my marriage, my lips married Jackie's the moment they touched in 1993 and we had our Fierce Queer True Love Union in 1996 at Black and Blue Tattoo. And a San Francisco legal one in 2004. We will be together forever and ever. A lifetime is not enough time for loving her, learning from her, learning about myself, laughing with her, hearing her stories and thoughts, discovering life together, creating a better world together and all that entails—the struggle and humor and brainstorming—feeling my skin prickle when she's near, feeling her arms around me, feeling her open me up body and soul with her lovin' hands. Screw 200 percent. Just being real, honest, in life now, feeling it, lightening the load for others and letting myself be helped as well is enough. In our slack-off, comatose, rushing-around-yet-not-really-getting-anything-that-really-counts-in-this-world-DONE, I realize that 100 percent love is more than I could ever ask for. I am so grateful for my blessings.

Keep yourself real. Pray for our public servants who are doin' the right thing. And pray for those who should. Blessings to all.

July 2004

The Femmepress Shar Rednour has been with her soul mate Jackie Strano since May 23, 1993. They run SIR Productions (www.sirvideo.com) and Rosita Van Productions. Shar shared her divalicious secrets in the righteous and hilarious (and very helpful) The Femme's Guide to the Universe.

Father/Son
Rick R. Reed and Nicholas Reed

Dear Son,

When you told me, a couple of years ago, that you were gay, I remember being surprised at my own reaction. I was kind of stunned, and maybe, just a little disappointed. I mean, don't most fathers want their sons to follow in their footsteps? I had imagined you being a writer, like me, although part of me hoped for a less volatile existence. The job description for professional dreamer doesn't always include the things we wish for our children, like security and avoiding the ugly specter of rejection. But I wasn't sure how I felt about you following in my footsteps as a gay man.

I've since grown used to the fact that you are who you are. And now I can look back with a wry smile at my initial reaction. A gay father is the last person one would expect to experience disappointment and shock when his son comes out to him. But I remember one of my first thoughts was, "Well, there go the dreams of dancing at my son's wedding." It's hokey, I know, but that doesn't change the fact that it was one of my initial thoughts.

A thought I did NOT have was, "Well, maybe that will change." It's amazing to me that as little as two summers ago, I didn't hold out much hope for watching you join up with someone special until death do you part. Oh sure, there was the possibility of a civil union, whatever that means. The prospect of dreaming about your kid's civil union just doesn't have the same cachet as imagining a wedding. Nor should it.

And now, here we are, on the brink of another summer, when the newspapers and airwaves are full of talk of gay people getting married. Only last month, gay people started to wed in Massachusetts (even though these weddings, legal as they are, don't hold the same power as a union "between one man and one woman"; one hopes that will change), and I began to think that maybe my disappointment at never seeing my son marry might not have been realistic.

So now I do what I can in the hopes that you will have the option of marrying one day. I speak out to family and friends, and try to convince them that the arguments against gay marriage are, at the root, hateful and discriminatory. I try to help them see that excluding a set of people from publicly declaring their love and commitment and enjoying the same legal rights as anyone else is wrong. I join groups like the Human Rights Campaign and *DontAmend.com*, all in the hopes that if we fight hard against right-wing bigotry and discriminatory legislation, you might have a different future than I have.

As you know, I tried the "one woman, one man" marriage thing (with your mother, whom I love and always will love) and, because of my orientation, it didn't work, with lots of people getting hurt in the process. While you're beyond the self-denial I went though, I'd like to make sure one thing you don't do like me is make the same mistakes.

Being able to marry the person you love and are sexually attracted to is a very logical hope I have for you. I don't think it's asking too much. You may choose never to get married, or your marriage may fail for different reasons. Or it may be just the sort of union I now have with my partner (whom I cannot marry, but gladly would), full of togetherness, commitment to one another's well being, and the choice we've made to spend the rest of our lives together. My hope for you is that you can find that kind of magic with another person...and that your own government recognizes your commitment and love…the same government that was, a long, long time ago, put in place to supposedly look out for your welfare, freedom, and happiness.

Of course, I hope that, when people start seeing that the fabric of civilization is not being ripped apart by gay couples running wild in Massachusetts, they will stop being so threatened. I hope that for myself, so that as I continue to build my future with my partner, we too will have the option of making a public, legal declaration of our commitment. But more, I hope it for you, the person in whose happiness and well-being I've always had the greatest investment. My life is probably more than half over; you're just beginning to make the journey. All I can do is continue to hope, to speak out, and to fight for the kind of future I know you're entitled to.

We always want what's best for our children. Your having the choice to marry, I know, is what's best.

Love,
Dad

Dear Dad,

When you told me you were gay, I couldn't have understood exactly what you meant; I was only five years old. After you had taken the time to explain it to me, the only thing I couldn't understand was why it was such a big deal to so many people. After all, you were still the same person you were before you had told me, with the same qualities—thoughtfulness, compassion, and gentleness—that I had come to respect and admire; and that I still emulate. In light of those virtues, my family's judgments of you as deranged and evil made no sense. Why they thought that pursuing what every human being needs—to love and be loved—was evil, I still don't know. I thought I would crack under the strain of their demands to either hate you or bear the stain of your sin, but I comforted myself with the illusion that this was some peculiar insanity of theirs; that in the wide world outside my grandparents' house everyone was rational and would see you the same way I did. I quickly learned that this was not the case.

In grade school I learned to be ashamed of you, if not inwardly at least outwardly. In a small Catholic school, the child of a single mother is an oddity, and the gossip and rumors about you started almost as quickly among parents, teachers, and clergy as it did among my classmates. When the truth found its way into the rumor mill, I learned what the world thought of you, and of me. It was bad enough that my classmates considered you diseased at best, worse that they thought of me as tainted by association, but the real betrayal came when parents, teachers, and clergy backed them up. At best they pitied me because of you; at worst they called me degenerate trash, or a mistake. It had been possible to stand up to the assaults from my family, but when a whole community turned on me, I caved. I denied the truth; I told people you had married a woman to try to regain some semblance of legitimacy. I told homophobic jokes, and used "gay" as an insult. It's awfully difficult to grow up ashamed of your origins; for a boy, a father is a map of the self. It only became more difficult as my own homosexuality emerged on a conscious level; my shame deepened.

Years later I have come to terms with all of this; I recognize now that homophobia is irrational, and on some level, insane. But looking back, I have to wonder how much easier it would have been to grow up the son of a gay man if people had valued the romantic love you had to offer instead of reviling you for it. That's why I get so angry now when I hear the champions of family values declaring that we cannot publicly recognize your love for the sake of the children. As a child, the only thing the ban on gay marriage protected me from was the feeling that I was a whole and legitimate person.

In the end though, marriage equality is not about the children. The simple facts that you want to marry, and that your marriage would not harm anyone, are reasons enough to allow it. This is a free country, and we are all better off when we are all truly free. I wish the best to you and your husband, and look forward to the day when everyone will recognize him as such.

Love,
Nick

Rick R. Reed's published novels include A Face Without a Heart, *which is a modern-day retelling of* The Picture of Dorian Gray, *and was nominated as best novel of 2000 by the Spectrum Awards. His books* Penance *and* Obsessed, *published by Dell, together sold more than 80,000 copies. Short fiction has appeared in numerous anthologies and magazines.*

Nicholas Reed is a junior at McGill University in Montreal, where he is majoring in English Literature. I Do/I Don't *marks his publication debut.*

Beneath the Glitter Ball:
Gay Marriage as Public Celebration
Alexander Renault

Defining "gay marriage" is no less difficult than defining "straight marriage," for what does it mean when *any* person promises to bind their life forevermore with another? The political aspects of this issue do, of course, concern an oppressed minority achieving equality in the eyes of the law, and procuring the right to enjoy the benefits this social and legal contract ensure.

Gay marriage becomes somewhat more mercurial when examined from a nonpolitical viewpoint: i.e., gay marriage as a public statement of commitment and celebration. Some argue that gay marriage is an assimilationist nightmare, the mimicking of our social and religious oppressors in order to be accepted by the mainstream. Be that as it may, any gay couple who has tied the knot and *really* made a real show of it will tell you that their experience and those of their heterosexual friends' are remarkably similar.

It is important to state that marriage is not for everyone, gay or straight. Human beings are not always monogamous creatures, and the notion of bonding for life is enough to make many people run for cover. Gay men in particular, *being* men, are often cursed/blessed with the "typically male" craving for sexual novelty. But there are those who are psychologically wired to bond with another, some for serial monogamy (like skipping a stone across the surface of a pond), some for a lifetime commitment to one person. Most of us crave some form of intimacy in our lives, but how we go about this is a full spectrum of behaviors. Some men are true-blue marriage material while others prefer promiscuity. Gay men will sometimes faze in and out between the extremes.

There are aspects of gay marriage that make its functioning a tricky endeavor, but most of the challenges for gay couples are identical to their straight counterparts. In fact, most of the differences faced by gay couples stem from the bizarre reactions we receive from people who are not quite so...*open-minded*, putting it kindly. For instance, while searching for a DJ to work at our reception, we did receive a voice mail from one of the most popular in our area who called to let us know he would not be available for our "function," quickly adding, "But congratulations anyway," with all the enthusiasm of a genital herpes diagnosis. Luckily, we ended up with a gay DJ who was fabulous. And, yes, a few people asked if we planned on topping our wedding cake with two little men. But my favorite question was: "You're not going to *kiss* at the end, are you?" to which I replied: "Yeah, a real deep soul kiss—with lots of tongue and spit."

But otherwise, the problems attached to our wedding celebration like barnacles were reflective of those inherent in any couple's Big Day beneath the big tent: financial arguments, family discord, managing the control freaks, ensuring that the seating arrangement will minimize the odds of screaming and crying and the smashing of rented dishes.

Robert's mother "couldn't make it" to our union ceremony because she had a "sore back," which did not deter me from having our DJ dedicate a song to "Alex's new mother-in-law" — "Polyester Bride" by Liz Phair. We get along much better now, but back then she had been convinced that I was after her money (even though Robert, a poor doctoral student when I first met him, gave no hint that he comes from any kind of money) and the song seemed appropriate.

Gay-marriage-slash-union-ceremonies allow same-sex couples to publicly profess their love and dedication to one another. Robert and I tied the knot at his American Baptist & Brethren church, in a minimalist ceremony before 150 of our dearest friends and family. We wanted to go "all out" on the reception and so rented a bed-and-breakfast for the weekend, complete with a surf-and-turf buffet, and a small dance floor that we had assembled in the open courtyard.

We were told that getting married could be a bit of a letdown, that people feel exactly the same after the ceremony as they did before it. That wasn't our experience. Robert was speaking to a woman on the bus one morning (after I confiscated his car that day) who was on her way to see her husband at the local nursing home. They had been married for over 40 years, and she went to stay with him every day, all day. Robert later told me that he did not completely comprehend marriage until speaking with this woman. When I asked him if that level of commitment made him nervous, he replied, "No," and I still believe him, eight years later.

Seeing my partner dance at our reception with my mother to Elton John's "Circle of Life" moved me profoundly. And dancing to the evening's finale — Pat Benatar's "We Belong," at midnight, the close of our Big Day — was not something often experienced by most gay people. Years of keeping secrets become ripped open with this kind of celebration — family, friends, neighbors, and co-workers, all these people who are often the gauntlet you must survive while initially coming out.

Robert would mince no words in telling you that preparations for a wedding and reception can be horrific because you are basically throwing the biggest party of your entire life, that the details can make you scream, or cry, or want to puke. But as hectic and draining as it was, the extravaganza took on an all-new meaning when four months afterward my mom was diagnosed with end-stage metastatic cancer. As she grew more and more ill, and up until her death two years later, we increasingly came to realize that the importance of our wedding had significance for more than just the two of us. It was a public celebration that our loved ones were invited not only to attend, but to *participate in*. Hearing Dad speak at our ceremony, seeing my sister and brother-in-law seated in the front row of the church, and watching Mom dance created the kind of memories that human beings take to — and beyond — their graves with fondness.

A public declaration of commitment also allows gay couples to show our families that we mean business. As was the case with my mother-in-law, an invitation to a gay wedding is a time to call everyone's hand. To put up or shut up. It's the great showdown, and not only for the couple publicly stating their covenant; it's a moment in time when all people, friends and relatives, are called upon to choose the right thing. Although our day was magical, my mother-in-law's absence was palpable. Who was to know, at the time, that our wedding celebration would be the sole opportunity for our mothers to meet in person? Sadly, the moment slipped away forever.

Politics can be brutal and gay politics, doubly so. Add to this recipe the controversy surrounding legalizing gay marriage and there one stands, holding a hand grenade while everyone around you struggles for control, grasping for the pin: the religious right, politicians, talk show hosts, pious Southern Baptists, radio commentators, "wicked" in-laws, and worst of all, the semiliterate, dodo bird president. You have to hold that grenade tightly in your hand, pull the pin yourself, and quickly decide where you want to throw it. Deciding to make ours a "love bomb," we tossed it directly into the center of our immediate circle with this message: Take cover if you must, but we're getting fucking married and there is no escape for any of you! Not even your absence will save you from the truth of our love!

So here we are. Robert and I have a little ranch house with a little wooden fence and two Boston terriers who fall asleep on our laps while we rock in our Gay-ZZZ-Boy recliners as we watch yet another dry, British film on DVD until it's time to go to bed, at which time we might—just *might*—exhibit the terrible and unrestrained sexual deviance that threatens our national security.

Some would say we've sold out on the great gay dream of freedom, have traded in our "edge" for complacency. But I believe that what bothers so many antiassimilation activists is the very normalcy of such a picture. Yes, we're different from other people in many ways. But we are far more similar than we are different. What some call an assimilationist nightmare is simply human nature *to us*, and I believe that at least some of these allegations stem from a fear of intimacy.

So, if it's true to who you are, have the guts to stand beneath that glitter ball and profess your love and dedication. Stand before everyone and celebrate your devotion. Throw the biggest party of your lives, swear to love one another, and dare to speak its name out loud.

Alexander Renault's (www.alexanderrenault.com) *work has appeared online at* Velvet Mafia, Mind Caviar, Ophelia's Muse, *and* Scarlet Letters, *as well as several anthologies. He is the editor of the self-published nonfiction collection* Walking Higher: Gay Men Write about the Deaths of Their Mothers. *His collection of sexuality essays,* It's Queerer Than You Think, *and his novella,* Soul Kiss: The Intimate Journal of a Gay Vampire, *are available through Renaissance eBooks.*

Marriage and Civil Disobedience:
Upping the Ante and Creating an Activist Movement
Eric Rofes

I joined thousands of people this past weekend and supported my city's mayor in standing up for California's constitution in a brazen act of civil disobedience. We didn't chain ourselves to a building, sit down in the middle of a crowded intersection, or occupy a public official's office until our demands were met.

We simply got married.

Following the vision of our city's new mayor, my lover and I on Valentine's Day joined almost 2,000 other couples in a peaceful, collective statement of our refusal to allow this central institution of democracy to continue to be used as if it were an elite private club. More than continuing to lend our voices to the rhetorical debates about marriage, we plunked down our cash, got our marriage license certified by our city clerk, and took vows under the rotunda of our City Hall. Some see this as status-quo liberal pandering to "heteronormativity." I see it as the start of catalyzing an activist movement on behalf of democracy.

For a long time, the drive for same-sex marriage has cried out for an infusion of civil disobedience. Democratizing the institution of marriage is precisely the kind of issue that benefits from peaceful acts of resistance by masses of ordinary people. Not only is same-sex marriage at core about justice, freedom, and the institutions of democracy, but the emotions and symbols surrounding marriage resonate deeply with Americans of diverse political stripes. Acts of civil disobedience are useful tools because they take abstract and highly charged issues and stamp human faces onto them. Yet unlike the media spinning of the marriage issue already underway by national legal and political groups, this new wave of civil disobedience involves masses of ordinary citizens who immediately bring the issue home to their families, co-workers, and neighbors.

During the past four days, San Francisco has produced over 3,000 ordinary citizens who are now public ambassadors on the issue in their day-to-day lives. While it was powerful to see the cover photo on the *San Francisco Chronicle* capturing the two gay men getting married while each held one of their infant twins or see the national television coverage of couples traveling swiftly from distant parts of the country to obtain a marriage license, even more powerful will be the work the newly betrothed take on in their home communities. To change the hearts and minds of the mushy middle of the electorate, we need them to feel a personal connection and a personal solidarity with this issue.

We arrived at San Francisco City Hall at 7:30 a.m. on Saturday morning, having turned on the local news a few minutes earlier and seen that several dozen people were already lined up, awaiting the 10:00 a.m. opening of the city clerk's office. Together with others on the line that soon surrounded City Hall, we took out cellphones and called friends and family from coast to coast, getting the word out about our participation in this historic action. We took photos throughout the four-hour process of waiting on line, receiving our marriage certificate, taking our vows, and filing the marriage with state authorities, and later that day, we sent them out online to family and friends, supporters and otherwise. Before we'd been married for 24 hours, our personal experience in this mass action had been shared with dozens and then passed on to hundreds of people in ever-expanding networks.

My lover does the work of public education on this issue with tremendous glee. On returning to work on Monday, he freely shared his ebullience with co-workers at his work site where he builds and maintains airplane engines. He's shown our marriage certificate to members of his work team—mechanics, engineers, and managers—who have long known he was gay but can now see that the abstract issue they might see on the television news is directly connected to a person with whom they feel some collegiality. He's phoned his company's human resources office to change my status from "domestic partner" to "spouse," and engaged in friendly musings with the personnel officer about whether the company's legal people have already determined how to handle our new (and perhaps, precarious) status.

Four years ago, I published an essay calling for queers and their allies to augment our legal and legislative efforts with a powerful direct action and civil disobedience strategy. While published in several dozen gay papers throughout the nation, then in the academic journal *Social Policy*, and finally in an anthology on political activism in the new millennium, I was disappointed that none of the national lesbian and gay political organizations took up the call and mounted a well-planned and carefully organized civil disobedience campaign focused on same-sex marriage. Instead, small collections of local activists and other ad hoc organizers have been the only ones moving in this direction. In the wake of San Francisco's daring leadership this past week, I'm eager to put forward ideas for additional organizing and civil disobedience. Especially, if we end up grappling with a constitutional amendment battle, it is critical for grassroots, activist organizing to be powerfully and strategically deployed.

First, efforts must be put into organizing dozens of other cities, counties, and states to take bold steps on behalf of same-sex marriage and to creatively examine their state's laws and policies seeking loopholes, silences, and contradictions that might provide opportunities to marry same-sex couples. If a renegade city clerk in Boulder, Colorado could issue marriage certificates to same-sex couples in 1975, why haven't the political leaders of that progressive center taken leadership today? Justice-minded residents throughout the nation and liberal political clubs should immediately pressure public officials to create a bandwagon behind San Francisco and continue to move this issue forward. (This recommendation was, in fact, taken up by leaders in diverse places, including New Paltz, New York; Multnomah County, Oregon; a rural town in New Mexico; Asbury Park, New Jersey; and several other sites.)

Second, the incredible legal and legislative victories in Massachusetts, ground zero of the marriage fight this year, must be buttressed and infused with creative and strategic approaches once that state begins issuing marriage certificates to same-sex couples in May. This will require the kind of sensitive coalition work that has rarely happened in contemporary queer organizing, where local organizers understand that their efforts have tremendous national implications and merit more than a narrow consideration, and national organizers are sensitive to the priorities and investments of Massachusetts activists. Should we organize campaigns to encourage queers throughout the nation to get married in Massachusetts? If Massachusetts is to be home to a statewide vote to change their constitution to keep lesbians and gays from marrying, should we initiate "Freedom Summer" types of efforts to engage in mass face-to-face dialogue all over the state?

Third, efforts must be directed to support people who are central to the marriage process in America and who, if organized and supported, might be part of additional strategic interventions in support of same-sex marriage. In particular, strategic efforts might be made to identify and organize independent county, city, and town clerks who are willing to join in an organized effort to stand up for justice. Progressive members of the clergy of all denominations seem poised on the brink of breaking out and participating in additional acts of resistance, if only some group would take on the task of organizing a strategic and adequately resourced effort.

It's tough to guess which major organization would take up this task and perhaps coordinate with the local and ad hoc activists already initiating direct actions on behalf of same-sex marriage. While liberal and Left organizations wrap themselves and their fundraising letters in nostalgic narratives of bus boycotts, campus sit-ins, and ACT UP sieges at federal agencies, they've ceded most street organizing, confrontational actions, and civil disobedience to ad hoc collections of unaffiliated activists. Hence we find ourselves today on the marriage issue at a moment where public officials seem more willing to be daring and deploy these tactics than organizations who describe themselves as activist. While lobbying, media spins, and conferencing remain valuable facets of movement building, if we want to transform same-sex marriage from an issue to a movement, some organization's got to get us all moving.

February 2004, San Francisco

Eric Rofes is a longtime organizer and community activist. He is a professor of education at Humboldt State University in Arcata, CA, where he teaches courses on teaching for social justice, community-organizing skills, and sexuality and schooling. He can be reached at eerofes@aol.com.

Why I Want to Celebrate Our Love with a Wedding Ceremony
David Rosen

Later this afternoon, Robb and I are going to a little card shop in Park Slope, Brooklyn, to order the invitations for our wedding. Tomorrow is the third anniversary of the day we met (over a business lunch, in which Robb presented me with proofs of Harvey Fierstein's fab children's book, *The Sissy Duckling*, can you believe it?)—and we are about two and a half months away from our wedding day. On October 2, 2004, at the Brooklyn Society for Ethical Culture, we'll be surrounded by some 100 of our closest friends and family—to mark, declare, and celebrate the miracle of our love and commitment to each other.

How did we get here? Why are we doing this?

One answer: We fell in love. Doesn't it sound so simple?

I am not unmindful of all of the religious, social, political, personal—and might I add, familial—ramifications of our wedding. I never actually thought about having a wedding before I met Robb. I've had a couple of "meaningful" relationships (including one that lasted for more than 15 years!) before, but never thought about a ceremony. I have had friends who had lovely ceremonies. *Not for me*, I always thought.

But something changed. Robb and I (and our friends and families—yes, there is much pressure here from our families!) have been toying with the idea of a ceremony (and rings) since a few months after we became, for lack of a more-meaningful word, *boyfriends*. Everyone who knows us really really really wants to celebrate our happiness together—at a ceremony and a party. Why?

How heterosexual! How traditional! Has the whole world gone topsy-turvy?

I, who have just turned 45, came of age and came out after no small degree of personal turmoil and triumph in the shadow of the great protest and civil rights movements of the '60s and '70s. I grew up in Buffalo, New York, and can honestly say I never thought I saw another openly gay man ever—ever! (Liberace does not count)—when I was growing up and when I was always secretly in love with my best friends (who were often athlete/bodybuilder kinds of guys).

In my professional life, I have worked with and befriended some of the great pioneers of gay liberation. How lucky I am to have so many teachers! I know firsthand—and I have learned from folks like Mark Thompson, Felice Picano, Patricia Nell Warren, Karla Jay, Andrew Holleran, Katherine V. Forrest, Edmund White, Christopher Bram, Minnie Bruce Pratt, and so many others—how difficult it was/and still is to come out, and how our struggles for equality—and plain old human dignity—are fought each minute and each hour of each day.

So, one has to wonder: Why would I ever want to have a wedding? In essence, why would I ever choose to mimic the very institutions that have so virulently railed against, rejected, and restricted the happiness of our Queer lives? Well, for one thing, as is the case with us using the word *queer*: There is much power in us making marriage our own.

I've just met Evan Wolfson, who in many ways is the Patron Saint of the gay-marriage battle. I urge you to read his new book *Why Marriage Matters*. It is a revelation. George Chauncey's *Why Marriage?* is equally significant, powerful, inspiring.

So, why will I marry Robb? My answer: Because it is right. It now fits me. Now is the time. Now is the time for us—with our circle of family and friends surrounding us—to take the plunge and to declare in our unique and meaningful way: We matter. We love.

How far we've come. How far I've come. Hallelujah!

David Rosen (www.insightoutbooks.com) is co-founder and editor-in-chief of InsightOutBooks. His work has appeared in several publications, including The Advocate, Lambda Book Report, *and several other publications. He has received the GLAAD Media Award, the Lambda Literary Pioneer Award, and has been inducted into the Saints and Sinners Literary Hall of Fame.*

The Pros & Cons
Rob Rosen

Fine, I didn't vote for Gavin Newsom. I mean really, I couldn't in good conscience vote for a man that was prettier than me. Shallow? Yes. So sue me. Besides, who could have guessed that shortly after winning the election he'd give us the right to marry; albeit with nary a shred of legality?

Of course, he did put me in a bit of a pickle. There I was, rolling merrily along, never even giving the idea of marriage a second thought, when *WHAM!* I was all of a sudden given the option. Being gay has so many advantages to being straight. No kids, no burdensome wife, and certainly no legal ties. None of that crap. Basically, I can concentrate on my tan, wait for the next Madonna album to come out, and continue on with my life, free and easy.

Oh sure, I love my partner and all, but I always had an out. A means of escape. Yes, I suppose there's always the risk of a palimony suit, but, unlike Liberace, I neither had the ways nor the means to make my partner rich; though I'm fairly certain my life-size, autographed, cardboard cutout of Miss Grace Jones would fetch a hefty sum on eBay.

But now, thanks to this liberal schmuck, hunky though he may be, I'm able to be seemingly just as trapped as my straight counterparts. Thankfully, there are no women involved, but you get my point.

So what was I to do? Was Jerry even expecting a proposal from me? Or worse yet, should I have expected one from him? And how would I respond, given the chance? So I sat down and made one of those Pro/Con lists you're supposed to make in these instances.

Con: No easy way out for me. And a life of legally binding, humdrum coexistence with him.

Pro: No easy way out for him. Ten years of living together has destroyed my girlish figure. What were the odds of finding anyone else who would want me after so long a hiatus from the market? And I doubted I had the energy to even bother looking for new and probably even-more-zaftig-than-me partner.

Con: A potentially costly and bitter divorce.

Pro: I already have half of everything Jerry owns with options for upgrades. Perhaps we'd even retire together someday and move to Palm Springs: Geezer Gay Mecca. And in terms of the bitter thing, I think you can see that I've clearly reached that point already.

Con: Living a life similar to a straight man.

Ugh. What an abominable thought that is. I can't think of a corresponding Pro for that one, but I have a feeling it doesn't matter. Gay men will always be more fabulous than straight men, with or without a binding piece of paper. Besides, I doubt we'd ever be all that similar. The lack of an opposite-sex partner would see to that, thank goodness. Two sexes, like two wrongs, don't usually make a right. Right?

Con: He could say no.

Pro: He could say no. Then I'd be back to the free and easy life; though, lately, Madonna's albums have been kind of lacking. Okay, **Pro:** He could say yes.

Fine, I was back to square one. Now what? Does all this nonsense really matter all that much, anyway? I love Jerry and he loves me. We already share a great life together. How would a measly piece of paper change anything? Do I really want or need to be accepted by my government? Should straight society's choices reflect my own? Doesn't seem like it's done them a hell of a lot of good. Just look at Britney or J. Lo-Almost Combs-Judd-Almost Affleck-Anthony. And let's not forget, God love her,

Ms. Taylor-Hilton-Wilding-Todd-Fisher-Burton-Burton-Warner-Fortensky. Please, Mary. This marriage thing is just one big joke to them. So why should it matter so much to me?

But I suppose it does, or there wouldn't be any of this waffling. If I really didn't care, I'd simply say to hell with it and move on to more pressing matters: like when the next Madonna movie is coming out, though I think I can wait a while on that one judging by her last endeavor. Okay, so maybe I do want that whole marriage thing. That whole "stand up in front of my friends and family and profess my undying love and devotion for my man Jerry" thing. It sure as hell worked for my mom and dad. Why not me?

Screw it. I guess I'll take the plunge into the choppy waters of marriage after all. To quote the indomitable Ms. Gabor-von Anhalt-O'Hara-Ryan-Cosden-Hutner-Sanders-Hilton-Belge-De Alba, "A man in love is incomplete until he is married. Then he is finished."

And, now, so am I.

Rob Rosen lives, loves, and works in San Francisco. Unlike the narrator in this piece, he is happily and quite legally domesticated to his partner Kenny, who he simply adores with all his heart. His first novel, Sparkle: The Queerest Book You'll Ever Love, *was published in 2001 to critical acclaim, and his short stories regularly appear on more than two dozen literary sites. Feel free to visit him at his website* www.therobrosen.com *or email him at* robrosen@therobrosen.com.

Super Marriage
Roxxie Rosen

Tuesday President George W. Bush proposed a constitutional amendment that would ban gay marriage, in part a response to the gay and lesbian couples who've been getting married in my hometown, San Francisco.

So my girlfriend asked me, over dinner, if I thought that having legal civil unions should be enough for us. "Honey," she said after the appetizers, "do you believe in gay marriage, too?"

I had to think. Could I, someone who has lived outside of the world of legally sanctioned relationships her entire life, actually decide to care? I suppose that the words "Marry me!" whispered in a moment of love must mean something. But after 40-plus years of living "in the life," "worshiping at the church," wearing black pants in the '70s to signal that I was a lesbian, and slipping in and out of gay and lesbian bars, not to mention trying to avoid job discrimination, harassment on the streets, or becoming a victim of homophobic violence, I wasn't sure I'd ever really considered it.

I could now get some of what my straight friends have. Our lives are so different, though.

I was speechless for a moment as I considered whether or not my straight women friends had my problems. Did they ever have to worry that their partner would wake up in the morning and wear their shoes, take their last tampon, or run off in their clothes?

Do my straight friends have the same mating issues? The statistics for heterosexual coupling are kinder. If 10 percent of the population is gay or lesbian, straight women and men get to interact in the other 90 percent. That's huge!

For lesbians, the oh-so-narrow dating pool has consequences. If you live and love in this tiny world, and the rest of the country is somewhat hostile to it, then you also have a much smaller group of people to share your friendships with. In other words, if you are homosexual, if your relationship doesn't work out, you may still need these people in your lives as friends. That's pressure.

You have to carefully consider who you will date, how you date them, and also how you break up. Sound tricky? It is. My now-deceased friend, the San Francisco artist, writer, and genius Kris Kovick, once drew a cartoon about a lesbian softball team. It was a drawing of all the women on the team. She called it "The Girlfriends." It was followed by the same drawing, same women, identical. It was called "The Ex-Girlfriends."

I've walked down to San Francisco's City Hall and cheered on the stream of couples flooding into Mayor Gavin Newsom's brave but probably temporary parting of the Red Sea preventing gay marriage. I've watched those quick enough to get there slip through and get their marriage licenses. These marriage licenses certainly are fun, but the truth is that it is harder for homosexuals to be joined in a lasting union.

The odds that these newlyweds will get bashed, heckled, or attacked walking down the street are still higher than for their straight friends. Watching one couple descend the City Hall steps in Hers and Hers tuxedos, I had to ask myself how challenging it has been for each of those getting married to have survived all their years together. Many had flown in from other parts of the country and didn't even have the benefits and freedoms we enjoy in San Francisco. I wished I could give them all medals.

Gavin Newsom has done a beautiful thing. Most people in the country by now have heard about the rush of gay marriages in San Francisco. I know it must be confusing, because it is something new for all of us. Is marriage the answer? Yes and no. We homosexuals need a bond greater than marriage. Our unions are much riskier.

By the time our main dishes had arrived, I told my girlfriend, "We can't just stop at marriage. We need to ask for more. We need marriage-and-a-half. We need to take any benefits of civil unions, add them to the benefits of marriage, throw in something to make up for homophobia and discrimination, and add something extra for gay men for living through the AIDS crisis. We need Super Marriage, a new hybrid form beyond the strength of regular marriage."

These folks rushing to San Francisco's City Hall know that. After growing up in love-that-dare-not-speak-its-name America, they now have their names printed and registered on marriage licenses. And if they are serious about keeping their marriages, they will have a long legal challenge ahead. We better have a really big party to celebrate after this is all done.

Roxxie Rosen, a writer who lives in San Francisco, is the founder of Girljock Magazine *and editor of* Girljock: The Book.

First appeared in *Newsday* and *The Fort Worth Star Telegram*. Reprinted by permission of the author.

Marriage Is Radical Enough
Richard J. Rosendall

We are crossing a major demarcation line in the history of the gay-rights movement. After May 17, 2004, gay marriages in America are a legal reality (if only in Massachusetts at first), not just a private commitment or an act of civil disobedience. To be sure, the fight will continue in courts and legislatures for many years, but that does not diminish the magnitude of this moment. The long struggle between gay liberation and integration has essentially been decided, and integration has won.

The conservative nature of this development has not been lost on the liberationists. Their antiassimilationism is rapidly becoming obsolete, as gay couples across the country demand full inclusion in the central institution of our society.

As with all Lost Causes, some diehards resist recognizing their defeat. In an August 2003 article for *The Boston Phoenix* decrying the "marriage rights mania," Michael Bronski dismisses marriage rights as "crumbs." The social benefits of marriage aside, few would regard the 1,138 rights and privileges associated with marriage under federal law, or the additional hundreds under state laws, as mere crumbs.

Bronski treats marriage as if it hasn't changed in 50 years. In fact, legalized contraception and abortion, no-fault divorce, and the rise of marriage as an equal partnership have left the institution far different from the oppressive patriarchal tool he portrays. His grim portrait, including his unsubstantiated claim of an "ongoing epidemic of domestic violence among straight and gay couples," reads more like Peter Pan appealing to Wendy to stay in Never-Never Land than a serious discussion of real families.

To hear some gay radicals tell it, this wedding season sounds more like a funeral. By adopting the strictures of marriage, so their thinking goes, our community will give up its freedom and lose its fabulousness. Many such qualms are reported by Michael Powell in a March 31, 2004 article in *The Washington Post*.

These lamentations remind me of the Lina Wertmuller film *Swept Away...*, in which a desert island is the only place where love can flower for the socially mismatched protagonists. Once they are rescued, their love is doomed. While I honor our movement's pioneers, I do not share this romantic view of our historic social isolation. Just as with the demise of the old Chitlin Circuit, which nurtured many great black performers before mainstream venues were desegregated four decades ago, few will reject the new freedom because it brings challenges along with opportunities.

For years, when faced with gay opponents of marriage, I have argued that their personal aversion was one thing, and opposing my right to choose for myself was quite another. Ten years ago, when I tried to persuade a gay-friendly DC mayoral candidate to endorse equal marriage rights, she pointed out that the gay community itself was divided on the issue. Indeed, Evan Wolfson, one of the earliest and staunchest gay-marriage advocates, was often subjected to blistering verbal abuse by gay people who resented his rocking the boat for something they didn't even want.

The climate has now irrevocably changed. There is no longer any serious division in our community on the question of civil marriage rights. From coast to coast and across the political spectrum, we were thrilled by the rush of City Hall weddings set off by San Francisco Mayor Gavin Newsom in February. The allure of alienation is melting away amid the joyous nuptials; the politics of victimhood is losing its grip even amid the antigay backlash; and gay families are adjusting their expectations upward. There is a growing recognition that, while the victory is far from won, the tide of history is with us.

It is only natural that such a change would take some adjusting. I can understand the nostalgia that some feel for the early years after Stonewall, when life at the margins of society brought with it a certain freedom. During the gay community's first "out" years, the lack of institutional signposts provided endless opportunities for creativity. But that was the freedom of people roaming uncharted territory. Thirty years ago, the bar scene was one of the few social options. There were no gay choruses, no gay film festivals, no gay chambers of commerce. The idea of openly gay politicians was outlandish even in the most liberal cities. Other than a few classical allusions, gay literature mostly consisted of lurid paperbacks and a magazine that was kept behind the counter at the newsstand.

Today, the number and variety of gay organizations and services is vastly greater. Whatever your interest or need, you're a quick Google search away from finding someone to share it or fill it. The truth is that we are infinitely more free than we were in the "good old days," simply by having more choices.

Twenty years ago, playwright Harvey Fierstein talked about the "perpetual adolescence" of the urban gay milieu, in which sowing one's wild oats became for many a lifetime occupation. The tragedy of AIDS forced our community to grow up, leaving us stronger and more responsible. Marriage is the next step—not just for particular couples as a legal option, but for our community as a social norm and aspiration.

Marriage isn't for everyone, of course. This is as true for gay people as for heterosexuals. But simply by becoming a realistic goal and part of the social landscape in which gay children grow up, it will give them the freedom to color with all the crayons in the box, as gay children before them never could. Imagine being a child again, and being able to blurt out your foolish dreams unself-consciously, the same as your siblings and playmates. Imagine receiving encouragement for those dreams, and taking that encouragement for granted. Imagine the wondrous ways a child may grow if properly nurtured. That's a radical enough vision for me, and making it come true will be pretty fabulous.

Richard J. Rosendall is an activist and writer whose work has appeared on Salon.com *and the* Independent Gay Forum (www.indegayforum.org). *He wrote and officiated at a gay wedding ceremony in 1994. Some of his writing is collected at* users.starpower.net/ rrosendall/.

First published as "Marriage: A Dream Open to Everyone" in *Liberty Education Forum,* May 2004. Reprinted by permission of the author.

From This Day Forward
Michael Rowe

On Sunday, June 15th, I legally married my partner of 19 years, Brian McDermid, in a private ceremony at St. Mark's United Church in Scarborough, Ontario, officiated by the Rev. Alan Hall. It was my second wedding, though unlike some other members of my family, it was to the same person the second time around. This time, I am taking my spouse's last name legally, as a testament of our legal conjoining.

The first one, which occurred on August 24, 1985, at the Metropolitan Community Church, was our "real" wedding, the anniversary we celebrate. It held all of the truest and most honest ingredients required for a union of two people declared before God: an expressed intent to make a life together, to care for each other through the hardest times, and to celebrate each day with the other as best we both could. As a Christian, it was important to me that it take place in a church. The difference was that the state didn't recognize it and that Brian and I spent the years between 1984 (when we met) and 2003 in a committed marriage, with all its attendant sacrifices, and none of its protections or sanctioned benefits.

Eighteen years from the day I took my first wedding vows, my day still begins when I see Brian's sleeping face on the pillow next to mine as I get up to feed Harper, our yellow Lab. Brian goes off to his medical practice, and I repair upstairs to my study to write. We both have full lives, with satisfying work and a broad group of friends and extended family, and yet, as saccharine as it may sound to some, the highlight of my day, every day, is the sound of Brian's key in the lock at night and Harper's mad scrabbling on the hardwood floor, as he, incoherent and surging with Labrador love, greets Brian at the door.

These moments, and many more in between, are what we took to the altar on that gold-green summer Sunday afternoon at St. Mark's, the year that Canada decided that Brian and I were full citizens, and entitled to the same rights and dignities as any other Canadian, in every way.

In the past few months, I've been asked many times what the point of a "gay marriage" might be. Anyone who has been married for many years would recognize the thousand threads that are woven together in the fabric of a marriage: the incalculable pride in your spouse's achievements; the helpless, hollow desperation of seeing them in pain, or sick, or troubled, and of not being able to relieve them with a touch or a whispered encouragement; the mornings you look at them and wonder how you could be so lucky as to have found someone who completes you like they do; and the mornings (far less often, one hopes) when you wonder what on earth you were thinking when you agreed to walk down that aisle in the first place. There is a moment at the end of the film *On Golden Pond* when Norman (Henry Fonda) suffers a heart attack. Believing that she is about to lose her husband of 50-plus years, Ethel (Katharine Hepburn) imagines him lying in his coffin. It's one of the most brilliant moments in Hepburn's film oeuvre, and it always makes me cry when I watch that film. While Ethel's words are reasonable, if poignant, her face tells another story. The titanic grief of losing her husband and partner reflected there in that moment is a vast awfulness that is instantly recognizable to any of us who have made a life with someone. It cuts across gender and sexual-orientation lines. It's a terror that lives in the very heart of what marriage and family mean, and it is the acknowledged Faustian bargain you make when you love someone more than you love yourself.

Brian and I have made that bargain, our parents (upon whose example our marriage is based) have made it, and millions of married couples, gay and straight, have made it. That's what marriage costs. I know every line of Brian's hands and face, every variegated timbre of his voice, and I know what every shift of his body means. I feel his pain and his joy and I safeguard his walk through life in every way I can. I would die for him, and I believe I would kill anyone who attempted to take him before his time. I defy any married man or woman to tell me they don't know what I mean.

None of these things seem to occur to the people asking that question. It's as though the idea of love itself was ultimately divided into rigidly segregated categories and marriage was a "gated community of the heart" whose primary purpose was to keep out the undesirables, which, in this case, means people like Brian and me. The more liberal among them suggest that the word itself is the problem and if we called our marriages something other than marriages—a "same-sex civil union" perhaps, separate but equal in the eyes of the law—it wouldn't be as difficult for society to deal with. None of them seem eager to get the ball rolling, though, by offering to redefine their marriages as "opposite-sex civil unions." Separate but equal never means "separate but equal"; it means separate. No one would think to ask a straight couple why they felt they "needed" to get married (and have it called a marriage) instead of remaining a "committed couple." But our straight friends who elect to bypass the rituals that, for many of them, seem outdated and unnecessarily patriarchal do so with the full knowledge that any time they change their minds, the societal marriage machine, with all its attendant rights and responsibilities, is there for them. They don't need to prove themselves "deserving" of the "special" right to marry the person they love; they just do it. Conversely, straight couples who elect not to marry and still raise families are considered "progressive" at best, and at worst "irresponsible." Gay couples in a similar situation are just occupying the space that the legal system in our society has allocated for them, period. Not a legally recognized couple, not a family, just roommates of 10, 20, 30, 40, 50 years.

I was raised by parents who were, above all, individuals. My father was a maverick of sorts whose career began in radio and television and culminated in a distinguished diplomatic career that took our family all over the world. My mother was a progressive American schoolteacher who gave up her U.S. citizenship as a declarative rejection of American paranoia and bigotry in the McCarthy era of the 1950s. A few years ago, my father suffered her loss. They had been married for over 40 years, and my father's bereavement was annihilating. Watching him endure it was a foretaste of what I will someday have to endure when I lose Brian, and my father's memories of his and my mother's life and adventures were an indirect injunction to celebrate each day and live deliberately. My mother's detailed, elegantly written obituary tribute in *The National Post* noted that "when one of her sons announced he was living with another man, she threw them a party." That son was me. She loved Brian and never didn't think of him as her son-in-law. My mother would have been proud on June 15th, not just of Brian and me, but of her adopted country which, in the same summer that American gays and lesbians were celebrating the end of antisodomy laws, was becoming the third country in the world to legalize gay marriage.

And in the United States, while waiting for the laws to change, more and more of us are getting married. Ironically, the gay couple's decision to marry, to publicly declare their intention to make a life together in spite of daunting odds, gets to the very heart of the meaning of marriage. While the people who would deny us the right to marry wallow in the Punch-and-Judy brutality of Anne Coulter and Rush Limbaugh, or the sideshow vulgarity of Jennifer Lopez and Ben Affleck's on-again/off-again engagement, or Britney Spears' 48-hour nuptials, or *The Bachelorette*, many gay men and lesbians are reaching for the solemnity of publicly announced vows and the sanctity of marriage, claiming it as an inalienable right in the same way that widowhood is borne with such dignity by those who lose their partners to AIDS without society's validation of that widowhood. The ability to live, love, and raise families of our own without the laws that support our straight friends is a reason to be proud, as is the notion of not waiting until the laws change to get on with the business of making our marriages. The laws will change, because the laws are illogical and cruel and future generations will see them for what they were.

The movement of life is forward, and, as George Bernard Shaw said, "the greatest truths begin as blasphemies." The right of gays and lesbians to marry is in the same line of ideological descent, for instance, as the right of women to vote, the right of Jews to hold public office, and the right of blacks to marry whites—all things that we take for granted today, but which were trumpeted as destructive to society when they were first presented. Allowing your fellow man to live well and prosper in love doesn't cost society anything but goodwill.

My mother would have laughed at anyone who told her that allowing her son the dignity of marriage was destructive to the notion of "family," and would likely have sent them packing with the same blistering tongue-lashing she once gave a missionary who urged her to turn away from her son, and impress upon him that he was going to hell for his "lifestyle."

My mother knew, as I know, that we are no threat to "the family."

We are the family. We are sons and daughters, brothers and sisters, and entering a blessed union with the one you love above anyone on this earth is the oldest family ritual in the human race's history.

Michael Rowe is an award-winning journalist and essayist whose most recent book is the essay collection Other Men's Sons. *In 2003, Rowe and his partner, Brian McDermid, became the first gay couple in history of the United Church of Canada to marry inside a United Church, as well as one of the first gay couples in Canadian history to legally marry. He lives in Toronto, and is at work on a novel. His website is located at www.michaelrowe.com.*

This piece first appeared as "True, Honest, and Finally Legal" in a slightly different form in *The United Church Observer*, September 2003. Brief portions originally appeared in *Hero* magazine, August 2000. Reprinted by permission of the author.

Red Tape, White Veil
Lawrence Schimel

During my first weeks in Madrid, I was having coffee with a well-known Spanish novelist who is openly gay. While we're talking, a woman comes up and says hello to him. This is not an uncommon occurrence, given that various books of his have been made into films, and he's a regular contributor to the daily newspapers, not to mention innumerable radio and television programs. He's easily recognizable.

The same cannot be said of her, and he's at a loss as to why she greets him so familiarly.

Distraught, she says: "You don't remember me? But you were the *padrino* at my wedding!"

After she's left, he explained the situation to me: she'd been paid to marry his (previous) Eastern European boyfriend, in order to get him his legal papers, but had gone to the wedding dressed in white, in a veil and everything. Even though it was all a legal fiction, she wasn't going to miss this opportunity to be the star attraction of getting married.

Half a decade later, despite having been turned down for residency because all of the gay literature I've published here was considered "irrelevant and of null interest to Spain" according to the right-wing Partido Popular government, I'm still living in Madrid—but how far things've come since then! Especially in the past five months. Spain has a new socialist government, which has not only instituted the only gender-balanced parliament in the E.U. along with Sweden, but has been pushing gay marriage forward from the outset—no more discussions, no more pussyfooting around, within a year it's to go through.

I used to have long arguments with my ex-boyfriend, who was against the various gay collectives and the work they were doing—work which is at long last paying off—not because of any reasoned principles, but because he was too young and too enamored of being the enfant terrible. For all of the infighting and other problems that these collectives, in their particular cases, might have, the idea and the ideals of the collective are still concepts I argued for as being valid and valuable. He was too young to realize how the social liberties he enjoyed came, in large part, to work these collectives had been doing for years—since long before he was born, since before Franco's death.

"When I get deported because you and I can't get married," I would always conclude, "we'll see if you change your tune." (This was a great way to always get the last word in these arguments.)

I didn't get deported, obviously, and he and I broke up last year—on Valentine's Day, of all possible dates. (In Spain, Valentine's Day means less than it would back in the U.S. Here—at least in Catalunya—Sant Jordi on April 23rd is celebrated as the Spanish equivalent, and one is supposed to gift a book and a rose to one's loved ones. How can that not be a writer's favorite holiday? And people wonder why I moved to this country...)

And suddenly that legal sanction that otherwise haunts binational couples is now within our collective grasp, and I'm single.

Friends jokingly ask if I'm going to get married now, to resolve the legal situation of my status here—still in limbo, after all these years—and if I were to get married for the sake of legalities, like the above-mentioned wedding that for far too many binational gay couples in many countries is and has been the working definition of "gay marriage" for years, I'd want to do so with another gay man. I'd received marriage offers over the years, usually from lesbians, but I'd always been dubious of the idea. I guess I'm really a romantic at heart. While I think that the whole notion of marriage should be abolished in favor of more reasonable forms of renewable, short-term social contracts, if and when I do get married, I want it to be for love.

And if I'm forced to rely on marriage as a way of cutting through the red tape and resolving my legal status, I'm definitely wearing white, with a veil and everything. Something my own *padrino*, whoever he is, shouldn't forget.

Lawrence Schimel (New York, 1971) has published over 70 books in a wide variety of genres, including PoMoSEXUALS: Challenging Assumptions About Gender and Sexuality *(Cleis),* The Drag Queen of Elfland *(Circlet),* Found Tribe: Jewish Coming Out Stories *(Sherman Asher), and* Vacation in Ibiza *(NBM), among others. He lives in Madrid, Spain.*

Withholding Creates Tension, Acknowledgment Creates Relief (And This Is Why We Are Talking about Gay Marriage)
Sarah Schulman

I am writing this one week after gay marriage was legalized in the state of Massachusetts. Yes, we all agree that all human beings should have the same legal rights. Okay, that's out of the way. Here is my question, What does gay marriage really mean? Why do people want it so badly? Is it really all about taxes, extending the special privileges that people receive for being in couples to gay couples as well?

The propaganda campaigns for gay marriage usually feature a perfect couple: they've been together forever, they have good solid incomes, one or more happy children. They are perfect, and their perfect union deserves to be protected from the state. The examples are offered over and over of ways this perfect love is vulnerable to the state—if one is sick the state can keep the other from visitation. If one dies the state can seize the other's belongings. Bad state.

Reaffirming, as I said above, that everyone should have the same legal rights, marriage has never really been about protecting the relationship from the government. Really, the purpose of marriage has been to protect women and children from male abandonment. Legal marriage was intended to force consequences (third-party intervention) on men who tried to violate their promises and dishonorably abandoned their responsibilities to women with whom they had shared love, kindness, friendship. Even though the state always disadvantaged women, when it came to marriage, there was some sense that married men do have some accountability to the women they have loved.

This, I think, is at the core of the desperate desire for relationship recognition that has spearheaded the campaign for gay marriage. Gay marriage does not so much protect the couple from the state, as it protects the couple from each other. It is a third-party acknowledgment and recognition that people who have shared love have basic responsibilities toward each other. These responsibilities include going through a process to change a relationship. Frankly, I think that this is a basic human responsibility and right: to not be dehumanized by abandonment, shunning, pretending you have never loved. Legal marriage tries to create a framework, a process, a forced negotiation and forced communication that are inherent human responsibilities.

A second true motive, I believe, for galvanizing energy around gay marriage, is to force the state to legitimate the emotional life of the gay person as a balance to the deprivation of recognition created by the family. A father may not believe that his daughter is a person, but the state gives her the right to vote. Ha ha. The diminished gay person now has a new standing of status and recognition imposed by the state on the family. The state becomes an agent of third-party intervention, forcing the denying family into a state of acknowledgment against their will, but transforming the social standard around them. Now, every person who is forced, by law, to recognize a gay marriage, carries that new knowledge into their family. It is social pressure to change personal behavior.

In these ways, gay marriage is a strategy to prevent or dilute the tension created by withholding and shunning, both from family, and from lover.

Have you ever said hello to someone on the street and have them not reply? It creates tension. If the person stopped, said, "Hello, Sarah. How are you?" then we could experience human acknowledgment, the essential responsibility of people who know each other. But if they refuse that acknowledgment, and instead choose shunning, they create a relationship of tension and conflict, which then needs to be resolved. In a way, this is the situation of gay people in America. We want the mutual relationship with the culture, but the culture refuses to respond. That refusal creates the tension, and it creates the urgent need on our parts to relieve the tension. Political movements are the product of the moment when the tension of exclusion or shunning is no longer bearable.

Let me restate this idea in other terms: People do things for reasons. Those reasons are located in earlier experiences. In that way, each moment is created by the previous moment. There is no behavior that is not in some way created by earlier experience. For this reason, the truth of any situation can be discovered in the sequence of events. What happened first? What followed? Awareness lies in identifying the core action and determining the sequence of its consequences. That's why people need to talk, so that the sequence of events can be understood. Too often we point to the consequences themselves without looking at the originating action that caused them. Gay people are upset; they are angry. Is this because they are inherently pathological? Or is the anger a result of someone else's originating action? An action that may be hard to describe or identify because it has been repeated so many times that it looks falsely neutral, i.e., nonexistent, when it is in fact The Cause. Gay people are uncomfortable as a consequence of the exclusion. They are responding to the originating action of oppression/ cruelty/ dehumanization/ diminishment/ humiliation/ deprivation of rights—however you wish to describe it. The cause is the shunning; it forces an urgent need for solution. Some people feel this solution to be gay marriage.

Back to the withholding person on the street. She is the lady who is emblematic of the culture. The next time I see her, I ask "Why are you angry, Culture? Lets sit down and talk it over." She refuses to answer and keeps walking. Her action CREATES a relationship far more intimate than the appropriate kindness would have created. Her action creates a relationship that is fraught and oppressive. It forces me to seek a solution, thereby deepening the connection between us, while she doesn't try to make things better. I am now forced to think about her, notice her, see what she is like, why she does what she does. In order to relieve the mysterious shunning, I must think like her in order to try to understand what she knows but will not communicate. I have to think on her terms in order to liberate myself from her shunning by ending it, to resolve it. As a result I know her better than she knows me. I know her ways. If I have humane empathy and she does not (as a consequence of privilege or trauma), I can see the justifications for her ways. I can see it from her point of view and my point of view. She thinks I don't have a point of view. I can see why she does what she does. This is both an expression of and source of love—the effort to understand. After being forced, by the oppression, to think about her so much, I develop a familiarity that makes her marriage acceptable to me while my homosexuality remains unacceptable to her. Partially as a consequence of this one-sided identification, gay people increasingly wish to get married.

When we ask the culture why gay people must be constantly diminished, it often does not bother to answer at all. For example, I would like to know why literature with primary lesbian content can no longer be published with consistency in the United States. But I cannot get an answer. I would like to see a forum in the *New York Times Magazine* on this question, but there will not be one. If I ask someone, they don't respond. Charlie Rose will not raise it with his guests, even the lesbian ones. And they won't raise it either, or they wouldn't be on *Charlie Rose*. No play or movie will ask this question. It is a nonquestion, because the people at stake are being treated as though we do not exist and have never existed. That we are not human, do not deserve representation, i.e., literature. In fact, we do not even have the right to discuss why we cannot have these things. This creates tension. The tension in turn creates an urgency for change. The silent exclusion creates the anxiety, which in turn creates the need to act for change; one causes the other. When a person refuses to discuss why they are shunning you, when they give no reason and have no terms for reconciliation, it is because to actually talk about it would be to reveal their own behavior. And their power lies in the ability to command silence about their own behavior. They can only pretend to be neutral if the mechanics of the moment are not discussed. Once sequence and substance are laid out starkly, their responsibility is revealed. Hence, no conversation.

Right now, half of America believes that gay people are not human enough to deserve the right to get legally married. They have idealized ideas about themselves and about marriage, and distorted beliefs about us, what we're like and how much we can bear. What makes this moment more disturbing than 20 years ago is that now, most of these people actually know gays and lesbians. More of us are out now, and so they hold their position with more viciousness, since it is aimed at human beings whose names they know.

They cling to this idealization of themselves for the same reason that more liberal people, who may support gay marriage, won't allow lesbian literature to exist. I believe it is because the dominant group (both the conservative and liberal wing) is deeply invested in seeing themselves, falsely, as neutrally objective and value free. If, in fact, other world views were treated as equally legitimate, their sense of themselves as naturally superior would be dismantled. They don't want this. So, they maintain the exclusion and the silence around that exclusion as a way to falsely construct themselves as deserving of that power to shun. And this impulse is instinctive, not conscious. I believe that if there were an open, complex discussion of the exclusion this answer would come to the forefront, and that is why there is no such discussion.

This is why, perhaps, my friend on the street won't discuss why she is angry. Because then her own cruelty would be revealed, and she wouldn't be able to pretend neutrality. Shunners believe that they are doing nothing, or God's will, or maintaining the status quo, but actually their exclusion of us is very active, which is why it is so unbearable. If her own motivations would be visible, her actions might be exposed as unjustified. She, the culture, needs to maintain the refusal to discuss as a way to hide her own inadequacy.

Let's say the woman on the street does provide an answer. Perhaps she gives "It's God's will. It's not natural. Marriage is a covenant between a man and a woman" as her reason for keeping me out. Or, let's say she explains her shunning by saying "You broke into my apartment, stole my money, and used it to buy drugs. I will not speak to you again until you have three years of sobriety." If this drug thing is in fact what happened, my acquaintance is in the right. She has a clear, legitimate CAUSE for her action. Her action is appropriate. It is justified. It is how I deserve to be treated by her. And furthermore, she has terms for reconciliation. This, too, is a basic human responsibility. If I comply with her terms, then we can sit down and negotiate. Of course, if I don't comply with her terms, she has the right to hold off contact until that changes. But to shun without terms is the definition of insanity. Once a person gives up on the possibility of human negotiation, they become apocalyptic. But, what if that drug answer, in fact, has no relationship to who I really am? I don't use drugs, I don't steal money, I have never committed the crime for which I am now being punished by silence. It is a false accusation. She is mistaken. Or deliberately lying to cover up something else in her life that she can't face. The burden, unfortunately, is now on me to reveal that she is mistaken, so that there can be relief for both of us. I don't have to be subjected to the pain of being on the receiving end of shunning, and she doesn't have to live with the poison of anger that is not rooted in the real. The consequence of her action on me is that I need the truth to become clarified so that she and I can both have better lives.

When gay people do get an answer as to why we are being excluded or separated, it is often not justified, not appropriate, and not how we deserve to be treated. It is most often a false accusation. I don't need to reiterate here all the reasons people give as to why we are lesser than they are. Suffice it to say that I have never heard one that is true.

Wait, I've changed my mind! I do want to tell you some cruel justifications that I have heard, because as I write this, those memories have become irrepressible. And, after all, writing (making art) is for me the only refuge from and antidote to the pain of experience. I never have to express the consequences of kindness; I simply enjoy them. It is only the cruelty that forces me to write—that forces me to make medicine from poison. If people treated me fairly and with love, I would never have to write a thing.

This is a true experience that I expressed in my novel, *Rat Bohemia*. I was on the way to my parents' house, but first I went to visit my friend Stan Leventhal. This story takes place in the 1980s or '90s. Stan was very sick. His apartment was a disaster; he was shaking, sweating. He gave me some books that he wanted me to have after he died. It was a stark, truthful moment. I think I was in my early thirties. I had already experienced many deaths. He shit in his pants. It was embarrassing and upsetting. I stayed with him longer than I anticipated. I arrived late at my parents' home. My sister was there with her boyfriend. I told my family why I was late. My mother said, "You only like men when they're dying. I had always hoped that you would grow up to be a productive person who was community oriented, but instead you put yourself in this mess." My sister and her future husband sat there and said nothing. These were false accusations used to justify my exclusion, and they were nonnegotiable.

Let me analyze the many traumatic components of this experience.

1. Stan's pain. His helplessness, his abandonment, his physical torture. Our open acknowledgment that he would soon die. The knowledge that his death was caused by societal neglect. The pain of his love for the book he gave me, *Jesus' Son* by Denis Johnson.
2. The cumulative pain of experiencing mass death of the helpless. My friends.
3. Having to explain this experience to my family—people whose privileges protected them from the true knowledge.
4. The lack of empathy or care from my family in the face of this experience.
5. My mother's insistence that my friends were not fully human. That they did not constitute a "community," and that, therefore, loving them did not constitute being connected to other humans. Her false accusation that I wish men to suffer and die because I am a homosexual.
6. The erasure of my productivity and accomplishments
7. The complicity of my sister and her future husband by remaining silent. The enjoyment of their privilege as a heterosexual couple in that room, and their privileges of not having to experience the mass death of the young. Their decision to exploit those privileges instead of risking them to create a more humane family.
8. The false characterization of the truth of the AIDS crisis, "this mess," as something one chooses to experience. Not, in fact, something that one chooses to deny.

So my family members excluded me from their world of people whose feelings matter. They separated themselves from me. That is a punishment, and its consequences are brutal. The ability to be interactive with other human beings is the gift of life. Choosing to disconnect from others is either a pathological act of cruelty, or a consequence of being on the receiving end of that cruelty. Withholding is never the positive choice. Like the representative shunning woman on the street. Why would I want to be separated from her? To forever be punished for buying drugs I never bought? To forever be faced with silence when I say "What did you do today?" To forever be denied the human experience of facing and dealing with problems with her, of the treasure of negotiation? To let her feel so badly and be so angry when there is no justification? To live forever on the receiving end of that unjustified anger?

I've been gay for a long time, 30 years this April, and I have met thousands of gay people around the world from all kinds of backgrounds, living in all kinds of conditions. Something I've noticed over and over again is that one of the most significant consequences of what we have endured is the creation of our various national and global subcultures. These subcultures are the highest stake in the gay-marriage debate. Some of us have CHOSEN to avoid the pain by living in subculture in order to minimize contact with the official culture and its people. When we make this choice we don't socialize with them that much, we don't read their bad books, we try not to be subjected to their false ideas about us. Others of us have tried to transform them and failed; we've gone head to head with the glass ceilings, bad thinking, ignorance, cruelty, and then, if we're defeated, we are FORCED back into subculture simply because they won't let us into the big world. We have commitment ceremonies and publish with marginal presses. There is also the third intention, that of choosing to live in the subculture as a place to prepare to force change. And this is where so many gay people of my generation have lived. Viewing our subcultural commitments as a way of strengthening ourselves for the task ahead of changing the big structures so that we can live inside them, alongside straight people, without being distorted by them. That is the most utopian, most difficult, and yet most inspiring option. So far, it has not been successful. The desire for gay marriage is, in many ways, a refusal of all of those subcultural positions. For, in some ways, gay marriage is a sign of spiritual exhaustion. A way to get out of the trenches, the white flag of surrender that can bring the tired soldier to a hot shower and a bowl of gruel.

So now I see gay and straight people getting married and, as a consequence, I look at their relationships. These are supposed to be good relationships that enhance the world; that's why the world is cheering them on, right? But I see many relationships that frighten me. One thing I have seen is talented, exceptional people hooking up with simple, more-limited people so that the relationship can be built entirely around the centrality of the more-gifted partner. This upsets me. I find it disappointing and somewhat monstrous. I also see people who can stay together because the connection is superficial; they fear a depth of understanding. Some of them have been traumatized, and truly reaching another person triggers, falsely, fear of violation. I see many relationships that are boring, not fun, repetitive. Is this truly what these people would want given a state of nature? And will they produce follow-the-leader children, who will in turn make the rest of us miserable? So little is right about how we live today, and relationships are the microcosm of the society. Stalin noticed that "the family is the building block of Socialism," and he was right. Relationships keep the social order, and what about when the social order sucks? When it is social imperative, convenience, and shallowness that cement the bond, do we have to say "Mazel Tov"? I hate to open up this can of worms, but do destructive relationships and their consequential impact on those around them deserve a party? George Bush's marriage re-enforces and protects him so he can destroy other people's lives everyday. Many relationships allow people to stay cruel, dishonest, cause havoc and pain. We'd be better off if these were dismantled, not re-enforced.

Conversely I see breakups that never should have happened. That are wrong, symptoms of mental illness, alcoholic behavior, untreated post-traumatic stress. I have also experienced and witnessed lesbian breakups rooted in the devaluation of one partner from outside the relationship, and the power of suggestion on the other, similarly devalued partner. Once someone learns that no one cares how their lover is treated, and also that no one cares how they themselves behave, they too can act out their fear and anger on the same person being scapegoated by the culture, the person before them. If there was gay marriage, perhaps this would be somewhat reduced. That woman shunning me on the street? If she was my legal wife, she wouldn't be able to just stop speaking to me one day; she'd have to negotiate something, say a few sentences. The law would mandate it. The law would care, and I think that would be a good thing. If a gay person knows that the law cares about how they treat their lover, perhaps they would be slightly kinder. If they felt that their lover was considered to be a human, and not lesser than, perhaps they would be able to negotiate and express instead of just destroy. If gay marriage would make her have to "show cause," I am for it.

I recently had a dinner party at my house with four friends from San Francisco. Wine collectors. On bottle four, one of them, Alice Hill, said, "Gay marriage is like abortion. Whatever you think of it, you have to have the right." Okay, I can go along with that. But my enthusiasm ends there. What I really want is for the shunning to end, so I can stop thinking about how I have to change myself to make the shunning stop when I know it's unjustified in the first place. I want to see you on the street, say "How are you?" and have you smile and let me know. I want my books to be equal to your books. I want my deaths to be equal to your deaths. I want my feelings to be equal to your feelings, and my place in the family to be equal to yours. And when you're mad about something, I want it to be for real reasons, that can be articulated, and then I want us to sit down and solve them together. If I had these things, I would not need gay marriage.

Sarah Schulman is the author of nine novels: The Mere Future *(forthcoming),* The Child *(forthcoming from Carroll & Graf),* Shimmer *(1998),* Rat Bohemia *(1995),* Empathy *(1992),* People in Trouble *(1990),* After Delores *(1988),* Girls Visions and Everything *(1986), and* The Sophie Horowitz Story *(1984); and three nonfiction books:* The Twist: Familial Homophobia and Its Consequences *(forthcoming),* Stagestruck: Theater, AIDS, and the Marketing of Gay America *(1998), and* My American History: Lesbian and Gay Life During The Reagan/Bush Years *(1994). Her plays include* Manic Flight Reaction *(forthcoming),* The Burning Deck *(La Jolla Playhouse),* Carson McCullers *(Playwrights Horizons), and a theatrical adaptation of Isaac Singer's* Enemies, A Love Story *(forthcoming). Awards include: Guggenheim in Playwrighting, Fullbright in Judaic Studies, two American Library Association Awards (Fiction and Nonfiction), Stonewall Award for Improving the Lives of Lesbians and Gays in the U.S., Revson Fellow for the Future of New York, and Finalist for the Prix de Rome. She was born in New York City, 1958.*

Marriage & The Shape of Things
D. Travers Scott

Marriage, from my point of view while growing up, was in poor shape. It seemed a rickety frame for love: My parents trial-separated, then divorced before I hit five. My mother remarried a couple more times, none lasting. My father's remarriage did succeed, and she was also a divorcee. My grandparents were dead, widowed, or a couple that should have divorced instead of suffering through addiction and abuse in order to uphold the institution. Marriage also seemed irrelevant: I was the homogay. Add art school, and I sniffed a whiff of patriarchal capitalism wafting from matrimony. Gay marriage has never been an issue that raised my fervor, especially because, at some times in my life, it wouldn't have helped any.

What Went Down

While I was away on book tour, my boyfriend confessed via telephone that he had become enamored of another. Glad to hear this, I encouraged him.

Not that I was looking for a reason to break up—not that I thought anything of the sort. Throughout the past six of our eight years together, Carl and I had assiduously negotiated an open relationship. During some of Carl's work trips, I'd wallowed in crushes with "surrogate boyfriends," all the while clearly communicating its limitations to the smit-object and steadfastly resisting any entanglements that might threaten my primary relationship. Enough currents of Montessori hippiedom course through my past to support the idea that my heart is capable of embracing more than one person at a time.

Carl invited Erik to my hometown book launch. We had drinks a couple of times; he spent a platonic night on our couch.

One night at a Mexican restaurant Carl caught me staring off, forgotten nacho poised midair.

"Hey—what's with you?"

I sighed dreamily. "Erik is...adorable!" Bang-zoom, Erik moved in within days.

Radical Dudes

Living in a triad was radical. Dude. Coming six years or so after my activist and performance art days, it was heady to feel so avant-garde again, our day-to-day existence scoring us lefty points for increasing the visibility of nontraditional relationships. Carl and I went to Erik's work parties; Erik and I went to Carl's art openings. At conferences I whipped out from my wallet photo-booth strips of the three of us. We all cosigned a lease on a new apartment with only two bedrooms— and made it clear to the landlord one would be an office. Erik's astonishingly liberal parents included us in all family gatherings almost immediately. We were popular photo targets at Gay Pride that year: our smiling, tattooed love bundle. One day Carl laid claim on a nearly new king-size mattress at a yard sale, waiting until Erik and I could arrive to test it out. The three of us precariously navigated the mattress and box springs home atop a swirly-wheeled grocery store cart, rattling down the steep slope of Olive Way, our new group bed hanging over the sides, flopping up and down like albatross wings.

Sometimes, more is better. I had more people to share good times with: playing Monopoly, decorating Easter eggs, carving jack-o'-lanterns. We all had someone to introduce to new experiences: the Seattle Aquarium, *Breakfast at Tiffany's*, Frito pie. Much akin to showing off your hometown to tourist friends, sharing enriches an experience as you see it through multiple perspectives and the unique subjectivity of others.

If you are not alone when you're in a relationship, you're even less alone when you're in a relationship with more than one person. Now I had someone with whom to share good things that had previously been private, such as surprises for each other: Carl and Erik got to share in the fun of scheming up a romantic picnic to circumvent my stubborn refusal to have a birthday celebration. Carl and I got to schoolgirl-out over which stuffed piranha Erik would like best for Christmas. I also had a ready outlet with whom to kvetch with about the relationship: *No, you're not being hypersensitive; Carl did pick the worst possible guy outside the relationship to sleep with. No, you're not being an ass; Erik has conveniently found ways to avoid helping with the move.* (And I'm sure together they carped about me.) Unlike with friends, I could talk with someone also experiencing it. I could receive empathy rather than sympathy.

Our triad was liberating, an additional boyfriend giving me more time and emotional resources for individual pursuits. I could go to Italy for a month knowing I wouldn't be abandoning Carl. When Erik needed advice on whether or not to glue his stretched ear lobes shut for a job interview, or Carl wanted someone to go help pick out a clothes hamper, it was a relief to let the other guy deal.

Our triad also encouraged independent thinking. There's something absolute and hermetic about a binary: black/white, on/off, right/wrong. For years Carl and I had been meshed in our private world. We'd grown to speak collectively of things that used to be singularly subjective: *We were so bored by* Pulp Fiction, *we walked out. We buy frozen orange juice with no pulp and whole bean coffee, but the store brand, not the expensive kind. We think marriage and military service are ludicrous goals for queer liberation.* But in a triad, love goes Cubist, multidimensional. Multiple partners add perspectives to the me/you, subject/object binary of a two-person relationship. The you-and-me-against-the-world mindset of a couple can too easily let assumptions go unchallenged, but all of the sudden there's another person asking, "Why?" It's simply much more difficult to get three people—especially three fags—to agree to anything. This challenge increased my critical thinking, evolving from "This is the what we think" toward "What do I think?"

An unexpected effect of the triad was higher values. When only us two, I had that sense of "no one's looking." With three, there was a witness. Two people could have a secret, but with three it became a conspiracy, which was much trickier to propose, let alone wrangle. Carl and I once abandoned two cats we couldn't find homes for before moving out of state. It's something I'm guilt-ridden about to this day and never wanted Erik to discover. If the situation had arisen with the three of us, though, I'm certain we would've handled it more nobly. Would three of us have dined-and-dashed at the sidewalk café in DC during the March on Washington? Something about the group dynamic of a triad inspired me to keep my nose cleaner.

Being connected to two people doubled the stakes of the relationship, made me hold myself to a higher standard. Previously I'd avoided problems until they'd exploded; with Carl and Erik I became a real whiner, bringing up problems as soon as I saw them: *I was hurt you didn't wait to go to the Science Center until I could join you; I felt left out of sex this morning; Even though we don't pay rent as building managers, you need to contribute by helping us out with those duties.* I was more honest, exposed, and vulnerable in communicating my needs and feelings than I had been in any other relationship.

All of these benefits could apply to any triad, but—pardon the homo snobbery—I felt a same-sex triad combined the subversion of polyamory with homosexuality's potential to undermine social power structures. Harry Hay, probably one of the 20th century's most influential gay liberationists, wrote about "subject/subject consciousness" as a unique experience of same-sex love. You don't see your beloved as a sexual or romantic object, an Other separate from you. Because they are the same as you, you are more conscious of their subjectivity as well. While I think Hay conflates potential and practice, a same-sex triad does add a heightened degree of shared subjectivity, further breaking down the authoritarian, materialistic potential of long-term relationships. In mixed-gender relationships, binary or polyamorous, there is always the cultural history of woman-as-property and the structures of male privilege, to lend greater power to the male(s). In a relationship of homogenous gender, this dynamic is thrown into question.

I've always savored those little moments when a same-sex relationship flummoxes the patriarchy: waiters who don't know to whom to bring the check, or who will taste and approve the wine. In my same-sex triad, the motel clerk not only didn't know who to give the bill to, he also had to deal with our insistence that the three of us only needed one bed.

I felt our relationship was on the radical edge of polyamory because we were exploring a true triad as opposed to a love triangle. Nietzsche wrote, "Marriage *cannot* be founded on 'love'—it is founded on sexual impulse, on the impulse to possess property (women and children as property), on the *impulse to rule*..." As hetero porn and fundamentalist Mormons evidence, when a man is the focal point of a heterosexual three-way (a V), it can be a deeply sexist model in which polyamory simply means one man possesses more than one woman. Taken to the extreme: harems or slavery.

The triad also helped me be less of a control freak. I'd hooked up with Carl when I was 20, and, in youthful naïveté mixed with homo insecurity, thought he was the only man who would ever love me. Add my divorce-kid fear of abandonment, and I could become a nasty little control queen: acting out parental behaviors of reprimand and punishment to confirm that I controlled him. If I controlled him, I could keep him from leaving. He could never be allowed to leave, because he was the only person that could ever love me. In *Marriage and Love*, Emma Goldman calls marriage "an insurance pact." While she refers to economics, you can apply the same idea to emotions: the driving force of a relationship being the protection against irrational fear of being alone. Feeling loved by Erik went a long way toward breaking this cycle. I was worthy of love. Carl wasn't the only person capable of loving me. Hey, I didn't have to keep Carl on such a tight leash, then, because he wasn't the only person who could ever love me.

But if Carl wasn't the only guy I could have a relationship with, then suddenly there was room for this question: Was he really the right relationship for me? Could I do better?

Bad Share Days

My year in a triad definitely had regressive as well as progressive elements. F. Scott Fitzgerald wrote, "The test of a first-rate intelligence is the ability to hold two opposing ideas in the mind at the same time and still retain the ability to function." While living in a triad was a fantasy come true, realizing a fantasy is frequently the recipe for its destruction.

The simplest aspect of my disillusionment with my triad was purely mathematic. Sure, I got double dick, support, love, income, assets, experience, friends, etc., but I also had twice as much competition, insecurity, complaints, processing, in-laws, jealousy, and all the other shit of a relationship. I had twice as many people to have sex with, but also twice as many people to not be in the mood, so I ended up eventually having less sex than when I'd been in a couple.

Flush with success at shattering those patriarchal paradigms, it was dismaying to witness the oldest of paradigms reassert itself: the family. In *The Mass Psychology of Fascism*, Wilhelm Reich writes, "The family is the authoritarian state in miniature, to which the child must learn to adapt himself as a preparation for the general social adjustment required of him later."

One night two friends—former sexmates of Carl's and mine who'd begun dating—leaned over a bar table with sly looks.

"So," one said, "with you and Carl and Erik. Who's who in the family?"

"Who's Mommy, who's Daddy, and who's Junior?"

We were sex radicals, not the Huxtables!

"Obviously," one said, "Erik's Junior. You both dote on him, and he gets away with murder."

"Carl's Dad because he's all emotionally unavailable—"

"And Dad and Junior fight all the time."

"And you're Mom, because you're like the peacemaker trying to keep everyone together."

I hotly defended my lovers from this most insulting assessment, but I walked home in a daze, stunned, accepting its accuracy.

For a while the triad energized Carl and me. Like interpersonal ozone, the air crackled, ripe with the possibility of change. Carl opened up emotionally in bed, with sex that was less rushed and more emotionally connected. I blamed Carl less for my fears: Previously I'd thought I could never leave Carl for a month at a writer's retreat, now I was doing it and planning another in Brazil.

Eventually I realized that, while the triad gave me tools to solve problems, it didn't solve the problems. Just as they follow you when you move to a new city, Carl's and my problems followed us into our new relationship with Erik.

Despite publicly championing open relationships, in the last few years of mine, I'd had a sinking feeling. We'd been saying for years we were going to spend less time in bars and more on friends and art—but sex and drink had a powerful pull. One Saturday night, when I found again myself staking a corner of a leather bar and quickly downing that first beer so I could start having fun, only now with two boyfriends instead of one, it hit me hard. Things had changed. Things had stayed the same.

One morning Erik and I were at home, with Carl at work. Erik had laryngitis and couldn't speak, but somehow we entered into a conversation. He wrote notes to me on the Mac, about his problems with Carl. I watched his furrowed brow and grave concern as he typed. The words shocked me, almost identical to things I'd thought privately over the years or confided to friends. When I saw this and other patterns repeating, despite the many differences between Erik and me, I lost my optimism for the triad, and questioned my relationship with Carl. A heavy realization settled that our problems weren't going to change, no matter how avant-garde of a relationship Carl and I put ourselves into. I felt optimism, albeit tinged with fear. I felt I could do better. I could change.

Cracking Up

Although Carl had met Erik first, and their intense spark had initiated our triad, it was their relationship that deteriorated the most. I'm still not sure what went wrong, but Carl's anger ran high in the final months. It seemed Erik had done something Carl couldn't forgive, but it was never clear what that was. Although Carl had possessed the dream situation—a new lover welcomed by the current—he carried a palpable air of resentment into the months after the breakup, when Erik and I continued seeing each other.

Maybe Carl should have just broken up with me and pursued Erik from the beginning. Maybe he was afraid to hurt me—or to risk the change. Sharing Erik seemed an ideal compromise. Maybe sharing had turned out to be harder than expected. Maybe he should have kept us separate: I've known men seemingly happy with their vanilla, long-term domestic partner and their spicy, outside partner(s). Secret or not, this arrangement never appealed to me. It seemed a paragon of the traditional—a replay of the wife/mistress scenario.

Basking in the transgressive thrill of a nontraditional relationship, I'd grown arrogant. I'd found myself feeling so far above and beyond the mainstream, I'd slipped into the oversimplified, binary thinking I was supposedly counteracting: us/them, queer/straight, radical/mainstream, superior/inferior, subversive/assimilationist, insider/outsider, etc. However, my triad and its aftermath coincided with my Saturn Return (for you astrology buffs out there), and this thinking did not survive that period of introspection. Humility was definitely my character trait that increased most during this period—acknowledging how few answers I had. I came to accept my relationships and myself as complicated, messy, overlapping, and contradictory. That strengthened and more realistic sense of self is one of the biggest reasons I don't regret my year in a triad.

Carl, Erik, and I are all now in new relationships. We're still friends, although Carl has moved to another city. I'm happy now, years into in my monogamous binary, yet I still think well of triads. My partner and I socialize with Carl, Erik, and their new partners; snapshots of the three of us are in the mix of my screen saver. Friends rush off to Portland or Massachusetts to marry; my partner and I debate what to do on our fifth anniversary. Commitment ceremonies sound so '90s now, don't they? And yet, I'm still not sure what marriage means to me.

The triad seems distant, part of that heady yet increasingly alien life *before*: Before turning 30, the millennium, 9/11, the 2000 election, anthrax, the dotcom bust, the recession, the Iraqi bloodbath. That world seems gone, out of reach, unreal. My critique of aspects of a triad is not, I hope, a conservative reaction to today's anxious times. No, now we need love more than ever, in its multiplicity of incarnations, married or unmarried. We need each other more than ever, and we need to love each other well.

Ultimately the power of a relationship is determined not by its shape but by what goes on within that shape. A monogamous, heterosexual binary couple who truly respect and support each other as equals, who work past the patriarchal legacies of ownership and possession, whose trust combats jealousy and fear, can be more subversive and transgressive than more baroque arrangements. It is through the content of our relationships—not the structure—that we improve the world.

D. Travers Scott's next novel, One of These Things Is Not Like the Other, *will be published in 2005 by Suspect Thoughts Press. Previously he wrote* Execution, Texas: 1987, *edited* Strategic Sex: Why They Won't Keep It in the Bedroom, *and guest-judged* Best Gay Erotica 2000. *Otherwise he has cropped up in places such as* This American Life, Harper's, *and* Best American Gay Fiction 2. *He lives in Seattle and runs 9099 Media, a regional micropress. He can be found at* www.dtraversscott.com.

Will Shank

Today I spoke words that I had always supposed were written for someone else. For richer, for poorer. In sickness and in health.

It all had a surreal aspect, because it came upon U.B. and me so quickly. We were still unclear on the concept of exactly how our new mayor, Gavin Newsom, had pulled off such a fast one. Was the much embattled national gay-marriage issue really that easy to overcome? How was it that several hundred same-sex couples had been able to fill in actual marriage certificates at San Francisco's City Hall yesterday, without anyone raising a ruckus?

Over coffee this morning, we considered the possibilities. "You wanna go to City Hall today, hun?" I said. "Is that a proposal?" he asked back. When we found out that our old friend, Supervisor Aaron Peskin, was available to perform the wedding ceremony for us this afternoon, we lost no time in emptying our calendars of everything else (including an *Advocate* press deadline! Perish the thought!)

For years we had considered asking Aaron to dub us "San Francisco Domestic Partners," a title that the State of California already bestowed on us just before the arrival of our daughter Stassa last year. But there was little incentive, other than the knowledge that our seven-year relationship, and a shared mailing address, coupled with a piece of paper from City Hall, made us sort of like other married folks. Besides, we had felt just a bit empty after the "ceremony" for our state DP designation. The clerks and the notary at the postal supply store in the Castro had cheerfully tossed packing peanuts at us, and we got a certificate in the mail from Sacramento. But it was mostly an essential part of the adoption procedure that we were about to complete, legitimizing our couplehood in the only way that the state of California knew how.

More meaningful to us was an evening at a candlelit Parisian restaurant in the Marais where, on a gray December night five years before, we had exchanged gold bands after dessert. We had considered ourselves married in every way except the legal one, since Pearl Harbor Day of 1998. But today, suddenly, the M-word was in the air everywhere in San Francisco.

Because Supervisor Peskin represents the essentially nongay neighborhoods of North Beach and Fisherman's Wharf, he was not in great demand, as was, say Tom Ammiano, our own supervisor in the Mission, or Bevan Dufty of the Castro. So he was delighted to say the vows for us, and his wife Nancy offered to serve as witness. As it turned out, a handful of our best friends also dropped everything and raced to City Hall to form an impromptu wedding party. (Luckily there was no time for bridesmaids' gowns.) We were joined by Greg and Ellen, whose own wedding in Tiburon some years back showed us how hard a straight guy could cry. U.B.'s sister Leslie showed up with a butter-cream-slathered cake from nearby Citizen Cake. And both our straight friend Katherine and our gay bud Jim were delighted not to have to jump for a wedding bouquet. Aaron read our vows in the elegant, empty Supervisors' Chambers, and we took off our Paris rings and put them back on each other's ring fingers. We cried as we each answered him, "I sure do!" And the supervisor's voice cracked as he pronounced us Spouses for Life (rhymes with "Man and Wife"). I think it was the first one of these things he had ever done. A group of third-graders, on a tour of City Hall, watched quietly from the front row as the docent let them know that they were witnessing history.

The energy in the air buzzed around City Hall like a beehive as 900 other couples performed the same ceremony that we had. In every nook and cranny of the soaring stone building, queers were saying their vows and being declared Spouses for Life by every city official available.

It felt to me just like the first Pride Parade I'd ever attended, about 30 years ago. Who knows what value the signed, sealed, sort of DMV-looking documents that we received today may have in the future. The deed was done. And there will be thousands of us ready to face whatever opposition may come in the future. By the time we got home a right-wing group was calling the San Francisco weddings an act of "municipal anarchy." As if that was a criticism! Thank God we live in a city that, in this time of reactionary American timidity and fear, leads the charge toward the future for those of us who have had enough of being second-class citizens!

April 13, 2004

Will Shank (www.willshank.com) was trained as an art historian and art conservator, and served as head of conservation at the San Francisco Museum of Modern Art throughout the 1990s. He is an arts writer for numerous publications, including the Bay Area Reporter, The Advocate, *and London's* The Art Newspaper. *He is also the recipient of the prestigious Rome Prize in Conservation/Historic Preservation for 2005. He and his family will be in residence at the American Academy in Rome for six months next year. Currently, he is working on several books about artists' techniques and his own photography.*

Here We Go 'Round the Hanukkah Bush
Simon Sheppard

There hasn't been much sex at my gym. Not lately.

Once upon a lust-drenched time, the steam room was reliably cruisy, with plenty of gropings, sometimes blow jobs, occasionally even a high-temperature spurt of cum or two. (One guy whom I cruised in the shower, whose asshole I fingered beneath the streaming water, turned out—somewhat embarrassingly—to be a well-known editor; I'd submitted a story to him a while before. In the months that followed that shower, he turned down my submission but took my fist.)

But then the Sex Police swooped down. The steam room's single dim bulb was replaced by two dim lights, then three bright ones; the farthest corners of the big room became as glaringly bright as a nighttime tennis court. Gym employees periodically patrolled the sauna, on the lookout for hard-ons and hanky-panky. It's not a gay gym, so perhaps some straight men truly were offended, though most of the time the action stopped as soon as a stranger walked in (and I'm pretty damn sure that more than one married man gladly got his dick stroked in the sauna). The rumor—one that a number of queers I spoke with found utterly plausible—was that the gym staffers behind the crackdown were gay.

So the other day it came as a pleasant surprise when I went into the sauna and the only other guy there started playing with his cock. Mid-forties, with a body so lean and muscular that the veins on his legs popped out. Shaved head, handsome, slightly ravaged face. Nice dick. The sauna has two-level seating, and he was on the upper tier, his crotch at my eye level, just across the room.

"Your dick always get hard like that," he asked, "without your touching it?" His cock, pretty as it was, hadn't reached full erection. Mine had, quickly.

"Depends on the stimulus," I flattered.

"You a top or bottom?" He was, clearly, getting right down to it.

"Mostly top, but sure not exclusively."

"I'm usually a top…" stroke stroke stroke "…but looking to be a bottom." Aha.

He patted the wooden bench beside him, a "come sit" gesture. I obliged, dick bobbling in the dry heat. There was a bottle of baby oil on the bench. He put a little oil in his hand and reached for my dick. It felt good, but after a second I told him I had no great desire to be busted by the gym staff. He took his hand away, I squeezed his now-hard dick briefly, and then we started talking.

We got around to discussing our primary relationships.

"Mine's pretty much completely open," I said. "We don't have any of the usual open-relationship rules, things like 'Only one time with each partner,' 'Not in our own bed,' or 'Only when one of us is out of town.' The only constant is mutual respect and consideration."

His had a few more rules than my extremely successful, extremely long-term relationship has. But he understood completely.

"What are you doing tonight?" he asked. He was still beating off, had been all along.

"Busy."

"Then let me give you my phone number."

Of course.

On the way out of the gym, I ran into my friend Phil, a longtime queer activist.

"So what do you think of this gay marriage hullabaloo?" Phil asked.

"Right fight, wrong time?" I offered.

"I'd say 'wrong battle, wrong time,'" Phil countered. "How did what started out as a radical challenge to stupid sexual norms become so intent on aping a flawed heterosexual institution?"

I thought that was a little harsh. After all, my buddies Ian and Greg had just gotten hitched, and they were hardly unimaginative assimilationists. Still, I knew what he meant.

A few years ago, my partner and I had taken part in a mass domestic partner commitment ceremony at San Francisco City Hall, long before the rotunda became ground zero for the slavering attack dogs of the Religious Right. Downstairs, where the reception was held, was a photo display titled something like "Love Makes a Family." All the photos—*all* of them, as far as I recall—featured beaming same-sex couples and their kids. My particular honey and I, who have not the slightest desire to raise children, felt nowhere represented. The fix was in: *Want to be a loving queer couple? Conform to the standard child-rearing model, okay?*

At that time, conservagay writer Andrew Sullivan was railing about queer promiscuity, positing same-sex marriage as the solution, saying something like "The gay movement should procure full marriage rights, then just dissolve." (This was before he was caught with his hand in the, um, cookie jar, posting ads on a barebacking website.) And that was when Rosie O'Donnell was still making jokes about being a "Lebanese," before she finally came out—for the sake, she told us, of queer parents raising kids. Still, you could pretty easily tell Sullivan and Rosie apart: Sullivan denounced gay radicals as "Stalinists," while O'Donnell called them "Nazis."

Now Sullivan is on TV defending George Bush's war, and O'Donnell and her honey have been wed in San Francisco, just like scads of other happy couples. My partner and I, though, are opting out of the corsage-and-rice routine. I have less desire to be just like Mom and Dad than to be entitled to my sweetie's Social Security, should he go first. Unromantic? Actually, we have a very romantic relationship. It's just one where *we've* invented the rules.

Much of the general discourse around same-sex marriage centers on sexual fidelity. "Gay men are naturally promiscuous," the Christian Ayatollahs intone, "so why do they pretend they're interested in marriage?"

"But," the good gays respond, "society has always told us that we're sluts. Give us a chance to be husbands and we'll settle down, honest."

Well, okay. Those who want, truly want, to be monogamous, out of love and not fear or jealousy, have my blessings. But monogamy's simply not a prerequisite for a good relationship; where I put my dick is not necessarily where I put my devotion. It's a rare, brave voice that reminds us, as an article in the *San Francisco Chronicle* did, that, "the consensual, non-monogamous agreements some gay couples have are honorable and preferable to the typical straight version of affairs and cheating."

When I was growing up in an overwhelmingly Christian suburb, some of the Jewish parents put up "Hanukkah bushes" for their kids. They were Christmas trees in drag, designed to make Junior feel less like an outcast. No matter that Judaism had its own glorious traditions, and that Christianity had been, as often as not, an enemy to those traditions. Those Hanukkah bushes were part consolation, part assimilation, part wishful thinking, part self-betrayal. I doubt that even the kids were fooled. And lately I've been thinking that the public face of queer marriage—with its straight-aping, "forsaking all others" facade of monogamous stability—is maybe, whatever its many possible virtues, our very own Hanukkah bush.

Tomorrow, history willing, still more queer couples will head down to San Francisco

City Hall to get hitched, and I wish them a hearty *Mazel tov* and all the happiness in the world. Political qualms aside, we all deserve nice, shiny presents under our Hanukkah bushes.

And that hunk from the gym? I've got a date to go over to his place and fuck his beautiful ass.

Simon Sheppard is the author of Kinkorama: Dispatches From the Front Lines of Perversion, In Deep and Other Stories, *and the soon-to-be-published* Sex Parties 101. *His work has appeared in over 100 anthologies, and his column "Sex Talk" appears in queer papers and on the Web. He and his partner of 30 years live in nonmonogamous bliss in San Francisco. He's at* www.simonsheppard.com.

This column originally appeared on *Gay.com*, April 2004. Reprinted by permission of the author.

The New Gay and Lesbian Wedding Traditions
Bob Smith

Over the centuries a large collection of proverbs, superstitions, and traditions has built up about love and marriage. Unfortunately most of these traditions assume that marriage is limited to a man and a woman. Since queer marriages can be considered a new innovation in matrimony, it seems reasonable that we should try to create our own wedding traditions.

• On the day of the wedding, it's bad luck for the two grooms to see each other at the gym.

• Traditionally at gay weddings the parents have an open bar *during* the ceremony.

• Gay wedding tradition dictates that both grooms refuse any cake because it's all carbs.

• It's considered bad luck for either of the grooms to have dated the priest.

• During the first dance it's considered in poor taste for the grooms to dance shirtless and use glowsticks, flags, or handheld lasers.

• For good luck at the nuptials of a drag queen, the bouquet is always thrown in the face of a hated rival.

• During the ceremony it's ill-advised for either of the grooms to sing or display any other "talent."

• At lesbian weddings, the brides are never given away—they take what is rightfully theirs!

• Traditionally at a Jewish gay wedding, instead of breaking a wine glass, the happy couple stomp on the tackiest gift for good luck.

• At *very* traditional lesbian weddings, the guests throw brown rice at the couple as they depart.

• Traditionally the father of the bottom pays for everything.

Born in Buffalo, Bob Smith (www.literati.net/Smith) has the distinction of being the first openly gay comedian to appear on The Tonight Show *and also have his own HBO Comedy half-hour. Bob's Lambda Literary Award–winning collection of essays* Openly Bob *was published to acclaim by Rob Weisbach Books/William Morrow, and his most recent Lambda Literary Award–nominated book* Way to Go, Smith! *was published by HarperCollins. He's written for Amblin Films, The MTV Video Awards, Dennis Miller, Roseanne, and Fox's MADtv. Bob is a regular contributor to* Out *magazine where he writes the popular monthly list column and feature articles. He's currently working on his first novel, a comedy set in Los Angeles and Alaska.*

First published in *Out* magazine, June 2002. Reprinted by permission of the author.

But Will Gay Marriage Make the World Safer for Blow Jobs in the Bushes?
Horehound Stillpoint

Busted!
While half of Queertown USA is getting gay married at City Hall
My butt's in the mud
A complete stranger is sitting three feet away
His ass is grass as well
We got caught
Now we're under the eye of a park ranger in a smart brown uniform
Waiting for some sergeant and a cop
The sergeant will decide if we are to be arrested
The cop will write the ticket
If we cooperate
Give truthful information
And do not try to run away
I ain't going nowhere
Just trying to keep a smile off my face
Trying not to look at the generous bulge in those park ranger trousers
Doesn't he know the script?
He's supposed to pull it out, force us to blow him, eat his ass, fuck him and
Fuck him and
Let him fuck us
This is Bad Boy Beach, after all
When the Black and White pulls up
It's obvious they got their own script
It's just a chore for the sergeant and the cop
The orgy will not be uprising
"We can't have this kind of behavior," one uniform informs,
"What if a kid wandered into these bushes?"
"I've blown and been blown by a hundred guys in these bushes,
And I've never seen a kid wander in"
This is what I do not say
I know my job is not to speak
Not to say: the only couple I've ever seen actually fucking out in the open
    Under the big sky, for God, and little children alike, to see
        Consisted of a heterosexual man and woman
        And they were not looking over their shoulders
I've been waiting for the cops to arrive
Ever since I turned 13
When I started having sex in library toilets, department store johns, and
parking garages
I wish I could have found some bushes
Believe me—I was looking
Even before that... Hell, when I was nine
The language police came for me right in the middle of a school day
For teacher and all the other kids to see

Shoved me into speech therapy sessions
Trying to get rid of (what no one called) my gay accent
I don't even know if this is my voice
I wish the words "Gay Marriage" had been floating on the wind when I was a kid
Maybe I would have found the courage to ask Brian Dove to the prom
Instead of Mary Matonick
Found ways to demonstrate love instead of disguising it
Being so desperate for touch
I would do anything, with any guy, anytime, anywhere
As long as he was someone I didn't know and would never see again
I wanted to be no man's man but one
But I got off on the wrong foot, on the wrong path
With head and heart and cock all going off in different directions at once
It was a miracle I found a man who loved me and whom I could tolerate
An artist, hippie, weightlifting, rock 'n' roll loudmouth
The man I would sleep with every night for the next 15 years
We called each other lovers, not husbands
We called it an open relationship and proceeded to drive each other crazy
He called me "Brat" most often
I called him with my last two dimes, when I did get arrested, in the eighties,
First words out of his mouth were: "Morals charge?"
I told him it was for smoking pot in a storefront doorway
He sounded surprised and annoyed
He died years ago of you-know-what
Now I fear I will never get my butt out of this mud
I keep my hands in plain sight and a "Sir" on the tip of my tongue
A lot of people are in jail for having adult consensual sex of the outlaw kind
We end up with tickets for disorderly conduct
    & creating a physical offensive condition
"Hey," I want to say, "there was nothing disorderly about it,
That was a very polite blow job"
Not to mention the incorrect grammar and sociological quagmire
That "creating a physical offensive condition" brings up
But I pay the ticket, I am not ashamed to say
My revolution is slow as evolution
I'm an old school fag and I believe I deserve everything I get
Including that guy in the bushes
He wasn't that cute, nor particularly built, just an ordinary guy
But, man, he tasted like grass and lakes, like sunshine and dirt
Fuck, they don't let us date, don't let us get married, don't let us love,
don't let us live
Then they're surprised we find each other in the forest at twilight
At the end of the world
Gay marriage is coming, but meanwhile they're policing Bad Boy Beach
This may be San Francisco, but it's still America
Land of the free, home of the brave, o'er the ramparts and through the woods
You know, some gay kid is dying...just dying to find these bushes
Even if I am what America fears: a solitary queer
In the dark, waiting, ready to pounce

I fear America
And America should be ashamed

Horehound Stillpoint is a writer/waiter punk-ass poet in San Francisco and his wanky words can be found in many anthologies of poetry and queer erotica, including Bullets and Butterflies *(Suspect Thoughts Press, 2005) and* Quickies 3 *(Arsenal Pulp Press, 2003).*

Choosing Family
Meg Stone

I used to be against same-sex marriage. At the time I was a single woman struggling to find recognition and understanding of the complex network of friends and biological relatives that made up my support system. I was frustrated that members of GLBT communities were fighting to assimilate, to gain legal status that would solely benefit monogamous partnerships when chosen families took so many forms. I was also working as a domestic-violence advocate and saw that batterers used the divorce process to prolong manipulation and emotional abuse. If not for legal marriage, I reasoned, there would be fewer barriers to leaving abuse.

I've changed my opinion about marriage but nothing else—I now support legalizing same-sex marriage because of my strong belief in chosen family and abuse prevention. The care we get from loving partners gives us the confidence and openness to work for change that benefits our whole communities, and strong and present communities can help counter the isolation in which family violence thrives.

My partner Mal and I decided to have a wedding ceremony shortly before the Massachusetts Supreme Judicial Court made its historic ruling. Our decision had nothing to do with legal rights or responsibilities, because we assumed we'd never have them. For me, getting married was not about making promises about forever. It was about affirming what is already true—that we dearly love each other and have created a home together that is a haven for the family we've created. I am marrying Mal because I trust that the warmth, ease, and partnership we have now will endure. I want to create a single community of the families we came from and the families we chose.

The way I initially justified our decision to get legally married was an appeal to pragmatism. If anything went wrong, we would have a clearly defined legal relationship that at least in Massachusetts would entitle me to make medical decisions, visit her in the hospital, and make necessary financial arrangements. Though these practical considerations are important, gaining societal recognition of our partnership is more than insurance for a worst-case scenario. It's a step toward a society in which legal recognition of family relationships more closely resembles families as we actually experience them.

The publicity same-sex marriage has received since last November has changed the conversations I have with the family I came from and the people in their world. Family friends I've known since childhood are asking me about gay rights for the first time ever. They express more anger about discrimination and antigay attitudes because those beliefs threaten my marriage. People who love me but never understood my life choices understand marriage. I never got this kind of support around employment discrimination, hate crimes, or other issues that affect me as a lesbian. Social change is made up of a few great victories like the *Goodridge* decision followed by the thousands of smaller connections and revelations those great moments catalyze.

Many people whose lives have diverged from their families of origin have a strong need to create a support network of people whose values, lifestyles, and politics resemble their own. Having a chosen family of people who understand me because they are like me makes it easier for me to love the family I came from, and through my marriage to Mal, I am also joining tradition and nontradition, where I came from with who I am. Creating a ritual to affirm what our relationship means to us is important, as is sharing that ritual with all the people we love. We are getting married in a nature preserve, and the money we spent to rent the venue supports environmental education programs for children. Our caterer is socially responsible. Our gift registry is a combination of fair-trade products and a list of social-change organizations to which people can donate in honor of the wedding. The joy surrounding our wedding is opening people's hearts to conversations about fair trade, recycled paper, and the political struggle we face as women who want to marry each other.

I have not stopped struggling with the fact that legal marriage is only a partial recognition of difference in family structures. As the right wing argues for legislation that explicitly defines marriage as a union of one man and one woman, there are parts of my community in which defining "man" and "woman" is far from simplistic. Marriage rights will only benefit those whose primary families are comprised of partners and children, but even this arguably narrow redefinition of legally recognized family is causing outrage and protest. This shows me how far the rest of the world is from accepting family diversity.

During a lobby day in which activists from both sides of the marriage issue convened in the Massachusetts State House, Mal, her mother, and I found ourselves sharing the waiting room outside her representative's office with a Catholic priest. Without thinking, we referred to him as being from the "pro-family" side, and it scared me to think that all the conservative family-values rhetoric had affected us. Without realizing it, we had conceded the definition of family, and I want to take it back. I will talk about my relationship with Mal in a way that it can be understood outside our immediate community because I want people who are undecided about marriage rights to be able to relate to us. It is just as important to me to create a connection through a common experience of partnership as it is to reject the majority of capitalist, patriarchal wedding conventions. I want other people who believe that family is about love, warmth, home, mutual respect, and shared responsibility to be able to relate to me, and by extension my struggle for equal rights, even if their lives look nothing like mine.

Meg Stone is a public health practitioner creating programs that address the health and economic effects of abuse. She and her partner were featured in a Boston Globe *story about their upcoming wedding.*

I Met My Wife at a Lesbian Sex Party
Jackie Strano

I met my wife at a lesbian sex party.

Our chemistry was off the charts and the first kiss was a mind-blower.

What started as an intense connection has deepened into a bond that no clergy or president can subjugate, legislate, or obliterate.

I love her goodness and open heart, her passion, compassion, and creativity, her gentle spirit, not to mention her beauty, loveliness, sexiness, and fierceness.

We fell in love pretty quickly and dramatically. It just felt right, easy, and simple. She and I are meant to walk this life together. Everything before her was black and white, now I could see in Technicolor. I had been in love before but that was young love, first love, this is real love and true love that can only come with feeling at peace, like you have finally found your way home.

Eleven years later we're still crazy about each other, still in love, she still turns me on and makes me laugh. Money comes and goes; you know we got our priorities straight.

Eight years ago we decided to get married. I had proposed to her 3 years before after being together for only 50 days. We were at the cable car turnaround down near Ghiradelli Square in San Francisco. I bought $5 silver rings for both of us off an old Chinese lady working one of those jewelry carts on the street. The vendor got real bossy about what rings were wedding-type rings. She handed me a thick band and a thinner one for Shar. Whether I passed as a man to her at the time or she was just A-OK with gay marriage back in 1993, I will never know, but she smiled at us and genuinely looked happy for us after I popped the question on bended knee with the foghorns over the bay as our backdrop.

Our engagement lasted for three years because we kept waiting for the right time—as in when we would have enough money to really do it up. Of course we knew it wasn't legal, but our love is above the law, outside of the law. We were proud to be outlaws after all. We somehow felt comforted in thinking that it didn't matter what the law said anyway. I wasn't too concerned with marriage rights back then; I wasn't asking for a government-sanctioned union anyway. Our spirituality was above and beyond that. We got each other's name tattooed on each other's ring finger after having a ceremony in the back of Black and Blue Tattoo in the Mission. We had family members, bio and chosen, assembled to witness our vows to each other. One of Shar's vows was to always be honest; I vowed to love her forever.

It was private, it was emotional, and it was permanent.

We knew from that day forward that things were different.

We were two individuals but now those lives were forever joined and a promise was made. From now on I got your back, baby; you go down, I go down, but together we are gonna fly. Anything you want, anyone you love, anywhere you wanna go, I am here now with you, in you, loving the day you were born and always trying to be the best person to walk beside you.

Our reception was held at Kimo's on Polk Street. Friends and family showered us with love, glitter, music, food, flowers, and a never-ending supply of good drag and sexy mofos. Shar and I know how to throw a party!

In our hearts we were married. Not just for orgies, three-ways, dance floors, and parties. We were also married for bouts of poverty, illness, depression, homelessness, joblessness, and touring. Anyone who has traveled to support their art by doing it all themselves knows exactly what I am talking about when I say touring. You want to test a relationship, go on and do it, I dare ya!

And yes, we have gone through all of the above together. Sometimes it was and is rough around the edges, but we always try to create a safe landing for each other and keep our sense of humor intact. We have enough tragedy on both sides of the family to understand how short life truly is.

Well, fast-forward to February 13, 2004. We stood on the steps of City Hall and did it all over again. This time my mother got to be there, and our nine-year-old nephew was our ring bearer. This time we once again ceremoniously used rings as the tattoos are still there. It was emotional all over again, and this time the added component of making history was a little intense. I never thought I would be standing on the steps of City Hall for anything other than a protest. My favorite part was seeing the gleeful and satisfied grins on the city clerks as they oh-so-willingly filed all our papers. A young straight couple came in to see the line and looked dazed. The woman was obviously very pregnant and the groom-to-be was wearing his best rock T-shirt for the occasion. When they saw what was going on they gave us all the universal rock 'n' roll salute that also looks like the I LOVE YOU sign in American Sign Language. It made everyone happy. The deputized clerk who married us got choked up during our vows. It was his very first ceremony to officiate at, and he teared up with us. He told us how much he loved his wife and how happy he was for us. We always knew what we were to each other, but now we had a genuine document in the hall of records that said in black and white that we were spouses for life. It was a great big pie in the face of every right-wing politician and religious leader that I had adamantly opposed for most of my life. As a grandchild of war refugees, I know full well to never trust the government to always protect you, but damn if it didn't feel good to have thousands of folks smiling around you celebrating love; that's it pure and simple…love.

I love to introduce Shar as my wife. I love using the word "wife" to describe who she is to me. Girlfriend sounds like someone you go have lunch with. Partner sounds like someone you play chess with. Wife says we fuck, we pay bills together, and we have seen each other at our absolute pretty ugly and we still want to fuck each other. Talking about my wife in public to everyone from the telemarketer to the grocery clerk is always an interesting anthropological study. You find out real quick who is cool and who is not. Just the other day I was talking to some AOL billing department customer-service guy, and I was explaining that the other email addresses on my account belonged to my wife. The young man on the line in Bangalore, India, all of the sudden was supernice and all familiar-sounding. My name is Jackie which in some cultures is an andro type name and my voice can be husky and deep for a woman on the phone sometimes; I am butch but there is no mistaking that I am a woman.

He told me how he always dreamed of coming to San Francisco. Oh yes, Mary, that's right. You just get here, to be, to be free. Oh yes Mary, America the beautiful. We embrace all of God's children, especially if you are white, rich, not queer, and HIV-negative.

George Bush can kiss my bulldagger ass. No one can tell me that some felon sitting in jail for raping and killing has more of a right than me to legally marry. But guess what? It's true. Some drunk girl like Britney Spears can drive to Vegas at a moment's notice and tie the knot with a total stranger and every state of the union will recognize all the rights and privileges associated with legal marriage. There are over 1,000 rights you can automatically expect and enjoy once the Elvis impersonator is done with the ceremony and the papers are signed. What happens in Vegas doesn't stay in Vegas; that marriage is a marriage in all 50 states and around the world.

We always considered ourselves on the outside of society, outlaws in some ways; so one of my favorite rights about legal marriage is that your spouse can't be forced to testify in court against you.

And to those queers and aging hippies who are antimarriage because they want to be antiestablishment, I can't even imagine what aping the patriarchy and assimilation would look like. If Shar and I are assimilating by demanding our marriage rights, then I invite anyone to live my life for a few days, especially in the small town we currently live in, and tell us how much we look and act like the mainstream, straight or gay. There is no comfort in knowing that some of the radical left's apathy around gay marriage makes the organized right-wing political-action groups very happy. For example, I can't imagine keeping silent or not caring about a women's right for a safe and legal abortion just because I am not sleeping with men, no matter what my personal opinion about having an abortion is.

Take a listen to talk radio as you drive through this fair country of ours and you will be chilled to the bone as you listen to what a lot of people outside of the coastal cities are thinking and doing. Same-sex marriage is the lightning rod of the 2004 election year. The bloody and heinous American occupation of Iraq, exposed as the insidious crime that it always was, will hopefully drum Bush back to Crawford, Texas; but America is about so-called morals remember, and there is going to be a showdown here as we get closer to November.

The guy who stole the 2000 election, uh, I mean George Bush…well, he wants a constitutional amendment that says that marriage is to be between a man and a woman. There is momentum in Congress about this right now.

In the bible a widow is supposed to marry her dead husband's brother. There are also polygamous marriages in the bible yet you see these hate-mongering fools on TV say that allowing same-sex couples to marry will lead to condoning marrying an animal or multiple-partner marriages.

No, masturbation does not put hair on your palms and gays getting marriage certificates won't make it okay for your neighbor Fred to legally marry his pet goat. As for multiple partners, the Mormons already have a corner on that child-bride baby-making market…leave us out of that one for now, please. Give gays a chance to ruin the institution! C'mon! We want our dramatic divorces too; we want to marry our cousins; and we want to go to the little wedding chapel in Vegas! Domestic partner sounds like a robotic dog, and it only covers your ass in California. What happens if we are touring in Florida and one of us is in an accident? The other is not considered next of kin and depending on the mood of the nurse that day, you either get to be allowed to stay by the bedside of your beloved OR you are barred and banned from any visitation, consultation, and decision-making in regards to treatment, prognosis, and condition.

The love revolution started in San Francisco this past February was an amazing educational action. I was surprised at how many people I talked to, including extended family members who thought that it was already legal for Shar and I to be married. Just because *Will & Grace* and *Queer Eye for the Straight Guy* are on people's TVs doesn't mean a thing. Well, it confirms what we always knew was true: that queers have more fun and have a better sense of humor and everyone loves a cute fag hag who sometimes goes both ways.

I certainly don't want a blessing from someone like George Bush, I am not asking for permission, I am not wanting to be part of the mainstream…I already know my love is different and special…I am demanding what is just and fair and rightly deserved. I love my wife, I love our life, and you can't amend that.

Jackie Strano is a 39-year-old butch dyke musician and porn star dubbed a local vocal legend by the San Francisco Bay Guardian. *Strano has rocked from coast to coast, from The Fillmore to CBGBs, opening for countless kickass bands sometimes with her band The Hail Marys and sometimes solo. When not playing and writing music, Strano runs S.I.R. Video Productions, with her partner in crime, Shar Rednour. S.I.R. stands for sex, indulgence, and rock 'n' roll — to find out more visit* www.sirvideo.com.

Moving the Mountain:
A Love Story
Ron Suresha

The March 15, 2004 cover illustration for *The New Yorker*, "Dress Reversal" by Mark Ulriksen, depicts two attractive betrotheds trying on identical wedding gowns in adjoining mirrors. On the right stands a young female, the traditional blushing bride. On the left, a definitely bearish male, sporting a trim van Dyke and curly, chestnut brown chest hair, gazes at his own seductive image in the mirror. The woman is astonished not by her own gorgeous reflection—but by that of the other, hirsute, bride-to-be.

I can imagine myself as that goateed, hairy-chested bridegroom in lace. I can construct myself as wearing a wedding gown because genderfuck is a typically queer expression of my homomachobearish psyche. Whether I look better in a gown or a tux—or in a silver lamé jumpsuit, for that matter—is someone else's entirely subjective opinion. But this vision of myself as bride/groom doesn't reflect some unconscious desire to buy into an essentially classist, sexist, capitalistic 1970s American dream of domestic bliss. Two or more same-gender folks getting hitched just seems more subversive than conformist, even if by having weddings many of these couples are blindsided by the wedding industry into buying into some exurban Barbie-doll bliss.

Until recently, I too would rather have said "I don't" than "I do." Several life-changing events unfolding over the past three years, however, have forced me to reconsider my singleness. Eventually, I surrendered my precious solitude by praying to find a worthy partner. My desire eventually took form in silent supplications to my Indian-born spiritual teacher and to the divine power, Shakti. I figured I'd go right to the top with this request, because I am an unusually particular and peculiar fellow. For me, the problem was not settling down so much as settling on a suitable candidate for a lifetime spiritual companion.

Last year, the journey to gay marriage seemed as unlikely as my traveling to Sri Lanka—a distant sub-subcontinent halfway around the world, where apparently many people live happily, but is neither accessible nor desirable to me. My long-established appetite for sexual variety complemented a solitary temperament: the greater the frequency one changes partners, I argued, the easier it is to retreat as necessary. I enjoyed nearly three decades of gay sex, with a cornucopia of boyfriends and tricks. Why sacrifice that for one single man?

Not that I had much space or energy in my already-chaotic existence to sacrifice for the demands of romance. Over five years, while serving as a primary caregiver for, and then burying, my dad, I successfully navigated two contentious legal battles with family. I also launched my writing career by compiling three books and going on a demanding 36-city book tour.

Forty-three years old and single ("family-free," I joked), I felt that I had already experienced more than my share of midlife crises. But some momentum kept my life careening dramatically in unexpected directions. While mending emotionally from the breakup with a particularly promising boyfriend, I finally sold my house after two failed attempts and moved from Boston to Providence, then moved again locally ten months later because of landlord problems.

On April Fool's Day 2003, I found a dime-sized lump in my neck. No kidding. Within six months, as it became infected and swelled, I underwent a painful biopsy of my left salivary gland, then surgery to remove the golfball-size mass that the final pathology diagnosed as a rare but treatable cancer, then six weeks of radiation. In this short time, I felt as if I'd been swallowed whole into a wormhole, chewed up, and spat back out into some parallel universe.

Cancer surgery and treatment shifted my view of my mortal, sexual body. This and other factors—curiosity about nonmale sexual encounters, perception of how queers create nontraditional families, becoming good friends with a bisexual married bear, and recognition of a very real sexual attraction to a woman who had been a female childhood friend—nudged me toward an appreciation of my long-standing feelings of attraction to women. To call my heterosexuality latent felt bizarre yet true. I had quietly regarded myself a Kinsey 5 as long as I could recall, and, as I now considered myself possibly bisexual, I felt no compelling reason whatsoever to further deny my erotic and affectional desire for certain women. Coming out as bisexual correlated also with my mistrust of allying myself with a singular partner. I have since discovered that bisexuality excludes neither marriage nor promiscuity; rather, it embraces marriage in a greater vision of sexual relations and family.

Still, I was familiar enough with homosexuals' biphobia to wonder what gay guy would fall in love with another gay guy who wants to start having sex with women?

At the ripe age of 45, even if I could pass the mountain of accumulating midlife crises, I thought it unlikely I'd ever meet an available, dear, trustworthy companion. Even though I had faith in the cancer treatment, I thought I'd run out of luck. Who would want an already-high-maintenance boyfriend—undergoing cancer treatment?

Ten days after surgery, I attended the Lambda Literary Festival conference in Provincetown, Massachusetts, where I met a handsome bearish literature lover and fledgling poet from Connecticut. Turns out I had heard of this doctor, Rocco, six months earlier, when looking for a gay physician in Providence. Interestingly, Rocco knew of me as well: his previous partner had shown Rocco a copy of my book *Bears on Bears*. That night, after a delightful dinner together, while we were walking home, I led Rocco to a bench by the shore. We sat quietly absorbing the cool moonlight refracted in the gentle motion of the water over the bay. We held hands, laughed, and kissed tenderly. Returning to Rocco's hotel room, we made passionate love.

Long story short, this incredible guy waltzed into my life and swept me off my feet. Without hesitating, he offered unrestricted kindness during my cancer treatment. He offered me his time and talent, his wit and humor, his love and devotion.

What can you say about someone who brings you flowers when you feel utterly crappy? Someone who makes up erotic verse for you at the end of a hellish day? Someone who drives an hour to take you to the seashore and hold your hand while you cry at the beauty of a sunset?

Six months later, in early May 2004, I found the right words. Rocco and I were participating in the Saints & Sinners GLBTQ litfest in New Orleans. We both attended an excellent make-time-to-write workshop, during which the facilitator advised us to ask our partners in a loving way to affirm their support for our writing efforts. Ostensibly, she meant, "When you get home." As we exited, though, Rocco unexpectedly pulled me to him in close embrace and kissed me. He said with utter sincerity, "I want to affirm to you my complete support for your writing. I will do whatever I can in any way to help you in your work."

Gratitude flooded my senses and, after parting, I walked dazedly to my next workshop. My heart expanded further in gratitude to the divine power, Shakti, for hearing my prayers to find a worthy partner.

That evening, after fun tramping with writerly pals all over the French Quarter, Rocco and I were in our room, knee-to-knee on the bed, naked and aroused. We kissed and rubbed each other's body in sheer delight. I squeezed Rocco's meaty paws in mine, gauging the size of his fingers. I was praying it would fit, but I couldn't be sure.

I slipped from my hand the ruby-and-two-tone-gold ring my father wore before he died. Then I gazed into his eyes and, with every drop of blood in my heart, I asked him, "Rocco, would you marry me?"

If I thought for even a nanosecond that he would say no, I wouldn't have asked. But lucky me, he cried out, "Yes!"

In that sacred moment, as Rocco and I shared joyful tears, we were married in the eye of the Universal Being.

For the many privileges I am accorded as a U.S. citizen, I am exceedingly grateful. Even though self-employed most of my working life, I dutifully pay my taxes to the federal government, and I expect them to deliver to me the same inalienable rights as all other taxpayers.

Not to sing the blues ad infinitum, but I'll just say that I've paid my dues to sorrow as well. I've survived dysfunctional family, constant bullying during childhood, depression and suicide attempts, an adulthood of spotty employment, spiritual searching, community service, AIDS around me, and cancer inside me.

So, in terms of whatever privileges that I may be entitled to by signing on to the admittedly archaic, religion-steeped, patriarchal institution of marriage, I say, "Bring 'em on!"

Marriage embodies an essential spiritual worldview. In Indian traditions, the householder was considered one of the four instituted stages of life, or *ashramas*. One was a student, then had a family before becoming a renunciant, and finally a forest-dweller. Admittedly, dwelling in forests is not viable for many of us, but why deny anyone, regardless of age, gender, or any other physical characteristic, access to a stage of life of such significant human value?

Recently the religious hypocrisy of the supporters of the Federal Marriage Amendment struck me dramatically as I was proofreading for Shambhala Publications on the Gospel of Thomas, just days before I went to Provincetown to do interviews for May 17th, the first day of legal gay marriage in Massachusetts. In Thomas 48: "Jesus said: If two can make peace between themselves in a single house, they can say to a mountain, 'Move!' and it will move." And in Thomas 106: "Jesus said: When you make the two into one, you will be called sons of men ['children of humanity']. When you say, 'Move, mountain!' it will move."

These aphorisms fairly leapt out at me from the page and filled me with joy and understanding. It seemed to apply to every aspect of my life, especially the prospect of creating a harmonious domestic life with my partner. If we can join our purposes, obstacles will be cleared for us to commit our lives to each other, and everything else will follow.

Rocco and I know that nobody's exactly rolling out a red carpet for us to stroll in matching leather tuxes (or lace dresses) down the aisle toward wedded bliss. We joyously witnessed the initiation of gay marriage in Massuchusetts, and are optimistic about the favorable reciprocal legislative support in Rhode Island and Connecticut and the overall political landscape. Though the fight for GLBTQ civil rights is far from over, we both have felt particularly welcomed to the option of coming to the table.

Traditional marriage *should* be queered as part of its transformation into something far greater. By queering marriage, we queer culture, government, and religion in the service of dismantling gender. The best way a gay/bisexual/queer man such as myself can prove my point is to get married to another similarly minded person. Although the striving of sisters, brothers, and others toward civil marriage has strengthened my political beliefs, Rocco's and my genuine desire to bond in a substantially intimate relationship, however, remains our focus.

Marriage strikes me as a lifelong mutual spiritual responsibility of two or more folks committed to each other, but not in exclusion to the world. If I can find or create singularity of purpose in my relationships—through some combination of solitude and harmonious solidarity with another—I will arrive at marriage. Marriage is a continent where I may arrive only after having passed through many other land masses along the way.

Much more has happened, politically and personally, since I proposed to Rocco in New Orleans. At present we plan to hold a private civil ceremony in Provincetown this October on our anniversary, in front of the bench where we first kissed—maybe wearing matching silver lamé jumpsuits, who knows? As we come closer to a mutual agreement about joining our lives together, we affirm our mutual love and long-term goals. As the Gospel of Thomas sayings illuminate, those whose prayers are united—who achieve consistent effort together—can accomplish anything.

Ron Suresha (www.suresha.com) *is the author of* Bears on Bears: Interviews & Discussions, *and the editor of several anthologies.*

Civil Union for All
Steve Swayne

In 1968, Spence Silver, a 3M research scientist, accidentally created an adhesive with properties that were then novel. It was spherical; it had the thickness of a paper fiber; it did not dissolve; it did not melt; each individual sphere was very sticky. But when many spheres were brought together onto a tape backing, they didn't adhere very well.

For five years, Silver pitched his discovery to folks at 3M, but no one thought much of his creation. Finally, in 1973, an application was found: movable bulletin boards. But it was hardly an earth-shattering application.

Enter Art Fry, a new-product development researcher at 3M. He had learned about Silver's adhesive, and he thought to himself: If I could put some of that adhesive on the back of a piece of paper, I could create a more reliable bookmark for my church hymnal instead of the scraps of paper that keep falling out. He brought his idea to 3M. Some initially tried to kill the project; why compete with something that already exists and works so well already? But Fry and others persisted. They eventually went to Richmond, Virginia, to see if they could sell this notion of scrap paper with an adhesive edge. People were interested, and in 1980—a dozen years after Silver's discovery—3M launched the Post-it Note.

With all the hue and cry about civil union and its alleged inferiority, I ask myself: Do the people who accidentally created this new adhesive have any idea how powerful their invention is? I don't think they do.

So let me offer an application for their creation. Since October of 2001, I've been proposing a different way to move forward in our struggle toward marriage equality. The dominant voices from our community have demanded marriage for gays, and marriage has been the rallying cry ever since we came so close in Hawaii. But some of us want to see something that is at once more radical and more conservative: civil union for all.

It's clearly more radical, because no nation on earth has ever abandoned civil marriage and adopted an alternative. In a debate with an advocate of same-sex marriage, my proposal of civil union for all was dismissed as being so much wishful thinking. We will always have civil marriage, I was told. Really? This same advocate cautioned against filing marriage lawsuits too soon, for fear of suits that may be unwinnable in the courts of law and public opinion. All the while, she cited Hawaii— the suit most gay legal thinkers thought was premature—as the beginning of the current push for gay marriage.

Fifteen years ago, few of us fully envisioned the possibility of gay marriage. Dismissing civil union for all out of hand similarly represents a failure of imagination on the part of leaders in the gay community and elsewhere. After all, civil marriage cannot trace its lineage to the beginnings of ancient civilization. So who's to say that a nation might not one day adopt civil union for all?

And what better nation to do this than the United States? American exceptionalism is part of our birthright. If any nation is poised to reinvent legal relationships on a large scale, it is our great and innovative land. Liberty, justice, and civil union for all.

The other complaint I hear from the champions for same-sex marriage is: We didn't get civil union by asking for civil union. I was up here in Vermont when we got civil union, and to be honest, none of us were all that happy that we didn't get marriage. But at the same time, few of us conceived anything like civil union. It's awfully hard to ask for something that does not yet exist. Who would know to ask for a Post-it Note that hadn't yet been invented? Now that we have civil union for gay couples, it's not so unimaginable to ask for civil union for all couples, is it?

And this is what makes my proposal conservative. By saying that all couples, gay and straight, get a civil union, we solve a number of issues simultaneously. Take polygamy, for example. The defenders of traditional marriage wail that polygamy is right around the corner if society allows same-sex marriage. We all know, though, that marriage has long been associated with polygamy, and granting or denying same-sex marriage won't affect that history one whit. Civil union, in contrast, has no history. So let's define it: two people who are unrelated by blood and above a certain age are eligible for governmental recognition of their relationship and the benefits and obligations that come from that recognition. Poof! No polygamy.

And talk about the separation of church and state! Has anyone you know pontificated about the sanctity of civil union, about the need to protect traditional civil union? Of course not.

The champions of same-sex marriage think they can finesse the church-state issue by talking about civil marriage and how no religious body would be forced to conduct a gay wedding. These gay leaders have no idea how integral marriage is to the theology of many religious persons in the United States and elsewhere.

Time for some self-disclosure. I was formerly the chaplain of a conservative Christian college. I know the religious right fairly well. For many Christians, it's not just the sanctity of marriage colliding with strictures against homosexuality. Marriage is a mirror that reflects the relationship that Christ has with the Church. And if this metaphorical marriage consecrates two men or two women, who gets impregnated with the Spirit of God? The religious objection is far deeper than simply maintaining the status quo. It subconsciously (and sometimes consciously) reaffirms the distinction between the sexes and the traditional subservience of one gender to the other.

Who can forget how gender-bound our understanding of marriage is? Think of the sentences that are forever wed to the wedding ceremony. "I now pronounce you man and wife" (i.e., master and property). "You may kiss the bride" (more preferential treatment for the groom). For the life of me, I do not comprehend why gay people, of all people, want to buy into this history. Call one another "husband" and "wife" if you choose, but notice how straight couples are beginning to abandon this language in favor of something more egalitarian. There are no gendered expectations in civil union; it skirts the sex-specific baggage of religious marriage. In my book, that's an improvement.

Time for some more self-disclosure. I'm black. And am I the only one to notice that black clergy stayed pretty much out of this struggle until gays won the legal right to use the *M*-word? In Massachusetts, the Black Ministerial Alliance did not make their voice heard until after the advisory ruling that said that civil union would not do. That was when they stood in opposition, and not a moment before. Those of us who are black and gay often feel that we have to choose which community we will call home. As the battle for the *M*-word escalates and as more black clergy speak out against same-sex marriage, I know of one black gay man who is feeling torn between two communities he loves and treasures.

Call me deluded, but I happen to believe that most of the black clergy who are rallying against same-sex marriage would give civil union a pass. We don't know if they would, though, because we haven't asked them. Instead, we cluck our tongues at these unsympathetic black leaders: don't they recognize prejudice when they see it? But maybe we're so blinded by our dogged pursuit of the *M*-word that we don't see there are other ways of securing equality for all.

So here's my pitch. Civil union won't work if it's only for gays and straights can get married. That's called segregation, and segregation is illegal in America. And I certainly am not opposed to marriage for all. I just happen to prefer civil union for all.

A straight woman asked me: what about straight people who want to say they're married? I asked her: who's stopping them? Gay couples have been using the *M*-word for quite some time now; we've not waited for the government to give us permission. No one is thrown in jail for saying they're married or civilly united or whatever they choose. Indeed, the champions of same-sex marriage infantilize gay couples by making us feel we are incomplete until Big Brother calls us married. Hogwash. And to those who accuse me of harboring internalized homophobia, I say: look in the mirror, sweetheart. I don't need the *M*-word; why do *you* need it?

What I *do* need that I don't have now are the 1,138 benefits that the federal government gives to straight married couples. (You do realize that all those fabulous couples who got married in Massachusetts since May 17, 2004, don't have these benefits, don't you?) I need it to be portable, so that it is recognized from state to state. And the idea that only marriage will give us this is laughable. Besides, there's portability and there's portability. Will the married gay couple from Boston be recognized as married in Baghdad?

Last bit of self-disclosure. I am a practicing Episcopalian. And while I live in Vermont, I've followed closely the story of the Rev. V. Gene Robinson, Episcopal bishop of the neighboring diocese of New Hampshire. Robinson was once asked for his take on gay marriage. "If gay and lesbian people are full citizens of the country and state in which they live, they should be accorded the same rights as other couples. I don't think it matters whether you call it marriage or civil union as long as the responsibilities and the benefits are the same." Now, what would a man who had a heterosexual marriage, fathered two children, divorced, joined his life to that of another gay man well over a decade ago, conducted many, many marriages as an Episcopal priest, signed many, many marriage licenses as a deputy of the state, counseled couples prior to marriage, in marriage, and before divorce, and now oversees the Episcopal church in New Hampshire: I mean, what would he know about marriage?

All the same, Robinson may concede more than I want to concede. I would not be content with civil union for gays and civil marriage for straights. It's all one or the other for me. So like Monty Hall (remember him?), I say: Let's make a deal. Make it civil union for all, and we'll drop our insistence for marriage. And if the other side won't settle for civil union, then I guess I'll have to settle for marriage.

But I really would prefer civil union for all. After all, we gay people created it. It's a cultural makeover not even *Queer Eye for the Straight Guy* could engineer. It's simple and elegant at the same time. It takes religion out of the picture. It's new and improved. So let's make it ubiquitous as well.

Like that little piece of scrap paper with the weird adhesive on its edge. Who would have thought in 1980 that the Post-it Note would become so common? I didn't. And who imagines today that civil union for all could become universal? I do.

Steve Swayne is an assistant professor of music at Dartmouth College. He writes extensively about gay civil rights. Some of his work can be found at www.indegayforum.org/authors/swayne/.

Freedom to Bury
Mattilda, a.k.a. Matt Bernstein Sycamore

The Next Bill Clinton?

The above heading appears on the July 2004 cover of *GQ* magazine. Inside, an article follows San Francisco Mayor Gavin Newsom to a promotional event where he shoots hoops (not guns!) with residents of the Bayview/ Hunter's Point district, just days after several nearby murders. The article fails to mention paramilitary-style police maneuvers in the Bayview just days later, during which strong-arm police tactics gave new meaning to the phrase, "Driving While Black." In the course of a weekend, police stopped over 600 motorists, mostly people of color—34 were arrested and 262 were ticketed, most for minor infractions.

The Bayview is the latest frontier in the San Francisco gentrification wars. The central core of San Francisco has become almost fully yuppified, and real estate profiteers are looking for new zones to "redevelop" with luxury loft properties. The Bayview, home to a large number of San Francisco's poor black residents, is perched right at the edge of the new biotech industry corridor, where San Francisco's elite hope that the next economic "miracle" will occur (biotech will be even better than dot-com!). Gavin Newsom, who got elected by promising to criminalize San Francisco's homeless, is only too happy to prepare new territories for "revitalization."

GQ, of course, wasn't necessarily interested in asking hard questions about the politics of San Francisco gentrification. Instead, they wanted to know whether Gavin Newsom, San Francisco newest big-money mayor, will be the next Democrat to carry "idealistic" values all the way to the White House. Newsom had already emerged from a narrow victory in San Francisco's mayoral election, to see his popularity ratings soar immediately after he directed city clerks to issue same-sex marriage licenses.

While Gavin Newsom's election was no surprise, his slim margin of victory blatantly revealed the existence of conflicting San Franciscos that rarely meet. I confess that I've spoken to only one person who expressed any intent to vote for Gavin Newsom, and that was someone I met on a phone-sex line. The beauty (and danger) of San Francisco is that if you have enough mobility, you can choose to interact only occasionally with people you hate.

The choice to escape is not available to many who grow up in San Francisco's poorest neighborhoods, though these same neighborhoods are now gentrification battlegrounds. Just before the police incursion into the Bayview, San Francisco police officers gunned down Camerrin Boyd, an unarmed, disabled 29-year-old black man, in front of a public housing development in the Western Addition. The area was once a thriving black neighborhood, but is now white yuppie territory, with islands of subsidized housing where black people live.

Though some poor people of color voted for Newsom, there is no question that his goal is their expulsion, removal, or murder to make way for higher property values. Matt Gonzalez led a formidable campaign to defeat Newsom's agenda, bringing together a coalition of progressives, leftists, hipsters (and a few slumlords), but he failed to defeat the guy whose father manages the $2 billion Getty family trust (yes, oil money takes you all the way to the top!). When a victorious Newsom immediately spoke about bridging the gap between two cities, everything could have exploded. Instead, Gonzalez, a supposed political outsider, demonstrated his insider skills, and echoed Newsom's rhetoric. Other than a small "funeral" at Newsom's inauguration, organized by Gay Shame, a radical queer activist group, few publicly challenged Newsom's rule. Even when news media exposed that city workers were paid to walk precincts for Newsom, Gay Shame was called "immature" for daring to confront *La* Newsom so early in his term.

When, three months after the election, Newsom pulled the ultimate risk-free political stunt and "legalized" gay marriage, throngs of gay people from across the country descended upon City Hall at all hours of the day and night, camping out, sharing snacks and wine, and toasting Gavin Newsom as the vanguard leader of gay civil rights. If Gay Shame organizers already felt marginalized for continuing to protest Newsom after his election, now we felt like pariahs. It was obvious to us that if gay-marriage proponents wanted real progress, they'd be fighting for the abolition of marriage (duh), and universal access to the services that marriage can sometimes help procure: housing, health care, citizenship, etc. Instead, gay-marriage proponents want to fundamentally redefine what it means to be queer, and erase decades of radical queer struggle in favor of a sanitized, "we're just like you" normalcy (with marriage as the central institution, hmm...sounds familiar). Just the fact that challenging the gay-marriage bandwagon became immediate heresy exposes the silencing agenda of gay-marriage proponents as they move steadily toward assimilation into the imperialist, bloodthirsty status quo.

For nonmainstream queers, these are dangerous times. Just two blocks from my apartment, a block of Polk Street known for street-hustling and speed-dealing has been transformed into the site of not one, not two, but four yuppie straight (or "mixed") bars—all replacing lower-end gay bars. My Place, a South of Market gay bar known for decades as a cruising hole, was shuttered by the Department of Alcoholic Beverage Control, sending shock waves through South of Market leather bars who now police their premises to root out sex deviants. As middle-class gay people of all political affiliations, ethnicities, and social backgrounds rush to tie the knot, they are discarding a queer identity that demands fundamental changes in the dominant culture, *not inclusion*.

Back in February 2003, Gavin Newsom's first gesture of goodwill to the "gay community" was to hold a lavish fundraiser for the LGBT Center, a blatant (and successful) attempt to pander to San Francisco's gay elite in order to bolster his looming mayoral campaign against several gay candidates. Gay Shame gathered to protest Newsom's closeted right-wing agenda and to call attention to the hypocrisy of the Center for welcoming Newsom's dirty money instead of taking a stand against his blatantly racist and classist politics.

We found out about the event at the last minute, and therefore had little time to plan much more than a banner drop and a flyer, though one flourish involved handing out hot pink bags of garbage to smiling patrons (the event was called "Hot Pink." Attendees, thinking perhaps we were part of the festivities, even agreed to pose for pictures while holding the delicately arranged trash. In spite of the tame nature of our protest, police officers, called by "our" Center, began to bash us as soon as they escorted Newsom inside. One officer hit a Gay Shame demonstrator in the face with his baton, shattering one of her teeth and bloodying her entire face. Four of us were arrested; one arrestee was put into a choke hold until he passed out.

The press loves blood, and the spectacle of the SFPD bashing queers outside of San Francisco's LGBT Center was not lost on local media. Police violence became a cover story in local gay papers and even arose in corporate newspapers, as well as on network news channels. With the arrests of antiwar protesters ten days later (as war on Iraq loomed), Gay Shame was unable to use this public outcry much to our advantage in indicting either the police or the Center. Neither Newsom nor the Center has ever made a statement condemning the police violence.

GQ neglected to mention that Bill Clinton actually flew out to San Francisco to campaign for Gavin Newsom. A friend and I stumbled upon press vans from every TV station in the city, and immediately telephoned everyone we knew, succeeding in amassing ten people to scream in Clinton's face. At such short notice, we couldn't think of chants more clever than RACIST or KILL BILL, but we did succeed in getting so close to Clinton that we could see the blank look in his eyes as he waved at us like we were fans. Gavin Newsom, who marched within the police contigent at Pride this year (for fear of a confrontation with Gay Shame), has not yet mastered the presidential gaze.

But let's get back to the original question about Bill Clinton. I confess that I actually voted for him. It was 1992, and though I was 19, I was not naïve enough to think that this would result in any social change. Instead, I bought the line that voting for someone as slimy and sickening as Clinton was still important, in order to "get Bush out." When Bill Clinton succeeded in dismantling welfare to an extent that Ronald Reagan and George Bush only dreamed of, I knew that I could never again vote for a lesser monster.

So let's reframe the original question: Will Gavin Newsom follow Bill Clinton's steps in order to hack away at social programs and dismantle systems of care? Undoubtedly.

Forget Feminism: Why Your Wife Should Take Your Name

Yes, the above is a cover heading from another national men's magazine. This time it's *Details*, December 2003. The article actually starts by mentioning that in August 2003, *The New York Times* "did something revolutionary" by opening its "Vows" section with the faces of smiling gay couples. The article, however, does not answer the burning question from the cover.

When 80-somethings Del Martin and Phyllis Lyon became the first smiling gay couple to marry in honor of Gavin Newsom, a chorus of oohs and ahhs erupted from liberal bedsides across the nation. As spokesmodels for gay (and lesbian!) marriage, Martin and Lyon, old enough to be grannies, (or even great-grannies!) exuded safety, and set off the avalanche of voices who proclaimed Gavin Newsom as the savior of gay civil rights.

Though Martin and Lyon have never been radicals, there is no doubt that by starting The Daughters of Bilitis, the first U.S. lesbian rights organization, in 1955, they inspired generations of queers with their work. This makes it all the more embarrassing that they are jubilantly serving as the poster children for a straight, ruling-class man almost 50 years their junior, whose first gesture for "gay rights" involved bashing queers.

Soon after Gavin Newsom's marriage stunt, a forum took place to thank "Saint Newsom" for his hard work (the Sisters of Perpetual Indulgence, a drag troupe who dress up as nuns, later performed a canonization ceremony at their annual Easter celebration). The gay press was uniformly fawning. Even more embarrassing was a cover series on gay marriage in the March 17, 2004 issue of the *San Francisco Bay Guardian*, San Francisco's progressive weekly. The subheading of *Bay Guardian* editor Tim Redmond's article read, "Newsom, Gay Marriage, and the Politics of the Revolutionary Gesture." In the article, Redmond compares Gavin Newsom's decision to direct city officials to grant same-sex marriage licenses with "AIDS activists who crashed meetings to demand action [and] pacifists who tried to shut down the war machine." At the time of Redmond's article, AIDS services were being gutted due to a state budget that slashed health care to the most vulnerable, and Newsom had made no attempt to save these services. Nor has Newsom ever made any statement condemning the U.S. war in Iraq; in a city overwhelmingly against the war, we can only assume that Newsom's silence means he supports it.

Newsom's marriage charade is anything but a "revolutionary gesture." It's a risk-free giveback to the gays who got him elected, and a ploy by a power-hungry, ruling-class politician to get national attention. The rush by the straight left to jump headfirst onto the marriage bandwagon exposes a lack of understanding about progressive or radical queer politics, and even a lack of commitment to left "values." Marriage is still a central institution of patriarchy, right?

The fight between promarriage and antimarriage queers is not a disagreement between two segments of a "community," but a fight over the fundamental nature of queer struggle. When Newsom weighed in on one side, he gained not only the loyalty of assimilationist gays, but the support of liberals across the sex-and-gender spectrum. As former foes of Newsom capitulate to this newfound "unity," resistance can seem all the more futile.

Gay Shame has struggled to respond to the shifting political allegiances in San Francisco. We made a flyer proclaiming, GAY SHAME OPPOSES MARRIAGE IN ANY FORM. We also wrote an op-ed in one of San Francisco gay papers, the *San Francisco Bay Times*. Our latest effort is a sticker that imitates the ubiquitous red, white, and blue heart-shaped "Freedom to Marry" sticker. Our sticker proclaims, "We All Deserve the FREEDOM TO BURY," and continues, "How many Iraqis were murdered while you were getting married?" These stickers are hastily removed by angry gays.

The level to which gay marriage proponents will go to obscure queer antimarriage messages was especially evident when the *Bay Area Reporter* (*BAR*) ran a cover photo of a banner hanging from the LGBT Center, which originally thanked Newsom for his "Leadership, Courage and Commitment to Equality," but had been covered with dripping red paint. The *BAR* failed to address this obvious critique of Newsom's gay marriage, instead choosing to quote Center Director Thom Lynch as saying, "it shows that even in San Francisco, we can be attacked."

It is no coincidence that queers who oppose gay marriage are shut out of the picture, since we expose the gay-marriage "movement" as a grab for privilege, rather than a civil rights issue. While not all gay-marriage proponents may want the freedom to slaughter Iraqis, the gay-marriage "debate" allows straight, white, male ruling-class politicians like Newsom, George Bush, and John Kerry to fight over a fake issue while the real goods stay in their pasty palms, and the U.S. government bombs away. While not all gay-marriage proponents may advocate rampant police brutality against people of color, their blind support for Newsom allows him to go ahead with his real agenda: the displacement of anyone who gets in the way of property development. And while not all proponents of gay marriage may favor a rabidly assimilationist gay identity, their prioritization of gay marriage as the central issue for queer struggle narrows the options for everyone else.

Mattilda, a.k.a. Matt Bernstein Sycamore, is the editor of That's Revolting! Queer Strategies for Resisting Assimilation, *the author of* Pulling Taffy, *and the editor of* Dangerous Families: Queer Writing on Surviving *and* Tricks and Treats: Sex Workers Write About Their Clients. *Mattilda is an instigator of Gay Shame: A Virus in the System, a radical queer activist group that fights the monster of assimilation. Visit* www.mattbernsteinsycamore.com.

tranny punk sell-out
zak szymanski

It's June 2003, a panel of black-robed white men and a coupl'a token-somethin-somethins just declared that ass-fucking is as all-American as gettin high, and there is great rejoicing.

Here, anyway. Other places they're calling some of the biggest saints sinful; in the woods of Blah-Blah-ville, a squinty Christian is pilfering pennies from old ladies and sayin he'll pray for me.

We're a threat to their rubber stamped rubbers-damp smug-fuck. Hetero-sex makes you holy despite your own damned self, but this supreme court ruling puts the bible in blowjobs, makes middle-fat-merica have to work harder.

The Castro is packed with rows of hairy butt-jammers in peephole briefs and leather mommies with their bois in chains but the evening news will be all mock turtleneck lesbians reciting the constitution. In comes the bitch-fem couple with the wedding dress and tux, not too butch to be a babe and not done up enough to be a dyke, and they're screaming their nuptials into the rally as if good old fashioned anal tissue ripping has anything to do with their registered silverware.

I'm so sick of these media images of gays; it's no wonder the public hates us. Who wants to associate sex with a mango-faced girdle-rider? I want fair representation, show those Mardi Gras frat boys doing Jell-O-shots from genitals that we're just as hot and perverted and rancid and shameless as they are.

Months pass, it's winter, the season when it becomes my duty to save a lost soul from the hopelessness she lives by. She's dark out, and inside, a fierce ethnic loyalty to wherever in Europe her dad sold muffins…and she's just getting out of a battle-kissed home-wreck, or she is one, or she sees what I need to possess.

It's February 12, 2004, and news breaks around the globe that San Francisco has begun performing same-sex marriages.

Within the hour, it is announced that long-term partners Barbie and Ken have broken up.

In February 2004 Mayor Gavin Newsom created civil unrest—and broke the law—when he allowed hundreds of gay and lesbian couples to camp out overnight at City Hall, a direct violation to his own anti-homelessness Propositions N and M.

Hundreds of workers give up the next Monday to make marriages happen before the court says no more.

My own morning starts with alarm-bytes of song I try to hum in sleep-cycle until the cheese-rock refrain. Hit snooze before the neighbors can laugh and make me live my worst nightmare: to be known as "adult contemporary."

Forget to take antidepressant again, although that doesn't belong here yet because it's not on the radar. How does one chronologize forgetting? Put order to absence? This comes later when it's realized, but really it comes now when it isn't.

Stagger downward to see there's 30 minutes to get to the dermatologist. My gender illness means I'm always at the doctor—even if I'm just sick of the recurring pus-pouch where my man-oil shots collect—so I leash the dog, run downstairs, let him pee on his feet, turn and run back up, lock the door, and run to the subway, where all the ticket machines are broken and there is nobody sitting in the glass help-me box. I jump the turnstile. Escalators are moving the wrong way again, as if the people getting off the damn train need to make it to the exit before I need to make it to the closing doors. I miss the train, wait six minutes, arrive at Powell Street and the man with the NO ILLEGAL SEX sign is in his regular spot, clocking all the sinners.

"One man, one woman," he yells after me on his bullhorn, thinking I'm a loose teenage boy on the prowl. "No sex before marriage, no sloppy seconds."

Skin doc keeps me waiting for an hour, then fits me into a 3-minute sermon on how things go bad and get worse when I touch them.

"Stop picking," he scolds. "I'm going to inject you. Hold still."

It ain't nothing, that 25-gauge tiny needle, but I'm convinced he didn't hit the right spot, and he leaves me alone with my acne, frustration, and kleptomania. I pocket the vial of his zit-potion, rummage around for syringes, and take off, then spend the rest of the afternoon injecting my boil again and again like a benzoyl peroxide addict turned hardcore.

Then it's onto my plastic surgery appointment where I learn that boy nipples are different, there's a whole mathematical formula to position them.

"How many do you want?" jokes Doctor Rob, and I say six across, so my lovers can milk me like a cow. You know in a few years you're gonna have people asking for horns and saying they're goats trapped in people bodies, I tell him. "That means we'll be removing horns," he says. "And getting sued for putting horns on heads."

My pecs are healing nicely after surgery and this is the final touch, nipples attached through two separate grafts and areolas tattooed with what looks like a blow torch. I suck in my bloated tummy and sit high on my ass to make my legs tiny when they drape above Rob's working posture, all to be how America wants me when I'm sodomizing women into loving me back. If I wanted to, I could marry anyone. Just a flick of a consonant and I dissolve.

Heterosexual marriage is so sacred that my lover can only leave hers on Wednesdays, where she waits for me in the sunlight and I smolder.

So, says her stare. And *so* I say back and it's worth all the violence in heaven, this red sullen grog. Pelvis seeping through the cracks of my face, suspects tunneling through the pitfalls of her groin.

She's face down, knees grinding broken vows on church steps. We're on blank worship-wood, her spine to cold prayer bench, contrasting the hot drops my wrist wrings from inside her.

And who says I can't have her,
lady of unfastened eyes
salt mouthed mirror
where she stings
first asks later

when her grip stamps
my mind with her hips
scuffing mine
a thousand times harder
than boyhood to bone.

I miss her hourly, but I can't cry these days, not since I upped my T-dose and went from mess to self-made man-thing.

Or so I'm telling her and myself just minutes after I've pissed my face off on the steps of City Hall: a prom dress, hip hop spousal garb, a stranger who brought soup in the rain. The revolution of rose petals is here and I've realized: I'm not anti-gay-marriage.

I'm anti-gay-marriage-spokespeople.

zak szymanski spent several consecutive days at San Francisco's City Hall during the marriage revolt, launching a website of photographs (www.authenti-city.com) that was circulated around the globe, and a video that premiered at the SF International LGBT Film Fest in June. When not earning a buck as a journalist, he is a creative writer.

In Between, Again
Cecilia Tan

Oh my goodness, what's a partnered bisexual to do these days? We thought we were being so progressive and forward-thinking when my partner and I refused to bow to family pressures to get married. I mean, just because I'm biologically female and he's biologically male (psychologically we are a whole 'nother story, of course), we thought we were being so radical by insisting that we wouldn't live under a fake-ass social convention just to make other people happy.

What we did do was buy a house together and have a big "house warming party" so that we could still get all the gifts. We bought a house in Cambridge, Massachusetts actually, where you find liberated sexuality activists debating literature in coffeehouses with left-wing political science professors all the time. We have ethnic diversity and curbside recycling, and so few republicans that in most elections that party doesn't even field a candidate. We love living here.

And on an early summer night recently, people lined up outside Cambridge City Hall waiting for midnight, when marriage licenses would be issued for the first time in Massachusetts history to same-sex couples. The Pride Parade in Boston a few weeks later featured many vehicles with "Just Married" signs, and more cans than our recycling center. I love it. It's touching. One couple, both in tuxedos, who had been in that midnight line at Cambridge City Hall, carried a sign that read "49 Years Together — Finally Married!" I cried when I saw it.

Believe me — getting the right to marry is one of the biggest steps forward in "same-sex lib" in my lifetime. I am all for it.

But, geez, guys and gals, did you stop to think about the pressure you're putting on us unmarrieds of all kinds? Here poor Marshall Miller and Dorian Solot finally get the Alternatives to Marriage Project off the ground, and the next thing you know, a thousand phones are ringing in a thousand bisexuals' homes, as parental voices cajole, "So, what's your excuse now?" You can hear it, can't you? "Those nice lesbians down the street just had the most beautiful ceremony with a white horse-drawn carriage and an open bar. Why can't you?"

And how embarrassing is it to realize that all our carefully constructed opinions about how marriage is a meaningless (to us) social convention that perpetuates the patriarchy, which were formerly so progressive, are now so...twentieth century? Marriage among sexual outlaws is now hip! Holy double bouquet, Batman!

It is back to square one for queer unmarrieds now, as far as explaining to our families why we've made the life choices we've made. It's that or give in, just to get the gifts.

Cecilia Tan is the author of Black Feathers, The Velderet, *and* Telepaths Don't Need Safewords. *She is a bisexual S/M switch with transgender tendencies who needed to combine science fiction with her erotica in order to get all her creative needs met. She is the founder/editor of Circlet Press, Inc. Find out more at www.ceciliatan.com.*

Untying the Knot
Tristan Taormino

"Dick's daughter sold out to help Dick run again." That was the tagline of a series of Internet ads launched by the Equality Campaign to target Vice President Dick Cheney's lesbian daughter, Mary Cheney. With simple stick figure images, the animated ads tell the story of how Mary Cheney came out, recruited gay, lesbian, bisexual, and transgender voters for George W. and her father in 2000, and continues to be a key, paid figure in their re-election campaign—all this despite the fact that her dad and his buddy want to make her and her partner second-class citizens. If you're queer, chances are you've got a complicated relationship with your parents, or at least it was temporarily complicated when you came out. Some gays are estranged from their parents, others are tolerated but not embraced, and still others have wonderful relationships. But what if your parents had the power to effect real change on a national level that touched you personally? That's why many of us cannot imagine how a daughter not only stands by her dad but actually supports him when his party and his administration want to deny her basic rights simply because of who she is and who she loves.

"Marriage in the United States shall consist only of the union of a man and a woman. Neither this Constitution, nor the constitution of any state, shall be construed to require that marriage or the legal incidents thereof be conferred upon any union other than the union of a man and a woman," says the text of the proposed Federal Marriage Amendment. It's a testament to the LGBT civil rights movement that we continue to be a prime target of the right wing; our visibility, activism, and progress have made us a true threat. The fact that they're freaking out at all is a small victory, but the war is far from over. Oh, and speaking of war, isn't it convenient that Republicans are whipping Americans into a frenzy over same-sex marriage, making it the hot-button issue of the election, so they can avoid addressing the economy, education, Medicare, and oh, that nasty little disaster called the war in Iraq?

Once again right-wingers are better organized than their lefty counterparts, mobilizing anti-LGBT groups to bombard senators with emails, phone calls, and letters encouraging them to vote for the FMA. (Pick up the phone or log on, people.) In another "you don't even want our money?" moment, a study by the Congressional Budget Office concluded that gay marriage would be worth $1 billion a year to the United States economy, but Republicans could care less. The right has swung into action, but what it has not done is make any compelling argument against same-sex marriage. Like a traditional yet out-of-touch mother of the bride, the conservative agenda has given us:

Something old: The Bible condemns homosexuality, and God does not believe in queer nuptials.

Something new: The FMA introduces hate and discrimination into a document that is supposed to be about rights.

Something borrowed: More moderate Republicans, as well as plenty of Democrats—shame on you, John Kerry—support LGBT civil unions. Separate-but-equal, gee, that sounds familiar.

Something blue (as in out of the blue): Pundits argue that if same-sex marriage is legalized, the floodgates will be open to bigamy, polygamy, incest, bestiality, you name it. It will be the end of marriage as we know it.

Well, that last part—about the end of marriage as we know it—is not far off. Conservatives are trying to hang on for dear life to this pretty idea of a heterosexual two-parent nuclear family, which is a true dying breed. They are attempting to give marriage this mythic status, one we know is totally false. If we stick to the headlines, marriage is the territory of reality-show weddings, talk-show paternity tests, cheating, separation, divorce, custody battles, domestic abuse, and murder. Less cynically put, marriage is not the '50s archetype anymore; the American family has evolved into a diverse picture of single-parent households, kids with two moms or two dads, stepparents and half-siblings, and the list goes on.

Queer Nation raised my baby dyke ass, feeding me direct-action tactics and clothing me with "Assimilate my fist" stickers in the early '90s. Yet I still cannot get behind the argument that no self-respecting queer person should want to marry because marriage is a patriarchal, heterosexual institution that we should neither support nor subscribe to. First, I can be in favor of the right for other queer people to marry but make the personal choice not to. Second, marriage does not have to be patriarchal or heterosexual, and it won't be once we're through with it. It'll have the most fabulous *Queer Eye* makeover yet. When we marry, we don't have to simply mimic the hetero-nuclear family. By being queer, we fuck up marriage to begin with, we redefine it, we challenge it, we move it forward, something you're not going to read a lot about in the Human Rights Campaign literature. I do not have to be a monogamous, gender-appropriate, conformist lesbian Stepford wife just because I walk down the aisle in a white dress and vow in front of friends, family, and the universe that I am committed to my genderqueer trannie boyfriend.

Even if the FMA is defeated, we still have to fight for same-sex marriage. I will fight for my right to marry because I'm a citizen who votes, pays taxes, and contributes to this country as much as any other citizen. I will fight for my right to marry because my relationship with my partner deserves the recognition, respect, and the 1,049 benefits that straight couples can get by going to City Hall today. I will fight for my right to marry because my gay father did not have that right. I will fight for my right to marry, and I will untie the old knots to free marriage from its conservative stranglehold.

Tristan Taormino is the author of True Lust: Adventures in Sex, Porn and Perversion, Down and Dirty Sex Secrets, *and* The Ultimate Guide to Anal Sex for Women. *She is series editor of the Lambda Literary Award–winning* Best Lesbian Erotica, *columnist for* The Village Voice, *and editrix of* www.Puckerup.com.

First published in *The Village Voice*, June 28, 2004. Reprinted by permission of the author.

The Story of an Almost Marriage
Robert Taylor

Dearly beloved:

We are gathered here today so I can tell you a story: about my almost marriage, the closest I was able to come, given the times and places in which I found myself.

For the picture to be complete, we need to go back in time and across an ocean to Vietnam. I spent a long and difficult year there, from the fall of 1966 to the fall of 1967, as a captain on the Intelligence staff of the Commanding General, U.S. Army Vietnam. Yes, I was one of the dreaded "gays in the military," carefully hidden away, protected by my pretending.

Soon after I arrived in Vietnam, I barely avoided yet one more lie-detector test — this the one that would have exposed and ruined me, sending me either back home in disgrace or off to prison as a threat to national security. As a result of this narrow escape, I spent that next year living in fear, not just of being killed, as we all were, but of being "discovered." From that second fear, I learned, there was no refuge.

Once I'd made it home, alive, I thought, *No more. If my survival means anything, it must be that I should start living the life I want, not some poor substitute dictated by the expectations of others.* My country had taught me to face down fear, and face it down I would.

I tried loving the first man I met, on a dark street in Georgetown in Washington, DC, where men went in those days, very late at night, to find each other. They, I'd been told, were looking for sex, first with one and then another. I was looking for love — that I hoped would last forever. The man I met there was, by some miracle, looking for the same.

"Hi, cutie," he said. "Let's go somewhere." And we did. We went to a park, where we lay under a tree on a blanket he kept always ready in the trunk of his car. A few nights later, we went to the apartment of a friend of his, when the friend wasn't home. Then, after my roommate got married and moved away, we went to my apartment and lived there for seven years.

Two of them were happy enough, four were spent on cruise control, and the last I spent gathering up the courage to leave. Much as I wanted the stability, the dailiness, the monogamy of our life together, I wanted it not to be with him. He was generous and loving, but he left my mind — and later my heart — untouched.

Most of all, I see now, I was becoming restless. I was feeling hemmed in by the propriety of the closeted life he believed we had to lead. ("No one must know," he insisted, though of course everyone knew.) This was the early '70s, and I'd had to watch from the sidelines as the Stonewall Revolution unfolded. Men like me, no longer afraid, were out there on the streets with their arms around each other, thumbing their noses at those who chose to mind.

I should be out there, I thought. *I should be right out there with them.* So I left. I moved across town to a tiny but wonderful apartment in the basement of a row house on Capitol Hill. And then, as soon as I was settled, I staged my own revolution. I told everyone — family, friends, co-workers — who I really was and the way I intended to live from then on.

"Take it or leave it," I said. Some took it; some left it. I didn't care. I had found the courage, at last, to break the bonds of fear and self-doubt that had held me prisoner for much too long, and I honest to god no longer cared. Most surprisingly of all, I felt no guilt — a great shock and disappointment, I have no doubt, to the generations of fundamentalist Protestants who produced me. But the guilt and shame they would have insisted upon somehow eluded me. All I felt was joy and pleasure at being free.

Not long afterward, I joined the Gay Activists' Alliance, where I found that sexual freedom was every bit as important as the political and personal kind. Fine with me. I leapt wholeheartedly into the wild and crazy bar scene and started having sex with everyone in sight. I danced and flirted and hopped from bed to bed, but my goal was the same as it had been on that dark street in Georgetown. I wasn't looking simply for naked bodies to enjoy and then replace. I was looking for love to last a lifetime.

On Gay Pride Day, in June of 1975, I was standing in a booth I'd helped build, handing out literature about GAA and its activities. I heard a deep voice say, "So how much is a kiss?" I turned. He was tall, strong shoulders, broad chest. Very masculine, very sexy. "I beg your pardon?" I said. He smiled. My knees went weak. "I said, how much is a kiss? Isn't that what you're here for?"

"Indeed not," I said. "We're changing the world here. Let me give you some information. Want to sign a petition?" He laughed. "Yeah, yeah," he said. "That may well be, but I still want to know: how much is a kiss?" "For you," I said, taking a break from changing the world, "absolutely free." And I kissed him.

Love at first sight? Love to last a lifetime? Romantic illusions, some would say. The truest truth I know, I would say. I loved Ted at that moment, and I love him still, almost 30 years later. Sure I love him more. I know him better. We've spent almost half our lives together, and during that time, I've learned a lot—what his hopes are, what makes him afraid, what makes him laugh, the part of him that's fragile, the part that somehow survived years of loneliness and misunderstanding. I know all of that now. But the seeds of everything were there at the beginning. I loved him from the second I laid eyes on him.

Would I have married him then, if that had been a possibility? In a heartbeat. But since it wasn't, we set about creating our own kind of marriage.

We agreed that, tempting as all those other naked bodies might be, we would love—and make love to—only each other. *Forsaking all others* was the only thing that made sense. Anything else would have been a distraction from what we were trying to build. That, at least, was the philosophical reasoning. I see now, however, that there was a far deeper truth: making love with Ted came to define for me what closeness and physical intimacy were all about. Once I'd had that experience, I was certain that nothing else could ever come close. During all the years we've been together, I've never had the occasion—or the desire—to test this theory, but in a way that only proves how true it is.

From the beginning, Ted and I combined all of our assets into one big pot—*for richer, for poorer*. No more his, no more mine, only ours. I couldn't help noticing that the part he was putting in was much larger than the part that had been "mine," but before long, all of that was immaterial. Everything we had was ours, and it was more than enough.

We bought a house. We bought rental property. We invested in stocks and bonds and mutual funds and gold and utilities and god only knows what all. That side of it was fine—productive and financially rewarding. The downside was that we had to spend enormous amounts of time and effort making sure that both of us were protected. That if something should happen to one of us, the other wouldn't lose any of this big pot we thought of as "ours." Had we been married in a legal sense, of course, those protections would have been automatic, and we wouldn't have had to worry. But we weren't, so we did have to worry.

For 20 years, neither of us had had any medical problems to concern us. Although friends all around us had been dying—young friends, too many to count—we were both fine, saved in a perverse way by that long-ago pledge of faithfulness. Then, suddenly, we learned what it meant to care for each other *in sickness and in health*. Out of nowhere, we discovered that Ted's arteries were almost completely clogged. In the space of four terrifying days, we went from an angiogram to see how much blockage there was through a weekend in intensive care to surgery at the crack of dawn on a Monday morning. (I say "we" because I was by his side, holding his hand, every minute he wasn't sleeping or being examined.)

While I sat in a waiting room, surrounded by family and friends, a team of surgeons created five bypasses around Ted's heart. They stopped his heart from beating, put him on a heart-lung machine, operated for six hours, took him off the heart-lung machine, and restarted his heart. That heart with which he had loved me so thoroughly and so well.

Though they were not required by law to recognize who I was or what this patient meant to me, though they would have been justified in holding me at arms' length as no more than an interested bystander, the staff at this hospital in Bangor, Maine, chose to be generous. They not only let me stay with him hour after hour, day after day, they also called me from the operating room three times to let me know how he was doing. And the nurse in the recovery room called to ask me to come there just as he was beginning to stir.

"I thought you'd like to be here when he wakes up," she said. Therefore, a few minutes later, when he opened his eyes, I was sitting beside him, holding his hand, smiling at him. Seeing my face, he says now, was the way he knew he was still alive.

So you see, I've had a marriage—a solid, sustaining, and thoroughly happy marriage—in every sense except for the "legal" one. I have spent most of my adult life with a wonderful and witty, strong and sexy man who has made everything possible for me. I have cared for him and been cared for by him. Laughed with him, cried with him, dreamed with him. He has *been* my life, and no piece of paper could possibly have made me love him more.

Even so, would I now, all these years later, stand with him in front of a gathering of those who mean the most to us and pledge to him—and to them—that I will continue to love him forever, *till death us do part*?

You bet your sweet life I would.

Robert Taylor is the author of two novels, The Innocent *and* All We Have Is Now, *and a collection of short stories and a novella, called* Revelation and Other Stories. *A new novel,* Whose Eye Is on Which Sparrow? *will be published in October 2004 by The Haworth Press.*

I Do
Richard Tayson

I bought the rings at R.J. White Jewelers
from the old man with cataracts
who handed me the black velvet tray,.
like a silver tureen reflecting black
orchids at the reception after
we'd kissed. I took
the tray and as I started to shake,
he told me to try one on for size,
then turned his back and blew
dust and dried rose petals
from the mantle. "Been in business
forty years," he said, rubbing
his finger over a smudged
mirror. So I chose the one
with tiny grooves etched
along the edge, I put it on
my ring finger, left hand — what
was I doing, this was not something
I could have planned for
or foretold, once done
it could never be cancelled.
"That's nice," he said, and told me
how he'd opened the shop in 1963,
same location, two hundred thirty dollars
to spare and a love of metals
that alchemized to liquid gold
under fire. "Back then
there weren't too many boys like you
buying rings, no sir. This was
before Stonewall, of course."
It had been years since I was called
a boy, and I thought how I was seven
the day in 1969 those men
in skirts and high heels stood up,
three blocks away, for the lives
of people like me who would one day
walk into a shop and buy a ring
for another man's finger. "You sure
this will fit him," I asked, looking
down at that perfect gold
circle, like a halo that would taste
of fire if I put it on my tongue
and swallowed. He patted my hand,
the way a grandmother would
and said, "If it doesn't, bring him in

and I'll serve the champagne I keep
chilled in back for special occasions."
He winked then, and a white poodle
appeared from where R.J.'s finger
pointed, as if the dog knew
those syllables of drink by heart,
and I supposed they'd been living there,
alone, since 1963, watching the years
go by like the parade passing
down Christopher each fourth
Sunday in June. *Let us not*
to the marriage of true minds
admit impediments, so I gave him
three hundred eighty-six dollars
and held the velvet case in my hand,
soft as my lover's palm, and went
to the Stonewall Bar to pay
my debt of gratitude with two
sips of gin and the feel
of names carved in the countertop:
Michael loves Robert,
Bill and Guillermo forever.
I started to get sentimental,
so I took the F train home and found
him on the couch in his underwear,
I held him for a long time, kissed
his lips and the room crowded close
around us, everyone we loved
took a seat, relatives alive
and dead, friends alive
and dead, everyone who had been
imprisoned for kissing in public,
the ones who were tortured
and had their tongues cut out,
the ones kept in boxes
the size of the body, the ones
tied to a fence and beaten
in the name of God. In front
of them all, I held the hand
of the man I loved
and said I wanted him in my life
for as long as I have my life.
His eyes welled up, and I tasted
salt in the corners of my mouth,
then I tasted his salt inside
my mouth as we
married each other
in front of the Van Wyck Expressway

at 6:15 on June 8th, a Tuesday
which will never repeat itself.

Richard Tayson's first book, The Apprentice of Fever, *won the Wick Poetry Prize. He teaches at Rutgers University, where he also directs the Writers at Rutgers reading series.*

First published in *Bloom* (Vol. 1, Issue 1), Winter 2004. Reprinted by permission of the author.

Assimilation
Dylan Vade

I believe in assimilation. Everyone should be queer.

Queer people have a lot to teach the world. We explore ourselves, our sexualities, our souls, our own bodies, and other people's bodies. We explore what it means to live and love in this world. Some of us live monogamous lives with one sweetheart. Some of us have several lovers—and live with all of them. Some of us have several lovers, live with none of them, and raise children with best friends. There are many different ways to be. That's beautiful.

Everyone can be queer. Everyone can explore and be intentional in their relations. That's a radical act, regardless if the relation is between three women and two transgender people, between an extended household, or between one woman and one man. Everyone can be queer. And, I want everyone to be queer. I want us all to see and make our world one of possibility and plenty in which there is space for everyone to truly be themselves, a world in which monogamy between two people is one among a million ways to live. Assimilation.

Assimilation the other direction doesn't sit so well with me. We are not the same as mainstream America. We are not like everyone else, with a tiny difference. Our difference is big.

That is my gut reaction to gay marriage. It's assimilation in the wrong direction.

The recent proliferation of gay marriages has also had quite an impact on my work. We've all heard the criticism that we need to be careful about how we allocate resources—we can't spend all of our energy and money working for a symbolic victory while there are many of us who have concrete needs like housing, shelter, food, work, health care, safe school and home environments, and more.

This criticism is for real. I'm an attorney at the Transgender Law Center. In the recent months, I've frequently heard "I'm really sorry, I don't have time right now, I'm working on marriage." Marriage has taken over. Is that what we want? Is this how we want all of us to spend all of our time?

And—is this how we want to spend our time at all? That question I hesitate to even ask. I want to be supportive of and rejoice with those thousands of people who are celebrating their partnerships. I also want to look at other options. Can we celebrate differently? Do we want to enter an institution that has historically and is presently harming women? Could we push to have domestic partnerships available everywhere and for everyone? How about replacing marriage with domestic partnership? Assimilation in the queer direction.

Practically speaking, this is possible. All of the rights and responsibilities of marriage are contractable—between people and/or between people and establishments. We could create a smorgasbord of rights and responsibilities that two, three, four, any number of people could contract. This would allow many more options to form relations—and to have those relations be protected legally.

I like expansion. I'm all for expanding how we do relations. I don't want to take away monogamous two-person relations. But—I do need more options. I need to see more role models of different ways to be. Yes—gay marriage might move us more in that direction—it could be the first in many opening expansive steps to come. But, it could also be an end point. I fear that once mainstream queers have gotten a victory, the less mainstream will be left behind—donations will stop, support will stop, the work will be marginalized. I fear that gay marriage will make the world less queer—and that makes me sad.

Dylan Vade is a queer transgender FTM-ish attorney and activist who co-founded and co-directs the Transgender Law Center in San Francisco. (His views here are his own and do not reflect those of the Transgender Law Center.) Dylan believes there are infinite ways to be, an infinite number of beautiful sparkly genders—a gender galaxy. He'd like to see the law recognize and protect the gender galaxy. If you want that too, please visit the Transgender Law Center (TLC) at www.transgenderlawcenter.org and People in Search of Safe Restrooms (PISSR) at www.pissr.org.

I'm (Not) Getting Married in the Morning
Jim Van Buskirk

On the morning of February 12, 2004, a friend called to tell me about California's first same-sex marriage, held at San Francisco City Hall. I was surprised to be learning about it from this man who'd been a founding member of the Mattachine Society in Los Angeles in the early 1950s, and now lived a quiet life in the suburbs of San Jose.

How perfect that Del Martin and Phyllis Lyon, leaders in the gay and the lesbian communities for decades, had been chosen to be the first couple to be legally married. I couldn't imagine a more appropriate pair to advance the cause for equal civil rights for gays, lesbians, bisexuals, and transgendered individuals. Nor a more appropriate date, two days before Valentine's Day, the most romantic day of the year, and the anniversary of their meeting over 50 years ago. How commendable and courageous of Gavin Newsom to confront California state law as his first act as mayor.

Suddenly the floodgates had opened, and couples were lining up to get married. The next afternoon, Friday the 13th, my friends Will and U.B. called, inviting me to come over and meet them as they stood in line for a 2:00 p.m. appointment to be married by Supervisor Aaron Peskin. I arrived at San Francisco City Hall to find it filled with a positive energy that was absolutely palpable. Couples of all ages, sizes, colors, shapes filled the rotunda with their friends, their children, flowers, and finery. Some pairs carefully dressed identically, some in considered high butch/femme, some dashed over in their street clothes. Everyone was jubilant. They were finally getting what they had always wanted. I was happy for them, sincerely. It was a momentous occasion, on many levels.

I quickly found my friends and held their eight-month-old daughter, Stassa, while they signed the papers. U.B.'s sister had brought a beautiful cake, other friends appeared with a bottle of chilled champagne. We all sped upstairs to Supervisor Peskin's office, where I relinquished Stassa long enough for her to be changed, and dressed in her wedding togs. Suddenly Aaron burst into the office.

"Don't look at the clock," he commanded. Of course we all did: it was exactly 2:00. "There's a hearing being convened right now, and at any moment we could be served an injunction to stop the proceedings." I had noticed the antimarriage demonstrators outside City Hall, but had paid little attention. Peskin's announcement dramatically heightened the urgency of this historic event.

Newly revised documents were quickly filled out and signed. When Aaron called for two witnesses, I was honored that Will and U.B. asked me to be one of them. I tried not to tremble as I signed my name on the form.

We dashed down the hall and slipped into the ornately carved Board of Supervisors' chambers where the simple ceremony was performed. I found myself choking up and fighting back tears, watching these two sturdy men look deeply into each others eyes, as Aaron pronounced them "spouses for life." Laughter, applause, and the flash of cameras punctuated the proclamation. As I blew my nose, in my head I heard the lyrics from *Sweet Charity*: "I love to cry at weddings. I walk into a chapel and get happily hysterical..."

Back into Aaron's offices the merriment continued over cake and toasts of champagne. "Are we supposed to take these back down to the office?" one of the new grooms innocently asked. After a flurry of confusion and contradictory information, it was determined that the forms must be taken downstairs and be filed immediately. U.B. set down his cake and champagne and flew out of the office. This was all so new that nobody knew exactly what the procedure was.

The giddy celebration continued. "When are *you* getting married?" someone asked me. My response surprised me. "I don't believe in marriage." It was true. I realized that this was not, had never been, my issue. I wondered if my reticence was connected to the relationship I was currently in. No, I realized that I felt positive about my relationship with Allen, that after weathering a series of storms, we were continuing to grow together.

Despite the fact that we had watched the battle for marriage being waged across the country—Vermont, Hawaii, Massachusetts—Allen and I had never discussed marriage as a personal option. When George W. Bush announced his support of a constitutional amendment to define marriage as between a man and a woman, I was appalled. I realized that I believed more in the sanctity of the U.S. Constitution than in the institution of marriage. If this ridiculous legislation becomes law, who, I wondered, will define the terms of what is a man and what is a woman? Many of my friends identify as transgender, transsexual, transvestite, intersex, or some other category indicating the fluidity of their sexual and/or gender identity. Their legal sex may or may not be the one they know themselves to be.

With all the attention suddenly being paid to marriage, my perverse nature was provoked. A few days later, walking to City Hall one afternoon with Allen to attend another wedding, I confessed that I was getting into the spirit of things. I was feeling left out. I wanted to be able to say we'd participated in an event as significant as Stonewall. I have an idea, I told him. He listened for my plan. I'll marry my best friend, and you can marry your best friend. The look on his face immediately made me realize my mistake. He had been half-expecting a romantic proposal of matrimony, and I was looking for another way to subvert the system. Fortunately for me, he found the humor in my misguided scheme, and held my hand as we strode across Civic Center Plaza.

When I first came out as a gay man, my very first thought was: *Terrific, now I won't have to get married, live in the suburbs, and raise children.* The models in my middle-class upbringing hadn't been terribly positive. Despite repeatedly singing the chorus of "Get Me to the Church on Time," I realized that I would never hear those bells.

I have been in a series of romantic relationships, some short-lived, others long-term. Sometimes we lived together, sometimes separately. Sometimes we pledged monogamy, other times not. I watched my friends (straight and gay and lesbian—and bisexual) to see how they were constructing their relationships. I took notes. I tried to determine what was working for them and what wasn't. I couldn't quite figure it out. Sure, I knew about the importance of communication and commitment. But there seemed to be something more, an elusive ingredient that cemented the whole thing. I wanted my relationships to be bigger, better, different than the ones I was seeing.

In the early 1990s I registered as a domestic partner with the man I'd been living with for seven years. We signed the forms at City Hall along with another couple, toasted our happiness with champagne, and enjoyed a lovely dinner together. We sent out announcements, and received supportive cards and generous presents. There's a photograph of the four of us, somewhere. A year later, I had left that man, realizing that something was wrong, not knowing what, or how to work on the relationship. Splitting up our belongings was arduous. We argued about the house, cars, artwork, and household items that we'd purchased together. Minor possessions suddenly became valuable and important. We finally engaged a mediator to help us disentangle. I returned to City Hall to fill out the form, "annulling" the partnership. Even now, when I remember that I no longer own a specific book or dish or CD, I quip that "I lost it in the divorce." I certainly was not going to do that again, I vowed. I realized how much I loved living alone. More unsuccessful relationships followed. "I'm not going to participate in gay marriage, until I know there is gay divorce," one friend cynically quipped.

In *Pride 04*, this year's glossy bloated book of text and photos celebrating a month of GLBT activities, a letter from Gavin Newsom proclaims, "I believe strongly that all couples deserve to be treated equally under the law." Say what? I thought this country was based on equal rights for all *individuals*. Now, here is another legal/social reinforcement of dyadic relationships. Count me out. I had hoped that in the struggle for equal rights, marriage might be shown to be an antediluvian institution to be demolished, not emulated. I don't believe anyone should be able to get married. Or rather, I believe that everyone—straight or gay or somewhere in between, male or female or somewhere in between, monogamous or open or somewhere in between— should have the legal right to a civil union. Then, if desired, they can arrange for a religious wedding to supplement or buttress it. Marriage, the public endorsement of a private relationship, is something that can be done at a religious site, in one's backyard, or not at all.

And what about domestic partnerships? Even the term confuses me, implying as it does cohabitation. I have friends who have been in committed relationships for decades who prefer not to live together. How are their relationships categorized? And what about the people involved in, or open to, more than one primary relationship? My experience is more complicated than binary systems: male/female, married/single, black/white, straight/gay, assimilationist/activist, essentialist/ constructionalist...

Some days I see all this focus on marriage as rather sad aping of an outmoded heterosexist, patriarchal system. Other days I see it as old-fashioned activism, civil disobedience, a militant march down a flower-filled aisle for much-deserved human rights. I understand the need for protection of property, children, health care, immigration, and other tangible aspects of partnership. Perhaps this is the way to do it. I don't think so. I am watching more and more of my friends buying houses, raising children, and now, getting married. I support them wholeheartedly, just as I support equal rights for everyone. Just don't expect me to get married. During this presidential campaign it appeared that the religious right had hoped this might be an important issue; it seems like no one really cares. Still, it remains disconcerting to hear how our lives and our loves are able to be discussed and debated as if we were animals in a zoo.

I had hoped writing this essay might change my thinking, might move me from my position of profound ambivalence to one of greater empathy or understanding. Even now when I'm asked whether I support gay marriage, I wholeheartedly reply: "I do."

But I'm not getting married in the morning.

Jim Van Buskirk is co-author with Susan Stryker of Gay by the Bay: A History of Queer Culture in the San Francisco Bay Area (*Chornicle Books, 1996*), *and his writing has appeared in a variety of anthologies, magazines, newspapers, radio programs, and websites. He works as Program Manager of the James C. Hormel Gay & Lesbian Center at the San Francisco Public Library.*

That's the date when gays and lesbians will finally be legally allowed to marry in one state in the union: Massachusetts. Unfortunately, conservative Republican Gov. Mitt Romney has dusted off a 1913 miscegenation law that will keep nonresidents from pulling a San Francisco and getting married in the Commonwealth.

Still, it's a banner day, one that we've been waiting for for a long time.

Ever since gays and lesbians started marrying in Canada, same-sex marriage has dominated our news. Article after article has analyzed the likelihood and the implications. There have been stories on the history of marriage, stories charting the history of happy gay couples, stories explaining why same-sex marriage would lead to the downfall of society.

Same-sex marriage has become one of the main issues of national debate. Gays, lesbians, bisexuals, and friendly citizens of all stripes have thrown themselves into trying to make marriage history. Lambda Legal has filed lawsuits. HRC has lobbied legislators. Activists across the country have raised awareness — and hell.

Same-sex marriage is vital to us — for the symbolism and for the 1,138 rights and benefits marriage conveys.

Same-sex marriage is an important thing.

But it's not the only thing.

Lost in our national obsession with same-sex marriage are other issues that are essential to gays and lesbians. Issues like gays in the military. Issues like the right to not be discriminated against in employment. Issues like the right to equal health care.

The conversation about marriage is important, but it shouldn't exclude other conversations. Not every gay man and lesbian will — or wants to — get married. Of course we need those rights.

But equality is not just about marriage.

It's about safety in one's home, job, city. It's about being able to walk down the street without being hit with a baseball bat just because you're in a gay neighborhood and look gay. It's about being able to display a picture of your partner on your desk without worrying whether you'll be fired. It's about not having to worry that a new doctor will refuse to see you because you're a lesbian. It's about not being harassed and bullied in the hallways of your school or nursing home.

Here's a list of where we are on some current issues, lest we forget:

Don't Ask, Don't Tell. The national conversation about gays in the military should be at its peak now, when our country is involved in a desperate war. Yet the media has been virtually silent on this issue. Perhaps it's because gays have been quietly retained since the U.S. invaded Afghanistan. The Servicemembers Legal Defense Network notes in its most recent annual survey that gay-related discharges have dropped by 40 percent in two years. In 2001, 1,273 service members were dismissed for being gay. In 2003, that number was 787. It seems that gays and lesbians are good enough to serve during times of war — just not in times of peace.

Health care. Health care is a major concern for gays and lesbians. Especially gays and lesbians living in Michigan. This week, the Michigan House passed bills that could allow doctors and other providers to refuse gays and lesbians treatment "on ethical, moral or religious grounds," according to the Associated Press. Nationally, those with HIV are waiting for the passing of the Early Treatment for HIV Act, which would release Medicaid funds for those with HIV who don't yet have full-blown AIDS. And the Institute of Medicine has called for increased research on lesbian health, as our health concerns still seem to be a mystery. That might be because lesbians often avoid doctors, worrying that their answer to the infernal question, "Are you on birth control? Why not?" will lead their doctors to follow the lead of those in Michigan and refuse to treat them.

Employment discrimination. The Employment Non-Discrimination Act has still not been passed, despite strong poll numbers indicating that Americans are in favor of gays and lesbians keeping their jobs.

If you're gay in Zanzibar, you can spend 25 years in jail. In Saudi Arabia, you can be put to death. Yes, we Americans tend to be pretty States-centric, but as gay and lesbian citizens of the world, we also have the obligation to help our brothers and sisters in other countries fight their way out of persecution. More than 70 countries have declared homosexuality illegal—in nine, being gay is equivalent to a death sentence. Ever been tempted to visit Jamaica? Don't—at least not with your partner. "Most Caribbean states have very tough antigay laws and a very dangerous climate, gay people are routinely beaten and murdered in places like Jamaica," activist Peter Tatchell told the *London Observer*.

If you like to travel, you had better start caring about laws like that.

The same-sex marriage movement—the forward momentum of it, the possibilities of it—is exciting because change is happening so rapidly. There are small battles and large ones across the country, and we seem to be steadily winning, even when there are setbacks.

But let us also keep attacking on the other equality fronts. We need all of our rights, not just some of them.

Jennifer Vanasco is an award-winning, syndicated columnist in Chicago. Email her at vanasco@chicagofreepress.com.

First published in the *Chicago Free Press*, 2004. Reprinted by permission of the author.

Love, Freedom, and Marriage
Carmen Vazquez

This is what I think freedom is:

Someday, I want to step into the austere and grand silent passion of an ancient Catholic church in Isola Madre in Northern Italy. I want to kneel and breathe in centuries of hope and prayer and incense. I want to light a candle to warm and illuminate cold stone walls, and I want to never, ever fear for what might happen to me when I step out from the shadows of that church dressed in the clothes of a man. That day I will be free.

Marriage will not give me that freedom, but it is not freedom that I seek in pursuit of the right to marry. I seek equality under the law and social and economic justice. Personal freedom and love had absolutely nothing to do with the origins of marriage in western culture. Economic necessity and the state's interest in defining family are what framed the institution of marriage. They still do.

Of course, that's not what the movies or what passes for "mainstream" culture wants us to believe. No matter what history tells us, western culture stubbornly insists on tethering love to marriage. We love therefore we marry. We stop loving, we get divorced.

Oh, but don't we wish it were that simple?

Marriage begins in the western world with patrilineal lines of inheritance. The caveman comes in from the cold and claims a woman as his own. Now he can know the flowering of his seed and who to leave his carcasses and weapons to. Be fruitful and multiply, said the white male god with flowing beard, and so we did. Romance was not yet invented, Cervantes and Shakespeare coming much later. When the first "marriage" occurred is in dispute—give or take a few millennia. There is, however, little disagreement over the continuing cultural norm asserted by most conservatives and even many a liberal that this arrangement—one man, one woman—can be the only legitimate expression of love in marriage.

Really? Even if we did all get going on marriage a mere 200,000, 20,000, or even 5,000 years ago, isn't it time we accepted a little change? And isn't it also time that *we learned to separate the cultural* (including religious) import of the alleged "sanctity" of marriage from its legal functions? Why is it we need a rabbi, minister, or priest to marry us, but only lawyers and judges can divorce us?

There is no question in my mind or heart that same-sex couples will eventually win the right to choose civil marriage. Equality under the law will eventually win out, as it must in any secular democracy. We aren't the first people to seek fuller equality on the battleground of marriage. But I suspect it isn't civil marriage or equality we're butting heads over. It is, in fact, the hearts and minds of average people that we are— both right and left on this issue—furiously trying to win over. It is culture, the "heart" thing, that makes us all tanglefoots. The cultural implications of acceptance and even of honor implied in this ancient tradition set us apart from those of our friends, family, and co-workers whose sentimental attachment to the communal ritual of marriage blinds them and many of us to the shortcomings and benefits of this wounded and evolving institution.

Feminists are wary. Marriage has not been a site of liberation for most women. It has been and remains essentially an economic arrangement, and for many an economic necessity, made sweeter by the dew of romance, and hopelessly distorted by the moral attributions of religion, but an economic arrangement nonetheless. Were it not so, who would need prenuptial agreements and why would we need all those Armani-clad divorce lawyers to dissolve a sacred, moral commitment?

As cultural phenomena, traditional (man + woman) marriage is actually less appealing than ever:

> The US Census Bureau's newest numbers show that married-couple households—the dominant cohort since the country's founding—have slipped from nearly 80 percent in the 1950s to just 50.7 percent today. That means that the U.S.'s 86 million single adults could soon define the new majority. Already, unmarrieds make up 42 percent of the workforce, 40 percent of homebuyers, 35 percent of voters and one of the most potent—if pluralistic—consumer groups on record.[1]

As an economic arrangement, however, marriage has become *more and more* engaging:

> The notion that married people lose out because they pay more taxes through the oft-cited marriage penalty is only partially true. Dual income, high earning marrieds and low-income couples sometimes suffer the penalty, but for slightly more than half of all spouses, marriage actually slashes tax bills, particularly for those with children. That means, for example, that mega-salary executives with stay at home wives get subsidies that single working mothers don't... Indeed, the elements are in place for a new form of social welfare. That's because what's occurring is a wealth transfer to the married class which imposes an array of unseen taxes on singles—no matter how many people they care for or are dependent on them.[2]

We need love. I do. I need Carlie's warmth, sweet and strong to hold me through the night. I need her breath on my neck, her laughter in my heart. I need her to show me the horizon. I want to be with her, in sickness and in health, for richer or poorer, all that. Have I asked her to marry me? Several times. She says no, not until it's real and maybe not then either. But marriage won't free us or keep us together, and love won't repair the inequities of an institution that can and must be retooled for a new era. Only the law can do that.

As we struggle to find common political ground to fend off the true abomination that writing discrimination into the U.S. Constitution via a "marriage" amendment would be, and as we put shoulders together in the battle to win the right to civil marriage, it behooves us to remember that we have as many or more allies among the heterosexual "unmarrieds" as we do among the married. We need those people on our side. We need them to join us in challenging the orthodoxy of the right and its insistence that culture, religion, and marriage are immutable forever. They are not. Marriage is a legal contract and an economic arrangement, but it is also a reflection of a people's culture. Culture reflects the spirit and imagination of people; and cultures, like people, change.

We need to place marriage within the context of an evolving cultural revolution in how Americans create family and kinship structures that meet the needs of a generation that is global in its outlook and economic structures, a generation that creates virtual communities of political and cultural affinity that are as meaningful as the people they might share a bed and a life with. Calls for a stand in defense of same-sex civil marriage must not come at the expense of a reasoned critique of the institution itself and its cultural and economic underpinnings. Changes in social and

[1] "UnMarried America," *Business Week*, October 20, 2003
[2] Ibid.

economic policies to alleviate the burden of single mothers, elder couples, and other people who need support to care for their families and loved ones are as critical to the future of our queer sisters and brothers as is the right to civil marriage for same-sex couples. Consenting to sexual pleasure outside of marriage without legal or economic recrimination is a human right, not a privilege. It's not one or the other. A progressive vision for our movement and generations of queers to come must embrace both personal freedom and civil equality.

The playwright Tony Kushner reminds us, "The world only spins forward. We will be citizens." Yes, Tony, but let us not forget that we came as immigrants to the shores of equality and illegal ones at that. If we choose to be citizens, let us be responsible ones. Let us also be bold and imaginative. Let us demand the right to equality in civil marriage and let us also demand justice for all the people marriage won't protect. Let us understand that we are redefining family in western civilization and that is good.

July 7, 2004
New York City, NY

Carmen Vazquez is Deputy Executive Director of Empire State Pride Agenda (Pride Agenda) and formerly the Lesbian, Gay, Bisexual & Transgender Community Center's Public Policy and Government Relations Director, a post she held from June 1994 through November 2003. She lives in Brooklyn, NY, with partner Carlie Steen.

An earlier version first appeared on *Lesbian.com*, January 2004. Reprinted by permission of the author.

Kai Venice

I was out of town when I heard that the mayor was performing marriage ceremonies for the San Francisco GLBT community. At first, I was thrilled. *Finally!* I thought. *We're getting what we want!* After having some time to get over my initial elation, and really think about the situation, I realized, *Fuck, they aren't really giving us anything at all!* Bush has the power to make it all go away anytime he wants to. The mayors performing the marriage ceremonies could always say (especially during an election year, when trying to garner as much of the GLBT vote as possible), "I did what I could for the community. It's the President's fault that it now means nothing."

I realized that we were still being discriminated against by the use of the term "gay/same-sex marriage." Why does it have to be labeled as "gay/same-sex"? When a Caucasian couple gets married, it isn't called a white wedding. When an African American couple decides to tie the knot, they don't have a black wedding.

It's analogous to how we separate and teach history. There is just History, and then there is African American History. I'm not denying the pain and suffering that Africans were subjected to before finally becoming Americans. However, isn't it a part of everyone's history? What about the attempted genocide of the Native Americans? Why isn't that included as a part of our history?

I just consider the specific naming of a group of certain people, when they are finally acknowledged and allowed to be included within human society as a whole, as a deliberate act of separatism and discrimination. It really disgusts me. True, the experience of some segments of our society has been crueler and more devastating. I am not lessening that the power of their native beliefs and culture played a great part in their continued survival. However, if they have now been accepted by American society, then that should just make them "Americans."

Therefore, when I hear the term "gay/same-sex marriage," it just leaves a bad taste in my mouth. The term does not include us; it's similar to throwing the GLBT community a bone, and trying to make us believe that it is the entirely whole and nutritious meal that the heterosexual community is receiving.

A great many people believe it to be a giant step in the right direction, not realizing how the terminology includes us, yet subtly discriminates against us at the same time. As long as the ceremony is called a "gay/same-sex marriage" rather than just a "marriage," it can always be used against us. If Bush or some future president decides to declare "gay/same-sex marriage" illegal, it will be a simple task. If it was just "marriage," then in order to stop it from happening, ALL marriages would have to be considered illegal.

Another big problem with using the term "gay/same-sex" is that it is discriminatory within our community. "Gay" is a label that is usually representative of men. Might this not cause a further rift between the gay and lesbian communities? There is also question of the transgender members of our community. How do they fit in this equation? Likewise, the bisexual segment of our community, might not they feel even further discriminated against? They are already experiencing a great deal of trouble being completely accepted by our community AND the straight community.

Our community needs to wake up and smell the bullshit—realizing that what is being given to us could just as easily be taken away. We need to fight for the right to get married, plain and simple. We need to realize that as long as our getting married is called a "gay/same-sex marriage," it isn't truly real. It is still a pseudomarriage, which could be easily abolished at any time.

It's clear that this issue is a great deal more complicated than we've allowed ourselves to think. It is time for everyone in our community to join forces and come up with some fresher strategies in order to get what we really want. What is truly necessary is for us to fix the problems that are in our own community, so that we can present a completely united front to those who will challenge us. Let them know that we are not happy with the bone we've been given and will not rest until we have received our full and unassailable right to just get married, without prejudice and discrimination.

Kai Venice has appeared online at www.iceflow.com/doorknobs/DOORBODY2.html. *Other stories are included in* Quickies 2 *and* The Gay Times Book of Short Stories: The Next Wave.

A Lot of Hooey on Same-Sex Marriage
Gays Didn't Wreck Marriage
Norah Vincent

Conservatives are all for personal responsibility except, of course, when it comes to their own failures. And they're always in favor of less federal intervention until it comes to their most cherished institutions. Which is why marriage gets them coming and going. It's a double bind: a failure for which they refuse to take responsibility and a cherished institution for which they are seeking special federal protection.

Hence what has been mentioned as a possible 28th amendment to the Constitution, the "federal marriage amendment," the preliminary text of which reads: "Marriage in the United States shall consist only of the union of a man and a woman. Neither this Constitution or the constitution of any state, nor state or federal law, shall be construed to require that marital status or the legal incidents thereof be conferred upon unmarried couples or groups."

I should make it clear from the beginning that I am a natural enemy of this absurd codicil; I am a lesbian who favors gay marriage. Regardless of your point of view, you've got to bear in mind that both conservatives and liberals admit that matrimony is a mess. Some studies have reported that half of all marriages end in divorce. The antiestablishment contingent of the left wing tends to lay the blame for this sorry state of affairs on the institution itself, claiming that marriage is failing largely because it is repressive of women. Conservatives, on the other hand, say that the push for legalization of same-sex marriage is the last straw. Witness the July 23 cover story in *National Review* magazine, which opines that "legal recognition of same-sex marriage...would in effect abolish the institution by collapsing the moral principles at its foundation."

Of course, in the real world the scenario is that Mr. and Mrs. Right are living in a very old house called marriage, one that is, as old houses often are, beset by termites that have all but worn away the foundation. Naturally, they're very upset about this. They fear for the loss of their home, a fear that is made exponentially worse by the fact that the gay couple next door is happily building a brand new house.

In their despair, the Rights have gotten it into their heads that their neighbors are responsible for the termites. Unable to admit to themselves that if they had taken better care of their house from the beginning, they wouldn't now be facing the loss of it, they project the blame onto poor Adam and Steve. Though any sensible person can see that the one has nothing to do with the other, the Rights have nonetheless begun circulating a petition to clean up the neighborhood. And, well, you get the idea.

But why, you may ask, are conservatives so set on this insensate amendment? The answer is at once simple and complex. American conservatism always has been plagued by an irrational distaste for homosexuality, a robust and righteous hate for the sin that cannot help extending to the sinner. And this has made it weil-nigh impossible for the right to see anything but corrosive evil in the gay lobby's push for equal access to heterosexual privilege.

There is no good, objective reason to believe that legalizing gay marriage would adversely affect traditional marriage, just as there is no good reason to believe that restricting marriage to a man and a woman would resuscitate an institution whose problems are human, not cultural. The sex of spouses has nothing to do with why relationships fail. They fail for lack of love or, more precisely, for lack of understanding what love is and what it entails over the long haul.

A constitutional amendment that purports to protect marriage will do nothing for the chronic human inability to love in sickness and in health. To think otherwise is naïve. Moreover, to blame a third party for one's conjugal failings is exceedingly uncharitable, not to mention obtuse. But then, that's the nature of blind prejudice.

Norah Vincent is a writer living in New York City.

First published in the *Los Angeles Times*, August 9, 2001. Reprinted by permission of the author.

Wedding Dae
Jeff Walsh

Cradled on a beach, Dae kisses me, says he wants to spend the rest of his life with me, and produces a ring. We kiss as he slides it on my finger.

It is silver, made of two interlocking pieces, with a lattice-like inlay that can spin around my finger.

He wants to be my husband.

He wants us to spend our lives together.

He wants us to be a happy couple.

Marriage was never my goal. Sure, I've signed the petitions. Worn the stickers at Pride. I may have even held a gay marriage poster at a rally or protest. But it was always a conceptual support. You have to be dating to think one level beyond it, and I never am.

Part of me also thought it was aping heterosexual patterns and that we might be better off redefining it on our own terms. *We are a couple today because we want to be together, not due to some oppressive legal commitment.* It always just seemed like an aching need for approval from society at large, that part of us still hated to be seen as different.

Don't get me wrong. I'm pretty boring and conventional. I'm never going to have a commitment ceremony in matching chaps with a thwacking spank on my partner's bare ass signifying my "I do." I'm not saying *you* can't, just that I'll probably end up being in a two-tux situation if it ever comes to that. But hey, vanilla is a spice, too.

I can't see past body image. Overweight since junior high, my life has always been on pause. My present is always tentative, and my future is a growing list of things to do once I'm thin. Some days I don't know it the two will ever meet. Friends and family always go out of their way with sentences that start, "If they can't accept you for who you are..." but the problem is me. I don't accept me. No need to blame others just yet. To quote Woody Allen paraphrasing both Groucho Marx and Freud's *Wit and Its Relation to the Unconscious*, "I would never want to belong to any club that would have someone like me for a member."

I'm not saying any of this is healthy, just that it's true.

I met Dae at a gay bar on Ko Samui, an island in Thailand, where he works. I was drinking a Coke, and he offered to give me a Thai massage upstairs, the ending of which, he assured me in a delightful almost-singing tone, would be "happy-happy-happy." I refused his offer, despite the fact that effeminate Asian *really* works for me. *Really.*

The massage was cheap and Dae was cute and in his mid-if-not-late 20s, but I figure a more explicit sexual menu and price list will appear upstairs. I am also tired and, despite Dae's second offer, I go home alone.

When I enter the bar a week or more later, Dae was at my side within seconds, thinking I had returned for a massage. He is absolutely stunning in his black mesh tank top, and our interaction is far more familiar. He asks if he can tell me a secret, and as he leans into my ear, the entire message is in tongues as I stroke his broad back and smooth skin.

This time, I was at the gay bar just killing time before a nearby Thai boxing match. "You need boy for massage, not boxing," he says, smiling suggestively, and steering things back around.

As we continue to make out at the bar, the catty chatter of the Thai boys is obviously about us as they wait for other *farang* (tourists) to show up. Dae insists I come back later that night for a massage, and I lie and tell him I might. I am leaving the island in two days and figure I won't see him again. We hold hands as he walks me back to the main street, and my kiss goodbye, and his kiss goodnight, is out of proportion with our history.

Something changed with the gay-marriage debate this time around. Maybe it was just me, but it seemed to be framed in an entire new light. It wasn't about us just trying to get tax breaks or society's approval. It was about recognizing love and commitment.

San Francisco had a palpable energy as the line of couples snaked around the entire block of City Hall, and people shed tears after getting recognition they had wanted for so long. I felt equal amounts of communal joy and personal emptiness as I witnessed history. The tides had turned, and with thousands of legally recognized couples on the books we were finally setting the agenda.

"The debate will become how to tear gay couples apart, how to demean and marginalize them, rather than an abstract debate about theories of marriage," Andrew Sullivan said on his website, and it perfectly encapsulated what went right this time.

After leaving Ko Samui, I went to Ko Pha-Ngan, the next island over and a half-hour boat ride away. The island is famous for its monthly Full Moon Party, a beach rave with lots of alcohol, drugs, people, and dancing. The night was mainly heterosexuality and alcohol until one skinny Thai boy dancing on a stool served as the party's gay beacon.

As I spin around dancing to the relentless house music, Dae stands directly behind me. I eventually turn around and everything stops when I see him there, the portrait of beauty. He is wearing a white sarong with occasional pink flowers, no shirt, and a white bikini. We start kissing immediately. The alcohol in my system doesn't allow for any of my usual pushback. We dance together all night and every time we kiss, tourists smile and take photos.

Cradled on the beach, away from the music, he says he wants to be my boyfriend. He says he loves me. He says that his sister married a *farang* and she is very happy. The more he talks, I wonder if he even is a prostitute. He could possibly just want someone to take him out of Thailand. Most of our discussion is about seeking clarity despite our language barrier. There is a longing in him that I can't explain, but maybe he just sees mine and wonders why we don't get rid of them together.

He says he will come to USA, I will go to work, he will take care of me, and we will be happy and married. At this point, he removes his ring and slides it onto my finger. He says it is for me to remember him, that we will be married, that I will come back for him. I tell him I will take it to remember him, but nothing more.

Doesn't he know that I couldn't bring him home with me if I wanted? That if he were a woman, it would be different? I could marry a female prostitute in Thailand, and the U.S. would accept her as my wife, but if I actually fell in love with a guy in Thailand, he would never get any recognition as a result? Not that I am considering any of this, but it is odd being asked for something that is too soon to exist (my love for Dae, my desire to marry him, him living in the U.S.).

We stare out at the sea, the boats, the moon, everything. We kiss every so often, and he continues telling me about the life we would have together. He wants to email me every day to tell me he loves me until I return for him. He wants to come back to my bungalow and spend the night with me. He wants to go to Bangkok with me. He wants to spend his life with me.

His words are as intoxicating as the rum I am coming down from. They are words I like hearing, if only the context were different. If I met Dae in San Francisco and he had just moved here, who knows what would happen? When I ask him why he wouldn't want to stay in Thailand, he says he loves it here, but just wants to be with me more. He said I could move here and be with him, too.

A slight drizzle starts to come down on us, and I question whether I have another 90 minutes in me, or however long it is until the sun rises. But I don't want to just abandon Dae.

He is fixated that we will be boyfriends, and married, and together. So, I finally tell him that he makes me happy, but I need to go to America and find someone to make me happy, and he needs to stay in Thailand and find someone to make him happy.

Dae opened his heart, offered me his love without a trace of hesitation, and defied me to refuse it. It was misguided, but inspiring.

I do need to find companionship, to see myself through someone else's eyes, to pursue these human connections that bring meaning to life, instead of my more pessimistic standoffish inclinations.

When Dae's face and body deflate, I know he understands. The rain comes down harder as we kiss some more. We hug tightly and neither makes any move to pull out of the embrace as I kiss the back of his neck.

I tell him I need to go. He just pouts but doesn't ask to come back with me. He just seems sad. We walk to the boat and kiss some more.

There are no more plans, no more talks of our life together.

We are kissing goodbye.

Jeff Walsh founded Oasis Magazine (www.oasismag.com), *an online magazine for queer and questioning youth, in 1995; is an ACLU plaintiff to ensure gay youth continue to have access to online resources; and is working on his first novel.*

Marriage: The Ultimate Perk
Patricia Nell Warren

For months now, the news has echoed with angry sound bites from enemies of same-sex marriage. Homosexual nuptials, it's being said, will tarnish the "sanctity" of heterosexual marriage.

Gosh, do these folks ever read the newspaper? Or a history book? Marriage has already been deeply de-sanctified by centuries of festering heterosexual pragmatism.

Admittedly my views are colored by personal experience. For 16 years I tried to be the perfect straight wife...gave it the old college try. But I never felt sacred—just more and more stifled and dishonest. When my homophobic spouse finally found out, he told me I was "sick." My first and only visit to a shrink revealed that he shared my spouse's opinion. So I ran for my life—divorce and coming out.

Apologists for "traditional values" seem to forget the real history of marriage. Christian civilization was built by royalty and nobility who saw marriage as dynastic. People wedded for titles, wealth, feudal estates, vassals, heirs—to link empires and win wars. Lifelong compulsory monogamy and chastity belts were invented to ensure that a husband passed his power only to his genetic offspring. While these marriages were sprinkled in holy water by ministers of "heaven," many of them were made in hell—as the tortured histories of blue-blooded families can tell us.

When the American Revolution separated church and state, it also separated marriage from church control. Marriage became basically a civil arrangement. Today, many American nuptials still start with church bells. But the "sanctity" of civil marriage is arguable, since it boils down to a list of heterosexual legalities that judges can rule on. These include inheritance rights, tax breaks, hospital visitation, pensions, joint custody—all things that homosexuals want too, and are told they can't have, in the name of "sanctity." Since when do the arbiters of "holiness" include probate courts, hospital receptionists, company pension plans, and the IRS?

Americans also rely on marriage for certain perks and conveniences. For minors, getting married is a way of evading parental custody. For embarrassed parents of a pregnant teen, shotgun marriage (hopefully) preserves the family honor. Marriage can get you free airline travel, a dental plan, diplomatic privileges, free housing on military bases, U.S. citizenship, the boss' daughter, and slave labor in the form of lots of kids. Marriage routinely enhances a celebrity career, even serves as cover for some CIA intelligence work. Repeated marriage-and-divorce allows some folks to cloak sexual adventure in legality. Years of living together in "common law" can equal marital status, or at least get you a nasty "palimony" lawsuit. To the man or woman who marries for nice things, marriage may equal prostitution.

Are these profane perks protected by state and federal law? Yes. Are they sacred? Hardly. It is amusing to think how many heterosexual Americans would scream bloody murder if they lost their "right" to this array of conveniences. Yet they would turn around and deny those same perks to gay people.

Closet marriages go beyond perk, into prevarication. "Closet" is how homosexuals historically conformed to the old feudal mandate. Nobody tries harder to make marriage work than a fag or dyke or bi who is hell-bent to pass! We have even pumped out children to be cannon fodder for feudalism. Indeed, the gay community's love of drag and theater may be instilled in us by long centuries of performing with that sword held to our throat. But an Oscar-winning act is still an act, no matter how brilliantly sequined in "sanctity" it might be.

Interestingly enough, homosexuals don't have a monopoly on the closet. Marriage is a good place for certain straights to hide too. Like the prostitute with heart of gold who hides her past by marrying Mr. Respectable with heart of gold. Or the "missing person" who hides in a marriage to start a new life, and cover the trail. Or the straight military man who grudgingly marries to advance his career, because the brass don't like to promote bachelors to admiral.

Marriage has no global agreement about what makes it "sacred." It's social silly-putty, squished into a thousand shapes by bias and blind belief. To the Israelites of the Ten Commandments, "sanctity" of marriage included polygamy, and a man's right to kill his wife and children if they got out of line. To feudal lords, the "sacredness" of a serf wedding required the bride to give her virginity to the lord. To the American colonists, a woman could work her way into marriage through contract labor or being an indentured servant. To Southern slave owners, marriage was out of bounds for black people. To my Irish Catholic forebears, the marriage knot required a priest's "authority." To my Protestant forebears, Catholic sacraments were "evil popery," so only a preacher's words could authorize the knot. But to bride and groom on the high seas, a ship captain's authority is "sacred" enough.

Some of my native American forebears had more sensible views. A couple stood before Creation and married each other on their own authority as human beings. They had no concept of being married by the power of some other person's religion or authority. "Nobody tells a Cheyenne what to do," my cousins used to say. If things went bad, all the aggrieved person had to do was put the partner's moccasins outside the tepee door...with the toes pointing away.

Can today's American marriage overcome its sorry history as a list of perks? Can a person today make it sacred and wonderful? Yes, I believe so. Real sacredness is infused into any relationship only by the two people themselves, be they straight or gay. They build a balance between their own self-respect and their respect for each other—and for their children, if they have them. If this sacredness is not deeply felt on the personal level, no law or sermon or tax break can put it there! Not even God and Goddess!

Not every heterosexual wants this kind of relationship. Not every homosexual does either. But those who do deserve the best that marriage can offer.

So yes...marriage in the '90s is darkly tarnished. But denying marriage to gay men, lesbians, bisexuals, and transgendered people will not untarnish it!

Heterosexuals have to take responsibility for the mess they've made of marriage. They were the ones who wanted to have marriage. They have spent 3,000 years making it a juggernaut of Judeo-Christian empire, politics, patriarchy, property, including their "right" to control of wife, children, and genetic heritage. Now, in the ultimate paradox, heterosexuals may actually need the help of us homosexuals, if they want to put some sacredness back in marriage.

Update:

The foregoing observations are even truer in 2004 than they were when I first wrote them in 1996.

American homophobes have sunk even lower, if that's possible, in their efforts to deny the right to marry to gay men, lesbians, bisexuals, and transgendered people. In the last couple of years, a number of conservative state legislatures have actually neglected attending to more urgent matters, like budgets, employment, education, and health care, so they could spend time "protecting" marriage from those awful homos. Our redoubtable President Bush has assured us that he will take precious time away from battling global terrorism and keeping America safe in order to try passing a constitutional amendment restricting marriage to one man and one woman.

Oh my. When will these people—who are forever invoking the "Christian history of marriage" in support of their antigay bigotry—get honest about the *real* roots of marriage in the West?

To start with, bible-beaters can stop invoking the "2000-year tradition of Christian marriage." Marriage as a legal entity is a recent development, even in the Christian world. It wasn't till 1563 and the Council of Trent that the Roman Catholic Church looked beyond merely blessing a marriage in church and started taking the position that the nuptial mass married you legally as well as sacramentally. The Protestant Reformation followed suit with their own definition of marriage legality across Britain and northern Europe. It took another couple hundred years, but finally many Europeans were ready to rebel against the stifling effects of both absolutist Catholic and absolutist Protestant control of all aspects of human life. When that moment finally came, dissenters saw the screaming need to yank the "legal"/"civil" aspect of marriage away from church control. In North America, colonies that were controlled by established churches—like Virginia—still required that all colonists be married in the Church of England. But the more liberal colonies started permitting civil marriages that didn't take place in church.

On November 9, 1791, as events in France built toward revolution, the people of that nation yanked marriage away from the Catholic Church, and instantly recreated it as an exclusively civil institution. Church control of marriage in France had become a festering issue—sore enough for the French people to put an end to it even before they got around to cutting the heads off their royalty a few months later.

In the brand-new United States, that very same year, our own Revolutionary founders realized that they too had to eliminate established religion in the U.S. if our newborn nation was to avoid the religious bloodbaths that had torn Europe apart for centuries. Our founders did this by adopting the Bill of Rights, making it illegal for the individual states to continue imposing state churches on their citizens...which most of them had done since colonial days. With the Bill of Rights in place, marriage in the U.S. instantly became a matter of civil law for all the states, not an issue of religious mandate by federal government. From that point on, it was the marriage license issued by local government that made a U.S. marriage "legal," not the words pronounced by a minister in any church.

With time, as other European countries threw off the yoke of absolutist churchism, they too adopted civil marriage. Ireland started allowing civil and non-Catholic marriages in 1845. England lightened up about that time, and began allowing civil (meaning non–Church of England) marriages to take place. Spain, under fascism, persisted in limiting legal marriage to Catholic nuptials until 1975, when General Franco finally died, whereupon that country finally became a democracy with religious freedom. Not only did the Spanish people disestablish the Catholic Church from its position of primacy in Spanish government and law, but they legalized civil marriage for all.

It's so ironic that both Europe and the United States share a history of revolution against absolutist monarchy and absolutist religion. Why? Because Europeans today are a lot clearer than many Americans are about the need to keep marriage as a legal institution open and democratic for all. They know they must do this if their countries are to avoid returning to the dark and bloody religious evils of centuries past. To that end, the Netherlands and Belgium now allow gays to legally marry. Germany's justice minister has vowed to introduce legislation to permit same-sex marriages before the end of the summer, overriding the objections of the country's powerful conservative lobby. Spain is following close behind, with domestic partnerships now recognized in at least one of her semiautonomous regions. Our neighbor to the north, Canada, shares in this greater European enlightenment—she too now opens legal marriage to gay people in several provinces.

As I write these words, I just returned from Canada, where I attended the wedding of two dear friends. They took a year to make all their arrangements with the Canadian government, and on the appointed day, family and friends of both men gathered in a Toronto reception hall where Harvey Brownstone, Canada's only openly gay judge, conducted the ceremony and supervised the public signing of papers. The two men approached their legal union with a sense of sacredness and responsibility that a lot of straight Americans in this country—especially celebrities who see marriage as a perk that allows them an overnight fling—could learn from.

We must hope that the people of the U.S. remember their real marriage roots just in time, and act to prevent the church absolutists from amending the Constitution and the Bill of Rights. Making gay marriage an election-year issue is just part of the bigots' bigger game plan. They want to re-establish total church control of the United States. They've made that very clear.

Religious-righters insist that keeping marriage limited to "one man, one woman" is a matter of protecting their own religious freedom. To them, the ultimate marriage perk is being able to force their personal definition of marriage on others. But their issue is a bogus one. Other religions don't even agree with them on what "marriage" is. For example, the world's most populous religion, Islam, defines marriage as "one man, four wives," provided he can provide for them adequately. As America's Muslim community grows, our courts have yet to consider whether our Muslim male citizens are denied religious freedom by being limited to one wife. Meanwhile American Baptists, Catholics, Methodists, etc., already enjoy the "religious freedom" of limiting marriage to one man and one woman in their own church ceremonies. But they have no right to force their own church's definition of marriage onto other Americans.

As Western democracy continues to evolve, the right of gay people to enjoy any civil liberties at all should automatically include the legal right to marry. To put it another way—freedom isn't a perk, and neither is marriage.

Patricia Nell Warren is author of The Front Runner, The Wild Man, *and other bestselling books, as well as a widely published commentator. Her publisher is Wildcat Press. Her other editorials are archived at* www.patricianellwarren.com. *Email her at* patriciawarren@aol.com.

No Wedding Song
Tom Wilson Weinberg

We had no wedding, no ceremony
No matrimony, we're just we
No invitations, no rice, no flowers
No bridal showers, we're we

    There wasn't a minister, rabbi or priest
    Who wanted to bless our connubial feast
    Back when we fell in love we hid it
    We mark our anniversary from the night we first did it

No rented chapel, no usher or bridesmaid
No movies or slides made, we're just we
No Mendelssohn marches, no long-stem roses
No family poses, we're we

    Our marriage began with a whole lot of lovin'
    But no one gave us a toaster oven
    We couldn't find our place in the holy scripture
    We couldn't find a paper to run our picture

No silver service, no hostess or hosting
No bright clever toasting, we're just we
No wedding cake cutting, no spun sugar topping
No champagne corks popping, we're we

    Just him and me
    We are we

Tom Wilson Weinberg is a composer/lyricist whose musicals include Ten Percent Revue, Get Used To It, *and* Bruhs and Gean. *More? Google "Tom Wilson Weinberg."*

From the musical *Ten Percent Review*, 1987. Words and music © 1987 Tom Wilson Weinberg/ASCAP. Reprinted by permission of the author.

Marriage—It's Not All about You!
Judy Wieder

Gay marriage is all about equal rights, not gay marriage. The decision to marry is a personal choice that all couples—gay or straight—have the right to make in private.

Today, this battle cry, "gay marriage," is the latest chapter in our struggle for equal rights, or it should be. It doesn't matter whether or not I want to get married any more than it matters whether or not I want to go into the military—hell, I'm a peacenik from the '60s! I don't think anyone should be in the military, but that's NOT the point. If someone else has the right to be in the military, then I want the right to be in the military! And I will fight for that right.

It's no different with marriage. I do have a very strong feeling about being married, and you may not guess it at all. But I feel very private and protective about it. However, the right to get married, that I'd protest about on Mars if it would help.

So don't forget our history lessons. Once women fought to have the equal right to vote. Today it seems ridiculous. Every American citizen has this right. Don't forget Voltaire declaring, "I disapprove of what you say, but I will defend to the death your right to say it." He was fighting for free speech, even if the words he was hearing weren't his thing.

We too shouldn't get dragged off subject. We mustn't spend all our time fussing with each other about whether or not marriage is a good thing for gay people. That's not anybody's business but the people who want—or don't want—to get married. What's more, a straight voting public on the fence will look over and say, "Well, gays don't even know if marriage is all that important to them either. Some don't even like the idea."

The point—the only point—is our RIGHT to get married. And that we absolutely must have.

Judy Wieder is currently the senior vice president and corporate editorial director for LPI Media, the parent company of The Advocate, Out, The Out Traveler, *and* HIV Plus *magazines, along with Alyson Publications, the oldest gay and lesbian book-publishing company in America. She is also editor in chief of Advocate Books, an imprint of Alyson.*

Hope Chest
Robert Williams

Webster's New World College Dictionary defines hope chest *as "a chest in which a young woman collects linen, clothing, etc. in anticipation of getting married."*

My oldest sister's hope chest was cedar, and smelled like a campfire. In it she kept clove cigarettes, love letters from her boyfriend, trashy paperbacks like *Flowers in the Attic*, *Playgirl* magazines, and old Chippendales calendars (the fireman with the salt-and-pepper pubic hair was a particular favorite of mine). I used to snoop in the chest regularly—it was never locked. I would scan the paperbacks for the sex scenes, giggling at the mention of a nipple, and stare, mouth agape, at the perfect penises in *Playgirl*; why is it that the men's dicks were always at a 45-degree angle? The advice column made my own groin tingle. Who knew there were so many ways to say penis: Cock, dick, sausage, pole?

When I wasn't snooping in the chest I was sitting on it. It was at the foot of her bed, directly across from her record player. The only record player in the house—it was here that I first sang along to Blondie, swooned over the sexually ambiguous Gary Numan, and marveled at the Fleetwood Mac album cover for *Rumours*. I mean, who wasn't enticed—gay or straight—by Mick Fleetwood in breeches; two black balls, like bowlers, dangling between his legs?

I was only 11 when my sister, who was four years older, got her hope chest, but I was acutely aware that this was some sort of rite of passage for her and her alone. That this was special. My mother and my sister talked about it for weeks, if not months, before she actually got it. The long and careful planning that went into the acquiring of the hope chest instilled in me a sense that this big cedar box was going to change my sister's life. My mother had a hope chest of her own as a young woman, and so she wanted to pass the tradition on to my sister. A couple of sacred items that had been in my mother's hope chest, a patchwork quilt of intricately laced swatches of fabric, a near complete set of Red Poppy Mikasa dishes, were then going to be placed into my sister's new hope chest, to use when she got married, because, of course, one day *she was* going to get married.

Like any rational child, I wanted what my sister got; if she got a Barbie Dream House then I wanted something of equal value, say, a *Star Wars* Cantina set (Okay, I did want the Barbie Dream House, too). But one day, when I was sitting on my sister's hope chest, most likely singing along to the *Grease* soundtrack, I began to wonder when and how I was going to be getting a hope chest of my own. Where I was to put my supplies for the future with my husband—because surely I was going to get married too, wasn't I? I fantasized about the things I would put in my chest, in preparation for my marriage: soft, colorful towels and bed sheets from Sears, a crockpot or fondue set, my own *Playgirl* magazines. I thought about what kind of stain I wanted the wood to be. I decided I didn't care too much for the red cedar of my sister's chest and that mine would be darker wood and lacquered shiny and smooth.

I told my sister about my plan.

"Boys don't get a hope chest, you dork! A hope chest is just for girls," she said, shooing me out of her room so she could call her boyfriend.

"So, I don't get anything?" I whined.

"Umm..." She could see the hurt in my scrunched-up face, "sure, you get...something else. Just not a hope chest."

But what would I be getting if it wasn't a hope chest? A hope duffel bag? A hope toolbox? I had been in the wedding of a cousin of mine—I was the ring bearer—adorable in my oversized blue velvet bow tie, my blond cowlick slicked down with my father's Dep Gel. At the rehearsal dinner all of the men in the wedding, including myself, received a buck knife, and the women, a charm bracelet. Maybe that was supposed to be my *hope buck knife*? Or was I supposed to put that buck knife into my hope duffel bag for when I got married?

When my own birthday was nearing, I figured I would ask my mother about my chances for a hope chest.

"Don't be silly. It's just for young ladies," she said, "to prepare them for marriage."

"Well, how do I prepare for marriage?" I asked.

"You," she hesitated, for even then my mother must have had some inkling that her son was different. "You get..."

Her eyes darted around the room, searching for something to say.

She continued: "You know, it takes a wife to make a house a home."

Ah. So that was it.

There would be no hope chest for me. No hope duffel bag. No place to put my buck knife. No hope chest. No hope. But was it that all boys had no hope? Or just gay boys like me?

It occurs to me now that this brief, awkward exchange with my mother has stayed with me, ingrained in my memory like a photograph, albeit somewhat warped like a Polaroid.

Why is it that men, and young men in particular, aren't really given containers in which to keep things? Except perhaps a toolbox; but of course this means that young men must be interested in tools. Women, on the other hand, from a very early age, are given jewelry boxes, purses, beach bags, a makeup bag. When women go shopping they are often given large, bright, showy shopping bags in which to carry their goods. Even Tupperware, with its intricately organized plastics, is (or was) targeted exclusively toward women. But men aren't supposed to get, or be interested in these things. These are domestic things–signs, signifiers, and preparations for domesticity and housekeeping and, most especially, marriage. And as my mother so eloquently put it: it takes a wife to make a house a home.

And so I grew up, came out to family and friends, co-workers. I've had serious boyfriends, and not-so-serious boyfriends. Marriage, though, was put away in the back of my mind. Marriage and me, the only son, was an issue that was avoided or ignored, by my family; yes, but it was also an idea that I rejected. It was hidden, much like the *Playgirls* and clove cigarettes in my sister's hope chest. I grew up thinking that there would be no marriage for me, and thus I shouldn't plan for it, shouldn't prepare for it, shouldn't be excited by it—why bother? So I wouldn't be getting a hope chest, no, but more than that I grew up to believe that my relationships weren't valid, or important—to my family and to me. Certainly they were not as important as my those of my two sisters,' because with them there was the potential for marriage.

Nothing reinforced this notion more than the following experience: five years ago, after I was accepted to graduate school in New York City, I almost had to turn it down; I didn't have enough money to both move across country and put a deposit down on an apartment. My sister, the one with the hope chest, called my father, long divorced from our mother and a blurry part of our lives, except for some weekends and holidays. She told my dad, who had rarely helped us out financially (except for the mandatory child support which had ended years before), that he needed to send me some money so I could get to New York City and fulfill my dream of becoming a writer. "You have to do it," she bullied him, "think of this as a wedding present for the wedding that's not going to happen. You paid for my wedding, and he's not going to be getting married."

My dad sent me a check.

And what of my sister's hope chest? Where is it now? Or, for that matter, where was it when she got married? It was nowhere to be found.

I asked her recently.

"Oh that old thing? I haven't thought of that in years. I don't know what happened to it. I think I sold it at a garage sale after I graduated from high school. I guess I didn't need it for my wedding, did I?" she said with a laugh.

Cut to today, where I've now had friends, gay friends, who have gotten married. I've known same-sex couples who have had commitment ceremonies. I have friends who have rejected the ceremony, but have exchanged rings. And I have friends who aren't interested in marriage or commitment at all, which is fine for them. I don't know what the future holds for me; I'm not even sure how I feel about it anymore. But I do know that with or without a hope chest, with or without marriage, my relationships are valid and important and deserve to be recognized.

Robert Williams was born in San Diego California and received his MFA in Fiction at Columbia University School of the Arts. He has been published in M2M: New Literary Fiction *and has a story forthcoming in the anthology* Fresh Men—New Voices in Gay Fiction, *selected by Edmund White. He lives in Brooklyn, NY, where he teaches English and writing. He has recently finished a story collection and is working on a novel.*

For Richer, for Poorer:
Same-Sex Couples and the Freedom to Marry as a Civil Right
Evan Wolfson

On the historic, horrific morning of September 11, 2001, John kissed his wife, Rosa, goodbye before heading to his job as an office-cleaner in the World Trade Center's North Tower. Rosa never heard from her husband again. After searching frantically for days, Rosa accepted the reality of his disappearance. She filed for a death certificate and arranged her husband's memorial service. Rosa received Workers' Compensation from the state and a small Social Security death benefit from the federal government. She contacted John's former employer, who arranged for receipt of his pension. Because John and Rosa had few assets, they had never seen the need for a will, nor did they have the financial means to hire a lawyer to prepare one. Nonetheless, John's assets, which included a small savings account, their home, and a car, were given to Rosa by law.

That same morning, Juan kissed Ryan, his partner of 21 years, goodbye and headed to his job as a file-clerk in that same North Tower. Like Rosa, Ryan never heard from Juan again. Ryan applied for Workers' Compensation and Social Security, but, unlike Rosa, he was told he was not eligible for those benefits because he was not Juan's legal spouse. Even though Juan and Ryan had taken some precautions to protect their commitment – such as registering as domestic partners, designating one another as beneficiaries on insurance policies, and executing health care proxies and powers of attorney – and even though Juan paid the same taxes as John, Ryan was not automatically entitled to any of the compensations given to Rosa. In addition to his emotional devastation, Ryan was financially devastated as well.[1]

Why did Rosa have an economic safety net, while Ryan did not? The answer can be summed up in two words: "*I do.*"

By getting married, John and Rosa gained access to critical legal protections and benefits for couples and their children that provided for them in their time of need. Married couples are entitled to literally hundreds of rights and protections that permeate their financial relationship, both in extraordinary circumstances such as the one mentioned above, or in everyday matters, like simply renting a car.

A 1996 government study found that there are at least 1,049 such protections, rights, and responsibilities that come with marriage under federal law alone. These protections include access to health care and medical decision making for a partner and children, parenting and immigration rights, inheritance, taxation, Social Security and other government benefits, rules for ending a relationship while protecting both parties, and the ability to pool resources to buy or transfer property without adverse tax consequences.

Juan and Ryan, however, like all same-sex couples, were denied the freedom to legally marry and were eligible only for the limited protections they could arrange privately.

Throughout the United States – regardless of how long they have been in a committed relationship, no matter how much they and their loved ones, often including children, need the protections that come with marriage – same-sex couples are denied the safety net that is automatically in place for couples like Rosa and John.

Exclusion from the protections that come with marriage, and the attendant social and legal inequality, affects all gay people, regardless of sex, race, religion, ethnicity,

[1] John, Rosa, Juan, and Ryan are representative of the experiences that real-life people, gay and nongay, have had in the aftermath of the September 11, 2001 terrorist attacks. For true and detailed stories of the hardships and discrimination experienced by gay 9/11 survivors, see *www.lambdalegal.org*.

or physical ability. Like with most civil injustices, marriage inequality falls particularly hard on those living on the margins: the poor, less educated, immigrants, the elderly, the ill, and those otherwise most vulnerable.

A landmark study of African American lesbian, gay, bisexual, and transgendered people in the U.S., *Say It Loud: I'm Black and I'm Proud*, released in March 2002 by the National Gay & Lesbian Task Force Policy Institute, found that marriage/family protections rank among the three most important issues facing LGBT communities of color alongside HIV/health care access and protection against violence. Ending the exclusion of same-sex couples from civil marriage would provide especially significant protections to LGBT people of color.

Although the struggle to win the freedom to marry is at least as much about love and equality as it is about law and economics, let's take a closer look at the important protections, benefits, and responsibilities that come with civil marriage.

Marriage Makes Life Together More Affordable

Marriage makes almost every aspect of a relationship less expensive. Without money, a lawyer, or any forethought, married couples receive the benefits of a complex set of legal rules that create default choices most couples would select anyway. Thus:

• Spouses are allowed to make life-saving decisions for each other without drafting powers of attorney or other complicated legal documents;
• Spouses presumptively inherit each others' estates without the need for intricate wills;
• Spouses may cohabitate in public housing units;
• Divorce laws protect both members of the relationship and minimize the power of one partner to keep the other in a situation of domestic violence;
• The spouse of a U.S. citizen may obtain residency in the United States without a long legal battle;
• Married people may adopt the children of their spouses easily and cheaply;
• Dependent health benefits are tax-free for a married couple, whereas an unmarried couple is taxed;
• By filing jointly, married couples in which one partner has a much higher income pay significantly less tax than similarly situated unmarried couples.

Ending sex discrimination in civil marriage is the only means of providing same-sex couples equal treatment by our own government. Beyond that, inclusion in civil marriage is an important step to assuring the benefits that the private sector offers to married people. Some of these are lower insurance rates; availability and lower cost of loans from banks; employer-sponsored events; free and reduced tuition for spouses of university employees; and family discounts.

Marriage Discrimination Harms Poor and Otherwise Disadvantaged Couples

Compared with the relatively cheap option of marriage, the creation of a legal web meant to simulate some of the protections of marriage is an expensive and time consuming project that simply cannot serve as a viable alternative for people of lesser means.

Working and middle-class same-sex couples who cannot afford legal services are therefore without the ability to properly plan for:

• Medical emergencies—Living wills and powers of attorney are intricate and expensive legal documents to draft. Doctors can leave same-sex partners out of critical decision-making processes without these documents. Marriage eliminates the need for any legal documents because spouses are not only allowed, but indeed expected, to make these important decisions for one another;

• Divorce—Unmarried partners cannot take advantage of the benefits of the forum of the divorce court to "wind-up" their relationships. Even without substantial assets to divide, issues of child support, childcare, and partner support arise that poor people will not have been able to plan for in advance through sophisticated legal mechanisms;

• The death of one partner—Even the lowest wage workers, if legally employed, pay to support the Social Security system. Unmarried partners, though, cannot receive the Social Security survivor benefits that married partners do, and may therefore be left without any means of supporting themselves.

In addition to important tax benefits, other governmentally provided rights and privileges are simply unavailable to same-sex couples because they are unable to marry, disproportionately impacting the poor. These include:

• Health care available to married couples—Allowing same-sex couples to marry would extend Medicare and Medicaid spousal benefits and would allow for the tax-free provision of benefits by an employer to the same-sex partner of an employee;

• Housing Benefits—Same-sex couples do not receive the protections of joint rental leases with automatic renewal rights. In highly competitive public housing slots, families can lose their homes.

• Immigration Benefits—A foreign-born national has a presumptive right to a green card when married to an American citizen or legal permanent resident. The spouse may then obtain a work permit and eventually become a U.S. citizen. Spouses of U.S. citizens and lawful permanent residents also face a far shorter waiting period. These spousal rights even trump the United States' ban on immigration for HIV-positive individuals. Same-sex partners are denied the family respect that otherwise governs immigration law.

• Social Security Benefits—No spousal benefits, including survivor benefits and disability benefits, are available to same-sex couples.

Marriage Discrimination Harms Children

Marriage protects the economic interests of children by providing an economic safety net to their families, and the kids themselves.

• The children have automatic and undisputed access to the resources, benefits, and entitlements of both parents.

• Married couples do not have to incur any expenses, legal or otherwise, to ensure that both parents have the right to make important medical decisions for their children in case of emergency.

• The children of legally married couples are automatically eligible for health benefits from both parents, as well as child support and visitation from both parents in the event of separation.

• If one of the parents in a marriage dies, the law provides financial security not only for the surviving spouse, but for the children as well, by ensuring eligibility to all appropriate entitlements, such as Social Security survivor benefits.

This economic safety net is critical for children in families of lesser means. However, the children of same-sex couples, whose marriages are unrecognized by law, do not have such a safety net. They suffer from their parents' lack of access to all the rights and entitlements that maximize their economic well-being. They are deprived of economic protection in case of death, disability, divorce, or other life-changing events. These disadvantages have a disproportionately high impact on children in families of lesser means. A 2000 report out of Stanford University surveyed the legal and economic landscape and concluded that because same-sex couples are denied the freedom to marry, "the children living with same-sex partners are made to suffer." These and other significant disadvantages for the children of same-sex couples prompted the prestigious American Academy of Pediatrics, in February 2002, to issue a strong call for full legal recognition of same-sex relationships.

Beyond Legal and Economic Concerns, Ending Marriage Discrimination Is a Matter of Civil Rights, Equality, the Pursuit of Happiness, and Love

During the lifetime of many Americans, there were major and hotly contested changes in the institution of civil marriage, including the legal declaration of women's equality in marriage, the allowance of married and unmarried people to make their own decisions regarding contraception and reproduction, and divorce reform. Each of these steps toward inclusion and respect was fiercely contested, often with the same arguments we see today against allowing gay people to marry.

During the congressional debate on the federal antimarriage law, the so-called "Defense of Marriage Act," aimed at shutting down the emerging civil rights discussion around marriage equality, civil rights movement hero John Lewis, now a Congressman from Georgia, decried the right-wing's attacks on gay people's freedom to marry. Congressman Lewis noted that the exclusion from marriage "denies gay men and women the right to liberty and the pursuit of happiness," and declared:

> Marriage is a basic human right. You cannot tell people they cannot fall in love. Dr. Martin Luther King, Jr. used to say when people talked about interracial marriage and I quote, "Races do not fall in love and get married. Individuals fall in love and get married."... Mr. Chairman, I have known racism. I have known bigotry. This bill [the proposed federal anti-marriage law of 1996, adding an overlay of federal discrimination against same-sex couples] stinks of the same fear, hatred and intolerance. It should not be called the Defense of Marriage Act. It should be called the defense of mean-spirited bigots act.

Despite this attack measure and the well-organized opposition of right-wing organizations, the landscape has begun to change dramatically. A 2001 Kaiser Family Foundation poll found that more than two-thirds of the American public has come to support extending "marriage-like" inheritance rights (70 percent) and Social Security benefits (68 percent) to lesbian and gay couples. More than two-thirds of the American public believes gay people will win the freedom to marry. A June 2002 poll in California showed that opposition to the freedom to marry for same-sex couples had dropped below 50 percent for the first time ever, and in April 2003, the front page of the *Boston Globe* reported that a majority in Massachusetts now supports ending discrimination in civil marriage with huge majority support among young and middle-aged voters.

In June 2002, a landmark lawsuit for marriage equality was filed on behalf of seven gay and lesbian couples in New Jersey—the same state where, in another high-profile lawsuit, the state's highest court ruled in favor of a gay scout leader's challenge of the discriminatory policies of the Boy Scouts of America. Meanwhile, the Massachusetts high court has before it now a case involving seven couples denied marriage licenses—*and could rule as soon as this summer!*

A victory in either court will mean same-sex couples can get married, but the United States will still be far behind countries such as the Netherlands and Belgium, and most likely Canada, which seems poised to end marriage discrimination within the next few months.

Marriage, of course, is not the only form of relationship or family deserving respect, and not every same-sex couple should or would choose to marry, just as not every heterosexual does. But lesbians and gay men willing to take on the commitment and responsibilities of civil marriage should not be denied the opportunity to build a life together and pursue happiness with the partner they love. Nor should their children and families suffer the economic hardships and disadvantages that come with exclusion from marriage.

We all hope to never again experience any semblance of tragedy like September 11th, and we cannot alter the damage of what has already occurred. What we can do, however, is change the way families like Juan and Ryan are protected and treated in the future by ending discrimination in civil marriage.

Allowing same-sex couples to marry would in no way destabilize or devalue marriage for other couples, nor would it tell any religion or person what marriages they must themselves celebrate. Rather, ending discrimination in civil marriage would properly hold America to its commitment to be a country where everyone has the right to be both different and equal—and where no one has to give up her or his difference to be treated equally.

June 2003

Evan Wolfson is the author of Why Marriage Matters: America, Equality, and Gay People's Right to Marry *and executive director of Freedom to Marry, a new gay and nongay partnership working to win marriage equality nationwide. Before founding Freedom to Marry, Mr. Wolfson served as marriage project director for Lambda Legal Defense & Education Fund, was co-counsel in the historic Hawaii marriage case,* Baehr v. Miike, *and participated in numerous gay rights and HIV/AIDS cases. Citing his national leadership on marriage equality and his appearance before the U.S. Supreme Court in* Boy Scouts of America v. James Dale, *the National Law Journal named Mr. Wolfson one of the 100 most influential lawyers in America. For more information on the fight for marriage equality and Freedom to Marry, please visit* www.freedomtomarry.org *or call 212-851-8418.*

First published on *www.drummajorinstitute.org*, June 1, 2003. Reprinted by permission of the author.

About the Editors:

Ian Philips (www.IanPhilips.com) *is the editor in chief (and mama bear) of Suspect Thoughts Press. He is also the author of two collections of literotica:* Satyriasis *and the Lambda Literary Award–winning* See Dick Deconstruct. *On February 19, 2004, he married heartthrob author-publisher Greg Wharton in San Francisco's City Hall. On August 12, 2004, the California State Supreme Court annulled their marriage. He is uncertain whether this annulment, like Henry VIII's in days of old, means he is also a virgin once more. He's having a hard time distinguishing, let alone separating, church from state these days.*

Greg Wharton is the publisher of Suspect Thoughts Press. He is the author of the collection Johnny Was & Other Tall Tales *and the editor of numerous other anthologies including the Lambda Literary Award Finalist* The Love That Dare Not Speak Its Name: Essays on Queer Desire and Sexuality. *He lives in San Francisco with his brilliant and sexy husband Ian Philips, a cat named Chloe, and a lot of books. For more information about the press or Greg visit www.suspectthoughtspress.com.*